Historical Archaeology of the Delaware Valley, 1600–1850

I0223052

Historical Archaeology
of the Delaware Valley, 1600–1850

Edited by Richard Veit and David Orr

THE UNIVERSITY OF TENNESSEE PRESS / KNOXVILLE

All Rights Reserved. Manufactured in the United States of America.
Cloth: 1st printing, 2014.
Paper: 1st printing, 2018.

Library of Congress Cataloging-in-Publication Data

Historical archaeology of the Delaware Valley, 1600–1850 / edited by Richard Veit
and David Orr. — First edition.
        pages cm
Includes bibliographical references and index.

ISBN 978-1-57233-997-2 (hardcover) — ISBN 978-1-62190-426-7 (paperback)

1. Delaware River Valley (N.Y.-Del. and N.J.)—Antiquities.
2. Delaware River Valley (N.Y.-Del. and N.J.)—History, Local.
 I. Veit, Richard Francis, 1968–
II. Orr, David Gerald, 1942–

F157.D4H56 2013
974.9—dc23
2013010717

Contents

ILLUSTRATIONS

Figures

Tables

Acknowledgments

We are indebted to a number of people and organizations for their assistance during the preparation of this book. We particularly appreciate the assistance of Lu Ann De Cunzo and an anonymous reviewer who helped us refine our arguments and better organize the volume. The patience and guidance of editor Thomas Wells was invaluable as we moved this volume toward publication. Michelle Hughes prepared the index. We also appreciate the endless encouragement of our students and colleagues at Monmouth and Temple universities as we discussed various aspects of this volume. We also owe a debt to our colleagues and friends, whose research on the Delaware Valley and its archaeological history inspired this work, especially, Bernard Herman, Anthony N. B. Garvan, John Cotter, Herbert Kraft, Robert Schuyler, and Marshall Becker. The volume was improved by our discussions with Sherene Baugher, Michael Gall, Adam Heinrich, and Michael Stewart. Finally, the support and forbearance of our wives, Terri Veit and Linda Orr, and our families, as we spent our days with the shades of Dutch settlers on Burlington Island, pirates and their lasses in Marcus Hook, Ben Franklin and the Great American Incognitum, Casper Wistar and his glassblowers in South Jersey, William Hamilton at The Woodlands, African-Americans fighting for their freedom at Timbuctoo, and many others, is truly appreciated.

INTRODUCTION

Historical Archaeology of the Delaware Valley, 1600–1850 is meant to be a selective reader on the archaeology of one of colonial America's great cultural hearths. Historical archaeologists have been studying sites in the Delaware Valley for over a century (see Abbott 1892, 1894; Mercer 1897; Cadzow 1936; Allen 1991), and several excellent books have been published on the historical archaeology of the region's major city, Philadelphia (Cotter, Roberts, and Parrington 1993; Yamin 2008). Much of the research that has occurred and is ongoing in the region, however, is buried in technical reports or has been presented only in ephemeral conference papers. Other important articles appear only in the journals of state and regional archaeological organizations with limited circulations, e.g.: Archaeological Society of New Jersey, Society for Pennsylvania Archaeology, New York State Archaeological Association, Middle Atlantic Archaeological Conference, Council for Northeast Historical Archaeology, and more recently on the web site of the Philadelphia Archaeological Forum. Although there are synthetic volumes on the archaeology of New Jersey and Delaware during the Historic period, e.g. *Digging New Jersey's Past* (Veit 2002) and *People, Places, and Histories of Delaware: An Historical Archaeology of the Cultures of Agriculture* (De Cunzo 2004), this is the first volume to examine the historical archaeology of the Delaware Valley. It complements earlier state and local works and draws together the results of significant recent research in Philadelphia, Southeastern Pennsylvania, New Jersey, and Delaware. Although it is neither encyclopedic nor all encompassing, it does endeavor to represent the diversity of approaches, both theoretical and methodological, that archaeologists working in the region employ. It was inspired by other regionally focused volumes such as Paul Shackel and Barbara J. Little's *Historical Archaeology of the Chesapeake* (1994) and David Hurst Thomas' volumes on the Spanish Borderlands (1989, 1990). It also builds from a long tradition of regionally focused prehistoric archaeological syntheses (Abbott 1876; 1907-1909, 1912; Volk 1911; Spier 1913; Kinsey 1972; Kraft 1974, 2001; Custer 1996; Stewart 2007) and the occasional volume that treats both prehistoric and historical archaeology (Levine, Sassaman, and Nassaney 1999).

The Delaware Valley is a distinctive region within the larger Middle Atlantic culture area. Defined literally, the region is enormous, as the Delaware River runs 410 miles from the Capes of Delaware to its headwaters in upstate New York. Our focus here is on the heart of the Delaware Valley, the areas bordering the middle and lower stretches of the river, to the north of Delaware Bay. This area has long drawn the interest of scholars. Historians (Wertenbaker 1938; Weslager and Dunlap 1961, 1967; Fischer 1989), geographers (Kniffen 1965; Lemon 1976; Stansfield 1998; Wacker 1975, Wacker and Clemens 1994), folklorists (Glassie 1968), architectural historians (Lanier and Herman 1997; Lanier 2004; Sheridan 2010, 2012), and as previously noted, archaeologists, have all written about the Delaware Valley. Most archaeologists have, until recently, focused on the region's rich prehistory. However, this volume focuses on the region's historical archaeology, a period stretching from the earliest interaction of explorers and colonists with Native Americans in the seventeenth century, through the colonial period, and beyond. It ends in the early nineteenth century, but historical archaeologists are busy documenting even more recent sites.

In the seventeenth and eighteenth centuries, the Delaware Valley was a fascinating place where Native Americans, English, Welsh, Scotch-Irish, French Huguenots, Swedes, Finns, Dutchmen, Africans, Jews, Quakers, German Pietists, and transplanted New Englanders came together and began to form a new and distinct American culture (Merrell 2000). Though somewhat less studied than New England's Puritans and the Chesapeake's planters and slaves, the Delaware Valley and its diverse inhabitants foreshadow later developments in American society. Thanks in part to William Penn's successful experiment with religious freedom, the Delaware Valley welcomed settlers of diverse backgrounds and faiths (Bronner 1978; Fischer 1989). Philadelphia, one of the largest cities in early America, was a center for trade, commerce, culture, industry, the arts, and science. In the early seventeenth century, the Delaware Valley played into the imperial ambitions of the Dutch and Swedes and was coveted by New Englanders to the north and Virginians to the south. The valley was the center of Quaker settlement in the New World, with major centers at Burlington City and more famously Philadelphia. Philadelphia subsequently grew to be one of the largest cities in the British Empire and a major hub for commercial activities. Other smaller commercial centers also developed along the Delaware at Trenton, New Castle, Wilmington, and to some extent at Salem and Greenwich.

The Delaware Valley played a vital strategic role during the American Revolution. At the conclusion of the successful British campaign for New York in 1776, Washington escaped with his battered and bruised army to safety on the Pennsylvania side of the Delaware Valley (Lefkowitz 1999). From there, he and his troops would cross the Delaware and win a series of stunning victories at Trenton and Princeton, allowing the revolution to continue. In 1777, the British succeeded in taking Philadelphia, after fighting their way up the Delaware (McGuire 2006, 2007). Congress fled the city, and the Continental Forces spent that winter encamped at Valley Forge. However, capturing the de facto capital of the young United States failed to snuff out the revolution. The next year the British abandoned Philadelphia and crossed the Delaware only to be intercepted on their way to New York at the Battle of Monmouth. This battle has seen considerable archaeological study (Stone, Sivilich, and Lender 1996). Though not treated here, as it occurred a bit to the east of our study area, Monmouth was a major political victory for the Americans and highlighted the growing strength of the Continental Army.

Philadelphia briefly served as the nation's capital from 1790 until 1800. It was also one of American's great intellectual centers for much of the late eighteenth and early nineteenth centuries and has even been called the Athens of America (Richardson 1982).

Prominent scientists and intellectuals such as William Penn, John Bartram, David Rittenhouse, Benjamin Franklin, Samuel Morton, Joseph Leidy, and numerous others resided in the Delaware Valley and participated in debates of international importance. Naturalists such as John and William Bartram, John James Audubon, Peter Kalm, and Charles Lucien Bonaparte cataloged specimens of fauna and flora. A good example of the latter is William Hamilton of the Woodlands who was an avid horticulturalist. Artists, such as Charles Wilson Peale, Thomas Sully, Charles Bird King, and Thomas Birch, called Philadelphia home. It was in the Delaware Valley that early archaeologists such as Montroville Dickeson, Charles Conrad Abbott, Henry Chapman Mercer, and others worked at unraveling American's ancient past.

In addition to their obvious historical importance, the Delaware Valley and its dominant city, Philadelphia, have been central to the growth and development of North American archaeology (Fowler and Wilcox 1983). In the late nineteenth century pioneering archaeologists Charles Conrad Abbott and Henry Chapman Mercer, both briefly associated with the University of Pennsylvania Museum, began to delve into the region's history through artifacts. Abbott conducted a very early excavation on Burlington Island, New Jersey, looking for the first European settlement in the Delaware Valley (1892, 1894). Meanwhile Mercer amassed an unparalleled collection of Americana: tools, stove plates, whale boats, and pottery, all representing the growth of our national culture, which Mercer believed was rapidly fading (Mercer 1897b, 1914). The Great Depression spurred another group of archaeological researchers, most notably Donald Cadzow in Pennsylvania (Allen 1991) and Dorothy Cross in New Jersey (1941, 1956), who in addition to excavating prehistoric Native American sites also examined historic sites. Indeed, Cadzow studied both the Printzhof, home of Johan Printz, governor of New Sweden, and Pennsbury Manor (Allen 1991). They were followed, in turn by John L. Cotter who devoted his career to putting Philadelphia's historical archaeology on the map (Roberts and Orr 2007). Cotter and his colleagues tested scores of sites in Philadelphia and its hinterlands. More recently Barbara Liggett, David Orr, Dan Roberts, Rebecca Yamin, Wade Catts, Doug Mooney, Judson Kratzer, and others have expanded our understanding of the region's rich archaeological heritage (see Yamin 2008). Large scale excavations in and around Philadelphia, most notably those associated with the construction of the National Constitution Center, Independence Mall, the Sugar House Casino, and the highways that traverse the city, have made significant contributions to our understanding of that city and its populace.

This volume is inspired by these previous works and builds on them. *Historical Archaeology of the Delaware Valley* brings together some highlights from the most recent scholarship on the historical archaeology of the Delaware Valley. Organized chronologically, it begins in the seventeenth century and runs through to the beginning of the nineteenth century. Several themes are also emphasized. The first three chapters focus on the early colonial history of the Delaware Valley. Michael Stewart, one of the leading authorities on the prehistory of the Delaware Valley, begins the volume with his chapter "An Archaeological Perspective on Native American and European Contact in the Delaware Valley." This chapter looks at how the Delaware Valley's first inhabitants, Native Americans, and particularly the Lenape/Delaware accommodated and resisted the changes brought to their land by European traders and settlers. Stewart argues that trade items were imbedded into longstanding social systems and that there was considerable persistence of Native stone tool and ceramic technologies. With the noteworthy exception of burial contexts, European trade goods are relatively scarce on contact period Native American sites in the Delaware Valley. Small dispersed communities of Native Americans relocated within their territories and continued to be a presence well into the eighteenth century and beyond. Stewart's work is important not just for its meticulous detail but also because it serves as a corrective to previous studies that have deemphasized the amount of cultural continuity among Native American groups in the historic period.

Charles Bello, Carolyn Dillian, and Richard Veit examine a different aspect of the colonial experience and at the same time reveal a curious chapter in the history of Delaware Valley archaeology through their reanalysis of Charles Conrad Abbott's 1880s excavations on Burlington Island. This island, situated between Bristol, Pennsylvania and Burlington, New Jersey was the site of the first European settlement in the Delaware Valley, a Dutch trading post and settlement established in 1624. Although the small group of settlers placed on the island by the Dutch West India Company was soon withdrawn to the more famous Manhattan Island, Dutch and Swedish settlers continued to use the island as a locus for trade, and later in the seventeenth century Dutch officials developed it as a plantation. In the 1880s, Charles Conrad Abbott, physician, natural scientist, and self-trained archaeologist, found seventeenth-century Dutch artifacts on the island's sandy shore. Abbott turned his considerable intellect to understanding the artifacts he had found and, over the course of several years, excavated the site which he called the Dutch Traders House. Bello and his co-authors through careful historical research trace the course of Abbott's excavation and reexamine what remains of his artifact collection, providing us with a glimpse of one of the Delaware Valley's earliest sites as well as insights into the work of the region's first archaeologist, C. C. Abbott.

Despite the early settlement of the Delaware Valley and Abbott's pioneering excavations, archaeological sites dating from the seventeenth century remain elusive, but archaeologists in Delaware, excavating at the site of Captain John Avery's plantation are beginning to fill this gap in our knowledge. A rather different glimpse of life during the early colonial period in the Delaware Valley comes from Joseph Blondino and Temple University's excavations at the Marcus Hook Plank House. Plank houses, which are constructed from carefully hewn timbers and dovetailed together like a large chest, are rare architectural gems. The Marcus Hook structure is the finest plank log house known and the only one to survive in such an excellent state of preservation. It is even more interesting due to its folkloric association with pirates, especially the mistress of the notorious Blackbeard. The house was, until the spring of 2004, hidden in plain sight. Then, a restoration project revealed that what was rumored to be an early house was, in fact, a most exceptional structure. Volunteer excavations led by the Society for Pennsylvania Archaeology and Temple University have revealed much about the evolution of the structure while, at the same time serving to introduce local residents to the value of historical archaeology. Moreover, ongoing excavations in Marcus Hook have subsequently revealed more early structures, reminders of this small community's historical importance as a gateway to Philadelphia. Blondino and his colleagues' work at Marcus Hook is also an excellent example of public archaeology.

Chapters 4 and 5 deal with sites associated with German émigrés. Both examine rural industries and the integration of German immigrants into the diverse cultural mélange which made up the colonial Delaware Valley. In their article on the Wistarburg Glassworks, William Liebeknecht and Damon Tvaryanas examine one of early America's most famous industrial sites. Begun by Casper Wistar and a group of skilled German craftsmen, it proved to be the birthplace of America's glassmaking industry. Archaeological excavations at the site have revealed quite a bit about the manufacturing complex and are providing considerable information about the range of products produced there.

Small-scale farm-based industries were also a common way for upwardly mobile farmers to supplement their incomes. Patricia Gibble examines a small rural Pennsylvania German distillery at the Alexander Schaeffer Farm/Distillery. This is an important study of an otherwise overlooked industry. Moreover her work points to a German refuse disposal pattern different from that seen on sites associated with other cultural groups. Gibble employs several types of material culture to understand the consumer choices made by three generations of the Schaeffer Family who occupied a 103 acre plantation in southeastern Pennsylvania from 1758 to 1807. Unlike previous assumptions that depicted the diverse ethnic groups settling in the province as adopting British cultural status markers in an effort to improve their rank in society, her interpretations indicate an effort to maintain some ethnic practices while adapting some aspects of English society to their own cultural patterns.

A very different sort of rural lifestyle is represented by Teagan Schweitzer's article, "The Archaeology of Food in Colonial Pennsylvania: An Historical Zooarchaeology of Foodways on the Stenton Plantation." Stenton, located five miles outside Philadelphia, was the country home of James Logan, William Penn's secretary and one of the most influential individuals in early Philadelphia. A cistern on the property excavated in the 1980s by Barbara Liggett yielded some 22,000 artifacts dating from the mid-eighteenth century. Over 8,000 animal bones were recovered. This assemblage provides a revealing glimpse of eighteenth-century foodways among one of Pennsylvania's wealthiest families in the years before the American Revolution.

Trade and maritime commerce were critical to the region's development. Daniel Griffith shares some of his findings from a British trading vessel en route to Philadelphia that wrecked and sank near Lewes, Delaware. His case study is an example of archaeological serendipity. The *Severn* was accidentally rediscovered when a dredge clearing the channel in the Delaware encountered the forgotten ship's remains and began spewing artifacts onto the shore. Although some of those artifacts were lost, many others were saved, and underwater archaeologists salvaged thousands more from what survived of the shipwreck. The *Severn* seems to have been something of a floating Wal-Mart, and excavations of the site have revealed a stunning array of consumer goods destined for merchants in the port of Philadelphia in the years just before the American Revolution. Griffith's article provides strong physical evidence about the dimensions of Trans-Atlantic commerce in the burgeoning Atlantic World.

From industries and trade, the volume changes tacks and looks at Philadelphia, the valley's commercial and social hub. Particularly emphasis is placed on understanding the role of Quakers in Philadelphia. Philadelphia's influence was widespread and pervasive, shaping cultural fashions in architecture, clothing, commemoration, and foodways. John Chenoweth's article "The Archaeology of Quakerism in Philadelphia and Beyond: Identity, Conformity, and Context" is a detailed reexamination of one of the Delaware Valley's most well-known cultural groups. Although past archaeology on Quaker sites has focused on how the Friends either hewed closely to their doctrinal value of "plainness" or, alternatively, how they rejected their own rules and participated more fully in the broader society, Chenoweth argues that the historical and archaeological evidence supports both conclusions. Looking at sites from Philadelphia and the Northeast, as well as elsewhere, Chenoweth wisely argues that a serious reconsideration of archaeological expectations regarding Quaker behavior is in order. Furthermore, he emphasizes the role of the individual in Quaker practice and how individuals and families elected to participate in the Society of Friends community. His thoughtful perspective has the potential to move us towards a more nuanced understanding of one of colonial America's most influential cultural groups.

William Hoffman and Deborah Miller's article, "The Baker and the Quaker: Ongoing Research from the National Constitution Center Site" examines the creation of Independence Mall as a green space in the middle of Center City Philadelphia during the 1950s and the more recent rediscovery of the archaeological remains of the neighborhood that once stood there. They focus particularly on the massive excavations at the site of the National Constitution Center, which spanned three quarters of a city block as well as included 115 house lots and 250 features that resulted in the recovery of over one million artifacts. This project is also an exceptional example of public urban archaeology as the processing, cataloging, and study of the artifact collection has taken place in a laboratory, staffed in part by local volunteers, which is on view to visitors exploring historic Philadelphia. The area that Hoffman and Miller examine developed rapidly in the late eighteenth century. A relatively poor neighborhood, the area was home to shoemakers, tailors, blacksmiths, and laborers. Some of these individuals were members of a burgeoning free African American community. Later, the area became increasingly industrialized. Hoffman and Miller's study is a detailed examination of both a neighborhood and the people who lived in it. Using assemblages from two privies—associated respectively with Godfrey Minnick, a baker, and the largely anonymous working class families who once lived on Cresson's Alley—we get a glimpse of middle-class life in the early republic.

Next, Patrice Jeppson introduces us to that quintessential Philadelphian, Benjamin Franklin, and traces the history of excavation at several sites associated with his life. Through these projects, we glimpse the scientific and patriotic activities of this founding father and famous Philadelphian. At the same time, we learn about the role that science and especially long-extinct mastodons played in the development of a sense of national identity in colonial America.

Another surprising glimpse of life in early Philadelphia is provided by archaeologist Mara Kaktins and faunal analyst Sharon Allitt. Their excavations at Philadelphia's City Almshouse (1732–1767) focused on the contents of a single privy. Philadelphia's City Almshouse was one of the first in North America. It opened in 1732. In 1767 due to overcrowding it was relocated, and the property was sold and redeveloped. Astonishingly, the almshouse privy survived beneath a later eighteenth-century structure and was carefully excavated by the intrepid Kaktins. The excavation of this privy revealed an astoundingly rich archaeological deposit that provides information about the health, medical practices, diet, and recreational activities that occurred at the almshouse, as well as the craft activities that the residents engaged in to support themselves. It is an intriguing study of institutional culture in early America.

While the poor were laboring away at craft industries in almshouses, other individuals were living quite well. Sarah Chesney's article, "The Root of the Matter: Searching for William Hamilton's Greenhouse at The Woodlands Estate, Philadelphia, Pennsylvania" examines one of Philadelphia's great country houses, the Woodlands in West Philadelphia. Several generations of the Hamilton family owned the house before William Hamilton decided to redesign the property following the latest trends in English landscape design. Hamilton, one of late-eighteenth-century America's great botanists, collected exotic plants by the thousands and erected an extensive greenhouse complex to nurture his prized horticultural collection. Chesney's investigations of the property provide an unprecedented opportunity to explore how scientific botany and private estates served to introduce the public to new types of landscapes and plants.

Hamilton was not alone in his horticultural exploits. Just upriver from Philadelphia in the riverside community known as Bordentown, Joseph Bonaparte, elder brother of Napoleon Bonaparte and former King of Naples and Spain, created another lavish Delaware Valley estate. Joseph fled to the New World after his brother's defeat at Waterloo and lived in the Delaware Valley from 1816 until 1839. The focus of this paper is on his palatial country estate, Point Breeze, in Bordentown. At Point Breeze, Joseph erected a pair of magnificent houses. The first, which stood on the site from 1816–1820, is a primary focus of this article. The authors argue that Joseph built his house as a grand stage upon which to play the role of a king in exile. As discussed by Richard Veit and Michael Gall, archaeology is revealing this extraordinary building and informing us about its trappings and the life of a king in exile whose passions for art, culture, and landscape design enriched the cultural life of the Delaware Valley.

Despite its well known moniker of the Garden State, New Jersey is well known for its industrial heritage. Richard Hunter and Ian Burrow introduce us to the historical archaeology of Trenton, New Jersey's capital and a former industrial powerhouse of the Delaware Valley. Trenton has probably seen more archaeological study than any other city its size in the eastern United States. Hunter and Burrow are masterful tour guides to the city and its heritage. Although the work in the city has been almost entirely conducted as part of a series of cultural resource management studies, their work is exceptionally scholarly. They examine Trenton in comparison to other North American towns and cities and employ a landscape archaeology approach. The temporal span of the article is broad, ranging from the ancient Native American settlements of the Abbott Farm National Historic Landscape through early industries—especially potteries and eighteenth-century military sites, such as the iconic Trenton Barracks. The article also contains an invaluable map of Trenton's archaeological sites.

The final article in the volume, "It Takes a Village: Archaeology and Identity at Timbuctoo," is authored by Christopher Barton. He examines a topic of great interest to archaeologists, historians, and the general public alike: the plight of African Americans—free and enslaved—in nineteenth-century America. New Jersey was the last northern state to abolish slavery. It did so in 1804 through a well-intentioned but clumsily implemented gradual emancipation act that served to keep many individuals in servitude well into the nineteenth century. Facing enormous challenges, free African Americans, sometimes with the help of Friends, created their own communities. At Timbuctoo, recently freed African Americans built a community that was organized in a manner similar to some West African communities. Whether this reflects a cultural survival or a circle the wagons mentality designed to help fend off rapacious slave catchers is unclear. That the community survived and indeed thrived in an era of intense racism and limited economic opportunities for African Americans is a tribute to the fortitude of those who settled there. Barton is giving voice to this important and overlooked story from nineteenth-century America.

The essays in this volume largely speak to the continuing conversation scholars have with questions of identity (regional or otherwise) and diversity. In her discussion of cultural landscape, Gabrielle Lanier argues that, "With its remarkable ethnic, sectarian, and cultural diversity in the early national period, the Delaware Valley—*in many ways the new nation writ small*—provides a unique laboratory..." (Lanier 2005:xviii). As we have seen in Gibble's essay, for example, the definition of the Pennsylvania German community that evolved from the late seventeenth century into the first quarter of the nineteenth century is fraught with challenges (see also Cooper and Minardi 2001:26 and McMurry and Dolson 2011:1-9).

No single ethnic group "dominates" the region in the time spans discussed in this book. Even the Scots Irish, one of the largest ethnic groups in the Delaware Valley, were part of a broader "shared experience" of diversity and mobility in the region. (Griffin 2001:156 and passim). This work demonstrates the rich variety of ethnicities, origins, and even racial backgrounds present in the Delaware Valley.

The American Revolution also contributed to notions of regional and national identity. Experiences like Valley Forge shaped the identity of many of the valley's inhabitants. Indeed, according to Riordan, "Revolutionary conflict in the Delaware Valley intensified people's awareness of the public importance of a diverse range of local identities, and their centrality to everyday life in the region helped to establish the conditions within which the nation was created there" (Riordan 2007:272). In the Delaware Valley, a wide range of questions persist in our own times as to the origins of American "identity or character." We believe that the essays in this volume deepen our understanding of regional identity despite the fact that its ultimate definition remains elusive.

At the same time, *Historical Archaeology of the Delaware Valley* highlights some of the most interesting and revealing archaeological excavations that have taken place to date in this region. They range in date from the seventeenth through nineteenth centuries and reveal the cultural diversity of the region, the influence of Quakers, the region's major cultural hub, Philadelphia, and the role of smaller communities such as Trenton, Schaefferstown, and Marcus Hook in defining practices of everyday life. Identity is a major theme running throughout the volume, whether it is the identities of Native Americans caught in the maelstrom of change in the seventeenth and eighteenth centuries, or the settlers: Dutch, Quaker, German, and Irish who increasingly displaced them. Even a king, such as Joseph Bonaparte, settled in the Delaware Valley. There he created a garden that harkened back to European antecedents and allowed him to play the role of an unofficial cultural attaché in the early republic.

Appropriately, many of the papers serve to complicate rather than simplify the issue of identity in early America, highlighting the active role that individuals played in shaping their own destinies. Furthermore, these sites in their diversity reflect the diversity of early American life, where individuals of varied ethnicities, divergent social classes, and myriad religious belief systems came together—much like George Washington's Continental Army at Valley Forge—to form a new American culture.

Industries and commerce are also examined as is landscape archaeology at Joseph Bonaparte's Point Breeze and The Woodlands. A variety of archaeological approaches from the careful reading of the historic landscape seen in Hunter and Burrow's article, to the faunal analyses of Mara Kaktins, Sharon Allitt, and Teagan Schweitzer at, respectively, the Philadelphia Almshouse and Stenton, casts a spotlight on the types of information that can be drawn out of the analysis of food remains. Schweitzer, Jepson, Dillian, Bello, and Veit all highlight the potential of old and often forgotten museum collections to shed new light on important aspects of our shared heritage. Many of these case studies—including the Plank House, Point Breeze, and Timbuctoo—are examples of public archaeology, where community members are volunteering their time to help unearth and reconstruct the past.

Archaeologists working in the region are also busy unearthing the remains of President Washington's residence in Philadelphia and laying bare the lives of the African American middle class in nineteenth-century Philadelphia. All of these stories reflect our shared heritage as Americans. Broken crockery, shattered glass bottles, and food waste long ago tossed into the dustbin of history can and will, through careful study, tell the stories of earlier generations. Through these material remains. we can better understand our own society today and its origins, and perhaps, use this information to shape a better future for all. By so doing, we come a step closer to accomplishing William Penn's "Holy Experiment" where individuals with different beliefs and traditions live harmoniously together.

References Cited

Abbott, Charles Conrad

1876   *The Stone Age of New Jersey.* Annual Report of the Smithsonian Institution for 1875: 246–380.

1892   *Recent Rambles or In Touch with Nature.* J. B. Lippincott Company, Philadelphia.

1894   *Travels in a Tree Top.* J. B. Lippincott Company, Philadelphia.

1907–09   *Archaeological Nova Caesarea.* MacCrellish and Quigley, Trenton, New Jersey.

1912   *Ten Years' Diggings in Lenape Land.* MacCrelish and Quigley, Trenton, New Jersey.

Allen, Rebecca

1991   Historical Archaeology in Pennsylvania During the Depression. *Pennsylvania Archaeologist* 61(2):18–30.

Bronner, Edwin B.

1978   *William Penn's "holy experiment": The Founding of Pennsylvania, 1681–1701.* Greenwood Press, Westport, Connecticut.

Cadzow, Donald

1936   Archaeology and the Works Progress Administration in Pennsylvania. *Pennsylvania Archaeologist* 5(4):99.

Cooper, Wendy, and Lisa Minardi

2011   *Paint, Pattern, and People: Furniture of Southeastern Pennsylvania, 1725–1850.* University of Pennsylvania Press, Philadelphia.

Cotter, John L., Daniel G. Roberts, and Michael Parrington
1993   *The Buried Past: An Archaeological History of Philadelphia.* University of Pennsylvania Press, Philadelphia.

Cross, Dorothy
1941   *The Archaeology of New Jersey.* Vol. 1. The Archaeological Society of New Jersey and the New Jersey State Museum, Trenton, New Jersey.
1956   *The Archaeology of New Jersey,* Vol. 2. *The Abbott Farm.* The Archaeological Society of New Jersey and New Jersey State Museum, Trenton, New Jersey.

Custer, Jay F.
1995   *Prehistoric Cultures of Eastern Pennsylvania.* Pennsylvania Historical and Museum Commission, Harrisburg.

De Cunzo, Lu Ann
2004   *A Historical Archaeology of Delaware: People, Contexts, and the Cultures of Agriculture.* University of Tennessee Press, Knoxville.

Fischer, David Hackett
1989   *Albion's Seed: Four British Folkways in America.* Oxford University Press, New York.

Fowler, Don, and David R. Wilcox
2003   *Philadelphia and the Development of Americanist Archaeology.* University of Alabama Press, Tuscaloosa.

Glassie, Henry
1968   *Pattern in the Material Folk Culture of the Eastern United States.* University of Pennsylvania Press, Philadelphia.

Griffin, Patrick
2001   *The People With No Name: Ireland's Ulster Scots Irish, and the Creation of a British Atlantic World, 1689–1764.* Princeton University Press: Princeton, New Jersey.

Kinsey, W. Fred III, editor
1972   Archaeology in the Upper Delaware Valley. *Anthropological Series 2.* Pennsylvania Historical and Museum Commission.

Kniffen, Fred B.
1965   Folk Housing: Key to Diffusion. *Annals of the Association of American Geographers* 55(4):549–577.

Kraft, Herbert C.
1986   *The Lenape: Archaeology, History, Ethnography.* New Jersey Historical Society, Newark.
2001   *The Lenape-Delaware Indian Heritage: 10,000 B.C.–A.D. 2000.* Lenape Books, Elizabeth, New Jersey.

Lanier, Gabrielle
2004   *The Delaware Valley in the Early Republic: Architecture, Landscape, and Regional Identity.* Johns Hopkins University Press, Baltimore.

Lanier, Gabrielle M., and Bernard L. Herman
1997   *Everyday Architecture of the Mid-Atlantic: Looking at Buildings and Landscapes*. Johns Hopkins University Press, Baltimore.

Lefkowitz, Arthur S.
1999   *The Long Retreat: The Calamitous American Defense of New Jersey 1776*. Rutgers University Press, New Brunswick, New Jersey.

Lemon, James T.
1976   *The Best Poor Man's Country: A Geographical Study of Southeastern Pennsylvania*. W. W. Norton and Company, New York.

Levine, Mary Ann, Kenneth E. Sassaman, and Michael S. Nassaney
1999   *The Archaeological Northeast*. Bergin and Garvey, Westport, Connecticut.

McGuire, Thomas J.
2006   *The Philadelphia Campaign, Vol. I: Brandywine and the Fall of Philadelphia*. Stackpole Books, Mechanicsburg, Pennsylvania.
2007   *The Philadelphia Campaign, Vol. II: Germantown and the Roads to Valley Forge*. Stackpole Books, Mechanicsburg, Pennsylvania.

McMurry, Sally, and Nancy Van Dolsen, editors
2011   *Architecture and Landscape of the Pennsylvania Germans, 1720–1920*. University of Pennsylvania Press, Philadelphia.

Mercer, Henry C.
1897a   *Researches Upon the Antiquity of Man in the Delaware Valley and the Eastern United States*. Publications of the University of Pennsylvania Series in Philology, Literature, and Archaeology, Vol. VI. Ginn and Company, Boston.
1897b   *Tools of the Nation Maker: A Descriptive Catalog of Objects in the Museum of the Historical Society of Bucks County, Pennsylvania*. Bucks County Historical Society, Doylestown.

Merrell, James H.
2000   *Into the American Woods: Negotiations on the Pennsylvania Frontier*. W. W. Norton, New York.

Richardson, Edgar P.
1982   The Athens of America, 1800–1825. In *Philadelphia: A 300-Year History*, edited by Russell F. Weigley. W. W. Norton, New York.

Riordan, Liam
2007   *Many Identities, One Nation: The Revolution and its Legacy in the Mid-Atlantic*. University of Pennsylvania Press, Philadelphia.

Roberts, Daniel G., and David Orr
2007   *Witness to the Past: The Life and Works of John L. Cotter*. Society for American Archaeology Press.

Shackel, Paul A., and Barbara J. Little (editors)
1994   *Historical Archaeology of the Chesapeake*. Smithsonian Institution Press, Washington, D.C.

Sheridan, Janet
2010   "Colonial Timber Framing in Southwestern New Jersey: The Cultural Implications of Structural Logic." Paper presentation at the Vernacular Architecture Forum Annual Conference, Arlington, Virginia, May 19-22, 2010.
2012   "Marshalltown: Reconstructing a Fragmentary Historic Black Settlement." 2012 New Jersey Historic Preservation Conference, June 7, 2012.

Shields, S. David (editor)
2009   Introduction. In *Material Culture in Anglo-America: Regional Identity and Urbanity in the Tidewater, Low Country, and Caribbean*, pp. 1–14. University of South Carolina Press, Columbia.

Spier, Leslie
1913   Results of an Archaeological Survey of the State of New Jersey. *American Anthropologist* 15:677–679.

Stansfield, Charles A., Jr.
1998   *A Geography of New Jersey: The City in the Garden*. Rutgers University Press, New Brunswick.

Stewart, R. Michael
2007   Assessing Current Archaeological Research in the Delaware Valley. *Archaeology of Eastern North America* 35:161–174.

Stone, G. W., D. M. Sivilich, and M. W. Lender
1996   A Deadly Minuet: The Advance of the New England "Picked Men" against the Royal Highlanders at the Battle of Monmouth. *The Brigade Dispatch* 26(2).

Thomas, David Hurst
1989   *Columbian Consequences, Vol. 1, Archaeological and Historical Perspectives on the Spanish Borderlands West*. Smithsonian Institution Press, Washington, D.C.
1990   *Columbian Consequences, Vol. 3, Archaeological and Historical Perspectives on the Spanish Borderlands East*. Smithsonian Institution Press, Washington, D.C.

Veit, Richard F.
2002   *Digging New Jersey's Past: Historical Archaeology in the Garden State*. Rutgers University Press, New Brunswick, New Jersey.

Volk, Ernest
1911   The Archaeology of the Delaware Valley. *Papers of the Peabody Museum of American Archaeology and Ethnology 5*. Harvard University, Cambridge, Massachusetts.

Wacker, Peter O.
1975   *Land and People: A Cultural Geography of Preindustrial New Jersey: Origins and Settlement Patterns*. Rutgers University Press, New Brunswick, New Jersey.

Wacker, Peter O., and Paul G. E. Clemens

1994   *Land Use in Early New Jersey: A Historical Geography.* Rutgers University Press, New Brunswick.

Wertenbaker, Thomas Jefferson

1938   *The Founding of American Civilization: The Middle Colonies.* Charles Scribner's Sons, New York.

Weslager, C. A. in collaboration with A. R. Dunlap

1961   *Dutch Explorers, Traders, and Settlers in the Delaware Valley, 1609–1664.* Rutgers University Press, New Brunswick.

Weslager, C. A.

1967   *The English on the Delaware 1610–1682.* Rutgers University Press, New Brunswick.

Yamin, Rebecca

2008   *Digging in the City of Brotherly Love: Stories from Philadelphia Archaeology.* Yale University Press, New Haven.

1

AMERICAN INDIAN ARCHAEOLOGY OF THE HISTORIC PERIOD IN THE DELAWARE VALLEY

R. MICHAEL STEWART

Introduction

It is fitting that a discussion of American Indians be included in a volume focused on the historic archaeology of the Delaware Valley, or any region in the Americas. European explorers, traders, and waves of colonists did not enter an empty world, but one populated and shaped by a variety of Native cultures with deep and complex histories. The fullest picture of the past will only emerge when we integrate the history, ethnohistory, ethnography, human ecology, and archaeology of everyone involved. Likewise, analysis and interpretation must be done at different contextual scales, from individual communities and specific landscapes to ever-broadening social, economic, and political networks and geographic areas.

This chapter focuses on insights derived from archaeological studies of American Indian sites of the region from the sixteenth, seventeenth and eighteenth centuries. The Delaware River Basin and adjacent interior and coastal areas of New Jersey and New York comprise the traditional homeland of the Lenape, later collectively referred to as the Delaware Indians (Goddard 1978; Grumet 1989, 1995: 211–242). In traditional studies, the time of concern here is referred to as the contact period. Using the term "contact" to designate a chronological unit of study is somewhat misleading. As an event, contact between specific groups of Native peoples and specific groups of Europeans is highly variable in time and space. Inter-cultural contact is a theme throughout the long tenure of human beings in the region. While an appreciation of separate contact events is certainly of interest, more important is an examination of the processes of interaction, the ways in which groups on the many sides of the cultural divides that existed reacted, responded, and adapted to one another (Wilson and Rogers 1993).

In what follows, I eschew a substantial reliance on the documentary record and its interpretation. I take to heart C. A. Weslager's (1985:2) admonition, echoed in the work of others (e.g., Lightfoot 1995; Milner et al. 2001; Rubertone 2000; Silliman 2005), that care must be taken with how we use the work of other specialists in the interpretation of the American Indian archaeology of the historic period. In an ideal world, projects would be carried out by cadres of cooperating specialists debating and evaluating the data and interpretations of one another. As an archaeologist, I am not thoroughly grounded in reliable historical sources, and therefore, I use documentary evidence with caution. I want to avoid the pitfall of conflating observations of Native peoples made at different times during the historic period with archaeological evidence in order to create a fuller picture of American Indian life (Stahl 1993). Organizing our data and interpretations in the most discrete contexts possible is critical to the construction of a reliable view of the past and the cultural and social dynamics that we wish to chart and understand. In emphasizing documentary sources, there can be a subtle, if not conscious, promotion of the European side of the story, of colonialism, rather than a view of Native peoples doing things to maintain or redefine their identities (Silliman 2005).

An archaeological approach provides another perspective, one that is closer in some respects to the lived reality of American Indians. I do not deny the ultimate interpretive power of integrating archaeological research with that of other specialists, but the full benefit of such integration is in the future. For now, presenting basic archaeological observations and developing interpretations and hypotheses that can be evaluated and complemented with independent data sets from history, ethnohistory, and ethnography (Stahl 1993) seem to be the best ways to proceed. In fact, reconciling the tension and disparities that exist between the archaeological and historical records of the past (e.g., Gallivan 2004), as they will continue to be revealed, will allow us to fashion a more complex understanding of the people and the time.

Background

Setting

The Delaware River is over 200 miles long with tributary headwaters in the Catskill area of New York State (figure 1.1). The river's drainage basin is extensive, encompassing portions of New York, Pennsylvania, New Jersey, Delaware, and the extreme northeastern corner of Maryland. Physiographic provinces crosscut the basin in a southwestern to northeastern direction and include from west to east: the Appalachian Plateau, Ridge and Valley; the New England Province or Reading Prong; Piedmont; Inner Coastal Plain; and Outer Coastal Plain (Hunt 1967; Wolfe 1977). It is an incredibly diverse environmental region with a wide variety of natural resources of potential interest to human societies. Of the provinces, tidal portions of the Inner and Outer Coastal Plains are the most biologically productive. The environmental diversity of the Delaware River Basin is reflected to different degrees in the adaptations of the Indian peoples who inhabited the region prior to, and during historic times.

Areas of interior and coastal New York and New Jersey adjacent to the Delaware Basin are included in the present study, given their association with the territories typically ascribed to the Delaware Indians. Munsee-speaking groups inhabited the Upper Delaware Valley, northern and western reaches of the drainage basin, as well as northeastern portions of New Jersey extending to the mid and lower Hudson River Valley of eastern and coastal New York. Unami-speaking groups, which I will

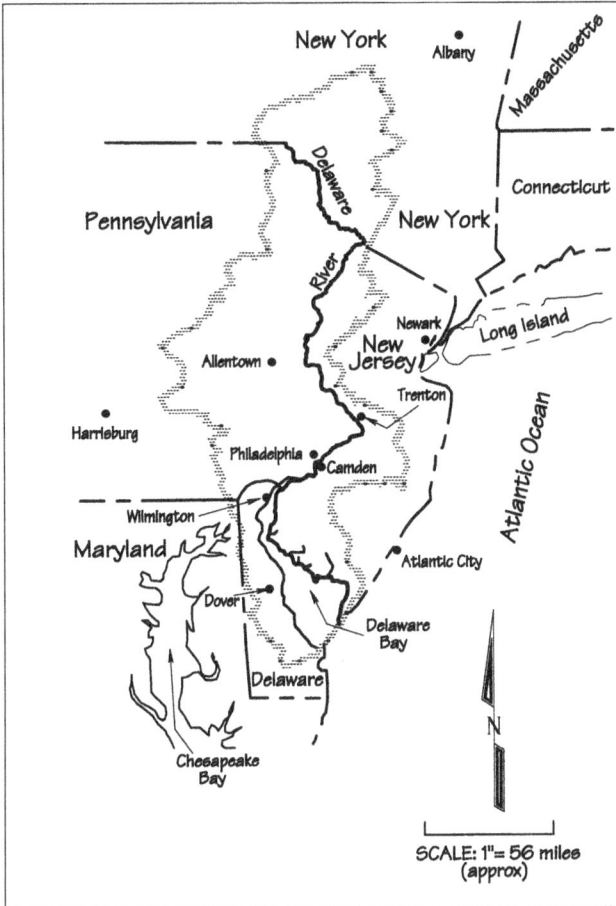

Figure 1.1. Regional location of the study area. The boundary of the Delaware River Basin is shown as a stippled line. Map by Allie Stewart.

collectively refer to as Lenape, occupied the mid and lower segments of the Delaware River Basin and portions of the Raritan River Basin south of Raritan Bay (Goddard 1978; Grumet 1989, 1995:211–242; Kraft 2001; Weslager 1972).

PRE-CONTACT NATIVE CULTURE AND DIVERSITY

Archaeological reconstructions of Native lifeways prior to the coming of Europeans provide a necessary basis for understanding the nature of Indian life and interactions during the historic period. This pre-contact era is designated as the Late Woodland period by regional archaeologists and is typically dated from AD 800–900 to 1609–1629 when initial European presence in the region becomes most evident. At the dawn of contact between Native Americans and Europeans during the early seventeenth century, a traveler beginning a journey in the Upper Delaware River Valley and passing downstream would encounter groups living in small farming communities as well as people for whom domesticated crops held little importance, each group possessing a slightly different material culture. Although there are common themes in the way of life of the indigenous people of the valley, there is also variability and diversity. The summary that follows draws on a variety of synthetic works that deal with the Late Woodland archaeology of the Delaware River Basin (Custer 1984, 1996; Grossman-Bailey 2001; Kinsey 1972; Kraft 2001; Moeller 1975, 1992; Mounier 2003; Stewart 1989a, 1990, 1993, 1998a; Stewart et al. 1986). It touches upon technology and material culture, community and settlement patterns, trade, and mortuary behavior—topics that also can be addressed with data from sites of the historic period.

The Late Woodland stone toolkit remains what it was during earlier times with three major exceptions: a stylistic change in projectile point form; the near disappearance of a formal bifacial industry exclusive of the production of projectile points; and a shift in the degree to which different types of tool-stone are used. The production of triangular projectile points represents the predominant bifacial industry evident on sites throughout the Delaware Valley. The decline of the production of bifacial knives and the heightened emphasis on a core and flake technology are trends evident in the greater region. I believe that the decline may be the result of changes in who made and used stone tools. My suggestion is that during Late Woodland times, the role of the stone tool specialist in Native communities faded. Instead, most stone tool production was undertaken by a larger segment of society, an "every-man/woman-for-himself/herself" type of strategy. Certainly the detachment of flakes from unprepared cores for use as expedient tools requires less skill and training than what is involved in the production of formal bifacial knives. The bipolar reduction of tool-stone is as well represented as free-hand reduction techniques (Stewart 1987a, 1989b). Formal tool types like scrapers and drills occur in Late Woodland assemblages and resemble those of earlier times. Pestles, mortars, manos, grinding platforms, and pitted stones represent stone-based milling equipment that persists throughout the period and has origins earlier in time. In middle and lower portions of the Delaware River Basin, there is a dramatic decrease in the use of argillite for tool production of any kind. Cryptocrystalline rock types fill in the gap, although they had been and remain the favored material for the production of formal scrapers and prepared flake tools. The most frequently encountered types of ornaments (pendants) are fashioned from various types of ground and polished stone. Beads are also fashioned from shell. Stone beads are rare.

Styles of pottery vary throughout the study area with vessels from upper portions of the Delaware Valley and adjacent areas (the equivalent of Munsee territory) sharing similarities with what cultures to the north are producing. This pottery, at least after AD1350, tends to be slab constructed. In more southerly portions of the study area (the equivalent of Lenape territory) all Late Woodland pottery tends to be coil constructed, sharing stylistic affinities with groups situated to the north and south along the Atlantic coast.

Late Woodland sites are situated in a wide variety of environmental settings including: the floodplains of high and low order streams; areas adjacent to wetlands of various types; rockshelters in a variety of settings; upland open areas associated with some type of surface water; and tool-stone quarries in a variety of lowland and upland environments. For large portions of the Delaware Valley and region, Late Woodland settlement patterns consist of small hamlets, often farming oriented, and task specific and seasonally focused camps. In the lower Delaware Valley, the farming of domesticates does not seem to be emphasized to any degree, although semi-sedentary settlements in alluvial settings can be noted (Allitt et al. 2008; Grossman-Bailey 2001; Messner 2008; Stewart 1993). In general, the Late Woodland subsistence base includes a variety of plants, animals, fish, and shellfish, although the importance of these food sources can vary within the region.

No hierarchy of Late Woodland residential sites exists, as might be expected if dealing with segmentary societies or chiefdoms. Variation in the size of residential sites can be related to the seasonal and functional differences of occupations, rather than as a fingerprint of administrative, political, or economic centers and their related outliers. The implication of these observations is that the Late Woodland ancestors of the Munsee/Lenape lived in relatively autonomous communities or small clusters of communities. To the degree that catchment analysis, the location of tool-stone sources, and the spatial distribution of pottery styles reflect the territory of a closely knit, interacting group, Late Woodland territories in the middle Delaware Valley range from 20–40 miles in a single linear dimension and involve areas on both the western and eastern sides of the river (Stewart 1998a, 2000). Similar analyses have not been carried out for other portions of the study area.

Relatively few community or intra-site patterns have been thoroughly documented. Late Woodland residential sites lack palisades. There is variation in the size of Late Woodland structures that may have implications for the size of households and thus social organization. Small, sub-rectangular, "longhouse-like" dwellings measuring up to 60 by 20 feet have been noted for Late Woodland sites, as have oval to circular structures 15 by 12 feet in dimension (Harbison 2007; Kinsey 1972:281–283; Kraft 1970, 2001; Moeller 1992; Stewart 1998a). Data are insufficient to determine if this variation reflects seasonal differences in site function or differences in the organization of the occupying group. There are no sites where different structure types co-occur and are demonstrated to be contemporaneous. While variations in house size between sites may imply differences in household organization, they do not seem to indicate differences in the economic, political, or social status of individual communities.

Where excavations have been sufficiently broad, Late Woodland pit features, which may have once been storage facilities, tend to be associated with individual structures or activity areas, and are not organized in what might be viewed as communal space. There are sites where large clusters of pit features occur, but evidence for structures is lacking. Assuming that storage takes place only at the level of the household implies that a relatively egalitarian form of social organization was in place. Nonetheless, this does not preclude the existence of differential access to rights, power, and resources on the basis of age or gender.

Late Woodland evidence for exchange or trade decreases dramatically in the Delaware Valley and Middle Atlantic Region relative to earlier times (Stewart 1989a). Notable is the continued movement of jasper tool-stone from sources in the Delaware Valley into the Northeast (Lavin 1983; but see King et al. 1997). Triangular-shaped, chipped stone projectile points fashioned from metarhyolite obtained from sources in the Potomac and Susquehanna valleys to the west are found occasionally in the Delaware Valley. There is a minor trade in pottery linking the Upper Delaware Valley with downstream portions of the drainage basin. The tremendous overlap in visual styles, however, makes it difficult to recognize short distance trade in pottery. Analysis of the technological style of Late Woodland pottery and clay provenance studies are attempting to resolve this problem (cf. Sidoroff et al. 2008; Stewart and Pevarnik 2008). Through the middle and upper sections of the Delaware Valley and areas farther to the north, the distribution of shell artifacts is suggestive of focused exchange (Stewart 1989a; also see Ritchie 1965:253–324). Trade in shell and shell beads seems to be brisk in many portions of the Middle Atlantic Region, linking coastal zones with the western and northern interior during the Late Woodland period (Stewart 1989a:63–64).

Graves of the Late Woodland period typically, but not exclusively, contain human remains in a flexed position, and infrequently contain obvious grave goods (Cushman 2007, n.d.; Cushman and Stewart 2008; Custer 1996; Kraft 2001). Graves appear adjacent to house patterns, hearths, and pit features, some of which may have been feasting pits associated with mortuary practices. Ordered cemetery space, spatially distinct from residential or work areas, do not seem to be a feature of Late Woodland mortuary practices. When intentionally placed goods are found in graves, they consist of what appear to have been personal items of the deceased, such as smoking pipes or an artisan's tool kit.

HISTORIC/ETHNOHISTORIC DATA

Space and personal expertise do not allow for a critical or comprehensive review of the literature dealing with documentary sources of evidence relevant to American Indians in the study area. Nonetheless, a useful sample of sources can be noted. Seventeenth-century observations include those of Adriaen van der Donck (Jameson 1937; van Gastel 1990), Johan De Laet (Jameson 1937), Peter Lindeström (Johnson 1925), Johan Printz (Myers 1912), David De Vries (Jameson 1937), Isaak De Rasieres (Jameson 1937), Daniel Francis Pastorius (Myers 1912), Jasper Danckaerts (James and Jameson 1913), and William Penn (Myers 1970; Weslager 1985). Often cited observations for the eighteenth century include those of David Zeisberger (Wellenreuther and Wessel 2005), David Brainerd (Dwight 1822), and John Heckewelder (1819, 1820).

Region-wide syntheses of documentary source material can be found in Brasser (1978), Esposito (1976), Goddard (1978), Grumet (1989, 1995), D. Kent (1979), Kraft (2001), Newcomb (1956), Richter (2005), Schutt (2007), Thurman 1973, Weslager (1972). Discussions of smaller segments of the region are provided by Appel (1991), Becker (e.g., 1983, 1985, 1986, 1988a), Boyd (2005), Flemming 2005, Grumet (1979, 1991), and F. Stewart (1932). Evaluation of historic maps and documentary sources locating American Indian settlements can be found in Cotter et al. (1992), Donehoo (1977), Dunlap and Weslager (1958), Kent et al. (1981), Rivinus (1965), and Weslager (1954, 1956). Contrary opinions exist about the documentary record of Delaware Indian settlement and subsistence patterns, group identity, and population estimates, including what is implied about pre-contact aspects of life (cf. Becker, 1984, 1988b, 1993a, 2006, 2009; Custer 1996; Goddard 1978; Grumet 1995; Kraft 2001; Stewart 1998a, 1999a; Thurman 1973; Weslager 1985, 1972).

The timeline shown in Table 1.1 conveys a sense of historical developments in the Delaware Valley and adjacent areas. Although extremely generalized, it provides another frame of reference for understanding the results of American Indian and European interaction as reflected in the archaeological record.

Previous Archaeological Research

Table 1.2 provides a comprehensive listing of known American Indian sites of the historic period and source references. The list builds upon the previous compilations of Cushman (n.d.), Grumet (1995:211–242), Kraft (2001:353–448), Pagoulatos (2007), Pietak (1995:Appendix A), and Santone (1999). It also includes sites gleaned from the electronic files of the Pennsylvania Archaeology Site survey (PASS). A thorough review of the New Jersey State Museum's site files has yet to be completed since Pagoulatos's (2007) study. An examination of the journals, *Pennsylvania Archaeologist, Bulletin of the New Jersey Archaeological Society,* and the *Journal of Middle Atlantic Archaeology* helped to supplement the list, as did a review of a variety of synthetic publications dealing with the time under consideration and a number of technical reports resulting from cultural resource management investigations. There are documented sites located to the west beyond the Delaware River Basin that can be attributed to eighteenth-century migrations of Delaware Indians (e.g., Pietak 1995, 1999:8–11). These are not included in table 1.2.

Overviews of the American Indian archaeology of the historic period for large portions of the study area are found in Becker (1980), Cushman (2007), Grumet (1995:211–242), Kraft (1974, 1984, 1989, 1991, 2001:353–448), Lenig (1999), Lenik (1989), Mounier (2003: 121–122,183–187), Pagoulatos (2007), Pietak (1995), Santone (1998), Williams and Kardas (1982). Of these, Pagoulatos (2007), Pietak (1995), and Santone (1999) are very helpful in providing thumbnail sketches of numerous sites, chronology, and history of investigation. Cushman's (n.d.) soon to be completed Ph.D. dissertation will also include extensive baseline data for

Table 1.1. Some Historic Developments of the Delaware River Basin and Environs.

1524	Giovanni da Verrazano sails along the Mid-Atlantic coast passing Delaware Bay and entering New York Bay.
1575–1600	Susquehannock Indians, who are trading with Europeans, interact with a variety of Indian groups throughout the Delaware River Basin and broader region.
1609	Henry Hudson sails into Delaware Bay.
1624	New Amsterdam established on Manhattan Island.
1620s–1650s	A series of forts and trading outposts established along the Delaware River as far upstream as Trenton.
1670s	After a series of Indian on Indian conflicts, the Five Nations Iroquois claim authority over the Lenape. The power of the Susquehannock Indians in relation to trade with Europeans comes to an end.
1670s–1680s	Colonial settlements established in the area of Trenton.
1674	The English supplant the Dutch as the colonial power on the Delaware and Hudson rivers.
1677	The Lenape could recall three smallpox epidemics that had affected their people.
1680s	Philadelphia established as a town.
1718s–1750s	Groups of Lenape begin migrations out of their traditional territories.
1737	The "Walking Purchase" concludes the colonial government's acquisition of the southeastern portion of Pennsylvania.
1746	Indian town of Bethel established in New Jersey.
1754	Governor Robert Morris of Pennsylvania offers cash bounties for Indian scalps and declared war on the Delaware Indians. The French and Indian War is in progress.
1755–1763	Series of frontier forts established in the Upper Delaware Valley.
1758	The Brotherton Indian Reservation established in New Jersey.
1765	Large portions of southern New Jersey (Pine Barrens) remain unsettled by Europeans.

Sources: Appel 1991; Cotter et al 1992; Custer 1996:Table 26; Flemming 2005; Grossman et al 2009; Grumet 1989; Hunter Research, Inc. 2009; Kraft 2001:353-448; Newcomb 1956; Revey 1984; Schutt 2007; Wacker 1982; Walling n.d.; Weslager 1972, 1978; Williams and Kardas 1982.

Table 1.2. American Indian Sites of the Historic Period in the Delaware River Basin and Environs*

New York (Delaware River Basin)	Van Etten, Orange County (Alterman 1996; Burmaster 1909; Cushman 2007; Heye and Pepper 1915; Pietak 1999)
Pennsylvania (Delaware River Basin)	36WY44 (Grumet 1995; **PASS files)
	Dayton Pond, 36Wy125 (Grumet 1995; **PASS files)
	Zimmerman, 36Pi14 (Cushman 2007; Werner 1972)
	Faucett, 36Pi13a (Moeller 1975, 1992)
	Manna, 36Pi4 (Kinsey 1972:1A; Perazio et al. 2003; Pietak 1995; Stewart et al. 2005)
	Krueger, 36Mr179 (Donald Kline, 2001 personal communication)
	Camp Ministerium, 36Mr8 (Donald Kline, 2010 personal communication)
	Wordsworth/Camp Wyomissing, 36Mr18 (Donald Kline, 1999 personal communication)
	36Mr27 (Stuart Bailey, 1988 personal communication; Basilik et al. 1989)
	Gemeinhaus National Historic Landmark, Northampton County (National Park Service 1987)
	Lehigh Gap Burials, Northampton County (Cushman n.d.)
	Martins Creek Burials, Northampton County (Cushman n.d.)
	36Lh188 (**PASS files)
	Saucon Creek Valley Burial, Lehigh County (Anderson 1992)
	36Bk357 (Grumet 1995; **PASS files)
	Ingefeld/Maxatawny, 36Bk450 (Becker 1980; **PASS files)
	Bluebead, 36Bk590 (Grumet 1995; **PASS files)
	Kutztown Cemetery, Berks County (Cushman n.d.)
	Vermuhlen, 36Bu20 (Grumet 1995; **PASS files)
	Overpeck, 36Bu5 (Forks of the Delaware, Chapter 14, 1980; Witthoft 1994)
	Diehl, 36Bu1 (Pietak 1995; Witthoft n.d.)
	Thousand Acre Rockshelter, Bucks County (Pietak 1995; Strohmeier 1985)
	Sweetwater, 36Bu57 (Grumet 1995; **PASS files)
	Pemberton Family Cemetery, 36Bu179 (Becker 1990; Witthoft 1951)

	Playwicki Farm, 36Bu173 (Moore 2007; Stewart 1999b)
	Pennsbury Manor, 36Bu19 (**PASS files; Witthoft 1994)
	Bristol Burial, Bucks County (Veit and Bello 1999)
	Unami Creek Rockshelter, 38Mg19 (Pietak 1995; Strohmeier 1980)
	Goods Field, 36Mg124 (Grumet 1995; **PASS files)
	36Mg219 (**PASS files)
	Schuylkill Crossing 2 Site, 36Mg395 (**PASS files)
	Hartenstine Heritage Site 3A, 36Mg346, (**PASS files)
	Rittenhousetown 207 & 207A, 36Ph104 (**PASS files)
	Governor Printz Park, Printzhof Site, 36De3 (**PASS files; Becker 1993)
	Caleb Pusey House, 36De4 (**PASS files)
	Sandilands House Site, 36De40 (**PASS files)
	Pyle, 36De126 (**PASS files)
	Broomall Rockshelter, Delaware County (Butler 1947; Cotter et al. 1992; Smith 1956)
	Montgomery, 36Ch60 (Becker 1978; Cotter et al. 1992; Pietak 1999; Weslager 1953, 1956)
	North Brook, 36Ch61 (Becker 1980; Pietak 1995; Weslager 1953)
	Darlington Corners Historical Complex, 36Ch608 (**PASS files)
	Horseshoe Rockshelter, 36Ch488 (McConaughy 2006; Pietak 1995)
New Jersey (Delaware River Basin)	Bevans Rockshelter, Sussex County (Cross 1948)
	Davenport, Sussex County (Leslie 1968)
	Minisink, 28Sx48 (Kraft 1978; Philhower 1953, 1954)
	Bena Kill Mine Road, 28Sx256 (Grumet 1995)
	Pratschler, 28Sx255 (Grumet 1995)
	Bell-Browning, 28Sx19 (Marchiando 1972; Puniello and Williams 1978)
	Friedman II, Sussex County (Marchiando 1970; Puniello and Williams 1978; Santone 1999)
	28Sx324 (Botwick and Wall 1994)

	Bell-Philhower/Ahalocking, 28Sx29 (Kraft 1978, Philhower 1953, 1954; Pietak 1995)
	Pahaquarra, Warren County (Kraft 1976)
	Harry's Farm, Warren County (Kraft 1975)
	Miller Field, Warren County (Kraft 1972)
	Zipser Lower Field, Warren County (Puniello and Williams 1978; Salwen 1972; Williams 1972)
	Calno School Burial, Warren County (Puniello and Williams 1978; Pietak 1995; Santone 1999)
	Mill Brook Findspot, Warren County (Becker 1990; Grumet 1995)
	Area D, 28Me1-D (Wall et al. 1996a)
	Sturgeon Pond, 28Me114 (Wall and Stewart 1996)
	Douglas Gut Archaeological Complex, 28Me273 (Hunter Research, Inc. 2002)
	Old Barracks, 28Me215 (Hunter Research, Inc. 1991, 1994)
	Abbott Farm National Landmark (AFNL), 28Me1: Excavation 2 (Cross 1956)
	AFNL, 28Me1: Excavation 9 (Cross 1956)
	AFNL, 28Me1: Excavation 12 (Cross 1956)
	AFNL, 28Me1: Excavation14 (Cross 1956)
	Lalor Field, Mercer County (Volk 1911)
	Rowan Farm, Mercer County (Veit and Bello 2001a; Volk 1911)
	Indian Burial Ground, Mercer County, Trenton (Veit and Bello 2001a, b)
	Bordentown, 28Me37 (Cross 1941)
	Thompson Park, 28Mi243 (Grossman-Bailey et al. 2009; Grossman-Bailey and Hayden 2009)
	Lenhardt-Lahaway, Monmouth County (Cross 1941; Cushman 2007; Veit and Bello 2002)
	Burlington Island, Burlington County (Veit and Bello 1999)
	Burr/Haines, 28Bu414 (Cosans-Zebooker and Thomas 1993)
	Grantberry Farm, Burlington County (Pagoulatos 2007)
	NJ-27, Burlington County (Pagoulatos 2007)
	NJ-28, Burlington County (Pagoulatos 2007)

	Sandhicky, Burlington County (Pagoulatos 2007)
	Murray, Burlington County (Cross 1941)
	Farnum Park, Camden County (Pagoulatos 2007)
	Marcel Haines, Camden County (Pagoulatos 2007)
	Gloucester City, 28Ca50 (MAAR Associate, Inc.1985; Thomas 1990; Thomas and Schiek 1988)
	Goose Island, Gloucester County (Cross 1941; Kier 1952)
	Salisbury, Gloucester County (Cross 1941; Kier 1952)
	Narraticon Village, Gloucester County (Kier 1948)
	Boni Farm, Gloucester County (Mounier 1974, 2003)
	Edwards Run, 28GL304 (Bourgeois et al. 2003; Grossman-Bailey and McEachen 2003)
	Nicolosi Farm, Salem County (Pagoulatos 2007)
	Ware, 28Sa3 (McCann 1950; Pietak 1995)
New Jersey (Atlantic Coastal Areas)	Brielle, Monmouth County (Pagoulatos 2007)
	West Long Branch, Monmouth County (Pietak 1995; Veit and Bello 2002)
	West Creek, 28Oc45 (Stanzeski 1996, 1998)
	Penella, 28Oc60 (Stanzeski n.d.)
	Johnson, Ocean County (Cross 1941)
	Mays Landing, Atlantic County (Pagoulatos 2007)
	Steel Site, Atlantic County (Pagoulatos 2007)
	Cape May Point Site, Cape May County (Cook 1969)
New Jersey (Adjacent Areas of New York)	Potake Pond, Rockland County, NY (Lenik 1987)
	Springhouse Rockshelter, Rockland County, NY (Grumet 1995)
	Ramapo Rockshelter, Rockland County, NY (Funk 1976)
	Todd Rockshelter, Sussex County (Cross 1941)
	Maple Grange, 28Sx297 (Santone et al. 1995)
	Monksville Reservoir, 28Pa136 (Lenik and Ehrhardt 1986)
	Apshawa Rockshelter, Passaic County (Lenik 1989)
	Echo Lake, Passaic County (Lenik 1976)
	LaRoe-Van Horn House, Bergen County (Lenik 1989)
	Darlington Rock House, Bergen County (Heusser 1923; Lenik 1989)

	Darlington Rockshelter, Bergen County (Bischoff and Kahn 1979; Lenik 1989)
	Wilder Mons, Bergen County (Lenik 1989)
	David Demarest House, Bergen County (Lenik 1985)
	Prospect Street, Bergen County (Lenik 1989)
	Stag Run I, 28Be171 (Cultural Resource Group, Louis Berger and Associates 1994)
	Wards Point, Richmond County, NY (Jacobsen and Grumet 1995)
	Rossville, Richmond County (Ceci 1977; Pietak 1995; Skinner 1909)
	Watchogue, Richmond County (Ceci 1977; Pietak 1995; Skinner 1909)
	Old Place/Tumissens Neck, Richmond County (Ceci 1977; Pietak 1995; Skinner 1909)
	Ryders Pond , Kings County, NY (Lopez and Wisniewski 1972-1973)
Delaware (Delaware River Basin)	Churchmans Marsh, 7NC-E-60 (Custer et al. 1998)
	7NC-E-42 (Custer 1982; Custer and Watson 1985)

*See Figures 1.2 and 1.3 for general site locations. Sites situated outside of the Delaware River Basin proper are included here owing to the territory traditionally ascribed to the Munsee, Lenape, or Delaware Indians. Sites attributed to migrations from original territories are not included in the listings.

**PASS = Pennsylvania Archaeological Site Survey

mortuary features and related sites from all portions of the Delaware River Basin and environs.

An overriding theme in many of the publications noted above is trade between Native peoples and Europeans. Pagoulatos's work is specifically focused on an analysis of settlement patterns. Becker (1980) conducted extensive surface surveys of historically documented Lenape summer stations. Cushman (2007, n.d.) and Pietak (1995, 1998, 1999) provide detailed analyses of mortuary behaviors, comparing and contrasting them with those of the Late Woodland period. Santone (1998, 1999) uses archaeological and ethnohistoric data to address the resiliency and maintenance of Munsee identity, also relying heavily on burial data. The archaeological recognition of American Indian families who adopted aspects of European colonial life is addressed by Cosans-Zebooker and Thomas (1993), Heite Consulting, Inc. (1997), and Heite and Blume (1999). Comparative analyses of sites and artifact assemblages are presented by Veit (1994), and Veit and Bello (1999, 2001a, 2002). Detailed studies of the stone tool technologies employed by Native peoples are rare in the region. The work of Moore (1999) and Picadio (1999) are examples of exceptions to this trend.

Historic period components were recognized on many of the sites included in Table 2 only as a result of intensive, large area excavations that eventually revealed the presence of a handful of European-made artifacts. Without the areal coverage and the chance finds, registering a historic component rather than a Late Woodland one would have been problematic if not impossible. Examples of sites where component separation was not as difficult include Minisink (Kraft 1978), Playwicki Farm (Moore 2007; Stewart 1999b), Burr/Haines (Cosans-Zebooker and Thomas 1993), Churchmans Marsh (Custer et al. 1998), and 7NC-E-42 (Custer 1982; Custer and Watson 1985).

The Insights of American Indian Archaeology

LOCATING RELEVANT SITES

There always has been a problem with studying the archaeological record of the American Indian side of contact and the historic period. Maps and documents indicate where settlements were generally located. The number of such settlements is substantial, yet the history of archaeological research reveals how difficult these sites are to find. The inventory shown in Table 1.2 is a very pale reflection of what could, or should, be awaiting discovery. Figures 1.2 and 1.3 illustrate the general distribution of archaeological sites in Pennsylvania and New Jersey.

The Susquehannock Indians, with primary settlements in the lower Susquehanna Valley, had access to European trade goods between 1575 and 1600 (Kent 1984). Susquehannock Indian pottery is found on sites throughout the Delaware Valley (e.g., Kraft 1975, 2001; Stewart 1998b), implying that the Lenape and Munsee probably had knowledge of Europeans and indirect access to their goods. Yet study area sites with assemblages that include Susquehannock pottery have played an insubstantial role in the definition of contact/historic period components and how their archaeology contributes to synthetic studies of the time.

Historic documents contain laundry lists of the variety and quantity of items that Europeans were trading to the Indians. Many of these objects are durable enough to be preserved in archaeological deposits. The list of exchanged goods from the 1682–1683 indenture between William Penn and the Indians in which the Indian town of Playwicky is mentioned serves as an example:

> 20 white blankets, 20 kettles (4 large), 40 hoes, 20 guns, 20 coats, 40 shirts, 40 pairs of stockings, 40 axes, 2 barrels of powder, 200 bars of lead, 200 knives, 200 small glasses, 12 pairs of shoes, 40 copper boxes, 40 tobacco tongs, 2 small barrels of pipes, 40 tobacco boxes, 40 pairs of scissors, 40 combs, 24 pounds of red lead, 100 awls, 2 handfuls of fishhooks, 2 handfuls of needles, 40 pounds of shot, 10 bundles of beads, 10 small saws, 12 drawing knives, 4 ankers of tobacco, 2 ankers of rum, 2 ankers of cider, 2 ankers of beer, 300 guilders of money (Myers 1970:73–74; Underhill 1934:10).

It is to our advantage that the material culture of American Indians and Europeans is so different; evidence of their interaction is more visible archaeologically. But therein lies the problem. For years the archaeological study of Native peoples during the historic period has been hampered by our assumptions of what relevant sites or deposits should look like. That is, we were looking for sites loaded with European trade goods and structurally different from their pre-contact precursors. The reality, documented by excavations throughout the study area, is that relatively few items of European manufacture are found on sites, and when they are found, occur in greatest frequency in mortuary features (Cushman 2007, n.d.; Cushman and Stewart 2008; Pietak 1995; Santone 1999; Stewart 1999b, 2006, 2009).

In referring to the territory of the Munsee and Lenape, Kraft states that, "Objects made from copper or brass are equally rare on any site in Lenapehoking. Not more than six brass pots are known from throughout Lenapehoking, mostly from the Bell Browning and Minisink sites in the upper Delaware River Valley" (2001:391). His observations are not unusual. Remarkably, the paucity of European trade goods on sites throughout the study area is not a reflection of haphazard surface surveys, small or insufficiently excavated areas. For example, the dense and extensive deposits of the Minisink, Bell-Browning, and Bell-Philhower sites are distributed over adjacent landscapes that have been the focus of intensive excavations for over 50 years. For over 100 years, the numerous sites encompassed by the Abbott Farm National Landmark near Trenton have been the focus of the most massive, spatially extensive excavations ever conducted in the Middle Atlantic Region. The small number of European trade goods resulting from this work led Cross (1956:164) to conclude that the area was abandoned by the Indians shortly after contact with Europeans, an interpretation not supported by later research. An excavation area measuring roughly 450 feet by 250 feet at 28Me1D produced a single European-made artifact, an iron spud, in a context radiocarbon dated to the eighteenth century (Wall et al. 1996a). At the Playwicki Farm, excavations sufficient to

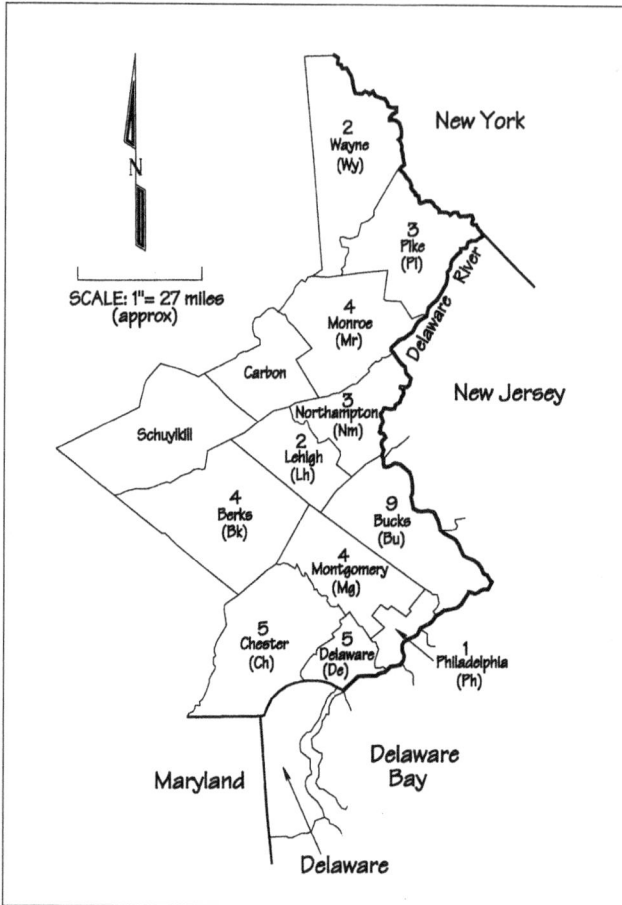

Figure 1.2. Pennsylvania portions of the study area showing counties (with abbreviations used in archaeological site designations) and the number of known historic period sites per county. Map by Allie Stewart.

delineate two structures nearly 40 feet in diameter and nearby features resulted in the discovery of a total of three artifacts of European manufacture (Moore 2007; Stewart 1999b).

The discrepancy between the documentary record dealing with Indian-European trade and archaeological expressions of this trade has been noted by archaeologists for quite some time (Kraft 1989; Lenik 1989; Pietak 1995; Santone 1998; Veit and Bello 2002; Williams and Kardas 1982). It is not clear, however, that these realizations have had an appreciable impact on field methods and archaeological systematics. As will be discussed below, American Indian sites of the historic period closely resemble their Late Woodland predecessors; without the presence of a smattering of European trade goods one could be mistaken easily for the other. This realization—coupled with attention to site formation processes, the use of independent data sets relevant to the age of contexts, and broad area excava-

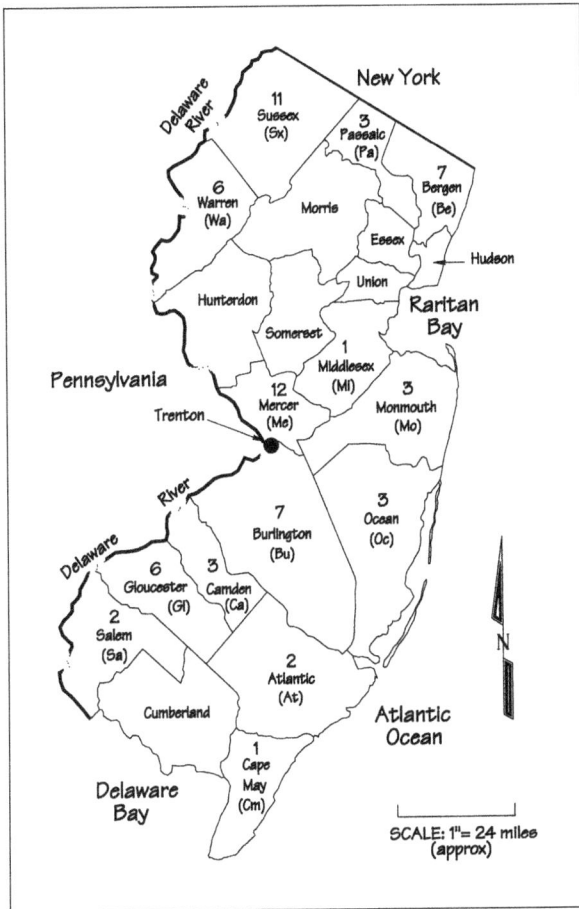

Figure 1.3. New Jersey portions of the study area showing counties (with abbreviations used in archaeological site designations) and the number of known historic period sites per county. Map by Allie Stewart.

tions—will increase the discovery and visibility of historic period sites. The existence of sites like Burr/Haines (Cosans-Zebooker and Thomas 1993) underscores the critical importance of adherence to archaeological systematics. At Burr/Haines, an assemblage of Native-made and English colonial artifacts is associated with a mid-eighteenth-century colonial structure. The deposit is interpreted as an American Indian household.

What remains to be understood is how European-made goods are being distributed, used, and integrated into American Indian craft traditions and society. Where are the missing trade goods? These and related issues are explored next.

TRADE

> We know that tomahawks, hoes, axes, adzes, awls, fish-hooks,
> guns, knives, beads, wampum, and a thousand other things were

> given the Indians by the whites, yet how rarely do we find an
> iron trade ax, a brass arrow point, or a glass bead . . . I cannot
> explain it [Skinner and Schrabisch 1913:30].

Major European outposts and settlements bracket and penetrate the territory of the Delaware Indians from the initial time of frenzied European interest in the fur trade to the establishment and maintenance of a colonial presence. If there ever was a time and place where trade goods should exist in profusion, the study area is it. Yet the reverse is what the archaeological record reveals.

Geographic proximity to European trading centers or settlements does not seem to be a factor influencing the frequency distribution of trade items. The Upper Delaware Valley may have been peripheral to more frequent interactions between Indians and Europeans, a refuge of sorts for Munsee-speaking groups, until well into the eighteenth century (Grumet1991, 1995; Santone1998:118, 1999:28). Yet the pattern of finding few items of European origin outside of mortuary contexts is seen in this area as well. Nor is the paucity of trade goods limited to a specific segment of the historic period; the pattern persists from the seventeen century well into the mid and late eighteenth century.

A number of factors have been proposed that may have impacted the degree to which the Indians had access to trade goods (Kraft 1989:22, 1991, 2001:347; Mounier 2003:121–122). Given the early presence of Europeans in the area as well as the ecology and relatively small size of the Delaware's territory, the Indians' ability to produce furs for trade may not have been maintained for any great length of time. Related to this may have been the Susquehannock's more dominant role in the trade of the region, and the variable nature of their relationship with the Lenape and others. The decline in regional populations, as a result of introduced diseases, may have also limited the size of the labor force that could participate in the hunting and production activities related to the fur trade. Sea level rise and urban development may have inadvertently destroyed sites of interest, too.

Some of these proposals have tentative support from a documentary perspective and could be tested with archaeological data in the future. However, even if we assume that the role of the Delaware Indians in the fur trade became insignificant early on, trade in deer hides, game meat, and maize would have continued to funnel European goods into Native communities (e.g., Becker 1995, 1999; Zimmerman 1966). Since the paucity of trade goods is a trend seen throughout the broader region and on sites in a variety of environmental settings, it is unlikely to be dramatically biased by the effects of sea level rise and urban development on archaeological deposits.

Schutt's (2007) discussion of the documentary record makes it clear how thoroughly European goods traded to the Indians were redistributed, regardless of the unique social and cultural background of individual recipients. Cultural notions of reciprocity, the maintenance of social relations, and alliance building meant that community representatives and heads of kin groups or households were circulating goods within and between settlements. Indian-to-Indian exchange of European goods employing traditional broad-based networks (Stewart 1989a) also would have served to disperse any initial concentrations of trade goods. Such redistribution, in a cultural milieu that prior to contact lacks rigid social ranking and the accumulation of material symbols of status, could go a long way in accounting for the frequency of European-made items on sites. In this vein, we should consider whether the quantity of European goods on a historic period site differs from the amount of Native trade goods that we would recognize on a Late Woodland site. My sense is that the quantities of trade goods will be similar, if we set aside what occurs in mortuary features of the historic period. Quantitative support of this relationship requires additional research.

The nature of non-ornamental trade goods recovered on archaeological sites reveals their curation as well as recycling and reuse, with final deposition often being in mortuary features. For example, flaked glass and mirrors found on the Harry's Farm and Pahaquarra sites were probably used as scrapers (Kraft 2001:382–381). Bottle and other glass flaked to create scraping margins also are found at Playwicki Farm (Stewart 1999b) and in Delaware at the Bloomsbury Site (Blume 1997; Heite Consulting, Inc. 1997).

Any European items gained in trade are integrated into longstanding Native technologies and the social relations in which they are embedded. Trade goods, whether of a practical, social, or ideological nature, are integrated into systems within which traditional material culture continues to function. Research on the contact or historic period throughout the country has shown that what was desired by Native peoples in trade with Europeans could be highly variable, and not just a matter of technology and function (Wilson and Rogers 1993:5). For example, in the Delaware Valley the color of cloth sought after in trade varied between Indian groups, many preferring red. Others desired cloth of blue and gray, maintaining that wearing red cloth hindered them in their hunting (Zimmerman 1974:65). Pietak's (1995, 1998, 1999). Research with bead color symbolism reveals cultural preferences in terms of personal ornamentation.

Owing to the difficulty in isolating the totality of historic period artifact assemblages on multi-component sites, a reliable assessment of what Native-made goods are being traded between Indian settlements is not possible. In the Delaware Valley, and the Middle Atlantic Region in general, trade in marine shell and shell artifacts continues from Late Woodland times (cf. Klein and Sanford 2004; Kraft 2001; Pendergast 1991).

The patterning of European trade goods in the Delaware Basin and its environs is different from what has been observed in other regions. In the mid Hudson Valley, which could be included in the definition of Munsee territory, the infrequent appearance of trade goods is replicated (Diamond 1996, 1999). Sites in the Susquehanna River Valley typically include greater quantities of trade goods in general, found in both mortuary and non-mortuary contexts (e.g., Custer et al. 1993; Kent 1984). The same can be said for the Upper Potomac River Valley (Wall 2004).

Discrepancies between Delaware Valley sites and sites to the north in Iroquois territory were noted long ago (Skinner and Schrabisch 1913:30).

The concentration of European goods in American Indian mortuary features is a behavior distinctive from the practices of the Late Woodland period and has implications for the nature of Native society. Together with an examination of traditional crafts that persist well into the historic period, the context for understanding trade with Europeans is enhanced.

TECHNOLOGY AND MATERIAL CULTURE

Statements regarding the abandonment of some Native crafts and the substitution of European goods for Native-produced ones can still be found in historical studies of the region (cf. Richter 2005:36; Strong 1997:146). The archaeological record, however, suggests otherwise. In fairness, some of these statements may be the result of generalizing about too broad of an area when more localized perspectives might reveal a variety of behaviors. As anthropologists and archaeologists, we accept that objects are integrated into cultural systems, are subject to manipulation, and serve technological as well as social and symbolic purposes. It is naïve, therefore, to assume that aspects of Indian material culture are readily abandoned and supplanted by European-made goods. Thought must be given to how the acquisition and acceptance of European tools and other goods affected the position and social relations of Native artisans, or anyone involved in aspects of the production of items of traditional material culture. Changes in the status quo are not to be taken lightly and might in fact be resisted by some.

Chipped stone and pottery technologies are represented on sites in all portions of the study area and date from the seventeenth century well into the mid-eighteenth century. For example, an assemblage dated between 1645 and 1680 from northern New Jersey basically resembles a Late Woodland one with the addition of small amounts of European trade goods (Lenik 1989:113). The Playwicki Farm in the valley's mid-section, estimated to date to the early eighteenth century, has an assemblage of projectiles, scrapers, flake tools, debitage, cobble tools, and pottery that are identical to the Late Woodland assemblages of the area. Detailed studies also reveal the use of bifacial and bipolar reduction techniques, the heat treatment of mediocre tool-stone, and tool-stone preferences that mimic those of the Late Woodland times (Moore 1999, 2007; Picadio 1999; Stewart 1999).

Farther downstream, a probable late-seventeenth- to early-eighteenth-century context at the Old Barracks in Trenton includes chipped stone projectile points and Native-made pottery (Hunter Research, Inc., 1991, 1994). The nearby deposits of the Douglas Gut Archaeological Complex, dated between 1620 and 1650, contain assemblages nearly identical to those of the Late Woodland occupations in the area, including large fragments of traditional pottery types (Hunter Research, Inc. 2002; Pagoulatos 2007: Table 2). The geographic diversity in Late Woodland pottery forming techniques—slab construction for upper portions of the drainage and coil construction the trend in mid and lower sections—is replicated in these and many other historic period sites.

From a national perspective, the survival of late prehistoric technologies following European contact occurs for incredibly different reasons; individual social, economic, and symbolic histories are critical to the eventual outcome (Cobb 2003a). Cobb (2003b:2) suggests that certain tools may do traditional types of work better than a European replacement. Alternatively, technology may be maintained because it is closely equated with cultural identity.

If the late prehistoric production of stone implements in the study area involved few or no specialists (i.e., individuals are producing tools for their own or household use), then trading for metal tools that could be used to do the same types of work during the historic period would not automatically undermine the social status of Native artisans. Trading for metal tools would also not require that the expedient manufacture and use of stone tools be abandoned, at least in situations where it was fairly easy to procure tool-stone. Metal tools would have made many forms of traditional work easier, and documents indicate that such implements were sought in trade by the Indians (Kraft 2001:377). The persistence of stone tool technology also might relate to the Indians inability to obtain sufficient numbers of metal implements capable of accommodating the amount of cutting, scraping, and chopping activities being undertaken.

Guns were difficult to come by, in part because of restrictions imposed by colonial law. The continued use of the bow and arrows with triangular, chipped stone heads makes sense in such a context. The maintenance and continued operation of firearms would foster continual Indian reliance on Europeans, if for no other reason than to obtain gunpowder and lead for the production of shot. The desire to avoid such relations on the part of some groups may have also contributed to the persistence of traditional weaponry.

Cobble-based tools, many of which may have been used for milling purposes, are the single largest artifact category (exclusive of flake waste) in the Playwicki Farm assemblage. They also are a common artifact on many sites assigned to the historic period. These implements, along with scrapers ostensibly employed in hide working, may be examples of traditional tools that performed as well as anything that could be obtained from Europeans. One need only look to the historic longevity of basketry and tree stump mortars and wooden pestles to realize that Indian peoples simply did not need or want certain things from Europeans (see illustrations in Feest 1978:Figures 5–8; Goddard 1978: Figure 6).

Are the quantities of European-made tools and implements found on a given site, including those in mortuary contexts, sufficient to satisfy the existing technological needs of a household or community? The minimum number of pots estimated for the late prehistoric/"tribal" components of the Faucett and Brodhead sites in the Upper Delaware Valley is 26 and 8 respectively (Kinsey 1972:171, 194–195,

259). In light of estimates like these, it is difficult to imagine how even one brass kettle per Indian household could adequately serve the container needs related to cooking, resource processing, hauling, and storage without recourse to domestically crafted pottery, baskets, bark, and wooden containers. Even considering preservation factors—and the fact that European tools might wear out less rapidly than Native equivalents made of stone, clay, bone, plant fiber, and wood—the answer to my initial question would be no. If this conclusion is accepted, than regardless of how or why Native peoples sought out or ignored European products, traditional crafts must have persisted to some degree.

Following Cobb (2003a:2), there seems to be no single explanation for the decline or survival of stone technologies, or any technology for that matter, that can be applied cross-culturally. The situation beyond the Delaware Basin is certainly variable. To the west in the Susquehanna Valley, Kent (1984:145) believes that the production of pottery ceased by 1690. To the north in central New York, the Onondaga Iroquois are thought to have abandoned stone technology by the mid-1600s (Bradley 1987). In southern New England, stone tools are in use by the Narragansetts and other groups well into the seventeenth century (Nassaney and Volmar 2003).

I have used the term persistence in the above discussion to refer to the existence of various American Indian crafts over a broad geographic area and spanning over 150 years. The data base of historic period sites is admittedly small, even smaller for sites where artifact assemblages are not inextricably mixed with those of earlier occupations. Because of this, it is possible that future, more chronologically fine-grained research could reveal localized cycles of craft decline and revival, rather than the overarching pattern of the continuity of craft traditions that current data support.

COMMUNITY AND SETTLEMENT PATTERNS

The same wide range of environmental settings in which Late Woodland sites occur is mirrored by the locations of American Indian sites throughout much of the historic period (cf., Pagoulatos 2001, 2007; Stewart 1987b; Stewart and Cavallo 1983; Stewart et al. 1986; Wall et al. 1996b:232–333). Most, if not all historic sites, contain pre-contact components. Nearly 100 years after initial contact, some Native groups continue to establish settlements and camps in areas where their ancestors did, while other groups have dramatically altered their use of the landscape (Stewart 1999, 2006). The extent and orientation of Indian paths (e.g., Boyd 2005; Wallace 1993), defined primarily on the basis of documentary research, implies the widespread interaction of Native peoples throughout the study area, and the Middle Atlantic Region, throughout the historic period.

Pagoulatos's (2007) settlement pattern study is useful for its documentation of sites and associated environmental settings within physiographic provinces. I am uncomfortable, however, with his attempts at using available data to define occupation types, subsequently employed in the modeling of settlement patterns. One assumption of his analysis, illustrated by his exclusive focus on New Jersey sites, is that the settlement movements of any American Indian group did not involve crossing the Delaware River. While this is in accord with Becker's (e.g., 1988a, 2009) various readings of the documentary record, it is an observation needing thorough testing with archaeological data. Pagoulatos's analysis also makes assumptions about the nature of individual occupations on sites where the non-European portion of artifact assemblages and features are difficult, if not impossible, to separate from those of the Late Woodland period. The observation that settlement systems of the Upper Delaware Valley characterize collectors and those of mid and lower segments of the drainage foragers (Binford 1980) relies on the presence or absence of what Pagoulatos terms Base 1 occupations with relative residential stability a key attribute. The absence of Base 1 occupations in lower sections of the valley is critical in Pagoulatos's assessment of regional differences in settlement patterns.

On the basis of published data, and taking into account caveats regarding the separation of components and the need for some intuitive leaps of faith, I believe that hamlet style settlements exhibiting relative residential stability can be found throughout the Delaware Valley. In the Upper Delaware Valley, the Minisink and Miller Field sites fit this characterization and date to the mid or late seventeenth century. In the valley's midsection, the size and intensity of deposits at the Overpeck site, and its association with a cemetery, could be construed as evidence of a relatively stable residential base (Cushman 2007, n.d.; Cushman and Stewart 2008; Forks of the Delaware 1980; Pietak 1995). Farther downriver at the transition from the Piedmont to Inner Coastal Plain, archaeological deposits at 28Me273 also resemble the house/living areas and associated features that characterize the Upper Delaware Valley sites and date to the mid-seventeenth century (Hunter Research, Inc. 2002). The presence of Native structures at the Printzhof Site (Becker 1993b), situated in the Lower Delaware Valley and possibly dating to the early historic period, might also represent a residential base. The sites that I have noted are situated in the floodplain or on terraces associated with the Delaware River in locations typical of Late Woodland hamlets or base camps.

The Playwicki Farm, a hamlet-like site, is located in the middle Delaware Valley and is an example of a dramatic shift in the location of such settlements (Moore 2007; Stewart 1999). The site dates to the early eighteenth century and is situated along a low order stream (Turkey Run). This type of setting is where archaeologists would typically find, at best, evidence of very small, temporary camps or short-term activities dating to pre-contact times. In contrast, the Playwicki Farm site contains the remnants of two, and possibly three large structures—what can easily be interpreted as a settlement meant to be occupied for a substantial period of time. In addition, the settlement exists in an area where there are many nearby colonial farmsteads and a town. In this context, the site's unusual setting cannot be explained as the relocation strategy of Native peoples in the face of European encroachment on traditionally settled landscapes.

Playwicki Farm also shows that elaborations are taking place in how Native people are constructing dwellings. The remains of two circular dwellings 40 feet in diameter were discovered, along with what may be a third dwelling of more traditional sub-rectangular size and shape comparable to the Late Woodland house patterns. The circular dwellings are built employing posts placed in an excavated wall trench, a technique unknown for earlier, pre-contact times, and not seen on any other historic period site in Delaware Indian territory. I have argued elsewhere (Stewart 1999) why the site should be affiliated with Delawarean peoples.

The Burr/Haines Site (Cosans-Zebooker and Thomas 1993) is another variation of American Indian settlement types of the eighteenth century. Easily mistaken for a colonial homestead, it reminds us of the role of human agency in response to colonial encounters.

The Area D Site (28Me1D), also dated to the eighteenth century, stands in contrast to Playwicki Farm and Burr/Haines in representing the long term use of a traditional setting (Wall et al. 1996a). The site is situated on fast ground in the freshwater tidal wetlands near Trenton. American Indians periodically camped in this spot for thousands of years, fishing and hunting. The location was still being used during the eighteenth century, more than100 years after first contact. Colonial settlements dating to the same period exist throughout the Trenton area (e.g., Hunter Research, Inc. 2009).

The archaeological record of historic period settlements is tantalizing but far from adequate for a full appreciation of how Native peoples organized their settlements and activities on the landscape. Nonetheless, data are sufficient to reveal that no single pattern will adequately characterize Delaware Indian behavior across time and space.

Mortuary Features and Implications for the Nature of Society

The most comprehensive treatment of these topics is found in the work of Cushman (2007, n.d.), Cushman and Stewart (2008), Kraft (2001:313–352), Lenik (1996), Pietak (1995, 1998, 1999) and Santone (1999). My brief summary cannot adequately convey the complexity of the data, analysis, and interpretations found in these sources, and readers are encouraged to consult them. Inferences gained from the biological analysis of human remains and burial populations are not addressed, although a relevant literature exists (e.g., Becker 1978; Byrne and Parris 1987; Clabeaux 1972).

Throughout the territory of the Delaware Indians, and evident during the entire span of the historic period, is the general (but not exclusive) pattern of interring individuals in the extended position. This contrasts with the general trend of body positioning seen in Late Woodland graves. Patterning in the orientation of the head and feet within the grave may serve to distinguish Munsee groups from Lenape. In the Upper Delaware Valley portion of Munsee Country (Grumet 1995:211–230), individuals are oriented with their heads to the west or southwest (Kraft 1978:55, 2001:345, 1999:26). An eastern orientation is typical of internments in portions of the study areas traditionally ascribed to the Lenape. These practices transcend the Late Woodland and historic periods revealing cultural continuity.

No clear explanations can be offered for the shift to the extended positioning of the dead. The shift is unlikely to reflect a Christian influence resulting from interactions with Europeans. The documentary record reveals that Native peoples reacted in highly variable ways to missionary efforts, and yet the change from flexed to extended forms of burial is a widespread pattern. In addition, grave goods representing Christian symbols are rare. The extended positioning of bodies may in some obscure way be influenced by the European use of coffins. However, the use of coffins is relatively rare among the Delaware, occurring only during the eighteenth century.

Historic period burials are more likely to be organized in a distinctive cemetery space, in contrast to the spatial patterning of mortuary features in and around residential and activity areas during Late Woodland times (Cushman 2007:155). The Overpeck Site (Forks of the Delaware 1980: Figure: 4) is probably the clearest example of this shift. The use of cemeteries may be signaling a change in the collective perception of the dead/ancestors and their role in maintaining and reaffirming Indian identity in the face of European encounters. Formal cemeteries could have also been used to mark and claim territories that were important to the Delaware because of the natural resources they encompass or provide access to or their socio-cultural significance (Cushman and Stewart 2008).

A greater number and variety of European goods are seen in the burials associated with historic period settlements than are found in general site contexts. Most of these objects were used in life, sometimes extensively, and were not just discarded anywhere, but saved for the grave. Prior to European contact, the extensive use of grave goods, especially items gained through trade, is not very common. Though the amount of goods in graves increases during historic times, on any given site roughly only one-third to one-half of the dead have associated grave goods, and these are typically European-made items (Cushman n.d.; Cushman and Stewart 2008).

There seems to be a shift in the perception of the value of material items taking place that we have yet to understand. European goods are used in secular/everyday contexts along with more traditional types of Native-made objects. Yet many of the European goods are deposited in sacred contexts (graves) while more traditional items are not. Native-made objects do occur in graves. But even these artifacts appear unusual in contrast to what is typically found in late prehistoric graves.

Utilitarian artifacts offered as grave goods often pattern by age and gender throughout the study area, indicating some shared beliefs when it came to appropriate grave goods. Ornaments are more frequently found in mortuary features than in general site contexts. Of those individuals buried with grave goods, females are just as likely as males to have them, and children often are more likely to have grave goods than adults. The reader should consult Cushman (2007, n.d.), Pietak (1995, 1998, 1999), and Santone (1999) for detailed discussions of burial associations.

If we accept the dramatic degree to which Native populations were decimated by introduced diseases or conflicts, then we must also consider that social relations and interactions within and between Indian communities were altered as a consequence (Ferguson 1993:53; Lightfoot 1995). The treatment of the dead provides one venue for assessing the nature of a society. Mortuary treatments need not directly reflect the status individuals had in life or broader social relations; mortuary behaviors are subject to manipulation by the living (Chesson 2001; Hodder 1982:10; Pearson 1999:32; Silverman and Small 2002). In fact, the "egalitarian" face of mortuary behavior could be viewed as a societal proscription preventing ritual from being used to promote the agendas of the living (Pearson 1982:110–112). The lack of grave goods might be a signal that public expressions of status or identity are controlled or limited, masking social relations evident among the living.

The increase in the use of grave goods during the historic period, many of European origin, and the degree to which children are associated with them, suggest that Delaware Indian society is becoming more differentiated, with a growing diversification of status roles (Pietak 1995; Santone 1999:27). That this diversification does not reach the level of ascribed status, I think, is seen in the quantitative nature of the data. If children with grave goods are a sign of ascribed status, then we would expect to see an equal segment of the adult population with grave goods since they would represent older members of a child's kin group. This complements the view of Pietak (1995) and Santone (1999) that expressions of status diversification are evident in the mortuary ritual itself but are masked by the closing of the grave and the lack of above ground distinctions within a cemetery. In such a scenario, the living relatives manipulate perceptions of social relations during an internment, but the lack of above ground symbols of status are a societal proscription preventing ritual from being used to promote the agendas of the living.

Following Santone's (1999) analysis of Bragdon's (1996) research in southern New England, the gifting of children with grave goods also could be viewed as a sacrifice promoting community renewal. Children serve to renew society, and removing valued items from circulation by placing them in graves is a sacrifice made in the hope of future social renewal (i.e., the birth or "rebirth" of children).

Beyond the study area, changes in American Indian mortuary ritual show interesting parallels with practices in Delaware Indian territory. In the Appalachian Highlands of south-western Virginia, Lapham (2006:135) sees an "increased importance placed on the expression of social differences in material forms, at least in funerary contexts." Children and adolescents are the primary recipients of grave goods, predominantly ornaments, in portions of Virginia and North Carolina (Boyd 2004:167). A similar pattern involving children is seen in the Potomac Valley of West Virginia and Maryland (Wall 2004). In southern New England, Narragansett territory, burial sites of the historic period are larger, more centralized and segregated from living areas (Turnbaugh 1993:145–146, 157). There are more grave goods in historic burials than previously, and children of both sexes are most frequently associated with grave goods. Higher rates of mortality owing to introduced diseases, and dispersed communities sharing a centralized burial space, are factors suggested to have influenced the location of cemeteries away from any given residential area. The increase in the use of grave goods and the focus on children is seen as a departure from the generally egalitarian treatment of the dead in pre-contact times.

A number of the distinctive patterns in mortuary practices seen in Delaware Indian territory also occur throughout the much broader American Indian world of the historic period. The implication seems clear. Behind the changes that have been documented are Indian peoples responding to similar circumstances in very similar ways. Testing the interpretations that we craft to explain local change against data sets from adjacent regions should be of great benefit in the future.

Final Thoughts

Contact and subsequent interaction between radically different cultures is a great laboratory for examining socio-cultural processes, cultural perceptions, human agency, human ecology, and the impact of historical contingencies. Historic period studies are in the unique position of integrating the insights of archaeological, historical, and anthropological research to provide multiple, complementary, emic/etic views of the past. No single model will accurately describe the "contact" and Indian-European experience, nor explain why things happened the way that they did. And while it is obvious that Indian peoples lost much as a result of European contact, they were not passive actors in the interactions that took place; they continued to maintain and elaborate upon pre-contact traditions.

American Indian culture in the Delaware River Basin and surrounding region is resilient throughout the seventeenth and eighteenth centuries. Many communities persist in their homelands long after major land sales, piecemeal migrations westward, the effects of introduced disease, and the often aggressive policies of the colonial government. Stone tool and ceramic technologies of Late Woodland/late prehistoric times persist through the seventeenth century and into the eighteenth century and are used in conjunction with European-made implements gained in trade. Items gained in trade are integrated into longstanding Native technologies and the social relations in which they are embedded. Trade goods, whether of a practical, social, or ideological nature, are integrated into the systems within which traditional material culture continues to function.

European trade goods are heavily curated and recycled, finding their most visible expression in burials. The nature and number of grave goods with a European origin reveals a shift in pre-contact Native mortuary practices. Mortuary features contain more grave goods, and goods of a more varied nature, than mortuary offerings associated with internments of the 1,000 years pre-dating contact with Europeans.

Burials tend to be placed in sacred spaces away from residential and work areas. The treatment of the dead indicates that social distinctions are becoming more marked.

The pattern in the use of European-made goods is one of the major reasons that archaeological surveys have failed to identify greater numbers of historic period settlements and activity areas dating to the time of contact with Europeans. Because such sites (excluding mortuary features) contain relatively few European goods, they are often mistakenly associated with the Late Woodland or late prehistoric period. The size and organization of individual settlements remain relatively consistent over time. However, the location and environmental setting of settlements, camps, and activity loci shift during the eighteenth century.

Throughout this chapter I have raised a number of issues that could and should be addressed with research in the future, and there are many more that deserve attention. One deals with the Indian intensification of hunting, whether for furs, hides, or game meat, in order to participate in European trade. This proposition is theoretically testable with archaeological data, and would involve comparative studies of faunal and tool assemblages from Late Woodland and historic period sites. If the production of hides or game meat is intensified because of their importance in trade, we should expect to see changes in the frequency, age, and sex with which certain species are represented in faunal assemblages as well as increases in the frequency of tools and implements related to their processing. Lapham's research (2004, 2006) provides an excellent model for structuring such endeavors. Productive intensification also has implications for gender roles in Native society if we accept that hide and game meat processing fell largely on the women of a community (Brasser 1978:84). Kraft (2001:372) assumes that intensification did occur, supported in part by European weaponry, and that it resulted in an ecological disaster and increased Indian reliance on European foodstuffs. Both of these assertions can be tested with well-established protocols for environmental reconstruction and dietary analysis. The laboratory analysis of human remains critical in such research, however, would need to be negotiated with the representatives of various Delaware Indian groups.

Finally, we should not forget that the Delaware remain a collection of thriving, vibrant communities throughout the Eastern Woodlands (Brown and Kohn 2008; Grant el al. 2007; Kraft 2001:531–578; Richter 2005) and that our research can have impacts beyond the scholarly realm. Let us renew or initiate efforts to share our individual concerns and work together in the future.

Acknowledgments

Many thanks are due to the individuals who provided information about relevant sites and sources including: Donald Kline (Mt. Bethel, Pennsylvania); Kurt Carr (William Penn Memorial Museum); Noel Stratton (Bureau for Historic Preservation, Pennsylvania Historical and Museum Commission); Ilene Grossman-Bailey (Richard

Grubb and Associates, Inc.); Greg Lattanzi (New Jersey State Museum); Jay Custer (University of Delaware); and Stu Bailey, Stroudsburg, Pennsylvania. Special thanks are owed Dustin Cushman (Temple University) for all of his insights and information on historic sites related to mortuary rituals. I am most grateful to Allie Stewart for drafting the graphics. I would never finish anything if not for her. Most importantly, I'd like to thank Rich Veit and Dave Orr for their encouragement and extreme patience while this chapter was being drafted.

References Cited

Allitt, Sharon, R. Michael Stewart, and Timothy Messner

2008   The Utility of Dog Bone (*Canis familiaris*) in Stable Isotope Studies for Investigating Prehistoric Maize Consumption: A Preliminary Study. *North American Archaeologist* 29(3–4):339–363.

Alterman, Michael

1996   The Van Etten Road Site: Native American and Dutch Settlement in the Upper Delaware Valley. Paper presented at the Annual Meeting of the Society for American Archaeology, New Orleans.

Anderson, David A.

1992   A Pewter Effigy Pipe from Pennsylvania in the Collections of the University Museum of Archaeology and Anthropology, University of Pennsylvania. *Pennsylvania Archaeologist* 62(1):73–78.

Appel, John C.

1991   Colonial-Native American Relations in Northeastern Pennsylvania, 1727–1787. In *The People of Minisink*, edited by David G. Orr and Douglas V. Campana, pp. 251–262. National Park Service Mid-Atlantic Region, Philadelphia.

Basilik, Kenneth I., Tom R. Lewis, Gale M. Treible, and David Rotenstein

1989   Archaeological Investigations at Shawnee-On-Delaware, Smithfield Township, Monroe County, Pennsylvania. Cultural Heritage Research Services, Inc., North Wales, Pennsylvania. Report on file, Bureau for Historic Preservation, Pennsylvania Historical and Museum Commission, Harrisburg.

Becker, Marshall J.

1978   Montgomery Site, 36–CH–60: Late Contact Lenape Site in Wallace Township, Chester County. Manuscript on file, the Pennsylvania Historical and Museum Commission, William Penn Memorial Museum, Harrisburg PA.

1980   Lenape Archaeology: Archaeological and Ethnohistorical Considerations in Light of Recent Excavations. *Pennsylvania Archaeologist* 50(4):19–30.

1983   The Boundary between the Lenape and the Munsee: The Forks of the Delaware as a Buffer Zone. *Man in the Northeast* 26:1–20.

1984   The Lenape Bands Prior to 1740: The Identification of Boundaries and Processes of Change Leading to the Formation of the "Delaware." In *The Lenape Indians: A Symposium*, edited by H.C Kraft, pp. 19–32. Seton Hall University Press, New Jersey.

1985   The European Contact/Early Historic Period in the Lenape Realm of Pennsylvania's Piedmont and Coastal Plain. In *A Comprehensive State Plan for the Conservation of Archaeological Resources,* Vol. II, edited by Paul Raber, pp. 41–52. Pennsylvania Historical and Museum Commission, Historic Preservation Planning Series No. 1, Harrisburg.

1986   Cultural Diversity in the Lower Delaware River Valley, 1550–1750: An Ethnohistorical Perspective. In *Late Woodland Cultures of the Middle Atlantic Region*, edited by Jay F. Custer, pp. 90–101. University of Delaware Press, Newark.

1988a   Native Settlements in the Forks of Delaware, Pennsylvania, in the Eighteenth Century: Archaeological Implications. *Pennsylvania Archaeologist* 58(1):43–60.

1988b   A Summary of Lenape Socio-Political Organization and Settlement Pattern at the Time of European Contact: The Evidence for Collecting Bands. *Journal of Middle Atlantic Archaeology* 4:79–83.

1990   The Origins of Trade Silver among the Lenape: Pewter Objects from Southeastern Pennsylvania as Possible Precursors. *Northeastern Historical Archaeology* 19:78–98.

1993a   The Lenape and Other "Delawarean" Peoples at the Time of European Contact: Population Estimates Derived from Archaeological and Historical Sources. *The Bulletin: Journal of the New York State Archaeological Association* 105:16–25.

1993b   Lenape Shelters: Possible Examples from the Contact Period. *Pennsylvania Archaeologist* 63(2):64–76.

1995   Lenape Maize Sales to the Swedish Colonists: Cultural Stability During the Early Colonial Period. In *New Sweden in America*, edited by Carol E. Hoffecker, Richard Waldron, Lorraine E. Williams, and Barbara E. Benson, pp.121–136. University of Delaware Press, Newark.1999
          Cash Cropping by Lenape Foragers: Preliminary Notes on Native Maize Sales to Swedish Colonists and Cultural Stability during the Early Colonial Period. *Bulletin of the Archaeological Society of New Jersey* 54:45–68.

2006   Anadromous Fish and the Lenape. *Pennsylvania Archaeologist* 76(2):28–40.

2009   Settlement Patterns of the Lenape and Their Neighbors in the Delaware Valley: Remembering Fantasies, Etc. *Newsletter of the Archaeological Society of New Jersey* 225:1, 4–7.

Binford, Lewis R.

1980   Willow Smoke and Dog's Tails: Hunter-Gatherer Settlement Systems
            and Archaeological Site Formation. *American Antiquity* 45(1):1–17.

Bischoff, Henry, and Michael Kahn

1979   *From Pioneer Settlement to Suburb: A History of Mahwah, New Jersey,*
            1700–1976. A.S. Barnes, South Brunswick, New Jersey.

Blume, Cara

1997   Artifacts from the Bloomsbury Site. Paper presented at the Annual
            Meeting of the Middle Atlantic Archaeological Conference, Ocean
            City, Maryland.

Bourgeois Vincent G., Charles R. Pennington, Steven E. Hardegen, Dennis Gunn,
            and Paul J. McEachen

2003   Archaeological Investigations, Weathervane Farms Residential De-
            velopment Plate 14, Block 1401, Lot 11, East Greenwich Township,
            Gloucester County, New Jersey. Manuscript on file, Richard Grubb &
            Associates, Cranbury, New Jersey.

Botwick, Bradford, and Robert D. Wall

1994   Prehistoric Settlement in the Upper Delaware Valley: Recent Survey
            and Testing in the Delaware Water Gap National Recreation Area.
            Journal of Middle Atlantic Archaeology 10:73–84.

Boyd, Clifford

2004   Evolutionary Archaeology: A Case Study from Virginia and North
            Carolina. In *Indian and European Contact in Context: The Mid-*
            Atlantic Region, edited by Dennis B. Blanton and Julia A. King,
            pp.149–171. University Press of Florida, Gainesville.

Boyd, Paul D.

2005   *Settlers Along the Shores: Lenape Spatial Patterns in Coastal Mon-*
            mouth County, 1600–1750. Ph.D. dissertation, Department of Geogra-
            phy, Rutgers University, New Brunswick, New Jersey.

Bradley, James W.

1987   *Evolution of the Onondaga Iroquois: Accommodating Change, 1500–*
            1655. Syracuse University Press, New York.

Bragdon, Kathleen J.

1996   *Native Peoples of Southern New England, 1500–1650.* The Civiliza-
            tion of the American Indian Series, University of Oklahoma Press,
            Norman.

Brasser, Ted

1978   Early Indian-European Contacts. In *Handbook of North American*
            Indians, Volume 15, The Northeast, edited by Bruce G. Trigger, pp.78–
            88. Smithsonian Institution Press, Washington, D.C.

Brose, David, Wesley Cowan, and Robert Mainfort

2001   *Societies in Eclipse: Archaeology of the Eastern Woodlands Indians,*
            AD 1400–1700. Smithsonian Institution Press, Washington, D.C.

Brown, James W., and Rita T. Kohn

2008   *Long Journey Home: Oral Histories of Contemporary Delaware Indi-
            ans.* Indiana University Press, Bloomington and Indianapolis.

Burmaster, Russell Evrett,

1909   Van Etten Site notes from the journal of Russell Everett Burmaster.
            Manuscript on file, New York State Museum, Albany NY.

Butler, Mary

1947   Two Lenape Rockshelters Near Philadelphia. *American Antiquity*
            12:246–254.

Byrne, Kevin B., and David C. Parris

1987   Reconstruction of the Diet of the Middle Woodland Amerindian Popu-
            lation at Abbott Farm by Bone Trace-Element Analysis. *American Jour-
            nal of Physical Anthropology* 74:373–384.

Ceci, Lynn

1977   *The Effect of European Contact and Trade on the Settlement Pattern
            of Indians in Coastal New York, 1524–1665: The Archaeological and
            Documentary Evidence.* Ph.D. dissertation, Department of Anthropol-
            ogy, City University of New York.

Chesson, Meredith S. (editor)

2001   *Social Memory, Identity, and Death: Anthropological Perspectives on
            Mortuary Rituals.* Archaeological Papers of the American Anthropo-
            logical Association No. 10. Arlington, Virginia.

Clabeaux, Marie Striegal

1972   Osteological Analysis of Disease in the Indians of New Jersey. *Bulletin
            of the Archaeological Society of New Jersey* 28:19–27.

Cobb, Charles R.

2003a   *Stone Tool Traditions in the Contact Era.* University of Alabama Press,
            Tuscaloosa.

2003b   Framing Stone Tool Traditions After Contact. In *Stone Tool Traditions
            in the Contact Era,* edited by Charles R. Cobb, pp.1–12. University of
            Alabama Press, Tuscaloosa.

Cook, Richard C.

1969   The Cape May Point Site: Ceramic Industry and European Trade Ma-
            terial. *Bulletin of the Archaeological Society of New Jersey* 24:19–20.

Cosans-Zebooker, Betty, and Ronald A. Thomas

1993   Excavations at the Burr/Haines Site, Burlington County, New Jersey.
            Bulletin of the Archaeological Society of New Jersey 48:13–20.

Cotter, John L., Daniel G. Roberts, and Michael Parrington

1992   *The Buried Past: An Archaeological History of Philadelphia.* University
            of Pennsylvania Press, Philadelphia.

Cross, Dorothy

1941   *Archaeology of New Jersey.* Vol. 1. Archaeological Society of New Jer-
            sey and the New Jersey State Museum. Trenton.

1948   The Bevans Rockshelter. *Bulletin of the Archaeological Society of New Jersey* 1:13–23.

1956   *Archaeology of New Jersey. Volume 2: The Abbott Farm*. Archaeological Society of New Jersey and the New Jersey State Museum. Trenton.

Cultural Resource Group, Louis Berger and Associates, Inc.

1994   Pahaquarra and Minisink Phases of the Late Woodland in the Ramapo River Valley. Report prepared for the New Jersey Department of Transportation, Trenton.

Cushman, Robert D.

2007   The Context of Death: Burial Rituals in the Delaware Valley. *Archaeology of Eastern North America* 35:153–160.

n.d.   *Death in the Valley: Cultural Change from the Late Woodland Through Historic Periods for the Delaware, As Inferred from Their Mortuary Rituals and Remains*. Ph.D. dissertation, Department of Anthropology, Temple University, Philadelphia, in progress.

Cushman, Robert D., and R. Michael Stewart

2009   Mortuary Practices and Social Complexity in the Delaware Valley of the Middle Atlantic Region. Paper presented at the Annual Meeting of the Society for American Archaeology, Atlanta, Georgia.

Custer, Jay F.

1982   The Prehistoric Archaeology of the Churchmans Marsh Vicinity: An Introductory Analysis. *Bulletin of the Archaeological Society of Delaware* 13:1–44.

1984   *Delaware Prehistoric Archaeology: An Ecological Approach*. University of Delaware Press, Newark.

1996   *Prehistoric Cultures of Eastern Pennsylvania*. Anthropological Series Number 7, the Pennsylvania Historical and Museum Commission, Harrisburg.

Custer, Jay F, Keith Doms, Adrienne Alleghretti, and Kristen Walker

1998   Preliminary Report on Excavations at 7NCE60, New Castle County, Delaware. *Bulletin of the Archaeological Society of Delaware* 35:1–27.

Custer, Jay F., and Scott Watson

1985   Archaeological Investigations at 7NCE42, A Contact Period Site in New Castle County, Delaware. *Journal of Middle Atlantic Archaeology* 1:97–116.

Custer, Jay F., Scott Watson, and Daniel N. Bailey

1993   Data recovery Investigations of the West Water Street Site, 36CN175, Lock Haven, Clinton County, Pennsylvania. Report on file, Bureau for Historic Preservation, Pennsylvania Historical and Museum Commission, Harrisburg.

Diamond, Joseph

1996   Terminal Late Woodland/Early Contact Period Settlement Patterns in the Mid-Hudson Valley. *Journal of Middle Atlantic Archaeology* 12:95–111.

1999   *The Terminal Late Woodland/Contact Period in the Mid-Hudson Valley*. Ph.D. dissertation, Department of Anthropology, State University of New York at Albany.

Donehoo, George P.

1977 [1928] *A History of the Indian Villages and Place Names in Pennsylvania*. Telegraph Press, Harrisburg, Pennsylvania.

Dunlap, A. R., and C. A. Weslager

1958   Toponymy of the Delaware Valley as Revealed by an Early Seventeenth-Century Dutch Map. *Bulletin of the Archaeological Society of New Jersey* 15–16:1–14.

Dwight, Sereno Edwards (editor)

1822   *Memoirs of the Rev. David Brainerd, Missionary to the Indians. . . Chiefly Taken from His Own Diary, by Rev. Jonathan Edwards, Including His Journal, Now. . . Incorporated With the Rest of His Diary*. S. Converse, New Haven, Connecticut.

Esposito, Frank J.

1976   *Indian-White Relations in New Jersey, 1609–1802*. Ph.D. dissertation, Department of Anthropology, Rutgers University, New Brunswick.

Feest, Christian F.

1978   Nanticoke and Neighboring Tribes. In *Handbook of North American Indians: Volume 15: Northeast* Edited by Bruce Trigger, pp.240–252. Smithsonian Institution Press, Washington, D.C.

Ferguson, R. Brian

1993   Explaining War. In *The Anthropology of War*, edited by J. Haas, pp.26–55. Cambridge University Press, Cambridge.

Flemming, George D.

2005   *Brotherton: New Jersey's First and Only Indian Reservation and the Communities of Shamong and Tabernacle That Followed*. Plexus Publishing, Inc., Medford, New Jersey.

Forks of the Delaware Chapter 14

1980   The Overpeck Site, 36BU5. *Pennsylvania Archaeologist* 50(3):1–46.

Funk, Robert E.

1976   *Recent Contributions to Hudson Valley Prehistory*. New York State Museum, Memoir 22, Albany.

Gallivan, Martin D.

2004   Reconnecting the Contact Period and Late Prehistory: Household and Community Dynamics in the James River Basin. In *Indian and European Contact in Context: The Mid-Atlantic Region*, edited by Dennis B. Blanton and Julia A. King, pp.22–46. University Press of Florida, Gainesville.

Goddard, Ives

1978   Delaware. *In Handbook of North American Indians: Volume 15: Northeast*, edited by Bruce Trigger, pp. 213–239. Smithsonian Institution Press, Washington, D.C.

Grant, Christine, Mariko Lockhart, Autumn Wind Scott, W. Cary Edwards, Henry
      Coleman, Nina Mitchell Wells, Lewis Pierce, and Megan Cordoma
2007   Report to Governor Jon S. Corzine. New Jersey Committee on Native
      American and Community Affairs, Trenton.

Grossman-Bailey, Ilene
2001   *The People Who Lived By The Ocean: Native American Resource Use
      and Settlement in the Outer Coastal Plain of New Jersey.* Ph.D. disser-
      tation, Department of Anthropology, Temple University, Philadelphia.

Grossman-Bailey, Ilene and Philip A. Hayden
2009   The Thompson Park Historic Site (28-Mi-243): Paper presented at a
      meeting of the Archaeological Society of New Jersey, Trenton.

Grossman-Bailey, Ilene, and Philip A. Hayden, with contributions by Michael J. Gall,
      Robert J. Lore, Adam Heinrich, Brenda Springsted, and Lauren J. Cook
2009   Phase II Archaeological Survey Monroe Township High School Block
      59, Part Of Lot 1.01 Monroe Township, Middlesex County, New Jer-
      sey. Richard Grubb and Associates, Cranbury, New Jersey. Report on
      file, Historic Preservation Office, Trenton, New Jersey.

Grossman-Bailey, Ilene, and Paul McEachen
2003   Mantua Creek Watershed Case Study. Paper presented at the Annual
      Meeting of the Eastern States Archaeological Federation, Mt Laurel,
      New Jersey.

Grumet, Robert S.
1979   *"We Are Not So Great Fools": Changes in Upper Delawaran Socio-
      Political Life, 1630–1758.* Ph.D. dissertation, Department of Anthro-
      pology, Rutgers University, New Brunswick, New Jersey.

1989   *Indians of North America: The Lenapes.* Chelsea House, New York
      and Philadelphia.

1991   The Minisink Settlements: Native American Identity and Society in the
      Munsee Heartland, 1650–1778. In *The People of Minisink*, edited by
      David G. Orr and Douglas V. Campana, pp.175–250. National Park
      Service Mid-Atlantic Region, Philadelphia.

1995   *Historic Contact: Indian People and Colonists in Today's Northeastern
      United States in the Sixteenth Through Eighteenth Centuries.* Univer-
      sity of Oklahoma Press, Norman and London.

Harbison, Jeff
2007   *Subsistence and Settlement in the Upper Delaware Valley: Excavation
      of the Shoemaker's Ferry Site (28WA278).* Master's thesis, Department
      of Anthropology, Temple University, Philadelphia, Pennsylvania.

Heckewelder, John G.
1819   *History, Manners, and Customs of the Indians Who Once Inhabited
      Pennsylvania and the Neighboring States.* Transactions of the Commit-
      tee of History, Moral Science and General Literature of the American
      Philosophical Society. Philadelphia.

1820   *Narrative of the Mission of the United Brethren Among the Delaware and Mohegan Indians from Its Commencement in the Year 1740 to the Close of the Year 1808.* McCarty and Davis, Philadelphia.

Heite Consulting, Inc.

1997   Archaeological Survey and Data Recovery in Duck Creek Hundred, Kent County, Delaware, for the Proposed Wetland Replacement in Connection with State Route 1. Draft report distributed as part of the symposium, Bloomsbury: Life on the Edge of Revolutionary Society. Annual Meeting of the Middle Atlantic Archaeological Conference, Ocean City, Maryland.

Heite, Edward, and Cara Lee Blume

1999   The "Invisible" Indians of Central Delaware. *Journal of Middle Atlantic Archaeology* 15:157–175.

Heusser, Albert H.

1923   *Homes and Haunts of the Indians.* The Benjamin Franklin Press, Patterson, New Jersey.

Heye, George G., and George H. Pepper

1915   *Exploration of a Munsee Cemetery Near Montague, New Jersey.* Contributions to the Museum of the American Indian, Heye Foundation 2(1). New York.

Hodder, Ian

1982   Theoretical Archaeology: A Reactionary View. In *Symbolic and Structural Archaeology*, edited by Ian Hodder, pp.48–53. Cambridge University Press, Cambridge.

Hunt, Charles

1967   *Physiography of the United States.* W.H. Freeman, San Francisco and London.

Hunter Research, Inc.

1991   Supplementary Archaeological Investigations at the Old Barracks, City of Trenton, Mercer County, New Jersey. Report on file, New Jersey Historic Preservation Office, Trenton.

1994   Additional Archaeological Studies in the Porch Area at the Old Barracks (28Me215), City of Trenton, Mercer County, New Jersey. Report on file, New Jersey Historic Preservation Office, Trenton.

2002   Archaeological Data Recovery Excavations and Monitoring, New Jersey Route 29, City of Trenton, Mercer County, New Jersey. Volume 1: Prehistoric Sites. Report prepared for the New Jersey Department of Transportation and the Federal Highway Administration. Trenton, New Jersey.

2009   The Abbott Farm National Historic Landmark Interpretive Plan: Cultural Resource Technical Document. Report prepared for Hamilton Township, Mercer County, Bordentown Township and the City of Bordentown, Burlington County, New Jersey.

Jacobsen, Jerome, and Robert S. Grumet
1995   Ward's Point Archaeological Site National Historic Landmark. *Bulletin of the Archaeological Society of New Jersey* 50:83–87.

James, Bartlett Burleigh and J. Franklin Jameson (editors)
1913   *Journal of Jasper Danckaerts, 1679–1680.* Charles Scribner's Sons, New York.

Jameson, J. Franklin (editor)
1937 [1909] *Narratives of New Netherland, 1609–1664.* Barnes and Noble, New York.

Johnson, Amandus
1925   *Geographia Americae, with an Account of the Delaware Indians, Based on Surveys and Notes Made in 1654–1656 by Peter M. Lindestrom.* Swedish Colonial Society, Philadelphia.

Kent, Barry
1984   *Susquehanna's Indians.* Anthropological Series No. 6, Pennsylvania Historical and Museum Commission, Harrisburg.

Kent, Barry, Janet Rice, and Kakuko Ota
1981   A Map of Eighteenth Century Indian Towns in Pennsylvania. *Pennsylvania Archaeologist* 4:1–18.

Kent, Donald H.
1979   *Pennsylvania and Delaware Treaties, 1629–1737.* University Press of America, Lanham, Maryland.

Kier, Charles F.
1948   A Narraticon Village Site in Gloucester County, New Jersey. *Bulletin of the Archaeological Society of New Jersey* 1:1–3.
1952   Return to Yesterday. *Bulletin of the Archaeological Society of New Jersey* 5:1–5.

King, Adam, James W. Hatch, and Barry Sheetz
1997   The Chemical Composition of Jasper Artifacts from New England and the Middle Atlantic: Implications for the Prehistoric Exchange of "Pennsylvania Jasper." *Journal of Archaeological Science* 24:793–812.

Kinsey, W. Fred, III
1972   *Archaeology in the Upper Delaware Valley.* Anthropological Series, Number 2. Pennsylvania Historical and Museum Commission, Harrisburg.
1975   Faucett and Byram Sites: Chronology and Settlement in the Delaware Valley. *Pennsylvania Archaeologist* 45(1–2):1–103.

Klein, Michael J., and Douglas W. Sanford
2004   Analytical Scale and Archaeological Perspectives on the Contact Era in the Northern Neck of Virginia. In *Indian and European Contact in Context: The Mid-Atlantic Region*, edited by Dennis B. Blanton and Julia A. King, pp.47–73. University Press of Florida, Gainesville.

Kraft, Herbert C.

1970   Prehistoric Indian House Patterns in New Jersey. *Bulletin of Archaeology Society of New Jersey* 26:1–11

1972   The Miller Field Site, Warren County, New Jersey. In *Archaeology in the Upper Delaware Valley,* edited by W.F. Kinsey, III, pp.1–54. Pennsylvania Historical and Museum Commission, Anthropological Series Number 2, Harrisburg.

1974   *A Delaware Indian Symposium.* Pennsylvania Historical and Museum Commission, Anthropological Series, No.4. Harrisburg.

1975   *The Archaeology of the Tocks Island Area.* Archaeological Research Center, Seton Hall University Museum. South Orange, New Jersey 07079.

1976   *The Archaeology of the Pahaquarra Site, Warren County, New Jersey.* Archaeological Research Center, Seton Hall University Museum, New Jersey.

1977   *The Minisink Settlements: An Investigation into a Prehistoric and Early Historic Site in Sussex County, New Jersey.* Archaeo-Historic Research, Elizabeth, New Jersey.

1978   *The Minisink Site: A Reevaluation of a Late Prehistoric and Early Historic Contact Site in Sussex County New Jersey.* Archaeo-historic Research, Elizabeth, New Jersey.

1984   *The Lenape Indian—A Symposium.* South Orange, NJ: Archaeological Research Center, Seton Hall University, Publication No. 7. South Orange, New Jersey.

1989   Sixteenth and Seventeenth Century Indian/White Trade Relations in the Middle Atlantic and Northeast Regions. *Archaeology of Eastern North America* 17:1–30.

1991   European Contact and Trade in the Lower Hudson Valley. In *The Archaeology and Ethnohistory of the Lower Hudson Valley and Neighboring Regions: Essays in Honor of Louis A. Brennan,* edited by Herbert C. Kraft, pp.193–221. Occasional Publications in Northeastern Anthropology No.11.

2001   *The Lenape-Delaware Indian Heritage: 10,000 BC to AD 2000.* Lenape Books, Elizabeth, New Jersey.

Lapham, Heather A.

2004   "Their Complement of Deer Skins and Furs": Changing Patterns of White-Tailed Deer Exploitation in the Seventeenth-Century Southern Chesapeake and Virginia Hinterlands. In *Indian and European Contact in Context: The Mid-Atlantic Region,* edited by Dennis B. Blanton and Julia A. King, pp.172–192. University Press of Florida, Gainesville.

2006   *Hunting for Hides: Deerskins, Status, and Cultural Change in the Protohistoric Appalachians.* University of Alabama Press, Tuscaloosa.

Lavin, Lucianne
1983   *Patterns of Chert Acquisition Among Woodland Groups Within the Delaware Watershed: A Lithologic Approach.* Ph.D. dissertation, Department of Anthropology, New York University.

Lenig, Wayne
1999   Patterns of Material Culture During the Early Years of New Netherlands Trade. *Northeast Anthropology* 58:47–70.

Lenik, Edward J.
1976   A Silver Brooch from Echo Lake. *Newsletter of the Archaeological Society of New Jersey* 102:6–7.
1985   Archaeological Investigations at the David Demarest House Site, River Edge, New Jersey. Manuscript on file, Sheffield Archaeological Consultants, Wayne, New Jersey.
1987   Cultural Resource Reconnaissance Survey of the Pierson Lakes Estates Property, Town of Ramapo, Rockland County, New York. Manuscript on file, Sheffield Archaeological Consultants, Wayne, New Jersey.
1989   New Evidence on the Contact Period in Northeastern New Jersey and Southeastern New York. *Journal of Middle Atlantic Archaeology* 5:103–120.
1996   The Minisink Site as Sacred Space. *Bulletin of the Archaeological Society of New Jersey* 51:53–63.

Lenik, Edward J., and Kathleen L. Ehrhardt
1986   Data Recovery Excavations in the Monksville Reservoir Project Area, Passaic County, New Jersey. Manuscript on file, Sheffield Archaeological Consultants, Wayne, New Jersey.

Leslie, Vernon
1968   The Davenport Site: A Study in Tocks Island Reservoir Archaeology. *The Chesopiean* 6(5):109–139.

Lightfoot, Kent
1995   Culture Contact Studies: Redefining the Relationship Between Prehistoric and Historical Archaeology. *American Antiquity* 60:199–217.

Lopez, Julius, and Stanley Wisniewski
1972–1973 The Ryders Pond Site, Kings County, New York. *New York State Archaeological Society Bulletin* 53 and 55.

MAAR Associates, Inc.
1985   Data Recovery at 28Ca50, Gloucester City, New Jersey. Report submitted to the National Park Service, Mid-Atlantic Region, Philadelphia, Pennsylvania.

Marchiando, Patricia
1970   Archaeological and Historical Survey and Selective Testing of Sites in the Tocks Island Reservoir. Manuscript on file, New Jersey State Museum, Trenton.

1972   Bell Browning Site, 28-Sx-19. In *Archaeology in the Upper Delaware
             Valley,* edited by W.F. Kinsey, III, pp. 131–158. Pennsylvania Histori-
             cal and Museum Commission, Anthropological Series Number 2,
             Harrisburg.

McCann, Catherine
1950   The Ware Site, Salem County, New Jersey. *American Antiquity*
             15(4):315–321.

McConaughy, Mark A.
2006   Horseshoe Rockshelter (36CH488). *Pennsylvania Archaeologist*
             76(1):20–47.

Messner, Timothy
2008   *Woodland Period People and Plant Interactions: New Insights From
             Starch Grain Analysis.* Ph.D. dissertation, Department of Anthropol-
             ogy, Temple University, Philadelphia.

Milner, George R., David G. Anderson, and Marvin T. Smith
2001   The Distribution of Eastern Woodlands Peoples at the Prehistoric and
             Historic Interface. In *Societies in Eclipse: Archaeology of the Eastern
             Woodlands Indians, AD 1400–1700,* edited by David Brose, Wesley
             Cowan, and Robert Mainfort, pp.9–18. Smithsonian Institution Press,
             Washington, D.C.

Moeller, Roger
1975   *Seasonality and Settlement Pattern of Late Woodland Components at
             the Faucett Site.* Ph.D. dissertation, Department of Anthropology, State
             University of New York at Buffalo.
1992   *Analyzing and Interpreting Late Woodland Features.* Occasional Pub-
             lications in Northeastern Anthropology 12. Archaeological Services,
             Bethlehem Connecticut.

Moore, Joseph
1999   Thermal Alteration Technology in a Historic Native American Village:
             Implications and Explanations from Playwicki. *Journal of Middle At-
             lantic Archaeology* 15:67–75.
2007   *Archaeological and Ethnohistorical Analysis of the Playwicki Farm
             Site, Pennsylvania.* Master's thesis, Department of Anthropology, Tem-
             ple University, Philadelphia.

Mounier, R. Alan
1974   An Archaeological Survey of a Section of the Pureland Industrial Park,
             Logan Township, Gloucester County, New Jersey. Manuscript on file
             with the author, Newfield, New Jersey.
2003   *Looking Beneath the Surface: The Story of Archaeology in New Jersey.*
             Rutgers University Press, New Brunswick, New Jersey.

Myers, Albert Cook (editor)
1912   *Narratives of Early Pennsylvania, West New Jersey and Delaware,
             1630–1707.* Scribners and Sons, New York.

1970 [1937] *William Penn's Own Account of the Lenni Lenape of Delaware Indians.* Middle Atlantic Press, Wilmington, Delaware.

Nassaney, Michael S., and Michael Volmar

2003   Lithic Artifacts in Seventeenth-Century New England. In *Stone Tool Traditions in the Contact Era*, edited by Charles R. Cobb, pp.78–93. University of Alabama Press, Tuscaloosa.

Pagoulatos, Peter

2001   Late Woodland Settlement Patterns of New Jersey. *Bulletin of the New Jersey Archaeological Society* 22(3):201–230.

2007   Native American Contact Period Settlement Patterns of New Jersey. *Bulletin of the New Jersey Archaeological Society* 62:23–40.

Pearson, Michael Parker

1982   Mortuary Practices, Society and Ideology: An Ethnoarchaeological Study. In *Symbolic and Structural* Archaeology, edited by Ian Hodder, pp.99–114. Cambridge University Press, Cambridge.

Pendergast, James F.

1991   *The Massawomeck: Raiders and Traders into the Chesapeake Bay in the Seventeenth Century.* Transactions of the American Philosophical Society, Volume 18 Part 2, Philadelphia.

Perazio, Philip., R., Michael Stewart, and Timothy Messner

2003   The Manna Site (36Pi4): Preliminary Report of the Temple University Field School. Paper presented at the Annual Meeting of the Eastern States Archaeological Federation, Mt. Laurel, New Jersey

Philhower, Charles A.

1953   The Historic Minisink Site. Part I. *Bulletin of the Archaeological Society of New Jersey* 7:1–9.

1954   The Historic Minisink Country. Part II. *Bulletin of the Archaeological Society of New Jersey* 8:1–7.

Picadio, Douglas

1999   Lithic Replication: Prehistoric Tool Technologies in the Historic Period, Bipolar Replication of Linear/Blade-Like Flakes from Playwicki Farm. *Journal of Middle Atlantic Archaeology* 15:55–65.

Pietak, Lynn Marie

1995   *Trading With Strangers: Delaware and Munsee Strategies for Integrating European Trade Goods, 1600–1800.* Ph.D. dissertation, Department of Anthropology, University of Virginia.

1998   Body Symbolism and Cultural Aesthetics: The Use of Shell Beads and Ornaments by Delaware and Munsee Groups. *North American Archaeologist* 19(2):135–161.

1999   Bead Color Symbolism Among Post-Contact Delaware and Munsee Groups. *Journal of Middle Atlantic Archaeology* 15:3–19.

Puniello, Anthony J., and Lorraine E. Williams

1978   Late Woodland Occupations in the Upper Delaware Valley. Final Re-
            port: 1974 Investigations at the Bell-Browning, Zipser Lower Field,
            Beisler, Heater II and Heater V Sites. Report submitted to the Inter-
            agency Archaeological Service, Atlanta, Georgia.

Revey, James, Lone Bear

1984   The Delaware Indians of New Jersey From Colonial Times to the Pres-
            ent. In *The Lenape Indian: A Symposium*, edited by Herbert C. Kraft,
            pp.72–82. Archaeological Research Center, Seton Hall University, Pub-
            lication No. 7, South Orange, New Jersey.

Richter, Daniel K.

2005   *Native Americans' Pennsylvania*. Pennsylvania History Studies
            No.28. The Pennsylvania Historical Association, University Park,
            Pennsylvania.

Ritchie, William A.

1965   *The Archaeology of New York State*. Natural History Press, Garden
            City, New York.

Rivinus, Willus M.

1965   *The Red Man in Bucks County*. Self-published, New Hope, Pennsylva-
            nia.

Rogers, J. Daniel and Samuel M. Wilson (editors)

1993   *Ethnohistory and Archaeology: Approaches to Postcontact Change in
            the Americas*. Plenum Press, New York.

Rubertone, Patricia E.

2000   The Historical Archaeology of Native Americans. *Annual Review of
            Anthropology* 29:425–446.

Salwen, Bert

1972   Test Excavations at the Zipser Lower Field Site, Warren County, New
            Jersey. *Bulletin of the Archaeological Society of New Jersey* 28:1–15.

Santone, Lenore

1998   Resiliency as Resistance: Eastern Woodland Munsee Groups on the
            Early Colonial Frontier. *North American Archaeologist* 19(2):117–
            134.

1999   Selective Change and Cultural Continuity Among the Munsee on the
            Colonial Frontier. *Journal of Middle Atlantic Archaeology* 15:21–34.

Santone, Lenore, Rhea J. Rogers, Henry M. R. Holt, and Ronald Kearns

1995   Phase III Archaeological Data Recovery, Maple Grange Road Bridge
            Site (28–Sx–297), Maple Grange Road, Vernon Township, Sussex
            County, New Jersey, for Maple Grange Road Bridge Replacement and
            Relocation. Cultural Resource Group, Louis Berger, Inc. Report pre-
            pared for the New Jersey Department of Transportation, Trenton.

Schutt, Amy C.
2007   *Peoples of the River Valley: The Odyssey of the Delaware Indians.* University of Pennsylvania Press, Philadelphia.

Sidoroff, Maria, George Pevarnik, William Schindler, and R. Michael Stewart
2008   An Experimental Approach to Understanding Clay Selection by Ancient Potters in the Delaware Valley. Paper presented at the Annual Meeting of the Society for American Archaeology, Vancouver, B.C.

Silliman, Stephen
2005   Culture Contact or Colonialism? Challenges in the Archaeology of Native North America. *American Antiquity* 70(1):55–74.

Silverman, Helaine, and David B. Small
2002   *The Space and Place of Death.* Archaeological Papers of the American Anthropological Association No. 11. Arlington, Virginia.

Skinner, Alanson
1909   The Lenape Indians of Staten Island. *American Museum of Natural History Anthropological Papers* 3:3–61.

Skinner, Alanson, and Max Schrabisch
1913   A Preliminary Report of the Archaeological Survey of the State of New Jersey. *Bulletin of the Geological Survey of New Jersey.* No. 9. MacCrellish and Quigley: Trenton, New Jersey.

Smith, Robert A., Jr.
1956   The Broomall Rock Shelter Sites. *Pennsylvania Archaeologist* 26(1):37–42.

Stahl, Leslie
1993   Concepts of Time and Approaches to Analogic Reasoning in Historical Perspective. *American Antiquity* 58:235–260.

Stanzeski, Andrew
1996   Two Decades of Radiocarbon Dating from the New Jersey Shore. *Bulletin of the Archaeological Society of New Jersey* 51:42–45.
1998   Four PaleoIndian and Early Archaic Sites in Southern New Jersey. *Archaeology of Eastern North America* 26:41–53.
n.d.   Archaeological Perspectives on the New Jersey Shore. Manuscript in possession of the author, Camden, New Jersey.

Stewart, Frank H.
1932   *Indians of Southern New Jersey.* Gloucester County Historical Society, Woodbury, New Jersey.

Stewart, R. Michael
1987a   Middle and Late Woodland Cobble-Based Technologies in the Delaware River Valley. *Bulletin of the Archaeological Society of New Jersey* 42:33–43.
1987b   Gropp's Lake Site (28Me100G), Data Recovery. Trenton Complex Archaeology: Report 2. The Cultural Resource Group, Louis Berger and

Associates, East Orange, New Jersey. Prepared for the Federal Highway Administration and the New Jersey Department of Transportation, Trenton.

1989a   Trade and Exchange in Middle Atlantic Region Prehistory. *Archaeology of Eastern North America* 17:47–78.

1989b   Micro-cores and Blade-like Flakes from Cobbles in Middle and Late Woodland Assemblages. *Bulletin of the Archaeological Society of New Jersey* 44:47–50.

1990   The Middle to Late Woodland Transition in the Lower/Middle Delaware Valley. *North American Archaeologist* 11(3):231–254.

1993   Comparison of Late Woodland Cultures: Delaware, Potomac, and Susquehanna River Valleys, Middle Atlantic Region. *Archaeology of Eastern North America* 21:163–178.

1994   Late Archaic through Late Woodland Exchange in the Middle Atlantic Region. In *Prehistoric Exchange Systems in North America*, edited by Timothy Baugh and Jonathan Ericson, pp. 73–98. Plenum Press, New York.

1998a   The Status of Late Woodland Research in the Delaware Valley. *Bulletin of the Archaeological Society of New Jersey* 53:1–12.

1998b   *Ceramics and Delaware Valley Prehistory: Insights From the Abbott Farm.* Trenton Complex Archaeology, Report 14. Special Publication of the Archaeological Society of New Jersey and the New Jersey Department of Transportation, Trenton.

1999a   Native American Fishing in the Delaware Valley. *Bulletin of the Archaeological Society of New Jersey* 54:1–6.

1999b   The Indian Town of Playwicki. *Journal of Middle Atlantic Archaeology* 15:35–54.

2000   Indian Territories in the Delaware Valley: Problems and Prospects of Identification. Paper presented at the Annual Meeting of the Society for American Archaeology, Philadelphia, Pennsylvania.

2006   An Archaeological Perspective on Native American and European Contact in Pennsylvania and Surrounding Areas. Paper presented in the symposium, *Exploring Pennsylvania's Native American Heritage.* The State Museum of Pennsylvania, Harrisburg.

2009   Finding American Indian Sites of the Contact Period. Paper presented at the symposium, *Early Colonial Period Archaeology of the Delaware Valley*, New Castle, Delaware, sponsored by the Delaware Division of Historical and Cultural Affairs.

Stewart, R. Michael, and John A. Cavallo

1983   Cultural History. In Abbott Farm National Landmark, Phase II Cultural Resource Survey and Mitigation Plans (2 vols). The Cultural Resource Group, Louis Berger & Associates, East Orange, New Jersey. Report on file, New Jersey Department of Transportation, Trenton.

Stewart, R. Michael, Chris Hummer, and Jay Custer
1986   Late Woodland Cultures of the Middle and Lower Delaware Valley
            and Upper Delmarva Peninsula, In *Late Woodland Cultures of the
            Middle Atlantic Region*, edited by Jay Custer, pp. 58–89. University of
            Delaware Press, Newark

Stewart, R. Michael, Philip Perazio, and Timothy Messner
2005   Reinvigorating Indian Archaeology in the Upper Delaware Valley. Pa-
            per presented at the Annual Meeting of the Society for Pennsylvania
            Archaeology, Morgantown, Pennsylvania.

Stewart, R. Michael, and George Pevarnik
2008   Artisan Choices and Technology in Native American Pottery Produc-
            tion. *North American Archaeologist* 29 (3–4):391–409.

Strohmeier, William
1980   The Unami Creek Rockshelter. *Pennsylvania Archaeologist* 50(4):1–12.
1985   Two Bucks County Rockshelters. *Pennsylvania Archaeologist* 55(4):4–
            11.

Strong, John A.
1997   *The Algonquian Peoples of Long Island From Earliest Times to 1700*.
            Empire State Books, Interlaken, New York.

Thomas, Ronald A.
1990   Salvage Excavations at the Gloucester City Site (28CA50), Camden
            County, New Jersey. *Bulletin of the Archaeological Society of New Jer-
            sey* 45:43–52.

Thomas, Ronald A., and Martha J. Schiek
1988   A Late Seventeenth-Century House Site in Gloucester City, New Jersey.
            Bulletin of the Archaeological Society of New Jersey 43:3–11.

Thurman, Melburn D.
1973   *The Delaware Indians: A Study in Ethnohistory*. Ph.D. dissertation,
            University of California, Santa Barbara.

Turnbaugh, William A.
1993   Assessing the Significance of European Goods in Seventeenth-Century
            Narragansett Society. In *Ethnohistory and Archaeology: Approaches
            to Postcontact Change in the Americas*, edited by Daniel J. Rogers and
            Samuel M. Wilson, pp.133–160. Plenum Press, New York.

Underhill, Sarah Gilpin
1934   *The Indians of Bucks County Pennsylvania Two Hundred and Fifty
            Years Ago*. Bulletin of Friends Historical Association, Philadelphia.

Van Gastel, Ada
1990   Van der Donck's Description of the Indians: Additions and Correc-
            tions. *William and Mary Quarterly* 47:411–421.

Veit, Richard
1994   Contact Period Artifacts from Burlington County, New Jersey in the
            Collections of the University Museum. *Bulletin of the Archaeological
            Society of New Jersey* 49:77–78.

Veit, Richard, and Charles Bello

1999   A Unique and Valuable Historical Indian Collection: Charles Conrad Abbott Explores the Historical Archaeology of the Delaware Valley. *Journal of Middle Atlantic Archaeology* 15:95–123.

2001a   Tokens of Their Love: Interpreting Native American Grave Goods from Pennsylvania, New Jersey, and New York. *Archaeology of Eastern North America* 29:47–64.

2001b   A Small Collection of Bird-shaped Pendants from the "Indian Burial Ground", Trenton, New Jersey - Collections of the Peabody Museum of Archaeology and Ethnology, Harvard University. *Bulletin of the Archaeological Society of New Jersey* 56:96–97.

2002   "Sundry Species of Trading Goods": A Comparative Study of Trade Goods Represented in Colonial deeds and Archaeological Sites from Monmouth County, New Jersey. *Bulletin of the Archaeological Society of New Jersey* 57:66–71.

Volk, Ernest

1911   *The Archaeology of the Delaware Valley*. Papers of the Peabody Museum of American Archaeology and Ethnology Vol. 6. Harvard University, Cambridge.

Wacker, Peter O.

1982   New Jersey's Cultural Resources: AD 1660–1810. In *New Jersey's Archaeological Resources from the Paleo-Indian Period to the Present: A Review of Research Problems and Survey Priorities*, edited by Olga Chesler, pp. 199–219. Office of Cultural and Environmental Services, New Jersey Department of Environmental Protection, Trenton.

Wall, Robert D.

2004   The Chesapeake Hinterlands: Contact-Period Archaeology in the Upper Potomac Valley. In *Indian and European Contact in Context: The Mid-Atlantic Region*, edited by Dennis B. Blanton and Julia A. King, pp. 74–97. University Press of Florida, Gainesville.

Wall, Robert D., and R. Michael Stewart

1996   *Sturgeon Pond Site (28Me114), Data Recovery*. Trenton Complex Archaeology: Report 10. The Cultural Resource Group, Louis Berger and Associates, Inc., East Orange, New Jersey. Prepared for the Federal Highway Administration and the New Jersey Department of Transportation, Trenton.

Wall, Robert D., R. Michael Stewart, John A. Cavallo, and Virginia Busby

1996a   *Area D Site (28Me1-D), Data Recovery*. Trenton Complex Archaeology: Report 9. The Cultural Resource Group, Louis Berger and Associates, Inc., East Orange, New Jersey. Prepared for the Federal Highway Administration and the New Jersey Department of Transportation, Trenton.

Wall, Robert D., R. Michael Stewart, John A. Cavallo, Douglas McLearen, Robert Foss, Philip Perazio, and John Dumont

1996b   Prehistoric Archaeological Synthesis. Trenton Complex Archaeology: Report 15. The Cultural Resource Group, Louis Berger and Associates, Inc., East Orange, New Jersey. Prepared for the Federal Highway Administration and the New Jersey Department of Transportation, Trenton.

Wallace, Paul A. W.

1993   *Indian Paths of Pennsylvania*. Pennsylvania Historical and Museum Commission, Harrisburg.

Walling, Richard S.

2005   *Bethel Indian Town of New Jersey: Its History and Location Revealed*. Printed by the author, East Brunswick, New Jersey.

Wellenreuther, Hermann, and Carola Wessel (editors)

2005   *The Moravian Mission Diaries of David Zeisberger, 1772–1781*. Pennsylvania State University Press, University Park.

Werner, David J.

1972   The Zimmerman Site, 36-Pi-14. In *Archaeology in the Upper Delaware Valley*, edited by W. Fred Kinsey, III, pp. 55–130. Anthropological Series, No. 2. Pennsylvania Historical and Museum Commission, Harrisburg.

Weslager, C. A.

1953   *Red Men on the Brandywine*. Hambleton, Wilmington, Delaware.

1954   Robert Evelyn's Indian Tribes and Place Names of New Albion. *Bulletin of the Archeological Society of New Jersey* 9:1–14.

1956   Delaware Indian Villages at Philadelphia. *Pennsylvania Archaeologist* 26(3–4):178–180.

1972   *The Delaware Indians: A History*. Rutgers University Press, New Brunswick, New Jersey.

1978   *The Delaware Indian Westward Migration*. The Middle Atlantic Press, Wallingford, Pennsylvania.

1985   Lenape Ethnology from William Penn's Relation of 1683. *Bulletin of the Archaeological Society of Delaware* 18:1–28.

Williams, Lorraine E.

1972   Excavations at the Zipser Lower Field Site. *Bulletin of the Archaeological Society of New Jersey* 28:16–18.

Williams, Lorraine E., and Susan Kardas

1982   Contact between Europeans and the Delaware Indians of New Jersey. In *New Jersey's Archaeological Resources from the Paleo-Indian Period to the Present: A Review of Research Problems and Survey Priorities*, edited by Olga Chesler, pp. 185–198. Office of Cultural and Environmental Services, New Jersey Department of Environmental Protection, Trenton.

Wilson, Samuel M., and J. Daniel Rogers
1993   Historical Dynamics in the Contact Era. In *Ethnohistory and Archaeology: Approaches to Postcontact Change in the Americas*, edited by J. Daniel Rogers and Samuel M. Wilson, pp. 3–18. Plenum Press, New York.

Witthoft, John
1951   The Pemberton Family Cemetery. *Pennsylvania Archaeologist* 21(1–2):21–32.
1994   The Direct Historical Approach to Lenape Archaeology. *Pennsylvania Archaeologist* 64(1):65–69.

Wolfe, Peter. E.
1977   *The Geology and Landscapes of New Jersey*. Crane Russak, New York.

Zimmerman, Albright G.
1966   *The Indian Trade of Colonial Pennsylvania*. Ph.D. dissertation, Department of History, University of Delaware, Newark.
1974   European Trade Relations in the Seventeenth and Eighteenth Centuries. In *A Delaware Indian Symposium*, edited by Herbert C. Kraft, pp. 57–70. Pennsylvania Historical and Museum Commission, Anthropological Series, No.4. Harrisburg.

2

CHARLES CONRAD ABBOTT'S ARCHAEOLOGICAL INVESTIGATIONS AT A SEVENTEENTH-CENTURY FUR TRADER'S HOUSE ON BURLINGTON ISLAND, NEW JERSEY

CAROLYN DILLIAN, CHARLES BELLO, RICHARD VEIT, AND SEAN MCHUGH

Introduction

Charles Conrad Abbott was an innovative man. He was an archaeologist who worked in New Jersey and Pennsylvania in the late nineteenth century and is most well known for his theories about the origins of Native Americans (Abbott 1872a, 1872b, 1873, 1876, 1881, 1892a, 1907, 1912; Hinsley 1985, 2003; Meltzer 2003, 2005). Abbott proposed an independent evolution of modern *Homo sapiens* in both the New World and the Old World, a theory that although initially well received (Dawkins 1883; Putnam 1888; Wright 1881) ultimately garnered a great deal of criticism in the academic press (Holmes 1893, 1898; Mercer 1892, 1893, 1894; Mercer et al. 1897; Putnam 1888; Shaler 1893). He based his ideas on the form of crude argillite bifaces and cores that he termed "paleoliths" and their stratigraphic positioning below presumably glacial gravels in the Delaware Valley (Abbott 1873, 1892a). The artifacts' presence in a major river valley was reminiscent of findspots for similar artifacts in Europe (Meltzer 2005:436). After years of rancorous debate, which has been called "The Great Paleolithic War" (Meltzer 2005:436), Abbott's theory of the concurrent evolution of *Homo sapiens* in the New and Old Worlds was proven incorrect. Nevertheless, his archaeological techniques were pioneering. At a time when many of his peers were simply accumulating antiquarian collections, Abbott was trying to understand geomorphology, create artifact typologies, and apply them to his understanding of the past.

What many do not know, however, is that Abbott was also innovative as an early historical archaeologist. This chapter focuses on the investigations that Charles Conrad Abbott conducted from approximately 1891 to 1894 (figure 2.1) at the site of an alleged seventeenth-century Dutch fur trader's house on Burlington Island, New Jersey. This large island (approximately 350 acres) lies in the Delaware River between Burlington City, New Jersey and Bristol, Pennsylvania (figure 2.2). Abbott's excavations there make up one of the earliest documented instances of historical archaeology in the Delaware Valley.

Figure 2.1. Professional photograph of Charles Conrad Abbott. Charles Conrad Abbott Papers, Manuscripts Division, Department of Rare Books and Special Collections, Princeton University Library.

According to Abbott's diaries, which are housed in the Manuscripts Division, Department of Rare Books and Special Collections, Princeton University Library, he and his son Dick frequently explored the Delaware River, including several of the islands in the middle of the river. Burlington Island, also referred to as Matinakonk Island (Bisbee 1971:39; Dankers and Sluyter 1867), Koomemakonokonk, or Tenneconck (Bisbee 1971:39), was one site where Abbott explored for prehistoric Native American artifacts, and he recovered many objects, including a large cache of netsinkers. It was also here that Abbott, while walking along the banks of the island, serendipitously discovered a seventeenth-century site. Information recorded in Dr. Abbott's diaries, record books, and correspondence suggest that the amount of material excavated and surface collected from this site was relatively large. For instance, he noted the presence of over 500 pipestems (Abbott 1894:168). However, the collections that survive, or at least those known to us, are relatively small and only hint at the richness of the original assemblage.

Figure 2.2: Locator map showing Burlington Island, New Jersey. USGS Topographic Quadrangle: Bristol, P.A.-N.J., 1955 (Photo revised 1981).

Burlington Island History and Geography

Burlington Island is located nearly 100 miles from the sea, though not quite at the head of navigation on the Delaware River. Both the English and Dutch laid claim to the South or Delaware River in the very beginning of the seventeenth century, but no permanent settlements were established until the Dutch formed a small settlement on Burlington Island. In 1624, the Dutch ship *Nieu Nederlandt,* commanded by Cornelius Jacobsen Mey, deposited a small contingent of Walloon settlers, originally from Belgium, on the island. The settlement included a trading house, designed to capitalize on commercial opportunities with the local Native American population, and a palisaded fort known as Fort Wilhemus (Bisbee 1972:11; Weslager 1961:59).

In 1625, Willem van der Hulst, or Verhulst, was dispatched to New Netherland as Provisional Director. It appears that the island was to be the seat of government in New Netherland. As the Provisional Director's instructions note: "Willem Verhulst is to have his usual place of residence on the South [Delaware] River. . . . [H]e shall also from time to time as occasion may require, betake himself to the North River to regulate matters there" (Van Laer 1924:64). Verhulst's tenure was brief. In 1626 he was removed from office for mismanagement and returned to Europe (Jacobs 2004:108). Soon after his successor Peter Minuit was appointed as director of the Dutch West India Company in New Netherland, the population of Burlington Island was removed and consolidated on Manhattan Island as the new seat of Dutch occupation of North America (Bisbee 1972:12; Weslager 1961:68). Though Burlington Island was noted as having prime fertile land and ample timber (Van Laer 1924:48–51), it was more advantageous to consolidate the Dutch stronghold in Manhattan. For nearly thirty years, there were no permanent European settlements on Burlington Island.

In 1659, several decades after the transfer of government to Manhattan, Burlington Island was reoccupied by Alexander d'Hinoyossa, the vice-director of New Netherland (Bisbee 1972:14). D'Hinoyossa was reported to have "made it a pleasure ground or garden, built good houses upon it, and sowed and planted it" (Dankers and Sluyter 1867). Five years later, the English conquered New Netherland and the island was seized by Sir Robert Carr on behalf of the Duke of York, but the English ownership of the island lasted only four years. On December 15, 1668, the island was turned over to Peter Alricks (also known as Aldridge), a Dutch businessman, who hired others to cultivate the island in his absence (Weslager 1967:196). In 1671, however, local Native Americans attacked and killed Peter Veltscheerder and Christian Samuels, two of his Dutch servants (Bisbee 1972:15), a fact that figured prominently in Abbott's interpretations of his archaeological finds.

The murder of these two servants by Tashiowycan and Wyannattamo, the local Lenape men who were charged with the crime, was allegedly precipitated by the death of Tashiowycan's sister (Nelson 1886:214) and resulted in tension between Native Americans and European settlers. Ultimately, the local Native American community elected to execute the culprits themselves, rather than release them to English authorities. In 1672, Tashiowycan was shot and his corpse hung on display at New Castle (Smith 1765:72). This event was also discussed in other contexts, including a deposition recorded in 1686 (Reed and Miller 1944:68). Abbott, who was well read in the history of the Delaware Valley, probably knew of the event from secondary sources and incorporated this intriguing scandal into his interpretations of archaeological material on Burlington Island.

Burlington Island changed hands a number of times, but as a result of the Treaty of Westminster (1674), New Netherland, and with it Burlington Island, once again became a British possession. Edmund Andros, the Governor of New York. claimed the island but is not believed to have visited it. Instead, Peter Jegou and Henry Jacobs farmed there (Bisbee 1972:16). Jegou also operated a tavern at Leasy Point, just north of Burlington City on the New Jersey side of the river. Robert Stacey, a Quaker, apparently coveted the island, and he later evicted Jegou and Jacobs (Bisbee 1972:18). In 1682, the island reverted to public ownership, and the West Jersey Assembly acted to set aside all profits from the island for the education of the youth within the city of Burlington. During the early twentieth century, the island evolved into a popular resort with extensive picnic grounds, amusement rides, and bathing beaches. This park, serviced by steamboats, continued to draw large crowds until it was destroyed by fire in 1928.

After the amusement park era, a series of commercial enterprises, most notably the Warner Company, began mining and dredging portions of the lower section of the island for gravel. Roughly 100 acres of the southern tip of the island was removed in the 1950s, creating a large lake. We know that the site Abbott excavated was located close to the southeastern tip of the island. Based on historic map evidence, it is possible that it survived the dredging. Today, debate continues over the island's future. Plans have recently been put forward to build a golf course and hotel convention center on Burlington Island.

Charles Conrad Abbott's Research on Burlington Island

Abbott worked extensively on Burlington Island between 1891 and 1894, but despite voluminous writing on archaeology and natural history, he published very little on his Burlington Island work. Interestingly, Abbott's only published works relating to his excavations on Burlington Island are found in his literary volumes entitled *Recent Rambles, or In Touch with Nature,* published by J. P. Lippencott & Co. in 1892, and *Travels in a Tree Top,* also published by J. P. Lippencott & Co. in 1894. Both of these volumes contain musings on the natural world and are not devoted to Abbott's archaeological findings. Yet, in *Recent Rambles,* Abbott wrote of Burlington Island: "I found a yellow brick upon the sand; and, looking farther, another, and curious old red bricks, and bits of roofing tiles, and pipe-stems; scattered everywhere odds and ends that could only have come from some old house near by" (1892b:313).

From his diaries, it is also clear that Abbott conducted significant archaeological work on the island as well as historical research. In his own words, "Buried inches deep in gradually-accumulating soil rest the ruins of an ancient house: buried fathoms deep in the mouldy pages of forgotten books are records of stirring times, before Philadelphia was, when there were Dutch on the Delaware" (Abbott 1892b:312). For reasons known only to him, Abbott elected to chronicle his work in his diaries, rather than in his published scholarly works.

Abbott's diaries, record books, and personal correspondence are on file in the Manuscripts Division, Department of Rare Books and Special Collections, Princeton University Library. In an early entry on the subject, Abbott wrote:

> November 22 (Sunday), 1891 — Soon after breakfast Dick and
> I went to Burlington Island and on lower end of it found a lot of
> bricks, roofing tile and other matter of an old Dutch House, as
> I take it to have been. Brought back a good lot of the spoils and

busied myself all the forenoon in drying two large and perfect
tiles for roofing. Early in the afternoon studied these so far as
one or two books availed anything, and planned an article about
the place and its early colonial traces.

The next day, he recorded in his daily diary: "November 23 (Monday), 1891 — Busied myself mostly with looking up historical matters in reference to the bricks and
tiles found yesterday on the island" (Diaries, Charles Conrad Abbott Papers, Box 3,
Folder 2, Manuscripts Division, Department of Rare Books and Special Collections,
Princeton University Library).

Once Abbott's interest was aroused on the subject of a "Dutch fur-trader's
house" as he began to refer to the site on Burlington Island (Letter, Charles Conrad
Abbot to F. W. Putnam, March 22, 1894, F. W. Putnam Papers, Peabody Museum,
Harvard University), he spent a good part of his free time researching the background
and history, with a stated goal of publishing this work. Admirably, Abbott visited
numerous historical societies, libraries, and museums in order to gather background
information on the island and its history (for example, as noted in diary entries dated
November 27, 1891; November 30, 1891; and December 2, 1891 [Diaries, Charles
Conrad Abbott Papers, Box 3, Folder 2, Manuscripts Division, Department of Rare
Books and Special Collections, Princeton University Library]).

Despite Abbott's clear attempts to find accurate historical information on
the "Dutch fur-trader's house," he appears to have been a bit confused about the
chronology of its occupation. He stated in *Recent Rambles* that a tract of land was
purchased by Peter Jegou (1892b:314). However, our historical research indicates
that Peter Jegou with Henry Jacobs, were not the owners of the island but at best
tenants of the governor and perhaps merely squatters.

Regardless, Abbott was intrigued by his historical finds and particularly by
the historical account of an Indian attack in 1671, which resulted in the death of two
servants of Peter Alricks' living on the island. He unfortunately conflated many of
these historical accounts, likely for the sake of drama, and stated in *Recent Rambles*:
"About the same time, the two men living in the island house were murdered. I was
delighted, and hurried back to the island. To think of murder and a state of siege
and all the wild tumult of midnight surprises having happened so near to home!"
(1892b:315). On December 13, 1891, Abbott wrote in his diary that "Dick [his son],
Ingersoll, and I went over to Burlington Island and disentombed a Dutchman" (Diaries, Charles Conrad Abbott Papers, Box 3, Folder 2, Manuscripts Division, Department of Rare Books and Special Collections, Princeton University Library). This find
further fueled Abbott's interest in the murder of two men on the island. A more recent analysis of skeletal remains unearthed by Abbott on Burlington Island, and now
housed at the Peabody Museum indicated that these remains are likely to be Native
American and not of European ancestry.

In fact, Abbott's penchant for drama was also evident in his stated plans to write an opera based on the historical and archaeological findings on Burlington Island, and it was in his evolution from historical fact to operatic fiction that the details of his "Dutch house" findings transformed into something that combined several different and unconnected historical details. By April 19, 1893, Abbott stated in his diary entry that he "told [Owen] Wister about my plan of an opera based on Dutch House." He continued visiting Burlington Island and collecting "Dutch House" artifacts through 1893–1894 and was frequently accompanied on these expeditions by family and friends (Diaries, Charles Conrad Abbott Papers, Box 3, Folders 2 and 5, Manuscripts Division, Department of Rare Books and Special Collections, Princeton University Library).

Yet it appears that the Dutch House opera never materialized, and Abbott instead decided to turn his writings on the subject into a lengthy poem, entitled "Island Tragedy" populated by characters whose names were chosen from a Native American dictionary (diary entry on February 27, 1896, Diaries, Charles Conrad Abbott Papers, Box 3, Folder 5, Manuscripts Division, Department of Rare Books and Special Collections, Princeton University Library). By March 7, 1896, according to his diary, the poem was completed and read before a one-person audience who "expressed herself as delighted with it, using a great many emphatic expressions of approval."

Despite its favorable reception by one of Abbott's personal friends, the poem received little interest from publishers. It was rejected by *Century Magazine* on May 6, 1896. Abbott edited the poem and on June 4, 1896 stated that he completed a new conclusion and "wrote a new song for the children that gather within hearing of the heroine's tent. Then took a nap" (Diaries, Charles Conrad Abbott Papers, Box 3, Folder 5, Manuscripts Division, Department of Rare Books and Special Collections, Princeton University Library). Abbott also commissioned illustrations for the poem from Oliver Kemp, though to date, we have been unable to locate these in any archive. After several rejections, Abbott dropped the idea of a long poem based on the archaeological finds on Burlington Island. He stated on April 22, 1897, that he received a rejection letter that was "severe on my text. . . and condemned the pictures." He further stated that "It is an unjust decision as to the drawings. . . as to my ability to write a narrative poem, that is another matter, but I am going to try again, or perhaps, re-tell the story in prose. . . ." However, we have never been able to find a published, or unpublished, version of the "Island Tragedy."

Burlington Island Artifacts

What we have relocated, however, are Abbott's collections of archaeological artifacts, now housed at the Peabody Museum at Harvard University, and his diaries and correspondence pertaining to the collection. According to Abbott's diaries, the collection was sent on April 2, 1894. He included a note to Frederic Ward Putnam, then Director of the museum in which he said,

> I . . . send the balance of "Dutch House," less one brick, which
> shall only go out of my possession to go into the museum. This
> one big box sent to-day completed the shipment and I earnestly
> hope that when received, the contents of the two boxes already
> sent and that of the one sent today will be placed in a case and
> labeled (ultimately) in accordance with the marks on the smaller
> objects, and the general label of Relics of a Dutch Fur-Trader's
> House Built in 1668 on the lower (S.E.) End of Burlington
> Island, Delaware River. House plundered and partly destroyed
> by Indians and fur trader murdered in 1670. House reoccupied
> by English a few years later: when destroyed (by fire) not now
> known, but previous to 1776. Discovered and ruins excavated
> by Dr. Charles C. Abbott, in 1892–1894 (Letter, Charles Conrad
> Abbot to F. W. Putnam, May 8, 1894, F. W. Putnam Papers, Pea-
> body Museum, Harvard University).

The collection, unfortunately, may have aroused less interest than Abbott had hoped. According to records in the archives of the Peabody Museum, the collection was not catalogued and accessioned until 1952.

In fact, Abbott hoped for some pecuniary remuneration for his efforts but noted that he had turned down other offers, since the Burlington Island artifacts were most appropriately to be included with the rest of Abbott's archaeological collections at the Peabody Museum. Abbott stated in a letter to Putnam on April 6, 1894, that

> I was so severely swindled in Philadelphia [by the University of
> Pennsylvania Museum, Abbott's former employer] that I am now
> desperately poor and will be until September but hope not to die
> of starvation and nakedness before the day of relief. In spite of
> this, I refused an offer of $100 for the "Dutch House" collection
> because my collection at Cambridge seems to be its proper place
> (Letter, Charles Conrad Abbot to F. W. Putnam, April 6, 1894,
> F. W. Putnam Papers, Peabody Museum, Harvard University).

In fact, all of the Burlington Island artifacts were ultimately remitted to the Peabody Museum, with the sole exception of a single tile housed at the University of Pennsylvania Museum of Archaeology and Anthropology. The object is curated and labeled as "Pan Tile, Dutch trader's house Burlington Island" and was relocated by one of the authors of this paper (R. Veit) in 1995 while working as a research as-sistant in the American Section collections. No other records or artifacts associated with Abbott's Burlington Island excavations have been found at the University of Pennsylvania Museum.

Abbott wrote in *Travels in a Tree-Top* of his excitement regarding the artifacts. He stated:

> I could enthuse, without being laughed at, over what to others was but meaningless rubbish, and I found much that, to me, possessed greater interest than usual, because of a mingling of late Indian and early European objects. With a handful of glass, porcelain, and amber beads were more than one hundred of copper; the former from Venice, the latter the handiwork of a Delaware Indian. With a white clay pipe, made in Holland in the 17th century, was found a rude brown clay one, made here in the river valley. Mingled with fragments of blue and white Delft plates, bowls, and platters, were sundried mud dishes made by women hereabouts during, who can say how many centuries? How completely history and prehistory here overlapped! (1894:171).

The artifacts recovered from what Abbott simply designated as "the Dutch trader's house" date primarily to the mid- seventeenth century. Although comprising only 196 items, it is one of only a handful of collections representing this early phase of European colonization of the Delaware Valley. The collection is composed of trade goods and other early colonial artifacts reflective of the European occupation of the site.

The catalog begins with two (undecorated) copper tinklers—one still retaining a trace of a rawhide thong, preserved intact by the copper salts. Copper tinklers or tinkling cones are not temporally diagnostic, except in the broadest sense. Made from small fragments of copper, sometimes reworked from kettle fragments (Beauchamp 1903:19; Ehrhardt 2005:119–120; Kraft 1975:154; Wray et al. 1990:249), they were used by Native Americans to ornament clothing.

Iron objects include a fragment of a sickle blade and 18 hand-wrought iron nails and spikes. A large fragment of a cast iron kettle was also recovered It has a triangular lug and resembles seventeenth-century European specimens recovered from the Burr's Hill Cemetery in Rhode Island (Dilliplane 1980:79). According to Alaric and Gretchen Faulkner, cast iron kettles are common on seventeenth-century English sites but not on French sites (Faulkner and Faulkner 1987).

Glass artifacts include 16 dark green "black" bottle glass fragments representing a minimum of two hand-blown bottles with different profiles—one a bulbous shape characteristic of late seventeenth and early-eighteenth-century bottles, the other has a more vertical profile, indicative of an 18th-century date (Noël Hume 1970:63–68). Additionally, there were nine window glass fragments present. They are crown glass and show evidence of devitrification. They most likely pre-date the

1840s (Scharfenberger 2004). Seventeen glass trade beads were found in the collection (figure 2.3). Most of the beads are similar to those listed by Kidd and Kidd (1970). Fifteen of the beads are round beads with redwood bodies and compound stripes. Similar beads have been found on Dutch sites dating from 1630 to 1730 (Karklins 1983:111, 115).

Four unglazed pottery roof tile fragments were also found in museum collections, two of which are housed at the University of Pennsylvania Museum, and two at Harvard's Peabody Museum. The University of Pennsylvania Museum's fragments mend to form a nearly complete tile which measures ca. 35 cm long, 20 cm wide. While these tiles generally seem indicative of the early colonial period, they do not allow the site's chronology to be determined with a great deal of accuracy. Similar tiles were employed on buildings in upstate New York, Maryland, Virginia, and throughout the Caribbean (Cotter 1958:171; Moser et al. 2003:206; Thomas

Figure 2.3. Glass beads from the "Dutch Fur-Trader's House" collection, reproduced courtesy of the Peabody Museum of Archaeology and Ethnology, Harvard University (Peabody ID#52-46-10/3409.1, Digital File 98600079).

1985:IV-40). Comparable tiles have also been found in Albany, Kingston and Manhattan, New York (Meeske 2001:185–186).

The most chronologically diagnostic artifacts recovered by Abbott were the tobacco pipes (figure 2.4). Although 500 tobacco pipes were said to be recovered, only 61 fragments are present in the collection. Of these, 56 were manufactured in Europe from white ball clay. The remaining five were made from reddish clay. Several maker's marks are present. Some have heels marked "EB," most likely the products of Edward Bird, an English-born pipemaker who worked in the Netherlands and was active between 1635 and 1665 (Dallal 1995:99; Huey 1991:76; Miller 1991:76). Another was marked "IS," possibly the mark of John Sinderling, active from 1668 to 1699 in Bristol England (Hurry and Keeler 1991:68–69). There was one specimen with the cartouche of Robert Tippet on the bowl. Although the first Robert Tippet was active between the 1660s and 1680s, two subsequent generations of Tippets manufactured tobacco pipes, and their wares are found on archaeological sites dating as late as the American Revolution (Walker 1977:1493). Two stems were marked with a fleur-de-lis, and one was marked "VBAK" possibly for TVBAC or tobacco (Diane Dallal, personal communication 1998). The two pipes displaying impressed fleur-de-lis within conjoined diamonds on their stems are likely Dutch, and similar pipes are common on seventeenth-century sites in Manhattan (Meta Janowtiz, personal communication 1998). Of the pipes identified by maker, 15 were of Dutch origin and two were of English origin. The majority (39) could not be definitively identified as to place of manufacture, although those with embossed stems may also be Dutch. Although the collection is quite small to be subjected to statistical analysis, when the Binford formula is applied to this collection, it gives a date of 1660, which corresponds fairly well with both the maker's marks and the historical information available about the site.

In addition to the ball clay tobacco pipes, there are fragments of red clay pipes. They include three stems, one stem and bowl fragment, and one bowl. The stems show what appear to be whittle marks, possibly from removing excess clay left in the molding process. None of the pipes are marked. All have bore diameters of 8/64ths of an inch. Two bowl fragments show rouletting around the lip of the bowl, a typical Dutch characteristic. These pipes are the most enigmatic objects that Abbott recovered. A note in Abbott's own handwriting was found with the single intact pipe. It reads, "This is a pipe made in New Jersey about 1700, and probably the first pipes for smoking tobacco made in this country. The clay same as that of tile for roof." It is worth noting that similar pipes, often designated terra-cotta pipes, have been widely recovered from seventeenth-century sites in Maryland and Virginia where they are known as terra cotta tobacco pipes (Deetz 1993:92; Emerson 1988; Henry 1979:14–37). They are also known in smaller numbers from New England (Baker 1985:22; Cranmer 1990:78).

Abbott also recovered a small collection of pottery that included 13 fragments of Delft or Dutch faience, some with blue underglaze decoration. The other ceramics in the collection included: redware, stoneware, porcelain, and curiously two fragments of whiteware. The whiteware fragments may well be intrusive. Unfortunately, the ceramic fragments were too small to allow them to be confidently assigned to various vessel forms. The absence of certain ceramic types which were common during the mid and late eighteenth century is also noteworthy. No fragments of Staffordshire slipware, white salt-glazed stoneware, creamware, or pearlware were recovered from the site. Their absence hints at a seventeenth-century occupation.

There were also a small number of prehistoric artifacts in the collection, including two spear-thrower weights, two small hematite objects, a chipped chert knife, and most interestingly, a catlinite disc pipe. Although the catlinite or redstone pipe was not closely examined by the authors, as it could not be located during their visit to the Peabody Museum, it has apparently been found as it is illustrated in the museum's online catalog. Similar pipes have been found on late-seventeenth- and early-eighteenth-century Seneca villages in western New York State (Kirk 2003:54). It is an exceptionally unusual find for a Delaware Valley site and may indicate trade with Native American groups from other parts of North America. Such pipes are well known from protohistoric sites in the Mississippi Valley (Brown 1989).

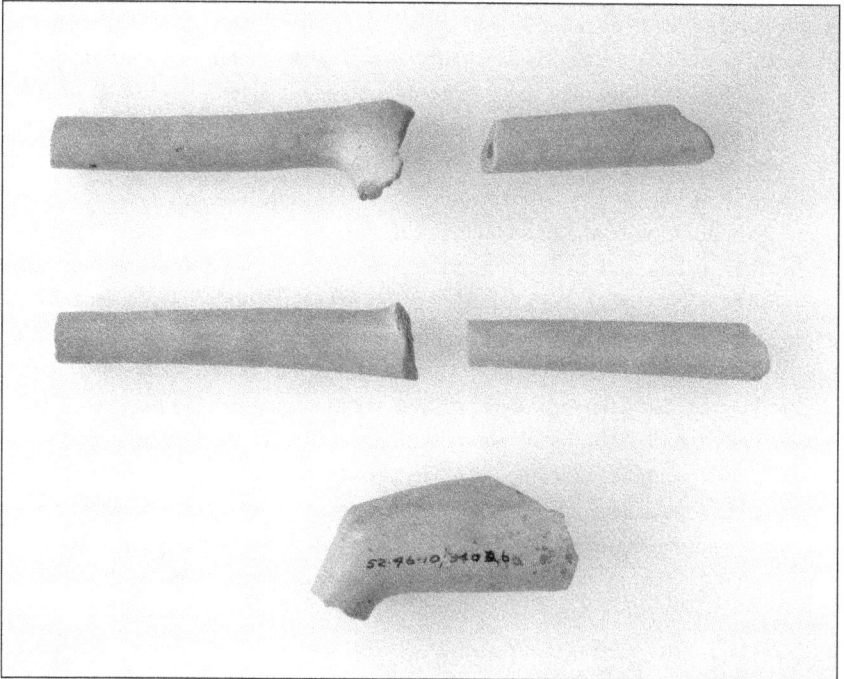

Figure 2.4. Terra cotta tobacco pipes from the "Dutch Fur-Trader's House" collection, reproduced courtesy of the Peabody Museum of Archaeology and Ethnology, Harvard University (Peabody ID#52-46-10/34026, Digital File 60740884).

The skeletal remains recovered by Abbott are also held in the Peabody's collections. Although the skull is missing, much of the post-cranial skeleton is present. Analysis indicates that the skeleton is probably not that of an adult man, but a subadult, who was most likely Native American. This is in direct contradiction to Abbott's belief that this was one of the unfortunate servants killed on the island in 1671.

In addition to the artifacts still present in the collection, Abbott claimed to have recovered yellow or Dutch bricks. While none of these are present in the collection, similar small yellow bricks have been recovered at seventeenth- and eighteenth-century sites in the Delaware and Hudson valleys (Becker 1977:112–118; Huey 1991:49; Veit 2000).

The bulk of the collection dates from the last third of the seventeenth century. Although Native American artifacts are present, including the catlinite tobacco pipe and the tinkling cones, evidence for trade is somewhat limited. Moreover, some of the artifacts, particularly the pan tiles, seem more evocative of a well-finished domestic structure than a simple trading post. Perhaps they relate to the island's occupation by Alexander D'Hinoyossa or Peter Alricks (1973:31).

Modern Investigations of Burlington Island

Our historical and archaeological investigations of Burlington Island, and specifically of Abbott's research on the island, have been ongoing for more than ten years. Abbott's work at Burlington Island first emerged as a research topic with the discovery of the pan tile in the collections of the University of Pennsylvania Museum. Subsequently, two of us published an article that outlined much of the history of Abbott's work at Burlington Island and analyzed artifacts from the collections of the Peabody Museum at Harvard University (Veit and Bello 1999). More recently, we have examined the possibility of archaeological materials associated with Abbott's "Dutch fur-trader's house" remaining *in situ*. Historic and modern maps, soils data, and site inspections suggest that intact archaeological strata may exist on Burlington Island, though portions are likely buried under extensive dredge spoil deposited in the middle of the twentieth century.

One of the earliest maps of Burlington Island, originally drawn in 1679, was published in the *Journal of a Voyage to New York and a Tour of Several of the American Colonies in 1679–80* (Dankers and Sluyter 1867). The map shows Burlington Island, labeled as "Matinakonk Eyland" with a structure located to the southern end of the island, in the vicinity of where Abbott conducted his excavations of the "Dutch fur-trader's house" (diary entry November 22, 1891, Diaries, Charles Conrad Abbott Papers, Box 3, Folder 2, Manuscripts Division, Department of Rare Books and Special Collections, Princeton University Library). Dankers and Sluyter did not note the presence of a Dutch trading post, but the island had reverted to English ownership in 1674. Instead Dankers and Sluyter recorded that:

This Island, formerly, belonged to the Dutch governor, who had
made it a pleasure ground or garden, built good houses upon it,
and sowed and planted it. He also dyked and cultivated a large
piece of meadow or marsh, from which he gathered more grain
than from any land which had been made from woodland into
tillable land. The English governor at the Manathans, now held
it for himself, and had hired it out to some Quakers, who were
living upon it at present (1867:174).

Dankers and Sluyter's hand-drawn map appears to be the only surviving detailed
map of Burlington Island that could have depicted the location of the "Dutch fur-
trader's house" excavated by Abbott.

Later maps—including the 1872 topographic map of Burlington County,
New Jersey (Beers 1872) and the 1876 atlas of Burlington Township (figure 2.5) and
Burlington City, New Jersey (Scott 1876a, 1876b)—depict Burlington Island, but
they do not show any structures on the island. However, a useful attribute on these
maps is the inclusion of a delineation of swampy land on the southeastern edge of
the island, which was later covered with dredge spoil in the mid-twentieth century.
Abbott's description of the site location places it on high ground on the southern end

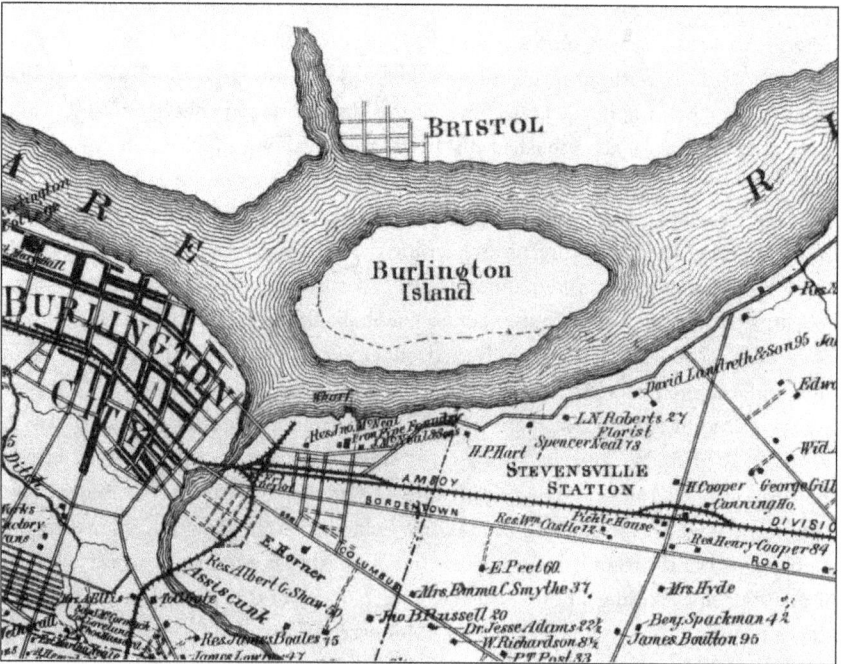

Figure 2.5. 1876 Map of Burlington Island from J. D. Scott (1876b) *Combination Atlas Map of Burlington Township, New Jersey.*

of the island, above the swampy areas, allowing us to pinpoint the site location with further accuracy.

The USGS Topographic map of 1893 depicting Burlington Island (figure 2.6) also provides some guidance as to the location of the original shoreline. In 1893, no structures were depicted on the USGS Topographic map, but the map does show the swampy ground on the southeastern edge of the island, which helps pinpoint the approximate location of Abbott's excavations, referenced as being on the southern tip of the island on dry ground above the swampy areas. Abbott's diaries and notes do talk about collecting artifacts near chicken coops on the island, but these are not depicted on the map from 1893, though it would have been drawn during the years that Abbott was excavating there.

By 1906, the USGS Topographic maps depict several houses on Burlington Island, which may have been built after Abbott's excavations were completed, as he

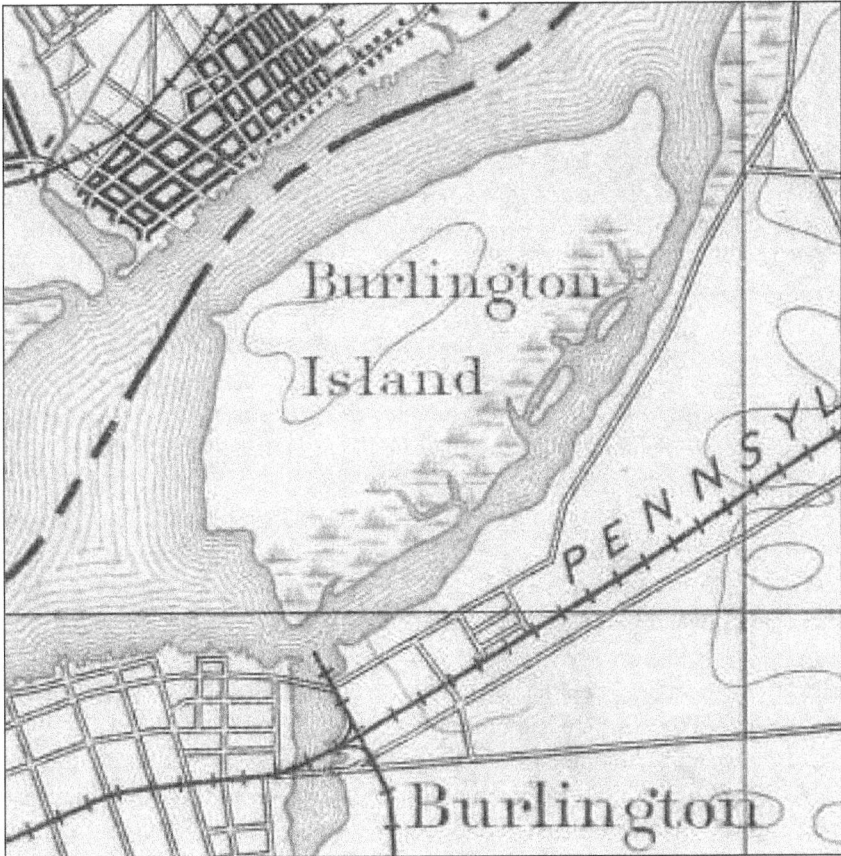

Figure 2.6. 1893 USGS Topographic Quadrangle: Pennsylvania-New Jersey, Burlington sheet, October 1893 (reprinted September 1904).

Figure 2.7. December 29, 1937 aerial photograph of Burlington Island from the USDA Agricultural Adjustment Administration.

does not discuss any structures other than chicken coops being present on the island. The map also depicts a pier on the western side of the island facing Bristol, Pennsylvania. In the early 1900s, an amusement park was operating on Burlington Island, drawing several thousand people each day during the summer (Bisbee 1972:26), and a ferry transported park-goers to and from the island.

An aerial photograph from December 29, 1937, provides the best view of Burlington Island prior to the gravel mining and dredging that began in 1955 and vastly transformed the appearance of the island. A comparison of the 1937 aerial photograph (figure 2.7) with a modern aerial photograph (figure 2.8) shows the extent of filling that occurred since 1955. Specifically, swampy areas to the south and east of the island have been filled, and sand and gravel mining has created a large internal lake in the southern half of the island.

According to Abbott's notes and diary entries, the "Dutch fur-trader's house" was located at the southern tip of the island, on high ground above the swampy areas on the southeastern shoreline. If so, the site may have escaped damage from the sand and gravel mining that took place in the middle of the twentieth century, impacting approximately 100 acres within the southern half of the island.

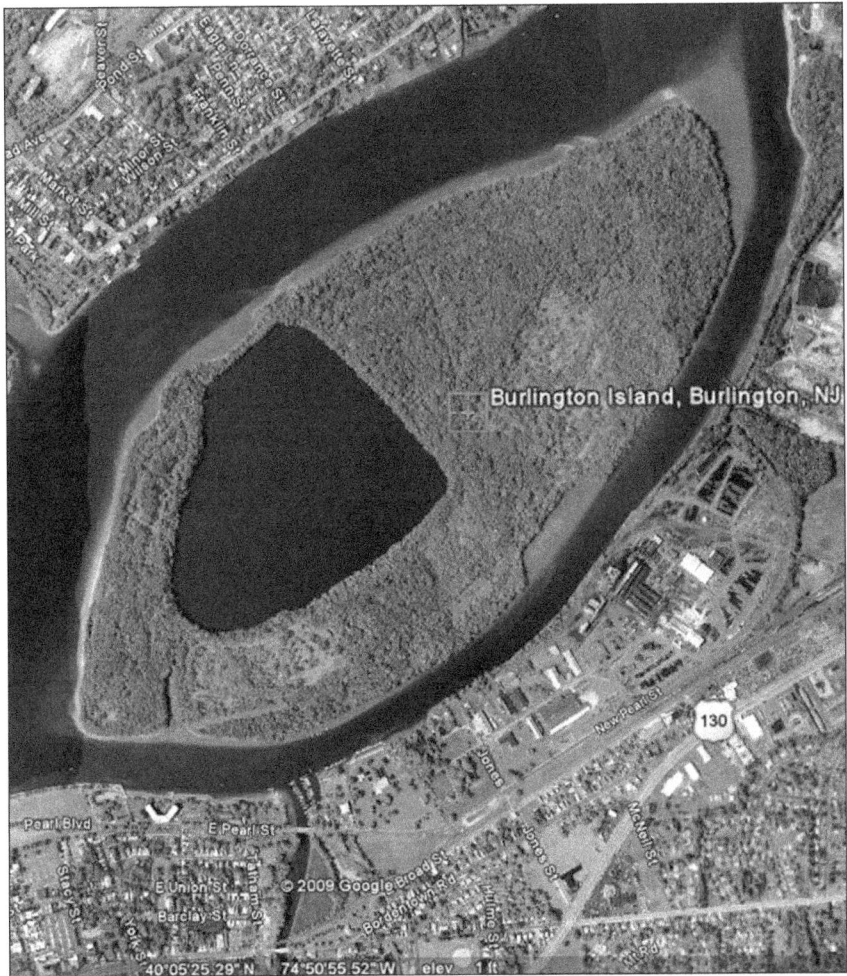

Figure 2.8. 2009 aerial photograph of Burlington Island from Google Earth imagery.

Because Abbott did not create a map of the site, we have no exact location, but his written description does suggest the approximate locale.

After a review of map data, the authors of this paper conducted a site visit to Burlington Island in August 2008. Surface inspection of the landscape in the vicinity of Abbott's excavations did not reveal any artifacts on the surface or within erosional faces along the river bank. Extensive dredge spoil piles were observed across most of the area, filling any low-lying swampy areas that were visible in the 1937 aerial photograph and capping higher ground across much of the remainder of the island.

Interestingly, during the site visit we also observed an area of apparently intact, undisturbed ground situated at the southeastern edge of the lake, in an area visible on the aerial photograph as located between areas of dredge spoil. The approach to this area from the New Jersey shore of Burlington City was possible through a partially water-filled ravine that ran between visible dredge piles. No artifacts were visible on the ground surface, and subsurface testing was not performed during the site visit. However, we maintain that there is a strong potential for undisturbed strata in this area, and it could correspond with the location where Abbott conducted his excavations of the "Dutch fur-trader's house." Unfortunately, at the time that this study was conducted, we were unable to obtain permission for formal archaeological excavation on the island.

Today, our work on Burlington Island continues Charles Conrad Abbott's early tradition. Extensive dredging and sand mining on the island has likely buried or destroyed much of the archaeological material that may have remained. However, an analysis of historical and modern aerial photographs reveals that a small pocket of intact ground may remain at the south end of the manufactured lake in the center of the island. Furthermore, this location once corresponded to the southern tip of the island during Abbott's time, and it may be the exact location where the "Dutch House" once stood. Unfortunately, the yellow bricks, red bricks, roofing tiles, ceramics, copper, and pipe stems, identified and collected by Abbott were not observed. Yet we hope that future historical research, additional archaeological survey, and a better understanding of the more recent and extensive disturbance on the island may yield new clues as to the "Dutch Fur-Trader's House" on Burlington Island.

Conclusion

Despite Abbott's fanciful interpretations of the history of Burlington Island and his assertion that his finds were associated with a "Dutch fur-trader's house," there is little explicit historical evidence for a trading post located on the island. Fort Wilhemus, built in 1624, functioned as settlement, garrison, and likely center for interactions with the local Lenape population. It seems likely that the inhabitants of this settlement traded with Native Americans. However, this collection is much later, dating from the last third of the seventeenth century. Abbott conflated many of the historical accounts, superimposing the murder of Alrick's servants, which occurred in 1671, with the trading activity likely associated with Fort Wilhemus. Nonetheless, the archaeological artifacts do clearly show a Dutch presence in the seventeenth century and include items that would have been traded with Native Americans such as tinkling cones, beads, and tobacco pipes. It is particularly noteworthy that the artifacts do reflect an occupation of the island at approximately the time when Alrick's servants were murdered. Perhaps recognizing this, Abbott conflated two good stories to make one better story.

However, it is also important to note that much of Burlington Island contains archaeological materials from a range of time periods, including ample evidence for long-term prehistoric occupation of the island (Skinner and Schrabisch 1913:62). During the contact period, Native American populations may have continued to live on Burlington Island while trading with early explorers and settlers of the Delaware Valley, resulting in European-made goods in Native American archaeological sites.

Yet, Abbott's work at Burlington Island remains noteworthy as an early example of North American historical archaeology. Though there are a few earlier examples, including excavations by the Pilgrims in the seventeenth century (Schuyler 1977:1), eighteenth-century excavations on St. Croix Island in Maine (Cotter 1994:16), and mid-nineteenth-century excavations of Miles Standish's house (Deetz 1996:39), Abbott was innovative in his attempts to understand contact period history. It is worth noting that in 1853 the New Jersey Historical Society had attempted to relocate the site of Fort Nassau, another early Dutch outpost on the river using maps, historical diaries, and landscape features. They did not, however, carry out any excavations (Mulford 1853). Abbott provided a model which would not be imitated locally until Donald Cadzow and his WPA work crews investigated Pennsbury Manor and other historic sites in Pennsylvania in the 1930s (Cotter et al. 1992:362).

Though Abbott's interests remained focused largely on the rise of *Homo sapiens* and his theories of an independent evolution in the New World, Abbott demonstrated an admirable ability for historical research and a strong understanding of archaeology and history in his work on Burlington Island. Today, we aspire to relocate Abbott's site of the "Dutch fur-trader's house" and resume his investigations into this fascinating element of contact period history.

Acknowledgments

A special thanks to all of the individuals who have helped us with our Burlington Island research over the years. We also particularly appreciate the assistance shown us by William Wierzbowski, Associate Keeper, and Lucy Fowler Williams, Keeper of the American Section Collections at the University of Pennsylvania Museum. Douglas Haller and Alex Pezzati, archivists at the Museum and Charles Kline, photo archivist are also thanked for their help. At the Peabody Museum of Archaeology and Ethnology, we are grateful to: Susan Haskell and Viva Fisher, Gloria Polizzotti Greis, Brian Sullivan, Susan Bruce, David Schafer, and Scott Templin. Our interpretations benefited from discussions with Meta Janowitz, Diane Dallal, Paul Huey, Marshall Becker, and Paul Schopp. This research was supported by grants from the Archaeological Society of New Jersey, the Friends of Princeton University Library Research Grant, and the Princeton University Grants in the Humanities and Social Sciences (#209–2310). Any errors remain ours and ours alone.

References Cited

Abbott, Charles Conrad

1872a　　　The Stone Age in New Jersey. *The American Naturalist* 6(3):144–160.

1872b　　　The Stone Age in New Jersey (Concluded). *The American Naturalist* 6(4):199–229.

1873　　　Occurrence of Implements in the River Drift at Trenton, New Jersey. *The American Naturalist* 7(4):204–209.

1876　　　The Stone Age of New Jersey. *Annual Report of the Smithsonian Institution for 1875*:246–380.

1881　　　*Primitive Industry.* G. A. Bates, Salem, Massachusetts.

1892a　　　Paleolithic Man: A Last Word. *Science* 20(515):344–345.

1892b　　　*Recent Rambles or In Touch with Nature.* J. B. Lippincott, Philadelphia.

1894　　　*Travels in a Tree Top.* J. B. Lippincott, Philadelphia.

1907–1909　*Archaeological Nova Caesarea.* MacCrellish and Quigley, Trenton, New Jersey.

1912　　　*Ten Years' Diggings in Lenape Land.* MacCrelish and Quigley, Trenton, New Jersey.

Aiello, Lucy

1973　　　Burlington Island. *New Jersey History* 352 (Spring):24-35.

Baker, Emerson W.

1985　　　*The Clarke and Lake Company: The Historical Archaeology of a Seventeenth-Century Maine Settlement.* Occasional Publications in Maine Archaeology, No. 4. Maine Historic Preservation Commission, Augusta.

Beauchamp, William M.

1903　　　Metallic Ornaments of the New York Indians. *New York State Museum Bulletin*, 73, Albany.

Becker, Marshall J.

1977　　　"Swedish" Colonial Yellow Bricks: Notes on Their Uses and Possible Origins in 17th Century America. *Historical Archaeology* 11:112–118.

Beers, F. W.

1872　　　*Topographical Map of the Northern Part of Burlington County, New Jersey.* F. W. Beers, New York.

Bisbee, Henry

1971　　　*Sign Posts: Place Names in History of Burlington County, New Jersey.* Alexia Press, Willingboro, New Jersey.

1972　　　*Burlington Island: The Best and Largest on the South River, 1624–1972.* Heidelburg Press, Burlington, New Jersey.

Brown, Ian W.

1989　　　The Calumet Ceremony in the Southeast and Its Archaeological Manifestations. *American Antiquity* 54(2):311–331.

Cotter, John L.
1958   *Archaeological Excavations at Jamestown Colonial National Histori-cal Park and Jamestown National Historic Site, Virginia.* Archaeological Research Series No. 4, National Park Service, U.S. Department of the Interior, Washington, D.C.
1994   Beginnings. In *Pioneers in Historical Archaeology: Breaking New Ground,* edited by Stanley South, pp. 15–27, Plenum Press, New York.

Cotter, John L., Daniel G. Roberts, and Michael Parrington
1992   *The Buried Past: An Archaeological History of Philadelphia.* University of Pennsylvania Press, Philadelphia.

Cranmer, Leon E.
1990   *Cushnoc: The History and Archaeology of Plymouth Colony Trad-ers on the Kennebec.* Occasional Publications in Maine Archaeology, No. 7. The Maine Archaeological Society, Fort West Museum, and the Maine Historic Preservation Commission, Augusta.

Dallal, Diane
1995   "The People May Be Illiterate But they Are Not Blind," A Study of the Iconography of 17th Century Dutch Clay Tobacco Pipes Recovered from New York City's Archaeological Sites. Unpublished Master's the-sis, Department of Anthropology, New York University.

Dankers, Jaspar, and Peter Sluyter
1867   *Journal of a Voyage to New York and a Tour of Several of the American Colonies in 1679–80.* Translated by Henry C. Murphy. Memoirs of the Long Island Historical Society, Vol. 1. Brooklyn, New York.

Dawkins, W. B.
1883   Early Man in America. *North American Review* 137:338–349.

Deetz, James
1993   *Flowerdew Hundred: The Archaeology of a Virginia Plantation, 1619–1864.* University of Virginia Press, Charlottesville.
1996   *In Small Things Forgotten: An Archaeology of Early American Life.* Doubleday, New York.

Dilliplane, Timothy L.
1980   European Trade Kettles. In *Burr's Hill, A 17th Century Wampanoag Burial Ground in Warren, Rhode Island,* edited by Susan G. Givson, pp. 79–84. Haffenreffer Museum of Anthropology, Brown University.

Ehrhardt, Kathleen L.
2005   *European Metals in Native Hands: Rethinking Technological Change, 1640–1683.* University of Alabama Press, Tuscaloosa.

Emerson, Matthew Charles
1988   Decorated Clay Tobacco Pipes from the Chesapeake. Unpublished Ph.D. dissertation, University of California, Berkeley.

Faulkner, Alaric, and Gretchen Faulkner

1987   *The French at Pentagoet, 1635–1674: An Archaeological Portrait of the
            Acadian Frontier.* Special Publications of the New Brunswick Museum
            and Occasional Publications in Maine Archaeology, Maine Historic
            Preservation Commission.

Henry, Susan L.

1979   Terra-Cotta Tobacco Pipes in 17th Century Maryland and Virginia: A
            Preliminary Study. *Historical Archaeology* 13:14–37.

Hinsley, Curtis M.

1985   From Shell-Heaps to Stelae: Early Anthropology at the Peabody Mu-
            seum. In *Objects and Others: Essays on Museums and Material Cul-
            ture,* edited by George W. Stocking, Jr., pp. 49–74. University of Wis-
            consin Press, Madison.

2003   Drab Doves Take Flight: The Dilemmas of Early Americanist Archaeol-
            ogy in Philadelphia, 1889–1900. In *Philadelphia and the Development
            of Americanist Archaeology,* edited by Don D. Fowler and David R.
            Wilcox, pp. 1–20. University of Alabama Press, Tuscaloosa.

Holmes, William H.

1893   Are there traces of man in the Trenton gravels? *Journal of Geology,*
            1:15–37.

1898   Primitive man in the Delaware Valley. *Proceedings of the American As-
            sociation for the Advancement of Science* 46:364–370.

Huey, Paul R.

1991   The Dutch at Fort Orange. In *Historical Archaeology in Global Per-
            spective,* edited by Lisa Falk, pp. 21–68. Smithsonian Institution Press,
            Washington, D.C.

Hurry, Silas D., and Robert W. Keeler

1991   A Descriptive Analysis of the White Clay Tobacco Pipes from the St.
            John's Site in St. Mary's City, Maryland. In *The Archaeology of the
            Clay Tobacco Pipe, XII. Chesapeake Bay,* edited by Peter Davey and
            Dennis J. Pogue, Liverpool Monographs in Archaeology and Oriental
            Studies No. 14, BAR International Series 566, pp. 73–88.

Jacobs, Jaap

2004   *New Netherland, a Dutch Colony in 17th-Century America.* Brill Aca-
            demic Publishers, Bedfordshire, United Kingdom.

Karklins, Karlis

1983   Dutch Trade Beads in North America. In *Proceedings of the 1982 Glass
            Trade Bead Conference, Research Records No. 16,* edited by Charles F.
            Hayes III, pp. 111–126. Rochester Museum and Science Center, Roch-
            ester, NY.

Kidd, Kenneth E. and Martha A. Kidd

1970   A Classification System for Glass Beads for the Use of Field Archaeolo-
            gists. *Canadian Historic Sites: Occasional Papers in Archaeology and*

History 1:45–89, Parks Canada, Ottawa. Reprinted in *Proceedings of the 1982 Glass Bead Conference,* edited by Charles F. Hayes, Appendix, pp. 219–257, Research Records 16, Rochester Museum and Science Division, Rochester, New York, 1983.

Kirk, Matthew
2003   Out of the Ashes of Craft, the Fires of Consumerism: A 1797 Deposit in Downtown Albany. In *People, Places, and Material Things: Historical Archaeology of Albany, New York,* edited by Charles L. Fisher, pp. 47–56. New York State Museum Bulletin 499.

Kraft, Herbert C.
1975   *The Archaeology of the Tocks Island Area.* Archaeological Research Center, Seton Hall University Museum, South Orange, New Jersey.

Meeske, Harrison
2001   *The Hudson Valley Dutch and Their Houses.* Purple Mountain Press, Fleischmanns, New York.

Meltzer, David J.
2003   In the Heat of Controversy: C. C. Abbott, the American Paleolithic, and the University Museum, 1889–1893. In *Philadelphia and the Development of Americanist Archaeology,* edited by Don D. Fowler and David R. Wilcox, pp. 48–87. University of Alabama Press, Tuscaloosa.
2005   The Seventy-Year Itch: Controversies over Human Antiquity and their Resolution. *Journal of Anthropological Research* 61(4):433–478.

Mercer, Henry C.
1892   Pebbles chipped by modern Indians as an aid to the study of the Trenton gravel implements. *Proceedings of the American Association for the Advancement of Science* 41:287–289.
1893   Trenton and Somme gravel specimens compared with ancient quarry refuse in America and Europe. *American Naturalist* 27:962–978.
1894   The nonexistence of Paleolithic culture. *American Naturalist* 28:90–92.

Mercer, H. C., E. D. Cope, and R. H. Harte
1897   Researches upon the antiquity of man in the Delaware Valley and the eastern United States. *Publications of the University of Pennsylvania, Series in Philology, Literature, and Archaeology* 6:87–109.

Miller, Henry M.
1991   Tobacco Pipes from Pope's Fort, St. Mary's City, Maryland: An English Civil War Site on the American Frontier. In *The Archaeology of the Clay Tobacco Pipe, XII, Chesapeake Bay,* edited by Peter Davey and Dennis J. Pogue, pp.73–88. Liverpool Monographs in Archaeology and Oriental Studies No. 14, BAR International Series 566.

Mulford, Isaac
1853   The History and Location of Fort Nassau on the Delaware. *Proceedings of the New Jersey Historical Society* 6:187–207.

Moser, Jason D., Al Luckenbach, Sherri M. Marsh, and Donna Ware
2003   Impermanent Architecture in a Less Permanent Town: The Mid-
            Seventeenth-Century Architecture of Providence Maryland. In *Con-
            structing Image, Identity, and Place: Perspectives in Vernacular Archi-
            tecture IX*, edited by Alison K. Hoagland, and Kenneth A. Breisch, pp.
            197–214. University of Tennessee Press, Knoxville.

Nelson, William
1886   Some Notes on Matinneconck, or Burlington Island. *The Pennsylvania
            Magazine of History and Biography* X: 214–216.

Noël Hume, Ivor
1970   *A Guide to the Artifacts of Colonial America.* Alfred A. Knopf, New
            York.

Putnam, F. W.
1888   Paleolithic man in eastern and central North America. *Proceedings of
            the Boston Society of Natural History* 23:247–254.

Reed, H. Clay, and George J. Miller
1944   *The Burlington Court Book: A Record of Quaker Jurisprudence in
            West New Jersey 1680–1709.* The American Historical Association,
            Washington, D.C.

Scharfenberger, Gerard P.
2004   Recent Evidence for Broad Window Glass in Seventeenth- and
            Eighteenth-Century America. *Historical Archaeology* 38(4):59–72.

Schuyler, Robert L.
1977   *Historical Archaeology: A Guide to Substantive and Theoretical Con-
            tributions.* Baywood, Farmingdale, New York.

Scott, J. D.
1876a   *Combination Atlas Map of Burlington City, New Jersey.* J. D. Scott,
            Philadelphia.
1876b   *Combination Atlas Map of Burlington Township, New Jersey.* J. D.
            Scott, Philadelphia.

Shaler, N.
1893   Antiquity of Man in Eastern North America. *The American Geologist*
            11:180–184.

Skinner, Alanson, and Max Schrabisch
1913   A Preliminary Report of the Archaeological Survey of the State of New
            Jersey. *Bulletin of the Geological Survey of New Jersey,* No. 9, Mac-
            Crellish and Quigley, Trenton.

Smith, Samuel
1765   *The History of the Colony of Nova-Caesaria, or New Jersey: Con-
            taining an Account of Its First Settlement, Progressive Improvements.
            The Original and Present Constitution, and Other Events, to the Year
            1721. With Some Particulars Since; and a Short View of its Present
            State.* James Parker, Burlington, New Jersey.

Thomas, Ronald A.
1985   Data Recovery at 28CA50, Gloucester City, New Jersey. MAAR Associates, Inc., Newark, Delaware, Report prepared for National Park Service, Mid-Atlantic Region, Philadelphia.

Van Laer, A. J. F. (editor)
1924   *Documents Relating to New Netherlands, 1624–1626, in the Henry E. Huntington Library.* Henry E. Huntington Library and Art Gallery, San Marino, California.

Veit, Richard
2000   Following the Yellow Brick Road: Dutch Bricks in New Jersey, Facts and Folklore. *Bulletin of the Archaeological Society of New Jersey* 55:70–77.

Veit, Richard, and Charles Bello
1999   "A Unique and Valuable Historical and Indian Collection": Charles Conrad Abbott Explores a 17th Century Dutch Trading Post in the Delaware Valley. *Journal of Middle Atlantic Archaeology* 15: 95–123.

Walker, Iain C.
1977   *Clay Tobacco Pipes with Particular Reference to the Bristol Industry.* History and Archaeology, nos. 11 A-D. Parks Canada, Ottawa.

Weslager, C. A.
1961   *Dutch Explorers, Traders and Settlers in the Delaware Valley 1609–1664.* University of Pennsylvania Press, Philadelphia.
1967   *The English on the Delaware 1610–1682.* Rutgers University Press, New Brunswick, New Jersey.

Wray, Charles F., Martha L. Sempowski, and Lorraine P. Saunders
1990   *Two Early Contact Era Seneca Sites: Tram and Cameron.* C. F. Wray Series in Seneca Archaeology, Vol. 2, Rochester Museum and Science Center, Research Record 21, Rochester, NY.

Wright, G. F.
1881   On the Age of the Trenton Gravel. *Proceedings Boston Society of Natural History* 21: 137–145.

Primary sources

Diaries, Charles Conrad Abbott Papers, Box 3, Folders 2, 3 and 5, Manuscripts Division, Department of Rare Books and Special Collections, Princeton University Library, New Jersey.

Correspondence, Charles Conrad Abbot to F. W. Putnam, F. W. Putnam Papers, Peabody Museum, Harvard University, Cambridge, Massachusetts.

3

Marcus Hook, Pennsylvania: Toward the Preservation of a Significant Historical Landscape

Joseph R. Blondino

Introduction

Known as the "Cornerstone of Pennsylvania," the borough of Marcus Hook has a long and fascinating history. Beginning with the arrival of the first colonists in the mid-seventeenth century and continuing through the early twentieth century, "the Hook" was one of the most economically and strategically important locations in the lower Delaware Valley—its importance in some ways rivaling even that of Philadelphia in the early colonial period. However, with the destruction of many of the town's early historic buildings and the establishment of two major oil refineries there, the historical significance of this small Delaware County town was largely forgotten by the end of the twentieth century. Fortunately, the efforts of a few dedicated local citizens have begun to change that, and there has been a recent resurgence of interest in the rich history of this small town along the Delaware River.

The spark that ignited this renewed interest in the history of the borough was struck in the spring of 2004, when Marcus Hook residents Michael and Pat Manerchia purchased a small house at the corner of Market Street and Market Lane (figure 3.1). No longer having children at home, the Manerchias were simply looking to downsize from the house they lived in at the time. The little house at 221 Market Street seemed perfect—it was just the right size for two people and had been in Pat's family for years. As the property was threatened by development, they could not pass up the opportunity to purchase and save the property. The house needed some work, but Mike was up to the task. At the time, Michael and Pat had no way of knowing just how much work they were about to take on.

The Manerchias knew quite well that the little house was old. In fact, it was known to Marcus Hook residents as the oldest house in town. As such, it was of course also reputed to be haunted. In fact, many Hook residents still regale one another with ghost stories related to the house, and some will even tell you that as children they would cross to the other side of the street rather than walk directly in front of it. Additionally, local legend had it that a mistress of the notorious pirate Blackbeard had lived in the house and that the famed sea-robber himself stayed there frequently when in the area.

Figure 3.1. The Marcus Hook Plank Log House in a late-nineteenth-century photograph. Only the bay with the porch remains today.

Reports of the house's great age seemed to have been confirmed when the Manerchias began to do work on the structure. While beginning some remodeling work in the kitchen one day, Mike fell through the floor when some rotted floorboards gave way beneath him. Beneath the floorboards, he found what appeared to be an original dirt floor and, after removing the remaining flooring, began to recover artifacts from it. Although Mike had no background in archaeology, he reasoned that the artifacts he was finding must pre-date the wooden floorboards, which he recognized as dating at least to the nineteenth century by the cut nails used to fasten them. Mike then contacted a local historian, who promptly showed up with a couple of amateur preservationists and proceeded to cut a hole in one of the walls. This exploratory hole through the drywall and plaster revealed the original plank log construction of the home. It was then that the Manerchias began to realize what an architectural and historical treasure they had on their hands. They soon contacted local archaeologists and architectural historians, and Dr. David Orr and I, both archaeologists in Temple University's Department of Anthropology, soon became involved. The local chapter of the Society for Pennsylvania Archaeology was also contacted, and this group began excavations under the direction of chapter president Dr. Catherine Spohn.

In the same year, the Manerchias established the Marcus Hook Plank Log Cabin Association, a non-profit organization dedicated to the study and preservation of the house, and they donated the house and lot to the organization. The association has as its goal not only the study of this structure, but, as worded in its mission statement, "the interpretation. . . of significant historical features of Marcus Hook social and cultural life during the seventeenth through nineteenth centuries." The association is thus concerned with the history and archaeology of the town as a whole, not merely of its own property. Since 2005, the all-volunteer organization, now known more inclusively as the Marcus Hook Preservation Society (MHPS), has worked to promote the historical significance of this small town. I will now turn my attention first to a brief discussion of the history of Marcus Hook, and then to the work of the MHPS and some of the discoveries which have been made through their efforts.

An Abridged History of Marcus Hook, Pennsylvania

The town of Marcus Hook was occupied by Swedish and Finnish settlers as early as the 1640s, when it was part of what was then New Sweden. Peter Lindstrom's 1655 map of New Sweden (reproduced in Acrelius 1874) refers to the area now occupied by Marcus Hook as "Finlandh." As is often the case, the choice of this particular piece of land for early settlement may have been a simple matter of local geography. Smith (1862) points out that Marcus Hook, along with Chester, occupies one of the only areas on the Pennsylvania side of the Delaware River below Tinicum Island where there naturally existed a significant amount of fast and dry land directly abutting a navigable portion of the river itself. Marshes and tidal flats separate the river from other potential areas for settlement. The Dutch also had their eyes on the area in the mid-seventeenth century, and for a time the fledgling colonies of New Sweden and New Netherland vied for control of the lower Delaware Valley. The English also coveted the region, of course, and it was they who ultimately became the victors in the struggle for control of the Middle Atlantic colonies, finally securing the region for themselves in 1674 (Acrelius 1874). However, the earlier European colonists continued to maintain a significant presence in the area for some time, as attested to by a 1676 map of the lower Delaware by Arent Roggeveen (reproduced in Smith, 1862), which still refers to this strip of land along the river as "Laplandt."

By the early eighteenth century, the area was under uncontested British rule, and Marcus Hook was a bustling community and market town, a public market there having been chartered by William Penn in 1701 (charter reproduced in Smith 1862). By 1708, Marcus Hook rivaled the neighboring settlement of Chester in size, both places being described in period documents as having nearly 100 houses (Ashmead 1884). By the middle of the eighteenth century, Marcus Hook had become a major regional center for the building of wooden sailing ships (Acrelius 1874), and it remained so until the late nineteenth century when demand for larger-tonnage vessels began to outpace that for the smaller sloops and schooners built at Hook (Ashmead 1884). In fact, the only iron-hulled American merchant schooner still sailing, the Pioneer, was built in Marcus Hook in 1885 (Miller 2007).

Much of Marcus Hook's historical significance, in fact, comes from its identity as a maritime town. Marcus Hook was among the first ports of call for vessels traveling to and from Philadelphia from its earliest days and would become the farthest upriver that large ships could safely navigate without taking on a pilot possessing knowledge of the local shoals and tides. The Hook was also a haven for pirates in the early eighteenth century, when piracy plagued the lower Delaware River and Bay. The market at Marcus Hook would have provided sea-rovers with a place to sell plundered goods and re-supply for their next voyage while remaining a safe distance downriver from the watchful eyes of the authorities and customs officials in Philadelphia. In fact, eighteenth- and nineteenth-century maps show that what is now Second Street was originally called Discord Lane, apparently because it was the location of much of the pirates' revelry while they were in town (Ashmead 1884). Although there is currently no evidence to support it, there is a local oral tradition that the Marcus Hook Plank House was once the home of a mistress of the notorious pirate Edward Teach, better known as Blackbeard. Blackbeard cannot be said with any certainty to have visited the Plank House, especially considering the likelihood that the house was constructed sometime after his death in 1718. However, Blackbeard is known to have operated in the Delaware River during his piratical career and to have probably visited Marcus Hook. Ashmead's 1884 *History of Delaware County* mentions Blackbeard frequenting Marcus Hook, and John Watson's 1830 volume, *Annals of Philadelphia and Pennsylvania,* tells us of a "traditional story, that Blackbeard and his crew used to visit and revel at Marcus Hook, at the house of a Swedish woman" (1830:217).

Marcus Hook also played an important role in the early history of the United States. During the American Revolution, a line of cheveaux-de-frise was committed to be placed across the channel of the Delaware at Marcus Hook to provide the first line of defense for Philadelphia against British naval forces. These do not seem to have actually been emplaced there, however, as period documents seem to indicate that the use of cheveaux-de-frise did not extend any farther downriver than Chester (Ashmead 1884). Nonetheless, Marcus Hook represented a critical stretch of the Delaware River shoreline for the Continentals to defend—as the channel of the river was such that vessels coming upriver were forced to come "within musket-shot of the shore at and near Marcus Hook" and some local residents feared it would present an ideal place for British troops to be landed for an overland march to Philadelphia (Ashmead 1884). In 1781, the allied American and French forces marched through Marcus Hook on their way to Yorktown, following what is now known as the "Washington-Rochambeau route." In fact, it seems that it was at Marcus Hook that General Washington received the news that French naval forces had managed to enter the Chesapeake without being harassed by the British (Wiseley 2009). Marcus Hook again served as a defensive post along the Delaware when several thousand militia troops were stationed there in 1814, and an earthwork mounted with artillery was constructed just below town to help fend off British naval forces again (Smith 1862).

Later in the nineteenth century, the area around Marcus Hook and Chester became a center for commercial fishing, particularly of shad and herring (Ashmead 1884; Smith 1862). Sturgeon remains recovered archaeologically in Marcus Hook attest to these great fish once being plentiful in this part of the river as well. The older citizens of Marcus Hook report that sport fishermen and quail hunters also stayed in several of the resort hotels that had been established in and near town, as Marcus Hook's location provided easy access to both the Delaware River and the extensive wetlands around Tinicum Island and the area now occupied by Philadelphia International Airport. Similarly, Ashmead (1884) reports that the area around Chester was, at the time of his writing, a popular destination in the summer and fall for hunting "reed-birds" in the local marshes.

The town of Marcus Hook began to take on its modern character in 1901, when Sun Oil Company established a large refinery there (Miller 2007). Nine years later, Union Petroleum established a refinery on the other side of town, making the Hook one of the largest centers of petroleum refining in the country. In the same year, the American Viscose Company built a large industrial complex in Marcus Hook, and the producer of "artificial silk" gave the town the distinction of being the largest producer of synthetic fiber in the world at the time (Miller 2007). By the middle of the twentieth century, Marcus Hook was well-established as an industrial town, and it remains such today, still home to refineries of both Sunoco and Conoco Philips (formerly Union Petroleum).

The Marcus Hook Plank Log House

Until recently, few knew that in the midst of this industrial center a significant historical landscape survived. As briefly discussed above, this landscape began to be rediscovered when historians and archaeologists, both amateur and professional, became interested in the Marcus Hook Plank Log House. The "Plank House" itself is a one-and-a-half story, hall-plan house featuring a finished upper level and full cellar. The house is constructed using sawn planks fitted together with full dovetail joinery (figure 3.2) in a manner similar to that seen in one of the only other plank houses known in the region, the Christopher Vandergrift House in New Castle County, Delaware (Herman 1987). The spaces between the planks are caulked with oakum. Some of the original riven lath remains on the interior of the house, and the walls were likely finished with plaster at the time of construction or soon thereafter. The cellar reveals that the foundation of the house was constructed of irregular courses of undressed quartz and Wissahickon schist. A stone and brick relieving arch in the cellar supports the fireplaces and chimney stack. The upper level of the house, accessed via a winder staircase located in the northeastern corner of the structure, essentially mirrors the main room below except that it has an inclined garret ceiling, which follows rafters beautifully joined at the peak with trenail-pinned mortise-and-tenons. The dormer window in this upper level is currently gabled, but surviving nineteenth century photographs of the house show that it was originally shed-roofed. The upper room also features a fielded panel fireplace surround and overmantle, which is believed to be original. The architecture of the house indicates a probable construction date of 1730–1750 but likely on the earlier end of that range.

Early twentieth-century photographs of the Plank House also show another wing to the north that was apparently removed. This north wing appears to be roughly contemporaneous with the construction of the main portion of the house and was likely built at the same time or shortly thereafter. The Plank House also features an extant shed-roofed brick addition to the rear of the main part of the structure. We believe that this addition was also added relatively soon after the construction of the main portion of the house—probably within twenty years or so, as indicated by the relatively pristine condition of the original weatherboarding and corbels of the main house that are now covered by the addition. The addition seems to have been built to serve as the home's kitchen, and it has continued to serve in this capacity throughout the occupation of the structure. In the northeastern corner of this room is what is left of the hearth for a large hooded, or "walk-in," fireplace. Just to the right of center in the wall above this hearth is a now-infilled brick arch representing what was once the access to a beehive-style bake oven, one of the footers for which has been recognized archaeologically in excavations just on the other side of the wall.

Figure 3.2. An interior view of the Marcus Hook Plank house, showing the intricate dovetail work and carefully fitted timbers. Photograph by Joe Blondino.

The lot upon which the Plank House sits is depicted on a 1701 map of the town in possession of the Historical Society of Pennsylvania. On this map, the lot is associated with the name Roger Jackson, the earliest known owner of the property. William Penn's 1701 charter for a public market at Marcus Hook (reproduced in Smith 1862) makes reference to a house on the lot. In this document, Penn gives directions for the layout of the market place, the location of which is still apparent by the grassy median that currently occupies this area. Penn explains that the breadth of the marketplace should extend to "the house now of Roger Jackson." The fact that Penn refers to the house *now* of Roger Jackson may be an indication that there was already a structure on the lot when Jackson purchased it, and Penn's apparent familiarity with the town attests to its importance in the early colonial history of the area. Exactly when Roger Jackson arrived in Marcus Hook is unclear. He is certainly in the area, and quite possibly at the current site of the Plank House, by 1694, at which time court records show that he was one of "Twelve men of the neighborhood" appointed to appraise a tract of land located along the Delaware waterfront in "Chichester Town" now known as Marcus Hook (Chester County Court Records 1910).

Perhaps as interesting as the facts about the early history of the Plank House are the legends. As mentioned above, the Plank House is reputed to have been the home of the pirate Blackbeard's mistress (or at least the one he kept in Marcus Hook), although this is considered unlikely due to the dating of the house to the period after the notorious pirate's death. Another local legend associated with the house is that of the underground tunnels, which supposedly connected the house to the Delaware waterfront. Thus far, no evidence of these tunnels has been located, and they are considered unlikely to exist. However, legends like these die hard, and many local citizens insist upon their existence, with a few even claiming to have been in the tunnels. The stories of these underground passages may result from an erroneous interpretation of the function of the relieving arch for the fireplace and chimney in the cellar of the house. This is an architectural feature found in the basements of other eighteenth-century houses in town as well, thus possibly giving rise to the tales of a complex network of tunnels. The tunnels, of course, are supposed by some to have been used by pirates to hide their plundered goods from the authorities. A similar story is that they were used by smugglers to slip goods into port while evading tax and customs officials. Still others propose that they were a part of the Underground Railroad, which, of course, was figuratively but not literally underground, and that they were used to transport and conceal escaped African American slaves. Like the Blackbeard legend, the stories of the tunnels are as of yet unfounded in fact, but they certainly provide for another interesting aspect of the house.

Archaeology at the Plank House

Archaeological investigations at the Plank House began in May of 2005 when a group of volunteers from Chapter 21 of the Society for Pennsylvania Archaeology became involved, working under the direction of chapter president Dr. Catherine Spohn. Later that year, Dr. David Orr and I also began working at the Plank House with several student volunteers from Temple University. Our work at the site has continued since that time. The archaeological investigations began with a series of 5 foot square excavation units placed in the area north of the extant portion of the house to recover evidence of the structure's demolished north wing, referred to as the "Counting House" because of a local oral tradition regarding the function of this part of the structure. The foundation walls of this wing were exposed, as was a stone feature that represents one of the footers for the bake oven associated with the kitchen addition to the rear of the house. The archaeology in this area suggests that this addition was likely also of log construction, as very few nails were recovered from the destruction levels. This portion of the house is believed to have been constructed contemporaneously with the standing structure or only shortly thereafter, and clearly predates the construction of the kitchen addition.

In the spring of 2011, Temple University archaeologists opened an excavation unit in the southwest corner of this addition, where it joins the standing portion of the house. This unit was opened to facilitate the installation of below-ground electrical service to the house, as we felt that the overhead lines detracted from the historic aesthetic of the structure. Because the new electric service had to enter the north wall of the cellar, the installation trench had to come through the foundation for the "Counting House" addition. This required the removal of the foundation stones from this corner. While we were initially less than pleased about having to disrupt the integrity of the foundation, this turned out to be rather fortuitous. In the preserved surface beneath the large cornerstone that abutted the foundation of the main house, we recovered an object that we believe firmly dates the construction of this addition: a Spanish two *reale* coin dated 1737. While technically this only gives us a *terminus post quem* of 1737 on the addition, the location and condition of the coin (apparently circulated very little), suggest that it was likely placed beneath the cornerstone at the time of construction in order to date the structure. With the addition thus fairly securely dated, we can say with confidence that the 1730s date suggested by the architecture of the standing structure is reasonably accurate.

Two excavation units opened north of the "counting house" encountered an additional stone foundation, albeit one appearing to be less substantial in nature. This wall abuts the main foundation for the north wing of the house and was originally thought to have possibly supported a small porch on this end of the structure. However, a recently discovered photograph reveals that this was actually the foundation wall for a third wing of the house (see figure 3.1). Thus far we have not excavated a sufficient sample of this area to allow the date or mode of construction of this wing to be determined.

Among the most important findings in the excavations to the north of the Plank House was a preserved ground surface recognized in several of the excavation units (figure 3.3). This buried surface was found to contain primarily artifacts dating no later than approximately the mid-eighteenth century. Not surprisingly, prehistoric artifacts were also recovered from this level, including a Jack's Reef stemmed point, evidence of occupation at least during the Middle Woodland period. Given the probability that the Plank House lot was occupied prior to the construction of the standing structure, this preserved surface represents our best chance to locate seventeenth- and early-eighteenth-century deposits on the site. Future excavations farther from the house itself may reveal locations where this original surface has been minimally impacted by later occupations and activities.

Archaeological excavations have also been conducted inside the northern portion of the kitchen addition. These were focused on determining whether traces of an original floor level or ground surface possibly containing evidence of a structure predating the standing house were present. Unfortunately, any such evidence has been obliterated by the construction of tunnels in this area. However, these are not the tunnels that the locals tell stories about, but a complex network of tiny tunnels left behind by burrowing rodents. The archaeological deposits in this area were extremely artifact rich but contained a mix of object types dating from the Late Archaic period into the twentieth century, with the vertical integrity of the deposits almost entirely destroyed by the rodent activity.

Figure 3.3. The dotted line indicates the buried ground surface noted in the excavation units to the north of the house. Photograph by Joe Blondino.

In the spring of 2006, a geophysical survey of the property was conducted by Naeva Geophysics, Inc., who graciously donated their services to the project. The Naeva crew first investigated the yard area for electromagnetic anomalies using an EM-61 high-resolution time-domain electromagnetic metal-detector. Following this, they conducted a ground-penetrating radar survey, recording reflection slices on a 2-1/2 foot interval grid for optimal resolution (Hamajima 2006). It was felt that this transect spacing was sufficiently small to allow for recognition of most archaeologically significant features, while being large enough for all open areas of the Plank House lot to be investigated in a single day's work. We were unsure at the outset of this survey how useful the data generated might be, as much of the property is covered by a thick poured concrete slab lying just beneath the sod and relating to the use of the lot through part of the twentieth century as a parking area for tow trucks and other vehicles. Despite this, promising results were seen in the field as the survey was being conducted, and the subsequent analysis of the data showed a number of discrete anomalies lying beneath the concrete. Although the electromagnetic data by itself is not particularly telling, the ground-penetrating radar revealed the locations of several anomalies, some of which correlate with electromagnetic aberrations picked up by the EM-61.

Analysis of the cross-sectional profiles of the largest of the GPR anomalies reveals a strong reflection roughly 2–3' below ground surface and measuring approximately 20' by 30' in area (Hamajima 2006). This likely represents a structure remembered by Michael Manerchia's father as a building used in the twentieth century as the local polling place during elections. Although this may not seem to be a terribly exciting archaeological feature, it nonetheless demonstrates the utility of employing GPR at this site despite the impediment posed by the thick concrete slab. These encouraging results make other reflections seem promising indeed, particularly a few which appear to potentially be sized, shaped, and located consistent with our expectations for privies or other deep shaft features. Ground-truthing such anomalies revealed by the geophysical survey will be the focus of future field investigations in the yard area. We are deeply indebted to the Naeva crew for donating their time and effort to the project, and we look forward to using their data to guide future excavations.

To date, one of the anomalies located by the geophysical survey has been investigated. This was a strong anomalous reflection located approximately 25 feet from the back of the original, plank log section of the house and almost directly in line with the back door (Hamajima 2006). As this anomaly was located in what seemed a possible location for a well or cistern, it was at the top of the priority list for ground-truthing. A block of two contiguous 5 foot square excavation units opened over this anomaly revealed an unmortared brick pavement running roughly northeast. This pavement appears to represent a walkway, although it is unclear what it may have led to, and the notion that it may in fact represent the floor of an earlier structure cannot be entirely discounted without further excavation. Additionally, it is interesting to note that the orientation of this pavement is somewhat askew to that of the Plank House, another possible indication that it may be related to an earlier structure. While the construction date of this feature is uncertain, a third excavation unit opened adjacent to it revealed what appeared to be a ground surface that yielded many artifacts dating to the first half of the eighteenth century. Although this level also contained a fair number of later objects dating through the first half of the nineteenth century, it nonetheless represents the largest concentration of both tin-enameled and Staffordshire slipped earthenware as yet identified at the site. The expansion of excavations in this area of the site in an effort to trace out this possible original surface will continue to be a focus of archaeological investigations at the Plank House.

Public Archaeology and Volunteering at the Plank House

The Marcus Hook Plank Log House provides an ideal place to get the public involved in archaeology and train volunteers in archaeological field and laboratory methods. The location of the site, near the riverfront along Marcus Hook's main street, makes it a setting with high visibility to the public. This setting is perfect for conducting public archaeology, and we take advantage of the town's various festivals and parades to work in view of and interact with members of the public. Additionally, because our work at the Plank House is research-driven and the site is not threatened, we do not feel the pressure of having to meet deadlines or budgetary restrictions and can proceed at any pace we choose. This being the case, all of the archaeology at the site is done on a volunteer basis, with professionals and amateurs alike contributing their time to the project.

The nature of the deposits at the Plank House site also makes it an ideal place to train people in archaeological methods. The stratigraphy across much of the site consists of a series of fills deposited following the demolition of the north wing of the house. Underlying these fills is a relatively undisturbed eighteenth-century land surface, and this sealed context has proven to contain features as well as period artifacts. Most importantly with regard to our volunteer effort is that the profiles exhibit classic "layer cake" stratigraphy, which is very easy to recognize and thus allows us to demonstrate clearly to our volunteers the basic principles of archaeological stratigraphy. The clear boundaries between the strata allow volunteer excavators to proceed with confidence as they dig. Additionally, these layers of fill are loaded with artifacts dating from the seventeenth through the twentieth centuries, so the thrill of discovery is a constant presence for workers at the site.

Volunteers work side by side with professional archaeologists, who are always on site whenever any excavation is being conducted. Volunteers are constantly learning about how archaeologists work and the reasoning behind the methods we employ, and we invite anyone interested in the effort to participate, whether they become "regulars" or just dig with us for a couple of hours. Our volunteers are also given the opportunity to work in whatever capacity they choose. Thus, we have both excavators and lab crew, many of whom have at this point become quite knowledgeable in eighteenth- and nineteenth-century material culture. We also have volunteers who are primarily interested in doing documentary research, and it is through them that we have learned much about the history of the area and have uncovered several early photographs of the house. Our dedication to using volunteers at the site has been beneficial to all parties involved. Without them, we would not have been able to accomplish even half of the amount of excavation, lab work, and documentary research that has now been done, and we, in turn, provide them with an opportunity not simply to learn about archaeology and other aspects of historical research but to directly participate in the process.

Other Archaeological Sites in Marcus Hook

The Plank House is not the only site in Marcus Hook that has received recent archaeological attention. The lot fronting the river at 12 East Delaware Avenue has also proven to contain significant archaeological resources. This property, by the way, is also owned by Mike and Pat Manerchia. In fact, it is the house into which they moved after realizing the information potential of the Plank House and donating it for research. Not long after buying the new old house, which is believed to date to roughly 1790–1800, Mike recognized a drainage problem in the backyard, where he wanted to erect a storage shed. Mike's intended solution to this drainage issue was simple enough—he would dig up the poorly drained soil and replace it with a thick bed of gravel. To this end, he got a backhoe (Mike is a heavy equipment operator, and therefore potentially both the best friend and the worst enemy an archaeologist can have), and he began to dig a hole. Within minutes, he had hit a stone foundation. Fortunately, Mike falls into the "best friend" category, and so immediately stopped digging and contacted the Temple University archaeologists.

Excavation continued after we arrived to take a look and monitor the work. We eventually found ourselves in a cellar apparently predating the standing structure, and likely from the first half of the eighteenth century. The cause of Mike's drainage problem had been that water was unable to readily drain from within the mortared stone walls of the cellar. We simply did not have time to fully excavate this site, so after recording what we could, we had Mike carefully backfill the cellar in the interest of preservation.

Ever since finding the cellar in the backyard, we had joked that Michael Manerchia was a magnet for the eighteenth century—just give Mike a shovel and follow him around for ten minutes and you were bound to find something. In November 2007, Mike again proved that he really is blessed (or cursed, depending on your point of view) with the ability to discover archaeological sites. This time he was turning over soil for a future garden area in the side yard of his house when he encountered another stone wall. He again stopped and called the present author. Although the exploratory trench he dug after finding the wall provided only a very small window into this new site, I was able to determine that it probably contained another cellar which postdates the backyard foundation but predates the standing house. We had identified three generations of building on one small lot, and it is probably safe to assume that this is not an anomaly in Marcus Hook. There must be dozens of early- to mid-eighteenth-century, and possibly earlier, sites in Hook that go undiscovered or, if discovered, go unreported to the archaeological community. The sites that we have identified already would have been lost had Mike Manerchia not been educated about the importance of recording and preserving archaeological resources. This is exactly the type of responsibility and stewardship that the Marcus Hook Preservation Society strives to promote. Though he is now Marcus Hook's greatest patron of archaeological research, Mike Manerchia had no particular interest in history before getting involved in hands-on preservation efforts, and we believe that other people will be affected in the same way Mike was if only given the opportunity.

Recently, archaeological testing was conducted in the grassy median in the center of Market Street in Marcus Hook, opposite the Plank House. This median occupies the location shown on a 1701 map as the Market Place, and described in William Penn's charter for the public market, dated the same year. Historic maps of Marcus Hook reveal that the area occupied by this median remained an open public square or market throughout much of the town's history. As such, the modern median was assumed to have great potential to contain evidence of the early market, or at least to contain evidence of additional preserved early ground surfaces. In September 2009, a series of shovel tests was excavated down the center of the median by the present author and graduate and undergraduate student volunteers from Temple University (figure 3.4). Unfortunately, no evidence of original surfaces was observed in the test excavations, and it seems as though the original ground surface in the areas tested has been truncated and replaced by a series of fill deposits relating to various utility installation trenches, and possibly a trolley line. However, it is not unlikely that small windows into undisturbed early deposits remain undiscovered in this area, and these could potentially be located by more extensive testing than that which was carried out, which was done largely as a public archaeology demonstration during the town's annual "Riverfront Ramble" festival. Additionally, the failure of this testing to locate preserved surfaces in this area, initially considered to be one of the most promising localities in Marcus Hook to contain such deposits, only goes to reinforce further the significance of those eighteenth-century deposits that have been located to date. This is certainly not to say that early surfaces and other archaeological deposits do not exist in Marcus Hook, only that they have yet to be discovered. Moreover, this clearly demonstrates the immense importance of documenting sites such as the Plank House—sites which not only contain significant early deposits, but which are accessible to archaeologists.

Figure 3.4. Shovel testing in the median of Market Street in an effort to identify the Marcus Hook Market Place. Photograph by Joe Blondino.

The Future of Marcus Hook's Past

Anyone who has been involved in a grass-roots preservation effort similar to the one that has been undertaken at Marcus Hook can attest to how much of a struggle it can be to get such a program off the ground. When our work in Marcus Hook began, many people at first thought that we were merely treasure hunters looking for Blackbeard's gold. Some individuals even actively opposed our efforts for fear that we would somehow interfere with residential development projects. We fought for federal recognition as a non-profit, wading through the sea of red tape involved in proving ourselves deserving of that status. However, we have made great progress. Largely as a result of the efforts of the Marcus Hook Preservation Society, the borough is now taking an active role in promoting and preserving its newly rediscovered past. Marcus Hook now even hosts an annual Pirate Festival in celebration of its maritime history. In addition, the MHPS finally enjoys federal tax-exempt status and is actively seeking funds for the stabilization and ultimate restoration of the Marcus Hook Plank Log House, with the goal of making it the centerpiece of the borough's historic preservation efforts.

We envision the Plank House as being more than just another restored historic home, replete with period furnishings and interpreters in period costume. While this approach may offer visitors a more direct experience of history, it can also sometimes distract them from the real historical importance of a site by showcasing "typical" period dress and furnishings over the things that give a *particular* site its significance. Instead, we would like to showcase the uniqueness of the architecture of the structure, leaving sections of the walls "peeled back" layer by layer so that visitors can not only appreciate the mode of construction of the house, but they also see how we work to reveal such details of a building's history. We advocate a more holistic approach to the interpretation of the site that incorporates history, architecture, and archaeology to more fully flesh out the story of the site as not merely an old house, but a place where people lived, worked, and were active participants in their home and community.

In addition to telling the story of the Plank House and other sites in Marcus Hook, it is important to the members of the Marcus Hook Preservation Society that we tell our own story as well. It is through the work of organizations like the MHPS that the small treasures of our nation's history will be preserved—places that are important not necessarily because of a famous person or event, but simply because they are important. These are the places that history often overlooks, but in fact, tell the real story of the past. Furthermore, small, "do-it-yourself" preservation groups—working in conjunction with professional preservationists, historians, and archaeologists—are often our best option for saving the history of small town and big city alike. We have already had great success in spreading our passion for history to others and giving people a unique opportunity to share in the discovery of that history on days when we open both the Plank House itself and the archaeological excavations there to the public and allow them to observe, interact, and maybe even get their hands into a sifting screen for a few minutes to pull out a piece of our collective past themselves. Members of the MHPS are active in making presentations to other local historical societies, school groups, community organizations, and anyone else who is interested in what we are doing. We have involved scores of volunteers and students and will continue to welcome new people into our organization. It is our hope that we not only stimulate interest in local history and archaeology in southeastern Pennsylvania, but also that our efforts serve as an example to others of what a dedicated handful of volunteers can accomplish with perseverance and more than a little stubbornness. If you should ever find yourself in Marcus Hook, come visit us—we might get you "Hooked" as well.

Acknowledgments

Thanks are due to people too numerous to list, but among those who deserve special mention for contributing their time and expertise to archaeological and historical research in Marcus Hook are: Dr. Cathy Spohn and Chapter 21 of the Society for Pennsylvania Archaeology, Dr. Bernard Herman, Dr. Jeffrey Cohen, Craig Lukezic, Keith Doms, the crew from NAEVA Geophysics, Inc., and the late Penelope Batcheler. Also thanks to the Temple University students, both graduate and undergraduate, who have devoted so much time to the archaeology at the Plank House: Carin Bloom, Katie Cavallo, Matt Olson, Mara Kaktins, and many others. Thanks as well to all of the volunteers who may not be associated with any particular organization or institution—the contributions of our many "freelance" volunteers are as important as any. Paula Manerchia was invaluable for her efforts at organizing the volunteer effort, keeping everyone informed of the latest happenings at the Plank House, and making the house a comfortable and inviting place to work. Special recognition goes to Dr. David Orr of Temple University, who initially got the present author involved with the Plank House and interested in Marcus Hook. His passion for archaeology is unwavering and always inspiring, and he is valued as both a teacher and friend. My appreciation for the work of the Marcus Hook Preservation Society must also be expressed, although my gratitude to them pales in comparison to that of future generations, for whom the history of their town will remain alive due to the efforts of this remarkable group of people. Finally, very special thanks go to Michael and Pat Manerchia, without whom none of this would have been possible.

References Cited

Acrelius, Israel
1874   *A History of New Sweden.* The Historical Society of Pennsylvania. Philadelphia.
Ashmead, Henry Graham
1884   *History of Delaware County, Pennsylvania.* L.H. Everts, Philadelphia.
Chester County Court Records
1910   *Record of the Courts of Chester County, Pennsylvania, 1681–1697.* The Colonial Society of Pennsylvania. Philadelphia.
Hamajima, Hiromi
2006   Results of Geophysical Investigation, Marcus Hook Plank Log House, 221 Market Street, Marcus Hook Pennsylvania. NAEVA Geophysics, Inc., Congers, New York.
Herman, Bernard L.
1987   *Architecture and Rural Life in Central Delaware, 1700–1900.* The University of Tennessee Press, Knoxville.
Miller, Patricia Ann
2007   *Images of America: Marcus Hook.* Arcadia Publishing. Charleston, South Carolina.

Smith, George
1862   *History of Delaware County, Pennsylvania, from the Discovery of the Territory Included within Its Limits to the Present Time*. Printed by Henry B. Ashmead, Philadelphia.

Watson, John F.
1830   *Annals of Philadelphia, Being a Collection of Memoirs, Anecdotes, and Incidents of the City and Its Inhabitants from the Days of the Pilgrim Founders*. E.L. Carey and A. Hart, Philadelphia.

Wiseley, Laura
2009   "Marcus Hook recognizes historic Washington route." *Delaware County Daily Times*. September 6, 2009.

4

Unearthing Wistarburgh: America's First Successful Glasshouse

Damon Tvaryanas and William B. Liebeknecht

Introduction

On September 9, 1738, two vessels made their way with the tide slowly up the Delaware River. Having dropped their sheets, the *Glasgow* and the *Two Sisters* tied up at Philadelphia's wharves and completed a long transatlantic crossing. Both vessels had last touched ground at the small port of Clowes in southeastern England and had sailed in company, weathering the broad Atlantic until they passed between Capes Henlopen and May and into the protected waters of the Delaware Bay. The merchantmen were packed with people. In addition to her master and crew the *Glasgow*, the larger of the two vessels, carried 349 Palatine Germans while the smaller *Two Sisters* carried 110 Palatines. Commanded by James Marshall of London, *Two Sisters* was a "snow," a type of brig that shipped extra sails abaft the main mast. Below deck she carried 41 men, 30 women, and 39 children as passengers (Pennsylvania State Archives , RG-26 53 A-B, 54 A-B). Most were peasants. A few of the more prosperous men had experience in a trade or craft. Within this last group were four highly skilled individuals recruited by the wealthy Philadelphia merchant, Caspar Wistar. These were the German glassmakers: Johann Wilhelm Wentzel, Martin Halter, Caspar Halter, and Simeon Griessmeyer. The four men carried with them skill, knowledge, and tradition; assets which would find legacy in the fiery furnaces of American glasshouses. They would provide the technical expertise for America's first successful glass making enterprise at Wistarburgh in Alloway Township, New Jersey and would make southern New Jersey the epicenter of the American glass industry for several generations.

In a populous, metropolitan state like New Jersey, one might expect that strong cultural connections with the distant past would have long ago been eroded, wiped away by the homogenizing force of suburbanization and the influx of new populations as farm land was converted to green lawns, backyards, and strip malls. However, deep in southern Jersey the past lingers. It lives long upon the face of the landscape and in the memories of the people. It would be wrong to suggest that the colonial period landscape of the farm belt of Salem, Gloucester, and Cumberland Counties survives unchanged. A great many eighteenth-century buildings, particularly the ones built of wood rather than brick and stone, have long since passed beyond memory. Other buildings have been erected as landmarks to nineteenth-and twentieth-century periods of personal and community prosperity; dirt roads have been replaced by concrete and asphalt highways. But a surprising number of eighteenth-century buildings survive, and these seem to visually dominate the still largely agricultural landscape. The area has happily remained something of a backwater and thus has escaped many of the harsher episodes of development that have recast so much of the physical and cultural landscape of the rest of New Jersey. The process of suburbanization has not yet wiped the old slate clean.

The story of Wistarburgh has long been embraced by the region's people and has become a building block of their cultural heritage. The glass industry loomed large over southern New Jersey's economy for the better part of two centuries. Many of today's residents can boast of ancestors who first settled in the area during the seventeenth and eighteenth centuries and of fathers, grandfathers, and great-grandfathers who spent hot days toiling in the nineteenth- and twentieth-century glasshouses of Salem, Millville, Bridgeton, and Glassboro. Some still earn their wages in the few plants that remain. Nearly to a person, long time residents understand this legacy of glass and know that it all began at a place known as Wistarburgh.

The founding of Wistarburgh in Alloway Township in Salem County, New Jersey is recognized among scholars of America's colonial past as being a significant early episode in the maturation of the colonial economy and the emergence of domestic manufacturing. Wistarburgh represents one of the earliest American examples of the transformation of craft activity into industrial process. The glassworks is also equally, if not even more famous, to scholars of early technology and to antique collectors and connoisseurs of the decorative arts. While there were a few earlier attempts at manufacturing glass in the New World, Wistarburgh was the first American glasshouse to make domestically produced window glass readily available within the colonial market. Until that point, fragile panes of glass had to be carefully packed and shipped across the Atlantic Ocean. Wistarburgh's window glass was advertised to be less expensive than imported glass and was more readily available in custom sizes and thus, facilitated the use of more and larger windows in colonial buildings (Palmer 1989:14).

Wistarburgh was also the first American glasshouse to produce bottles and tableware in substantial quantities. The handful of surviving glass vessels firmly identified as having been produced in Wistarburgh's furnaces belong to the earliest group of glass objects manufactured in America and have consequently been highly sought after by museum curators and collectors of early American glass for well over a century. Scientific wares were also produced, including tubes for electrical experiments and distillation equipment.

Thus, the history of the glass factory at Wistarburgh has long been of interest to many. The first historical discourse on glassworks appeared in print in Cushing and Sheppard's *History of the Counties of Gloucester, Salem and Cumberland of 1883*, and R. M. Acton's article, "A Short History of the Glass Manufacture in Salem County, New Jersey," which was published in *The Pennsylvania Magazine of History and Biography* in 1885. Since the dates of these publications, the colonial records of

Salem County and Philadelphia have been sifted on many occasions by historians, scholars, and researchers looking to shed ever more light on the activities of the glassmakers at Alloway. The tale of Wistarburgh has figured prominently in nearly every published history of the American glass industry and every work on early American blown glass. But the focus, almost exclusively, was on what information had been gleaned from the archival record and from glass vessels in the hands of museums, collectors, and families that had been attributed (correctly or not) to the hands of Wistarburgh's craftsmen. Much less scholarly attention was focused on the site of the glasshouse itself and on what it could tell us.

Acton described the site of the glasshouse as it appeared in 1885:

> On what in some of the old surveys of this section is called "The great road to Pilesgrove" from Salem, by the way of Thompson's Bridge (now Alloway), but little more than a mile from the latter place, stands an old dwelling, built of logs neatly squared and dovetailed at the corners, carrying the scars where the joists have been sawn off, which at one time extended several feet beyond the first story to support the projecting roof, so common to the homes of the early German settlers. This was the principal residence of Wistarburgh. The kitchen of one story attached to the west end of the house has been removed within the last forty years.

The interest connected with the locality arises from the fact that here, it is believed, the first glass works that were successfully operated in the United States were erected. The store for the sale of merchandise (the removal of which has been of comparatively recent date) stood on the edge of the highway, on the same side as the dwelling and about fifty yards west of it, shaded by the stately sycamores still standing on the opposite side of the road, with the factories perhaps one hundred yards in the rear (Acton 1885:343–344).

The fact that scholars paid less attention to what could be learned through physical investigation of Wistarburgh than they did to the archival record is not to say that no one had taken a shovel to the site. Over the years, many holes were dug in the alfalfa field where it was believed by many that the glasshouse had stood. Most of these holes were excavated by collectors seeking, quite improbably, to unearth a bottle that had somehow survived the destruction of the factory and more than a century of agricultural plowing. None of these treasure hunters is known to have been successful. In the end, they all seem to have been content with making souvenirs out of the relatively small shards of glass, which could so easily be picked up from the plowed surface of the field. A few individuals actually came seeking information rather than buried antiques. Most of these, however, were interested in learning more about the extent of Wistarburgh's range of products and were relatively unconcerned with acquiring information about the factory itself. It is rumored that at least once digging was undertaken under the auspices of a college but no records of these activities have been identified, and there is no reason to believe that the digging was extensive or systematic.

It was not until 1996 that any serious consideration was given to the professional archaeological investigation of the glasshouse site. In that year, a group of interested individuals coalesced with the express purpose of actually figuring out how much information about the Wistarburgh Glasshouse survived beneath the ground's surface. This group included local residents, glass collectors, archaeologists, and museum professionals. Working in conjunction with the Museum of American Glass at Wheaton Village, a fundraising effort was commenced and an archaeological consulting firm, Hunter Research, Inc., was engaged to undertake the work. As is almost always the case in such circumstances, the monies raised by the group were relatively limited. Enthusiasm, however, was high—after all Wistarburgh was legend. No one involved with the project expected that a comprehensive investigation of the site could be undertaken. It was obvious from the start that the budget just would not bear the cost. However, with significant concessions and donations of time, materials, and equipment, it was determined that the available funds could be stretched sufficiently to support a short program of targeted fieldwork. The work would be aimed at assessing the extent and integrity of surviving archaeological remains rather than on thoroughly excavating large portions of the site.

It was hoped that, ultimately, the archaeological investigation of Wistarburgh could help us to better understand its full story. The founding and subsequent success of the glasshouse at Wistarburgh cannot be reduced to either a simple tale of the achievements of the four hardworking craftsmen from the Palatinate (Johann Wilhelm Wentzel, Martin Halter, Caspar Halter, and Simeon Griessmeyer), or, as it is more often told, an important chapter in the rags to riches tale of its more famous financial backer, Caspar Wistar. Rather it must be presented as a complex account of interwoven colonial social, political, and economic forces; as the immigration of Wistarburgh's German glassblowers was, in itself, part of a much larger story. Driven at first by war and famine, the migration of Palatine Germans to Pennsylvania had begun with an initial influx of individuals in 1709. Once commenced, the exodus from the Palatinate proved surprisingly enduring. The spring of each year witnessed the arrival of a new batch of prospective immigrants to the refugee camps that had been established at Rotterdam and Amsterdam. These were the primary embarkation points. The year of 1738, which witnessed the immigration of the four glassmakers, quickly proved to be a year beyond all expectations with regard to the number of new arrivals. Over 6,000 immigrants left Germany for the New World in 1738. Most previous yearly totals had been measured in the low hundreds rather than the thousands (Wust 1998).

Few of these emigrants were wealthy enough to finance their own journey. Most were forced to bind themselves into indentured servitude in order to pay English shipping companies for the cost of their transport. Wistarburgh's four glassblowers were neither wealthy nor forced to sell themselves to other masters. Instead, the four men appear to have journeyed to colonial Pennsylvania on the basis of a preexisting understanding. Their passage was to be paid by Caspar Wistar, the wealthiest of Pennsylvania's German citizens. In return, they agreed to partner with Wistar in the establishment of an American glass manufactory and to share with him the technical expertise necessary to erect a glasshouse and to make glass from sand. But the art of glassmaking took more than just knowledge. Wistar's four German glassmakers would also provide the skill necessary to blow bottles and table glass and to shape and size window panes. They would work in the factory shaping glass and training others in the craft.

In addition to paying Captain James Marshall for the glassmakers' passage, Wistar provided capital and land, approximately 2000 acres in the hinterlands of southern New Jersey (on which the glasshouse would be constructed and from which the requisite vast reserves of firewood could be harvested). Through stores in New York and Philadelphia, Wistar would also provide retail outlets in large urban markets for the products of the endeavor.

Better than most, Caspar Wistar understood both the problems and the opportunities facing new immigrants. Decades earlier, a much younger Wistar found himself almost four thousand miles away from home and family with no friends and little money. The details of Wistar's journey from the Palatinate to America did not differ greatly from that later experienced by his four glass blowers. In May 1717, a twenty-two-year-old Caspar Wüstar left his family's home in the village of Waldhilsbach and traveled first to the regional center of Heidelberg and thence by boat down the Rhine to Rotterdam. He crossed the English Channel to London in an English transport and then made the long sea voyage to Philadelphia (Beiler 1994:187). Unfortunately for Wistar, unlike the glassblowers he would subsequently sponsor, no wealthy patron awaited him on the wooden docks of Philadelphia. With more resources than most of his fellow passengers, young Caspar was able to pay his own fare, but he had arrived in the rapidly growing city on the Delaware with very little left in the way of additional funds and without any readily marketable skills.

Caspar was the son of Hans Caspar Wüstar, a forester in the service of the Elector of the Palatine. Foresters and hunters were in effect feudal environmental bureaucrats who together oversaw the natural resources of tracts of lands (principally forests, marshes, and beaches) held by the elector. Caspar Wistar's grandfather and quite likely his great grandfather had also been foresters. Young Caspar, himself, had apprenticed as a hunter which was potentially a step in the direction of following in his father's and grandfather's footsteps if a posting as a forester or hunter opened up in one of the neighboring districts. However, Wistar was coming of age at a time when the numbers of forestry officials were being reduced and pay was often slow in coming. Wistar's prospects for finding a stable place in the system that had provided a strong livelihood for many of his forbearers would not have seemed particularly bright. Undoubtedly, this fact weighed heavily in his decision to abandon the German woods for a future in the New World (Beiler 1994:17, 27, 40–41, and 68–71).

In Germany, Casper had been trained in the management of forests. His profession was valued in a land where natural resources were limited and thus were carefully exploited by those who controlled them. In America, land was cheap and forests were endless. There was little call for the skills of a young man with such a background. For over a year after landing in Philadelphia, Wistar worked for a soap maker. It was the only job he could find. He rendered fat, boiled soap, carted ashes, and undertook whatever tasks needed to be done.

According to his own account, the turning point in Wistar's life came when he was taught the art of brass button making. In a city where such simple luxuries were often extremely difficult to obtain because of the need to import them from England, Wistar was able to quickly parlay the practice of such a basic craft into wealth. He established himself as an entrepreneur and merchant and began building important business and social relationships with elite members of Philadelphia's Quaker establishment. These links were reinforced when Wistar took a Quaker wife, Catherine Jansen, and joined the Philadelphia Monthly Meeting of Friends (Beiler 1994:216–220).

Although Wistar would proclaim his profession to be that of button maker and brazier throughout his adult life, most of his fortune seems to have been derived from international and domestic trade and, probably more importantly, land speculation. It was with regard to his investments in land that he was finally able to apply the experience of his youth in Germany. Wistar was uniquely well positioned to understand that America's riches lay in its land and knew from generations of family experience how to exploit it. In the 1720s, during an economic downturn, Wistar utilized his connections with prominent Quaker financiers to pool money to begin investing in devalued real estate. Later, Wistar began purchasing large tracks of land from the Penn family (Beiler 1994:223–229).

By the time of his death in 1752, Wistar had received patents for or purchased close to 23,000 acres in Philadelphia, Bucks, and Lancaster Counties. Wistar sold much of this land to German immigrants and their families. A large part of his financial success lay in his ability to serve as a patron for the rapidly growing number of German immigrants, functioning as the leading business, social, and political figure of Pennsylvania's ethnic German population. Pennsylvania Germans due to language barriers, economic status, and religious and ethnic traditions found themselves isolated in many ways from the broader Anglo-Pennsylvanian population. Wistar was accepted and trusted as a member of both Philadelphia's Quaker elite and the Pennsylvania German population and thus was uniquely positioned to be a cultural intermediary (Beiler 1994: 236–238).

Wistar did much both to help and to profit from new immigrants. He extended badly needed credit, provided personal character references, supplied aid and advice, and frequently engaged immigrants as indentured servants when they lacked the funds to pay for their passage. Perhaps most lucratively, he sold them land and granted them mortgages. He maintained business communications with the Palatinate and thus was able to serve as bridge between immigrant Germans and their homeland. He was trusted by Germans in both America and Europe to handle the transatlantic transfer of monies, the resolution of estates, debts, and other basic legal and personal matters. Undoubtedly, it was through these European connections that he was able to recruit his four glassmakers.

Important research into the life of Caspar Wistar undertaken by Rosalind Joy Beiler and documented in her dissertation entitled "The Transatlantic World of Caspar Wistar: From Germany to America in the Eighteenth Century" (1994) and her book *Immigrant and Entrepreneurs: The Atlantic World of Caspar Wistar 1650–1750* (2008) has demonstrated that Wistar almost certainly had direct contact with at least one glasshouse prior to becoming involved with the Wistarburgh enterprise. This would have occurred during the period that he served as a hunter's apprentice in the Palatinate. Wistar's master, Georg Michael Forester, oversaw the use of natural resources by, and collected fees from, the Peterstal glasshouse, which was located not far from Wistar's family home. Wistar almost certainly visited the glasshouse and was in the process of being professionally trained in what resources it needed access to in order to successfully operate. He would have been familiar with the glasshouse, its workings, and the amounts of timber and the kind of sand necessary for its operation (Beiler 1994:293–296).

There were further ties between the glasshouse Wistar knew at Peterstal and the one he would erect at Wistarburgh. Wistar's glass blowers seem to have all had some link to Peterstal. Johann Wilhelm Wentzel may well have been a close relative of Johann Peter Wentzal, the operator of the Peterstal glassworks. Simeon Griessmeyer's father and uncle served journeymen glassblowers at Peterstal. and Halter, the surname of the remaining original Wistarburgh glassmakers, was a common family name in the area surrounding the Peterstal glassworks (Beiler 1994:294–295). Peterstal likely served as an important model for Wistar and his partners when they established their works at Alloway.

In the Palatinate that Caspar Wistar had known, the use of natural resources was regulated and taxed to an extraordinary extent. Most tracts of open land were held by the state and overseen by the foresters. Would be entrepreneurs could rent such lands for substantial fees but rarely if ever could they purchase them outright. Duties were assessed for the use of all resources, including the right to cut firewood or lumber, to mine minerals and clays, to hunt game, and to forage livestock. All such activities were closely monitored and tightly controlled. The situation was vastly different in British North America. In Pennsylvania and New Jersey, where almost all land was held privately, there were almost no limits placed on the use of real estate and its resources, and relatively few taxes were assessed. Wistar was uniquely suited to understand the opportunities that wide open American private property rights presented (Beiler 1994:20–21, 294, 311).

The new glasshouse in Salem County, New Jersey was erected quickly, and glassblowing commenced in 1739. In 1744, Wistar codified the details of his arrangement with the four glassmakers in the form of a written agreement, which created "the United Glass Company of Salem County, New Jersey." The United Glass Company was actually an "umbrella" company for three smaller concerns. Overall, the four German glassmakers were to pay one-third of the total costs of operating the glassworks, and Wistar was to contribute the remaining capital. The actual manufacturing of glass would be undertaken by three separate companies, each of which would own and operate an oven served by its own staff of craftsmen and laborers (Beiler 1994:317–319). Johann Wilhelm Wentzel and Caspar Halter each owned shares in separate companies in conjunction with Wistar. Both Wentzel and Halter paid one-third of the costs of operating an oven, and each received one-third of the profits of that company. Together, Johann Martin Halter and Simeon Griessmeyer shared the expense of the third company with each paying one-sixth of the expense of operating their oven, and each receiving one-sixth of the profits. Upon any termination of their agreement, the glassmakers would retain rights to the ovens and apparatus associated with the individual companies to which they belonged. Items owned jointly by the whole company, such as the kettles in the potash house, would be divided up with Wistar receiving a two parts share and the rest of the glass-makers one part (Beiler 1994:318).

Caspar Wistar and the United Glass Company operated Wistarburgh successfully from 1739 to 1752. Wistarburgh's products were marketed through Wistar's store in Philadelphia, through stores at Wistarburgh, and probably also through his son Richard's store in New York City (Palmer 1973:76).

Following the death of his father and all of the original German glassblow-ers and faced with an array of personal and financial difficulties caused by the Revolutionary War, Richard had a difficult time keeping the glassworks in operation. In 1780, he unsuccessfully sought to sell most of his father's southern New Jersey real estate holdings including Wistarburgh. Richard died the following year with the glass factory apparently still in operation (Murschell 2007:136–137). Little, however, is known about the final days of Wistarburgh and what happened when its fires were extinguished for the last time. In 1885, R. A. Acton wrote "that after the business was discontinued at Wistarburgh the hamlet gradually disappeared, except the debris of the factories, the old dwelling being the only reminder of what once had been" (Acton 345). This dwelling, described as the "mansion house" in old documents, had been at various times occupied by members of the Wistar family and by managers of the works. Most of the land reverted to agricultural uses, but by 1849, brickyards with their associated clay pits had been opened nearby. Thankfully, from an archaeo-logical perspective none of the pits impacted the core of the site.

In 1928, the glassworks site and 140 surrounding acres were purchased by Joseph Marish. Marish was a Pennsylvania coal miner who aimed to trade a life working underground for one spent in the open fields of South Jersey. The former miner moved his family into the mansion house and became a dairy farmer. The Marish family has occupied the property, living in the old log house from that time until the present and farming the lands on which the glasshouse complex once stood. One of the leading members of the group behind the archaeological excavations, Donald Kohler, was a boyhood friend of Leon Marish, Joseph's son. Through this friendship, Donald was able to convince Leon and his wife to permit access to the property. By spring 1998, everyone involved in the investigation was excited, and all expectations were that the plowed fields of the Marish Family farm would soon provide new insights and flesh out the body of knowledge concerning Wistarburgh's past.

There was never much doubt about where to start looking for the remains of the glasshouse structure. Highly developed skills of sleuthing were not required. It is true that Caspar Wistar once controlled close to 2,000 acres of land in the area, thus, at least in theory, it might have been difficult to figure out exactly where on that great tract of land the hamlet of Wistarburgh had once stood. After all, the village was largely abandoned after the last batch of glass was blown in the early 1780s. and the intervening two centuries would have provided a good deal of time for its location to have become obscured. But such was not the case.

Wistarburgh had never been forgotten by those who resided nearby. At some point during the first half of the twentieth century, an ornate cast iron historic marker had been erected beside the road near the supposed location of the glass manufactory. The factual nature of the information provided by such roadside markers should never be taken for granted, but in this case, there was no reason to doubt its accuracy. There were plenty of physical clues. Among the most obvious of these was the small rural road named "Glasshouse Lane" which terminated at the reported location of the glassworks. The location of the manager's house was another indication. Although reduced from its original eighteenth-century height by a full story and covered in vinyl siding, the old squared log walls of the original home still survived within the much altered outer shell.

The builders of the house would have sited it in very close proximity to the glasshouse. It would have been just far enough away for the family who lived in it to have been spared some of the dirt, smoke, smells, and noise, but close enough that activities at the works could be easily observed from its windows. The small field which extended to the north and west, behind the manager's house, was scattered with glass shards and small bits of broken brick. In its midst, a low oblong mound rose a foot or two above the surrounding landscape. It seemed obvious to everyone involved that this undulation must represent the location of the remains of one of Wistarburgh's primary buildings and probably represented the footprint of the glasshouse itself. This was the most logical place to begin looking for buried structural remains.

The primary goals of the archaeological investigations were: to establish the location and state of preservation of the foundations of the glasshouse, to define the overall limits of the manufacturing site, and to assess the appropriateness of future archaeological investigation at the site. A detailed field plan was needed in order to assure that the stated goals would be met with an economy of effort. Moving large volumes of dirt archaeologically is extraordinarily expensive. The process of digging is, in itself, slow and labor intensive, but every hour logged by an archeologist with a trowel in hand must be backed up by many more in the completion of paperwork; the taking of photographs; the creation of plan and profile mapping; the care, conservation, and analysis of artifacts; and the production of reports. As was stated earlier, the funding for a large-scale effort simply did not exist. Archaeological excavation is also inherently destructive in nature. An archaeological site can only be fully excavated once and then, in most cases, it survives only in the form of the records of the excavation. It was not deemed to be appropriate to sacrifice large portions of the site given the preliminary nature of the investigations. If the project was to meet all of its declared goals, was to be completed on time and on budget, and was not to be overly destructive, it was critical that a well thought out and highly targeted excavation plan be developed.

In part to facilitate the formulation of just such a plan, a geophysical investigation of the site was proposed. It was intended not only to confirm what seemed so obvious from the superficial inspection of the site—that a sizable building or structure had once been located in the field behind the mansion house where the low mound now stood—but also to locate other areas of potential archaeological sensitivity that might not be easily identified from inspection of the field's surface. Timothy and Felicia Bechtel, the owners of Enviroscan, Inc., a geophysical survey company based in Lancaster, Pennsylvania, were contacted in this regard, and they very kindly agreed to donate their services. On May 4, 1998, Timothy Bechtel conducted a magnetic survey of the field behind the mansion house using a high resolution cesium vapor magnetometer. Magnetometers are instruments that measure localized changes in the strength of the earth's magnetic field. Usually these changes or "anomalies" are related to buried concentrations of ferrous material or areas where activities involving intense heat have altered the natural magnetic field. These variations can be entirely natural or caused mundanely by buried electric lines, pipes, or tanks.

In our instance, it was hoped that the survey would show evidence of the archaeological remains of buildings, possibly the glasshouse itself, or evidence of other buildings, structures, or activities associated with the operation of the eighteenth-century glassworks. The survey was successful in identifying a number of magnetic anomalies in the field. Some of these had small footprints and were of relatively low magnitude. Others were somewhat stronger and could possibly have been interpreted as being related to buried iron objects or small historic cultural features. However, one, much stronger magnetic anomaly was identified, which was described by Enviroscan's report as being consistent in nature with "an intact foundation remnant or remnants, or a voluminous pile of jumbled or misorientated remnants" (Enviroscan 1998). The location of this anomaly corresponded directly with the highest point of the rise in the middle of the glass field. After the results of the geophysical survey, there was little debate about where the program of archaeological testing should be focused.

The primary goal of the fieldwork was to attempt to confirm the presence of archaeological structural remains related to the glasshouse. The physical and symbolic core of the Wistarburgh glasshouse would have been its glass furnaces. These were the large masonry stacks in which the raw sand and other ingredients were heated and worked. In 1747, in a letter to Thomas Darling of New Haven, Connecticut, no less an authority than Benjamin Franklin described Wistarburgh's glass furnace as "being approximately 12 foot long, 8 wide, 6 high, has no grate, the fire being made on its floor. . . . On each Side in the furnace is a Bench of Bank of the same materials with the Furnace, on which the pots of Metal stand, 3 or 4 of a side." Franklin also noted that Wistarburgh's furnace was constructed of bricks of white clay, which needed to be replaced after each blast (Palmer 1989:11).

Arlene Palmer, one of the leading Wistarburgh scholars and an expert in historic American glass, has suggested that as it was described in Franklin's account the Wistarburgh furnace was typical of Germanic glass furnaces of the period and was of a type that would have been very familiar to Wistarburgh's four original glassblowers. This familiarity should come as no surprise as they would have been responsible for the design of Wistarburgh's glasshouse and probably oversaw its construction first hand (Palmer 1989:11).

Indications from the archival record are conflicting with regard to how many furnaces once stood within the walls of the Wistarburgh's glasshouse. In Caspar Wistar's written agreement with his four initial glass blowers, it was implied that each of the three separate glass blowing companies that together formed the United Glass Company would be responsible for the ownership and maintenance of its own furnace. Although the agreement that was struck would seem to imply there were at least three individual furnaces at Wistarburgh, this would have been an unlikely scenario given the cost of erecting three separate furnace stacks and the size which the glass house would have needed to be in order to encompass the footprints of three such structures.

Franklin consistently referred to the furnace at Wistarburgh in the singular as in his above referenced communication. However, in the same year (1747) that Franklin penned his description, Wistar wrote in a letter to New Jersey's colonial governor Jonathan Belcher that "the clay for the Furnace bottoms was but poor and often gave way" suggesting that, by that date, there was actually more than one furnace on the site (Palmer 1989:12). The reference may, however, also refer to the bottoms of fritting, annealing, and flattening furnaces, which were sometimes contained within secondary chambers inside of the primary furnace stack. Fritting was the process of preliminarily heating the mix which was to become the glass batch, annealing ovens slowly cooled finished vessels to insure they did not crack, and flattening ovens removed the curve of window glass produced through the cylinder method (figure 4.1).

It is certainly possible that the number of furnaces at Wistarburgh was different at various points in time. Furnaces regularly had to be rebuilt. Brick and other components deteriorated quickly in the intense and constant heat to which they were subjected. These necessary episodes of reconstruction may have also been opportunities for implementing change. Other than the fact that the glass factory at Wistarburgh

Figure 4.1. An image from *Diderot's Encyclopedia* showing an eighteenth-century glassworks producing cylinders for windows. Courtesy of Hunter Research, Inc.

was relatively long lived, little is known about its actual financial success. Over the forty plus year span during which the enterprise was in operation, more furnaces might have been constructed to meet the needs of an expanding market or underutilized furnaces may have been demolished.

Changes in the organizational structure of the ownership and operation of the enterprise may also have been reflected in alterations to infrastructure. Following the death of Caspar Wistar in 1752, the structure of the company was reconfigured so that Richard Wistar, Caspar's son and chief heir, would pay half of the company's total expenses and Johann Martin Halter and Johann Wilhelm Wentzel would each pay one-quarter (Beiler 1994:317–319). Simeon Griessmeyer had died in 1748, and Caspar Halter had withdrawn from the ownership structure. What this actually meant in terms of how many furnaces would have been required for the effective operation of the business is unclear.

By 1780, near the end of Wistarburgh's period of operation, it is apparent from a newspaper advertisement that there were two furnaces in the main glasshouse at Wistarburgh. One would have been utilized for the manufacture of window glass and the other for the production of bottles and other vessels. It is likely that twin furnace stacks would have been located at the center of the building with auxiliary ovens at each of the four comers of each furnace stack. Additional fritting and annealing ovens may have been arranged around the perimeters of the rectangular building. This is an arrangement that was documented during the excavation of the late eighteenth-century glass furnace known as Amelung at New Bremen, Maryland.

Unless some intrepid scholar discovers some heretofore unknown period description of the glasshouse at Wistarburgh, the chronology of any changes to the number of Wistarburgh's furnaces and the configuration of the glasshouse's structure and work floor are important pieces of technological information that will only be definitively revealed through archaeological investigation of the site. The retrieval of such data, data which will allow a much better sense to be developed of what the glasshouse was actually like and how it operated, is ultimately one of the prime reasons for expending time, money, and effort in investigating the site of the glassworks. It is why everyone was so excited when the start of warm weather in spring 1998 permitted the digging to commence. But it should be understood and remembered that the work planned for that initial field campaign was never intended to answer these questions but rather was targeted at assessing whether the site still possessed sufficient archaeological integrity in order to do so.

A field strategy was developed that involved the excavation of 30 shovel tests and 2 trenches. Shovel tests are simply test holes of approximately 18 inches in diameter excavated to the maximum depth to which it is feasible to dig such a hole with a long handled shovel. Their purpose is typically to identify quickly locations of archaeological sensitivity (or insensitivity) through observations made with regard to the soil stratigraphy observed while digging the hole and through the dating of artifacts retrieved by screening the earth removed from each soil layer encountered during this process. Twenty-three shovel tests were laid out at 50 foot intervals in two transecting lines that met atop the low knoll. These tests yielded large numbers of artifacts associated with the glass manufacturing process including glass drips and waste, vessel fragments and flat glass shards, furnace related ceramics (fragments of glass melting pots and ceramic shelves from within the furnace structure), and other related materials (figure 4.2).

Four additional shovel tests were excavated on the peak of the rise where the greatest likelihood of encountering structural remains was anticipated on the basis of topography and the results of the geophysical survey. These tests encountered a clay loam layer with charcoal, brick, and mortar inclusions immediately beneath the plowzone and what appeared to be evidence of brick structural remains. Three more shovel tests were excavated on the sites of strong secondary magnetic anomalies. One of these, located on the western edge of the mound, also encountered what appeared to be an intact brick surface, possibly a floor or other working surface.

Although the pattern of shovel tests produced thousands of artifacts and at least some indication that identifiable building remains might survive, no clear cut evidence of well preserved walls or foundations or footings was encountered. To further investigate whether data might be present that would be useful in interpreting the size, footprint, layout, and method of construction of any building or buildings

Figure 4.2. Fragments of ceramic pots used to melt glass and fragments of blowpipes. Courtesy of Hunter Research, Inc.

that may have formerly stood in this location, the excavation of two large trenches or "excavation units" on the highest part of the knoll was planned. These trenches were dug where the magnetometer had logged its strongest readings and where shovel tests had encountered some evidence suggestive of the possible survival of structural remains. The first trench, which measured 2.5 feet by 15 feet was placed directly in the center of the magnetic anomaly. A total of 5,181 artifacts were recovered, 99 percent of which were retrieved from the plowzone. Beneath the plowzone, the mortared remains of a portion of what was almost certainly a limonite foundation were encountered. The foundation remains were very shallow and consisted, for the most part, of a single course of stones. The upper stones had been scavenged for other uses or removed by deep plowing.

Limonite is a sedimentary stone formed by a natural biological process. Common throughout many areas in southern New Jersey and very high in iron content, it was frequently utilized as a building material during the eighteenth- and nineteenth-centuries. Not easily given a fine finish and very susceptible to weathering when exposed to the elements, the stone was most often used in the construction of foundations and footings. Most of the houses in the area of Wistarburgh built before the widespread introduction of concrete had limonite foundations. The uncovering of these foundations provided the first strong evidence that if a large enough area was archaeologically excavated, it might be possible to discover the size and shape of the footprint of the building that had once occupied the crest of the mound. More excitingly, it was noted that the mortared limonite foundation remains showed strong evidence of reddening. Limonite, which naturally occurs in several shades of brown, turns red when exposed to intense heat. This characteristic of the stone has long been known. The region's prehistoric Native American population had heated the stone in very hot fires in order to reduce it into a red pigment. The reddening of the limonite of the foundation noted in the first trench excavated at Wistarburgh suggests that the foundation had been subjected to substantial heat. One quite plausible explanation for this is that the feature represents the remains of the glass furnace itself or one of its associated secondary ovens. This was an important discovery, especially since the second trench, a 2.5 foot by 10 foot unit excavated along the northern edge of the magnetic anomaly, yielded over 2,700 artifacts related to the manufacture of glass in the plowzone but no similar evidence of structural remains (Tvaryanas et al. 1998:3–6).

Building on the success of the first trench, additional funds were raised to excavate a third unit on the site of the shovel test on the western side of the mound that had revealed what had appeared to be a brick floor. This 10 foot by 10 foot excavation was undertaken as a second excavation effort in the spring of 2001. A brick floor was not uncovered as expected. The brick layer encountered during the excavation of the shovel test turned out not to be a neatly laid horizontal level but rather a jumbled deposit of decayed brick, possibly related to the collapse of a nearby structure. Evidence of the eighteenth-century ground surface associated with the operation of the glasshouse was identified along with chunks of charcoal, partially burnt wooden planks, and bits of mortar. A total of 15,133 artifacts were recovered during the excavation of this single shallow unit. The deposits were rich in waste from the glassworks and included fragments of glass-coated-refractory fragments, glass, glass-waste, slag, and vessel glass. However, over 40 percent of the artifacts recovered were fragments of mostly pale green or aqua flat glass, almost certainly window glass (Liebeknecht et al. 2001:4–8).

All of the flat glass fragments recovered during the excavations were small but of even thickness, suggesting they were manufactured using the cylinder method. Cylinder glass was also sometimes referred to as "German" sheet glass as this method was commonly used to produce window glass in Bohemia and Germany (Charleston et al. 1975:4). Its use at Wistarburgh could well be evidence of the continuing influence of Wistar's German trained glassmakers, however, attempts at manufacturing cylinder glass in Great Britain's North American colonies have been traced back as early as 1683 when a window glass factory was established in the Northern Liberties area of Philadelphia. There is no evidence of any Germanic ties with regard to the owners or craftspersons connected with this early enterprise (McKearin and McKearin 1941:77; Palmer 1973:22).

Cylinder glass was made, as the name would suggest, by the blowing of large cylinders of glass in the glasshouse. These cylinders would then be slit lengthwise and, while still hot and flexible, opened up and flattened in secondary ovens. Later, glasscutters would cut the sheets into individual panes. Archival references to the presence of flattening ovens at Wistarburgh provide additional evidence that this was the primary method of window pane production utilized at the site (Palmer 1973:117). The remarkable abundance of flat glass window pane or light fragments in this trench suggests this area may be the location of the factory's glass cutting house. Many fragments exhibited cut and score marks identifying them as scraps left over from the cutting of panes (figure 4.3).

By the time the last of the three excavation units had been backfilled in the middle of April 2001, it was clear that despite generations of plowing, the repeated

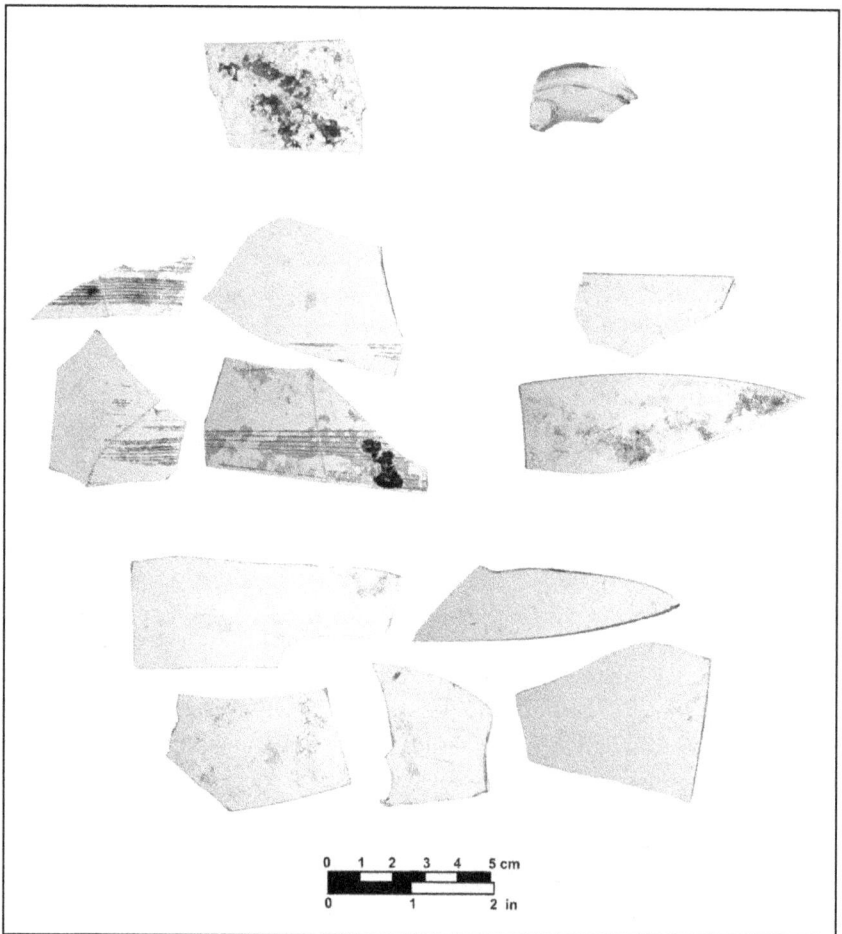

Figure 4.3. Glass shards from the manufacture of cylinder glass. Courtesy of Hunter Research, Inc.

looting of the site by glass collectors and amateur historians, and the removal of stone and brick in the early twentieth century, structural evidence associated with a building connected with the Wistarburgh Glassworks had been uncovered on top of the low rise in the middle of the glass strewn field behind the manager's house. The remains encountered were not particularly substantial, but they were there. Given the limited nature of the digging involved, these were not insignificant results.

The importance of the discoveries of the fieldwork campaigns of 1998 and 2001 would be fully revealed a few years later when a significant new piece of archival information came to light. In 2001, Gayle Wistar, the widow of a direct descendant of Caspar Wistar, placed a mid-eighteenth-century map of the Wistarburgh real estate holdings in the care of the Salem County Historical Society. Held closely by the Wistar family for generations and unknown by historians, the map depicts the little nucleated community of "Wistarburgh" at the intersection of the roads known today as Commissioners Pike and Glasshouse Lane. Atop a small rise, in the field north and west of the mansion house, the cartographer drew an image of a large gable roofed building surmounted by a central chimney or cupola (figure 4.4). In a fluid cursive hand, the mapmaker labeled this building "The Glass House." It is worth noting that the author of the map took particular care to sketch in the low mound on top of which the glasshouse had been erected. There is little doubt that the low hill shown on the map and the gentle rise that still exists in the field behind the mansion house are the same topographical feature, and thus that the structural remains uncovered by the archaeological investigations of 1998 were indeed associated with Caspar Wistar's legendary glasshouse, the industrial core of the Wistarburgh complex. Very little of the historic fabric of the Wistarburgh Glasshouse, perhaps only the lowermost stones and a few work surfaces, remains. A good probability exists, however, that future archaeological investigations could discern the building's footprint and its internal layout and thereby contribute much to our knowledge about the birth of the American glass industry.

When access to the mid-eighteenth-century survey map became available, it brought an important aspect of Wistarburgh into clearer focus. Wistarburgh was more than just a single building; it was a manufacturing complex and a crossroads village. Indeed, it was an entire, long vanished, community. The archaeological explorations completed up until that point had focused most of their efforts on the site of the glasshouse alone. A good idea of the true presence of the complex on the landscape can be garnered from an advertisement for the sale of the property placed by Richard Wistar in the *The Pennsylvania Journal* of October 11, 1780:

> The GLASS MANUFACTORY in Salem County, West Jersey, is for sale, with 1500 Acres of Land adjoining. It contains two Furnaces, with all the necessary Ovens for cooling the Glass. Drying Wood &c. Contiguous to the Manufactory are two flattening Ovens in separate Houses, a Store-house, Pot-house, a House

fitted with Tables for the cutting of Glass, a stamping Mill, a
rolling Mill for the preparing of Clay for making of Pots; and at
a suitable distance are ten Dwelling houses for the Workmen; as
likewise a large Mansionhouse, containing six Rooms on a Floor,
with Bakehouse and Washhouse: Also a convenient Store-house
where a well assorted retail Shop has been kept above 30 years;
is as good a stand for the sale of goods as any in the county,
being situated one mile and half from 2 navigable creek where
shallops load for Philadelphia, eight miles from the county town
of Salem, and half a mile from a good mill. There are about 250
Acres of Cleared Land within fence, 100 whereof is mowable
meadow, which produces hay and pasturage sufficient for the
large flock of cattle and horses employed by the Manufactory.
There is Stabling sufficient for 60 head of cattle, with a large
Barn, Granary, and Waggon-house. The unimproved Land is well
wooded, and 200 Acres more of meadow may be made.

 The situation and conveniency for procuring materials,
is equal if not superior to any place in Jersey.

 For Terms of Sale apply to the Subscriber in Philadelphia.

 Richard Wistar

This description provides something like a window into the past but just like the
rippled, green tinted panes manufactured at Wistarburgh, the view is somewhat unclear. The description provides an inventory of the factory's infrastructure but tells
us very little about how it was all arranged, where each of the buildings was located,
and how they related to each other.

 To the best of our knowledge, the extant farmhouse is the much altered remains of the mansion house (Acton 1885; Maxwell 1951). Little early fabric is visible
from the exterior of this heavily modified structure, but evidence of the original squared
log walls can be observed on its interior, and the large stone fireplace on the building's
northeastern wall is further evidence of a relatively early date of construction.

 As to the locations of the barn/granary, stables, and wagon house mentioned in the advertisement, it would seem likely, but not certain, that the historic
focus of the factory's agricultural facilities lay in the general vicinity of the farmstead's current barn and outbuildings. A brief examination of the existing large
timber-framed barn showed that this structure contains framing elements consistent
with an eighteenth-century date of construction, but these same features could just as
easily reflect a construction date in the early nineteenth century. Local tradition holds
that the factory's ten workers' houses were located on what is now the southern side
of Commissioners Pike, generally opposite the existing farmstead. Richard Wistar's
advertisement notes only that the houses were located at "a suitable distance" from
the glasshouse.

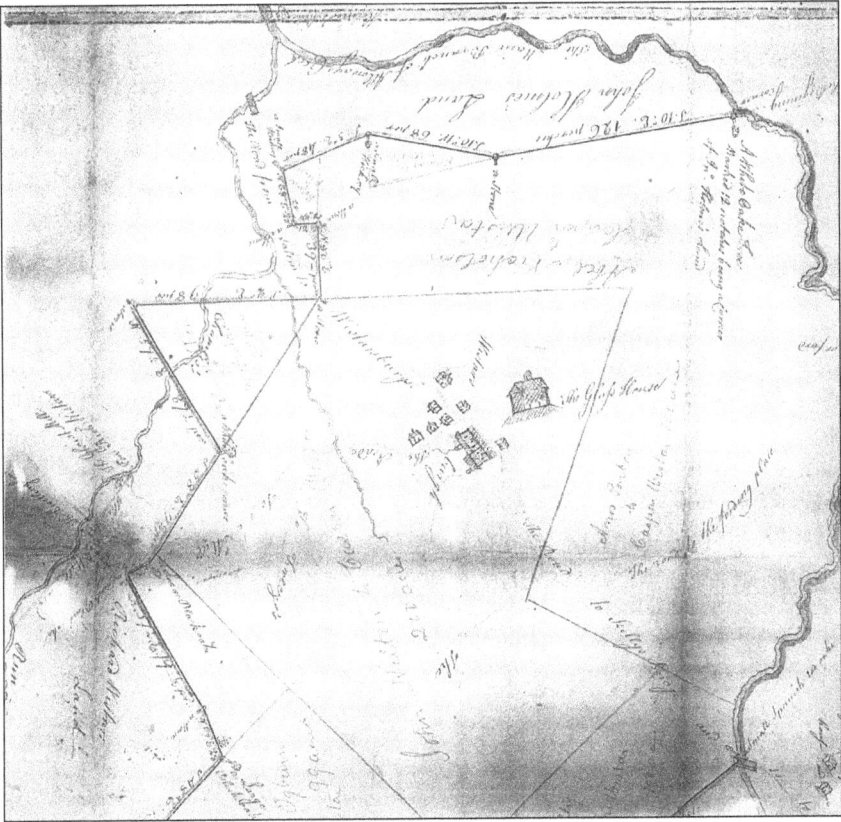

Figure 4.4. A mid-eighteenth-century map showing the glass house and other structures associated with the Wistarburgh glassworks. Courtesy of the Salem County Historical Society.

If the locations of the numerous buildings and structures mentioned in the advertisement could be ascertained, the archaeological investigation of their remains almost certainly would prove enlightening in a host of ways. The Wistarburgh glass factory was a remarkable social and cultural phenomenon. It began its life as an outpost of newly migrated German glassmakers in a rural landscape otherwise largely dominated by wealthy English Quaker farmers. The manufactory had a considerable staff. Richard Wistar stated in the mid-1750s that the glass house required a staff of 28 people in addition to the teams of wood cutters that worked to keep the furnaces supplied with fuel. Archaeology may provide material evidence concerning the lifestyle and the gradual acculturation of this group of persons through the excavation and analysis of the sites of the workers' housing and other buildings. In order to address these issues, a program of supplemental shovel testing was undertaken to investigate the archaeological sensitivity of the entire nucleated Wistarburgh complex.

Seventy additional shovel tests were excavated in rows paralleling both sides of Commissioners Pike. These tests covered many of the areas in which buildings appeared on the survey map, but permission was not received to access some of the properties on which the map suggests that buildings formerly stood. Unfortunately, for the most part, these supplemental tests proved less than successful in identifying the locations of additional buildings from the village. Eighteenth-century artifacts were identified in many of the tests but, disappointingly, only in one instance was evidence of an actual eighteenth-century building or structure found. This building was a no longer extant wing of the mansion house. The wing is depicted on the eighteenth-century survey map as a second block to the building but had been demolished by the start of the twentieth century when the first detailed descriptions of the property began to appear in print. Two shovel tests excavated in close proximity to the existing portion of the mansion house revealed remains associated with the stone foundation of the structure. On the basis of this information, a 3 foot by 6 foot excavation unit was placed in such a fashion so as to straddle the probable location of one of the exterior walls of the structure. The stone foundations walls had been pushed into an open cellar hole following the destruction of that section of the mansion house. Based on the dating of artifacts recovered from the unit and evidence of charring, it seems that the wing was knocked down following a fire, which seems to have occurred at some point during the mid- to late 1860s.

Although the quest to find evidence of the houses, shops, and other buildings that formed the larger Wistarburgh community ended without spectacular results, other efforts undertaken at the same time were far more successful. A second field effort commenced in November 2001 and began with a new phase of surface collection. The field in which the glasshouse site is located had been planted in alfalfa. Alfalfa is a grass that is cut every year but only very infrequently replanted. Reportedly, the glasshouse field had not been plowed in over twenty years. A repeat surface collection had not been planned but upon arriving on the site, the team found to its astonishment that the farmer had chosen that fall to replace his ageing plants and that the field had been deeply plowed only a week before. As the damp morning sun cast its raking light across the field, its freshly churned soils glittered with freshly exposed shards washed clean by recent rains. As had been the case with the previous episodes of surface collection, there were far too many bits of glass on the surface of the ground to be picked up and processed considering the time and the funds available. Instead, only recognizable parts of vessels, shards displaying unusual treatments, finishes, or colors, or other significant objects were retrieved. Thousands, if not tens of thousands, of shards could have been picked up from the fields. By and large, the glass fragments that were recovered on this day were among the largest and most diagnostically useful artifacts to be retrieved from the ground surface on the glasshouse site in recent years (figure 4.5).

Wistarburgh is best remembered today as the legendary source of the some of the most desirable and sought after early American blown glass objects. Much of the broader interest in the archaeological investigation of the site is derived from the desire to extract sufficient knowledge to firmly discriminate between surviving

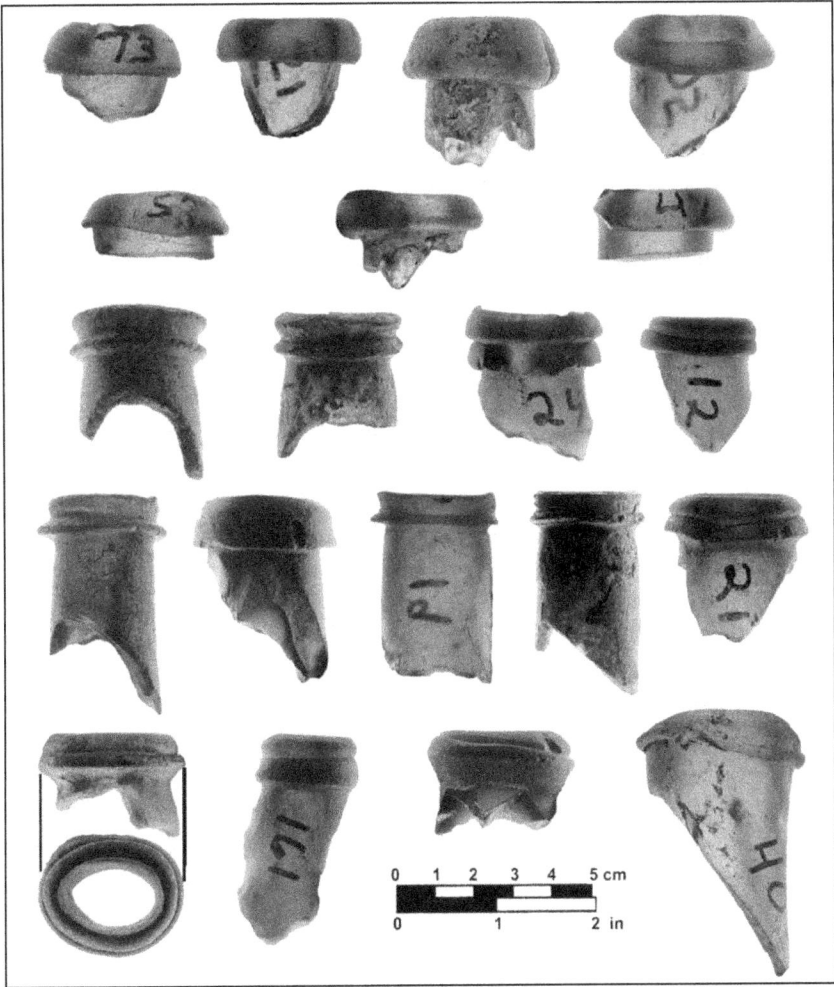

Figure 4.5. Select bottle finish fragments recovered from the Wistarburgh site. Courtesy of Hunter Research, Inc.

examples of eighteenth-century American glass. In other words, to know which actually came from Wistarburgh and which came from the other less famous factories that sprung up later. Very few, if any, objects with an ironclad Wistarburgh provenance have come onto the open antiques market in the last half century. Most glass vessels with Wistar family attributions or other strong links to the site have long ago passed into the collections of museums and historical societies. One recent study has attempted with apparent success to identify a unique profile for the chemical composition of glass produced at Wistarburgh through the analysis of waste shards removed from the site and surviving vessels with Wistarburgh associations (Owen 2004:683).

Collectors avidly compete for bottles, bowls, and pitchers that fit the popularly held conceptions of what Wistarburgh glass should look like. These conceptions have become more refined over time. During the first half of the twentieth century, almost any type of glass manufactured in the broad South Jersey tradition was marketed by antique dealers as having been made at Wistarburgh, regardless of what should have been obvious clues with regard to form, color, style, and decoration.

The initial impetus for acquiring and collecting American antiques, including Wistarburgh glass, was tied closely to the birth of the American Colonial Revival movement. The Colonial Revival is often said to have sprung out of the patriotic fervor induced by the great spectacle of the Centennial Exhibition of 1876 in Philadelphia. Among the centennial's most popular exhibits were displays honoring both the nation's "Founding Fathers" and the lives of more humble early "settlers." The deepest roots of the Colonial Revival movement can, in fact, be traced back to before 1876, but the centennial served as the mechanism for its pervasive spread throughout popular American culture.

The Colonial Revival, like the English Arts & Crafts and the American Craftsmen Movements, was, in part, a reaction to the challenges of a rapidly industrializing and urbanizing world. These movements represented a romantic longing for the "simpler" life of bygone times. However, the early days of the collecting of American antiques were dominated far more by the activities of the social and economic elite rather than by the American factory worker who actually might have had better cause to reminisce about a preindustrial existence. Only the truly privileged had both the free time to devote to the search for colonial artifacts and the wealth to spend previously unimagined sums on antique furniture and heirloom china. There is actually a certain irony in the fact that Wistarburgh glass was so highly sought after. It could, after all, have been viewed as the harbinger of the beginning of the American industrial age.

The interest of the rich and well-to-do in acquiring the trappings and detritus of America's colonial past was not really rooted in any desire to revive the "quaint" days of chamber pots and open hearth cooking. Rather it was an effort, conscious or otherwise, to solidify social status through the acquisition of rare and coveted objects. Such treasures linked their owners conceptually to America's founding generations and its bluest blood lines regardless of whether the antiques had descended for generations in the family or had been purchased from the most prestigious galleries in New York or Boston.

Frederick William Hunter was one such independently wealthy collector and was personally responsible for popularizing both many of the truths and the widely held misconceptions about the glass Wistarburgh produced. He was a graduate of Columbia University and a lawyer who moved in New York City's social circles but made his home in Freehold, New Jersey. A *New York Times* notice concerning the sale of Hunter's collection following his death in 1916 revealed that his interests spanned the full range between English ceramics and Chinese snuff bottles.

The report also noted that among the vast display of valuable items that were to be auctioned off: "The most interesting section for many collectors will be that devoted to eighteenth century Stiegel Glass and the Millville and Wistarburgh Glass of New Jersey, the interesting and old shapes, strong color, and simple decoration having steadily increased in favor with the increase in difficulty in obtaining good examples" [New York Times 1920].

F. W. Hunter was one of the first serious collectors of early American glass, but unlike many contemporaries who simply chased rare objects, Hunter expended some effort in trying to understand them. It was this process that ultimately led to the publication of one of the more influential early studies of the subject, Hunter's *Stiegel Glass* of 1914. As its title would suggest, the book was primarily devoted to the two Lancaster County, Pennsylvania glass factories founded by Henry William Stiegel in the third quarter of the eighteenth century. Hunter was primarily concerned with being able to securely identify Stiegel's products, and in order to do so, he had to study the output of Stiegel's only serious contemporary competitor, Wistarburgh. Hunter traveled to both Lancaster County, Pennsylvania and Salem County, New Jersey scouring the stock of local antiques shops and visiting with families to study heirloom sugar bowls and bottles. More significantly, he gathered artifacts directly from the glasshouse sites.

In 1913, in the company of his brother-in-law J. B. Kerfoot, Hunter conducted informal excavations at the site of the Wistarburgh factory. Based on the fragments of broken glass garnered from these sites, conversations with local historians, and his own, sometimes prejudiced, observations, Hunter characterized the products of the two operations as representing two distinct seminal traditions of American glassmaking. According to Hunter, the glassmakers at Wistarburgh concentrated on the production of relatively crude bottles, utilitarian vessels, and window glass. Wistarburgh's output reflected the long standing traditions of the German glasshouses from which Caspar Wistar had so wisely solicited his talent. Stiegel glass, on the other hand, was manufactured in a conscious attempt to compete with the refined engraved, molded, and enameled tablewares being produced in England and Venice and purveyed by Philadelphia and New York's more exclusive merchants and importers.

In defining these two competing schools of colonial American glass manufacture, Hunter was clearly guilty of oversimplification and selectively interpreting facts to support his working thesis that the glass produced in these factories reflected the character of their owners. Hunter portrayed Wistar as a stoic German Quaker and Stiegel as a flamboyant entrepreneur and innovator. Hunter also ignored the well documented fact that Stiegel hired artisans trained at Wistarburgh's fires, a detail that suggests transference of style and technology. Hunter's assessment was misguided in a number of ways, but in general, he appears to have been largely on target with regard to his assessment of the types of products produced by the two glassworks, particularly with regard to Wistarburgh. The fragments of glass collected during the course of the most recent investigations at the Wistarburgh site and those known to have been retrieved by others over the course of the twentieth century indicate that the glassworks at Alloway focused its activities largely on the manufacture of window glass and utilitarian bottles. With that said, there is also clear evidence that tableware was regularly made and strong indications that attempts were undertaken to manufacture refined and decorated wares.

Hunter's characterizations shaped the way Wistarburgh glass has been viewed for close to a century, and his book was largely responsible for generating an increased interest in the general collecting world for the products of South Jersey's glass industry. For many years, Hunter's *Stiegel Glass* remained the best known publication on the subject of early American blown glass. Since his work addressed only the manufacturing activities of the Wistarburgh and Stiegel works, the popular perception it fostered was that all early American glass belonging stylistically to the South Jersey or Germanic traditions was likely produced at Wistarburgh. Later works such as N. Hudson Moore's *Old Glass European and American* (1924) and, most importantly, Helen and George S. McKearin's *American Glass* (1941) attempted to correct this misconception by providing information concerning the large number of other American glass factories in existence during the eighteenth and early nineteenth centuries. But Wistarburgh still loomed largest in the minds of collectors, and many highly suspect attributions were made.

In disputing the ascription of early American blown glass to Wistarburgh, the McKearins, who were perhaps the most highly respected experts of their generation, went so far as to state that they were not aware of a single surviving glass vessel that could be firmly linked to the glasshouse. Since the date of the initial publication of the McKearins' landmark book, a small number of apparently American-made eighteenth-century glass objects with strong Wistar family associations have come to light, but the McKearin's point was ultimately well taken by many. Considerable caution should be exercised before attributing any glass vessel as the work of the glassblowers at Wistarburgh. Today, most serious collectors and dealers are much more knowledgeable than they ever were, but the issue of attribution is still a difficult one. Many of the items now held in private collections and proudly identified by their owners as being the product of the Wistarburgh glasshouse may well have been blown there. But they also could just have likely been blown in any one of the more than a dozen American glass manufactories that opened during the second half of the eighteenth century.

With regard to what could actually be learned through the study of the glass fragments retrieved from the Wistarburgh Glasshouse site, it was observed during the archaeological investigations during earlier walkovers that there were a few large clusters of shards of similar types. An extensive deposit of dark green glass was noted near the eastern end of the glasshouse mound. A concentration of light green and aquamarine bottle fragments were noted near the central portion of the mound while a large quantity of clear or lightly colored flat glass shards was identified on the northern edge of the mound just west of its center. These concentrations, which were of sufficient density to have survived generations of the mixing and dispersive nature of plowing, may relate either to the locations of specific manufacturing activities or storage sites.

Pale green, aquamarine, olive, and dark green are the most common colors found among the glass shards retrieved from the Wistarburgh field during the walk-overs and from the archaeological excavations. Not coincidently, these are the colors most commonly associated with the known products of Wistarburgh and the early South Jersey glass tradition. For the most part, the varying shades of greens are caused by iron impurities inherent in the locally available sand. Potash was added to the glass mix in order to counteract the effect of ferrous sands. It was produced by collecting wood ash from all of the furnace ovens and soaking them in water. The water was then allowed to evaporate leaving potash behind. Untreated ashes were sometimes added directly to mix. The use of unsoaked or undersoaked ash typically produced the green glass of differing shades, which is so often associated with the crudest products of the early American and European glassworks. In one area near the glasshouse mound, it was noted that the deep plowing activity had turned up a large deposit of wood ash extending for approximately 60 feet in width and about 40 feet in length. Interspersed with glass fragments, the upturned wood ash may have represented the remains of a storage pit or ash pile associated with the glass manufacturing process.

Although much of the more subtlety green tinted glass may have been produced unintentionally, glass of darker shades of green was probably produced deliberately for use in forming bottles. In some cases, darker shades of green glass would have been produced simply by not adding any potash to the glass batch. The darkest shades may have been the product of coloring agents deliberately introduced into the mix.

Earlier researchers have assumed the most strongly tinted green glass found on the site (usually referred to as "black" glass because of its nearly opaque character) was brought to the site as cullet produced from European bottles. During the seventeenth, eighteenth, and nineteenth century, glass of this type was utilized primarily in the production of bottles and only very rarely is encountered in other vessel types. "Black" glass bottles were historically preferred for the storage of certain light-sensitive types of alcoholic beverages. Very dark green glass is most easily produced in the extremely oxygen reduced atmospheres of coal-fired furnaces. For this reason, it has been suggested that eighteenth-century "black" glass bottles must be European in origin as coal-fired glass furnaces were not in use in North America or other parts of the world during the eighteenth century. It has recently been shown, however, that glass of this shade was produced in the seventeenth and eighteenth centuries in wood-fired furnaces. "Black Glass" could result from the serendipitous presence of natural impurities in glass sands or through the purposeful introduction of iron furnace slag or marl (Van den Bosssche 2001:392–394). Both of these materials were available in southern New Jersey during the eighteenth century. The very large volume of black glass present on the Wistarburgh site, the retrieval from the site of black glass fragments from partially formed vessels, and the identification of a few whole black glass bottles with possible historical connections to Wistarburgh considerably strengthen the case considerably that black glass bottles constituted a notable part of Wistarburgh's product line.

Small quantities of amber (also the product of iron rich sands), clear/uncolored and green glass fragments were also documented. The production of "white" or clear/uncolored glass is documented in the surviving records of Wistarburgh and was probably achieved through the introduction of manganese oxide to the batch (Palmer 1976:89). In addition to the above mentioned colors, a few much rarer anomalies were also encountered. These include several fragments of blue glass and one piece of amethyst glass. There are only three known surviving blue vessels with firm Wistarburgh attributions—two blue candlesticks and a small handled bucket. All were at one time owned by members of the Wistar family (Palmer 1976:93–97; 1993:300). The piece of amethyst glass is a thin grooved rod.

Pieces of window glass were more numerous than vessel shards although some fragments of flat sided case bottles may have been lumped in with the window glass because of the difficulty of distinguishing between them. Among the fragments of glass vessels recovered, pieces of bottles were by far the most numerous; parts of bowls, jars, and mugs were also identified along with the handle of a glass letter seal, fragments of tubes, a funnel, and handles from unidentified vessel types. Pieces of slag and drips are the byproducts of glass production and were found throughout the site. How representative this selection of glass shards is of the broader production of the Wistarburgh manufactory is questionable. The majority of finished products would have been shipped to market while broken or defective products would have been recycled within the factory. In addition, the glassworks site had been picked over for generations prior to the commencement of archaeological investigations. Scavengers would have targeted the more eye-catching and recognizable portions of the vessels with the remaining material increasingly reflecting a disproportionate volume of waste as opposed to pieces representative of finished forms.

Additionally, there was always the question of cullet. Cullet were shards of broken glass which were recycled by being added to the glass batch in order to introduce certain chemicals that they contained into the mix. Glass factories frequently obtained cullet from outside sources and thus have clouded the ability of determining what types of glass and what types of glass objects were manufactured at a glasshouse site by analyzing fragments recovered from the site. On this basis, it is difficult to say with any absolute certainty if particular vessels and vessel forms actually represent Wistarburgh products. Some glass fragments collected at the site almost certainly were either cullet or the remains of glass objects brought to the site for their own use. These include a clear/uncolored nonlead glass fragment that displays red and yellow enameled decoration in the Germanic style and three clear lead glass stem fragments—one with a double knop decoration, an air bubble stem, and an opaque twist stem. The records of Caspar and Richard Wistar indicate that they were importing English glass for personal as well as commercial purposes (Palmer 1976:83). Caspar Wistar also owned engraved wine glasses known to have been blown in Germany (Palmer 1989:10).

Three fragments of green glass were identified as exhibiting evidence of cutting. The color and fabric of the glass strongly suggest that they are Wistarburgh glass and not cullet, and the shapes of the pieces suggest that they are the byproducts of the manufacture of a cut vessel and not the result of the production of window glass panes. This is significant because the documented history of Wistarburgh makes no clear reference to the production of cut glass at the site, and the possibility that such work was undertaken there has been downplayed by authorities who have traditionally classified Wistarburgh as the producer of utilitarian products and only on rare occasions of relatively crudely formed tableware. There are, however, a few hints that more refined work was taking place on site, particularly with regard to cut or engraved glass. A Wistarburgh employee, Christian Friede, is identified in the historic record as having been a glasscutter (Palmer 1973:171). He may simply have been employed in cutting window panes to size as has been previously suggested. or he might have been undertaking more decorative pursuits. Caspar Wistar also received a compliment from a German friend regarding his successful "Glasschnitten," which translates literally as glasscutting (Palmer 1973:17). Arlene Palmer felt that this quote may have referred to etched glass, but it could also have referred to cut glass. Palmer has identified two etched glass tumblers made for Caspar Wistar's daughter, Margaret. Fashioned in a clearly Germanic tradition, these glasses may well have been manufactured at Wistarburgh (Palmer 1989:11).

Although the core of the glasshouse site has been picked over and looted over the years, larger shards of Wistarburgh glassware (for example, pieces taken home by glasshouse employees, items discarded from storehouses, or bottles discarded in privies or middens) may well be found in adjacent areas. Such was the case during the investigations of 1998 when artifacts were retrieved from the plowed surface of the field that occupies the southwest corner of the intersection of Glasshouse Lane and Commissioners Pike. The mix of eighteenth-century domestic English and Continental ceramics and glassware fragments of Wistarburgh type suggests that this location may have been the site of buildings associated with the glass factory. Buildings are, in fact, shown in this approximate location on the mid-eighteenth-century survey map of Wistar family's holdings discussed above. The glass fragments collected in this location were of a larger size and represented a range of forms not found during the course of excavations on the site of the glasshouse itself. Taken as a group, they provide an important body of knowledge concerning handle and foot shapes utilized on some of Wistarburgh's more sophisticated products.

To date, the archaeological study of the Wistarburgh Glasshouse site has provided evidence concerning the glassmaking complex, the technologies it employed, and the glass that it produced. Additional support has been generated for some long held beliefs—Wistarburgh does seem to have been primarily concerned in the production of window glass and utilitarian bottles. However, new evidence has been developed, which strongly suggests that very darkly tinted green glass bottles were manufactured at Wistarburgh in spite of the fact that it has been previously suggested by scholars that such bottles were only produced by European manufacturers. Evidence, although fragmentary, has also been developed to show that Wistarburgh's glassblowers did undertake to produce a range of products that extended beyond windows and bottles. Scholars have never questioned that the craftsmen at Wistarburgh produced a limited amount of tableware and ornamental glass, but since most of the examples that survived today have come down to us as family heirlooms, it has been difficult to say to what extent these more showy objects belonged to the glass manufactory's commercial product line. Based on the small numbers of such pieces known today, they could quite simply have been occasionally produced as whimsies or gifts for friends and family.

A substantial number of glass shards were recovered during these investigations which display handworked decorative treatments, molded patterns, and unusual colors. Lead glass fragments were also identified as well as handles, feet, and decorative elements associated with more sophisticated tableware forms like mugs and sugar bowls. Although some of these shards may well represent cullet and although the numbers of such atypical shards are relatively low in comparison with window glass and bottle glass fragments, the volume of such material that was encountered is probably greater than what one would have expected if more refined or decorative pieces were being produced only as special objects for glassworkers, themselves. Even these pieces, however, fall technologically and stylistically within the broader Germanic tradition of glass blowing. Relatively little evidence was observed of glass objects displaying more of the refined and sophisticated characteristics of the English and Italian glass industries, which were often thinner walled and of higher quality, clearer glass than their German counterparts.

Most importantly, the archaeological investigations of the glasshouse site have proved that Wistarburgh survives. This was the first goal of the undertaking and the most basic and the most significant information which could have been garnered from the site. The site of the glasshouse is not just a gently rolling empty field where some distant historic event once took place but rather a tangible historic resource that survives beneath plowed fields.

The importance of the tangible and, to some degree, the visceral experience of history, must also be recognized alongside the scholarly and the academic quests to acquire more knowledge. This is something grasped innately by most visitors to archaeological sites but all too often overlooked or actually downplayed by archaeologists seeking to protect the image of the discipline as a pure, analytical scientific pursuit. Although most archaeologists were drawn to the field by the thrill of discovery and the chance to touch the past first hand, many professionals shy away from such public admissions out of the fear that they are dark shadows—the unscientific or unscholarly motivations of the treasure hunter and the looter.

Archaeologists, instead, are taught to evaluate the significance of sites in terms of how much can be learned through their physical study. This is an approach that evolved in part from the need to create standardized evaluation criteria to justify the investigation and/or preservation of archaeological sites of particular scholarly merit. Archaeologists are far less comfortable with evaluating a site on the basis of its modern day cultural significance and meaning. However, we must not lose sight of the importance of these factors just because they cannot be as easily pigeonholed into a comparative evaluative framework. No one would suggest that the value of a historic house lies only in what we can learn from it through the study of its fabric. Historic buildings have value, in part, because they contribute to our collective cultural heritage, so do many archaeological sites.

A lone hand molded, red clay brick excavated from the remains of the Wistarburgh glass furnace might have little to tell us scientifically about the technology of eighteenth-century glass manufacture or the lives of glassworks employees, but it can still be an incredibly valuable artifact if it is placed in the hands of a child. It is in this manner that links with the past are forged. The more that one understands and feels connected to the history and traditions of the place in which one lives, the more one feels a pride in that place and a sense of living in a community with a unique and special identity with its own history, culture, and traditions. These are the communities to which residents are proud to belong, communities which we are inspired to celebrate, and communities in which we are willing to invest financially and emotionally. Ultimately, this is why the archaeological investigations undertaken at Wistarburgh to date have been so significant. It is true that they have expanded our knowledge of the past in some very narrow and specific ways, but more importantly they have proved that one of the building blocks of a region's cultural identity still survives. The glass industry shaped large aspects of life in southern New Jersey for over two centuries. Wistarburgh was its birthplace, the starting point. Our work proved that Wistarburgh still exists today—and not just as a nondescript location in the landscape but more tangibly as archaeological remains that can be explored, documented, touched, and experienced.

References Cited

Acton, R. M.

1885   A Short History of the Glass Manufacture in Salem County, New Jersey. *The Pennsylvania Magazine of History and Biography* 9:343–346.

Beiler, R. J.

1994   *The Transatlantic World of Caspar Wistar: From Germany to America in the Eighteenth Century.* Ph.D. dissertation, Department of History, University of Pennsylvania, Philadelphia.

2008   *Immigrant and Entrepreneur: The Atlantic World of Caspar Wistar 1650–1750.* Pennsylvania State University Press, University Park.

Cushing and Sheppard
1883   *The History of the Counties of Gloucester, Salem, and Cumberland New Jersey*. Everts and Peck, Philadelphia, Pennsylvania.

Enviroscan
1998   Final Report, Geophysical Survey Wistarburgh Glassworks Site, Salem County, New Jersey. Submitted to Hunter Research, Inc., Trenton, New Jersey.

Hunter, F. W.
1914   *Stiegel Glass*. Houghton Mifflin, Boston.

Liebeknecht, William, Damon Tvaryanas, Rebecca White, and Michael Murphy
2001   Archaeological Investigations at the Wistarburgh Glassworks Site (28Sa134), Alloway Township, Salem County, New Jersey.

Maxwell, F. C.
1951   Wistarberg, Yesterday and Today. *Antiques* 60:190–192.

McKearin, G. S., and H. McKearin
1941   *American Glass*. Crown Publishers, New York.

Moore, N. Hudson
1935   *Old Glass: European and American*. Tudor Publishing, New York.

Murschell, Dale
2007   Wistarburgh: Window Tiles, Bottles and More. Self Published. Springfield, West Virginia.

Owen, J. Victor
2004   Geochemistry of Wistarburgh Glass (ca. 1739–1777): Implications for Batch Recipes and Distinction from Other South Jersey Wares. *Canadian Journal of Earth Sciences* 41: 683–697.

New York Times
1920   Art Notes; Collection of the Late Frederick William Hunter on View. 1 January:14. New York

Palmer, A. M.
1973   *The Wistarburgh Glassworks of Colonial New Jersey*. Master's thesis. University of Delaware, Newark.
1976   Glass Production in Eighteenth-Century America: The Wistarburgh Enterprise. *Winterthur Portfolio* 11:75–101.
1989   *The Wistars and Their Glass*. Wheaton Historical Association, Millville, New Jersey.

Pennsylvania Archives
n.d.   Ships' Lists of German Passengers, 1727–1808 (Record Group:26.36)

Survey of the Lands of Richard Wistar.
c. 1760   On file, Salem County Historical Society, Salem, New Jersey.

Tvaryanas, Damon, William Liebeknecht, and Christy Roper Morgenstein
1999   Archaeological Investigations at the Wistarburgh Glassworks Site, Alloway Township, Salem County, New Jersey. Wheaton Museum of American Glass, Millville, New Jersey.

Van den Bossche, W.
2001   *Antique Glass Bottles: Their History and Evolution (1500–1850)*. Antique Collectors' Club, Suffolk, England.
Wust, Klaus
1998   The Year of the Destroying Angels—1738. *Beyond Germania* 10(1)

5

TRANSCULTURATION AND ETHNOGENESIS: MATERIAL CULTURE FROM AN EIGHTEENTH-CENTURY PENNSYLVANIA GERMAN FARMSTEAD/DISTILLERY

PATRICIA E. GIBBLE

Introduction

Culture contact or interaction between diverse ethnic groups, whether forced by conquest or instigated by people themselves, results in a dynamic interplay of negotiation, acceptance, and/or resistance to another's cultural practices. Individuals as well as groups do not wholly accept cultural domination and assimilation but exercise human agency in choosing what they will absorb, what aspects of culture they will manipulate to fit their own cultural patterns, and how they will resist the dominant ideology.

Cusick (1998) provides an extensive critique of twentieth-century anthropological theories on interaction and culture change as well as application of these concepts to archaeological research. For social scientists in the early twentieth century, interpreting cultural interaction from ethnographic studies was largely based on the anthropological paradigm of acculturation. More recently, social scientists have begun to question some of this paradigm's assumptions (Cusick 1998:126–140). For example, some researchers assumed that the flow of cultural transmission was unidirectional, only from a dominant to a subordinate group (Alexander 1998:478; Cusick 1998:132). Some held the bias that Western cultural values were superior to native cultural features, while other scholars saw small changes in a cultural system as indicating alterations in the entire cultural identity of a group. And subordinated groups were seen as passive actors in exchange, absorbing the dominant culture's characteristics such that the subordinate society would become almost indistinguishable from the dominant culture (Alexander 1998:478–479; Cusick 1998:126–140). Past interpretive models (such as assimilation, adaptation and dependency, evolutionary theory, and world system theory) ignored the unequal levels of group acculturation. especially evidenced in private vs. public spaces or in demonstrating a subordinate group's influences on the traditions of the colonizing society (Cusick 1998:131; Deagan 1998:31). In spite of some shortcomings, scholars recommend that models of acculturation should not be completely abandoned but critically examined and in many cases revised as a basis for future research (Cusick 1998:136).

Anthropological and archaeological researchers at the end of the last century sought to demonstrate the autonomy of subordinated groups to make decisions on aspects of a dominant culture as well as to prevent outside influences from producing cultural disruptions and/or creating a new identity. For example, Alexander (1998) points to processes in cultural interaction resulting in a variety of responses such as the blending of some cultural features and processes that maintain ethnic distinctiveness in some fundamental elements of a society (Alexander 1998:476–483).

Specifically focusing on culture contact studies in the Spanish American colonies, Deagan (1998) has identified two perspectives for conceptualizing interaction in the archeological contexts: transculturation and ethnogenesis. The former is a term coined by cultural anthropologist Fernando Ortiz in his studies of the diverse ethnic origins of the Cuban culture, which emphasizes symbiosis and resistance to some aspects of assimilation (Deagan 1998:27). Ethnogenesis refers to the purposeful alteration and reforming of a new cultural identity in response to cultural contact with the "other" (Deagan 1998: 27–28). She notes that employing these concepts in a post-processual approach to understanding cultures in contact avoids some of the pitfalls of past acculturation studies (Deagan 1998:27–30).

J. Daniel Roger's (1990) inquiry on culture change in historic Arikara society is seen as a promising example of the archaeological application of the concept of acculturation and the use of material culture to interpret specific site contexts (Deagan 1998:27). Roger's approach emphasizes cultural processes at work in specific historical contexts wherein an ethnic group contemplates several avenues of choice when encountering hegemonic influences. Demonstrating both autonomy and human agency, a contacted group may maintain some or most aspects of their culture, add individual cultural elements from the other society, completely replace components of their society with cultural features from the other, or reject portions of a dominant ideology. In all cases, some transformation of a subjugated society may occur just from the experience of cultural interaction. These proposed processes are seen as bridging arguments between the archeological record from a site and historical documentation of events associated with the archaeological record (Deagan 1998:27).

Following this model, comparison of the archaeological record from the Alexander Schaeffer Farm/Distillery to the site's built environment and contemporary historical documents allows a unique opportunity to explore the extent of these dynamic acculturation processes on a German-speaking household in a largely Anglo-dominated societal context. In this case study, comparison of these data sources addresses several questions. First, as part of the largely English trade network, what material goods were available to the three generations of a Pennsylvania German yeoman family (c. 1760–1810) who occupied this hinterland plantation? Can the recovered material culture and extant farmhouse style suggest the acceptance of the dominant British ideology, especially in terms of public display, as a way to demonstrate socioeconomic status? What aspects of material culture suggest the maintenance of conservative pan-German values by this Pennsylvania family?

Pan-German Settlement

As a result of his distribution of promotional broadsides throughout England and continental Europe, emigration to William Penn's newly chartered province in North America began soon after 1682 (Dunn and Dunn 1986:43). Penn focused not only on attracting wealthy British investors who would bankroll his investment, but he also hoped to entice yeomen, day laborers, and craftsmen from all European centers to settle in his colony (Soderlund 1983:63). Farmers and producers of handcrafts would supply the needed food stuffs, domestic goods, and services to make the colony flourish. Because of deteriorating economic circumstance, religious strife, and the exigencies of recent European wars, large numbers of German-speaking citizens sought economic opportunities in "Penn's Woods." The first German-speaking immigrants settled in the Lower Delaware Valley in Philadelphia, Bucks, and Chester counties. Later arriving German and Swiss groups bought available land holdings in surrounding Montgomery, Berks, and Lancaster counties.

By 1750, Penn's entrepreneurial efforts resulted in over one hundred thousand German speakers making the arduous transatlantic crossing to establish a new homeland in the region (Beiler 1997:73–75). Board of Trade Censuses commissioned by London ministers during the early years of European exodus erroneously labeled all German-speaking immigrants as coming from the Palatinate region, when in fact family groups and individuals came from dozens of European principalities. Emigrants hailed from numerous German villages along the Rhine as well as Holstein, Thuringia, and Swiss territories located some distance from Rhineland centers (Otterness 1999:9). Upon arriving in the colony, new immigrants encountered the first pressures to assimilate. They were required to declare an oath of allegiance to the English king and royal family, and in some cases, renounce the jurisdiction of the papacy (Schelbert 1983:50; Fogleman 1991:365–372). As early as 1698, English Navigation Laws were enforced by a special Vice-Admiralty Court in Pennsylvania. These regulations allowed only manufactured goods from England into the colonies, thus protecting eighteenth-century British economic interests (Schelbert 1983:53–56). The court's judgment often resulted in the confiscation of the immigrants' household goods brought with them on the ocean voyage to begin a new life in North America (Schelbert 1983:53–56).

The majority of German-speaking immigrants tended to settle in enclaves populated by people from similar ethnic backgrounds in and around Philadelphia and surrounding counties. Selected segregation was the trend even into the latter half of the eighteenth century, enabling immigrants to maintain aspects of their unique cultural traditions and language, while at the same time negotiating their identity as part of the dominant Anglo-America society (Fogleman 1996:82–83). Fueled by commercial trade of imported British commodities in exchange for local agricultural products, German-speaking populations regularly interacted with Anglo citizenry in small villages and larger towns (Wenger 2008). Schaefferstown (originally known as Heidelberg) offers an example of a rural Germanic settlement and the direct social and commercial relationships with the larger Anglo-American population in North America.

Initially designated as part of Lancaster County, the Alexander Schaeffer Farmstead/Distillery (36LE480) lies in a fertile valley in Lebanon County, 80 miles northwest of Philadelphia. Historic Schaefferstown, Inc. (HSI), a non-profit educational and historical society, purchased the farm property in 1966 and since that time has preserved the homestead as an example of Pennsylvania German cultural heritage. Extant buildings on the property include a two and one-half story limestone farmhouse with a centralized chimney (figure 5.1). Although professional architectural analysis is ongoing, the original portion of the structure reflects a medieval German/Swiss multi-purpose house that served both domestic and economic functions (Noble 2009). The ground-floor room boasts a large fireplace and workroom, with the second and third floors used as living space for the farm family. Existing outbuildings on the homestead include a late eighteenth-century smoke house, pig sty, circa 1890 summer kitchen, a large bank barn, and remnants of a springhouse located 168 feet south of the farmhouse.

Three types of resources inform this inquiry regarding Germanic culture and aspects of culture change. First, archaeological excavations at the Schaeffer homestead have yielded a rich artifact assemblage, contributing to our understanding of the material culture used and discarded by yeoman citizens in settlements outside the Philadelphia region at the end of the eighteenth and into the beginning of the nineteenth century. Other contemporary written sources such as colonial wills, probate records, and merchants' daybooks and bills of sale delineate the availability of

Figure 5.1. Crew excavating outside the original section of the Alexander Schaeffer Farm/Distillery (36LE480). Photograph by Patricia Gibble.

imported commodities and socioeconomic status of the site's occupants. Eighteenth-century farmhouse renovations provide clues regarding the display of socioeconomic status and resistance to culture change in the built environment. Comparison of these data leads one to question the assumption proposed by some scholars: that with the acquisition of wealth, all citizens (including German speakers) wished to acquire social status indicators such as high-end imported ceramics, Georgian-style houses, and other material culture associated with status in early American society (Falk 2008).

A Brief History of the Farm

Extant deeds indicate that the property now known as the Alexander Schaeffer Farm (36LE480) was first owned by German land speculators John and Katherine Miley who sold the plantation to an immigrant "Switzer" family in 1736. Headed by Durs Thommen, the family hailed from the Basel District of Waldenberg, Switzerland (Dibert 2006; Schelbert 1983). In 1758, forty-six-year-old Alexander Schaeffer purchased 103.5 acres of property from Thommen's sons, Durs, Jr. and Martin, nine years after their father's death (Weiser and Neff 1987:v). Schaeffer had arrived in Penn's province in 1738 with his young family and sisters from the market town of Schriesheim, located in the Palatinate region of Germany (Weiser and Neff 1987:v). Around the same time that Schaeffer bought the plantation from the Thommens, he purchased another 440 acres one-quarter mile east of the homestead. On this land parcel he laid-out a European-style village around a town square, naming his newly organized village Heidelberg after the historic university-town near his Palatinate home (Weiser and Neff 1987:vii).

As a savvy entrepreneur, Alexander Schaeffer strategically located his town at the crossroads of the Philadelphia road, artery to Lancaster town, and roads to the Cornwall Iron Furnaces and the German Tulpehocken settlement. Building at this prime location meant that he could take economic advantage of the constant flow of traffic by teamsters, iron furnace workers, farmers, and travelers. At the corner of Main and Market Streets, he constructed a multi-story limestone tavern/store and began distilling apple whiskey in the basement workroom of his nearby farmhouse to supply beverages for his tavern customers. Account books show that Schaeffer paid Michael Meyer for his work as early as 1762. Meyer is later identified in a notation of August 17, 1965 as a gatshel brenner or distiller (Weiser and Neff 1987:131). Like many Pennsylvania farmers, Schaeffer realized that it made good economic sense to turn grains and fruits grown on the farm into alcoholic spirits to meet the large demand for alcoholic beverages. Alcohol consumption during this period was based on European traditions that advocated the regular imbibing of spirits as part of a healthy diet and cure for some physical ailments (Rorabaugh 1979:25).

As founder of the town that later bore his name, successful farmer, merchant, innkeeper, and leading church elder, Schaefferer achieved high rank and status among his peers. His estate inventory shows that he not only owned several large farm properties and wooded tracts, equipment, farm animals, household goods, and a store/tavern, but he had an annual income from the sale of town lots and collection of annual ground rents on those tracts. His probate inventory enumerates monies owed him before his death by friends and neighbors, amounting to over £1200 and cash lent to local businessmen and merchants totaling £400. In 1779, he demonstrated his patriotism for the fledgling American nation by helping to finance the Revolutionary War through the purchase of two Loan Office Certificates from the Constitutional Congress amounting to £1400 (Dibert 2001). Other generous donations to the Heidelberg community contributed to his standing in the eyes of town citizenry. He donated town lots to the Dutch Reformed and Dutch Lutheran congregations for a cemetery to be used in common (Weiser and Neff 1987:vii) In 1763, Schaeffer deeded the land tract at the southern edge of town to homeowners on Market Street; the parcel held the town spring that supplied fresh water to the households on the street. He had previously constructed a gravity-driven water system of interlocking wooden pipes to convey spring water from this reservoir to the troughs outside his tavern at the corner of Market and Main Streets (Brendle 1901:14; Weiser and Neff 1987:vii–viii).

During the mid-1770s, Schaeffer's only surviving male heir, Johann Heinrich (Henry), set up his own household on one farm property with first wife, Anna Eva Schweitzer. Alexander and his wife formally conveyed the deed for the property to young Henry in November 1775 for £1800 with payment of this debt deferred until his father's death in 1786 (Dibert 2006).

Archaeological and documentary evidence confirms that Henry expanded the seasonal distilling operation by adding a second still firebox in the basement workroom to increase apple whiskey production (Gibble 2006). Henry also constructed a water system consisting of interlocking wooden pipes that conveyed fresh water from the spring house located south of the farmhouse to the basement distilling room. His 1803 probate inventory lists the necessary distilling equipment for alcohol manufacturing such as two copper pot stills, worm tubes, other copper vessels, hogsheads, five tierce (barrels) with whiskey and various other distilling utensils (Dibert 2000).

Samuel Rex, one of several Heidelberg storekeepers operating retail establishments during the last quarter of the eighteenth century, kept account records that reflect both Henry Schaeffer's distilling activities and the economic links between small Pennsylvania rural towns, the larger network of trade, and incipient capitalist markets in Post-Revolutionary America (Wenger 2008). In one daybook entry dated December 4, 1798, Rex sold over 330 gallons of apple whiskey for Henry "Sheffer" to Philadelphia merchants, Dubs and Earl, who operated a shop on High Street in Philadelphia (Wenger 2008:190). Henry was paid 65 pounds, 4 shilling, and 6 pence for his domestically produced alcoholic spirits (Samuel Rex Daybook #6). In 1802, one year before his death, he bought large quantities of rye whiskey, a primary ingredient in apple whiskey, from Rex every week beginning in July through the end of September (Samuel Rex Daybook #20). Shortly after, Rex records that he "sent Squire Schaeffer one load apples from Rex & Valentine [Rex's store with partner Michael Valentine] and one by Rex to be stilled for the shares. . ." (Samuel Rex Daybook #20). Henry also purchased nine hogshead barrels in September for storing the apple whiskey and shipment of the product by wagon to Philadelphia.

As the son of the town's founder, Henry Schaeffer may have been ascribed automatic respect and status by the local town residents. His inheritance comprised multiple parcels of valuable real estate including the Schaeffer farm, properties in Lancaster and Berks counties, and the tavern/store (Dibert 2000). He achieved business and political prominence through a lifetime of work on the plantation, seasonal commercial distilling, his service as Justice of the Peace (1793), and appointment as an Associate Justice of the Court of Dauphin County (Record of Indenture for Gartrout Sweitzer 1793; Dibert 2006). During the Revolutionary War, Henry distinguished himself as captain of a militia company known as Flying Camp that traveled to Amboy, New Jersey (Dibert 2006).

Following the southwestern German tradition of partible inheritance that parceled land holdings between male heirs (Güterzersplitterung), in his will of October 1803 Henry divided his real estate between his two sons (Fogleman 1996:24). His eldest son, Johannes, inherited the Schaeffer farmstead, two other large land tracts, some of his father's clothing, farm equipment and animals, and other personal possessions (Dibert 2000; Henry Schaeffer's Will and Estate Inventory 1803). Henry, Jr., the youngest child of Henry, Sr. and second wife, Margaret Hoffman, also received substantial bequests from his father's estate including several land parcels, the annual ground rents from the village lots, and the Schaeffer tavern/store (Dibert 2000; Henry Schaeffer's Will and Estate Inventory 1803). Each of Henry's three oldest daughters inherited £700, with a lesser amount of £300 left to daughter, Anna Maria, because her husband had previously borrowed funds from his father-in-law to buy a nearby farmstead.

Johannes Schaeffer was twenty-one at the time of his father's death and would have grown up learning both agrarian pursuits and the distilling business. He continued these economic ventures up to his untimely death at the age 25 in September 1807. Abraham Rex, who like his brother Samuel engaged in the mercantile trade, operated a store in Mount Pleasant, a village 10 miles southeast of Schaefferstown (Wenger pers. comm.). On Dec 11, 1804, Johannes Schaeffer bought goods at Rex's store, where Abraham identifies him as a "stiller" and lists Schaeffer's purchases of "oil, molasses, rum, coffee, alum, madder, allspice, indigo . . . logwood" (Abraham Rex Daybook #7).

No will or estate inventory distributing Johannes' property has been found thus far. At the time he passed away, Johannes was survived by his wife, Esther Weisz Schaeffer, and a four month old infant son, John (Johannes Schaeffer's Gravestone, Schaefferstown Cemetery). Under Common Law, if a man died intestate (as Johannes Schaeffer had), his widow was entitled to dower or one-third of his property and possessions for her lifetime or until she remarried (Salmon 1986:16, 143–146, 162–163). As Johannes' only male heir, his infant son, John inherited the bulk of his father's property upon reaching maturity as well as his mother's portion when she remarried or passed away. John, Jr. received formal title to his father's property in1830 when he came of age (Lebanon County Land Indenture 1830). Sometime before 1810, Widow Esther Schaeffer married David May, settling in nearby Manheim, Pennsylvania (Sowers 2008:13; Ancestry.com, U.S. Census Records 1810).

No archival documents have survived indicating the continued occupation of the farmstead by any Schaeffer family member or tenant farmers between the time of Esther's remarriage and the sale of the property in April 1842. In that year, John Schaeffer, Jr. and wife Susan conveyed the farmstead to John Steinmetz (Dibert 2006). By mid-life, John Schaeffer had become a successful entrepreneur, first as a tavern owner and later as a merchant, eventually establishing a book printing and publishing company in Lancaster, Pennsylvania (*Lancaster Saturday Evening Express* March 24, 1866; *Lancaster Intelligencer Journal* March 24, 1866; Manheim Boro Tax Records 1847–1854; Rapho Township Tavern Application 1837; 1860 Map - Borough of Manheim). Upon John's sale of the plantation, the farm ownership passed out of the Schaeffer family. For the next 124 years, the agricultural property was owned by eight different farm families who continued cultivation and animal husbandry until in 1966, when Historic Schaefferstown, Inc. purchased the tract (Dibert 2006).

Comparison of Material Culture

THE ARCHEOLOGICAL RECORD AND ARCHIVAL DOCUMENTS

In 2004, archaeological investigations began at the Schaeffer Farm sponsored by Historic Schaefferstown, Inc. (HSI), a Historic Preservation grant from Pennsylvania Historical and Museum Commission (PHMC), and generous private donations. During the initial season of archaeological excavations, our research design centered on discovering any tangible evidence of colonial alcohol production remaining in the basement workroom. Excavations uncovered bases for two terra cotta tile and brick fireboxes, located directly adjacent to the openings in the back of the basement's hearth walls (figure 5.2). The stratigraphy surrounding these features, however, proved to be highly disturbed by a complex of rodent tunnels resulting in a temporal mix of mid-eighteenth- through twentieth-century material culture (Gibble 2006). Dr. Robert Sternberg, Professor of Geosciences at Franklin and Marshall College, collected brick samples from the features for archaeomagnetic dating. This chronometric dating strategy held the possibility of defining when the fireboxes were burned for the last time. Preliminary testing results indicate that firebox #2 was used for the last time between1790 and 1810, coinciding with the time period when both Henry and Johannes Schaeffer had died (Sternberg 2006).

Figure 5.2. Exposed eighteenth-century brick and tile firebox bases uncovered within the farmhouse basement distilling room. Photograph by Patricia Gibble.

Subsequent seasons of archaeological investigation (2005–2007 and 2010) continued on both the interior of the distilling room and exterior areas adjacent to the house's southern façade. Another feature associated with the distilling activities at the site was uncovered consisting of a circular, three foot diameter, brick and limestone lined opening located directly outside a break in the house's southern limestone wall. Because of its shallow depth (less than 2.5 feet to subsoil), the feature was determined to be a settling tank or catch basin, whose probable function was to receive slop, water, and distilling debris flushed from the workroom area (Gibble 2006). The basin would have been used when the copper stills and other distilling equipment were cleaned between production episodes.

Hundreds of datable household items had been thrown into the catch basin during its deconstruction. Portions of English case bottles, blown wine bottles, animal bones, redware, imported ceramics, nit combs, pewter and tombac buttons, clay pipe bowls and stems, bricks, terra cotta roof tiles, an eighteenth-century horse shoe, and iron nails had been recovered from the feature (Noël Hume 1969) (figure 5.4). Diverse classes of material culture reflective of a domestic context were recovered from all other excavation units as well. A large portion of the assemblage equates to the occupation of the plantation by three generations of the Schaeffer family beginning when Alexander first purchased the homestead (1758) until Esther Schaeffer departed the farm to remarry sometime before 1810. The artifact assemblage

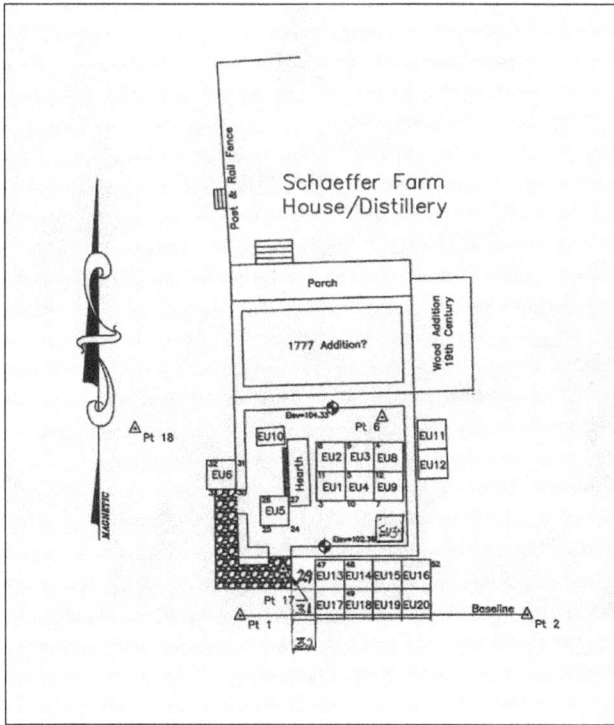

Figure 5.3. Excavation grid showing five foot square units investigated within the basement distilling room and farmhouse exterior. By Patricia Gibble.

represents a limited amount of the multigenerational material goods owned by the Schaeffer household, but they may still provide clues to socioeconomic status of the residents and their intentional consumer choices (Spencer-Wood 1987:13; Spencer-Wood and Heberling 1987:48–49).

After the artifacts had been processed by community volunteers at weekly HSI artifact clinics, sherds of many ceramic vessels and blown glass bottles from units dug on the eastern side of the farmhouse (Units 11 &12) could be mended with sherds from southern elevation units (Units 13, 14,15,16, 17 30, 31) (see figure 3). Eighteenth-century Germanic farming households typically discarded broken or unwanted household debris by throwing their garbage into the surrounding farmyard or garden. Based on ceramic, pipe stem, and button analysis, the majority of assemblage coincides to a time when Henry and Margaret Schaeffer's family occupied the farmhouse and the short period that Johannes and Esther Schaeffer lived there (Gibble 2006).

As Wheeler points out from her research into early-nineteenth-century deposit episodes on New England sites, "the responsibility for the discard of refuse will fall to the succeeding household, but the acquisition and use of the material themselves will be associated with the departing group . . . " (Wheeler 1999:43). At the Schaeffer farm site, the large deposit of reconstructable household items repre-

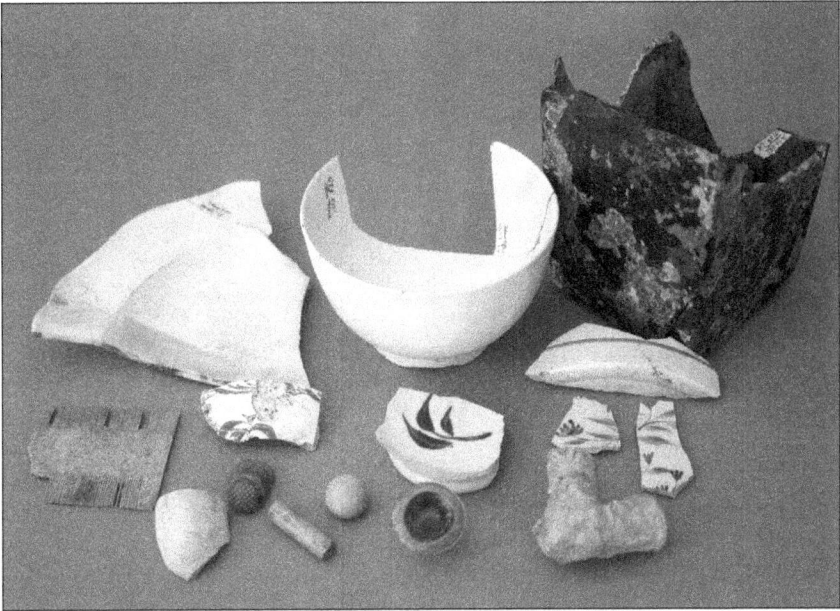

Figure 5.4. Artifacts from a sheet midden deposit including plain and decorated creamware, case bottle, hand-painted pearlwares, portion of a hand-made pipe, neck of a medicine vial, clay marble, kaolin smoking pipe, brass thimble, and nit comb. Photograph by Patricia Gibble.

sents three generations of Schaeffers but especially material debris tossed out after Margaret and Esther Schaeffer left the property. Since no archival evidence has confirmed other residents on the property up to when John, Jr. sold the farm to John Steinmentz in 1842, one can conclude that the possessions of both Margaret and Esther were discarded around this time. Table 5.1 summarizes the material culture categories identified in the sheet midden deposit.

Domestic and imported ceramic vessels, manufactured from the mid-eighteen century to the second decade of the nineteenth century, were recovered from the sheet midden deposit and catch basin feature. A total of 94 possible ceramic vessels have been identified with reassembling of the wares underway (table 5.2). Typical for a domestic context, the majority of ceramics recovered from this deposit consisted of redware pottery (figure 5.5). The Schaeffer wives and daughters turned kitchen garden, orchard produce, and grains into consumables using the earthenware vessels recovered from archaeological contexts. The assemblage includes plain-glazed redware vessels that functioned as food and beverage storage, hygiene, and food preparation forms (Gibble 2001). Butter pots, medium and large pots, patty pans, an earthen bottle, and large pottery bowls were used by farm women to process and store dairy products such as milk, cheese, butter, and puddings. Three slip-decorated mugs, slip-decorated plates, a plain glazed porringer, chamber pots, and thumb-size

Table 5.1
Material Culture from Contiguous Deposits, 1760–1810

Ceramics	Armaments	Architecture	Bottle Glass
Plain glazed Redware	Musket Ball	Brick	Blown Wine Bottle
Dec. Redware	Gun Flints	Window Glass	Blown Case Bottles
Creamware/Queensware		Wrought Nails	Medicine Vials
Hand-painted Pearlware		Early Cut-Nails	Beverage Vessels
Shell-edged Pearlware		Clay Roof Tiles	
Mocha		Latches, Hinges	
Dec. Creamware		Iron Shutter Hook	
Porcelain		Iron Door Pulls	
Stoneware			

Personal	Smoking	Farm Equipment	Dietary	Fuel
Shoe Buckle	Kaolin Pipe Bowls	Iron Horse Shoe	Shellfish	Charcoal
Brass Pins	Kaolin Pipe Stems		Bird Bone	
Metal Buttons			Small, Medium, & Large Mammal Bone	
Clay Marbles				
Sleeve Buttons				
Bone Nit Combs				
Slate Pencil				
Thimbles				

cosmetic or galley pots were also recovered (Gibble 2001). Since colonial redware potters rarely signed their work, the pottery collection cannot be accurately dated or attributed to any specific regional craftsmen, but several local potters producing earthenware marketed their wares at Schaefferstown general stores during this temporal period (Wenger 2008).

Sherds from two imported stoneware storage vessels and imported English teaware forms are part of the assemblage. Plain and decorated creamware vessels and almost equal amounts of hand-painted blue and white, shell-edged, and polychrome pearlwares were recovered along with a scant number of fragments from a small mocha bowl (Miller et al. 2000; Noël Hume 1972:242; Sussman 1997). None of the more expensive English transfer-printed pearlwares were identified in the assemblage, and only two sherds of undecorated porcelain were inventoried. Although their husbands were considered prominent by contemporary socioeconomic standards, ceramic analysis of the sheet midden deposit suggests that the Schaeffer wives did not invest the family funds in the higher priced imported ceramics. Instead they chose middling-priced and medium quality ceramics for tea consumption.

No matched dining sets or large plates are among the recovered assemblage dating to this period, but Alexander's and Henry's estates inventories provide some

Table 5.2
Ceramic Types and Forms, 1760–1820

Form	Red-ware	Decorative Redware	Stone-ware	Plain Cream	Deco-rative Cream	Deco-rative Pearl	Edge-ware	Porcelain
Food and Beverage, Preparation and Storage								
Butter Pot	12		1					
Medium Pot	2		1					
Large Pot	7							
Patty Pan		8						
Bottle	1							
Large Bowl		3						
Health and Hygiene								
Chamber Pot	4							
Galley Pot	2							
Food and Beverage, Consumption								
Mug		3				1		
Cup								
Tea Bowl				4	1	9		1
Tea Pot					1			
Small Plate				3			2	
Large Plate		4						
Slop Bowl				4		6		
Porringer	2							
Unknown	6	4						1
Total by Type	36	22	2	11	2	16	2	2

clues as to the dining vessels used by both generations. Alexander's probate inventory (1786) listed large numbers of pewter plates, dishes, a pewter teapot, cream jug, and various sized pewter mugs (Dibert 2001). No imported refined earthenware of any kind is recorded in his inventory even though as a storekeeper he would have had access to more expensive imported wares available at the time from venders in Philadelphia. Among Henry's goods and chattels inventoried in 1803 were "sixteen pewter plates, 4 basons [sic], 5 dishes and pint and quart mugs valued at over three pounds" (Dibert 2000) Some ". . . Queensware Plates and Bowols [sic]" were

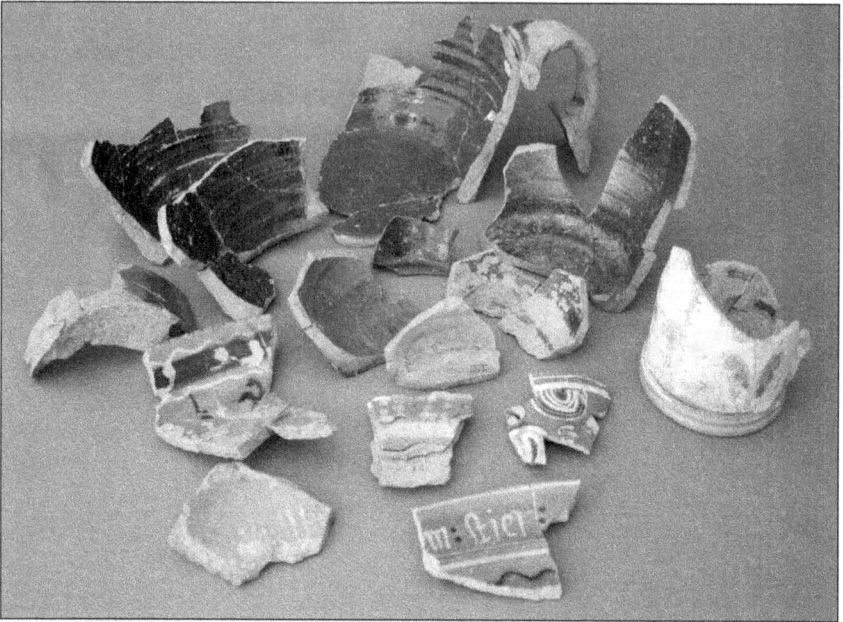

Figure 5.5. Slip-decorated and plain glazed domestic redware including storage and butter pots (*background*), mugs, small plates, patty pans, and a coggled-edged dish (*foreground*). Photograph by Patricia Gibble.

recorded, but these vessels were among the least costly imported wares at the time of his death during the first years of the nineteenth century (Dibert 2000; Miller 1991). To the prosperous, but frugal father and son and their wives, the initial expense for sturdy pewter vessels made better economic sense in contrast to the purchase of expensive and fragile imported dishes. And while pewter vessels were a staple for food and beverage consumption throughout their subsequent occupations of the farm, Henry's household did purchase the least costly imported cream-colored vessels to enjoy their morning tea.

Henry's purchases at Samuel Rex's store in preparation for his daughter Anna Maria's wedding to Fredrick Oberly indicate the family's continued emphasis on the practicality and longevity of metal tablewares. The entry also gives some hints to the family's socioeconomic standing in 1798. Among the long list of housewares, Henry bought his daughter over 38 lbs. of pewter valued at almost seven pounds as well as a half dozen pieces of china teaware at six shillings, and a half dozen sets of lesser priced common tewares for 4 shillings, 6 pence (Samuel Rex Daybook #6). China was a ubiquitous term used by country shopkeepers that may have referred to a variety of imported wares such as porcelain, creamware, pearlware, or other refined earthenwares (Noël Hume 1973:231–232). Along with bedding and other household items, these vessels were among the portable estates that young women brought to their marriage as their specific possessions and a visible symbol of the prosperity of the wife's natal family (Wheeler 1999:41). The ledger shows that Henry Schaeffer had accumulated enough wealth to be able to make a substantial investment in more expensive pewter vessels and some tea equipage for his daughter's upcoming marriage.

Ceramic evidence for the Schaeffer's occupation of the plantation suggests the site's occupants had chosen to incorporate the European trend of consuming Oriental teas into their foodways. The evidence does not necessarily indicate, however, that the German-speaking family wished to mirror the other socially competitive traditions of wealthy Anglo American citizens by equipping their households with more expensive matched sets of expensive teawares and tablewares.

Merchants Accounts Books

Several factors influence consumer choice such as access to markets, socioeconomic status, intrinsic ethnic traditions, historical events, and trends in consumer fashions (Baugher and Venables 1987:31–53). These influences in turn will impact the types of material culture that may be recovered from an archaeological site. Everyday ceramics used continuously are more likely to break and be discarded than the better housewares that are used for only special occasions. If ceramic evidence suggests that the Schaeffer household held middle income tastes in ceramics for the home, was their ceramic choice governed by preference? Were more expensive transfer-printed and porcelain teas and matched dining sets available for purchase by the German-speaking residents in the Pennsylvania settlement? Analysis of two country shop-keepers' account books and wholesale bills of sale from Philadelphia ceramic dealers suggest some answers relevant to this inquiry.

Samuel Rex operated his Schaefferstown store from 1790 to 1807, selling domestic and imported alcoholic spirits, English and German books and Bibles, groceries, buttons, cloth, smoking pipes, pottery and ceramics, tools and farm supplies, meat, sewing notions, and paper and writing implements (Wenger 2008:177–185). Rex made frequent buying trips to Philadelphia wholesale merchants to purchase commodities that would meet the needs and desires of his customers. His store accounts record that he employed a standardized set of terms to enumerate his ceramic inventory for sale. In the majority of Rex's entries, he designates the sale of various hollowwares and flatwares using only functional nouns such as teaware, tea cup, plate, teapot, cream jug, pots, and jars. In a few entries, he lists sets of teaware prefaced by the adjective common, which probably refers to the least costly imported cream-colored ceramics available at the time (Sam Rex Daybook #6; Miller 1991:39). Only twice does he employ descriptive terms (china and delft), explicitly identifying the style and quality of wares sold to local clientele (Wenger 2008:179).

Extant bills of sale from two Philadelphia wholesale merchants document storekeeper Rex's buying excursions to Philadelphia to stock his village establishment with ceramics during the 1790s. James Gallagher, a china/glass wholesaler who operated his business at 5 South Second Street, sold Rex large quantities of ceramics (Wenger 2008: 191). From 1790 to 1794, Rex purchased dozens of different sized "... Coll. [colored] ... White, Blue & White, and Enameled cups and plates ... White bowls, . . . White & Blue and Sky Blue quart mugs. . ." (Gallagher Invoices 1790, 1791, 1794). Gallagher charged Rex one pound, seven shillings for 24 sets of cups and saucers, while the same number of Blue & White teawares cost the retailer two pounds, 14 shillings or double the price (Gallagher Invoice 1790).

Rex made ceramic purchases in 1799 from another Philadelphia vender, Elizabeth Collringer, who sold him dozens of white and enameled cups, teawares, white and enameled teapots, " . . . Nests of dishes, . . . Second size plates, . . . [and] doz. of enameled pint mugs. . . ." (Collringer Invoice 1799). Comparison of Collringer's invoice (1799) to Gallagher's earlier bills demonstrates that the whole-sale cost of enameled vessels continued to be twice that of "white" wares, indicating stable pricing for these ceramics throughout the last decade of the eighteenth century. Storekeeper Rex appears to have offered common cream-colored (or white) wares to village consumers, the least costly imported ceramics during the period and also made available the higher priced hand-painted or enameled English vessels to his backcountry customers.

Just twelve miles east of Schaefferstown, German immigrant Adam Konigmacher operated a store and stocking weaving business in a similarly-sized farming community called Ephrata where he had built up a flourishing business from 1783 until his death in1793 (Spohn 1989:5). After Konigmacher died intestate, his wife, Christina, and two eldest sons, Abraham and Jacob, received letters of admin-istration that were required by the Pennsylvania Courts for them to continue opera-tion of the store (Spohn 1989:6).

Although Christina's store account books have not survived, records of her wholesale purchases from Philadelphia merchants show that the family patronized two other city venders on their buying trips. Ceramics dealer Adam Morris used a similar vocabulary as observed in Gallagher's bills to describe items he sold the Konigmachers. They bought "white quart mugs, collard [sic] quart mugs, large collard bowls, red bordered bowls, and sets of large collard cups . . ." (Christina Konigmacher Account Book 1793). In the same year, Richard Humphreys was more explicit in his descriptions of the wares he sold to the Ephrata merchants using modi-fiers such as "blue-edged, flowered, green-edged, octagon shaped dishes, . . . enam-eled teas pots . . . and china . . ." (Christina Konigmacher Daybook 1793). Taking into consideration the temporal context of the Konigmacher's purchases and the pricing of ceramics on this bill, one can conclude that vender Humphreys referenced hand-painted English ceramics such as shell-edged and the more elaborately hand-painted pearlware (Noël Hume 1973; Miller 1991:39). Like storekeeper Rex, the Konigmacher retailers do not seem to have purchased any ceramics that are explicitly described in the bills of sale as porcelain or transfer-printed (Miller 1991).

George Miller's (1991) extensive research into decorative style, manufac-ture, and cost of imported English ceramics from extant potters' pricing lists is useful for making tentative inferences on availability and consumer preferences in the south central Pennsylvania region during the last decade of the eighteenth century. His analysis shows that up to 1780, manufacture and export of "CC" or undecorated cream-colored vessels dominated continental European and North American ceramic markets (Miller 1991:38). After this point, hand-painted designs on white-bodied vessels surpassed the cream-colored wares in price and popularity. The complexity of hand-painting (or enameling) designs on a refined earthenware body determined the market price. Minimally decorated wares, including shell-edged, sponge decoration, banded, and mocha types, cost more than common creamware but were less expensive than the more elaborate polychrome hand-painted vessels. Polychrome wares displayed intricate painted flowers, leaves, stylized Chinese landscapes, or geometric motifs that required increased labor and skill by design decorators (Miller 1991:39–40).

In the 1790s when Samuel Rex sought large lots of white and enameled ceramics to sell in his hinterland store, a new technological innovation had emerged in the English ceramics industry that streamlined the decoration process on refined earthenwares. Instead of the time-consuming hand-painting of decorative patterns on white-bodied vessels, potters created templates that could be easily transferred to refined earthenware forms, making possible the manufacturing of matching sets of tablewares and tea wares (Miller 1991:40). At the close of the eighteenth century, underglazed transfer-printed patterns cost 3 to 5 times as much as painted wares, becoming the most fashionable tablewares in elite European circles (Miller 1991:40).

The paucity of regional wholesale and retail documents available in this study precludes firm conclusions on which ceramic classifications were available to or desired by consumers in the Schaefferstown/Ephrata region, but the existing evidence does allow some tentative inferences. First, both merchants obtained hollowwares and flatwares from some Philadelphia ceramic dealers who consistently use modifiers for vessels such as white, collard [sic], blue & white, and blue. Miller demonstrates that by the second half of the nineteenth century, English pricing lists referred to CC or cream-colored wares as "common" or "white" (Miller 1991:39). In addition, in a missive to his partner, Thomas Bentley in March, 1779, English potter Josiah Wedgewood calls their newest painted ceramic style "blue & white" based on comparison of a cream-colored plate to a plate of their hand-painted ware which appeared "...another degree whiter and finer..." (Wedgewood in Miller 1991:51).

While anecdotal at best, two inferences emerge from this inquiry. First, vendor invoices suggest a pattern in the lexicon used during the 1790s wherein wholesalers in Philadelphia distinguish creamware (as white) from decorated pearlwares (blue & white, collard, shell-edged, or flowered). Second, some country storekeepers may have not stocked their retail shops with porcelain or printed vessels because these ceramics were either not readily available at the time or there was little demand for the wares. Due to the time lag between production, shipment, and distribution of transfer-printed wares to American cities and towns, these wares may have not been available to American rural markets until the first decade of the nineteenth century (Samford 1997:3–4). In farming communities like Schaefferstown and Ephrata, hinterland households may have preferred to apportion extra income for the lowest and median priced vessels instead of the costly porcelain or printed wares.

ARCHITECTURAL ANALYSIS

Late-eighteenth-century renovations made to the built environment at the Schaeffer plantation show the family's pragmatism regarding architecture and resistance to demonstrating wealth and status through housing styles. Alexander Schaeffer and his wife probably occupied the farmhouse for a short period of time; they eventually moved into the residential quarters on the upper floors of the store/tavern in order to closely oversee the business. By the time Henry married in the late 1770s and set up housekeeping at the Schaeffer Farm, Alexander's four daughters had also left home to establish their own domestic households. The elderly parents had no need or incli-nation to build a new, fashionable house but could adapt the residential space on the second floor of the tavern for their later years.

Some scholars have concluded that the residential space (or second floor) of the original Schaeffer farmhouse conforms to a modest, three room "Flurkuchen-haus" plan spatially organized around a *küch* (kitchen), *stube* (parlor) and *kammer* (bedroom) (Berengren 2004:24–31; Nobel 2009:6). The third floor garret provided more storage space and extra sleeping quarters for family members (figure 5.6). Many log and stone homes of the same period in back-country Pennsylvania com-munities are of the Flurkuchenhaus type, a building tradition favored by German-speaking yeomen (Bergengren 2004:23–35; Long 1971:81–85).

In the late 1770s, Henry Schaeffer made extensive renovations to the original dual-purpose house in order to provide additional domestic space for his burgeoning family that eventually included four daughters and two sons (Griggs 2010:4; Weiser and Neff 1987:vii). A stone vaulted cellar (*gewelbkeller*) was added onto the north end of the original house, adjacent to the ground-floor workroom (Long 1972:101) (figure 5.6). This space provided cold storage for dairy products and consumables but also added increased storage space for barrels of apple cider in close proximity to the distilling room. An expansive kitchen was constructed directly above the cellar including a seven foot long hearth with squirrel tail oven that was situated just outside the eastern end of the kitchen on a small porch.

Around the time Henry Schaeffer and first wife, Anna, renovated the farm-house, some residents of the merchant ranks in south central Pennsylvania were constructing traditional residences following a Germanic style called *Durchgangi-gen* (Bergengren 2004:32–34). Bergengren delineates examples of this center hall-through-passageway style house including the Samuel Rex house on the Schaeffers-town square and the Philip Erpff house on South Market Street. He believes these structures underwent some creolization of exterior elements at the end of the eigh-teenth century, thus mimicking external features of English Georgian-styled homes.

Figure 5.6. Original section of the Alexander Schaeffer Farmhouse with central chimney (*right*) and northern addition added by Henry Schaeffer circa 1774–1775 (*left*). Photograph by Patricia Gibble.

While these examples displayed exterior façades "making the houses indistinguish-able from the standard Georgian houses," most retained interior elements from the functional Germanic style including a kuche cooking fireplace that fed a stove in the front parlor and a rear facing stairway (Berengren 2004:33). Extant Germanic ver-sions increased social display on the exterior or public face of the house while retain-ing the private spatial organization and the functionality of a traditional Germanic household (Bergengren 2004: 30).

For Henry Schaeffer's family, the choice to simply expand the footprint of the farmhouse to provide more living and storage space demonstrates human agency and an effort to maintain a traditionally pragmatic and functional architectural scheme. Given the family's prominence, socioeconomic status, and consistent inter-action with Anglo citizens, their decision to replicate a Germanic housing tradition could be considered an example of resistance to culture change and the assimilation pressures of the late-eighteenth-century period.

Discussion

Three types of historical data have been compared in this inquiry to establish the socioeconomic rank of a German family that occupied the Schaeffer Farm for almost

40 years. Understanding the lineage's level of prominence through time and space contributes to an interpretation of their decisions as consumers in this largely German-speaking region of Pennsylvania and their responses to cultural interaction under British hegemony. This case study highlights the concepts of transculturation or the social dynamics inherent between dominant Anglo and subordinate German groups in the Pennsylvania province. Comparison of material culture demonstrates the concept of ethnogenesis, or the intentional reforming of an immigrant German culture into a unique German-American identity by one extended rural family.

Evinced in primary documents of the period, the Schaeffers negotiated their position by choosing to incorporate aspects of British/Anglo society in public political and economic contexts. At the same time, they maintained other Germanic customs in private or domestic spaces. For example, Henry Schaeffer became an active participant in the post-Revolutionary government as Justice of the Peace and later as an Associate Justice for Dauphin County Court. Each of these bureaucratic positions required Henry to have a command of the English language and an extensive knowledge of American law. He and his son Johannes engaged in the burgeoning capitalist network by shipping hundreds of gallons of apple whiskey to Philadelphia merchants. Store ledgers also indicate that the family regularly purchased exotic, imported commodities and sold domestically produced goods such as butter for shipment to the city. In each case because these activities were socially or economically advantageous, they made the choice to incorporate aspects of the dominant culture in their own cultural milieu.

Successive generations of this German-American lineage maintained their distinct ethnicity in less public, domestic contexts. They preferred to follow the pragmatic German tradition of supplying the household with sturdy pewter vessels and limiting their acquisition of more fragile, imported wares. Henry Schaeffer's house renovations followed an asymmetrical vernacular style that increased living, storage, and work space; renovations were not made to mimic the English Georgian architectural design or signal an improvement in social standing. Their decisions show that in domestic contexts, these citizens eschewed the British philosophy of symbolic display of socioeconomic improvement thereby negotiating their distinctly German-American ethnogenesis.

Interpretation of this family's material culture preferences demonstrates that viewing culture change employing assimilation principals alone is problematic. Surveys of Germanic artifacts held in museum settings and extant colonial housing styles may delineate some examples of British influences on eighteenth-century German material culture, but archaeological evidence from existing and demolished buildings and artifact assemblages would provide a more representative sample of transculturation for interpretation.

References Cited

Alexander, Rani T.

1998   Afterward: Towards an Archaeological Theory of Culture Contact. In *Studies in Cultural Contact: Interaction, Culture Change, and Archaeology*, edited by James G. Cusick, pp. 476–495. Southern Illinois University Occasional Papers No. 25. Center for Archaeological Investigations, Carbondale, Illinois.

Baugher, Sherene, and R. W. Venables

1987   Ceramics as Indicators of Economic Class in Eighteenth Century New York. In *Consumer Choice in Historical Archaeology*, edited by Susanne M. Spencer-Wood, pp. 31–54. Plenum Press, New York.

Beiler, Rosalind J.

1997   Distributing Aid to Believers in Need: The Religious Foundations of the Transatlantic Migration. *Pennsylvania History* 64:73–87.

Bergengren, Charles

2004   Pennsylvania German House Forms. In *Architecture and Landscape of the Pennsylvania Germans*, 1720–1920, edited by Nancy van Dolsen, pp. 23–46. The Vernacular Architectural Forum, Harrisburg, Pennsylvania.

Borough of Manheim

1860   *Rapho Township Map: 1860*. Lancaster County Historical Society, Lancaster, Pennsylvania.

Brendle, A. S.

1901   *A Brief History of Schaefferstown*. Dispatch Publishing Co., York, Pennsylvania.

Cusick, James G.

1998   Historiography of Acculturation: An Evaluation of Concepts and Their Applications in Archaeology. In *Studies in Cultural Contact: Interaction, Culture Change, and Archaeology*, edited by James G. Cusick, pp. 126–145. Southern Illinois University Occasional Papers No. 25. Center for Archaeological Investigations, Carbondale, Illinois.

Deagan, Kathleen

1998   Transculturation and Spanish America Ethnogenesis. In *Studies in Cultural Contact: Interaction, Culture Change, and Archaeology*, edited by James G. Cusick, pp. 23–24. Southern Illinois University Occasional Papers No. 25. Center for Archaeological Investigations, Carbondale, Illinois.

Dibert, James A.

2000   The Will and Estate Inventory of Henry Schaeffer. *Historic Schaefferstown Record* 33:3–4.

2001   The Will and Estate Inventory of Alexander Schaeffer. *Historic Schaef-ferstown Record* 34:1–2.

2006   A Chronology of the Alexander Schaeffer Farm. *Historic Schaeffers-town Record* 37:31–45

Dunn, R. S., and M. M. Dunn

1986   *The World of William Penn*. University of Pennsylvania Press, Philadelphia.

Falk, Cynthia G.

2008   *Architecture and Artifacts of the Pennsylvania Germans: Constructing Identity in Early America*. Pennsylvania State University Press, University Park, Pennsylvania.

Fogleman, Aaron Spencer

1996   *Hopeful Journeys: German Immigration, Settlement, and Political Culture in Colonial America 1717–1775*. University of Pennsylvania Press, Philadelphia.

Gibble, Patricia E.

2001   *Continuity, Change and Ethnic Identity in 18th Century Pennsylvania Red Earthenware: An Archaeological and Ethnohistorical Study*. Ph.D. dissertation, Department of Anthropology, American University, Washington, D. C.

2006   Preliminary Summary of the Archaeological Investigations at the Historic Alexander Schaeffer Farm 2004–2007. *Historic Schaefferstown Record* 37:1–30.

Griggs, Carol

2010   Dendrochronological Dating of the Schaeffer Farm in Schaefferstown, Pennsylvania. Unpublished report on file at Historic Schaefferstown, Inc., Schaefferstown, Pennsylvania.

Headstone: Johannes Scheffer

1807   Schaefferstown Cemetery. Schaefferstown, Pennsylvania.

Konigmacher, Christina

1793   Daybook. Historical Society of Cocalico Township, Ephrata, Pennsylvania.

Lancaster Intelligencer Journal

1866   Death of John Schaeffer, Esq. p.2. 24 March, 1866. Lancaster County Historical Society. Lancaster, Pennsylvania.

Lancaster Saturday Evening Express

1866   Death of John Schaeffer, Esq. p.2. 24 March, 1866. Lancaster County Historical Society, Lancaster, Pennsylvania.

Long, Amos, Jr.

1972   *The Pennsylvania German Family Farm*. The Pennsylvania German Society, Breinigsville, Pennsylvania.

Manheim Borough
1847–1854 Tax Records. Lancaster County Historical Society, Lancaster, Pennsylvania.

Miller, George L.
1991 Classification and Economic Scaling of 19th Century Ceramics. In *Approaches to Material Culture Research for Historical Archaeology*, edited by Ronald L. Michael, pp. 37–58. The Society of Historical Archaeology, California, Pennsylvania.

Miller, George L., Patricia Stanford, Ellen Shlasko, and Andrew Madsen
2000 Telling Time For Archaeologists. *Northeast Historical Archaeology* 29:1–22.

Neff, Larry M., and Frederick S. Weiser
1979 *Friedrich Heinrich Gelwicks, Shoemaker and Distiller: Accounts, 1760–1783*. The Pennsylvania German Society, Breinigsville, Pennsylvania.

Noble, Tim
2009 National Historic Landmark Nomination: The Alexander Schaeffer Farm. Copy on file at Historic Schaefferstown, Inc., Schaefferstown, Pennsylvania.

Noël Hume, Ivor
1969 *A Guide to Artifacts of Colonial America*. Vintage Books, New York.
1973 Creamware to Pearlware: A Williamsburg Perspective. In *Ceramics in America*, edited by Ian M. G. Quimby, pp. 217–254. University of Virginia Press, Charlottesville, Virginia.

Otterness, Phillip
1999 The 1709 Palatinate Migration and Formation of German Immigrant Identity in London and New York. In *Explorations in Early American Culture*, edited by William Pencak and George W. Boudreau. The Pennsylvania Historical Association, University Park, Pennsylvania. (66):8–23.

Rex, Abraham
1804–1820 Daybook and Ledgers. Historic Schaefferstown, Inc. Archives, Schaefferstown, Pennsylvania.

Rex, Samuel
1790, 1791, 1794, 1799 Bills of Sale. Leon Lewis Collection. Lebanon County Historical Society, Lebanon, Pennsylvania. Reel 6:section AS 107.
1791–1802 Daybooks and Ledgers. Historic Schaefferstown, Inc. Archives, Schaefferstown, Pennsylvania.

Rorabaugh, W. J.
1979 *The Alcoholic Republic*. Oxford University Press, New York.

Samford, Patricia M.
1997   Response to a Market: Dating English Underglazed Transfer-Printed Wares. *Historical Archaeology* 31:3–4.

Schaeffer, Henry
1793   Record of Indenture for Gartrout Sweitzer. Historic Schaefferstown, Inc. Archives, Schaefferstown, Pennsylvania.
1803   Will and Estate Inventory. Historic Schaefferstown, Inc. Archives. Schaefferstown, Pennsylvania.
1830   Lebanon County Land Indenture. Lebanon County Court Archives, Book D, 638. Lebanon, Pennsylvania.

Schaeffer, John
1837   Petition for Tavern License. Rapho Township. April 1837. Lancaster County Historical Society, Lancaster, Pennsylvania.

Schelbert, Leo
1983   On the Power of Pietism: A Documentary of the Thommens of Schaefferstown. *Historic Schaefferstown Record* 17(3 & 4): 42–74

Soderlund, Jean R.
1983   *William Penn and the Founding of Pennsylvania 1680–1684*. University of Pennsylvania Press, Philadelphia.

Sowers, Gladys B.
2008   *Court of Common Pleas Records, Lebanon County 1813–1820*. Masthof Press, Morgantown, Pennsylvania.

Spohn, Clarence E.
1989   The Konigmacher Family of the Cocalico Valley. *The Journal of The Historical Society of the Cocalico Valley* 14:4–6.

Spencer-Wood, Susanne
1987   Introduction. In *Consumer Choice in Historical Archaeology*, edited by Susanne Spencer-Wood, pp. 1–20. Plenum Press, New York.

Spencer-Wood, Susanne, and Scott D. Heberling
1986   Consumer Choices in White Ceramics: A Comparison of Eleven Early Nineteenth Century Sites. In *Consumer Choice in Historical Archaeology*, edited by Susanne Spencer-Wood, pp. 55–84. Plenum Press, New York.

Sternberg, Robert
2006   Preliminary Report on Archaeomagnetic Dating of Brick Samples from the Alexander Schaeffer Farm/Distillery. Unpublished Report on file at Historic Schaefferstown, Inc., Schaefferstown, Pennsylvania.

Sussman, Lynne
1997   Mocha, Banded, Cat's Eye, and other Factory-Made Slipware. In *Studies in Northeast Historical Archaeology*, edited by Lorinda B. R. Goodwin, No. 1. Council for Northeast Historical Archaeology, Boston.

U.S. Bureau of the Census

1810   *U.S. Census Records for Manheim Borough, Rapho Township, Pennsylvania*, http://www.Ancestry.com (accessed August 26, 2009).

Wenger, Diane E.

2008   *A Country Storekeeper in Pennsylvania*. The Pennsylvania State University Press, University Park, Pennsylvania.

Weiser, Frederick S., and Larry M. Neff

1987   *Records of the Purchases at the King George Hotel, Schaefferstown, Lebanon County, Pennsylvania 1762–1773*. The Pennsylvania German Society, Birdsboro, Pennsylvania.

Wheeler, Kathleen L.

1997   Contributions of Women to the Acquisition, Maintenance, and Discard of Portable Estates. *Northeast Historical Archaeology* 28:43–56.

6

THE ARCHAEOLOGY OF FOOD IN COLONIAL PENNSYLVANIA: HISTORICAL ZOOARCHAEOLOGICAL EXPLORATION OF FOODWAYS ON THE STENTON PLANTATION

TEAGAN SCHWEITZER

Introduction

This chapter relies on zooarchaeological and documentary research to investigate the foodways of the households living on the Stenton plantation, located five miles outside of Philadelphia, in the mid-eighteenth century. Discussions of food center around the meat, fowl, fish, shellfish, and even reptiles that made up the food landscape for the Logan families who lived at Stenton during this period. Information derived from the analysis of animal bones discarded in a cistern on the property provides the zooarchaeological data, and several documentary sources from this period relating to the Logans provides historical data. Importantly these two types of sources about past foodways offer slightly differing pictures of the food landscape of the farmstead and thus, when combined, facilitate a more nuanced and well-rounded view of foodways at Stenton.

Stenton: The House and Plantation

Stenton is the name of the plantation originally owned by James Logan, secretary to William Penn and one of the wealthiest and most influential individuals in early Philadelphia. Located to the north of the colonial city, the Georgian-style home once stood on approximately 500 acres of land. Today the house operates as a museum in which the eighteenth century is evocatively interpreted to visitors (figure 6.1).

As was the case with many wealthy gentlemen in the eighteenth century, James Logan owned both a city and a country home. Stenton served as a place of respite from the hubbub of city life. It was also an important place of escape, especially during the sweltering summer months in Philadelphia and particularly towards the end of the eighteenth and early nineteenth centuries when yellow fever epidemics occurred almost annually and killed up to as much as 10 percent of the population.

Stenton was named after James Logan's father Patrick's birthplace in Scotland: "I have proposed to call ye place Stenton after the Village in E. Lothian where our father was born . . ." (Logan 1730). Construction of the house at Stenton began in 1728, and the Logans took up residence there in November 1730 (Shepherd

Figure 6.1. South-facing façade of the Stenton main house. Photograph by Teagan Schweitzer.

1968:16). The finished abode was indeed worthy of Logan's lofty status within the colony with descriptions such as "the first monumental colonial country house in Pennsylvania" (Engle 1982) and "one of the first large country estates created by wealthy Philadelphians intent on living the life of the landed English gentry" (Cotter et al. 1992:332).

At first, Stenton was occupied mainly as a summer residence, but it did eventually become the Logans' permanent residence. In 1732 James began signing his letters "James Logan of Stenton" (Logan 1899:28–9). Once the family was living permanently on the plantation, John Steers was hired as a plantation manager, and a series of tenant farmers worked on the land (Engle 1982). There were also roughly ten indentured or hired servants and enslaved Africans working at Stenton at any given time (Tolles 1957:188). As the transition to the countryside occurred, state business, of necessity, took place in the house as well. If Logan was not in the city to take care of his affairs, they would have to travel to his doorsteps at Stenton (Logan 1899:28–9). Thus the house had a nearly continual stream of social and political visitors throughout the time that the Logans were in residence.

As James approached the end of his life, the running of the plantation was passed down to his eldest son, William, who officially took up this responsibility upon the death of his father in 1751. The house remained in the Logan family until the early twentieth century. In 1899, The National Society of Colonial Dames of America in the Commonwealth of Pennsylvania, through a lease with the Logan family, agreed to manage the property. This group continues to play an essential role in the preservation of the property to this day.

James and William Logan

James Logan, a Quaker, was born in Lurgan, County Armagh, Ireland on October 20, 1674. At the age of 23, he decided to pursue a career as a merchant in London; it was at this time that he made the acquaintance of William Penn, who eventually hired James as his personal secretary. In 1699, Logan immigrated to Philadelphia with Penn. When Penn returned to England in 1701, permanently as it turns out, he put James in charge of his affairs in Pennsylvania. Logan held a number of appointments during his day including clerk of the council, secretary of the province, commissioner of property, mayor of Philadelphia (1722–23), member of the governor's council, recorder of the city, president judge of common pleas, chief justice of the supreme court of Pennsylvania, and president of the council. He made his fortune as a merchant, a commissioner of property, and an Indian agent—a post that allowed him to invest heavily in the fur trade. In part because of the connections he cultivated while in these positions, by 1748 he owned 18,000 acres of prime land in Pennsylvania and New Jersey (Bronner 1982:41; Cotter et al. 1992:332; Salade 1925). "Logan dominated the political and cultural life of the colony and city for almost half a century" (Bronner 1982:40). James married Sarah Read in 1714. They had a total of seven children of which four survived into adulthood: Sarah (1715–44), William (1718–76), Hannah (1719/20–61), and James, Jr. (1728–1803) (Penney 1927:19). James (the elder) eventually died at Stenton at the age of 77 on October 31, 1751. "Easily the most considerable man in the Delaware Valley in his lifetime, he was . . . one of the three or four most considerable men in colonial America" (Tolles 1957:6).

As mentioned above, William Logan inherited the Stenton property upon the death of his father. During William's tenure, Stenton functioned mainly as a summer residence, the family living in Philadelphia the rest of the year. By the mid-eighteenth century, he was a successful Philadelphia merchant. When he assumed the responsibility for the plantation, William gave up his commercial interests to focus on agriculture and became one of the leaders in the development of scientific agriculture in the United States (Tolles 1958). He also held a seat in the Provincial Council and had some involvement in other political affairs. William married Hannah Emlen in 1740, and they had six children together. When he died in 1776, the house was unfortunately left at the mercy of a negligent caretaker for the remainder of the Revolutionary War years.

Archaeology at Stenton

In 1981 and 1982 archaeological excavations took place at Stenton under the direction of Barbara Liggett, who was at the time the Director of the Division of Archaeology at the Atwater Kent Museum in Philadelphia. She was contracted "to excavate the east garden wall, George Logan's c. 1793 privy, and the portion of the rear courtyard thought to be the location of Logan's original 1720's outbuildings" (Miller 2006:16). During the course of these excavations a cistern, Feature 14, was located and excavated in the rear courtyard space. The animal bones from this feature are discussed here in relation to evidence for the foodways of the Logan household during the period represented by the artifacts in the feature, namely circa 1740–1770.

An important but unfortunate fact about the excavations directed by Liggett in the 1980s is that she failed to leave behind the original excavation documentation including field journals, maps, and photos. In addition, she never produced a final report of her findings: "A short draft report, the transcription of a 1984 lecture, and limited correspondence are the only sources of written documentation from the excavations, and provide contradictory information at best" (Liggett 1970,1978,1984a/b; Miller 2006:16). Thus the original context of these artifacts has been lost, compromising any interpretations of the recovered materials.

The rear courtyard, where Liggett's excavations took place, was thought to have been the original location of James Logan's kitchen and service buildings that were subsequently demolished. Today the yard is flanked to the west by a kitchen, greenhouse, and carriage house that were built in the mid-eighteenth century and to the south by the main house (figure 6.2). At the time of James's death the main house was attached to a network of outbuildings including the "kitchen and washhouse, a shingled barn, a chaise house, a plant house, a dairy, possibly a smokehouse, and certainly a necessary" (Shepherd 1968:30). Three other features or foundations were uncovered by Liggett and her team during the 1981–1982 excavations in the courtyard. The features excavated in this area may represent the above-listed buildings, however, without the proper excavation documentation, it is impossible to tell for sure (Miller 2006:17).

Feature 14 was a mortared brick vault with mortared limestone floor, which measured 9 foot by 5 foot by 8 foot with a slotted opening in the ceiling of approximately 15 inches in width and capped by a limestone slab. Although there has been some debate as to the function of this feature, it was most likely a cistern due to its overall design, its proximity to a number of structures on the property associated with domestic chores, and the lack of stains, odors, or other identifiers that might indicate its use as a privy, a suggestion made by Liggett in her notes about this feature (Miller 2006:19–21). A cistern of similar design and construction was built on the Hill-Physick-Keith property on the corner of Fourth and Chestnut Streets in Society Hill, Philadelphia sometime around 1786 (Cotter et al. 1992:189).

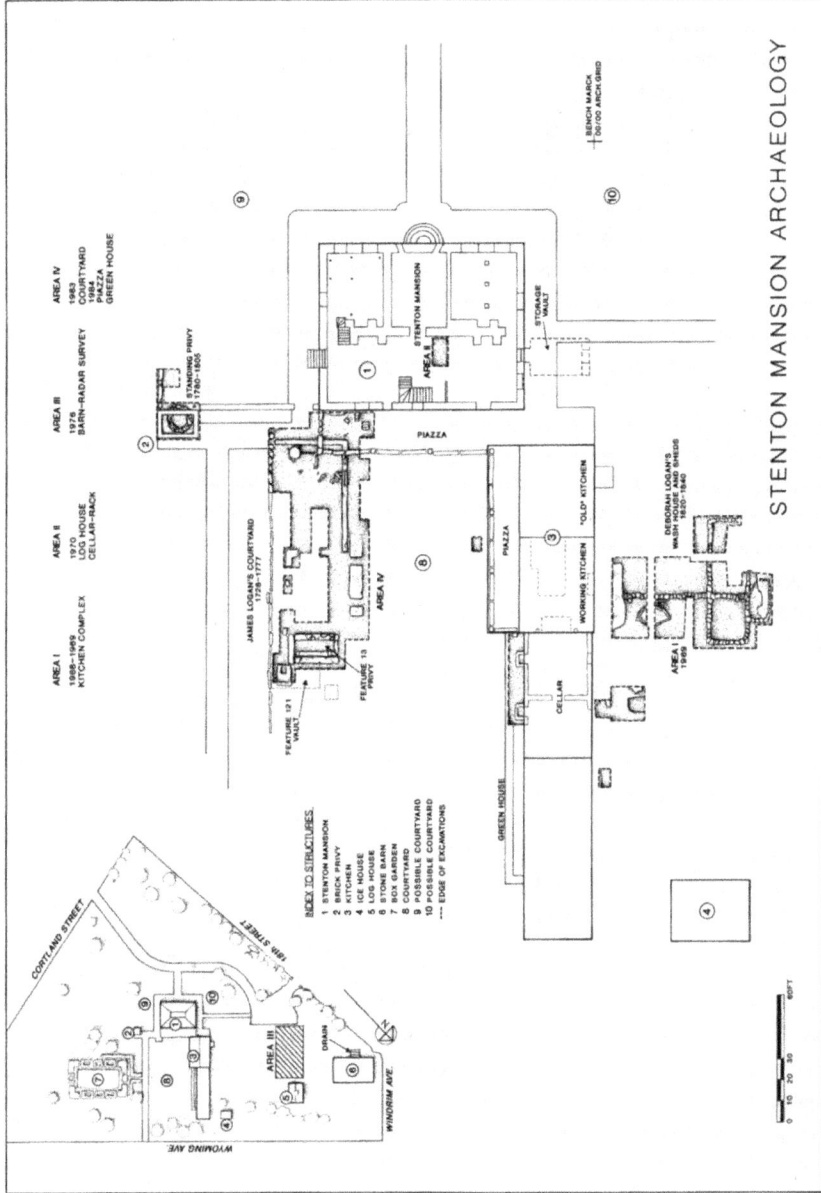

Figure 6.2.
Stenton archaeo-
logical site plan
(source: Cotter et
al. 1992:333).

STENTON MANSION ARCHAEOLOGY

AREA I
1988–1989
KITCHEN COMPLEX

AREA II
1970
LOG HOUSE
CELLAR-BACK

AREA III
1976
BARN–RADAR SURVEY

AREA IV
1983
COURTYARD
1984
PIAZZA
GREEN HOUSE

INDEX TO STRUCTURES:
1 STENTON MANSION
2 BRICK PRIVY
3 KITCHEN
4 ICE HOUSE
5 LOG HOUSE
6 STONE BARN
7 BOX GARDEN
8 COURTYARD
9 POSSIBLE COURTYARD
10 POSSIBLE COURTYARD
--- EDGE OF EXCAVATIONS

JAMES LOGAN'S COURTYARD
1728–1777

STANDING PRIVY
1780–1805

FEATURE 121
VAULT

FEATURE 13
PRIVY

AREA IV

PIAZZA

STENTON MANSION

AREA I

STORAGE
VAULT

WORKING KITCHEN

"OLD" KITCHEN

PIAZZA

DEBORAH LOGAN'S
WASH HOUSE AND SHEDS
1830–1840

CELLAR

AREA I
1989

GREEN HOUSE

BENCH MARK
0d/00 ARCH.GRID

CORTLAND STREET

19th STREET

AREA III

DRAIN

WINDRIM AVE.

WYOMING AVE.

0 10 20 30   60FT

Feature 14 contained over 22,000 artifacts including ceramics, metals, glass, and animal bones, which appear to reflect the occupation of James Logan (1730–1751) and his son William (1753–1776) at Stenton. Ceramics and glass found in the vault date the fill episode to circa 1765–1770 (Miller 2006:23–24). Due to the lack of field notes, it is impossible to tell whether there may have been multiple fill episodes, though crossmending of ceramics from the feature may help to answer this question. Many of the goods recovered from Feature 14 appear to have been in perfect condition when they were discarded, thus it has been suggested that these materials were goods from James's household that were disposed of by William when he assumed responsibility for the farmstead. William may have been updating his new home to reflect the very latest social and material trends, consequently jettisoning the outdated pieces that his father had owned (Miller 2006:19–24).

Of the 2,212 pieces of ceramic recovered from the feature, the bulk of which date to the 1740s and 1750s, the largest proportion were Chinese export porcelains. These pieces, valued second only to James Logan's collection of silver in his probate inventory, were among the best tablewares available in the eighteenth century. Affordable only to the wealthiest citizens, they were a distinct symbol of social and economic status (Miller 2006; Tolles 1958). The majority of the porcelain ceramic forms were associated with tea service and would have been used when guests visited Stenton and enjoyed tea in the parlor (Miller 2006:27–9). Salt-glazed stoneware comprised ten percent of the total ceramic assemblage. A variety of forms were represented, including plates, pitchers, tankards, creamers, saucers, and teapots (Miller 2006:29–31). Tin-glazed earthenwares, also known as "delft," made up roughly ten percent of the ceramic assemblage as well and were primarily decorated in underglazed blue against a white dipped body, a style that attempted to mimic Ming porcelains exported from China. Both refined earthenwares and stonewares were purchased by the upper classes but were also found in middle-class homes. Many of these wares were produced specifically to emulate the more expensive and, to some, financially out of reach, porcelains (Miller 2006:31,57). Staffordshire wares, an earthenware manufactured in Staffordshire County, England, accounted for less than one percent of the total ceramic assemblage and included less refined slipware examples dating to the early eighteenth century (Miller 2006:32–4). The remainder of the ceramic assemblage, approximately 16 percent, were redwares, which would have been produced locally in Philadelphia, Germantown, or elsewhere by immigrant potters, unlike these other ceramic types that were imported. The wares tended to follow the design elements found in English and Germanic potting traditions and were primarily coarse slip decorated red-bodied earthenwares. These vessels would have functioned as utilitarian pieces in the form of platters, pots, pans, and jugs and would likely have been the everyday wares for the Logans when dining without guests (Miller 2006:34).

A brief note here about teapots. A total of eleven teapots were uncovered in Feature 14, a large number in relation to the other ceramic forms. Nine of these were block molded white salt-glazed stoneware and two were Staffordshire manu-

factured earthenwares; each was uniquely decorated (Miller 2006). The sheer number of teapots from this assemblage speaks to the importance of the tea ceremony in
the Logan household during the mid-eighteenth century, a trend on the rise in Britain
contemporaneously, and parallels the wealth demonstrated in the whole ceramic assemblage. It appears that the Logans were serving their guests with the most fashionable teawares of the day.

English and French wine and case bottles dominate the glass bottle assemblage from the feature though American examples were present as well. The glassware also included a variety of wine glasses, tumblers, and other drinking glasses.
The collection suggests that the Logan household was well stocked with English and
French bottles and decanters filled with Madeira, port, and other spirits; beverages
that could be served into delicately decorated wineglass (Miller 2006:36, 37, 58).

The Logans imported many of their ceramics and glasswares, and they appear to have had the latest and best goods available as befitted their high social status
and wealth. This would have been aided by the fact that both James and William
Logan were longtime Philadelphia merchants and were well connected in the world
of trade goods— local, national, and international.

A number of additional items were recovered from Feature 14 including
tobacco pipe stem and bowl fragments, pharmaceutical bottles and vials, tin-glazed
earthenware or "delft" ointment pots, several horn and bone combs, a bone tooth-
brush, straight pins, a pair of scissors, buttons, iron hooks and eyes, bar enclosures, a
pair of gold sleeve links (with the initials "L" and "S" suggesting that they belonged
to Logan's eldest child Sarah), jaw harps, undecorated brass finger rings, bone cutlery
handles, thimbles, pins, needles, gunflints, and architectural materials such as mortar,
brick, plaster, flooring tiles, nails, and wood fragments. The architectural materials
may have been the remnants of William Logan's post–1751 renovations of the main
house and construction of the new kitchen (Miller 2006:39–46).

FEATURE 14, THE FAUNAL ASSEMBLAGE

A total of 8,050 animal bones were recovered from the excavation of Feature 14.
Of these, 6,979 were recovered from the interior of the cistern. These bones will
be the center of the following discussion about the foodways of the Logans in the
mid-eigtheenth century from a zooarchaeological perspective. Although the other
categories of artifacts have potential to contribute to our knowledge about Stenton's
historic foodways, faunal remains provide the most direct evidence for specific foodstuffs available to and possibly consumed by the Logans.

Examining the cistern assemblage as a whole, bird bones dominated in Feature 14, comprising almost 65 percent of the total number of identified specimens
(NISP) (table 6.1). Mammals were the second most prevalent animal class represented at roughly 25 percent and reptile bones, mainly turtles, were also relatively
abundant in this feature at just over 5 percent.

The predominance of birds in this feature was somewhat surprising. Given the fact that Stenton was a working farm, it might be expected that domestic mammals such as cows, pigs, and sheep would have made up the majority of the deposit. However, bird-heavy archaeological features are not unprecedented. Several features from nineteenth-century Philadelphia contained similarly high bird bone-dominated faunal assemblages, including Block 1 Feature G (AS I) (TPQ 1825) where 56 percent of the assemblage NISP was birds, and Block 2 Feature B (ASII) (TPQ 1820) where bird bones comprised 44 percent of the total NISP (Milne 2004:53). In these other features, increased presence of birds has been associated with higher social status (Milne 2002:4). This association also aligns well with the eminent Logan household.

Taphonomy

In assessing any zooarchaeological assemblage, it is important first to consider the taphonomic signature(s) on the bones. By addressing the ways in which bones have been altered since death, archaeologists are better able to understand the processes that impacted the assemblage composition and condition, as well as the depositional environment. These considerations help researchers to tease out the processes which create, alter, and destroy bones.

The number of unidentifiable bones in Feature 14 was relatively small at roughly 4 percent and is a function of the fact that there was a low fragmentation rate amongst the recovered bones, both pre- and post-depositionally. The storage of these bones in Stenton's basement meant that little damage occurred after they were recovered from the ground. Very few bones in the assemblage showed any signs of charring, less than half of a percent. Of these burned specimens, all were mammal bones and most were calcined. It should be noted that charring of bones is not an indication that the bones were cooked since the temperatures required to cause bones to change colors are much higher than would be present in typical cooking environments (Asmussen 2009; Nicholson 1993; Shipman and Schoeninger 1984). Surprisingly few bones in the assemblage showed any signs of gnawing, particularly given the fact that there was a minimum (MNI) of 28 rats in the cistern. Approximately 0.3 percent of the bones had gnaw marks on them, and the majority of those were ravaged by dogs rather than rats. All bones with gnaw marks belonged to mammals, suggesting that either the ravagers had a preference for mammal bones, perhaps because of their higher density and therefore greater pleasure in chewing, or that the gnawers were not given access to the bird bones. The bird bones may also have been directly discarded into the cistern while at least some of the mammal bones could have been deposited for a time in a location accessible to dogs and rats. This circumstance suggests that perhaps a portion of the mammal bones may be the result of secondary deposition.

The assemblage as a whole showed little signs of weathering. There was evidence that a few bones had been exposed on the surface long enough to cause loss

Table 6.1. Distribution of Bones in Feature 14.

Bone type	NISP	% total NISP
amphibian	2	0.0
bird	4487	64.3
fish	100	1.4
mammal	1704	24.4
reptile	378	5.4
shellfish	27	0.4
unid	281	4.0
Total	6979	99.9

of the exterior layers of bone, but this was a minority of the assemblage and seems to suggest that the bones were minimally exposed to weathering forces. Slightly less than 3 percent of the bones in the assemblage had cutmarks on them. This small percentage is due, in large part, to the overwhelming number of bird bones in the feature, which often do not exhibit many cutmarks. Of the bones with cutmarks, 58 bones or 28 percent appeared on bird bones, 146 or 70 percent occurred on mammal bones.

BIRDS

A wide variety of birds were represented in Feature 14, including chicken, guinea fowl, turkey, Northern bobwhite, duck, goose, pigeon, dove, songbird, American woodcock, killdeer, green heron, Cuban parrot, red-shouldered hawk, eastern screech owl, and woodpecker. It is unlikely that the heron, parrot, hawk, owl, or woodpecker bones represent the remnants of meals, thus they will not be discussed further here. But their presence in the cistern does provide additional evidence about the landscape around Stenton. Many of these birds, including chickens, guinea fowls, turkeys, ducks, geese, pigeons, and doves may have been raised in the poultry yard at Stenton, which would have been the responsibility of the lady of the house (Sarah and then Hannah Logan). Others, such as ducks, geese, pigeons, doves, Northern bobwhites, American woodcocks, and killdeers could have been hunted in the surrounding landscape or possibly purchased in the marketplace.

Chickens (*Gallus gallus*) were the most frequently identified bird bones in the feature. One difficulty that arose with the chicken bone analysis was the simultaneous presence of guinea fowls (*Numida meleagris*) in the cistern assemblage. Guinea fowl bones closely resemble chicken bones in both size and shape. However, there do exist certain bone elements that are distinct between the two species including the skull, scapula, coracoid, sternum, pelvis, radius, and carpometacarpus. Male guinea fowl also do not possess spur cores on the tarsometatarsus (MacDonald 1992). Chicken and guinea fowl bones are not distinguishable in their immature state since the relevant boney characters are not yet visible on the bones at this early developmental stage, and there were a large number of immature chicken or guinea fowl bones in the assemblage. Of the mature medium-sized galliform bones recovered, the scientific order into which both chickens and guinea fowl are classified, a minimum of five guinea fowls were identified. This suggests that the number of chickens at Stenton most likely far outstripped the number of guinea fowl.

Chicken bones in the feature represented the full range from very immature up to fully mature, suggesting that the Logans were slaughtering these birds at a variety of different stages of maturity. Both roosters and capons (castrated males) appear to have been present. There were also at least two different breeds of chicken, one of a crested fowl variety—illustrated by the presence of a skull with a cranial hernia (Brothwell 1979). Crested fowl were some of the fancier breeds available in colonial Pennsylvania, and their identification here suggests that the Logan women may have had a preference for exotic poultry.

The zooarchaeological presence of guinea fowl at Stenton initially came as a surprise since these fowl were not listed in any of the nineteenth-century Pennsylvania bird books that were consulted (e.g. Gentry 1877; Turnbull 1869), nor were they mentioned in any of the available Logan family documents that recorded livestock holdings on the farm (Logan 1752). This latter piece of information is not conclusive, however, since poultry were considered to be part of the female realm and therefore were infrequently mentioned in farmyard inventories. A reference to the presence of the guinea fowl at Stenton was discovered in the journal of Charles Read, a friend of the Logan family who lived in New Jersey in the mid-eighteenth century. Read wrote in one of his agricultural notebooks "Guinea Fowls should be left to choose their nests and hatch as they please they will rear their Young & bring them home to you. [Wm. Logan, Esqr has proved this]" (Woodward 1941:327–28). It would appear from this note that, at least among Read's acquaintances, William Logan was the local guinea fowl aficionado. In descriptions of the bird, guinea fowls were often considered comparable to game birds in terms of flavor and texture. They were frequently suggested as good substitutes in recipes that originally called for game birds such as pheasant, grouse, quail, or partridge (Lawrence and Fessenden 1832:13).

Turkey (*Meleagris gallopavo*) was not particularly popular with the Logans since only a single turkey was identified amongst the bones in the cistern.

The ducks and geese (family Anatidae) identified in Feature 14 may have been raised in the poultry yard or hunted on the surrounding landscape. There were a minimum of two mature geese and thirteen mature ducks, with a large number of immature specimens. The fact that there were over one hundred immature duck bones in the assemblage suggests that at least some of these birds were likely being raised by the Logans, but this is not conclusive evidence. The range of lengths of mature long bones implies that, as with the chickens, the assemblage included several different species of ducks.

A minimum of three mature mourning doves (*Zenaida macroura*) and seventeen mature and three immature pigeons (family Columbidae) were identified in the cistern. According to nineteenth-century Pennsylvania bird books, the pigeons were most likely of the passenger pigeon (*Ectopistes migratorius*) variety. The presence of immature pigeon bones in the assemblage is evidence that the Logans were probably raising these birds on their farm because pigeons are very protective of their young and do not typically allow them out of hiding until they are fully mature in the wild. When raised in a domestic capacity, their nests are more vulnerable, and this is the most likely explanation for the presence of immature pigeon bones here.

The Northern Bobwhite (*Colinus virginianus*), also known as the Virginia quail or Bobwhite Quail, and frequently referred to as the partridge and sometimes the quail in nineteenth-century literature on Pennsylvania birds, was a commonly hunted game bird that was both "abundant and plentifully distributed" (Turnbull 1869:27). A minimum of three of these specimens were identified in Feature 14. Their presence suggests that the Logans did not rely solely on domestic poultry, but they also hunted birds on the surrounding landscape. Bent (1932:26) comments that the bobwhite "is undoubtedly the most universally popular of all North American game birds" and the fact that they preferred to live in close proximity to humans and their cultivated fields no doubt added to their appeal. Several authors commented on their tendency to become semi-domesticated or tame, that they occasionally could be found in the farmyard mingling with the poultry, and that they were known to nest in cultivated fields (Gentry 1877:318; Warren 1888:48).

A minimum of 70 songbirds (order Passeriformes) were identified from the cistern. Due to the large number and variety of songbirds in Pennsylvania, many of similar size and weight, these bones were not identified to species level. However, it was surprising to find such a large quantity of such delicate bird bones in the assemblage. Skulls were the most frequently recovered skeletal element. Given the generally fragile nature of skulls, particularly amongst small birds, their presence and completeness is a testament to the care of the excavation and storage processes. Surprising as it may sound, these birds may well have been consumed by the Logans. A number of recipes from period cookbooks describe preparations for small birds. Larks were the most popular variety of songbirds in England at the time and consequently are most often referenced in period cookbooks. English larks would have been of similar size to many of the birds recovered from the cistern. Other non-lark songbirds could easily have been substituted into the same recipes with equal success. Gulielma Penn, wife of William Penn, for example, had her cookery book transcribed to send along to Pennsylvania with her son, William, Jr., in 1703. The recipes are distinctly English and mainly from the seventeenth century, and she included one for "To Stew Larks" (Benson 1966). Priscilla Haslehurst published *The Family Friend, or Housekeeper's Instructor* in 1802, which included a recipe for "A lark pye." Special lark or bird spits were even manufactured for preparing these smaller varieties of birds.

Two kinds of shorebirds were identified in Feature 14. The killdeer (*Charadrius vociferus*) and the American woodcock (*Scalopax minor*) were each represented by a minimum of two individuals. Killdeer are a variety of plover, a plump-bodied shorebird. They are the only species of plover that breeds regularly in Pennsylvania and are the most common and most widely distributed plover in the state (McWilliams and Brauning 2000:148). The woodcock, also known as the "timberdoodle," is part of the sandpiper and phalarope family of shorebirds. It is one of the few birds in this family that breed in the state of Pennsylvania. This bird would have been hunted for its flesh, it being a popular game bird, though local hunting regulations restricted this practice beginning in 1839 (McWilliams and Brauning 2000:187).

MAMMALS

Mammal bones comprised slightly less than 25 percent of the total number of identified specimens in Feature 14. Small mammals, including cat, rat, shrew, mouse, rabbit, and squirrel bones, dominated the mammal bones in this assemblage. Most likely, only the rabbit and possibly squirrel bones contributed to the diet of the Logans. Other mammals present included the major domesticates—cows, pigs, and sheep— many of which were immature.

There were a minimum of nine suckling pigs recovered from Feature 14. These animals are typically a celebratory or feasting food so their presence in the cistern suggests that important formal meals were an integral component of the Logans' dining habits. This comes as no surprise given the high social status and political connections of the Logan family, who, even at their country farm, would have entertained often. Mature pig bones in the assemblage consisted of a minimum of four feet and a mandible. Heads and feet were amongst the first parts removed from pigs during butchery; these bones may be the remnants of early stages of butchering that took place on the plantation.

Both beef and veal bones were present in the cistern. The bones indicate the presence of at least one cattle older than and one younger than 18 months. The majority of the veal bones came from the foot (phalanges, metapodials, and tarsals). Other immature bones included a femur, tibia, and proximal radius. These bones were encompassed in the fillet, fore and hind knuckle, and blade bone veal cuts. Beef cuts represented by the bones in the assemblage included the leg, shin, edge, rump, thick flank, and rib cuts.

A minimum of two mature sheep and one lamb were represented by the bones in the cistern. The lamb bones included a scapula, humerus, ulna, radius, and two metapodials, which together represent a leg of lamb, along with a few skull fragments. Sheep's heads were used in eighteenth-century cooking for their high collagen content. The incomplete nature of the immature skeleton suggests that the Logans may have shared the lamb with their neighbors. This was standard practice on farmsteads at this time to ensure that meat from a slaughtered animal would be consumed before it became rancid. Mature sheep bones consisted of head, feet, and leg elements and denote leg, shoulder, breast, and scrag end of the neck mutton cuts.

A minimum of 12 bunnies and six mature rabbits were represented in the feature. The presence of both mature and immature rabbits may well indicate that they were being raised at Stenton, a common practice on both farmsteads and urban backyard spaces at this time.

A minimum of four grey squirrels were represented in Feature 14. Squirrels were not only abundant across the landscape, but they would have been among the varieties of wild animals that were considered acceptable provisions in the eighteenth century. Therefore, it is no surprise to find squirrels in this assemblage, and they may well have appeared on the Logan dining table.

TURTLES

Two species of turtles were identified in Feature 14—box and snapping turtle. Both of these turtles would have been available in and around the Stenton farmstead. A minimum of two snappers and four box turtles were recovered. Recovery of turtle bones suggests that turtle meat may have been used from these specimens in any number of turtle-related dishes for the Logans' table although their presence may also indicate that they were simply discarded whole into the cistern. Turtle preparations, including the well-known turtle soup (Schweitzer 2009), were quite popular in the eighteenth century and were considered to be a relatively high-status dish, certainly a preparation that would have demonstrated the elevated social status of the Logans. Although box turtles were more prevalent in Feature 14 than snapping turtles, the latter was the more likely candidate for culinary uses.

SHELLFISH

Shellfish were a minor part of the Feature 14 assemblage, contributing only 0.4 percent of the total number of identified specimens. A variety of species were represented, however, including oysters, hard shell clams, a blood ark clam, a local scallop, a Great Scallop, a lobster or crab claw, and a conch shell with the tip sawn off—possibly in the process of removing the meat or because it was used as a horn.

FISH

Only two varieties of fish were identified in this assemblage—catfish and striped bass. All identified catfish bones were from the post-cranial portion of the skeleton, implying that the heads of these fish were removed prior to discard in the cistern. In a traditional marketing situation, this bone pattern suggests that the fish were purchased as fillets or with their heads already removed. Given the location of Stenton, however, it is unlikely that the Logans were transporting these fish from Philadelphia since they would have been available in the rivers and streams nearer their property. Consequently, the lack of head bones is likely a reflection of preparation and discard behavior at Stenton.

Striped bass were prevalent in the Delaware and Susquehanna rivers in the spring when they would spawn, but they were also available throughout the year because they remained inshore. Meehan (1893:591–92) wrote that "The striped bass is a magnificent table fish. Its flesh is white, firm and flaky, and is rightly esteemed as one of our most toothsome food fishes." Thomas De Voe (1867:194) also wrote glowing culinary praises about the striped bass:

> These fish are highly prized by all who have eaten them. Those from a half to one pound weight are best to fry; above that weight to three pounds should be split for broiling, and from four to eight are the choice to boil. The very large fish are sometimes known as "green-heads," and are usually found coarse and rather dry eating, especially when above twenty-five pounds; then the best manner to prepare them is to boil and souse, or pickle the fish.

Although this fish was likely not available directly from the streams around Stenton, they were very popular and readily available in Philadelphia in the eighteenth century.

Summary

A wide variety of species were recovered from Feature 14 at Stenton; many of which would have been available locally in and around the farmstead. The Logans' food habits represented by the bones in the cistern point to a diet rich in fowl, including chickens, guinea fowl, turkey, ducks, geese, pigeons, and a few wild birds. The relatively small number of medium and large mammal bones recovered from this feature may indicate that the large domesticates being raised on the farm, including cows, pigs, and sheep, were not major contributors to the family diet. Alternatively, these larger bones may have been discarded elsewhere on the property since they would have filled up the cistern more quickly (Colaninno 2008:11). The prodigious number of fowl and suckling pigs recovered from Feature 14 suggest that the Logan household was eating well and entertaining often at Stenton in the mid-eighteenth century since these foods were associated with higher social status and lavish dining practices. This assemblage clearly demonstrates that the Logans had a diverse food landscape to choose from at Stenton.

Documentary Evidence

The faunal remains from Feature 14 dating to circa 1740–1770 provide one view of the food landscape at Stenton. The documentary record provides yet another. When combined, these two research perspectives help archaeologists and historians to construct more comprehensive reconstructions of food landscapes and foodways in the past. In order to best compare zooarchaeological and documentary resources, the following discussion focuses specifically on the documentary evidence for animals on the Stenton plantation. Two primary sources will be consulted in this discussion: William Logan's *Memoranda in Husbandry On My Plantation* (begun in 1752) and a manuscript cookbook associated with Stenton containing eighteenth-century recipes.

William Logan's *Memoranda in Husbandry On My Plantation* (1752)

In his memoranda, William Logan records a number of observations with regard to the workings of Stenton including tasks completed on the farm, livestock inventories, and culinary and medicinal recipes. Animals mentioned in the document include horses, cows, pigs, sheep, rabbits, muskrats, dogs, mice, fowls, geese, pigeons, and snakes. An inventory of livestock on the plantation in 1756 records the presence of 8 horses and mares, 23 horned cattle, 12 milch cows, 42 sheep, and 8 hogs. William also notes the purchase and slaughtering of livestock on or for his estate. For example an entry made in February of 1756 reads:

> I Killed a Sow Weighed. . . . 141lb @ 3d. . . . 1.15.5
>   total £37.8.7
> NB The Hide of the Ox mentioned above was Sent to Jacob
> Neagless
> It weighted (left blank)
> Total of Pork killed and laid in is 1393lb for the next years
> Provisions
> Total of Beef killed and laid in is 1873lb

From the memoranda. it is clear that William was slaughtering and purchasing new livestock annually, in addition to purchasing pickled pieces of dried beef for provisions on his farm. The document focuses on the large domesticates—i.e. cows, pigs, and sheep— since these were the responsibility of the men of the house and illustrates that a sizable amount of beef, veal, mutton, lamb, and pork would have been available for consumption at Stenton. This is quite a different view of the food landscape than was presented by the faunal remains in Feature 14. Foodways of the Logans based on this document suggest a much greater reliance on and availability of domestic meat products.

Stenton Cookbook

The Stenton archives contain a manuscript cookbook dating to the early eighteenth century, which includes 78 recipes, and appears to have been written by a single individual. An image of Queen Anne (1665–1714) on the cover of the book, a note stating that the blank notebook book was printed in 1715/1716, and the contemporaneous marriage of James Logan and Sarah Read in December 1714 suggest that this book may have been written for the use of the young Sarah as she took on the responsibility of running her own household for the first time. Unfortunately, this manuscript does not have a clear provenance so it can only tentatively be linked to the Logans.

Animal foods mentioned in the recipes in this cookbook include beef, veal, mutton, lamb, pork, venison, rabbit, hare, chicken, turkey, duck, goose, pigeon, lark, oysters, shrimp, lobster, eel, anchovy, and fish. The recipes are typical of the English cooking style in the mid-eighteenth century, mirroring those found in published cookbooks of the period. So, even though it is not possible to confidently associate the cookbook with the Logans, it is presumed that these types of recipes would have been prepared in their home at this time.

In addition, this cookbook is the only source, either documentary or archaeological, to indicate venison, shrimp, eel, or anchovy. Although remains of these animals were not recovered from Feature 14, this is not conclusive evidence that they were not eaten by the Logans. Not only does the cookbook broaden the scope of the Logan food landscape, it also provides important specifics about potential ways in which foods may have been prepared. At the present there is no way to distinguish how archaeologically recovered foodstuffs were cooked so these types of historical sources are integral to our understanding of past culinary practices.

Conclusion

This chapter has been an exploration of the process of historical zooarchaeological research focused on the elucidation of the foodways and food landscape of the wealthy and prominent Logan households living on the Stenton plantation in the mid-eighteenth century. Faunal remains excavated from a cistern feature on the property dating to this period suggest a diet rich in a variety of birds, a scenario typically associated with higher-status households, like the Logans. Domestic mammals in the faunal assemblage were mostly immature and dominated by a large number of suckling pigs, a preparation typically reserved for lavish dining. Snapping and box turtles, a small variety of shellfish, and catfish and striped bass also contributed to the food landscape evidenced in Feature 14.

Documents contemporaneous with this faunal assemblage sketch out a somewhat different picture of the food landscape at Stenton at this time. Domestic mammals, such as cows, pigs, and sheep, were much more visible in William Logan's *Memoranda* and suggest that a significantly larger portion of the Logan diet relied on these animals than was suggested by the faunal remains. An eighteenth-century manuscript cookbook associated with Stenton mentions several foodstuffs not found in these other sources, but it also provides potential preparations for many of the identified foods. This information is critical for understanding the full spectrum of the foodways sequence—from production, to preparation, to consumption, and eventual discard.

Ultimately this study demonstrates the importance of combining archaeological and documentary research in studying foodways and food landscapes in the past. No one source of data can be relied on to illustrate the complete picture of historic culinary practices. Through combining multiple perspectives, it is possible to formulate a more well-rounded and comprehensive reconstruction of food practices in the past. Through use of these techniques in this study of foodways on the Stenton plantation, it has been possible to construct a more complete picture of the food habits of the Logans in eighteenth-century Pennsylvania in a rural landscape just five miles from the bustling city of Philadelphia.

References Cited

Asmussen, Brit
2009   Intentional or incidental thermal modification? Analyzing site occupa-
             tion via burned bone. *Journal of Archaeological Science* 36(2):528–
             536.
Benson, Evelyn Abraham (editor)
1966   *Penn Family Recipes: Cooking Recipes of Wm. Penn's Wife, Gulielma.*
             George Shumway, York, Pennsylvania.
Bent, Arthur Cleveland
1932   *Life Histories of North American Gallinaceous Birds: Orders Galli-
             formes and Columbiformes.* Smithsonian Institution and United States
             National Museum Bulletin 162. United States Printing Office, Wash-
             ington, D.C.
Bronner, Edwin B.
1982   Village into Town, 1701–1746. In *Philadelphia: A 300-Year History*,
             edited by R. F. Weigley, pp. 33–67. W.W. Norton, New York.
Brothwell, Don
1979   Roman Evidence of a Crested Form of Domestic Fowl, as Indicated by
             a Skull Showing Associated Cerebral Hernia. *Journal of Archaeological
             Science* 6:291–293.
Colaninno, Carol
2008   Animal Remains from the Dock Street Theater Privy. Paper presented
             at the 43rd Annual Conference on Historical and Underwater Archae-
             ology, Amelia Island Plantation, Florida.
Cotter, John L., Daniel G. Roberts, and Michael Parrington
1992   *The Buried Past: An Archaeological History of Philadelphia.* University
             of Pennsylvania Press, Philadelphia.

De Voe, Thomas F.

1867   *Market Assistant, Containing a Brief Description of Every Article of Human Food Sold in the Public Markets of the Cities of New York, Boston, Philadelphia, and Brooklyn.* Hurd and Houghton, New York.

Engle, Reed Laurence

1982   *Historic Structure Report: Stenton, 18th & Windram Streets, Philadelphia, Pennsylvania for the National Society of the Colonial Dames of America in the Commonwealth of Pennsylvania.* John M. Dickey, Media, Pennsylvania.

Gentry, Thomas G.

1876   *Life-Histories of the Birds of Eastern Pennsylvania,* Vol. II. The Naturalists' Agency, Salem, Massachusetts.

Haslehurst, Priscilla.

1802   *The family friend, or, Housekeeper's instructor: Containing a very complete collection of original & approved receipts in every branch of cookery, confectionery, &c.* J. Montgomery, Sheffield.

Lawrence, J., and T. G. Fessenden

1832   *A treatise on breeding, rearing, and fattening, all kinds of poultry, cows, swine, and other domestic animals.* Lilly & Wait, Boston.

Logan, James

1730   Letter to William Logan of Briston, "15 10 mo 1730." Logan Letter Book Vol. IV, p. 208, Historical Society of Pennsylvania, Philadelphia.

Logan, Frances A. (editor)

1899   *Memoir of Dr. George Logan of Stenton by His Widow Deborah Norris Logan with Selections from his Correspondence.* Historical Society of Pennsylvania, Philadelphia.

Logan, William

1752   *Memoranda in Husbandry on My Plantation.* Stenton Archives, Stenton Museum, Philadelphia.

Liggett, Barbara

1970   Summary Report on Archaeology at Stenton, 1970. The National Society of Colonial Dames of America in the Commonwealth of Pennsylvania. Stenton Archives, Stenton Museum, Philadelphia.

1978   *Archaeology at New Market: Exhibit Catalogue.* The Athenaeum, Philadelphia.

1984a   Description of Discoveries: A Preliminary Report. Manuscript on file, Stenton Archives, Stenton Museum, Philadelphia.

1984b   Untitled lecture notes. Manuscript on file, Stenton Archives, Stenton Museum, Philadelphia.

MacDonald, Kevin C.

1992   The Domestic Chicken (*Gallus gallus*) in Sub-Saharan Africa: A Background to its Introduction and its Osteological Differentiation from

Indigenous Fowls (*Numidinae* and *Francolinus* sp.). *Journal of Archaeological Science* 19:303–318.

McWilliams, Gerald M., and Daniel W. Brauning
2000   *The Birds of Pennsylvania*. Cornell University Press, Ithaca, New York.

Meehan, William E.
1893   *Fish, Fishing and Fisheries of Pennsylvania*. E.K. Meyers, Harrisburg, Pennsylvania.

Miller, Deborah
2006   "Just Imported from London": The Archaeology and Material Culture of Stenton's Feature 14. Unpublished Masters thesis, Department of American Studies, The Pennsylvania State University, Harrisburg.

Milne, Claudia
2002   Appendix C: The Faunal Assemblages From The Block 2 Features. In *Hudson's Square—A Place Through Time: Archaeological Data Recovery on Block 2 of Independence Mall*, edited by Rebecca Yamin. Report to Day & Zimmerman Infrastructure, Philadelphia. John Milner Associates, Philadelphia.

Milne, Claudia
2004   Dining with the Ogles and Turnbulls on South Sixth Street: The Faunal Assemblages from the Liberty Bell Center Site. In *After the Revolution—Two Shops on South Sixth Street: Archaeological Data Recovery on Block 1 of Independence Mall*, pp. 41–58. Report to the National Park Service, Denver. John Milner Associates, Philadelphia.

Nicholson, R. A.
1993   A morphological investigation of burnt animal bone and an evaluation of its utility in archaeology. *Journal of Archaeological Science* 20:411–428.

Penney, Norman (editor)
1927   *The Correspondence of James Logan and Thomas Story, 1724–1741*. Friends' Historical Society, Philadelphia.

Salade, Robert F.
1925   *James Logan: A Famous Pennsylvanian*. Benjamin F. Emery Company, Philadelphia. Stenton Archives, Stenton Museum, Philadelphia.

Schweitzer, Teagan
2009   The Turtles of Philadelphia's Culinary Past—An Historical and Zooarchaeological Approach to the Study of Turtle-Based Foods in The City of Brotherly Love circa 1750–1850. *Expedition* 24(3):37–45.

Shepherd, Raymond V., Jr.
1968   James Logan's Stenton: Grand Simplicity in Quaker Philadelphia. Master's thesis, University of Delaware, Newark.

Shipman, P., G. Foster, and M. Schoeninger
1984   Burnt bones and teeth: an experimental study of color, morphology,
            crystal structure and shrinkage. *Journal of Archaeological Science*
            11:307–325.

Tolles, Frederick B.
1957   *James Logan and the Culture of Provincial America*. Little, Brown,
            Boston.
1958   Town House and Country House, Inventories from the Estate of
            William Logan, 1776. *The Pennsylvania Magazine of History and Bi-
            ography* 82(4):397–410.

Turnbull, William P.
1869   *The Birds of East Pennsylvania and New Jersey*. Henry Grambo,
            Philadelphia.

Warren, B. H.
1888   *Report on the Birds of Pennsylvania*. Edwin K. Meyers, Harrisburg,
            Pennsylvania.

Woodward, Carl Raymond
1941   *Ploughs and Politicks: Charles Read of New Jersey And His Notes on
            Agriculture 1715–1774*. Rutgers University Press, New Brunswick,
            New Jersey.

7

The Roosevelt Inlet Shipwreck, An Eighteenth-Century British Commercial Vessel in the Lower Delaware Bay: A Framework for Interpretation

Daniel R. Griffith and Charles Fithian

The Shipwreck

The Roosevelt Inlet shipwreck is the site of a wooden-hulled, commercial sailing ship lost in the lower Delaware Bay during the third quarter of the eighteenth century (figure 7.1). In the fall of 2004, a beach replenishment project struck a portion of an uncharted shipwreck. The dredge operations pumped sand and artifacts onto a nearby beach. The artifacts were reported to archaeologists working for the State of Delaware and the state responded by forming the Lewes Maritime Archaeology Project jointly with the Archaeological Society of Delaware and the Delaware Marine Archaeological Society. Over a three year period, nearly fifty thousand fragmentary artifacts were recovered from the beach while nearly thirty thousand additional artifacts were recovered by underwater archaeologists under contract with the Department of the Army, Corps of Engineers and the State of Delaware to investigate the shipwreck. The purpose of the research conducted was to determine both the precise location and condition of the shipwreck site and to determine the origin of the ship and its cargo (Griffith and Fithian 2006).

Shipwrecks are a highly significant window into the history of early America. Although typically salvaged shortly after the ship was lost, the remaining artifacts from the Roosevelt Inlet shipwreck offer an important window into the cargo of a specific ship participating in transatlantic trade and the connection the mid-Atlantic colonies had to that trade. The cargo was composed of a variety of goods that originated across the developed world at the time. The large quantity of artifacts recovered provides an opportunity to study material and physical dimensions of the British Atlantic World of the third quarter of the eighteenth century.

Identification of the Ship

Contemporary accounts describe the loss in the Delaware Bay of a British commercial vessel inbound to Philadelphia. On May 11, 1774, the *Pennsylvania Gazette* declared: "The ship *Severn*, Captain [James] Hathorn, from Bristol for this port, is ashore in our Bay, full of water, and is thought will be lost." The casualty listings in the *New Lloyd's List*, number 545, reported: "'The Severn,' Hathorn, from Bristol for Philadelphia, is on shore in the Delaware Bay, and full of water; the crew saved" (14 June 1774).

Archaeological and historical evidence that the Roosevelt Inlet shipwreck is the British commercial ship *Severn*, though indirect, is convincing. Underwater archaeological investigations of the shipwreck site by the Delaware Department of State, Dolan Research, Inc. and Southeastern Archaeological Research, Inc., recovered a wide range of cargo that can generally be characterized as retail commodities representing the second and third quarters of the eighteenth century. The cargo is representative of an in-bound commercial vessel from northern Europe or more probably Great Britain. Several specific artifact types recovered from both the beach and during offshore investigations narrow the time range by both their presence and their absence.

Two ceramic types point to a post 1760 loss of the ship. The first ceramic typed is a green and yellow, interior lead glazed, buff-bodied, flat bottomed, earth-

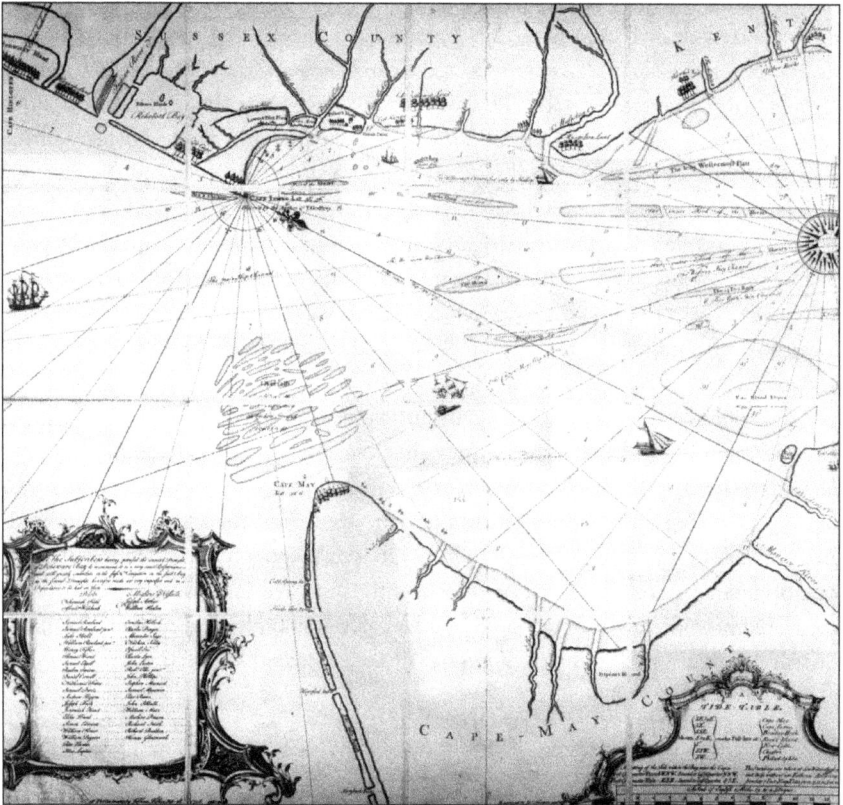

Figure 7.1: Fisher map from 1756 of lower Delaware Bay showing shipwreck location. Courtesy of Delaware Public Archives.

enware cooking pot. Nearly two hundred and fifty individual vessels have been identified from the beach and shipwreck site. It is known to Dutch and German archaeologists as Frankfurter Ware (figure 7.2). The ware was produced in the Rhine Valley of Germany starting in 1760 and heavily traded into the Dutch market (Bartels 1999:166). Its occurrence on a ship bound for Britain's American colonies is consistent with the reach of British North Atlantic commerce in the eighteenth century—though this is the first time this ceramic type has been identified from a site in North America.

Also recovered from the shipwreck site was an abundance of British cream-ware, first produced for retail markets in 1762. In addition to a large sample of un-decorated creamware, several creamware sherds with hand-painted, blue under-glaze designs were found (figure 7.3). Correspondence with British archaeologists indicates that hand-painted creamware indicates a post 1770 production (Barker 2006). Cor-roborating evidence comes from retail advertisements in Philadelphia newspapers of the early 1770s. The first clear notice of sale of hand-painted "Queensware," as it was then known, appears in 1772 (Pennsylvania Packet, 27 April 1772). An earlier retail advertisement appears to refer to hand-painted Queensware in the *Pennsylvania Packet,* December 16, 1771.

Thousands of Dutch tobacco pipes and fragments were recovered from the shipwreck site (figure 7.4). Many of the complete and partial pipe bowls and

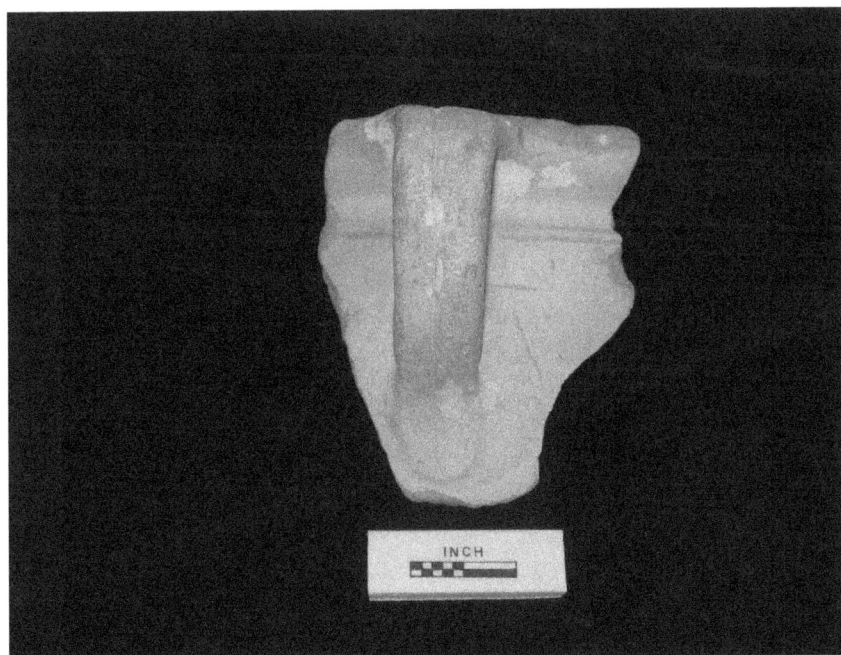

Figure 7.2: Photo of Frankfurter ware. Courtesy of Delaware Division of Historical and Cultural Affairs.

stems contained maker's marks, all of which were from Dutch pipe makers. One Dutch maker's mark in particular was informative. Garrett Maarling, makers mark "GLM," did not register his mark with the Dutch pipe-making guild until 1769 (Duco 2003:177), indicating a post 1769 date for the loss of the ship.

Determining the date of the shipwreck was aided by two dated artifacts recovered from the shipwreck site by Southeastern Archaeological Research, Inc. in October 2006. The first is a coin, a copper farthing, from Denmark, exhibiting the mark "Zelandia—1768." The second artifact is a copper alloy plated button. The button is molded and exhibits a human profile and the date 1772, indicating a post 1772 loss of the ship.

Efforts to determine the latest possible date of loss of the ship from the artifact analysis alone is more problematic, but there are some clues. Pearlware, a British ceramic type widely popular in early America was first produced in 1779. No pearlware was found at the shipwreck site or on the nearby beach.

The convergence of artifact evidence alone suggests that the shipwreck was lost no earlier than 1772 and no later than 1780. A wide range of other artifacts were recovered from the shipwreck site, and the dates of their manufacture and use are consistent with this date range.

Historical documentation points to the *Severn* as well. The ship *Severn* is the only reported commercial ship loss recorded in the Delaware Bay or the near shore of Delaware's Atlantic coast between 1772 and 1783. During the American War for Independence (1776–1783), 82 ship losses were reported between Cape Henlopen and the head of navigation on the Delaware. They were all military wartime losses. No commercial losses were recorded during the war (Cox 2005:A-2). Commercial ships during the war, mostly traveling between Britain and her West Indian colonies,

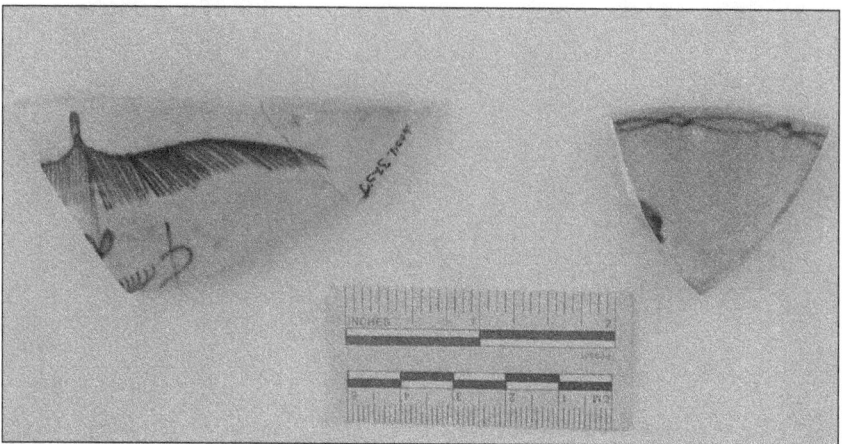

Figure 7.3: Photo of Hand Painted Creamware. Courtesy of Delaware Division of Historical and Cultural Affairs

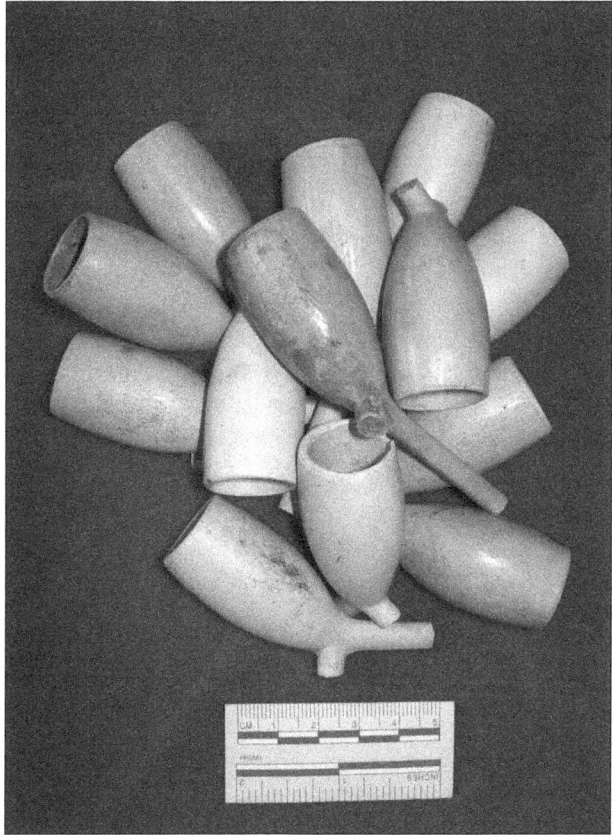

Figure 7.4: Photo of
Dutch Tobacco Pipes.
Courtesy of Delaware
Division of Historical
and Cultural Affairs

were frequently in an escorted convoy. Even then, the commercial ships tended to be lightly armed to fend off privateers if they were separated from the convoy. No defensive armaments, munitions, or related equipment were found at the Roosevelt Inlet shipwreck site.

The historical description of the loss of the *Severn* in one account states that she was "on the beach, full of water, and the crew was saved" (New Lloyds List, No. 545, 14 June 1774). The Roosevelt Inlet shipwreck is in 15 feet of water. A ship of the *Severn's* class would have been "full of water" at that depth and location, as the distance from the keel to the weather deck is approximately 15 to 16 feet. There were no human remains found at the wreck site, even though preservation was sufficient in some areas of the site to preserve organics, like wood, leather, and fragments of cloth. This observation is consistent with the 1774 report that the crew was saved.

The Ship Severn

The ship *Severn* is listed in Lloyds Register of Shipping in 1769. She was registered as a ship class vessel with a net tonnage of 200. The master was James Hathorn, and the registered owner was Thomas Pennington. The ship was also registered as belonging to the Port of Philadelphia. Historical research in Britain revealed that Pennington was an important merchant in Bristol and hired Hathorn as master of the ship *Prince George* in the mid-1760s prior to hiring him to master the *Severn* in 1769. Captain Hathorn, originally from Belfast, Ireland, changed his place of abode to Philadelphia when he became master of the *Severn* (Ship *Severn* Muster Roll; 23 May 1769 to 10 August 1769). An August 19, 1773, Bristol Customs Record lists the *Severn* as "British built" (British Customs, D. Harson, Esq. entry 271). Further research revealed that *Severn* was built in Philadelphia, consistent with the Bristol Customs Record listing the ship as "British built." Analysis of a heavy timber recovered from the shipwreck site shows it was made of white oak, a material commonly used for shipbuilding in the American colonies. At a reported net tonnage of 200, the *Severn* was typical of ships trading in Bristol at the time: "All of the transatlantic ships trading at Bristol in the eighteenth century were moderate in size, the average being under 200 tons" (Morgan 1993:45).

Commerce, Economic Policy, and Practice

A study of the ship *Severn*, its captain James Hathorn, and its owner Thomas Pennington offers an opportunity to examine British colonial commerce in the period of general peace between the close of the Seven Years War and the outbreak of the American War for Independence.

During the seventeenth and eighteenth centuries, European nations sought colonies as a means of gaining power through economic self-sufficiency (Stout 1973:1). British mercantilists talked of the British Empire as the best of all possible empires because its imperialism was primarily commercial (Fairburn 1945:314). The British North Atlantic trade included assembling goods manufactured in Great Britain and the transport of finished goods to British ports for re-export from suppliers in other countries as well as the transport of raw materials and agricultural products from the colonies to British ports. British colonies were primarily valued for these raw materials and agricultural products, and perhaps as importantly, the colonies provided markets for British manufactured goods. At the major colonial ports, like Philadelphia, imported finished goods were sold by retailers in the port city or redistributed over land or by water to consumers within the economic sphere of that port. A contemporary quote of the period clearly describes Britain's economic relationships with her colonies, "Pennsylvania, within 40 years, has made wonderful improvements, which has very much enlarged their demands upon us [the British merchants and manufacturers] for broad cloths, druggets, serges, stuffs and manufactures of all sorts. They supply the sugar plantations with pipe-staves, lumber, etc" (Gee 1738:25).

The likelihood that the Roosevelt Inlet shipwreck is a British commercial vessel is reenforced by the fact that the exclusive trade monopoly with her colonies held by Britain was upheld by a series of acts known collectively as the Principal Navigation Laws and Acts of Trade. The laws required that all goods, both export and import, had to be carried on English or colonial built ships manned and commanded by Englishmen (Fairburn 1945:161). Our research in Britain located a muster roll for the ship *Severn* dated 29 March 1771. The muster roll identifies Captain Hathorn and his crew of 28 as British, and it lists places of abode for the Captain and crew within the British American colonies (Muster Roll, Ship *Severn*, March 1771).

Shipping was the lifeblood of the Atlantic economy in the eighteenth century—shipping patterns were the arteries through which merchants and commodities of the North Atlantic trading world were drawn together into an international trading network (Morgan 1993:55). Philadelphia was the queen city of America and one of the largest cities in the British Empire (Stout 1973:74). As the chief port on the Delaware River, which served as the main outlet for Pennsylvania, Delaware, and portions of New Jersey, Philadelphia was the primary exporter of American bread and flour, largely to the West Indian market. It was also the largest American importer of British West Indian rum. In terms of European trade, Philadelphia had a particular connection with the British port of Bristol. One in five ships entering the port of Philadelphia was Bristol owned (Morgan 1993:36).

Bristol supplied a wide array of manufactured goods and processed raw materials to Philadelphia, yet received only modest direct trade in return resulting in a trade imbalance and indebtedness on the part of American merchants (Morgan 1993:112). The heavily populated colonies, like Pennsylvania, produced very little that England would buy; most of the Philadelphia shipping profits were made in sending lumber, lumber products, and foodstuffs to Britain's West Indian colonies. Bristol merchants extended liberal credit to American buyers but expected payments in full typically within 6 to 12 months (Morgan 1993:110). This placed American merchants in the middle, buying reasonably expensive manufactures from Britain while attempting to raise cash by selling bulk commodities to British markets. Retail advertisements in period newspapers illustrate this dynamic:

> Philadelphia—May 1, 1769—The ship *Severn* for Bristol has most of her cargo loaded and has excellent accommodations for [paying] passengers [Pennsylvania Chronicle, 1 May 1769].

> Philadelphia—June 8, 1772—Stocker and Wharton—Just imported on the ship *Severn*, James Hathorn, from Bristol—nails, pale ale in hogsheads, window glass in boxes, iron pots, rounded and flat [case] bottles, boxes and kegs of pipes, etc. [Pennsylvania Gazette, 8 June 1772].

On the outbound voyage from Philadelphia, *Severn* did not have a full cargo load to return to Bristol.

The *Severn* was in-bound to Philadelphia from Bristol when lost in the lower Delaware Bay on May 3 or 4, 1774. Interestingly, historic weather records report a severe coastal storm on these dates that produced widespread snow from Virginia to New England (Pennsylvania Gazette, 11 May 1774). Though *Severn* in her career visited the ports of Lisbon, Barcelona, and Leghorn (Italy), by the time of her loss she had settled into a regular, direct shipping route between Philadelphia and Bristol. Direct shipping routes were the safest way to deal with the risks and costs of long-distance seaborne trade (Morgan 1993:88). Shipowners, in their letters to correspondents in America, were especially anxious that vessels should not be idle or simply "trading in ballast" (i.e. returning empty) (Morgan 1993:70). Shipowners and merchants insured that each shipment from Bristol was well loaded, regardless of whether a colonial merchant had actually ordered the goods (Morgan 1993:118). Bristol merchant and shipowner Thomas Pennington assembled manufactured wares from Britain as well as imports from the continent and elsewhere at his leased portside warehouses in Bristol (Ancient Lease:1644/8, Bristol). However, most commodities sent to transatlantic markets were of English manufacture (Morgan 1993:91).

A partial list of goods of British manufacture recovered from the Roosevelt Inlet shipwreck is illustrated in table 7.1. Bristol merchants also re-exported manufactured goods from the European continent and elsewhere. In general, between 10 percent and 35 percent of British exports to the North American mainland were re-exports (Morgan 1993:93). Re-export items recovered from the Roosevelt Inlet shipwreck are listed in table 7.2.

Excess shipping space on outbound voyages from Bristol was frequently filled with crates of empty bottles and barrels of beer (Morgan 1993:98). In addition, excess space was filled with high weight and volume materials, like the bricks, millstones, and processed antimony recovered from the Roosevelt Inlet shipwreck. Bristol exporters made sure their ships were full.

"The expansion of British exports to North America . . . frequently led to flooding of the colonial market. Colonial merchants repeatedly complained about the glut of exports and were particularly concerned when British merchants saddled them with unsolicited goods" (Morgan 1993:118). The *Severn's* owner, Thomas Pennington, was not above such practices. Indeed, a Philadelphia merchant on receipt of too much earthenware and glassware found much of the cargo remained unsold, which led him to consider changing his Bristol correspondent from Pennington to Lancelot Cowper (Morgan 1993:118).

Growing Tensions and Trade

Overseas commerce between Great Britain and her American colonies should not be viewed only in the context of colonial market economies of a mercantilist system.

Table 7.1. Goods Recovered from the Roosevelt Inlet Shipwreck

Table Service	Architectural	Furniture	Sewing/Clothing	Bulk Containers	Miscellaneous
White Salt Glazed Stoneware	Iron nails	Upholstery Tacks	Brass Pins	Stoneware Bottles	Stone Mortars and Pestles
Creamware	Window Glass		Thimbles	Glass Case Bottles	
Table Glassware			Brass Pressing Iron		
Round Bottles			Glass Linen Smoothers		
			Buttons		
			Buckles		
			Faceted Glass Gemstones		
			Pressed Glass Gemstones		

Table 7.2. Re-export Items Recovered from the Roosevelt Inlet Shipwreck

Germany	Holland	China	South Africa
Blue Gray Stoneware	Tobacco Pipes	Porcelain	Constantia Wine Bottles
Frankfurter Ware	Tin Glazed Earthenware		
Stoneware Mineral Water Bottles	Woolen Blankets		

This commerce was also played out against a very real background of political tension between Great Britain and her American colonies, a tension that grew steadily more heated between 1764 and 1776.

Upon his ascension to the throne in 1760, George III demanded that all American colonies be made by force, if necessary, to conform to all English laws with respect to trade and taxation. After the general peace of 1764, England became determined to enforce its Navigation Acts and protect all British ships in their privileged, exclusive trade even "if it takes the entire British Navy to do it" (Fairburn 1945: 309). Both colonial government officials and Royal Navy officers were charged with enforcing the acts (Stout 1973:3). The British Board of Trade throughout its existence consistently attempted to keep the colonies in a state of political and economic subservience to England (Stout 1973:29). Beginning in 1763, the Royal Navy was called on to assist the Board of Trade in enforcing the revenue acts. The Royal Navy ship *Rainbow* was stationed between Cape Henlopen, Delaware and Cape Henry, Virginia, while the ships *Squirrel* and *Sardoine* cruised between Cape Henlopen, Delaware and Sandy Hook, New Jersey (Stout 1973:29). Both naval groups were enjoined to seize all vessels suspected of illegal trade. The *Sardoine* spent three years on the Delaware station during which time her boats examined every ship they sighted (Stout 1973:136). As noted by one author, "In Delaware, seizures were made of almost everything, including cloth and coffee" (Stout 1973:136). Indeed, "After an initial testing of the resolve of the Royal Navy between 1763 and 1766, merchants, traders and their investors found it safer and economically less risky to obey the law" (Stout 1973:77).

The regulatory features of the British Navigation and Trade Laws benefited both British and American merchants as it relates to the exclusivity of trade. Until 1764, the primary emphasis of the British Customs Board and the Royal Navy was the enforcement of the regulatory features. However, with the passage of the Sugar Act by Parliament in 1764 and the Townshend Act of 1767, the Navigation and Trade Laws were increasingly enforced as measures to raise revenue for Britain in her colonies (Stout 1973:12). The American reaction to such revenue pressure took the form of boycotts on certain classes of British goods, which resulted in British merchants increasing their trade with northern Europe (Schlesinger 1918:238). *Severn* owner Pennington and shipmaster Hathorn were well aware of the escalating tensions. In 1766, the cargo of the ship *Prince George*, owned by Pennington and mastered by Hathorn, was confiscated in New York by the "Sons of Liberty" and held for return to Bristol (Schlesinger 1918:81). With the repeal by Parliament of the Townshend Act in 1770, commercial ties with Britain and material prosperity increased rapidly until the passage of the Tea Act in 1773 (Schlesinger 1918:240). One well-known example of the American reaction to the Tea Act is the Boston Tea Party of December 16, 1773, which occurred nearly five months prior to the loss of the *Severn*. At the time of the Boston Tea Party, Captain Hathorn and the *Severn* were en route from Philadelphia to Bristol (Pennsylvania Gazette, 24 November 1773), while the Boston Port Act (closing the port of Boston) of March 1774 was adopted near the time of *Severn's* departure from Bristol. *Severn's* return trip to Philadelphia in the spring of 1774 was her last.

Transatlantic merchants and shippers were affected by the non-importation measures and adjusted where they could. Non-importation measures adopted in Philadelphia in the mid-1760s and early 1770s affected the mix of cargo imported into the colonies (Morgan 1993:93). Even after the repeal of the Townshend Act, merchants acquired manufactured items from other suppliers, mostly on the European continent, that either would not conflict with the non-importation measures, as they understood them, or were from suppliers on the continent where they had established good trading relationships during the American boycotts of British goods (Schlesinger 1918:238).

This dynamic it seems is reflected in the bottom of the Delaware Bay. The Roosevelt Inlet shipwreck site has an unusually large amount of utilitarian German and Dutch goods, goods that otherwise could have been obtained in Britain herself. We are not the first to make this observation. A 1773 letter from Royal Navy Admiral Montague from his station off the Atlantic Coast of America to British Admiralty states: "it would amaze your Lordships to see the great quantity of Holland goods that is run annually into Virginia, Philadelphia and New York" (Stout 1973:136).

Conclusion

The Roosevelt Inlet shipwreck and its cargo provide an excellent example of the physical and material expressions of British mercantilism as well as a window on the social and political dynamics between Britain and her American colonies on the eve of the American War for Independence. The examination of the vessel and her cargo leads us to broader questions about British culture and her empire while illuminating historical dynamics on a fine scale.

References Cited

Barker, David
2006   Personal communication regarding hand painted creamware, 2006.
Bartels, Michiel
1999   *Cities in Sherds 1*, Stichting Promotie Archeologie Swolle en de Rijks-
            dienst voor het Oudheidkundig Bodemon derzoek, Amersfoort.
Bristol Records Office
1762   Ancient Lease BCC/F/E/4292: 1644/7, Records of the Corporation of
            Bristol, Bristol Records Office, UK.
British Customs Records
1772   D. Harson, Esq., Entry 271; August 19. 1773, Bristol Records Office,
            UK.
Cox, J. Lee., Jr.
2005   *Phase 1 and Phase 2 Underwater Archaeological Investigations,
            Lewes Beach and Roosevelt Inlet Borrow Areas, Delaware Bay, Sussex
            County, Delaware,* Dolan Research, Inc., September 2005.
Duco, D. H.
2003   *Merker van Goudse pipenmakers 1660–1940.* Uit geversmaatschappij
            De Tijdstroom Lochem/Poperinge.
Fairburn, William Armstrong
1945–1955 *Merchant Sail,* Volume 1, L. Middelditch Co. Center Lovell, Maine.
Griffith, Daniel R., and Charles Fithian
2006   "Roosevelt Inlet Shipwreck; (7S-D-91A)." National Register of His-
            toric Places, United States Department of the Interior, National Park
            Service. Washington, D.C.
Gee, Joshua
1738   *British Merchant,* 4th Edition. Buckley, London.
Morgan, Kenneth
1993   *Bristol and the Atlantic Trade in the Eighteenth Century.* Cambridge
            University Press, Cambridge.
New Lloyds List
n.d.   Guild Hall Library, Manuscript Department, London.
Pennsylvania Chronicle
            American Historical Newspapers. http://infoweb.newsbank.com. Ac-
            cessed 26 October 2007.
Pennsylvania Gazette
            Americas Historical Newspapers. http://infoweb.newsbank.com. Ac-
            cessed 26 October 2007.
Pennsylvania Packet
            Americas Historical Newspapers. http://infoweb.newsbank.com. Ac-
            cessed 26 October 2007.

Schlesinger, Arthur M.

1918   *The Colonial Merchants and the American Revolution 1763–1776.*
            Columbia University Press, New York.

Bristol Records Office

1769   Ship *Severn* Muster Roll. 23 May 1769 to 10 August 1769. Port Books
            of Bristol, Bristol Records Office, Bristol.

Stout, Neil R.

1973   *The Royal Navy in America, 1760–1775, A Study of Enforcement of
            British Colonial Policy in the Era of the American Revolution.* Naval
            Institute Press, Annapolis, Maryland.

8

THE ARCHAEOLOGY OF QUAKERISM IN PHILADELPHIA AND BEYOND: IDENTITY, CONFORMITY, AND CONTEXT

JOHN M. CHENOWETH

Introduction

This volume is focused on the Delaware Valley and its archaeology, but I am going to take this region as my starting point and—as my title suggests—move beyond it to tackle larger issues with particular relevance to the Philadelphia area. While Dutch and Swedish settlers were the first non-Natives in the Delaware Valley, the Quaker-inspired settlement of Philadelphia was what made it a colonial-era hot spot. Considering the way Quakerism is bound up with the history of the Philadelphia, an archaeology of the Society of Friends would have many implications in understanding the past lives of the city's inhabitants.

Previous work on sites once owned or occupied by Quakers is not overly rare, but fewer works engage deeply with the issue of Quakerism, the forces which influence the material culture of Quakers, and how we might understand that culture through archaeology. At times, these works contain a debate between two opposing interpretations: that colonial-era Quakers kept to a doctrine of "plainness" and restricted themselves to necessities, or that Quakers followed the lead of their contemporaries and participated fully in the fashions of the day. Sometimes, these opposing views are given voice in the same article since the evidence encountered appears to lead to both of these conclusions in different ways.

It is my contention here that the apparent conflict between these two conclusions is the result of our assumptions about both Quakerism and about how the phenomenon of social identity functions and can be seen in material culture. Recent archaeological work has moved from seeing particular patterns or artifacts as being "of" a certain group to understanding material culture as being used in active negotiations of identity (see, most recently, Silliman 2009). Importantly, material culture is given meaning in the local social contexts in which it is deployed (for a discussion of this process centering on Quakers, see Chenoweth 2009).

This chapter will discuss the social contexts in which Quakers lived in colonial America and contemporary England—their concerns, unique difficulties, and priorities as they stem from both their religious and social lives—and how these may impact archaeological interpretations of Quaker-related sites. Before we turn to these issues, however, a brief introduction to Quakerism is in order, as is a discussion of some of the archaeological work that has been conducted on Quaker sites.

Quakerism

Born out of the economic and social turmoil of the English Revolution and late Reformation, Quakerism is considered to have its beginnings in the late 1640s, when several like-minded lay-ministers, including George Fox, James Naylor, Margaret Fell, and others began to wander the English countryside spreading their religious views. Properly known as the "Religious Society of Friends," members early on took ownership of the moniker "Quaker," the origin of which is a constant source of anecdotes and debates. Quakerism was initially one of the most extreme and fervent nonconformist movements of the late Reformation, often disrupting religious services and spurning social mores. The movement spread quickly in the 1650s and 1660s becoming geographically widespread across the Atlantic world before turning isolationist in the eighteenth century and suffering frequent schisms in the nineteenth. Though altered, Quakerism survives to this day in a varied group of about 350,000 members or "Friends." The group is probably best known today for its abolitionist efforts in the eighteenth and nineteenth centuries, and peace activism in the twentieth century, including the winning of the 1947 Nobel Peace Prize.

Quakers saw themselves not as religious innovators but as returning to an "authentic" gospel as they thought it had been practiced in the time of Jesus: a "primitive Christianity" from before it became adulterated by later innovations and human faults (Davies 2000; Penn 1696). George Fox, one of the movement's principal founders, encouraged his followers to dispense with all the "vain traditions, which they [i.e. most people] had gotten up since the apostles' days" (Fox 1952:36).

The fundamental tenet of Quakerism is that there is "that of God in everyone" and that all people can have an unmediated experience of God through the "Inner Light." This led to Friends' famous silent Meetings for Worship, wherein they gather together to "wait upon the Light" rather than engaging in more outward forms of religious worship, such as singing or praying aloud. It should be noted that this is quite diametrically opposed to the form of worship of the Shakers, with whom Quakers are often confused, and who practice a distant off-shoot of Quakerism. Following from the idea of the "Inner Light" is a belief that all aspects of life, however mundane, should be spiritual. Thus daily life for Quakers should be explicitly influenced by the tenets of Quakerism. Simplicity and modesty, pacifism, complete equality among people, and a strong sense of community and morality: these were all to be conscientiously maintained in every action.

Quakers came into frequent conflict with the rest of their society for these ideals. Many Friends spent time in prison, including George Fox (seven times for charges ranging from refusal of oaths to blasphemy), or were deprived of livelihoods and property for their beliefs. In the first dozen years of Fox's preaching, 21 of his associates or followers are known to have died in prison or otherwise as a result of their faith (Nuttall 1952:xix) and over 400 died throughout the course of the seventeenth century (Davies 2000:178). Though many certainly negotiated a "middle way" when conflicts arose, the nature of Quaker religious thought insisted that they continue to actively and publically proclaim their religion; one could not be a Quaker without practicing Quakerism. They could not hide their religion, whatever persecutions they might face.

This persecution is one of the influences that led to the foundation of Philadelphia. William Penn, an early follower of Quaker doctrine, planned a new colony as a "holy experiment" where all would have religious freedom (so long, of course, as they were Protestant). Many Quakers settled in and near Philadelphia at its founding in 1682, and for the next 70 years they held a great deal of political power, before more or less withdrawing from politics in the middle of the eighteenth century (Marietta 1984). Their values and philosophy greatly influenced the laws, architecture, education, social development, and material culture of Philadelphia and the surrounding region.

Previous Quaker Archaeology

Space prevents a complete listing of all Quaker-related archaeological reports, but the following will touch on many of the major published works that actively engage with the issue of Quaker religion as part of an archaeological analysis of a Quaker-related site. Other sites once owned or occupied by Quakers have been studied but not all reports give extensive consideration to Quakerism as it may have influenced life there. The following discussion should give an idea of the scope of works that attempt to engage with these issues.

One of the earliest works to consider Quakerism archaeologically is White's (1985) excavations at Quakertown, an early nineteenth-century community on the Pennsylvania-Ohio border founded by three families of Quaker settlers. A brief account of the project observes a "simple" lifestyle in the earliest deposits, but it also describes grand architecture in the Georgian-inspired fashion of the day and notes the presence of silver cutlery, fine ceramics, and other evidence of a "somewhat more than Spartan" existence (White 1985:29).

An often quoted dictum of Quaker life is that one should endeavor to have the "best sort, but plain" in all manner of things (John Reynell 1738, quoted in Tolles 1960:88): quality without opulence. McCarthy's (1999) study of the Dock street site in Philadelphia seems to support this. The author acknowledges a relatively small sample and focuses on methodological considerations, using the ratios of South's "functional groups" to identify the activities leading to each deposit. Considering Quakerism, McCarthy concludes that Philadelphia Quakers were well supplied but chose "less pretentious" ceramics. This is supported by the presence of fewer porcelain sherds than comparable sites and those being of good quality but less decorated. His documentary work on the early Philadelphia Quakers, however, complicates these observations, with Quaker "Grandees" providing examples of both tempering and excess in material culture (McCarthy 1999:147, 149).

Work on the home of John Bates, a Quaker shopkeeper in early eighteenth-century Virginia, seems to belie the "best sort, but plain" pattern (Samford and Brown 1990). Bates' store was extremely successful financially, but Bates himself seemed to have made use of the same stock as his lower- to middle-class patrons. In the case of fabrics, revealed through probate inventories, the expected pattern holds with there being some high quality silks but mostly in solid colors rather than the more fashionable stripes. The ceramics revealed archaeologically, however, show an opposing pattern: no evidence of any high-quality porcelain, yet the presence of several Chinoiserie Delfts which imitated porcelain's decoration at a lower cost (Samford and Brown 1990:35, 39). Additionally, Bates put on a show of his wealth in the creation of his public persona, and he seems to have participated equally in social trends of the day, such as the move towards partitioned space and variety in kitchen implements (Samford and Brown 1990:27, 41–42). Samford and Brown conclude that "Bates is an example of a man typical of his wealth category for early Chesapeake society. Despite his Quaker beliefs, Bates was actively participating in the acquisition of consumer goods which was beginning to distinguish the residents of the Tidewater region" (1990:44).

Porcelain was also in scant supply at the Reid Site, a small eighteenth-century farm in North Carolina, as were decorated pieces of all sorts (Gray 1989:64–5). The Pools, the site's Quaker occupants during the middle of the eighteenth century, seem to have preferred the middle- to high-quality but aesthetic simplicity of white salt-glazed stoneware. Anna Gray's use of South's artifact pattern analysis on the site suggested its similarity with other contemporary (non-Quaker) sites (Gray 1989:66). Elsewhere, Gray has written that Pool appeared to be of modest means but occasionally able to be "extravagant" (Gray 1997). Neither the similarity with other sites, nor the suggestion that the site can be characterized by occasional extravagance quite fits with our expectations for Quaker material culture.

My own archival work and archaeological discussions of part of the National Constitution Center site in Philadelphia has also unearthed conflicting evidence (Chenoweth 2006). The site was owned by a Quaker named Ebenezer Robinson, who was not prominent but was very active within the Quaker community. Documents reveal a man of solid financial acumen, trusted by his meeting with tasks as diverse as "treating with" members not living up to expectations, serving as a delegate to the Quarterly Meetings, and even managing financial transactions in the Meeting's name. Yet even as the local community railed against the dangers and sins of alcohol, Ebenezer rented one of his buildings to what has been revealed to be a low-class tavern. My analysis suggested that while tavern laws (written primarily by Quakers) attempted to force taverns to focus not on providing drink but on supplying shelter and food to travelers—services needed by the growing city—this particular tavern focused on serving alcohol. While the tavern did not survive long on this site, its association with Ebenezer Robinson could not have gone unnoticed, as he moved his family to this location shortly after the tavern closed, making the connection quite public, and yet his standing as a moral and proper Quaker did not seem to be affected.

One of the most substantial works on the archaeology of a Quaker-related site is Marley Brown's dissertation, which focused on four generations of the Mott family, a prominent Quaker family in Rhode Island during the seventeenth and eighteenth centuries (Brown 1987). Brown observed that his Quaker occupants participated in the same general trends observed throughout the colonies in the period. For instance, local vernacular building styles gave way to a "Georgian plan" house for the Motts much as they did in non-Quaker families although Brown considers Quakers "generally conservative" (Brown 1987:195, 197). Brown expresses doubt that Quaker "plainness" is accessible archaeologically, and he uses documentary evidence to suggest that the Motts may have bucked certain trends which more offended their religious beliefs than others: for instance the trend towards creating "parlors," more public areas of a house where finery was put on display, although he notes that other Rhode Island Quakers may have done otherwise (Brown 1987:283–4). Similar results are found in a comparison of clothing, use of credit and debt, and attitudes toward slavery. On the other hand, Quakers, including the Motts, Brown suggests, spent more money on some categories of material goods, such as bedding and other ways of making a home comfortable and warm, and on books (Brown 1987:290–300).

Cemetery studies make up a large fraction of Quaker-related sites to receive archaeological treatment and consideration of Quaker identity, and I will discuss four here: three in England and one in the United States. Based on their work on a Quaker burial ground in Alexandria, Virginia, Bromberg and Shepherd (2006:78; Bromberg et al. 2000) have argued that Quaker ideals are the cause of a comparatively low percentage of decorated caskets, though these are not absent altogether. Expectations for Quakerism's influence are complicated further by the presence of at least one burial vault, something expressly forbidden by Meetings elsewhere. The authors suggest that personal decisions and tastes are behind the variation present, which is likely true, but it is interesting to observe that personal taste seems to have had such free reign in a society that historians have long argued to be so prescriptive. For instance, historian James Walvin wrote that Quaker ideals were "enforced by a structure of management which was more intrusive and manipulative than many have recognized" (Walvin 1997:208).

Gwynne Stock (1998a, 1998b) has compared written meeting records and historical accounts with the actual practice of Quaker burial as seen through archaeology at a site in Bathford, England, and also found significant variability. Despite explicit "advices" from Meetings to the contrary and historical accounts of these being followed, Stock also encountered burial vaults, along with lead coffins, ornamental coffin hardware, and grave markers from the period 1717 to 1850 (when they were expressly forbidden). He also found more than a few instances of the use of named months on gravestones (avoided by Quakers in many contexts due to their pagan origin). Meanwhile, Quaker values seem to have been upheld at Bathford in terms of the variability of burial orientation and an efficient use of space, probably based in a goal of not being wasteful of the Meeting's property (see below for a discussion of Quaker attitudes toward waste).

More variation is introduced by the discussion of the Quaker burial ground at Kingston-upon-Thames (Bashford and Pollard 1998; see also Kirk 1998; Bashford

and Sibun 2007). Again, the authors encountered substantial vaults and lead coffins, presumably aimed at preservation of the body and thus counter to the "dust to
dust" mentality espoused by Quakers in written works of the period. They also document a concern in this particular Meeting's membership with disturbance of burials
(Bashford and Pollard 1998:156). This is born out archaeologically, as the authors
encountered a number of cases where charnel was carefully deposited in a special
pit at the foot of a new burial, and one where ashes may have been accorded special
treatment (Bashford and Pollard 1998:162). Quakers attempted to be respectful of
corpses but also to avoid "superstitious" concern with the bodies of the dead; focus
was to be on the soul of the departed. Coffins were again highly variable, possibly
reflecting social standing, and this variability reflected that seen in casket styles in use
by the general English public of the period. That is, Quakers followed styles in burial
patterns too, as Brown observed of the Motts and Samford and Brown of the Bates
in other aspects of material culture. Some measure of religiously inspired modesty
may be behind the lack of specifically funeral attire observed at this site, however
(Bashford and Pollard 1998:159).

The human remains at Kingston-upon-Thames also received a detailed
study (Start and Kirk 1998; Bashford and Sibun 2007). Not surprisingly, considering the historical evidence that Quakers of this time tended to be of the wealthier
merchant class, these remains reflected better than average health for the period with
fewer examples of dental caries and cavities and cases of rickets and anemia than
their counterparts as well as less bone damage resulting from physically demanding
work in life. In fact, the burials at Kingston-upon-Thames represent a generally "remarkably healthy post-Medieval population" (Bashford and Sibun 2007:142). But
even here all is not as would be predicted from a literal reading of Quaker advices
and historical accounts of Quaker lifestyles. One burial, skeleton 1098, died from
a long-term, advanced case of venereal syphilis, known even then to be a sexually
transmitted disease. Sexual immodesty would certainly have been seen as grounds
for "disownment" or removal from the Quaker community by many contemporary
Quakers, and thus probably exclusion from Quaker burial grounds. In life, this person received sufficient long-term care to survive for quite some time despite the difficult nature of the disease and the sinful way it may have been acquired, and in death
he was treated as any other member. Perhaps, though, this is what we should expect
from Quakers.

Work on another burial ground, in the west England town of Bromyard,
has also revealed a number of "Quakerly" patterns, including non-religious symbolism, simple patterns in coffin hardware, and at least one possible case of human remains receiving less than formal treatment: a burial (infant burial 138) was disturbed
by a later burial (number 40) and the charnel not placed in the new grave (Archenfield Archaeology 2004). On the other hand, as with the sites discussed above,
exceptions to expected Quaker practice were also found. As at Bathford, there was
a pre-1850 headstone, and there was one decorative name plate (although without

an inscription). There was also the existence of two separate registers of coffin hardware: some, being copper alloy, were "the best sort but plain" while others, being the cheaper iron, were simply "plain" suggesting a wealth-based differential (Archenfield Archaeology 2004:37, 41). Those buried in Bromyard represent a comparatively healthy group, despite higher incidence of trauma, arthritis, and caries and cavities compared to Kingston-upon-Thames; the latter two maladies may relate to the older ages in the Bromyard skeletons and the smaller sample (Archenfield Archaeology 2004:52).

Quaker "Rules" and Practices in Context

To be clear, I do not question the work or conclusions of any of these authors, but it seems that the archaeology of Quakerism is nonetheless in need of clarification. If Quaker practice varied so greatly, and Quakerism seems to have been so many things to so many people, how are we justified in referring to it as a unitary movement? Despite this variety in Quaker practice, Frederick Tolles, a noted Quaker historian, was able to write:

> If George Fox's greatest achievement was "the knitting together
> of Friends into a great religious society" [quoting Braithwaite,
> another well-known Quaker historian], then the consumma-
> tion of that achievement was the successful extension of the
> society across the Atlantic, making Friends wherever they found
> themselves—in Antigua, Jamaica, New Jersey, Maryland, Rhode
> Island, in London, Bristol, Yorkshire, Ireland, Holland—feel that
> they were all members of the same society [Tolles 1960:13].

So we have a contradiction: that unifying social identities, such as the Quaker religion, are created in daily practice (Chenoweth 2009), yet these practices vary locally. For Quakers, despite the very explicit nature of the general ideals that unite them, archaeology suggests that actual practices vary quite a bit. Yet historians argue with good reason that the group was extraordinarily unified. Quakers certainly considered themselves to be fundamentally united, and this belief certainly motivated their actions.

Fundamentally, Quakerism is rooted in an individual relationship with the divine, and as such entails a strong element of individual conscience. For Friends, religious decisions—such as how a guiding principle is applied in a particular real-life situation—were not to be handed down from a hierarchical structure and followed mechanically but were reserved for the small worship group and, ultimately, the individual (Philadelphia Yearly Meeting 1997:i, 175). That is, the practices associated with Quakerism were the results of a series of processes of deliberation, which occurred in a local setting. Historians have correctly argued that Quaker meetings held

enormous influence over their members' daily lives (Walvin 1997). I do not mean to
suggest the opposite, but it is important to remember that this influence was brought
to bear locally—by one's peers in each village, town, and Meeting—and was not a
universal, agreed-upon force in Quaker life.

Since the individuals, times, and places of each of these "rulemaking" processes vary so will the rules that result. We are speaking, now, not of a unitary entity
called "Quakerism," moving through time encapsulating people and declaring them
inside or outside a group, but of how the very defining traits of the social group are
constantly being redrawn by the active individuals who compose it. We are speaking
of the *agency* of these individuals or of these groups in articulating the practices that
define Quakerism. The practices create the group, rather than the group handing
down "rules" for daily practice.

This lends itself to a different view of identities like Quakerism as not being
a thing to be held or a box into which a person may be placed. This "pigeonhole" view
has been widely critiqued in archaeology over recent years (Meskell 2001; for more
discussion of recent theoretical conceptions of "identity" and the process of identification, see, for example, Chenoweth 2009; Voss 2006; Meskell and Preucel 2004;
Clark and Wilkie 2006; Wilkie and Hayes 2006; contributions to Conlin Casella
and Fowler 2004). Rather, "identity" can best be seen in practice as an active process:
that of identifying with or finding common ties with, and coming together to create
a group with, others.

This more fluid picture of identity may make the prospect of archaeological
analysis of social identities seem bleak. Quite the contrary, I believe that understanding the fluid nature of identity traits offers us a better window into social life than the
static conceptions we are working to move past. The non-hierarchical and explicitly
practice-based nature of Quakerism makes it an excellent group to explore this process. The material nature of many Quaker tenets suggests that archaeology is well
suited to conduct this exploration and provide insights into the often unconscious
habits of daily life, which are recorded nowhere else and yet which contribute to the
shape of social life so fundamentally.

A Changing Relationship of "Difference"

Traits do not come to be associated with social identity groups randomly but stem
from specific priorities and needs (Chenoweth 2009). In order to interpret practices
or objects as signs of or associated with certain groups, they must be seen in the
context of a matrix of relations both inside and outside of the group, where material
culture is one element of a complex dialogue. For instance, a group like the Quakers
wishing to set themselves apart and encourage group identity would not simply seek
to mark their "difference" but difference in a particular way.

Quakers saw their society as different from the majority of British and
American culture in that they dispensed with what they saw as vain and superstitious

religious practices that took the place of and interfered with true religiosity. Many of the traits that came to be associated with Quakerism, and that define Quakerism in the minds of both members and non-members (including modern archaeologists) are those which served to highlight this particular kind of difference. But neither among Quakers nor among their British and American counterparts were ideas of what was "vain" and what was "truly religious" static or universal. In the constantly changing relations of Quakers and non-Quakers, different material signs would take on and lose the ability to create and communicate the kind of difference that brought the group into being.

Quaker practices show an underlying unity of purpose, but since they are defined and redefined continually in response to the larger society in which Quakers live, they change through time and space—sometimes radically. Understanding of what it meant to be Quaker in seventeenth-century London or nineteenth-century Virginia, therefore, requires careful consideration of the context of each of these societies. This suggests that the variations noted in previous archaeology on Quakerism may not indicate a fragmented or inconsistent group. The context of social life affected the way Quakers signaled their Quakerness. Indeed, the context of life in the British Atlantic World actually helped determine what it meant to be Quaker.

The Social Context of Quaker Material Culture

If this set of relations within groups and between groups and outsiders plays such an important part in how a social group is created, maintained, and changed over time, it is worth discussing in a more detailed way the social context in which Quaker material culture was given meaning. This discussion is not, of course, meant to be exhaustive of the issues which have mattered to Quakers and affected their choices during the last 350 years, but it is meant to touch on several of the important factors which may be at play. As, at present, historians have done most of the work of considering this context; their works inform the balance of this discussion.

PUBLIC PERCEPTIONS OF QUAKERS

The 1797 edition of the *Discipline*, a book published by several Quaker "Yearly" Meetings on how to live a good, Quakerly life, contains a description of the procedure for "disownment"—the removal of a member from a Meeting and the greatest punishment Friends had for each other. Disownment may be considered for any member "given to . . . disorderly and indecent practices as shall occasion public Scandal" specifically as a means to "end that Scandal" if no other means—the member's confession and restitution—is available (Philadelphia Yearly Meeting 1797:34). However, "if the offence committed be only against the Church, and not of public scandal, in that case an acknowledgement and condemnation by the Party, under Hand [i.e. written], and the same entered on the Monthly Meeting Book, is sufficient" (Philadelphia Yearly Meeting 1797:35). This description makes it clear that one concern when a person's offenses are being judged is the damage done to the entire community's public image.

Historian Jack Marietta describes how, in addition to compensating any victims of a transgression, erring Friends had to put their sins in writing, have this writing approved by the Meeting, and then attend while it was read out publically to the entire congregation (Marietta 1984:7–8). This public declaration of transgression had to include a statement that "the evil action was not in accordance with Friends' principles" (Vann 1969:138). But this was only the start of the penitent's ordeal for the "Yearly Meeting ordered that the 'condemnation be published . . . in such a manner that it may reach as far and become as publick as the offense hath been'" (Marietta 1984:9). Marietta goes on to describe how this may have included posting on the meetinghouse door or in the public marketplace, communicating the paper to a specific group which had been wronged, and even—in extraordinary cases—having the condemnation printed and distributed as far away as New York, London, Barbados, and Antigua. Importantly, the reconciliation of a contrite Friend with the meeting was made public "not intend[ing] to humble the offender; [the publications] were rather designed to show that the evil deed was not in harmony with Friends' principles" (Vann 1969:138).

What is interesting about the discussion of disownment in the 1797 *Discipline* and the examples cited by historians Vann and Marietta is that they focus on external appearances to the *non-Quaker* public as a cause for concern over and above the actual damage done in the transgression. More public restitution was required of more public crimes, and correction was not primarily a religious or personal matter of atonement but something for public knowledge.

Quakers had a more than usual cause for concern about public disapproval. During the first four decades of the Quaker movement, from when George Fox began to preach in 1647 to the "Act of Toleration" in 1689, Quakers were subject to charges of heresy in their rejection of the established church and treason because of the relationship of the Church of England with the Crown. This resulted in frequent cases of what is often euphemistically referred to as "rough handling" by George Fox in his journal:

> And when they had led me to common moss [town green], and
> a multitude of people following, the constables took me and
> gave me a wisk over the shoulders with their willow rods and so
> thrust me amongst the rude multitude which then fell upon me
> with their hedge stakes and clubs and staves and beat me as hard
> as ever they could strike on my head and arms and shoulders,
> and it was a great while before they beat me down, mazed me,
> and at last I fell down upon the wet common [Fox 1952:127].

Such rough handling was not reserved for the leader of the movement; many of his followers were similarly attacked. Many spent time in prison, and as noted above, up to 400 Quakers may have died for their faith during the seventeenth century.

Magistrates and officials who disapproved of the troublemaking of early Quaker ministers could throw them into prison indefinitely, and, as noted in the preceding quote, Quaker preachers were often opposed by mobs of the general public. However, due to the nature of the Early Modern English legal system (see Herrup 1987), enforcement of laws against Quakers was very much a matter for the public, and there was often room to avoid these extreme results if enough people were sympathetic. In effect, good public relations could allow Quakers to continue to practice most aspects of their religion, even if they were at odds with the law.

What Vann refers to as the "constant emphasis on preserving the good name of Quakerism" was also a result of the tenuous nature of legal toleration, once begun at the end of the seventeen century (Vann 1969:140–1). Acts such as the Toleration Act and Affirmation Act allowed a more peaceful coexistence with "world's people," but the laws that established these exceptions explicitly required periodic renewal, and such renewal was conditional on Friends "behaving as responsible subjects" of the king (Frost 2002:25). This judgment would obviously be made of the group as whole, not individual members. Therefore, even long after active persecution of Friends ended, the public perception of Quakers was directly tied to their safety and their ability to continue to act within their consciences. While it is debatable how much of this danger still applied to Philadelphia Quakers a century after legal recognition of Quaker dissent, the above-noted concern with public image in the 1797 Philadelphia Meeting's *Discipline* implies that care was still being taken. While Philadelphia was founded as a Quaker colony, Quakers had withdrawn from political power by the middle of the eighteenth century and their need to maintain good relations with the rest of Philadelphian society is a matter for further consideration.

This concern with public relations had wide ranging implications for Quaker actions and priorities. Some have suggested that it was due to the uneasiness of this peace with "world's people" that Quaker Meetings exercised a great deal of oversight on their members. Walvin writes (1997:78–9) that Quakers acted as auditors for each other's businesses, explaining and revealing all aspects of their business history upon demand of their Meeting. Since this fact was public knowledge, it contributed greatly to the development of Quaker businesses, for "in eighteenth-century Britain—a society where the huckster, the rouge and the fraudster personified the world of commerce and trade—the Quaker stood out as the consumer's reliable, upright and trustworthy servant" (Walvin 1997:79).

Wealth, Waste, and the Family

For Friends, the family is central; it is the beginning and end of all Quaker values. "In the loving home and family, young and old learn about equality and its limitations,

simple forms of stewardship, integrity in its many guises, simplicity in all its complexities, and how hard but how satisfying it is to be peaceable" (Philadelphia Yearly
Meeting 1997:70). In other words, family was and is the central means for the
perpetuation of Quaker ideals. This was felt so strongly that marriage beyond the
faith—likely to produce children who were not brought up in the protection of a
Meeting—was strictly prohibited for the first two centuries of Quakerism and one of
the most frequent reasons for a member's disownment.

I have discussed Quaker attitudes towards alcohol in more detail elsewhere
(Chenoweth 2006), but it bears repeating that, although usually in favor of temperance, Quakers did not object to alcohol itself but to the sinful behavior and waste
resulting from its excessive use. One of the fundamental reasons for Quaker temperance was the danger "strong drink" was perceived to have for the family unit.
There was great fear that those who drink to excess "become like Ground fitted for
the Seeds of the greatest transgression" and that this ultimately leads to "the ruin of
themselves, their Wives and Families" (Philadelphia Yearly Meeting 1797:86). The
"ruin" that was feared was brought about through the usual mechanisms of violence
and infidelity—those acts of "greatest transgression" enabled by too much drink—
but also and centrally because alcohol was *wasteful*.

Waste was closely tied to alcohol because its production consumed large
quantities of grain better used to feed the hungry. Waste was considered a great sin
as it endangered a Quaker family's stability as well as being seen as sinful in itself.
Personal industry was godly, and William Penn himself wrote against religious mon-
asteries where monks engaged in "a lazy, rusty, unprofitable Self-Denial, burdensome
to others to feed their Idleness" (quoted in Walvin 1997:73). It was far better to be
productive and become wealthy (so long as wealth itself was not the goal) than to be
lazy—whether attributed to godliness or not—and consume resources yet contribute
nothing to society.

Although Quakers are often imagined as living monkish, Spartan lives
and rejecting the world's wealth, few ideas could be farther from the truth. As several studies, both historical (Walvin 1997) and archaeological (Cotter, Roberts, and
Parrington 1992; Brown 1987), have indicated, Quakers had no fear of financial success. On the contrary, the pursuit of wealth to some extent was required, for it was
only with a certain level of financial security that one could provide adequately for
one's family and thus perpetuate Quaker ideals. Quakerism is a religion of practice;
one cannot be a Quaker part of the time, but must always act within one's conscience. A home to shelter oneself and a full belly were seen as prerequisites to such
action as well. It is within this frame that Quaker material success must be viewed.
Ideally, money was pursued not as an end in itself but as a means of securing the stability of the family and so its ability to practice Quaker values and perpetuate them
in the next generation. Quaker pursuit of wealth was not supposed to be a matter of
amassing fortunes (although Quaker fortunes were certainly made) but of stability
and security; of course, the greater the wealth, the more stable the family's position,
and the more free a member would be to practice a Quakerly life.

The spending of money itself was therefore not considered to be a problem as long as it was not excessive, and "excessive" was seen to be very much a relative term. Spending more than one was able while still providing the important things in life would be excessive, as would living "of" the world and focusing too much on material things, no matter how much or little one possessed. Thus, "a family who showed up regularly for Meeting, contributed funds, and sent their children to Quaker school might receive more leeway even though their house appeared a little grand, particularly if the family could afford it. But woe be to them if after such indulgence the father got into financial difficulties" (Frost 2002:27).

Quaker Membership and Exclusivity

Anthropologists of all stripes have cited a generic need to form or strengthen social groups—often termed "solidarity"—as the reason behind peoples' actions in many contexts. But the simple act of drawing a line between those who saw themselves as being or were seen to be members of the Quaker religion and those who were not has proven difficult. If archaeologists are to consider the influence of Quakerism on their sites, including the many Quaker-related sites across the Delaware Valley, understanding the complexities of how membership in the Religious Society of Friends was defined is vital.

The organizational structure which arose for Quakerism plays an obvious role in the issue of how the community separated itself from the rest of society. In the 1670s, George Fox and other early Quakers organized their followers into a hierarchical structure of Meetings, not to hand down policy but to coordinate efforts. The principle work of Quakerism was still seen as individual and local, but local "Meetings for Worship" sent representatives to "Monthly Meetings," and these in turn to "Quarterly" and to "Yearly Meetings." Such a system in a religion which sets lack of hierarchy as an explicit goal is surprising, but it had several causes.

For one, the Church of England was so tied into daily life that removal from it posed many unexpected problems for Quakers. For instance, inheritance was confirmed by birth and marriage records kept by the parish, which also distributed poor relief to those in need. These roles would have to be taken up by the Quaker Meeting structure for members to continue to function in society. These efforts, directly or indirectly, have a number of implications for the question of who was a Quaker. Meeting records are an obvious way to identify those who are seen as members by each local community. However, turning to membership lists does not settle the issue as simply as one might hope. Membership was not an issue to the earliest Friends, nor did they maintain a self-image as a separate coherent body. "They were animated instead by the conviction that the direct operations of the Spirit of God [was] to supersede all existing religious institutions" in the near future (Vann 1969:123). Membership was irrelevant, since everyone would soon be reached by the Light and become like them. Everyone would soon be Quaker so there was no need to precisely define who was Quaker now.

Quakerism, of course, was not static, and the millennial fervor of the 1650s and 1660s faded in time. Eventually, Quakers themselves ran up against this very issue of who "belonged" and who did not, for instance in the question of poor relief. George Fox and Robert Barclay, two principle founders of the movement, explicitly argued that caring for the poor, elderly, and orphaned members was a necessity, and this was part of the justification for the creation of the membership structure of Monthly, Quarterly, and Yearly Meetings (Vann 1969:143). But the question of who should receive this relief hinged on who was actually a member of what meeting, for while "we were taught to do good unto all," Quakers' focus in charity should be "especially unto the household of faith [i.e. Quakers]" (Fox 1952:373).

Even so, Vann argues against a formalized notion of membership in seventeenth- and early-eighteenth-century Quakerism. Though determinations of membership had to be made when poor people with tenuous associations made requests, tacit, not explicit, signs were consulted for a determination. Membership needed definition only in particular cases, such as poor relief, and therefore occurred only in those cases and did so on an *ad hoc* basis (Vann 1969:148–150).

One final warning that should be made is that even those records which were kept by seventeenth- and eighteenth-century meetings were inconsistently maintained, occasionally omitting up to half the very events they were intended to record (Walvin 1997: 46; Vann 1969:160–1), such as births, marriages, and burials. One strategy that has been used in archaeological studies (Brown 1987; Chenoweth 2006) is to consider these records in a more qualitative light, assessing, for instance, the ways and number of times a specific person appears in Meeting minutes being given a task for the Meeting, a mark of respect but also of responsibility to the Quaker community. Those most closely tied to the Meeting would receive the most important and regular assignments while those on the fringes might be mentioned more often as needing support or "correction."

Quaker Membership and Practice

Quakerism is a faith of practice (Davies 2000: 2–3; Nuttall 1952: xxii). For members, "their faith was not put on hold the moment they left the meetinghouse, but entailed a consistent style of personal and social behavior" (Walvin 1997: 56). Vann argues that Quakers distinguished between "convincement" and "conversion" to Quakerism; many people attended meetings and felt "intellectual assent" with Quaker ideology, but true members had to undergo a conversion. This, too, was internally felt but became expressed by the "outward signs" or "public testimonies" for which Quakers are known. Quoting Theodor Sippell, Vann states that "Quakerism is above all a testimony; it is a permanently-declared appeal to the consciences of all men" (Vann 1969:188). Thus, the practices of Quakerism became a means of dividing Friend from non-Friend in a way as important as and more tangible than "belief."

These testimonies—specific directives on dress, style, speech, etc.—received increasing attention over the eighteenth century. In fact, Vann goes so far as to suggest that they came to stem not from internal holiness but became routinized (Vann 1969:189). "Conversion to Quakerism, at least insofar as it had to be judged by 'taking up a public testimony,' thus entailed the necessity of buying a new set of clothes; the pathway to heaven commenced in a tailor's shop" (Vann 1969:194). Whatever their consistency (a theological or psychological question) and practical uniformity (a more archaeological one), it is certainly true that the "public testimonies" of Quakerism contributed to the separation of Quakers from the balance of society.

Frost charts the development of these testimonies from the earliest days of Quakerism (when persecution was at its height), where he finds that they were inconsistently practiced (Frost 2002). This is consistent with the above-noted lack of concern for the boundaries of Quaker identity during the early years when the messianic fervor was most pronounced. Frost suggests that, while based on readings of the Bible, the particular expressions of Friends' faith were more influenced by economic and social impulses, such as reactions to the excesses of Restoration court life or the wealth gap between rich and poor or even personal life histories (Frost 2002:18–22). This picture of Quakerism is still "in the world" even in its reactions to the world.

It was only towards the end of the seventeenth century that these testimonies began to be codified, to receive disciplinary actions when violated, and to become more specific. Frost suggests that this emphasis on "the plain style," as this collection of external "testimonies" came to be known, stemmed from the increasing wealth of Friends, and also from an inward-looking tendency which followed acceptance and the end of persecutions: "No longer striving to reshape an entire society, Friends concentrated on improving themselves" (Frost 2002:25). Thus efforts to "create a Quaker culture," to divide Friend and non-Friend, came, both in motivation and in the form they took, from particular religious foundations.

Such public proclamations of difference, of course, cannot take place without ripple-effects. When in the mid-nineteenth century the group debated dispensing with the practices of endogamy and some of the more obvious testimonies of dress and speech, it was acknowledged on both sides that these habits served as a barrier between Quakers and wider society (Isichei 1967:169–170). But the question arose as to whether this continued to represent a good thing; those who lobbied for liberalization suggested that this barrier prevented "the ingress not of worldly principles but of potential converts" (Isichei 1967:170–171). This interesting debate suggests a rift among Quakers between those who saw the testimonies as founded in religious principles versus those who saw them simply as a practical tactic for the survival of the group, which could be dispensed with if the group was threatened. This tension in the understanding of Quaker practices—as religious ideals made manifest versus practical statements about identity—is visible even in my own discussion earlier in this chapter and probably will not be settled easily.

Quaker Social Context and Archaeology

In the particular context of the archaeology of the Delaware Valley, the issues and debates that confronted Quakers in their daily lives may have resulted in various practices and differing negotiations on the part of individuals. For instance, how Quakers viewed wealth, waste, and expense has obvious repercussions for purchased and discarded material culture. In addition, the issue of Quaker presence on a site is intimately tied up with that of what it meant to be a Quaker and who was accorded membership or felt themselves to be bound to the performance of "testimonies." Of course, what it meant to be a Quaker was contested as much by those in the past as by scholars in the present. Procedures for "disownment" and distancing the group from certain peoples' actions suggest that even while membership was complex and often unclear, even to Quakers, it was a vitally important issue. Ultimately, understanding the reasons behind the actions of Quakers—the habits, the separation of the group from the rest of society, and the changing religious perspectives—is vital to understanding any material traces they might have left.

A final important note is that, as discussed above, these various influences on Quaker life will be realized differently in different contexts because of the nature of Quaker "rules," which I have seen as practices taken in a local context. Like all social identities, "Quakerism" is created, changed, and maintained through the actions of individual agents, who each alter that identity as they perform it. This means that we cannot move from these observations to "checklists" of traits which Quaker sites can be expected to exhibit. Rather, we must interpret our findings in the context of the Quaker community's priorities and the conflicts and overlaps they had with broader British and American culture.

Conclusions and Future Directions

This chapter has reviewed the conclusions drawn by archaeologists who have considered what it meant to be Quaker in the past, and asked how it is that they have come to such varying answers. I have tried to suggest why such different results may have been met by previous studies attempting to characterize Quakerism archaeologically. To reiterate, Quakerism's practices are not, in fact, "rules" but various manifestations in daily practice of a unifying set of ideals. Quaker "rules" of practice are seen by members as being not prescriptive items in a checklist but the outward signs of inward states, and we can see these practices as being based on individual agents' interpretations of the general ideals which serve as a foundation to the religion. But these interpretations result from a corporate and often individual process of deliberation which occurs in a particular cultural, temporal, and geographic context.

Quakers rejected many of the habits and cultural patterns of contemporary society, but this was not merely an amoeba-like response—for as the archaeological studies of the Mott and Bates sites and the Kingston-upon-Thames excavations have shown especially clearly, Quakers did participate in trends and styles of their day. As the review of historians' takes on Quakers' social context shows, Quaker values and priorities were tied into the rest of the British and American society in which most of them lived in complex and deep ways. Quakers carefully negotiated their cultural contexts to hold themselves apart in certain important ways while continually working to remain integrated in others and find the best application of their ideals to the difficult real-life situations that they encountered.

Quaker "testimonies," financial practices, Meeting structure, public relations, and the other aspects discussed here are clearly tied together with the reactions of non-Friends in a web of causes and effects. All of these ultimately come under the umbrella of religious ideology that begins to define, but does not dictate, that "something visible, tangible, and uniquely discernible that makes 'Quaker-*liness*'" (Lapsansky 2002:6, emphasis in original) This quality was not just something "different" from non-Quakers, but different in particular ways. A consideration of the social priorities and difficulties of being a Quaker in the past has suggested some of those ways that may be important in the consideration of other Quaker-related archaeological sites.

Acknowledgments

I would like to thank Rich Veit and David Orr both for organizing the Society for Historical Archaeology conference session in Albuquerque, New Mexico, in which I presented a paper that forms the basis for some of this chapter, and for putting together the volume itself. Some of the ideas presented here have been discussed with and greatly informed by Ethan Shagan, Laurie Wilkie, Rosemary Joyce, and Christine Hastorf, and parts of the paper are based on research conducted for my master's thesis at the University of Pennsylvania, which was supervised and greatly aided by Robert L. Schuyler and Robert Preucel. I thank all of these people for their discussions and comments. Of course, any errors which remain are entirely my own.

References Cited

Archenfield Archaeology
2004   Tanyard and Burial Ground Report. Archenfield Archaeology, Hereford, United Kingdom.

Bashford, Louise, and Tony Pollard
1998   "In the Burying Place": The Excavation of a Quaker Burial Ground. In *Grave Concerns: Death and Burial in England 1700 to 1850*, edited by M. Cox, pp. 154–166. Council for British Archaeology, York.

Bashford, Louise, and Lucy Sibun
2007   Excavations at the Quaker Burial Ground, Kingston-upon-Thames, London. *Post-Medieval Archaeology* 41(1):100–154.

Bromberg, Francine W., and Steven J. Shephard
2006. The Quaker Burying Ground in Alexandria, Virginia: A Study of the Burial Practices of the Religious Society of Friends. *Historical Archaeology* 40(1):57–88.

Bromberg, Francine W., Steven J. Shephard, Barbara H. Magid, Pamela J. Cressey, TimothyDennee, and Bernard K. Means
2000 *"To Find Rest From All Trouble"*: The Archaeology of the Quaker Burying Ground, Alexandria, Virginia. Alexandria Archaeology, Alexandria, Virginia.

Brown, Marley R., III
1987 "Among Weighty Friends": The Archaeology and Social History of the Jacob Mott Family, Portsmouth, Rhode Island, 1640–1800. Ph.D. dissertation, Department of Anthropology, Brown University, Providence, Rhode Island.

Chenoweth, John M.
2006 "What'll Thou Have": Quakers and the Characterization of Tavern Sites in Colonial Philadelphia. *Northeast Historical Archaeology* 35:75–90.

2009 Social Identity, Material Culture, and the Archaeology of Religion: Quaker Practices in Context. *Journal of Social Archaeology* 9 (3):319–340.

Clark, Bonnie J., and Laurie Wilkie
2006 The Prism of Self: Gender and Personhood. In *Handbook of Gender in Archaeology*, edited by S. M. Nelson, pp. 333–364. Altamira, New York.

Conlin Casella, Eleanor, and Chris Fowler (editors)
2004 *The Archaeology of Plural and Changing Identities: Beyond Identification*. Springer, New York.

Cotter, John, Daniel G. Roberts, and Michael Parrington
1992 *The Buried Past: An Archaeological History of Philadelphia*. University of Pennsylvania Press, Philadelphia.

Davies, Adrian
2000 *The Quakers in English Society, 1655–1725*. Clarendon Press, Oxford.

Fox, George
1952 *The Journal of George Fox*, edited by J. L. Nickalls. Cambridge University Press, Cambridge, United Kingdom.

Frost, J. William
2002 From Plainness to Simplicity: Changing Quaker Ideals for Material Culture. In *Quaker Aesthetics: Reflections on a Quaker Ethic in American Design and Consumption*, edited by E. J. Lapsansky and A. A. Verplanck, pp. 16–40. University of Pennsylvania Press, Philadelphia.

Gray, Anna L.
1989 Be Ye Friend or Foe?: An Analysis of Two Eighteenth Century North Carolina Sites. M.A. thesis, Department of Anthropology, The College of William and Mary, Williamsburg, Virginia.
1997 Return to the Port of Brunswick: An Analysis of Two Eighteenth-Century North Carolina Sites. *North Carolina Archaeology* 46:69–83.

Herrup, Cynthia B.
1987 *The Common Peace: Participation and the Criminal Law in Seventeenth-Century England*. Cambridge University Press, Cambridge, United Kingdom.

Isichei, Elizabeth
1967 From Sect to Denomination among English Quakers. In *Patterns of Sectarianism: Organisation and Ideology in Social and Religious Movements*, edited by B. R. Wilson, pp. 161–181. Heinemann, London.

Kirk, Lucy
1998 The Excavation of a Quaker Burial Ground, 84 London Road, Kingston upon Thames. *London Archaeologist* 8(11):298–303.

Lapsansky, Emma Jones
2002 Past Plainness to Present Simplicity: A Search for Quaker Identity. In *Quaker Aesthetics: Reflections on a Quaker Ethic in American Design and Consumption*, edited by E. J. Lapsansky and A. A. Verplanck, pp. 1–15. University of Pennsylvania Press, Philadelphia.

Marietta, Jack D.
1984 *The Reformation of American Quakerism, 1748–1783*. University of Pennsylvania Press, Philadelphia.

McCarthy, John P.
1999 Eighteenth-Century Quaker Lifestyles: Philadelphia's Merchant Elite at the Front and Dock Streets Site. *Journal of Middle Atlantic Archaeology* 15:137–155.

Meskell, Lynn
2001 Archaeologies of Identity. In *Archaeological Theory Today*, edited by I. Hodder, pp. 187–213. Polity Press, Cambridge, United Kingdom.

Meskell, Lynn, and Robert W. Preucel
2004 Identities. In *A Companion to Social Archaeology*, edited by L. Meskell and R. W. Preucel, pp. 121–141. Blackwell, Malden, Massachusetts.

Nuttall, Geoffrey F.
1952 Introduction: George Fox and his Journal. In *The Journal of George Fox*, edited by J. L. Nickalls,, pp. xix-xlviii. Cambridge University Press, Cambridge, United Kingdom.

Penn, William.
1696   *Primitive Christianity Revived in the Faith and Practice of the People Called Quakers*. T. Sowle, London.
Philadelphia Yearly Meeting
1797   *Rules of Discipline and Christian Advices*. Samuel Sansom, Jr., Philadelphia.
1997   *Faith and Practice*. Philadelphia Yearly Meeting, Philadelphia.
Samford, Patricia M., and Marley R. Brown, III
1990   *The Bates Site: Investigation of a Quaker Merchant*. Colonial Williamsburg Foundation, Williamsburg, Virginia.
Silliman, Stephen
2009   Change and Continuity, Practice and Memory: Native American Persistence in Colonial New England. *American Antiquity* 74 (2):211–230.
Start, Helen, and Lucy Kirk
1998   "The Bodies of Friends": The Osteological Analysis of a Quaker Burial Ground. In *Grave Concerns: Death and Burial in England 1700 to 1850*, edited by M. Cox, pp. 167–177. Council for British Archaeology, York.
Stock, Gwynne
1998a   The 18th and Early 19th Century Quaker Burial Ground at Bathford, Bath and North-East Somerset. In *Grave Concerns: Death and Burial in England 1700 to 1850*, edited by M. Cox, pp. 129–143. Council for British Archaeology, York.
1998b   Quaker Burial: Doctrine and Practice. In *Grave Concerns: Death and Burial in England 1700 to 1850*, edited by M. Cox, pp. 144–153. Council for British Archaeology, York.
Tolles, Frederick B.
1960   *Quakers and the Atlantic Culture*. MacMillan, New York.
Vann, Richard T.
1969   *The Social Development of English Quakerism, 1655–1755*. Harvard University Press, Cambridge, Massachusetts.
Voss, Barbara L.
2006   Sexuality in Archaeology. In *Handbook of Gender in Archaeology*, edited by S. M. Nelson, pp. 365–400. Altamira, Walnut Creek, California.
Walvin, James
1997   *The Quakers: Money and Morals*. John Murry, London.
White, John R.
1985   Unearthing Quakertown. *Archaeology* 38(1):26–31.
Wilkie, Laurie, and Katherine Howlett Hayes
2006   Engendered and Feminist Archaeologies of the Recent and Documented Pasts. *Journal of Archaeological Research* 14:243–264.

9

THE BAKER AND THE QUAKER: ONGOING RESEARCH FROM THE NATIONAL CONSTITUTION CENTER SITE

WILLIAM HOFFMAN AND DEBORAH MILLER

Introduction

Since its creation, Independence National Historical Park has served as a patriotic bastion, a place where connections to our national origin can be experienced and explored. These sentiments are especially focused in the three blocks north of Independence Square where the potent symbols of Independence Hall and the Liberty Bell are in prominent view. It is from this vantage point that a present-day visitor can enjoy a view stretching along the three open city blocks of Independence Mall—a green void in the midst of the urban bustle of center city Philadelphia.

The mall was born out of the movement to create a safe and dignified setting for the shrine of Independence Hall. Efforts to preserve and restore the historic character of the area gathered momentum throughout the late nineteenth and early twentieth centuries as the once illustrious nature of the neighborhood was swept westward with the suburban expansion of the city. Left in the wake of this urban flight was a rundown, semi-industrialized area that, in the eyes of some contemporary civic leaders, threatened the once celebrated neighborhood that housed the founding of our nation.

This restoration movement culminated in a coordinated plan between the state and federal government to create a national park. Conceived in the postwar enthusiasm for urban renewal, the goal was to restore the area to its original colonial character as a remedy to the urban malaise. In a grand attempt to wipe the slate clean, Independence Mall was carved out of the surrounding urban fabric through the demolition of multiple city blocks between 1952 and 1959. This literal clearing of almost 15 acres and 143 standing buildings was intended to translate figuratively into a clearing of the air; to create a contemplative arena that would distill and convey the story of the founding of the nation (Gibson et al. 1994:3).

Although the founding mission of Independence National Historical Park was to interpret and "create a landscape that would accurately reflect the nation's earliest days in Philadelphia," the overall design of Independence Mall is very much an artifact of the mid-twentieth century (Cotter et al. 1992:77). More recent plans to modernize the landscape inadvertently broke the façade of Independence Mall and led to the discovery of the archaeological remains of a once thriving neighborhood.

Refurbishment of the Independence Mall landscape throughout the 1990s included construction of the Liberty Bell Center, the Independence Visitor's Center, and the National Constitution Center, all of which required large-scale archaeological investigations under section 106 of the National Historic Preservation Act (Yamin 2004; Yamin 2007).

These updates to Independence Mall bear a certain irony, palpable to the many archaeologists involved, as they led to the large-scale study of an area whose history was overlooked when the park was originally created (Yamin 2007:16). The archaeological investigations on Independence Mall are a study of everyday life in eighteenth- and nineteenth-century Philadelphia that provide a broader context for understanding this major city before and after the American Revolution.

This chapter considers the archaeological investigations at the site of the National Constitution Center (NCC), the largest excavation of the Independence Mall redevelopment project. Archaeologists from the firm of Kise, Straw and Kolodner conducted investigations within the building's footprint, which encompassed approximately three quarters of a city block and included 115 individual house lots, 250 features (including 25 excavated shaft features), and over 3,375 square feet of preserved historic ground surface from the backyard areas of these houses. Approximately one million artifacts were recovered from the excavation.

The project nearly faltered following the completion of fieldwork in 2003, but has been; revived under a renewed partnership between the National Park Service and the National Constitution Center. (Levin et al. 2009; Yamin 2008). Laboratory work is taking place in a unique National Park Service facility that not only functions to process, catalog, and study the artifact collection, but it also serves as an interpretive attraction that invites the public into the process. Through the efforts of laboratory staff, volunteers, students, contractors, and other partners, this work-in-progress is providing a glimpse into the everyday, and sometimes profound, lives of a diverse group of Philadelphians during the late colonial and early national periods. The NCC block is the archaeological study on the scale of an entire neighborhood and offers, in what has become the mantra of the project, a look into the lesser-recognized lives of "we the people." Although much work still lies ahead, this chapter highlights preliminary findings from two features currently under study as examples of the ongoing investigation of this Philadelphia neighborhood.

Block History

For much of the early eighteenth century, the NCC site was undeveloped land situated on the western outskirts of Philadelphia. Bounded by Fifth and Sixth and Arch and Race streets in the formal city grid, the block was initially divided into several parcels primarily held by absentee land owners in the late seventeenth and early eighteenth centuries. By the middle of the eighteenth century, the northern half of the block, was owned by the wealthy and well-connected Quaker George Emlen, who passed the tract to his daughter, Sarah Emlen Cresson. Sarah's children, Caleb and Joshua Cresson, inherited the tract in 1752.

Caleb and Joshua Cresson began systematically subdividing their land in the 1760s, advertising available lots for sale or ground rent in the *Pennsylvania Gazette*. They also facilitated the orderly development of the block by laying out a grid of equally spaced interior alleys. Their speculation paid off as the undeveloped lots, once referred to as "old pasture" in the original deeds, were completely built up by the 1790s. This surge of urban development was fueled by waves of European immigrants and the post-Revolution establishment of Philadelphia as the temporary capital of the United States. By the close of the eighteenth century, there was little open space remaining on the block.

The block is a prime example of how Philadelphia's urban spaces evolved into modern cityscapes during the early national period. Though elements of the old colonial walking city remained, with a mix of social classes and ethnic groups living and working in close proximity, the NCC site illustrates increasing socioeconomic segregation associated with the rise of the middle class (Upton 2008:22). A general pattern emerges of wealthier homeowners residing along the major streets while lower income rentals crowded the interior alleys and courts of the block. The majority of residents fell within the lower margins of the taxpaying population while a small group of wealthier occupants, including Caleb Cresson, were among the top percentile of taxable citizens.

The NCC site is located in Philadelphia's South Mulberry Ward, one of the poorest neighborhoods in the city during the second half of the eighteenth century. The ward became increasingly poorer and more crowded in the nineteenth century as the population continued to grow at a greater rate than the available housing supply (Smith 1990:164). As a result, the NCC site was home to a generally more humble population than the better-off households of merchants, civil servants, and even presidents who lived just two blocks to the south.

Initial background research into tax records, census records, and city directories paints a picture of a diverse working population generally composed of the middling to lower sorts with occupations such as shoemakers, tailors, bakers, saddlers, blacksmiths, laborers, and whitewashers among others (Toogood 2004; Smith 1990:5). In addition, the block housed a number of residents in building-related occupations including carpenters, joiners, and bricklayers who found work in the housing boom of the early national period. The block was also home to a burgeoning free African community that included notable leaders in the Free African Society and the independent churches born from this organization including the African Episcopal Church of Saint Thomas.

The block was also affected by the increasing industrialization of the city throughout the nineteenth century. By the eve of the Civil War, the walking city had almost been entirely replaced by new spatial patterns of class segregation and land use (Blumin 1989:163). Commercial and industrial properties replaced the homes of the wealthy who had moved west of the old city core into new suburbs. By the late nineteenth century, the NCC site was home to a brass foundry, a shoe factory, and a bookbindery while pockets of residential housing clung to the interior alleys. The block remained in this declining state into the twentieth century, bringing us full circle to the eventual demolition and development of Independence Mall in the 1950s.

While the original design of Independence Mall looked back to the founding of the nation for clarity during uncertain social times, these archaeological investigations have unearthed the material remains of, what turn out to be, equally uncertain times. The NCC block was never a static place but rather a neighborhood reshaped by shifting residential and occupational patterns that ushered in a period of social uncertainty during the late eighteenth and early nineteenth centuries. This period saw the emergence of a new middle class operating under different rules as people strove to define their lives within these changing surroundings.

Much of the study of the emerging middle class emphasizes the concept of gentility. This is considered through the various ways people defined and embodied concepts of polite behavior, and to what purpose it served them (Blumin 1989; Bushman 1992; Upton 2008:86; Waldstreicher 1997).

The rank and status foundation of eighteenth-century society, adapted from the court culture of Britain, required a willingly deferential population and a clear social order. Wealthy Philadelphians had long used architecture, material goods, and ritualistic behavior, especially the art of tea drinking, as a means of "convincing others, and themselves, of their own gentility and status" (Sweeney 1994:10). However, as more middling and lower class citizens began to adopt refined modes of living, this traditional version of gentility began to falter. In a city increasingly filled with strangers, outward appearances mattered more while the once clear social markers of family privilege and land ownership began to matter less. Once a "fraternal handshake" utilized by the elite to exclude others, gentility was transformed into something transparent that was readily described, analyzed, promoted, defended, and available to almost anyone (Upton 2008:86, 87). This change created great anxiety for those concerned with preserving social equilibrium. For others, this new form of gentility stabilized their identity amid the social confusion of the early nineteenth century (Bushman 1992:404).

The experience of the emerging middle class is unique, particularly in the context of a cosmopolitan city at the center of the new republic. Considering the extent to which these influences played on daily life provides an entry point into the study of "we the people" and illustrates one of many possible avenues of research into the archeology of an entire neighborhood. This chapter further explores these concepts through preliminary discussion of artifact assemblages from two privy features (figure 9.1). The features are considered as brief studies for these varied interpretations of middle-class ideology. We begin with a baker named Godfrey Minnick whose late-eighteenth-century townhome, and its complimentary material contents, mimic an idea of gentility that existed prior to the American Revolution. We then move to the crowded tenements on Cresson's Alley, where working families in the early to mid-nineteenth century were participating in a different interpretation of polite living that resembles something more uniquely American.

GODFREY MINNICK'S HOUSEHOLD

Documentary evidence suggests that the artifacts from Feature 193 are from the household of Godfrey Minnick, a German Baker whose family occupied the lot at 53 N. 6th Street during the last fifteen years of the eighteenth century. Minnick first appears in a 1765 passport application for "Conrad Miinch, of Mechtersheimer, near Speyer, his wife and his brother Gottfried Miinch" (Elliott 1916:387). Later that year on August 24, the passenger manifest for the snow *Polly* recorded Godfrey and Conrad Minnick's arrival in Philadelphia (Strassburger 1934). Like the tens of thousands of Germans who immigrated before and after him, Minnick found a large German community in Philadelphia with support networks that "partially replicated the pattern of life in the German territories" (Roeber 1991:252). These transatlantic networks made Philadelphia the primary center of German life in America—a place where prosperity was certainly attainable for new immigrants (Roeber 1991:257).

Figure 9.1. Two privy features from the NCC site during excavation. *Left*: Feature 91 associated with a series of tenements along Cresson's Alley. *Right*: Feature 193 associated with the Godfrey Minnick household. Courtesy of Independence National Historical Park.

During the post-Revolutionary development boom of the NCC site, Minnick purchased a "stable and Lot of ground situated on the East Side of Sixth Street" from Samuel Lewis in 1784 (Philadelphia Registry of Deeds 1784). He appears to have set about improving the lot, and three years later he was taxed £375 for a "Dwelling and Bakehouse" (Toogood 2004:76). He continued to pay taxes for both structures until 1789 when the bake house was excluded from the tax record, and a "New Brick Building" was listed in its place (Philadelphia County Tax Ledger 1787:54–59). Additionally, the 1790 Federal Census records him residing with three males under 16, five males over 16 and two females (United States Bureau of the Census 1790).

Minnick insured a "nearly new" three-story brick house in 1791 (Philadelphia Contributionship 1791). The house contained a finished back parlor and front chamber as well as a small shop on the first floor. This new house with its specialized rooms was fitting for the owner of real estate along a developing street located a little over two blocks from the commercial center of Philadelphia. Chappell (1994:186) has noted that it was "increasingly important to Americans with available capital and social pretensions to have at least one room that was large and well finished." Unlike the crowded, multi-family tenements at the center of the block, Minnick enjoyed the luxuries of a single family home where he could separate the spheres of work and leisure and privately enjoy the trappings of his success. This illustrates a general trend in development along this section of Sixth Street during the last decades of the eighteenth century when there was an increase in property ownership by modest investors with enough income to purchase and develop these lots (Toogood 2004:80).

Minnick continued to expand his real estate holdings on the east side of Sixth Street following the construction of his house. His 1798 will specifies ownership of an adjacent "Lot on the East Side of Sixth Street adjoining to my present dwelling house and lot" (Philadelphia Register of Wills 1798). This property likely housed additional structures that either supported the baking operation or provided supplementary worker and/or tenant housing. Throughout the 1790s, Minnick's property was regularly assessed at a higher value than his immediate neighbors, showing the return in his real estate investments. By the time of his death, his property, dwellings, and household were valued at more than £1500, an impressive sum for a man whose occupation rarely allowed for upward mobility (Philadelphia County Tax Ledger 1798:88).

Minnick's widow, Frances, greatly benefitted from her husband's success thanks to his well crafted will. German Americans were encouraged to produce written wills that followed traditional patterns of property distribution at the time of the head of household's death. In Pennsylvania, intestacy customs were more in line with the English practice of primogeniture, which transferred the bulk of an estate to the eldest son (Roeber 1991:267). To protect themselves, Germans often named their wives executrix of the will, as Frances Minnick was, to ensure the "faithful German woman" received the generous provisions due her, if not outright control of the estate (Roeber 1991:267). Frances Minnick was granted all future rental profits as well as the estate for the duration of her life unless she remarried. In 1799, she moved to a new home at Ninth and Cherry Streets where she was taxed as a "gentlewoman" with an estate worth approximately £1,900 (Philadelphia County Tax Ledger 1799:92). The Minnick family retained the Sixth Street home as a rental property until at least the mid-nineteenth century. The last known reference to the property lists a daughter, Catharine, as owner in 1857 (Philadelphia Contributionship 1857).

Minnick's life is a glimpse into the role that he and other neighbors like him played in the development of American culture. Minnick was a successful immigrant artisan who, through hard work and a likely touch of luck, became a considerable property owner within 20 years of his arrival in America. Minnick's home, located on the two floors above his shop, contained a bevy of disposable goods that symbolized his success and genteel aspirations. His "Back Parlour . . . finished with breast closets, Mantles- Surface and Skirting Round" was a multi-purpose space furnished with a walnut dining table, mahogany card table, walnut tea table, and an assortment of Windsor chairs that could be used in either private or public settings (Philadelphia Contributionship 1791; Philadelphia Register of Wills 1798). He built a home through his own personal industry but furnished it with fine things that followed acceptable models of sophistication. The artifact assemblage from Feature 193, as well as his surviving probate, points to a stable family whose consumption of fashionable, albeit affordable, goods created a comfortable living environment that effectively balanced their polished exterior and frugal core. By consuming goods in such a manner, the household blurred the lines between the worldly and vernacular but managed to capture the essence of genteel culture set against a backdrop of republican virtue (Bushman 1992:xvi).

The archaeological record of the Minnick household captures the material spirit of the emerging middle class in post-Revolutionary Philadelphia. The Minnick privy contained a mixture of moderately expensive and affordable ceramics, mostly in common forms with a few specialized exceptions. The Minnicks purchased multiple sets of teaware, the benchmark of a genteel household, but mixed and matched more humble forms for their private table. Missing from the archaeological record are highly specialized tablewares such as soup tureens, sauceboats, and covered dishes necessary for fine dining and entertaining. Perhaps most noticeably, the lack of large quantities of Chinese Porcelain in the assemblage, the most expensive ware available to consumers, clearly identifies the Minnicks as a middling family who valued the symbolic meaning of beautiful things but exercised restraint in their personal display of such goods.

Archaeological investigations of the Minnick lot identified three privies in the rear yard. Feature 193 is a brick-lined privy 5.5 feet in diameter located at the southeast corner of the lot. The feature contained several feet of compact brick and stone rubble that was possibly pushed into the privy during the demolition of the house in 1958. Beneath this fill was 4 feet of intact deposits containing late-eighteenth-century artifacts. Almost four thousand ceramic artifacts were recovered, with more than two hundred reconstructed vessels. Mean ceramic dates for these deposits indicate a late 1780s–early 1790s occupation period for the site, dating it to the occupation of Godfrey Minnick. The majority of the refined ceramics are of English manufacture, but the assemblage also includes Chinese export porcelain, Faience, German Stoneware, and locally produced red earthenwares among others.

The highest quality ceramics from the Minnick privy include Chinese and English porcelains in both underglaze blue and enameled decoration. Teawares are a substantial component of the porcelain assemblage with 11 vessels. Of the teawares, two teacups and three saucers have been identified as English soft paste porcelain. Four of the five are matching sets with a "cell" pattern printed at the rim above a molded body. The third saucer, with a pair of printed quail, is likely from the pottery of Seth Pennington or Pennington & Part in Liverpool (Godden 2004:331).

The high number of soft paste teawares is unusual when compared to other period lots on the NCC block that contain mostly Chinese porcelain in the "Canton" or "Nanking" patterns. By the late eighteenth century, the cost of Chinese porcelain had fallen sharply as a result of direct trade between America and China, making it available to most consumers (Roth 1988:452). Godden (2004:49) suggests that, at least in England, porcelains of English manufacture were primarily marketed to the ever-growing middle class. Their similarity to Chinese porcelains, coupled with a marketable price, made them desirable to a larger group of consumers. Minnick's examples are also unique in that they have printed designs. Perhaps the Minnicks saw their printed English porcelains as exotic alternatives to the standard market porcelains.

The Minnick assemblage also contains refined English earthenwares, including a matching china glaze tea and coffee set in the "Chinese house" pattern (figure 9.2). A well-executed creamware punchbowl with a chinoiserie landscape, along with smaller individual painted punch bowls, or possibly waste bowls, are also present. Produced between circa 1775 and 1800, these moderately expensive wares were targeted at the middling classes in England and America with a growing disposable income and taste for finer tablewares (Roberts 2006:9). Clearly inspired by Chinese porcelain, these beautifully naïve wares acknowledged the West's ongoing love affair with all things Chinese and served as important tools in creating a polite and genteel environment (Miller and Hunter 2001:157).

In addition to the china glaze tea set, creamware teawares, including two teapots with enameled floral decorations, including the well known "blowsy rose" motif, were also recovered. These sets are less ornate than the china glaze wares, but they further illustrate the significance of tea-drinking as a signifier of gentility. These wares also extended to the Minnick children, whose miniature teawares served as teaching implements and fostered an early understanding of the importance of polite behavior (Roth 1988: 450).

In contrast to the numerous sets of teawares of varying ceramic types present in the Minnick assemblage, tablewares are chiefly represented by plain creamware. Royal pattern dinner plates make up the majority, but octagonal plates with

Figure 9.2. China glaze wares from Feature 193. Courtesy of Independence National Historical Park.

molded diamond rims and feather edged plates are also accounted for in the assemblage. Heavy use wear on the plates indicates daily use in the Minnick household, perhaps over a number of years. Their condition, along with the quantities of creamware teawares, suggests that less expensive wares were employed in private settings by the household.

One object of note, a pearlware quintile or finger vase with blue-painted floral decoration is a distinctive reminder of the upward mobility of the Minnick family as it is an object used purely for public display. The quintile's sole function was to beautify the environment and symbolize "repose, polish, and economically useless knowledge" (Bushman 1992:264). Use of items like the quintile, particularly in specialized spaces like a parlor, illustrates the intentional creation of refined spaces. These spaces separated leisure space from work space, a place where the family could socially perform, even if the family bake house and shop were just a few steps away.

Like the ceramics, the glass assemblage from the Minnick lot contains a rich and diverse group of late-eighteenth-century table forms. Tankards, tumblers, stemmed drinking glasses with straight, knopped, balustriod, and air twist stems, firing glasses, dessert glasses, and footed salts underscore the Minnick's desire to maintain a fashionable table. One notable glass artifact is a colorless tumbler with "Liberty" engraved across the face. Similar to the famous "No Stamp Act" creamware teapots of the 1760s, the "Liberty" tumbler is a bold statement against oppressive forces and an object that clearly displays political loyalties. Minnick's military affiliations, if any, are unknown, but his trade and personal ambition made him a likely supporter of the Revolutionary cause. Schultz (1995:266) argues that "Revolutionary era artisans . . . were heirs, with working people in general, to a tradition of popular thought and political opposition that predates the Revolution by at least half a century." This tradition, coupled with Minnick's flight from a turbulent Germany, likely made him sympathetic to the ideas of social and personal liberty that the Revolution espoused.

Like the enterprising English potters and glassmakers who supplied the American market with goods bearing anti-English sentiments, Minnick may also have seen the Revolution as an opportunity to improve his quality of life. Unlike cabinet makers, cobblers, and other artisans, Minnick produced an invaluable commodity—bread—needed by both the native and occupying forces in war torn Philadelphia. The prices of commodities, particularly food related goods, skyrocketed in Revolutionary Philadelphia, leaving small fortunes to be made by the providential few who supplied them (Schultz 1995:266). Perhaps Minnick's "Liberty" tumbler served as a reminder of his personal struggles as well as his successes.

Caleb Cresson's Tenements

Feature 91 is a privy located in the rear yard of a series of tenement houses fronting Cresson's Alley. Study of this particular feature highlights two concurrent, but disparate, stories. The first, illustrated through the physical structures themselves, is one of Caleb Cresson, the wealthy namesake of the alley whose financial decisions dictated much of the development of the immediate area. The second, told through the household refuse that fills the privies and backyards of these tenements, is a story of the transient and relatively anonymous middling to lower sorts who made their lives in these rented properties. Feature 91 presents a through line that links the stereotypical image of prosperous Quakers of eighteenth-century Philadelphia to the working-class population of the nineteenth-century industrializing city. In some ways, we pick up where Godfrey Minnick left off, as these intertwined experiences carry our story out of the Georgian mindset and into emerging Victorian sensibilities.

As previously mentioned, Caleb and Joshua Cresson inherited the largely undeveloped northern portion of the NCC block in the 1760s. By 1764, they were advertising "sundry lots" ripe for building and opened an "alley of 20 feet wide . . . through said piece of ground east and west, on which will also be a number of lots to dispose of in manner abovesaid" that would allow their subdivision to develop in an orderly fashion (*Pennsylvania Gazette* 1764). Contemporary maps show the pace of this development. The 1762 Clarkson-Biddle map of Philadelphia shows the relatively open and undeveloped northern half of the site while the 1797 John Hills map illustrates a dense block with development along the interior alleyways (Toogood 2004:21). In a few short generations, we see land acquired through elite family connections, originally intended as a single lot in William Penn's "greene country towne," transformed into an investment subdivision inhabited by a mix of speculators, land owners, and renters (Cotter et al. 1992:34)

Caleb Cresson developed some of these lots for himself including his personal dwelling on Cherry Street. He also built a series of rental properties including

"Five adjoining tenements . . . Situate on the south side of Crefsons Ally" (later named Quarry Street) that backed his residential complex (Philadelphia Contributionship 1774). The tenements served as a source of income for Cresson by tapping into the housing boom fueled by a steady wave of immigration swelling the growing city during the early national period (Toogood 2004:19). Caleb Cresson died in 1816 a very wealthy gentleman, thanks in no small part to his real estate savvy. The five tenements remained in the Cresson family until the mid-nineteenth century when they were sold by his grandchildren.

Fire insurance surveys for policies taken out by Cresson and subsequent owners on the tenements trace the maintenance and improvements of these homes from their initial construction into the twentieth century (Philadelphia Contributionship 1774, 1848, 1851). The five adjoining tenements were originally constructed in 1774 as 11 foot by 14 foot, two and one-half-story buildings with shallow back yards. They were fairly modest with one room to each floor and contained minimal architectural embellishments including plain mantles and breast closets. New one-story kitchens were added to the rear of each property in 1848 and 1849. These tenements survived into the twentieth century without major alteration, as described in an insurance survey as "very old" and still "containing toilets in the yard" (Mutual Assurance Company 1917).

The flipside to the existing documentary record of ownership of these properties, however, is the fluid population of renters who moved through these tenements and whose lives are represented in the material culture of Feature 91. The precise makeup of each household over time is not known although tax assessments, census records, and city directories provide a snapshot of the occupants at various points through the close of the eighteenth and into the nineteenth century.

The 1780 tax ledger lists a tailor, a painter, a weaver, and two widows paying on behalf of the estate of Caleb Cresson (Egle 1897). By the 1790 census, 20 individuals are living in the five tenements with the household heads including a widow, a plasterer, a breeches maker, a laborer, and a currier (United States Bureau of the Census 1790). In the 1810 federal census, the tenements house a grocer, a paper hanger, two printers, and a tobacconist with 23 individuals listed as occupying those households (United States Bureau of the Census 1810). A cursory review of city directories reveals that few residents in the tenements paid to be listed (Kite 1814; Robinson 1816; Dawes 1817; Desilver 1828,1833; McElroy 1861). Identified residents include a printer in 1814 and 1816 and a sugar boiler in 1817. The widow Jane Norton, a nurse, appears in 1828 and 1833 at the same address within the tenements. Jane Norton is also in the 1820 census in a household with five other women, which may represent a rare occurrence of a long term resident. The demographic trend of artisans and unskilled professionals inhabiting these tenements continues through the nineteenth century as seen in a 1860s city directory listing a tailor, a porter, laborers, a grocer, and a carriage driver.

This group of occupants, as Billy Smith (1990:5) describes of many laboring Philadelphians, shared the fundamental similarity of "low wages, uncertain prospects of advancement, and, usually, a position of propertylessness that also meant disenfranchisement." The development of rental housing as a commodity "forced working-class tenants to move around to find accommodations within the price limits set by wages that had become their only means of livelihood" (Blackmar 1988:379). A high degree of mobility is seen in the occupants of Cresson's tenements, and other survival strategies were likely utilized including taking in boarders and sharing rent between multiple families at a single address.

By the 1790s, Caleb Cresson served as landlord for almost half of the properties along Cresson's Alley including the five tenements and a series of adjacent rentals known as "Cresson's Court." Cresson's private home on Cherry Street, a three-story brick house encompassing more square footage than the five tenements combined, was located just over the wall from some of these rentals, creating a striking circumstance of great socioeconomic disparity within a confined geographic space. Although Cresson's Quaker beliefs bred a distaste of ostentation, he lived a life very much driven by the eighteenth-century concepts of gentility that Godfrey Minnick strove to achieve. Cresson's 1816 will describes a well-appointed home with front and back parlors containing books, mahogany tea tables, silver coffee and tea sets, clocks as well as bed chambers with looking glasses and feather beds (Philadelphia Register of Wills 1816).

Cresson likely kept his distance from his tenant neighbors, both figuratively and literally. His diary from 1791–1792 describes his daily routines that include matters of moral and physical well-being, his Quaker faith, and a near obsession with his garden's grape vines (Cresson and Cresson 1887). Encounters with his tenants are rare in his diary, but the few interactions mentioned convey an air of enlightened virtuousness and moderation while dealing with unruly renters (Miller 1996:129). One such interaction includes a "spiteful and malicious spirit" named Boggs and another with a tenant who "evidently designed to impose . . . as long as he could" until he was eventually evicted (Cresson and Cresson 1887:103, 104). Cresson's ability to separate these social spheres is starkly illustrated in his descriptions of peaceful garden solitude with his grape vines and fruit trees a short distance from these tenements and their privies beyond the wall.

Three privies were identified behind the tenements fronting Cresson's Alley. Feature 91, the largest of the three, is brick-lined and 8 feet in diameter with a smaller 3 1/2 foot diameter interior shaft. The privy was constructed to an overall depth of 24 feet, exceeding the 16 foot maximum depth for this part of the city that was established by a 1763 act of the General Assembly (Benedict 2004:Figure B2). Privies of this style typically saw the placement of wood planking over the top of the smaller interior shaft. Some consider this "double shaft" feature to be an early-nineteenth-century technological innovation that kept solid waste in the upper shaft for periodic cleanings while allowing for drainage through the wooden flooring into the lower shaft (Benedict 2004:4,5; Roberts and Barrett 1984:111).

The privy was located in the middle yard of the five adjoining tenements indicating that is was shared by a number of the occupants. In terms of the diameter of the outer shaft, the privy is one of the largest from the NCC site, and it is also quite large when compared to other similar double-shafted features documented in Philadelphia (Benedict 2004:7). The volume of material recovered also suggests communal filling of the privy from numerous occupants over time. Almost 120,000 artifacts were recovered from this feature alone, roughly 30,000 of which are ceramic. To date, almost 1,000 vessels have been reconstructed from the ceramic assemblage.

The presence of some fragmentary eighteenth-century materials, including white salt-glazed stoneware and Whieldon-type wares, hint at the earliest opening of the privy and may represent leftover deposits from cleaning episodes. Lenses of lime in the upper portion indicate that at least some of the artifacts were deposited into the shaft during its use as a privy. A small void at the base of the upper shaft and general slumping of the soil levels reveals that the wooden planking collapsed at some point mixing the upper artifact bearing organic deposits with the sandy soils in the lower shaft. In general, the overwhelming bulk of the ceramic assemblage dates from the early to mid-nineteenth century. It is possible that the privy was closed when new kitchens were added to the tenements in the late 1840s.

The communal filling of Feature 91 blurs the individual families involved, but taken as a lump assemblage they can still say something about life inside these households. Although these tenants were quite low on the socioeconomic ladder when compared to Caleb Cresson and Godfrey Minnick, their poverty is, in some ways, relative. From the ceramic vessels reconstructed, we can glean elements of a material life that belies the simple, crowded housing and transient nature of the occupants. The ceramic assemblage shows, at least in a generalized way, that these tenants were not simply imitating their wealthier neighbors but were participating in their own version of a growing middle-class ideology (Bushman 1992:230). And while the eighteenth-century version of gentility that Godfrey Minnick strove to achieve was meant to make a clear distinction between gentlemen and ordinary people, the nineteenth-century gentility that influenced these renters served to secure one's identity along the lower reaches of the middle class and helped in establishing a valid place for ordinary citizens (Bushman 1992:404).

The ceramics from Feature 91 represent the complete spectrum of ware types available in this time period, from the modest to the expensive including utilitarian redware, cream-colored wares, shell edge, dipped, painted and transfer printed wares, white granite, and various types of porcelain from China, Europe, and America. The sheer volume of ceramic artifacts partially attests to the number of residents depositing refuse into the privy but also speaks to the changing context in which these ceramics were purchased and used. The massive discard of consumable goods, particularly ceramics, is a phenomenon observed on many urban contexts throughout the East coast during the early to mid-nineteenth century, and is influenced by the interrelated factors of falling ceramic prices and changing patterns of consumption (Shackel 1998:2). As Miller and Earls (2008:102) argue, it is supply that "was the driver in the nineteenth century" as the markets were flooded with surplus production. But it is within this framework that Brighton (2000:20) justly asks the question of why households of limited income would necessarily want or need this quality and quantity of ceramics.

Transfer printed wares comprise a large percentage of the ceramic assemblage. Although the most expensive decorative type, the price of these wares plummeted throughout the nineteenth century, likely attributing to their major presence in the assemblage (Miller and Earls 2008:96). In addition, access to these wares was not an issue for the residents of this major port city. The printed wares show some degree of style consciousness, although it is not discernable if this is within individual households or a product of the revolving households over time. Almost all stylistic genres of printed wares available in this period are represented and range from Chinoiserie, pastoral, historical, floral, classical, and gothic imagery. Many of the transfer printed wares are associated with tea drinking and consist of teapots or matching sets of tea bowls and saucers. These vessel forms, even if only in partial or mismatched sets, show the ongoing importance of tea drinking and its associated rituals.

Although these tenements lacked proper parlors, as seen in Godfrey Minnick's or Caleb Cresson's home, the teawares reveal a certain separation of the worlds of work and leisure. In many cases, the single rooms of these tenements likely housed multiple families or even served as work spaces. The preponderance of teawares indicates at least an attempt to partake in the social performance associated with tea drinking or elaborate food serving in these crowded households. Other unique vessel forms, such as a single soup tureen, evoke a much larger and specialized serving setting. Manufactured by Stevenson between 1813 and 1830, the tureen is printed with the British views of "Haughton Hall, Norfolk" with a lid in the "Ampton Hall, Suffolk" pattern (Coysh and Henrywood 1982:21). When seen in poorer households, single elaborate vessels like the tureen "may compensate for the presence or absence of the full set of objects associated with particular forms of behavior" (Herman 2005:200).

American scenic and patriotic views including Courthouse of Baltimore, City Hall New York, and Table Rock Niagara are also present in the transfer printed wares. Additionally, two other patriotic views manufactured by Enoch Wood depict French hero the Marquis de Lafayette at Washington's tomb and the peculiarly macabre Washington standing by his own tomb (Snyder 1995:16, 22). Less serious topics, though still manufactured primarily for the American market, are printed wares of the satirical cartoon Dr. Syntax in patterns of "Dr. Syntax and the bees" and "Dr. Syntax taking possession of his living" (Coysh and Henrywood 1982:108).

The ceramic artifacts also speak to the lives of children living in the five tenements. Cups, plates, redware coin banks, and miniatures demonstrate the use of the home as a training ground for polite behavior, even in these poorer households. In comparison to the Minnick household, they show changing attitudes towards childhood in the nineteenth century. Rather than the miniature version of adult forms, like the enameled creamware and China glaze tea bowls that the Minnick daughters had, these vessels include individualized forms and sayings geared specifically to children such as "A token of respect," "a prefent for my dear girl," "for a good child," and "for my dear boy" (figure 9.3). Also of interest is a matched set of eight octagonal children's plates printed with vignettes of Robinson Crusoe that are colorfully decorated with overglaze clobbering. They are copied from a popular 1840s J. J. Grandville printing of the tale (Riley 1991:88). Many attribute the prevalence of these children's cups to emerging Victorian ideals that encouraged individualism and instilled an appreciation for private property at an early age (Shackel 1998:8; Brighton 2000:27).

One final artifact recovered from Feature 91 offers a potent symbol of these changing nineteenth-century values of gentility and offers insight into the background of at least some of the tenants. A saucer with a transfer print of the Irish temperance movement leader Father Mathew, manufactured by William Adams and Sons between 1829 and 1861, points to Irish immigrants active in this Catholic temperance movement (Furniss et al. 1999:68). Study of a matching Father Mathew teacup recovered from the Five Points site in New York City highlights the significance of these ceramics (Reckner and Brighton 1999; Brighton 2008). Reckner and Brighton (1999:67) describe the temperance movement as a vehicle by which America's growing Irish immigrant community distinguished itself from the impoverished and degraded lower classes. These objects indicate that some of the residents were making middle-class inspired improvements to their lives and were participating in gentility as a means of stabilizing their communal identity. This saucer offers a contrast to the decorative objects of Godfrey Minnick's household such as the pearlware quintile. The quintile represents leisurely and economically useless activities in a household engaged in refined pursuits clearly separated from the working world (Bushman 1992:256). The Father Mathew saucer with its motto of "industry pays

Figure 9.3. Children's cups from Feature 91. Courtesy of Independence National Historical Park.

debts" embeds values of work and social advancement into these concepts of polite behavior. It also shows that while these tenants were not at the top of the socio-economic ladder, they were declaring that they were not at the bottom either—an important distinction in the densely packed housing of Cresson's Alley.

Conclusion

The public study of archaeological materials from the National Constitution Center site is a counterpoint to what is often expected at Independence National Historical Park. Rather than distilling the story of the nation's founding, we, the archaeologists, muddy the waters by introducing a new cast of characters that presents a dynamic, and often contradictory, depiction of the past.

The preliminary case studies presented here emphasize the changing view of what it meant to live in this neighborhood during the late eighteenth and early nineteenth centuries as considered through the lens of middle-class ideology. While the Minnicks bought into a worldview inherited from Georgian modes of sophistication, the transient tenants of Cresson's Alley reacted to the marginalizing circumstances of wage labor and their inability to afford property. This discussion is only one preliminary look into the lives of a few of the residents of the NCC site, and we hope to have your attention as we continue to learn more of how these people, "we the people," were living out their lives.

References Cited

Benedict, Tod
2004   Appendix B: Bricklayers, Well Diggers, Hod Carriers, Privy Cleaners, and Carters: The Construction and Maintenance of Brick-Lined Shafts in Philadelphia to 1850. In *After the Revolution—Two Shops on South Sixth Street: Archeological Data Recovery on Block 1 of Independence Mall*, pp. 1-48. Report to National Park Service, Denver. John Milner Associates, Philadelphia.

Blackmar, Betsy
1988   Rewalking the "Walking City": Housing and Property Relations in New York City, 1780–1840. In *Material Life in America, 1600–1860*, edited by Robert Blair St. George, pp. 376–377. Northeastern University Press, Boston.

Blumin, Stuart M.
1989   *The Emergence of the Middle Class, Social Experience in the American City, 1760–1900*. Cambridge University Press, Cambridge, United Kingdom.

Brighton, Stephen A.
2000   Prices That Suit the Times: Shopping for Ceramics at Five Points. In *Tales of Five Points: Working-Class Life in Nineteenth Century New*

York, Volume 2, An Interpretive Approach to Understanding Working-Class Life, edited by Rebecca Yamin, pp. 11–30, John Milner Associates, Philadelphia.

2008   Collective Identities, the Catholic Temperance Movement, and Father Mathew: The Social History of a Teacup. *Northeast Historical Archaeology* 37:21–37.

Bushman, Richard L.

1992   *The Refinement of America, Persons, Houses, Cities.* Alfred E. Knopf, New York.

Chappell, Edward A.

1994   Housing a Nation: The Transformation of Living Standards in Early America. In *Of Consuming Interests: The Style of Life in the Late Eighteenth Century*, edited by Cary Carson, Ronald Hoffman and Peter Albert, pp. 167–233. University Press of Virginia, Charlottesville.

Cotter, John L., Daniel G. Roberts, and Michael Parrington

1992   *The Buried Past: An Archaeological History of Philadelphia.* University of Pennsylvania Press, Philadelphia.

Coysh, A. W., and R. K. Henrywood

1982   *The Dictionary of Blue and White Printed Pottery 1780–1880.* Antique Collector's Club, Woodbridge, England.

Cresson, Ezra Townsend, and Charles Caleb Cresson

1877   *Diary of Caleb Cresson, 1791–1792.* Ezra Townsend Cresson and Charles Caleb Cresson, Philadelphia, PA. http://books.google.com.

Dawes, Edward

1817   *The Philadelphia Directory for 1817.* Edward Dawes, Philadelphia.

Desilver, Robert

1828   *Philadelphia Directory and Stranger's Guide for 1828.* Robert Desilver, Philadelphia.

1833   *Philadelphia Directory and Stranger's Guide for 1828.* Robert Desilver, Philadelphia.

Egle, William Henry (editor)

1897   *Supply, and State Tax Lists of the City and County of Philadelphia, for the Years 1779, 1780 and 1781.* William Stanley Ray, State Printer of Pennsylvania, Harrisburg.

Elliott, Ella Zerby

1916   *Blue Book of Schuylkill County: Who was who and why, in Interior Eastern Pennsylvania, In Colonial Days, the Huguenots and Palatines, Their Service in Queen Anne's French and Indian, and Revolutionary Wars: History of the Zerbey, Schwalm, Miller, Merkle, Minnich, Staudt, and Many Others.* Joseph Zerby, Pottsville, Pennsylvania.

Furniss, David A., J. Richard Wagner, and Judith Wagner

1999   *Adams Ceramics, Staffordshire Potters and Pots, 1779–1998.* Schiffer, Atglen, Pennsylvania.

Gibson, Deirdre, Mary Whelchel Konieczny, Kathy Schlegel, and Anna Coxe Toogood
1994   *Cultural Landscape Report Independence Mall.* National Park Service, Denver.

Godden, Goeffrey
2004   *Godden's Guide to English Blue and White Porcelain.* Antiques Collectors Club, Woodbridge, Suffolk, United Kingdom.

Herman, Bernard L.
2005   *Townhouse, Architecture and Material Life in the Early American City, 1780–1830.* University of North Carolina Press, Chapel Hill.

Kite, B. & T.
1814   *Kite's Philadelphia Directory for 1814.* B. & T. Kite, Philadelphia.

Levin, Jed, William Hoffman, Deborah Miller, and Douglas B. Mooney
2009   The National Constitution Center Site: The Archeology of "We the People." Paper presented at the 42nd Annual Conference on Historical and Underwater Archaeology, Toronto, Ontario, Canada.

McElroy, A.
1861   *McElroy's City Directory for 1861.* E.C. & J. Biddle, Philadelphia.

Miller, George, and Robert Hunter
2001   How Creamware Got the Blues: The Origins of China Glaze and Pearlware. In *Ceramics in America,* edited by Robert Hunter, pp. 135–161. Chipstone Foundation, Milwaukee, Wisconsin.

Miller, George L., and Amy C. Earls
2008   War and Pots: The Impact of Economics and Politics on Ceramic Consumption Patterns. In *Ceramics in America,* edited by Robert Hunter, pp. 67–108. Chipstone Foundation, Milwaukee, Wisconsin.

Miller, Jacquelyn C.
1996   An "Uncommon Tranquility of Mind": Emotional Self-Control and the Construction of a Middle-Class Identity in Eighteenth Century Philadelphia. *Journal of Social History* 30(1):129–148.

Mutual Assurance Company
1917   Cresson's Alley Fire Insurance Survey, Policy #1789. Microfilm Roll no. 28. On file, Independence National Historical Park Archives, Philadelphia.

Pennsylvania Gazette
1764   No title. 19 January. Accessible Archives. http://www.accessible.com.

Philadelphia Registry of Deeds
1784   Deed from Samuel Lewis to Godfrey Minnick, September 30, 1784. Book D, Vol. 10, p. 454). On file, Philadelphia City Archives, Philadelphia.

Philadelphia Contributionship
1774   Insurance Survey for Caleb Cresson, Policy S01827. Contributionship Digital Archives. http://www.philadelphiabuildings.org/contribution ship/search.cfm.

1791   Insurance Survey for Godfrey Minnick, Policy S02438. Contribution-
              ship Digital Archives. http://www.philadelphiabuildings.org/contribu
              tionship/search.cfm.

1848   Insurance Survey for John Thomason, Policy S01827. Contribution-
              ship Digital Archives. http://www.philadelphiabuildings.org/contribu
              tionship/search.cfm.

1851   Insurance Survey for John Thomason, Policy S09306. Contribution-
              ship Digital Archives. http://www.philadelphiabuildings.org/contribu
              tionship/search.cfm.

1857   Insurance Survey for Catharine Minnick, Policy S06924. On file, Phila-
              delphia Contributionship, Philadelphia.

Philadelphia County Tax Ledgers

1787, 1798,   County Tax Ledger, South Mulberry Ward. On file, Philadelphia City
1799   Archives, Philadelphia.

Philadelphia Department of Records

1931   508–518 Quarry Street. Department of City Transit Collection, Asset
              ID 51815. http://www.phillyhistory.org/PhotoArchive/Search.aspx.

Philadelphia Register of Wills

1798   Will of Godfrey Minnick. Book 2C:458. On file, City Hall,
              Philadelphia.

1816   Will of Caleb Cresson. Book 6:342. On file, City Hall, Philadelphia.

Reckner, Paul E., and Stephen A. Brighton

1999   "Free From All Vicious Habits": Archaeological Perspectives on Class
              Conflict and the Rhetoric of Temperance. *Historical Archaeology*
              33(1):63–86.

Riley, Noel

1991   *Gifts for Good Children, The History of Children's China, Part 1,
              1790–1890*. Richard Dennis, Somerset, United Kingdom.

Roberts, Daniel G., and David Barrett

1984   Nightsoil Disposal Practices of the 19th Century and the Origin of Ar-
              tifacts in Plowzone Proveniences. *Historical Archaeology* 18:108–115.

Roberts, Lois

2006   *Painted in Blue: Underglaze Blue Painted Earthenwares 1775–1810*.
              The Northern Ceramic Society, Newbury, United Kingdom.

Robinson, James

1816   *Philadelphia Directory for 1816*. James Robinson, Philadelphia.

Roeber, A. G.

1991   "The Origin of Whatever Is Not English among Us": The Dutch-
              speaking and the German-speaking Peoples of Colonial British Amer-
              ica. In *Strangers Within the Realm: Cultural Margins of the First British
              Empire*, edited by Bernard Bailyn and Philip D. Morgan, pp. 220–283.
              University of North Carolina Press, Chapel Hill.

Roth, Rodris

1988   Tea Drinking in Eighteenth-Century America: Its Etiquette and Equi-
            page. In *Material Life in Early America 1600–1860*, edited by Robert
            Blair St. George, pp. 439–463. Northeastern University Press, Boston.

Samford, Patricia M.

1997   Response to a Market: Dating English Underglaze Transfer-Printed
            Wares. *Historical Archaeology* 31(2):1–19.

Schultz, Ronald

1995   Small-Producer Thought: The Argument For Capitalism. In *Life in
            Early Philadelphia: Documents From the Revolutionary and Early Na-
            tional Periods*, edited by Billy G. Smith, pp. 265–279. Pennsylvania
            State University Press, University Park.

Shackel, Paul A.

1998   Classical and Liberal Republicanisms and the New Consumer Culture.
            International Journal of Historical Archaeology 2(1):1–20.

Smith, Billy G.

1990   *The "Lower Sort": Philadelphia's Laboring People, 1750–1800*. Cor-
            nell University Press, Ithaca, New York.

Smith, Billy G. (editor)

2004   *Down and Out in Early America*. Pennsylvania State University Press,
            University Park.

Strassburger, Ralph Beaver

1934   *Pennsylvania German Pioneers, Vol. I–II*. Pennsylvania German Soci-
            ety, Norristown.

Snyder, Jeffrey B.

1995   *Historical Staffordshire: American Patriots and Views*. Schiffer, Atglen,
            Pennyslvania.

Sweeney, Kevin M.

1994   High-Style Vernacular: Lifestyles of the Colonial Elite. In *Of Consum-
            ing Interests: The Style of Life in the Late Eighteenth Century*, edited
            by Cary Carson, Ronald Hoffman, and Peter Albert, pp. 1–58, Univer-
            sity Press of Virginia, Charlottesville.

Toogood, Anna Coxe

2004   Historic Resources Study Independence Mall, the 18th Century Devel-
            opment, Block Three, Arch to Race, Fifth to Sixth Streets. Manuscript
            on file, Cultural Resources Management, Independence National His-
            torical Park, Philadelphia.

United States Bureau of the Census

1790   First Census of the United States, South Mulberry Ward, Philadelphia.
            http://www.ancestry.com.

1810   Third Census of the United States, South Mulberry Ward, Philadelphia.
            http://www.ancestry.com.

Upton, Dell
2008   *Another City: Urban Life and Urban Spaces in the New American Re-*
              public. Yale University Press, New Haven, Connecticut.
Waldstreicher, David
1997   *In the Midst of Perpetual Fetes: The Making of American Nationalism,*
              1776–1820. Omohundro Institute of Early American History and Cul-
              ture. University of North Carolina Press, Chapel Hill.
Yamin, Rebecca
2004   After the Revolution—Two Shops on South Sixth Street: Archeological
              Data Recovery on Block 1 of Independence Mall. Report to National
              Park Service, Denver. John Milner Associates, Philadelphia.
2008   *Digging in the City of Brotherly Love: Stories from Philadelphia Ar-*
              chaeology. Yale University Press, New Haven, Connecticut.
Yamin, Rebecca (editor)
2007   *Hudson's Square—A Place Through Time: Archeological Data Recov-*
              ery on Block 2 of Independence Mall. Report to Day & Zimmermann
              Infrastructure, Philadelphia. John Milner Associates, Philadelphia.

10

Rediscovering Franklin: The Archaeology of Benjamin Franklin in Philadelphia

Patrice L. Jeppson

Introduction

Something unusual happened in the spring of 1953 in the Old City section of Philadelphia (figure 10.1). Men wielding shovels and pick axes tore up a stretch of sidewalk laying adjacent to a vacant lot on one of the neighborhood's cobblestone streets. Their work was part of an unusual archaeological experiment the objective of which was seeking the ruins of Benjamin Franklin's Philadelphia "mansion."

Two centuries before, Benjamin Franklin had directed that a house be built somewhere in the vicinity. It was there that Franklin's wife, Deborah, and daughter, Sarah, lived while Franklin worked overseas in England on behalf of various North American colonies. Franklin was in residence at the house during the pivotal year of the country's founding, 1775–1776, but was soon absent again, serving the new nation in a diplomatic posting to France. He returned to spend the final years of his life in the residence, from 1785 to 1790, during which time he made significant alterations to both the house structure and its surrounding property (figure 10.2).

Franklin's daughter had inherited the house upon her father's death in 1790 and, in the decades following, the "House-Mansion" remained identified with the renowned man while being rented out for various residential and commercial uses (see, for example, the August 29th, 1792, Philadelphia *General Advertiser* advertisement to "let" the home). In 1822, more than a decade after Sarah's death, her widower husband had the structure demolished, building in its place two rows of small but profitable tenant buildings. The stone and brick house rubble was used to fill in the subterranean, cellar floor-level of the once-standing "Mansion House" while some architectural elements were salvaged for use in the new constructions. The house ruins were then paved over by a cobblestone street, burying them in place but out of sight, where they were eventually forgotten.

As decades and then centuries passed, the street entombing the ruins was repaved and renamed and several of the overlaying tenant structures were themselves replaced. The horse carts that traversed the street gave way to automobiles, and buildings that served initially as residences evolved into factory workshops. Then, 140 years after the house had last stood, the archaeological investigation was launched to search for evidence of this lost American history. The goals of the excavation were to determine whether any physical evidence of the mansion survived the ravages of time and to identify specifically the location of where this house once stood.

The archaeological exploration was a joint project of the American Philosophical Society and the National Park Service (NPS). It was inspired by, and was undertaken in advance of, the 250th anniversary of Franklin's birth, which was to be celebrated in 1956. Lasting only a few days in the spring of 1953, with a short follow-up in 1955, the excavation was considered a success. The first day of digging revealed several marble steps presumed to be from the mansion's front entrance. The design element along the profile (front edge) of these steps was anomalous for the nineteenth-century. The steps also exhibited higher levels of wear than the entrance steps that fronted the extant nineteenth-century structures. The archaeological and architectural assessments at the time evaluated these steps as reused elements taken from the Franklin mansion when it was destroyed (Jeppson 2005, Schumacher 1953, Brandreth 1953). Soon after uncovering these steps, the brick floor and stone wall foundations of Franklin's eighteenth-century mansion cellar were discovered resting

Figure 10.1. The "X" indicates the location of the first excavations, undertaken in 1953, along a narrow street lined with nineteenth- and twentieth-century shops and warehouses. Independence National Historical Park Archives, Working Photo Collection: Franklin Court-1950's: "#153, Philadelphia, Franklin Court [Orianna Street] looking north toward Market Street showing east side of Orianna Street, [by] Fawcett, September 1950."

among and under the foundations for the nineteenth-century tenant structures. Using this original architectural fabric, the excavators were able to specify the exact location of the house—positioned within the center of the city block defined by 2nd and 3rd Streets and Chestnut and Market Streets—where it last stood graciously within a fine, French-inspired, courtyard.

This 1950s-era excavation proved to be only the first phase of a long archaeological legacy at the Franklin mansion site. In 1960-1961, and again (on and off) from 1969 through 1974, more extensive archaeological investigations were conducted at the site of the house. These research efforts sought to learn more about what the house might have looked like as no image of the structure is known to have survived. These subsequent research efforts also investigated the areas surrounding the house and collected artifacts found in association with the house foundations. NPS launched these later phases of study as part of their Master Plan for establishing Independence National Historical Park (INHP), a national historical park preserving resources associated with the birth of the United States. As a Founding Father, inventor, printer, scientist, diplomat, humorist, and entrepreneur, Franklin "personified the spirit, ideals, curiosities, and ingenuity of a developing America" and his home site was included in the park's mission (INHP 2007:8). The Franklin mansion archaeological discoveries came to form the basis of the Independence National Historical Park site of Franklin Court, which opened to the public in the American bicentennial year of 1976.

Figure 10.2. Conjectural drawing of Franklin's mansion by W.C. Campbell, circa 1963. Independence National Historical Park Archives, Franklin Court-Historic Structures Report 1, 1963.

The archaeological interpretation that NPS created for Franklin Court was pathbreaking in how it presented historical information for public consumption. The high level of detail needed to accurately restore or reconstruct the mansion remained missing so the outlines of the house were instead merely suggested by a framework of steel tubing placed over the archaeologically-exposed house foundations (see, among others, the Philadelphia Museum of Art 1976:639-640, *#539, Franklin Court: Garden Level Plan, Franklin Court Interior Plan*). (Figures 10.3 and 10.4.). This "ghost house" sculpture functions to symbolically outline the volume of the long absent brick building without creating false memory in the mind of the observer. Colored stones are used on the ground surface to demarcate the hearths, windows, and door piercings of the now absent rooms, the locations of which are known from the archaeological research. Glassed-in portals constructed on top of the excavated ruins allow visitors to the site to view this original evidence of the house where it once stood (*in situ*). These preserved in place ruins provide the visitor to Franklin Court with a tangible touchstone to both Franklin, the man, and his times.

Figure 10.3. The Franklin mansion "ghost house" sculpture framing the archaeologically discovered stone foundations. Colored stones mark the archaeologically defined house floor plan and viewing portals allow visitors to examine the original, excavated, house foundations. Independence National Historical Park Archives, Multiplex Slide Collection, "Events," 1963–1975, "Franklin Court" (9-4-5).

The property that surrounded Franklin's house is likewise richly interpreted. Independence Park historical architects discovered that several tenant structures designed by and constructed for Franklin during his last years in residence were still standing within the original property boundaries. These late 18th-century dwellings front the northern edge of Franklin's property along today's Market Street. The park used two of these buildings to interpret portions of Franklin's life history via a functioning, reconstructed, post office (as Franklin was the first post master) and a printing shop (reminiscent of Franklin's first career as a printer). Another structures was stripped down to its original structural elements to present a unique architectural display interpreting, among other building elements, Franklin's fireproofing innovations (as Franklin is credited with crafting the idea for fire insurance). This same structure holds the "Fragments of Franklin Court," an archaeological exhibit that contains many of the artifacts recovered during the various site excavations. Built underneath a large swath of the entire Franklin property is an "Underground Museum" displaying decorative art objects, scientific instruments, and information about Franklin and his role in the making of the modern world are presented. This below-ground design, novel for its time, was likely inspired by the subterranean nature of the excavations.

Now open for more than 35 years—since the nation's bicentennial year in 1976—Franklin Court currently receives more than 300,000 visitors annually. In total, although a very conservative estimate, more than 6 million visitors have learned about Franklin and his times from this archaeologically derived historical site and its interpretation. But is the archaeology at Franklin Court finished?

The Franklin Court archeological research, 1953-1974, represents a pioneering effort in urban archaeology (archaeological study of and in cities). Franklin Court is also a seminal site for both historical archaeology (the study of everyday life during the last 500 years) and public archaeology (the study of the public's engagement with the archaeological past). Franklin Court, moreover, forms a prototype case study for the NPS's historic preservation policy of "Better preserve than repair, better repair than restore, better restore than construct" (NPS General Restoration Policy, Memorandum, 19 May 1937, clause 3, as stated in Unrah and Williss 1983, Appendix 2). To this day, Franklin Court remains one of the most extensively researched and most publicly interpreted U.S. archaeological sites. So, is the archaeology at Franklin Court "all said and done?" Recent discoveries and re-discoveries "excavated from" the stored Franklin Court collections indicate that no, the archaeology of the site is not done and, indeed, will never be done. This understanding comes after a re-excavation of the Franklin Court site using the archaeological assemblages in the Independence Park museum collections and the archaeological site record collections stored in the Park's archive repository. This latest archaeological research at Franklin Court involves "collections reuse" and it demonstrates the value of researching and appreciating the history of archaeological practice overtime. This newest phase of site research forms a case study in "the archaeology of archaeology"—an archaeological methodology with implications not just for Franklin Court but for archaeological sites in the Delaware Valley, and for anywhere, far, beyond.

Excavating Franklin Court Anew

In 2002, fifty years after the first exploratory excavations at Franklin Court, and more than a quarter-century since the last excavations in the 1970s, legislation by the 107th Congress of the United States established the *Benjamin Franklin Tercentenary Commission Act (H.R. 2363)* to study and recommend activities to honor Benjamin Franklin on the 300th anniversary of his birth in 2006. As part of this commemoration, a consortium of five, Franklin-cofounded, Philadelphia institutions joined together to undertake celebratory activities—the American Philosophical Society, the Franklin Institute Science Museum, the Library Company of Philadelphia, the Philadelphia Museum of Art, and the University of Pennsylvania. For their tercentenary contribution, the consortium's team of curators and consultants produced a traveling museum exhibit, created an in-perpetuity database of Frankliniana (i.e., "a catalogue of all things Franklin"), and developed a comprehensive Franklin Tercentenary website (http://www.benfranklin300.org/advisory.htm). Between 2003 and 2005, all Franklin-related historical archaeology evidence known to date was surveyed for the needs of these three consortium projects. This archaeological assessment did not involve a full, formal, re-analysis of the previously recovered archaeological assemblages but rather studied and evaluated the previous findings and interpretations of others for the needs of the tercentenary commemoration activities (Jeppson 2005). Toward this end, only samples of artifact collections were reanalyzed with positive results and it is expected that other new information remains waiting to be discovered.

In the case of Benjamin Franklin, even a restricted assessment involved consideration of a particularly wide and deep range of previous archaeological research. It included analysis of a Philadelphia salvage study that was conducted in the mid-1970s at the sites of three Market Street houses where Franklin had once resided. These properties were originally investigated during a highway overpass construction project. Archaeological projects at the sites of two Franklin-associated French and Indian War forts—Fort Allen and Fort Franklin—were also researched. These fort sites had been explored in recent decades by avocational archaeologists and by the Pennsylvania State Archeologist, Stephen G. Warfel. Also surveyed were the results of an archaeological heritage management project conducted as part of tercentenary commemorative activities taking place in London, England. This involved assessment of an archaeological study undertaken at the house at No. 36 Craven Street, London where Franklin was a long-term lodger. A cache of coins discovered at the location of Franklin's childhood home on Milk Street in Boston was similarly assessed. Franklin's burial plot in Christ Church cemetery in Philadelphia has never been archaeologically excavated but the Tercentenary Consortium study considered the role this archaeological resource plays as a memorial site for the public.

The majority of the Consortium's tercentenary assessment study focused on the site of Franklin's Philadelphia mansion and involved assessing the multiple phases of archaeological research that has taken place at the site over the years. This research produced significant and substantive results, identifying three new types of archaeological information and making clear that the archaeological research at Franklin Court should not yet, or perhaps ever be, considered "done". First, new artifacts were "uncovered" when objects not recognized during the previous research efforts were now identified and interpreted. Second, some of the previously identified and analyzed artifacts had their interpretations updated. This was possible because the original artifact identifications were produced 30–50 years ago and, due to the passage of time and the subsequent development of archaeological understandings in the interim, some previously studied artifacts were found to be "under-analyzed" (in terms of how archaeology is practiced in the present). These new analyses resulted in new social meanings and historical associations for what were long-term, stored, archaeological collection materials. Lastly, the recent study identified entirely new resources that had not actually existed previously. This new evidence was discovered in the archived archaeological site documentation that was produced during the original excavation process. In short, the passage of time made once irrelevant information related to the 1950s, 1960s, and 1970s archaeological work itself relevant and useful for telling fresh stories. This includes an important historiographical story about the search for Franklin's mansion 200 years after Franklin's death.

New Findings from Some Old Archaeology

How does one "excavate" a site that was already excavated a long time ago? The Tercentenary Consortium's archaeological study re-excavated Franklin Court by investigating and evaluating the findings of the site's previous researchers. Different people undertook these previous archaeological studies at different times for different reasons, and the various resulting findings overtime reflect, to an extent, the objectives and goals of the different endeavors. For example, the initial 1950s excavations sought structural evidence to specifically relocate the house. The 1960s work was directed by architectural history concerns and mainly involved determining the footprint of the house and the original ground surface depth. At that time, objects (artifacts) were also formally sought in order to help date the foundation walls so as to secure structural evidence dating to Franklin's occupation. In contrast to these earlier dating efforts, the last phase of excavation, taking place during the late 1960s and early 1970s, reflected the interests of the (then) newly established field of historical archaeology—an anthropological approach to the study of the recent past that uses material culture residues to explore past everyday life experience. This phase of the site's study aimed to define the property's development over time (considering the property as a "landscape artifact"), to determine the "use areas" within the property's boundaries (so as to identify the locations of domestic and or commercial activities), and to flesh out the ordinary existence of the property's colonial-era inhabitants (to use items such as buttons, animal bones, and dish fragments to gain understanding about everyday life as it was lived on that property and in the colonial city).

Coming 50 years after the first excavations, and 30 years after the last, the Tercentenary Consortium's study considers each of these earlier phases of archaeological investigation as a new layer, or stratum, of cultural history at the Franklin Court site. The new research thus re-investigates the original archaeological work at the house while also investigating the different phases of site excavation as information. In doing so, the tercentenary-era study undertakes "the archaeology of the archaeology" at Franklin Court; the archaeological focus includes the archaeological excavation process itself.

The data employed in this kind of an archaeological exploration expands beyond the usual archaeological field and lab scenario where artifacts are excavated from a site and then cleaned, identified, inventoried, and interpreted. Undertaking the "archaeology of" archaeological field and lab work involves digging into the archaeological documentation housed in official archives and re-examining excavated archaeological assemblages stored in artifact repositories. In this case, the field work included "digging into" the original archaeological site documentation stored in the INHP Archives so as to re-excavate the site after the fact using the original archaeological site drawings, field notes, field photographs, photo logs, artifact catalogues, and preliminary and final reports. The study also involved assessment of the previously recovered and analyzed artifact specimens now on display in the Fragments of Franklin Museum, and the artifact assemblages stored in the INHP museum collections.

Beyond examining these "artifacts of the archaeological process," other NPS and Independence Park primary resources related to Franklin Court were consulted—everything from General Management Plans, to National Register Nominations, to taped and transcribed oral history testimony collected as part of the park's administrative history recordkeeping. In addition, academic studies evaluating aspects of Franklin Court's archaeology and its interpretation were perused, and interviews were conducted via phone and email exchange with several of the principals involved in the original excavations.

Likewise considered as artifactual evidence for the needs of this study were the historical interpretations for Franklin Court that INHP has presented to the public overtime. These "artifacts of archaeological interpretation" included popular period tourism publications, period newspaper clippings, slide and photograph collections documenting Franklin Court's development and ceremonial opening, and the park's interpretive training and outreach materials, including retired exhibition materials. Beyond this material evidence of past public interpretation practice, informal observations of present-day visitors to the site were made, and current information was formally gathered from Independence Park personnel who interface regularly with the public at Franklin Court. Lastly, the manager of the Independence Park web pages containing Franklin archaeology content was consulted for insight into the public's online access of Franklin Court archaeological information (Jeppson 2005).

This "archaeology of archaeology" research represents a highly positive use of existing archaeological resources. Such reuse of archaeological collections material is a topic of interest and concern within the discipline of archaeology as evidenced by the Maryland Historical Trust's Maryland Archaeological Conservation Laboratory project bringing 1 million artifacts to the public via internet access (see http://jefpat.org/2archaeology.htm) and the effort to expand research potentials via the Digital Archaeological Archive of Chesapeake Slavery (http://www.daacs.org/aboutDAACS/). Using existing archaeological resources for new research projects and new heritage interpretations is thought to be a cost-effective strategy that also helps to preserve archaeological resources (e.g., Bacharach and Boyd 2003; Ellick 2003; and King 2003). Digging a site is not only expensive but destructive as all that often remains after a site's excavation is the archaeologist's field documentation and the artifacts recovered from the location. (Hence the need to safely preserve these materials, in perpetuity and for posterity, in archives and museum collections.) In demonstrating the potential value of collections reuse in a broad sense of the word, the new Franklin Court archaeological study is not just a novel undertaking but an unusually instructive one. Here below are a few of the highlights from this most recent phase of archaeological research at Franklin Court.

FRANKLIN'S MONSTER

At the outset of the Tercentenary Consortium's assessment, it was assumed that, at a minimum, the passage of time and the bringing of a more mature historical archaeology to bear on 30–50-year-old research might mean that the previous Franklin archaeology efforts could be re-explored in new ways. While cutting edge—indeed truly innovative for their time—the earlier phases of archaeology at the site do not always represent the historical archaeology that has evolved overtime and is therefore practiced today. Moreover, taking place long before the digitization of Franklin's papers, the earlier research incorporated little of the rich body of Franklin documentary evidence because that information was not yet easily available.

This initial assumption proved true and is demonstrated here in the case of one particular artifact newly identified during the tercentenary-era research. The object in question is a fossil tooth originally recovered in 1959 by an electrician laying a conduit in the dirt floor basement of a nineteenth-century building on Market Street. This nineteenth-century building had several construction phases with additions built onto its back that extended into the middle of the block, over the location of where Franklin's eighteenth-century house lay buried as ruins. This fossil item was examined by a paleontologist upon its initial discovery, and it was eventually put on display, in 1976, in the "Fragments of Franklin Court" exhibit alongside a sign identifying it as a mastodon molar possibly from the Paris Basin fossil bed in France (figure 10.4).

Over the past 30 years much more information has become known about Franklin's scientific interests via the publication of the *Franklin Papers*, which are now searchable on CD-ROM. Paleontological insights since the 1970s have also evolved. Recent history of science research indicates that no European mastodon fossils were known of during Franklin's lifetime and Franklin's papers reveal how, as a natural philosopher, he was very intrigued by the creature now referred to as the mastodon. Franklin's correspondence indicates that he requested fossil mastodon specimens be sent to him from the Big Bone Lick fossil bed site (now in Kentucky), that he made comparative studies of mastodon teeth with elephant teeth from Africa, and that he sent and personally carried several mastodon specimens with him overseas to England and France. Taken together, this new analysis indicates that the Franklin Court fossil tooth is a North American specimen.

Added to this revised scientific insight is the past 30 years of specialization in Intellectual and Social History scholarship which lets us consider the Franklin Court mastodon tooth with a new cultural eye. Today this fossil specimen can be understood not just as evidence of Franklin's scientific curiosity but as a window into the social and political transformations that were shaping the modern western world and, importantly, forming the backdrop for the establishment of a new American nation.

Figure 10.4. The mastodon tooth discovered in 1959 on the Franklin property and a drawing of the now extinct *Mammut americanum* (INHP Museum Accession #315, Photograph by Peter Harholdt) for the *Benjamin Franklin Tercentenary's* Frankliniana Database, 2004. INHP mastodon tooth image a122, courtesy of INHP Curator Karie Deithorn and the Benjamin Franklin Tercentenary. Mastodon sketch courtesy of Sarah E. Jeppson.

Franklin lived during a time of fervent evolution in western thought known as the Enlightenment. Marked by scientific observations of the natural world and by rational thought, this age experienced and fostered a new philosophical understanding that countered the then existing classical, medieval, Christian explanation of the universe known as the "Great Chain of Being," or *scala naturae* (natural ladder). This older, theologically derived model of existence long operated with a notion of a fixed hierarchical order. The highest rank, the place of perfection, is the realm of God. Beneath this lies "physical existence" within which people represent the highest order. People are themselves hierarchically positioned with rulers over commoners and males above females. People are ranked above animals, which are, in turn, ranked above plant life, and so on, in a descending ladder of imperfection. The basic fundamental elements—dirt and minerals—fell at the bottom in this "mental template" of understanding "for all that was known". The emerging and evolving scientific ideas of Enlightenment science challenged the foundations of this fixed order of existence. The discovery of fossil mastodon bones in eighteenth-century colonial America forms an important chapter in this new, science-derived and driven age.

As part of this shifting theoretical and theological cultural backdrop, the mastodon came to serve as an important symbol for the new American nation (Semonin 2000). With no deep past to draw upon, North American residents turned to the majestic landscape and its unique natural history attributes in creating a sense of self and society (Semonin 2000). The *Incognitum*, as Franklin knew the mastodon, and its presumed great size (thought then to be greater than any known terrestrial animal), was taken to be a ferocious beast (Semonin 2000). This made it a potent symbol of national identity for the new Republic (Semonin 2000; Jeppson 2006a, 2006d, 2006e, 2005b). The newly discovered fossil bones emboldened the colonists by providing support for the idea of a grand history for a new continent (Semonin 2000).

Today we can recognize the Franklin Court mastodon tooth as more than just an interesting curio once in Franklin's possession. This "natural" fossil is also a "cultural" artifact. It was taken from its fossil bed for the needs of natural history study. This defines it as residue of the new scientific method of observation and hypothesis making that were transforming western European society. This new identification reinterprets the fossil tooth as residue of the, then, new scientific methods of observation and hypothesis making that transformed western society, creating a worldview quite different from the long-established, hierarchical, understanding of the world. This new explanation for the order of existence, in turn, formed an important backdrop for the formation of the new American nation. Rather than a social order based upon a strict hierarchy, the new explanation of existence allowed for a new social order where the revolutionary idea of democratic self-rule could be founded.

A new look at this fossil 30 years after its discovery at Franklin Court determines that this object is more than just a natural curio once in Franklin's possession. In redefining the Franklin Court mastodon, The Tercentenary Consortium's assessment study has identified a new "cultural" artifact. The mastodon tooth is now recognized as tangible material residue of western society's basic values and beliefs being restructured. It is a cultural artifact reflecting colonial American and Enlightenment-Age thinking and it is valuable evidence of Franklin's scientific role in helping to transform western worldview.

LEARNING FROM A RAT'S SKULL

Another new finding resulting from the tercentenary archaeological study involves the public's response to an artifact on display in the now, 30-year-old, Franklin Court archaeological exhibit in the "The Fragments of Franklin" museum (located in one of Franklin's original tenant structures at 318 Market Street). The tercentenary research found that one of the most popular artifacts in this museum is a rat skull. This microfauna specimen, or small animal bone example, is displayed along with several other rodent skeletal elements next to seeds and nuts (floral evidence) likewise excavated from the Franklin Court site.

The rat skull on display is indicative of the rodent population inhabiting the colonial-era seaport city of Philadelphia, or any city in past or modern times. Rats, of course, have a high "gross-out" factor, and that aspect was what was first thought to account for visitors' interest in this archaeological evidence. But the tercentenary archaeology assessment turned up another possibility for the skull's popularity, which in turn generated new understandings about how people learn about Benjamin Franklin.

In specific, the new study investigated the Franklin Court archaeological interpretations in relation to popular understandings about Benjamin Franklin's history. This relationship was relevant given the tercentenary celebration's planned museum exhibit (one of the purposes behind the assessment). Learning from the extant displays of archaeological evidence in the "Fragments of Franklin" exhibit could help to ensure that the tercentenary exhibit would be sensitive to the background and educational needs and interests of various projected audiences (school children, those with science interests, etc.). Studying the public's interest in the Franklin Court archaeology exhibit resulted in an unexpected finding made possible by the Franklin Court rat skull. It seems that hundreds of thousands of people over the past 63 years (3 generations) have learned about Franklin, in part, via a rodent! And this reality, in turn, in a round about way, likely plays a part in the visitor's engagement with the archaeology at Franklin Court.

The explanation for this understanding is based in the children's book by Robert Lawson entitled *Ben and Me: An Astonishing Life of Benjamin Franklin as Written by his Good Mouse Amos*. In this book, a small mouse named Amos comes to live with Franklin and turns out to be responsible for many of the inventions and ideas that Franklin is known for. First copyrighted in 1939, the book's copyright was renewed in 1967. The book has been continually in print since 1988.

With an awareness of the existence of this fictional "Amos" character, the tercentenary archaeology consultant contacted the book's current publisher seeking information about the public's consumption of the *Ben and Me* story. It turned out that 36,000 paperback copies of the book were sold the month that the archaeologist contacted the publisher. The inquiry resulted in an agent of the Time Warner Book Group being assigned to what had been a backlist book with automated ordering. Subsequent research undertaken by the agent (at the request of the archaeologist) revealed that the lowest sales number for the book at this publishing house was 23,000 copies for one month, in 1988, while the highest number was 41,000 copies—during the summer of 2003, as part of school textbook-distributor bulk purchasing (Bill Boedeker, of Time Warner Book Group, personal communication to Patrice L. Jeppson, December 16, 2004). According to the book's newly assigned agent, the average non-best-selling book typically only has an annual run of approximately 15,000 copies. This background research confirmed that the story of Franklin's rodent friend is likely active in the visiting public's popular memory.

But people learn about this story beyond the Lawson book route. Also investigated as part of the tercentenary study was the 1953, Disney-produced, animation-short based on the Lawson book. This popular movie was nominated for a "Short Subject" Academy Award, and, at the time of its release, Disney simultaneously published a Golden Book version of *Ben and Me*. Over subsequent decades, the rodent Amos was included among the costumed characters populating the Disney theme parks. At the time of the tercentenary research, a porcelain figurine of "Amos the Pint-Sized Patriot" was being marketed, for a limited time, through exclusive, independent retailers, as a 50th anniversary commemorative item. This animated movie, however, was created a generation ago. Could it still be part of the public's memory?

Research conducted at the Free Library of Philadelphia—one of the nation's largest lending libraries, and one begun by Franklin—provided the answer. A research librarian and the tercentenary archaeologist working together with the library's database records discovered that, system-wide (across the city), a VHS version of this video is the most checked out video that is not a current blockbuster release. So yes, cinematographic "Amos" too could be relevant to the public's interest in the rat skull on display at Franklin Court.

The investigation did not end there. Using the keywords "Ben and Me" and "curriculum," an Internet search was conducted that produced more than 470 viable hits (a large "return" for the internet in the year 2004). This research revealed that Lawson's book is used extensively as a curriculum resource by individual classroom teachers, by school districts, by home school consortiums, and by commercial education companies. The story is used for teaching subjects ranging from Language Arts (literacy, narrative writing, learning historical fact from historical narrative) to Science (learning how an inventor works, learning the idea that mistakes "can work") to History (American History, History of Science and Technology). *Ben and Me* is commonly part of everyday life experience in the nation's schools.

Figure 10.5. The Independence Park unit of Franklin Court interprets the architectural residues of Franklin's house and rental properties. Artifacts recovered from archaeological research at Franklin Court are on display inside the museum. Independence National Historical Park Archives, Multiplex Slide Collection, "Events," 318 Mkt, "Market St Houses" (9-1-1).

The popular history route to how people learn about Franklin—research triggered by the rat skull—was confirmed. *Ben and Me* is part of the popular understanding of Ben Franklin for this, and for recent, generations. But how is this popular history knowledge about Franklin relevant to the archaeology on display at Franklin Court?

Not to be overlooked is the rat skull's display context. The specimen is presented in a setting that very possibly links to an already existing "Franklin Memory" in the mind of many visitors. Amos' story (*Ben and Me*) is described to the reader at the outset of the book (in a contrived forward) as "a manuscript" discovered while "altering an old Philadelphia house." The forward goes on to explain that workmen found this manuscript (now in the reader's hand) when they uncovered a small room with "small articles of furniture all of the colonial period." This narrative links directly to the visitor experience in Franklin Court.

The rat skull is on display in the "Fragments of Franklin" exhibit, an architectural and archaeology interpretation located adjacent to the "ghost house" sculpture and the Franklin house foundations. This space displays the architectural history of Franklin's rental buildings with the walls and floors stripped down to expose the joists, beams, and brick (figure 10.5). The room is filled with fragments of colonial period objects, namely "mice-sized" bits of excavated ceramic and glass artifacts. One of the display cases includes the rat skull.

Displayed in this unique context, the rat skull very likely recalls in the minds of many of the visiting public the popular history of Franklin that they already know, even if that knowledge is by now subconscious, or even if it has been replaced by subsequent formal learning. While archaeologists rarely consider the process of learning (even though it is relevant to the process of acquiring historical memory), this is a realm of research being explored by educators interested in the development of sequential learning and by scientists studying the brain mechanics of creating memory. The scenario created in a visit to Franklin Court is likely an example of these processes in action.

Of course, no one with a concern for history or archaeology would ever advocate that this rat skull artifact be equated with Amos. But this artifact's popularity should not be ignored as it has a lesson to teach us. The Franklin Court rat skull provides a useful point of reference, or hook, for reaching a significant segment of the public with information about Franklin. By assessing the public's involvement with artifact interpretations at Franklin Court, the tercentenary study has discovered new information. Previously identified resources have been identified for a new use and, in the process, important understandings about how people learn about Franklin have been acquired.

A Measure of the American Experiment

One of the most interesting new findings from the tercentenary archaeology study makes use of what past archaeological research at Franklin Court "left behind." Archaeologists may study material culture residues from the past, but they also produce new residues during the process of an excavation. These residues are the artifacts of the archaeological process. They include the field notes, drawings, reports, and photographs that record the archaeological site work. These archaeologically created products are important because archaeology is a destructive science. The artifacts of the archaeological process stand in for the site after the dig is completed and the site no longer exists. The tercentenary study used these residues from the previous archaeological research phases at Franklin Court to bring forth a new Franklin Court interpretation. This new story allows a peek at Franklin's ideas for the nation 200 years into the American experiment.

These new artifacts came to light during the Tercentenary Consortium's assessment of the Franklin Court archaeological records, which are stored in the Independence National Historical Park Archive. The first notable specimens, discovered during the first day of the Tercentenary study, were some black and white photographs found glued into a 1956 site report authored by NPS archeologist Paul Schumacher. From these images it was learned that the individuals who initially relocated the Franklin house ruins were African American. A hand-typed, onion skin-paper contract, entitled "Estimate for Excavation of Benjamin Franklin's Court to locate and record all walls which may give us clues as to the location of Benjamin Franklin's home," revealed that these excavators were also members of the Laborers

International Union, Local 57, which is a construction and industry, or building trades, union (Schumacher 1953). This demographic history of the participants who searched Franklin Court archaeology is interesting given the passage of time. These once irrelevant details about who did what, when, recorded in the site's archaeological documentation are now potentially and potently useful data for telling not just the story of Franklin's mansion and its discovery—but more.

For example, some of these new artifacts are significant because of a new interest in Franklin's later life, the last five years of which were spent at Franklin Court. These years represent the pinnacle of Franklin's enlightenment thinking put into practice, including that which goes beyond his contributions to the American Revolution and independence. This period of his life is marked by participation in the American abolitionist movement. Once a slave owner, he later becomes President of the anti-slavery movement in the New World. He pens and submits to Congress unsuccessful anti-slavery petitions. He opens his house to the anti-slavery society for meetings and also lends his name and image to their cause, one of the first, if not the first, uses of American celebrity for a secular cause. In 1788, the first abolitionist cameos in the New World bearing the slogan "Am I not a man and a brother" were shipped from England to Franklin.

In recent years, Independence National Historical Park has expanded its interpretive themes, broadening the park's portrayal of the American experience to include the country's rich mosaic of diverse cultural and ethnic heritage (INHP 1997). This includes issues of religion, ethnicity, and race among the people of Philadelphia. The park has likewise amended its National Register nomination adding Franklin Court, along with other relevant park properties, as part of an Underground Railroad theme. The artifacts of the archaeological process discovered during the tercentenary study are useful toward this end. They demonstrate the story of Franklin the slaveholder and then abolitionist coming "full circle" (as was suggested to the author in 2005, by INHP Historian Anna Coxey Toogood). Figuratively speaking, the descendants of the community Franklin worked to help free, in turn, excavated Franklin's history for the needs of the American people in the creation of national historical memory.

But the contributions from the recent "archaeology of archaeology" study do not end there. The 1960s site documentation was equally informative and fascinating (Powell 1961, 1962a, 1962b). It indicated that the second phase of excavation, likewise conducted by African American laborers, was performed under the direction of two NPS archaeologists—one of whom was a Native American. An INHP oral history interview (conducted June 8th, 1977, by George A. Palmer [Cynthia P. McCollum transcriber]) recorded NPS Regional Archeologist John Cotter stating that "most archaeologists, of course, are doing work in Indian site explorations and [Jackson Ward "Smokey" Moore, Jr.] returned the favor by being an Indian who excavated in the historical area of one of our notable historical figures"—referring to Franklin Court (see INHP Archives, Constance M. Greiff Administrative History Project Working Files, 1939-1985: Series 1, Interviews and Biographical Data Files,

Box 1/28.) While this transcript identifies Moore as a Seminole, Mr. Moore identified himself as Chippewa during a tercentenary research oral history interview (Jeppson 2006c:32) (figure 10.6).

And there is more. The final phase of excavation in the late 1960s and early 1970s proved similarly revelatory, even though the period in question, occurring more recently, overlapped with greater living and institutional memory. This phase of Franklin Court research involved contracted teams of archaeologists that included several females—three of whom held supervisory positions (see, among others, Liggett 1971; Cosans 1972; Mish 1974). When juxtaposed against the previously detailed crew information, the gender aspect of the 1970s crew leadership, now not particularly significant, became highlighted. Such a leadership scenario is not usually found in archaeology projects of this date, nor is it commonly found in most other disciplines.

One can only guess what Franklin would have thought of this peek at American society, 1953-1974, but it seems fair to surmise that he would have been pleased. The artifacts of the Franklin Court archaeological process provide a measure of how Franklin's eighteenth-century ideas have worked overtime. These new artifacts contribute contextual richness to an understanding of American history and

Figure 10.6. Franklin Court field slide taken in 1962 showing, among others, NPS Archaeologist Jackson Ward "Smokey" Moore Jr. (in the white shirt). Moore, a Native American Chippewa, conducted a significant amount of early historical archaeology research at sites such as Appomattox Courthouse, Fort Fredericka, Fort Smith, Bent's Old Fort, and Fort Union Trading Post. Independence National Historical Park Archives, Multiplex Slide Collection, "Fr. House Privy Outside of Archway, Smoky Moore & Worker, John Cotter, no date" (FC 1:21, 5).

its history (i.e., historicity). The data helps assimilate and re-present Franklin Court for a new story that looks at the state of the American experiment 200 years after its founding (Jeppson 2005, 2006b, 2007).

Conclusion

New archaeological investigations began at the site of Franklin Court 30–50 years after the original excavations. This new study implemented an innovative, "archeology of archaeology" methodology based in researching archived archaeological records and stored artifact collections. With this novel "collections reuse" strategy, Franklin Court is again in the vanguard of archaeology.

This latest phase of archaeological study took a new look at the Franklin Court research findings using twenty-first-century eyes. Due to the evolution of the discipline of archaeology over time, the new study produced fresh data (new artifacts) relevant to the study of Franklin and his times. Beyond these new artifacts, this new research was also able to elicit insights into the process of making Franklin historical memory (Jeppson 2008, 2006d, 2006e, 2004). These new understandings were obtained through an "archaeology of archaeology" approach that takes into account both the context of, and the responses to, previous archaeological research. An additional historical interpretation for the Franklin Court site was also generated by the new study. This latest contribution is based in the archaeological story of the Franklin house rediscovery. (Jeppson 2007, 2006b, 2006c).

Obtaining such rich results from the reexamination of an already dug site is exciting. Importantly, this positive outcome is also a significant finding by itself. The research results demonstrate not just *how* but *why* the archaeology at Franklin Court remains unfinished—and why it should not ever be considered "done" (Jeppson 2008, 2006a). The new research results make clear that just as understandings about history are ever-evolving, archaeological research at a site is never truly complete. This is a point not often understood or appreciated inside, but especially beyond, the field of archaeology. This is also an understanding relevant not just for the site of Franklin Court but for any and all archaeological sites, be they still partially intact, *in-situ*, in the ground, or no longer extant except as collections in archaeological repositories.

The new historical insights highlighted here represent just a handful of the findings that came from the recent Tercentenary Consortium study, but these examples prove that Franklin Court remains a viable and valuable archaeological resource for further study, interpretation, and presentation of history. The same likely holds true for other stored Delaware Valley archaeological collections. The rediscoveries at Franklin Court illustrate that archaeological evidence is not just buried in the ground. Our archaeological heritage is also excavated and stored in archives and museum collections waiting to be *re*discovered.

Acknowledgments

Between 2003 and 2005, this research received significant assistance from Independence National Historical Park personnel including Karen Stevens (then Archivist), Andrea Ashby Leraris (Library Technician), Bob Giannini (Staff Curator), Mary "Missy" Hogan (then East District Ranger Supervisor), Thomas Degnan (Park Ranger), former NPS Architectural Historian Penny H. Batchelor, Anna Coxey Toogood (Historian, Division of Cultural Resources Management), Karie Diethorn (Chief Curator), Jim Mueller (then History Branch Chief), Renee Albertoi (Interpretation and Visitor Services Park Ranger), Charles Tonetti (Historic Architect, Division of Cultural Resources Management), Sue Glennon (then Supervisory Education Specialist), and Renee Albertoi (then Interpretation and Visitor Services Park Ranger). University of Pennsylvania Museum of Archaeology and Anthropology Archivist Alessandro Pezzati provided assistance with research undertaken in the John Cotter Papers. William (Bill) Henry, Dan Roberts, and Bob Giannini (contracted field crew during the 1970s-era excavations of Franklin Court), along with Betty Cosans-Zeebooker (site director), and Jackson Ward "Smokey" Moore (NPS Archaeologist at Franklin Court 1960–1961) provided interesting and important details about Franklin Court's archaeology. Betty Cosans-Zeebooker, the late William Hershey, and Dave Orr helped me to make sense of early Philadelphia historical archaeology research. The Tercentenary Commission's Page Talbott and Connie Hershey provided invaluable assistance and suggestions while Conover Hunt provided early useful direction and Anne Brandt facilitated early administrative aspects of this project. Jed Levin, Karen Lind Brauer, and Janet Asimov provided helpful feedback on earlier versions of this text prepared for conference presentations. I am grateful to Dave Orr and Rich Veit for inviting me to participate in a CNEHA session focusing on the archaeology of the Delaware Valley and for their willingness to shepherd to fruition an edited volume on this same topic.

References Cited

Bacharch, Joan, and Christine Boyd

2003   Out of the Basement: The Use and Accessibility of Archaeological Collections. Symposium presented at the 5th World Archaeological Congress, Washington, DC.

Bandreth, Charles

1953   Drawings of Steps, Franklin Court and Orianna Street Archaeology Project No. 4. On file, Independence National Historical Park Archives, Philadelphia, Franklin Court, Schumacher (1953) Archeology Field Notes, Franklin Court East Side, Project No. 4. Box 10, folder 3.

Benjamin Franklin Tercentenary

2008   *About the Tercentenary.* http://www.benfranklin300.org/about.htm, accessed January 2009.

Cosans, Betty
1974   Volume VI: 1974, Franklin Court Report. Catalog and Remarks. 1974.
              On file, Independence National Historical Park Archives, Philadelphia,
              Acc. No. 3926. Series I: Reports Box 15, Folder 12.
Ellick, Carol
2003   Collections and Education: The Potential of an Under-Used Resource.
              Paper presented at the 5th World Archaeological Congress, Washing-
              ton, DC.
Independence National Historical Park [INHP] [Staff]
2007   Independence National Historical Park Long-Range Interpretive Plan.
              On file, Independence National Historical Park Archives, Philadelphia.
1997   General Management Plan, Abbreviated Final Report. On file, Inde-
              pendence National Historical Park Archives, Philadelphia.
Jeppson, Patrice L.
2008   Rediscovering Franklin: A New story from Franklin Court. Paper pre-
              sented at the Council for Northeast Historical Archaeology Annual
              Conference, St. Mary's City, Maryland.
2007   Civil Religion and Civically Engaged Archaeology: Researching
              Benjamin Franklin and the Pragmatic Spirit. In *Archaeology as a Tool
              of Civic Engagement*, edited by Barbara Little and Paul Shackel, pp.
              73–202. Alta Mira, Lanham, Maryland.
2006a   Ben Underground: A Survey of Archaeological Evidence Related to
              Benjamin Franklin. Paper presented at the New Discoveries: The Ma-
              terial Culture of Benjamin Franklin Symposium. Center for American
              Art at the Philadelphia Museum of Art.
2006b   Which Benjamin Franklin—Yours or Mine?: Examining the Responses
              to a New Story from Franklin Court. *Archaeologies* 2(2):24-51.
2006c   Life, Liberty, and the Pursuit of . . . Archaeology: How the history of
              our own field offers a glimpse into the American Experiment. Paper
              presented at the Society for Historical and Underwater Archaeology
              Conference, Sacramento, California.
2006d   Projects in Parks: Independence NHP Archeology at Franklin Court.
              InsideNPS. National Park Service, U.S. Department of the Interior,
              Washington, DC.
2006e   A New Look at the Franklin Court Mastodon Tooth. *Franklin Gazette*,
              Quarterly Publication of the Friends of Franklin, Inc. Summer 2006.
2005   *Historical Fact, Historical Memory: An Assessment of the Archaeol-
              ogy Evidence Related to Benjamin Franklin: Historical Archaeology
              Research Undertaken for the Benjamin Franklin Tercentenary Consor-
              tium*. On file, Independence National Historical Park, Philadelphia.
2004   "Not a Replacement, But a Valuable Successor . . . ": A new story from
              Franklin's mansion in colonial Philadelphia. Paper presented at the So-
              ciety for American Archaeology, Montreal, Canada.

King, Julia A.

2003 A Comparative Archaeological Study of Colonial Chesapeake Culture. Paper presented at the 5th World Archaeological Congress, Washington, DC.

Lawson, Robert

2003 *Ben and Me: An Astonishing Life of Benjamin Franklin as Written by his Good Mouse Amos Discovered, Edited & Illustrated by Robert Lawson.* New York.

Liggett, Barbara

1971 Final Report, Archaeological Investigation at Franklin Court Independence National Historical Park, conducted by the University of Pennsylvania for NPS 1970–1971, in fulfillment of the terms of contracts #14-10-5-950-57; #14-10-5-391-022; and #14-10-5-391-025. On file, Independence National Historical Park Archives, Philadelphia, F.C. Field Documentation 1971, Report (1 of 2) INHP Box/File 11/16.

1970 Completion Report, Department of Interior Contract 14-10-5-950-57, Archaeological Work at Franklin Court. On file, Independence National Historical Park Archives, Philadelphia, F.C. Field Documentation, INHP Box 11/8.

Mish, Mary

1974a Franklin Court, INDE Archives: Mish, Acc. No. 2873. Manuscript on file, Independence Park Archives, Philadelphia, Series I: Reports Box 12 Folders 16–17.

1974b Franklin Court V, INDE Archives: Mish, Acc. No. 2873. On file, Independence National Historical Park Archives, Philadelphia, Series I: Reports Box 12, Folder 18.

Philadelphia Museum of Art

1976 *Three Centuries of American Art, Bicentennial Exhibition Catalogue.* Philadelphia Museum of Art, Philadelphia.

Powell, B. B.

1961 Franklin Court Collections: T-31, Orianna Street Trench, July–Dec. 1960, April–Sept. 1961. On file, Independence National Historical Park Archives, Philadelphia, Powell Acc. No. 696 (4). Series I: Reports Box 10, Folders 17-25.

1962a The Archeology of Franklin Court. On file, Independence National Historical Park Archives, Philadelphia, Powell, Acc. No. 696 (3). Series I: Reports Box 10, Folders 26-18.

1962b Problems of Urban Archaeology. *American Antiquity,* 27(4):580-583.

Schumacher, Paul J. F.

1956 Preliminary Exploration of Franklin Court, Archaeological Project No. 4, May–September 1953. On file, Independence National Historical Park Archives, Philadelphia, Acc. No. 59. Box 10 Franklin Court, Folder 4-8.

1953   Application for Archeological Excavation in Franklin Court. On file, Independence National Historical Park Archives, Philadelphia, Acc. No. 59. H2215, Box 10 Franklin Court, Folder 1-3, Archaeological Field Notes.

Semonin, Paul

2000   *American Monster, How the Nation's First Prehistoric Creature Became a Symbol of National Identity.* New York University Press, New York.

Unrah, Harlan D., and G. Frank Williss

1983   Administrative History: Expansion of the National Park Service in the 1930s. National Park Service. Denver Service Center. http://www.cr.nps.gov/history/online_books/unrau-williss/adhi.htm (accessed January 2010).

United States Congress, 107th

2002   *Benjamin Franklin Tercentenary Act, H.R .2362,* 107th, January 23, 2002. U.S. Government Printing Office. http://ftp.resource.org/gpo.gov/bills/107/h2362eh.txt.pdf (accessed January 2010).

Wilson, Gaye

2005   Doctor Franklin, Jefferson's "Beloved and Venerable" Friend. Thomas Jefferson Foundation, Inc., *Monticello Newsletter* 16(2):1. Charlottesville, Virginia.

11

THE EARLY POOR IN PHILADELPHIA: A PRELIMINARY REPORT ON THE PHILADELPHIA CITY ALMSHOUSE PRIVY EXCAVATION

MARA KAKTINS AND SHARON ALLITT

Introduction

This paper presents preliminary findings from the excavation of a privy associated with the first Philadelphia City Almshouse, in operation from 1732–1767. Excavations conducted by Temple University students recovered a wealth of artifacts relating to diet, task work, care of the infirm, and even recreation at the almshouse, providing information on colonial treatment of the poor and the daily lives of some of early Philadelphia's least documented citizens. The assemblage contains numerous artifacts, which would be expected from an institution of this nature, as well as many that were not, such as musical instruments, evidence of a surprisingly varied diet including tea consumption by inmates, and some intriguing initialed redware pots. The documentary and archaeological evidence suggest this short-lived almshouse was caught between the traditional methods of poor relief, which relied heavily on "outrelief" such as firewood or small amounts of money, and reforms that advocated the full institutionalization of the poor. Ultimately, the relatively small complex rapidly became overcrowded, and in the second half of the eighteenth century was replaced by a much larger structure called the Bettering House.

Few colonial-period institutions for the treatment of the poor have been examined archaeologically. The principal focus of archaeologists has thus far has been on late-eighteenth and nineteenth-century institutions. These include: the Falmouth, Massachusetts Almshouse, in operation from 1814 into the twentieth century (Spencer-Wood 2009); the Uxbridge and Hudson poor farm cemeteries of Uxbridge, also in Massachusetts (Bell 1990; Elia and Wesolowsky 1995); the cemetery of the Blockley Almshouse located in Philadelphia, which operated from 1835 until the twentieth century (Kimberly Morell, personal communication 2010); the Magdalen Society for the reformation of wayward women, also in Philadelphia (De Cunzo 1995); the 1886 Schuyler Mansion orphanage in Albany (Feister 1991, 2009); and the Destitute Asylum of Adelaide, Australia, which ran from 1849–1917 (Casella 2009). Two colonial American almshouses have been excavated to date: the relatively small 1696 Dutch-built Albany Almshouse (Huey 1991, 2001; Pena 2001) and the 1736–1797 New York City Municipal Almshouse complex (Baugher and Lenik 1997, 2001).

Brief Historical Background of the Philadelphia City Almshouse and Colonial Period Treatment of the Poor

The Philadelphia City Almshouse, operating from 1732 until 1767, was the city's first public poorhouse—although the city's Quakers had built their own private almshouse in 1713. Located in a section of Philadelphia now known as Society Hill, on the block bounded by Spruce and Pine and 3rd and 4th Streets, the City Almshouse was designed to house the city's poor, infirm, and insane. Construction began in 1730 after a suitable block of clear meadow ground was purchased from Alden Allen for £200, and the first inmates were accepted in 1732 (Lawrence 1905). Little is known of the almshouse building and complex itself. Few maps depict the almshouse; the most informative, by Clarkson and Biddle (1762), shows the main building's footprint and its orientation on the block, fronting on Third Street. No outbuildings are shown on the map, but there is a large building located at each end of the main structure. These do not appear to be connected to the main building although it is unclear if this reflects the actual layout of the complex or if it is only a function of the map being drawn as a "schematic" depiction. Errors contained within the original map make it somewhat difficult to know precisely how the almshouse complex was laid out with respect to the present block; however, when the 1762 map is scaled and superimposed over a modern aerial photograph, the excavated privy is seen to be located just within the northeast corner of the enclosure surrounding the complex (figure 11.1). There is but a single known possible image of this almshouse, a watercolor painted by David Kennedy in the nineteenth century based on of a now-lost sketch by Thomas Birch drawn in 1798. Given that even the original image was completed 31 years after the decommissioning of the Almshouse, which was torn down well before 1798, the accuracy of the depiction is in question (Hunter 1977).

The almshouse provided much in the way of out-relief in the form of money, clothes, and firewood (Wulf 2004). At least initially, this was likely the Philadelphia Almshouse's primary function, with only orphans, the elderly, and the very sick actually being admitted (Nash 1979). Limiting admittance to the almshouse served to keep needy families intact, fostered independence, and limited financial strain on the institution. In fact, the building was not originally designed to hold more than 40 or 50 residents at once. As Philadelphia's population swelled and the almshouse administrators began changing their strategy from giving out-relief to the poor to admitting more and more needy citizens in order to rehabilitate them, its population well exceeded 200 in its later years (Hunter 1977). There is a documented change in the role and administration of almshouses over time. Almshouses developed from a more "family" type model in which uniforms were not required, residents were able to leave the grounds, and large rooms housed individuals separated by sex (if that), into one of a "total" institution (Goffman 1970) in which inmates' lives were rigorously controlled, classified, and segregated, with a goal towards reforming the "failed"

Figure 11.1. Plan view showing the approximate location of the City Almshouse complex superimposed on a modern aerial photograph of Philadelphia.

poor, who were increasingly being seen as criminal (Rothman 1990; Spencer-Wood 2001, 2009). The first Philadelphia City Almshouse initially appears to have been set up as a "family" type model with no uniforms, substantial out-relief vs. admittance, communal rooms, and at least some freedom to leave the grounds (Wolf 2004; Rothman 1990). This is not to say that the living in the Philadelphia Almshouse was a pleasant affair or that no stigma was attached to receiving charity. Almshouses were seen as institutions of last resort by many who flocked to them during difficult times, especially the winter months, and many left or escaped as soon as they were able (Wolf 2004; Spencer Wood 2009). The Daily Occurrence Log of the second Philadelphia public almshouse is full accounts of escapees, recorded by a rather ornery clerk: "October 16th, 1790, Eloped: Rachel Davis and Sarah Smith—Two pregnant women, who last night both eloped, it is strange how they got away"; "October 19th, 1790, Eloped: Francisco Messerus—A silly or deranged Spanish lad who was admitted here being considerably recovered, hath by falsehood and deception effected his escape"' "November 3rd, 1790, Eloped: John Harkins, a very worthless young man who was admitted here 15th of September nearly naked and very ill—a shoemaker, he is recovered and well cloathed [sic], and scoundril [sic]-like ran away" (City Archives, Almshouse Daily Occurrence Log 1790). Most needy individuals would first turn to any existing kin networks or the numerous private charities set up by ethnic, religious, and trade groups that cared for their own unfortunate (Bridenbaugh 1962; Alexander 1980). People feared ending up in the almshouse; even those given out-relief were often stigmatized by being forced to wear red or blue cloth badges painted with letters identifying the citizen's city or country of origin, as was the case in Philadelphia and New York (Ross, 1988; Bridenbaugh 1938; Nash 2004; Lawrence 1905; Mohl 1971; Alexander 1980). This humiliating practice served to easily identify the recipients of alms in a city. As the eighteenth century progressed, attitudes began to change and mirror earlier English thinking that the poor need not just be fed and clothed but taught skills and reformed, as they were seen as poor as a result of inherent defects (Nash 1979). This led to many almshouses employing their tenants in attached workhouses where residents would be made to pick oakum, weave cloth, manufacture buttons, shoes, or linens, and other such activities, which would also hopefully serve to defray the costs of running the almshouse (Nash 1976). After the second quarter of the eighteenth century, admittance to the first Philadelphia City Almshouse increased steadily (a trend seen across the colonies) while out-relief dropped, as the managers insisted that more inmates be admitted to facilitate reformation. Increasing numbers of inmates were made to perform task work to generate revenue for the institution (Nash 2004). The first Philadelphia City Almshouse proved too small to handle changing attitudes towards poor relief, which increasingly shunned out-relief as "hand-outs" and equated poverty with moral deficiency requiring confinement and reformation.

In 1767, due to overcrowding caused by a growing homeless population resulting from increased immigration and the depression following the close of the French and Indian Wars, coupled with the aforementioned growing belief that all poor should be institutionalized, the almshouse moved to a larger complex at Tenth and Spruce Streets, sometimes referred to as the Bettering House (a fairly loaded name for the new almshouse). The Bettering House managers insisted that the overseers admit as many people as possible in order to reform them and generate revenue from task work done by its inmates (Alexander 1980). Shortly after it was decommissioned, the property on which the first almshouse was located, now prime real estate in a growing city, was subdivided and cross-streets put in, leading to the archaeologically fortuitous positioning of a house atop the almshouse privy around 1790. Luckily, the resident at the time of the archaeological investigations discovered the feature, contacted archaeologists, and was more than happy to allow excavation of the privy situated in her basement.

Archaeological Excavation

The privy is the only available archaeological evidence of the complex although additional features and foundations likely lie beneath the late-eighteenth and early nineteenth-century houses that dominate the present-day block. Doctor John Cotter, along with students from the University of Pennsylvania, conducted the first archaeological investigation of this privy in 1976. Cotter's work did not complete the excavation of the feature and never reached privy deposits; in fact, he initially identified the feature as a cistern associated with the extant house though he had suspicions as to its association with the first almshouse (Cotter et al. 1993). Cotter's efforts were abandoned after approximately 4 feet of excavation due to lack of time. Excavations by Temple University students and local volunteers resumed between February 2006 and September 2007.

The privy, consisting of a dry laid brick-lined shaft approximately 8.5 feet in diameter, is suitably large for institutional use, and was filled after abandonment with relatively clean local silty clays containing a small number of artifacts dating to the mid- to late eighteenth century. Upon reaching privy deposits and examining the artifacts recovered from them, all of which dated to the time period during which the almshouse was in operation, the feature was determined to indeed belong to the first Philadelphia Almshouse. It is estimated that this privy shaft would have extended approximately 15.5 feet below modern ground surface although it had been truncated by the construction of a house atop it around 1790, and extended at least 2½ feet below the present water table. The privy was clearly cleaned out prior to abandonment although approximately 2½ feet of privy deposits remained in the bottom of the shaft. Not surprisingly, all of these surviving deposits extended beneath the water table, indicating that the nightmen cleaning the shaft likely abandoned their efforts upon reaching water. In fact, once the fill in each of the quadrants was removed, shovel-pitting from the last efforts of the workers could clearly be seen in the compacted surface of the night soil.

The feature was divided into quadrants, the fill overlying the original privy deposits removed (approximately one-fourth of which was screened), and excavated by 6 inch arbitrary levels. Although it is of course preferable to excavate features by natural stratigraphy (Wheeler 2000), the location of all privy deposits below the level of the water table tended to obscure most of the natural stratigraphy. Faint thin bands of organics and possibly lime could be seen in profile immediately upon pumping the water out of the feature although these were all less than a quarter of an inch in thickness. All of the privy deposits were excavated and water-screened, while 50 percent were also put through 1/8 inch screens. One-gallon flotation samples were also kept from each quadrant and level. Preservation was excellent owing to the waterlogged and anaerobic conditions of the context. Cloth, eggshell with interior membrane intact, leather, wood shavings, insect remains, and hair survived in remarkable condition. Upon removal of one layer of privy material, a flattened but clearly discernable squash was noted—seeds still aligned on the interior and adhered to connective fibers. Although artifacts were noted in all quadrants and levels of the feature, the vast majority, approximately 90 percent, of the ceramics, glass, and metal, were recovered from Quadrant A. Complete or near complete vessels were recovered from this quadrant, consisting primarily of low-value items such as chamber pots, redware table and kitchenwares, wine and master snuff bottles, ointment pots, and medicine vials. This concentration of artifacts in a specific location within the privy indicate a possible dumping episode occurring toward the end of the almshouse's existence during which time items likely not considered worth transferring to the new complex were discarded. Excavations have recovered thousands of glass and ceramic sherds, as well as a few whole vessels, tens of thousands of seeds, hundreds of cloth and leather fragments, and thousands of wood shavings, as well as a multitude of small finds and metal items.

Artifact Analysis

For the present purposes, the results of preliminary artifact analysis are given with artifacts divided into functional groups consisting of task work, medical, floral/faunal, personal, kitchen, table, and teawares. Due to the fact that this study is ongoing and all of the 1/8 inch screen materials have yet to be processed, we are unable at this time to determine exact counts and percentages of most artifacts, however, approximate figures are given where possible.

TASK WORK

Task work was an integral part of almshouse life in the colonial period and well into the nineteenth century. Designed to help reform the idle poor through cleansing labor, this work also generated needed funds for the operation of the facility. The system usually failed on both counts, as inmates resented being made to work without compensation due to their perceived "moral deficiencies," and very little income was derived from the labor (Nash 2004; Alexander 1980). Common tasks included oakum picking and cloth and button manufacture. The first excavations of at New York City's first municipal almshouse complex revealed 26 bone button blanks from manufacture on-site by residents (Baugher and Lenik 1997; Baugher 2001) while recent excavations have revealed an incredible 979 fragments of button blanks (Alyssa Loorya, personal communication 2011). In addition, the late-seventeenth-century Albany Almshouse produced evidence of wampum manufacture by inmates (Pena 2001). The Walnut Street Jail prisoners in Philadelphia made buttons, nails, and other items in a nearby workshop (Cotter et al. 1988). Even the Pennsylvania Hospital required occupants to perform task work. Benjamin Franklin decreed upon establishing the Pennsylvania Hospital for the sick poor in 1751 that able patients were to perform simple task work and aid nurses as a goal towards reformation (Cohen 1954).

In 1749, the city authorized the Overseers of the Poor, a group of mostly middle-class local businessmen hired to be administers to the almshouse, to purchase raw materials for task work within the complex to supplement the institution's income, including rope for oakum picking and hemp, flax, wool, and yarn for weaving

(Nash 1976; Heffner 1913). Excavations of the almshouse privy produced numerous rope fragments, bone button discs with single holes drilled in them (a byproduct of button manufacture), and hundreds of cloth fragments and trim scraps including wool, linen, and even silk, thus supporting documentary evidence. Close to forty copper alloy wound-head pins have been recovered thus far, along with three thimbles and five pairs of scissors. Four pewter spoon fragments, some partially melted, may be indicative of another form of task work: recycling. Pewter is an unusual find on most archaeological sites, as it could be sold for scrap to be melted down and reused. Why would an almshouse on a strained budget discard valuable pewter? A fragment of a pewter spoon was also recovered from the New York Municipal Almshouse (Baugher 2001), and two were found in the seventeenth-century Albany Almshouse excavation (Huey 2001). Heffner (1913) indicates that the City of Philadelphia gave the overseers permission to purchase junk for recycling as well as other raw materials for the purpose of keeping the poor employed, and this may have included pewter. Upon decommissioning, some stray pewter fragments may have been discarded in the dumping episode along with other only slightly valuable items, rather than be transferred to the new Bettering House.

Thousands of recovered leather scraps are a byproduct of shoe manufacture at the almshouse. These fragments include large pieces with patterns cut out of them as well as numerous trim portions and a few punched out "hole" remnants. Nineteen partial shoes, mostly utilitarian and primarily for adult males, were excavated as well. Additionally, a tool that appears to be a spur or rowel missing the handle and wheel was recovered, which would have been used to impress stitch marks or outline patterns on leather. Although no documentary evidence has been found to date of leatherworking at the first Philadelphia City Almshouse, it is known that shoe cobbling was taking place at its replacement, the Bettering House (Nash 1979). Based on archaeological evidence, woodworking also appears to have been a task inmates engaged in at the first Philadelphia City Almshouse. Thousands of wood shavings and fragments were present in the privy; the majority of which are thin and curled, indicating they were removed with a plane while green, and sawn sections and scraps, which appear to have been removed with an adze were recovered as well. It is unknown at this point what end product was being produced from the woodworking activities, however, further document research and analysis of the fragments will hopefully provide the answer.

Care of the Infirm

Almshouses often contained infirmaries that administered to those who could not afford to hire private doctors or nurses or to visit city apothecaries. During the first half of the Philadelphia City Almshouse's existence, the poor of the city had no other choice but the almshouse infirmary should they become seriously ill. In 1751, the Pennsylvania Hospital was founded to treat the sick poor with the support of Benjamin Franklin and a multitude of local Quakers, doctors, and other prominent Philadelphians. While this institution was designed to serve the less fortunate, there were strict admission policies early on which resulted in many individuals such as unmarried pregnant women, incurables, those afflicted with venereal disease, and persons classified as "unworthy" poor, being turned away (Cohen 1954; Wulf 2004; Bridenbaugh 1962; Alexander 1980). As a result, the first Philadelphia Almshouse, as well as the subsequent Bettering House and later Blockley Almshouse, all had well-developed infirmaries to treat the sick poor that were turned away by all others. The Blockley Almshouse eventually evolved into Philadelphia General Hospital (Croskey 1929).

The infirmary of the first Philadelphia City Almshouse is represented archaeologically by six ointment pots, at least eleven glass medicine vials, one badly-decayed human tooth, and fragments of two bone lice combs. The ointment pots include three light blue tin-glazed examples, an unusual intact buff body ointment pot with a thick metallic black glaze, and two intact locally made redware pots with dark brown lead glaze, one with a pronounced firing defect in the base. This misfired pot exhibits a hole in the base with a thick glaze pool around it, rendering it useless for its intended purpose. It is possible that the almshouse was purchasing ointment pots in lots and that this vessel was acquired in this fashion. The two intact and viable ointment pots recovered lend support to the idea of a dumping episode having occurred towards the end of the almshouse's existence.

The medicine bottles from the privy are cylindrical and thin bodied with short necks and a flared finish, ranging from 5–6 inches in height. The two exceptions are a pair of smaller vials, one intact and 3 inches tall, with thicker bodies and similar flared finish. Again, it would appear that they were discarded upon the decommissioning of the almshouse; their value not deemed sufficient to warrant their transfer to the new complex.

A single human tooth recovered from the privy may speak to dental practices in the infirmary. This tooth, a molar, exhibits at least one drill hole, possibly two, and one badly decayed root. Clearly the tooth was in need of extraction given its advanced state of decay, and breakage along the crown may be evidence of damage during removal. The tooth would not likely have come out on its own due to the fact that one healthy root remained although it certainly would have caused extreme pain for its unfortunate owner. The offending molar was then unceremoniously thrown into the privy in an age before medical waste disposal was an issue.

Lice combs, a necessary tool in an infirmary, were also recovered. Fragments of at least two bone combs were excavated which resemble modern two-sided varieties with very closely spaced teeth on one side and slightly wider teeth on the other. One can only imagine that, in addition to delousing new inmates, the task of keeping lice out of an increasingly crowded almshouse was a daunting one. The clerk keeping the Daily Occurrence Log for the second public Philadelphia almshouse notes, in his unique tone, that many individuals admitted were in need of delousing: "October 9th, 1790, Admitted: John and Sarah Smith—a very worthless couple and constant autumnal customers as they then duly return, covered or wrapped up in rags swarming with filth and vermin"; "Saturday November 6th, 1790, Admitted: John Brown—a sick man wrap'd in filthy rags and swarming with vermine" (City Archives, Almshouse Daily Occurrence Log 1790).

FAUNAL/FLORAL ANALYSIS

Faunal analysis was conducted by Sharon Allitt with assistance from Michelle Cave, both of Temple University. The resulting data has revealed much about the diet of the almshouse occupants. To date, almost four thousand bone fragments have been analyzed. It should be noted that the 1/8 inch screen is largely responsible for recovering this remarkable number of faunal remains, and although only the 1/8 inch screened material from Quadrant A has been sorted, this has greatly elevated the number of recovered fish remains, as well as those of rodents, and small fragments of mammal and bird bone. Meadow (1980) notes the effect screen size has on the recovery of small faunal remains, and we have seen the impact careful screening can have with the first Philadelphia City Almshouse excavation, as sampling error would have been a major factor had less fine-grained recovery techniques been employed.

Fish bone was particularly prominent at the site, comprising 89.77 percent (n=1,158 bones and scales) of the identifiable animals thus far. The fish appear to range greatly in size, though exact species have yet to be determined. It is reasonable to suggest that fish represented a significant portion of the diet even though they obviously may contribute more bones per individual to the archaeological record than do mammals. This is not surprising given the location of the almshouse complex a few blocks from the Delaware River. In addition, Rothschild (1990) notes that after 1760 in New York City, fishing was becoming industrialized, leading to greater accessibility and decreased cost of fish, especially large varieties such as cod. The excavation of the contemporaneous New York City Municipal Almshouse Complex also revealed a large percentage of fish—56 percent, although this includes shellfish, which the Philadelphia percentage does not (Baugher 2001). Baugher indicates that the New York Almshouse leased portions of shoreline to fish and that the city government intermittently paid people to fish on behalf of the almshouse. Given the large percentage of fish in the assemblage, these are both possibilities for the Philadelphia City Almshouse, and further documentary research will be conducted with the goal of ascertaining how the complex obtained their fish.

Shellfish also appear to have been a significant component of the diet of residents of the first Philadelphia Almshouse. The majority of the shell hinges recovered were oyster, with a few quahog clams, a single fresh water river mussel fragment, and one saltwater mussel fragment. During the early years of the almshouse, oysters would have been primarily a food consumed by the lower classes, and in Philadelphia they would have been inexpensive and procured locally. As the eighteenth century progressed, they became a food enjoyed by all social groups (Rothschild 1990). Andrew Stanzeski conducted preliminary analysis of the oysters from the privy excavation in 2007. His findings indicate that around 30 percent of the almost one hundred oyster shells randomly pulled from all contexts of the excavation for study exhibit charring on the exterior, indicating that they were roasted open. Slightly over 10 percent show evidence of hacking while only a few examples may have been shucked. The majority of the oysters appear to have been opened via roasting, a technique requiring minimal effort. The average age of the oysters from the privy is six years, with the oldest being approximately thirteen years.

Mammal bones technically make up the largest category of faunal remains although the majority of these were small, unidentifiable fragments recovered from the 1/8 inch screen, and as such only identifiable species are included in the percentages. Avian bones make up slightly over 5 percent of the assemblage (n=82). With the exception of one pheasant and two turkey bones, these are mostly unidentifiable with regard to species due to their fragmentary nature. When minimum number of individuals (MNI) is examined for the almshouse assemblage, deer surprisingly dominate, with five individual deer represented by femurs. Although there were more bovine bones total, representing over 2 percent (n=37) of the assemblage, these only equaled a MNI of three. Only two fragments of sheep/goat bone were recovered, representing one individual, while the four pig bones and ten teeth similarly denote only one individual. Although the high MNI count for deer seems unusual, it should be remembered that the first Philadelphia City Almshouse was located in what was, at the time, the outskirts of the city in the countryside, where access to deer and other game may have been a ready and cheap source of food for the residents. There is further evidence that diet in the almshouse was supplemented with wild animals. Although not in nearly the same quantities as deer, the turkey and pheasant recovered may also represent exploitation of wild game, as may a single raccoon bone recovered from the privy. Raccoon, though not typically considered desirable meat, is nonetheless consumable (Rombauer and Becker 1975), however, it may also have been a nuisance animal trapped on the property and discarded. Non-food animals recovered from the privy include one bone each from a fox, skunk, and juvenile cat, in addition to 35 rat bones, including three skulls. The rat bones were in remarkably good condition, with vertebrae and jawbones still articulated at the time of excavation, having lain untouched since presumably having been killed on the grounds and discarded.

At this time, there is no documentary evidence for butchering on site. While the complex encompassed an entire city block and is known to have had gardens, and likely orchards, there is no mention in the historical records of pastureland for large animals, unlike the contemporary New York Municipal Almshouse (Baugher 2001), or purchases of whole animals for consumption. Archaeological findings support this, and it is estimated that no primary butchering and very little, if any, secondary butchering was taking place on the grounds. The cuts of meat identified from the privy are generally of poor quality and would have been best suited for stews and the like. While the pig bones are generally unidentifiable with regard to age, the bovine bones appear to be primarily from sub-adults. Both almshouses clearly relied heavily on fish to feed their residents although it would appear, at least initially, that the Philadelphia Almshouse's remote location and lack of pastureland for animal husbandry led to a slightly different strategy for feeding residents, which included supplementing the diet by exploiting the local game population.

An impressive number and variety of seeds and nutshell fragments have been recovered from the almshouse privy. All of the seeds have yet to be identified, although cherry, plum, grape, raspberry, apple, persimmon, peanut, chestnut, walnut, hickory, sunflower, peach, citrus fruit fragments, cucumber, and various squashes are known to be present, some in great quantities. As with the New York Municipal Almshouse (Baugher 2001), there is evidence that the first Philadelphia City Almshouse had gardens to supply the complex with fresh fruits and vegetables, as well as work for the residents, who likely would have maintained the grounds. Approximately 15,000 cherry pits have been recovered (which consistently clogged the inlets of the sump pumps used to remove water from the privy during its excavation!) from Quadrant A alone, along with approximately 1,600 plum pits and over 1,000 squash species seeds. Grape, raspberry, cucumber, peach, and apple seeds number in the hundreds. Given the overwhelming number of cherry and plum pits, it is likely that orchards were present on site in addition to the garden, and that an assortment of fruits and nuts were available at the complex that were grown on-site. While many would not expect a varied diet at a poorhouse, it would appear that the first Philadelphia City Almshouse provided inmates with quite a variety of foods.

SMALL FINDS AND PERSONAL ITEMS

A number of personal items were recovered from the privy, including jewelry, buttons, buckles, toys, and musical instruments. The most surprising of these finds was without a doubt the King Helmut conch (*Cassis tuberosa*) shell that had been converted into a horn. This large shell of a conch species native to the Caribbean clearly had the top portion of the crown removed and the resulting hole smoothed off. Based on the 1853 painting by Shepard Alonzo Mount entitled "The Breakfast Call," which depicts a girl with a similar horn, the almshouse horn may also have had a mouthpiece inserted in this modified end. The conch horn, although technically an instrument, would have likely functioned primarily as a novelty and may have been donated to the almshouse by a wealthy patron. Another possibility is that it could have been used to call inmates to meals. The horn is in a remarkable state of preservation, with a high polish on the interior, however, it exhibits a clear break on the side, likely from being dropped, which rendered it useless as an instrument and may have ultimately led to its discard. Given the context from which the horn was recovered, we have resisted the urge to see if it still produces noise. A mouth harp recovered represents a more everyday instrument, which was likely brought in by an inmate of the almshouse and played on the grounds. The harp may have been dropped accidentally into the privy although it is missing the thin strip of metal that would have run through the center of the piece and acted as its vibrating "reed" or "tongue," and it may have been discarded for this reason.

Children were certainly housed in the first Philadelphia City Almshouse. Most would not have stayed long, and many were bonded out to area citizens if their parents were found unfit to raise them, as most were. Those who bonded out children paid a fee to gain a child and promised to give them a basic education and usually teach them a trade before releasing them at the age of 18 for girls and 21 for boys. These age limits, however, were often not followed with regard to minority children, who appear to have been kept for much longer periods. This was the case with Catherine Biesmanin, listed as a mulatto bonded out on September 10, 1790, to "Michael Kraft of Northern Liberties for Housewifery, to read in the bible, write a legible hand, to sew plain work and at expiration of her time . . . for 26 years" and a "negro" boy only known as "Marsh" who on March 19, 1782, was bound to "William McMullen of Southward (the author likely meant "Southwark") to read and write the English tongue and all necessary employ for 25 years and 6 months" (City Archives, Indentures Made 1751–1787).

Given this information, it is unsurprising that so few toys were recovered from the almshouse privy. Among those that were recovered are three miniature vessels: a redware porringer, a redware cup with extensive use-wear on the interior, and a miniature white metal mug. All of these are of such a size that they could have been utilized by children, suggesting the possibility that these items were used to actually feed children, not necessarily for play, and even this possibility is not certain as these artifacts only fall into the "miniature" category but may not actually have functioned as toys, per se. The only definite toy is a pewter model pocket watch stamped with the face of an actual watch on both sides. Both the front and back of this toy watch were recovered. The hands of the watch point to a dial of Roman numerals surrounded by a floral motif and read twelve thirty. Remnants of what appears to be a hinge on either side of the watch indicate that it would have opened. Forsyth and Egan (2005) describe similar watches found in the mudflats of the Thames, noting that they had multiple components, including occasionally a winder key and ratchet ring. London pewter merchants began manufacturing these watches in the early eighteenth century, possibly as a secondary source of income during slow economic times. These pewter watches were likely marketed to the middle class, with wooden or paper toys being more affordable for the lower classes (Fritzsch and Bachman 1965). However, a child could be admitted to an almshouse with toys from better days, or toys may have been acquired by them through donations from wealthy patrons. A number of very similar pewter toy pocket watches were recovered from the late-eighteenth-century shipwreck of the *Severn*, a British merchant vessel likely dating to the 1770s and found in the Delaware River in 2004 (Lukezic 2007). The watch from the Philadelphia Almshouse likely belonged to a boy. Lois Feister (2009) states in her study of the Orphanage at Schuyler Mansion that, starting in the eighteenth century, children were encouraged to mimic adults with their toys and were given miniature versions of adult items so they could "play grownup" and define their gender roles early in life. Little girls were given dolls, small tea sets, and kitchenwares, while boys played with such items as pocketknives, miniature soldiers, watches, and even novelty white clay pipes (Zorn 1897). At present it is unknown how many of the children housed at the first Philadelphia City Almshouse were kept long term and how many were bonded out to other households. The later Bettering House did have an orphanage and schooled poor children, but it also bonded out a large percentage of children that came through their doors (James 1963, Wulf 2004, City Archives—Indentures Made 1751–1787). During the period of the first Philadelphia City Almshouse, orphanages as we know them were not in existence, and schooling of the lower classes was not a priority (Murray 2004). Therefore it is likely that most children at the first almshouse, primarily orphans, did not stay there long, resulting in the relatively small number of toys.

A variety of buttons and buckles, in a range of materials and sizes, were recovered from the privy. Buttons excavated include examples made of wood, bone, pewter, a single copper alloy button with what appears to be a gold gilt exterior, and a woven cloth button in perfect condition. The wood and bone buttons are in the majority and are found in an array of sizes. With the exception of the gilt button and the woven cloth button, none of the examples from the almshouse are ornate or decorated. Iron and copper alloy buckles were also recovered from the almshouse privy deposits. The iron examples were undecorated and in a variety of shapes and sizes. Being the least expensive material for buckles, these are the most likely to have belonged to the inmates. Fragments of two highly decorated copper alloy buckles are also present in the collection and may represent overseers, visitors, or managers that were present on the complex or donations from wealthier patrons. The wide range of materials, shapes, and sizes of buttons and buckles reinforces Baugher's (2001) observation that a variety of clothing ornamentation and fasteners should be seen archaeologically at an institution where uniforms are not required, such as the New York Municipal Almshouse. As mentioned above, the only type of identifier Philadelphia required of relief recipients during this time were the aforementioned cloth badges (Bridenbaugh 1938; Nash 2004; Lawrence 1905; Alexander 1980).

Not surprisingly, very little in the way of jewelry was excavated from the almshouse privy. A small faceted black glass bead was recovered from the 1/8 inch screened material, while the 1/4 inch screen picked up a relatively large blue glass rhinestone. This classic diamond-shaped jewelry component shows wear along the bevel and would likely have been mounted in a ring, necklace, or broach. A single intact pewter cufflink with simple stamped decoration was also recovered. The cufflink, in excellent condition, is of good quality and was almost certainly not worn by an inmate.

Initialed Redware Vessels

Three of the 58 redware vessels recovered from the first Philadelphia City Alms-house privy exhibit incised initials or symbols on their bases. Of the 22 chamber pots reconstructed thus far, one clearly displays the initials "CM" while another has a crudely but deliberately drawn "X" or cross on the base. A locally produced redware pitcher with dark brown lead glaze, one of six recovered, exhibits what appears to be the initials "EB," although it could be a series of tick marks followed by a "B." All marks were incised post-firing, and therefore were probably made by the users of the vessels rather than by their manufacturers. Manufacturers of redwares would also be unlikely to initial lowly chamber pots or pitchers; if by some small chance they did, they would likely do so prior to, rather than after, firing the vessels. The "CM" initials are the most elaborate and would have taken the most time to produce (figure 11.2). The "EB" on the pitcher is more rudely scrawled, as is the "X." All three vessels exhibit extensive use-wear on their bases. In the case of the "CM" chamber pot, it was worn to such an extent after being initialed that the final upright of the "M" was worn off. It should also be noted that the edges of the "X" on the other chamber pot are slightly worn away, indicating that the inscribing of this vessel was not the final act of the owner or user prior to discarding it (figure 11.3). This is an important

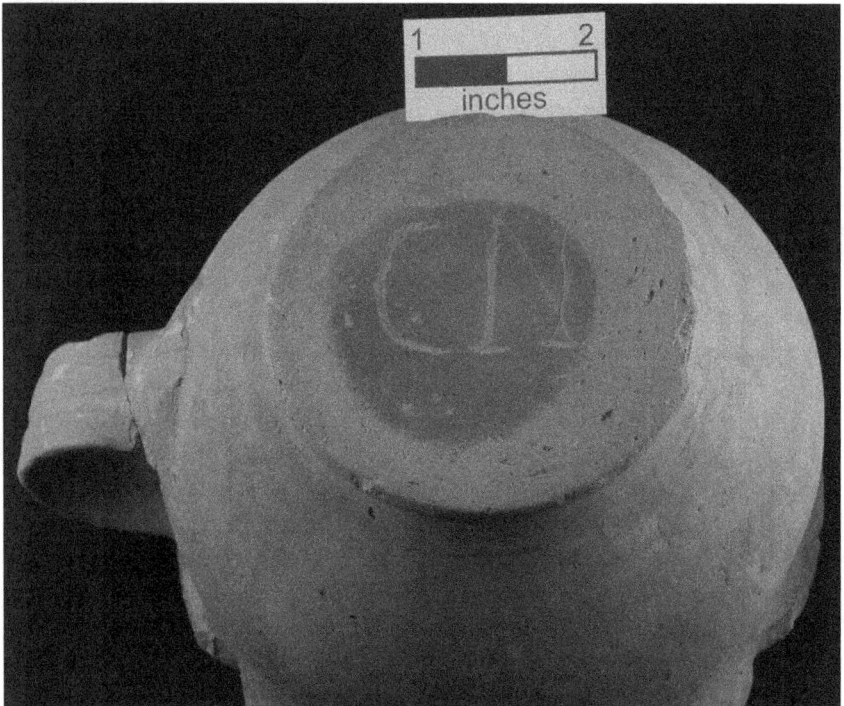

Figure 11.2. Base of a locally produced redware chamber pot incised with the letters "CM." The final bar of the letter M has been worn away.

observation if one is to consider the significance of inscribing an "X" on a pot before it is ritually killed in some African and African American cultures. The use wear on this vessel would seem to preclude this interpretation.

While these unusual artifacts do not necessarily indicate that inmates owned personal possessions, they may signify an attempt at ownership and a form of resistance by the inmates, who were supposed to be humble, poor, and diligent workers until they could be released and fend for themselves; hoarding and defacing almshouse property certainly would have run counter to the goals of the institution. Living in an environment where most (if not all) property was owned by the institution, it is human nature to try to reserve certain items for oneself. The initialed chamber pot is understandable: who wouldn't want his/her own pot in a crowded poorhouse? However, the pitcher is a communal vessel and would not have been utilized by one person, presumably making attempted ownership of this object more difficult unless it was owned (or claimed) by a family in residence at the almshouse. Ownership aside, inmates at the almshouse may have been acting out of boredom, frustration, or anger. Excavations at the contemporaneous Ephrata Commune, which operated from 1732 until the early nineteenth century, revealed similar initialed redwares. Almost thirty sherds of earthenware pottery with post-firing inscriptions on their

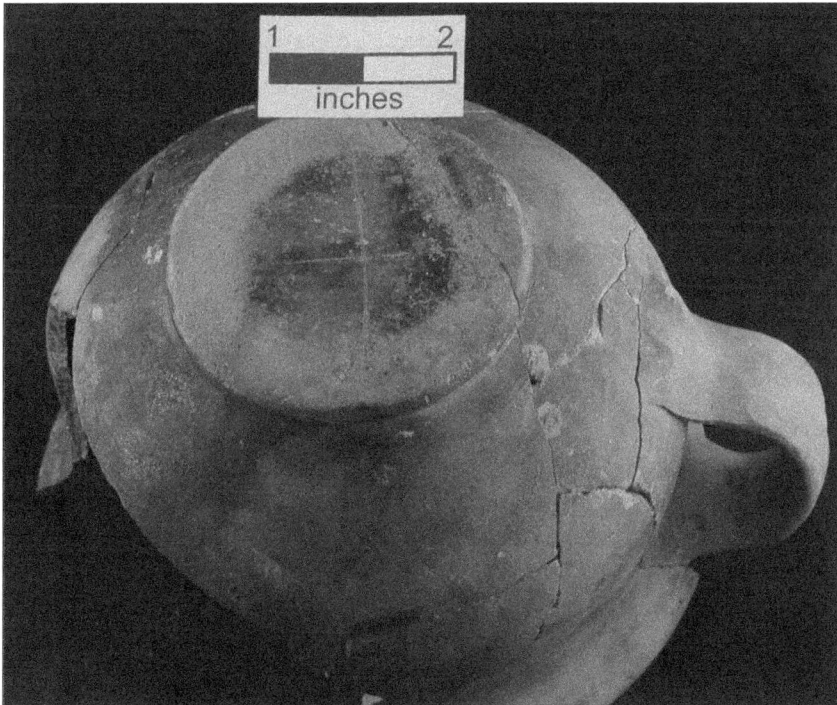

Figure 11.3. Base of a locally produced redware chamber pot, incised with the letter "X."

exterior bases were recovered from the brothers' dormitory area of the Commune (Warfel, 2009). These voluntary inmates of the Commune were taught to disdain private property but nonetheless still personally marked institution-owned vessels. Ultimately, this intriguing idiosyncratic behavior can never be precisely understood in terms of why these people decided to scratch what they did on each vessel. It is certain that this defacing of property or attempt at ownership of communal property is not unexpected in an institution although one can speculate for days on exactly why one decided to initial the base of a chamber pot. The owner of the initials "CM" would likely derive much amusement from the knowledge that it has caused so much contemplation.

TABLE, KITCHEN, AND TEAWARES

As might be expected, the majority of the 47 tablewares and kitchenwares are locally produced Philadelphia-style redwares with dark brown to black lead glazes and interior hollowed-out feet on the hollowwares. The few slipware dishes present are also locally made with typical trailed slip designs and distinctive green copper mottling. An almshouse on a budget would be expected to exploit the cheapest and most readily available ceramic resources, and this certainly seems to hold true for the first Philadelphia City Almshouse. In fact, only one imported British buff body slipware vessel is present in the assemblage, represented by a single sherd. The majority of the redware vessels exhibit extensive use-wear, and there is evidence from two mended chamber pots that the almshouse was purchasing seconds to further reduce their costs. The interior glaze of one of these did not fire properly, leaving a mass of slag-like material fused to the base, which must have made thorough cleaning of the pot tricky although it was apparently utilized extensively nonetheless based on the amount of use-wear present. Another chamber pot exhibits two large cracks in the interior that formed prior to or during firing, as glaze has seeped into them. This vessel exhibits relatively little use-wear, indicating that it probably soon broke along the cracks.

Of the coarse earthenware tablewares present, five bowls and nine porringers dominate over the flatwares, consisting of only three redware dishes. Obviously wooden or pewter dishes cannot be accounted for. As previously mentioned, the diet of the occupants likely consisted mainly of stews, porridges, soups, and the like, as reflected in the faunal assemblage. Cooking vessels from the assemblage include one redware pipkin with celery-shaped feet and a near-complete cast iron pot or cauldron. Looking at the six refined tablewares present in the collection, the opposite is true; there are five plates, one porcelain and four white salt glazed stoneware, all mismatched, and only one plain white salt glazed bowl. Inventories for the Bettering House also reflect similar vessel acquisitions. In 1781, the institution purchased 180 porringers versus only 24 dishes (City Archives, Weekly Receipt Book 1801).

Drinking vessels in the assemblage are made up mostly of redwares, including six tankards of various sizes and six pitchers, all in the Philadelphia style. There are a number of tin cups, at least four large and one miniature, as previously mentioned. The stem and foot of a wine glass and fragment of a glass handle, possibly for a small pitcher or mug, represent the only table glass excavated from the privy. Of great interest, though, is the preponderance of teawares present in the almshouse collection. A total of 18 percent of the total identified vessels identified are teawares, with ten teacups, four teapots, and four saucers recovered. The teawares occur in refined cream-colored earthenware, porcelain, and both plain and scratch blue salt glazed stoneware. Interestingly, a significant number of relatively high-status teawares were also recovered from the New York Municipal Almshouse excavation, comprising 18 percent of the tableware assemblage from that site (Baugher 2001). Huey (2001) also notes the presence of high-status wares such as porcelain and scratch blue stoneware from the Albany Almshouse excavation. Although some of the scratch blue teawares from the Philadelphia Almshouse exhibit similar motifs, such as swag and tassel and a floral design with herringbone border, none of them can be said to "match" and all the cups are of differing sizes. With this in mind, the 18 different teaware vessels recovered stand to represent up to 18 different tea "sets" from one almshouse privy (figure 11.4).

The obvious question is: how did so many higher-status teawares end up in a poorhouse privy? Baugher gives a number of explanations in her article on the

Figure 11.4. Fragments of a Scratch Blue stoneware tea set recovered from the Philadelphia Almshouse.

New York Almshouse excavation (2001). The first of these is perhaps the most obvious conclusion: the overseer, who was a middle-class member of society, would have owned a number of teawares. The overseer and his family would have lived on the grounds, and it is to be expected that artifacts associated with his presence would be found. However, as with the New York Almshouse assemblage, the variety within the Philadelphia collection precludes all of these teawares belonging to just the overseer and his family. Another possibility is that some teawares were kept on hand for visitors to the almshouse. Strange as this may seem, citizens of Philadelphia regularly toured the grounds of the almshouses for pleasure, took tea, and even had dinners while visiting (Cresson 1908; Smith 1954). Huey (2001) notes the trend of erecting lavish buildings to house the poor with elaborate ornamental gardens designed to impress. When the Bettering House replaced the smaller City Almshouse it was, at the time, the largest building erected in the colonies and featured the aforementioned gardens (Nash 2004). Again, however, while this explanation may account for some of the teawares and even some of the other high-status artifacts recovered from the excavation, it cannot explain all of them. Baugher (2001) suggests that inmates retaining remnants of their rosier pasts may have brought some vessels into an almshouse. While inmates were allowed to possess personal items in colonial period almshouses, there is documentary evidence that almshouses were last resorts—that they were places where diseases were spread and women were separated from their children, where people were frequently escaping and even stealing the donated clothes issued by the almshouse and selling them for whatever small amount of money they could get (Cray 1988; Wulf 2004; Nash 2004; Spencer-Wood 2009b). Given this information, it is unlikely that many individuals would enter an almshouse with valuable ceramics that they could have potentially sold to stave off admittance to the poorhouse.

That last and most likely explanation, also suggested by Baugher, (2001) is that the teawares are donations given by wealthy patrons of the almshouse. This would explain the mismatched nature of the assemblage. Given the apparent dichotomy between the utilitarian redwares clearly purchased by the almshouse and the refined teawares, it is likely that the teawares and other refined tablewares were not purchased by the almshouse. There is already evidence from the collection for donations by wealthy patrons. John Pole, a Quaker who emigrated from England to Burlington, New Jersey and then to Philadelphia, was involved with local charities. This would be expected of Mr. Pole, given his listing in the *Pennsylvania Gazette* as a successful pewter merchant (1741). Pole was a prominent citizen who signed the articles creating a group of Philadelphia firefighters called the Fellowship Fire Company in 1738 (Jordan 1903) and was in charge of 4,000 pounds sterling sent by the Pennsylvania Assembly to buy food for forces protecting Nova Scotia (Baumann 1973). Of particular interest is that a bottle with his personal seal dated 1750 ended up in the bottom of the first Philadelphia City Almshouse privy (figure 11.5). Aside from indicating that John Pole was a benefactor of the almshouse, which is not surprising given his documented good deeds and Quaker affiliation, this artifact lends

Figure 11.5. A wine bottle bearing the seal of John Pole, a prominent Philadelphia Quaker and benefactor of the Philadelphia Almshouse. The bottle is dated 1750 and may have been a gift from Pole to the Almshouse residents.

support to the practice of donating used items such as ceramics and even bottles to the institution for use by the inmates.

The idea of poorhouse residents consuming tea and chocolate may seem unusual, and was not a practice in English almshouses where this would be considered an extravagance (Huey 2001). It may be the case that tea was served to residents at the complex in an effort to include them in an eighteenth-century ritual that respectable citizens were expected to observe on some level (Yentsch 1990), rather than as a way to elevate them past their lower-class status. There is documentary evidence that tea and chocolate were purchased for residents of both the New York and Philadelphia almshouses (Shammas 1990). This evidence, along with the overwhelming number of teawares excavated, indicates that the first Philadelphia Almshouse inmates were engaging in the tea ceremony. The Bettering House also provided tea, coffee, and chocolate to inmates well into the nineteenth century. Inmates were issued daily allowances of their choice of tea, chocolate, or coffee with detailed records being kept as to amounts and types of beverages issued each inmate; in 1801, clerks record purchasing 314 pounds of tea and 210 pounds of coffee for the Bettering House (City Archives, Daily Issues 1805 and Daily Receipts 1801).

Conclusions

Investigations into the first Philadelphia City Almshouse stand to contribute significantly to our understanding of colonial period treatment of the poor and institutions for the indigent, sick, and insane, as well as the transitions that these institutions were

undergoing during the eighteenth century. The move from a familial-type organization to a "total" institution reflects a shift in public mentality towards the needy,
which led to a shift toward more and more applicants being forced to enter the
almshouses as opposed to obtaining out-relief; this can be seen through examination
of the first Philadelphia Almshouse and the subsequent Bettering House. Excavations have already revealed evidence for a surprisingly varied diet rich in fish and
supplemented with local game although one cannot speak to the actual amounts or
caloric intake provided to residents. Tens of thousands of seeds recovered confirm the
presence of orchards and gardens while thousands of leather and wood scraps and
other artifacts support documentary evidence of task work occurring on the grounds.
The large percentage of mismatched teawares, along with available documentary evidence, indicates that almshouse residents, the poorest citizens of Philadelphia, were
engaging in the tea ceremony. In addition to providing data on the almshouse, a
total of 58 locally produced mended redware vessels and hundreds of sherds stand
to contribute to our knowledge of regional ceramics while the initialed pots may be
a sign of how the stresses of institutional life are manifested physically on artifacts.
This study is ongoing, and much research is yet to be done, including more detailed
analyses of the artifacts and further research into primary documents. Regardless
of the work that lies ahead, initial findings indicate that the study of this relatively
short-lived almshouse will reveal much about the lives of the poorest and least documented citizens of eighteenth-century Philadelphia.

References Cited

Alexander, John K.
1980   Render Them Submissive: Responses to Poverty in Philadelphia, 1760–
            1800. University of Massachusetts Press, Amherst.
Baugher, Sherene, and Edward J. Lenik
1997   Anatomy of an Almshouse Complex. Northeast Historical Archaeol-
            ogy 26:1–22.
Baugher, Sherene
2001   Visible Charity: The Archaeology, Material Culture, and Landscape
            Design of New York City's Municipal Almshouse Complex. Interna-
            tional Journal of Historical Archaeology 5(2):175–202.
Baumann, Roland M.
1973   John Swanwick: Spokesman for "Merchant-Republicanism" in Phila-
            delphia, 1790–1798. The Pennsylvania Magazine of History and Biog-
            raphy 97(2):131–182.
Bell, Edward L.
1990   The Historical Archaeology of Mortuary Behavior: Coffin Hardware
            from Uxbridge, Massachusetts. Historical Archaeology 24(3):54–78.

Bridenbaugh, Carl

1938 *Cities in the wilderness; the first century of urban life in America, 1625–1742.* The Ronald Press Company, New York.

1962 *Rebels and Gentlemen; Philadelphia in the Age of Franklin.* Oxford University Press, New York.

Casella, Eleanor C.

2009 On the Enigma of Incarceration: Philosophical Approaches to Confinement in the Modern Era. In *The Archaeology of Institutional Life,* edited by April M. Beisaw and James G. Gibb, pp. 17–32. University of Alabama Press, Tuscaloosa.

City Archives

1751–1787 Indentures Made, Record Group 35.2

1790 Almshouse Daily Occurrence Log, Record Group 35.75

1801 Daily Receipts, Record Group 35.77

1801 Weekly Receipt Book, Record Group 35.78

1805 Daily Issues, Record Group 35.76

Clarkson, Matthew, and Mary Biddle

1762 *A Map of Philadelphia.*

Cohen, Bernard I.

1954 *Some Account of the Pennsylvania Hospital by Benjamin Franklin.* The Johns Hopkins University Press, Baltimore, Maryland.

Cotter, John, R. W. Moss, B. C. Gill, and J. Kim

1988 *The Walnut Street Prison Workshop : A Test Study in Historical Archaeology Based on Field Investigation in the Garden Area of the Athenaeum of Philadelphia.* Athenaeum of Philadelphia, Philadelphia.

Cotter, John, Daniel G. Roberts, and Michael Parrington

1993 *The Buried Past: An Archaeological History of Philadelphia.* University of Pennsylvania Press, Philadelphia.

Cray, Robert E. J.

1988 *Paupers and Poor Relief in New York City and its Rural Environs, 1700–1830.* Temple University Press, Philadelphia.

Cresson, Anne H.

1908 Biographical Sketch of Joseph Fox, ESQ., of Philadelphia. *The Pennsylvania Magazine of History and Biography* XXXII:175–199.

Croskey, M. D., and John Welsh

1929 *History of Blockley, A History of The Philadelphia General Hospital From its Inception, 1731–1928.* F.A. Davis, Philadelphia.

De Cunzo, Lu Ann

1995 Reform, Respite, Ritual: An Archaeology of Institutions; The Magdalen Society of Philadelphia, 1800–1850. *Historical Archaeology* 29(3):1–168.

Elia, Ricardo J., and Al B. Wesolowsky
1991   Archaeological Investigations at the Uxbridge Almshouse Burial
            Ground in Uxbridge, Massachusetts. *British Archaeological Reports
            International Series 564.*

Feister, Lois M.
2009   The Orphanage at Schulyer Mansion. In *The Archaeology of Institu-
            tional Life,* edited by April M. Beisaw and James G. Gibb, pp. 105–116.
            University of Alabama Press, Tuscaloosa.

Forsyth, Hazel, and Geoff Egan
2005   *Toys, Trifles, and Trinkets; Base-Metal Miniatures from London 1200–
            1800.* Museum of London, Unicorn Press, London.

Fritzsch, Karl E., and Manfred Bachman
1965   *An Illustrated History of Toys.* Abbey Library, London.

Goffman, Erving
1970   *Asylums: Essays on the Social Situation of Mental Patients and Other
            Inmates.* Aldine, Chicago.

Heffner, William C.
1913   *History of Poor Relief Legislation in Pennsylvania 1682–1913.* Holz-
            apfel Publishing, Cleona, Pennsylvania.

Huey, Paul
1991   The Archeology of Fort Orange and Beverwijck. In *A Beautiful and
            Fruitful Place: Selected Rensselaerswijck Seminar Papers,* edited by
            Nancy A. McClure Zeller, New Netherlands Publishing, Albany.
2001   The Almshouse in Dutch and English Colonial North America and its
            Precedent in the Old World: Historical and Archaeological Evidence.
            International Journal of Historical Archaeology 5(2):123–154.

Hunter, Robert J.
1977 [1955] *The Origin of the Philadelphia General Hospital, Blockley Division.*
            1977 Commemorative ed. Philadelphia.

James, Sydney V.
1963   *A People Among Peoples; Quaker Benevolence in Eighteenth-Century
            America.* Harvard University Press, Cambridge, Massachusetts.

Jordan, John W., William Callender, John Pole, Jno. Lukens, and Joseph Trotter
1903   The Fellowship Fire Company of Philadelphia, Organized 1738. *The
            Pennsylvania Magazine of History and Biography* 27(4):472–481.

Lawrence, Charles
1905   *History of the Philadelphia Almshouses and Hospitals From the Begin-
            ning of the Eighteenth to the Ending of the Nineteenth Centuries.* C.
            Lawrence, Philadelphia.

Lukezic, Craig
2007   *Pewter Toys from the Severn.* Unpublished.

Meadow, R. H.
1980   Animal Bones: Problems for the Archaeologist Together with Some
            Possible Solutions. *Paleorient* 6:65–77.
Mohl, Richard A.
1971   *Poverty in New York, 1783–1825.* Oxford University Press, New York.
Murray, John E.
2004   Bound by Charity: The Abandoned Children of Late Eighteenth-
            Century Charleston. In *Down and Out in Early America,* edited by
            Billy G. Smith, pp. 213–232. Pennsylvania State University Press, Uni-
            versity Park.

Nash, Gary B.
1976   Poverty and Poor Relief in Pre-Revolutionary Philadelphia. *The Wil-
            liam and Mary Quarterly* 33(1):3–30.
1979   *The Urban Crucible.* Harvard University Press, Cambridge Massachu-
            setts and London, England.
2004   Poverty and Politics in Early American History. In *Down and Out in
            Early America,* edited by Billy G. Smith, pp. 1–37. Pennsylvania State
            University Press, University Park.

Peña, Elizabeth S.
2001   The Role of Wampum Production at the Albany Almshouse. *Interna-
            tional Journal of Historical Archaeology* 5(2):155–174.
Rombauer, Irma S., and Marion R. Becker
1975   *Joy of Cooking.* Penguin Group, New York.
Ross, Steven J.
1988   Objects of Charity: Poor Relief, Poverty, and the Rise of the Almshouse
            in Early Eighteenth-Century New York City. In *Authority and Resis-
            tance in Early New York,* edited by William Pencak and Conrad Edick,
            pp. 138–172. New-York Historical Society, New York.
Rothman, David J.
1971   *The Discovery of the Asylum; Social Order and Disorder in the New
            Republic.* Little, Brown, Boston.
Rothschild, N. A.
1990   *New York City Neighborhoods.* Academic Press, New York.
Shammas, Carole
1990   *The Pre-Industrial Consumer in England and America.* Clarendon
            Press, Oxford, United Kingdom.
Smith, Robert C.
1954   A Portuguese Naturalist in Philadelphia, 1799. *Pennsylvania Magazine
            of History and Biography* 78(1):71–106.
Spencer-Wood, Suzanne M.
2001   Introduction and Historical Context to the Archaeology of Seventeenth
            and Eighteenth Century Almshouses. *International Journal of Histori-
            cal Archaeology* 5(2):115–122.

2009   A Feminist Approach to European Ideologies of Poverty and the In-
               stitutionalization of the Poor in Falmouth, Massachusetts. In *The
               Archaeology of Institutional Life,* edited by April M. Beisaw and
               James G. Gibb, pp. 117–136. University of Alabama Press, Tuscaloosa.

Stanzeski, Andrew

2007   *Almshouse Privy: Shellfish Component—Resident or Caretaker?* Un-
               published manuscript.

Warfel, Stephen G.

2009   Ideology, Idealism, and Reality: Investigating the Ephrata Commune.
               In *The Archaeology of Institutional Life,* edited by April M. Beisaw
               and James G. Gibb, pp. 137–150. University of Alabama Press,
               Tuscaloosa.

Wheeler, Kathleen

2000   Theoretical and Methodological Considerations for Excavating Priv-
               ies. *Historical Archaeology* 34(1):3–19.

Wulf, Karin

2004   Gender and the Political Economy of Poor Relief in Colonial Philadel-
               phia. In *Down and Out in Early America,* edited by Billy G. Smith, pp.
               163–188. Pennsylvania State University Press, University Park.

Yentsch, Ann

1990   Minimum Vessel Lists as Evidence of Change in Folk and Courtly Tra-
               dition of Food Use. *Historical Archaeology* 24(3):24–53.

Zorn, George

1989 [1892]   *George Zorn & Co. Pipes and Smokers Articles.* 5th ed. S. Paul Jung
               Jr., Bel Air, Maryland.

12

THE ROOT OF THE MATTER: SEARCHING FOR WILLIAM HAMILTON'S GREENHOUSE AT THE WOODLANDS ESTATE, PHILADELPHIA, PENNSYLVANIA

SARAH CHESNEY

Introduction

One of the most enduring images of Colonial and early Federal America is that of the elite country plantation consisting of a picturesque mansion house surrounded by landscaped grounds, formal gardens, and carefully placed outbuildings. Modeled after English country estates, these early American rural retreats were carefully planned by their owners to showcase not just their wealth but their complete control over the natural world and their understanding of complex design principles that reaffirmed their position at the pinnacle of colonial society (Chesney 2009; Leone 1984, 1988).

Some of the most elaborate examples of these early American country estates can be found in the Delaware Valley. The numerous plantations found in southern New Jersey and along the Schuylkill River in Pennsylvania functioned as second homes, where members of the Philadelphia elite and their guests could relax among landscaped grounds carefully designed to refresh and revitalize the shattered sensibilities of those whose business kept them in the midst of the crowded, dirty, and noisy city for much of the year (Brown 1937; Jacobs 2006; Long 1991). These country estates were havens for Philadelphia elites, providing a welcome respite from the city and a private space in which to pursue the lifestyle of an English country gentleman, including large-scale landscape design based on the latest European ideas (Betts 1979; Brown 1937; Heintzelman 1972; Jackson 1932; Jacobs 2006; Long 1991; Stetson 1946, 1949a; Wulf 2009).

The Woodlands, William Hamilton's late-eighteenth-century country estate on the west bank of the Schuylkill River in Philadelphia, was no exception. Like other men of his social standing, Hamilton inherited both income and property from his male relatives, including a small country estate four miles west of Philadelphia known as The Woodlands (Betts 1979; Boyd 1929; Fussell and Long [1998–2009]; Jacobs 2006; Long 1991; The Pennsylvania Horticultural Society [PHS] 1976; Rasmusson 1966). Here Hamilton was able to indulge his interests in architecture, landscape design, and botany to such an extent that he transformed The Woodlands into what was considered one of the most magnificent examples of an English country estate on this side of the Atlantic (Betts 1979; Fussell and Long [1998–2009]; Harshberger 1924; Huddleston 1969; Jacobs 2006; Jefferson 1944; Long 1991;

McLean 1984; Madsen 1989; O'Malley 1996; Schlereth 2007; Stetson 1949a; Ward 1879). But Hamilton's botanical obsession pushed him beyond his peers to create not just an exemplary English-style country estate outside of Philadelphia but also to amass the most extensive collection of rare and exotic flora in private hands in British North America (Fussell and Long [1998–2009]; Long 1991; Madsen 1989). This botanical collection was distributed across the entirety of The Woodlands estate, but the most exotic and fragile specimens were housed in Hamilton's extensive greenhouse complex. Since 2009, this greenhouse complex has been the focus of an ongoing historical and archaeological investigation that has begun to reveal not only the complex nature of Hamilton's botanical activities on his estate but also shed light on the close-knit world of Philadelphia botanical enthusiasts and their roles in the development of American botany.

Background

The early history of William Hamilton's country estate does not differ greatly from that of other country estates owned by members of the Philadelphia elite. The property was originally acquired in 1735 by Hamilton's grandfather, Andrew Hamilton I (circa 1676–1741), a former Pennsylvania Attorney General, who passed the estate to his son, Andrew II (William's father) (Allen 1885; Betts 1979; Fisher 1892; Jacobs 2006; Long 1991; Ward 1879). William inherited the estate at the age of two when his father died in 1747 (Jacobs 2006; Long 1991; Madsen 1989). In Hamilton's youth, The Woodlands estate functioned as many others did: it was a vacation home, a country seat of the Hamilton family, and a place of refuge in summer months but not the family's primary residence (Betts 1979; Boyd 1929; Jacobs 2006; Long 1991; Ward 1879). At the time of Hamilton's inheritance, the entirety of The Woodlands estate consisted of a modest house and 350 acres of farmland that was rented out to a tenant for much of the year (Betts 1979; Boyd 1929; Fussell and Long [1998–2009]; Jacobs 2006; Long 1991). As only one of a handful of properties owned by the Hamilton family, whose holdings included a Philadelphia townhouse where the family lived for much of the year, and another estate at Bush Hill that was owned by Hamilton's uncle, former Lieutenant Governor and Mayor of Philadelphia James Hamilton (1715–1783), The Woodlands was not the primary focus of the family's interest. The estate might even have faded into obscurity if not for William's inheritance and subsequent decision to turn it into a botanical paradise (Allen 1885; Long 1991; Neible 1908; Steiner 1897; Ward 1879).

As a young man, Hamilton was fascinated by botany and intrigued by the possibilities for landscape design and the display of exotic flora offered by a country estate such as The Woodlands (Jacobs 2006; Long 1991; Stetson 1949a). While a student at the College of Philadelphia in the 1760s (later the University of Pennsylvania) Hamilton made plans for the redesign of The Woodlands based on the latest trends in English landscape gardening and his own passion for exotic flora (Betts

Figure 12.1. Portrait of William Hamilton and Anne Hamilton Lyle. Oil on canvas. Reproduced by permission from the Historical Society of Pennsylvania.

1979; Boyd 1929; Jacobs 2006; Long 1991; Nash 2002; Thayer 1982; Tinkcom 1982). He continued to refine those plans as he discussed them with a growing number of acquaintances among the international botanical community, including such prominent botanists as Philip Miller, head of the Chelsea Physic Garden in London, and André and François André Michaux of the Jardin du Roi in Paris (Betts 1979; Jackson 1932; Jacobs 2006; Lockwood 1931; Long 1991; Madsen 1989; Schlereth 2007; Stetson 1946, 1949a). Hamilton's correspondence with these individuals only encouraged his obsession with exotic plants and his need to display them at The Woodlands. He began acquiring more land for the display of his exotics, creating extensive pleasure gardens and landscaped grounds that extended across the main area of the estate. Hamilton's improvements to the landscape included specially-arranged groves as well as a vast, 140 foot long greenhouse-hothouse complex that contained a lily pond and as many as ten thousand different plants (Boyd 1929; Fussell and Long [1998–2009]; Lockwood 1931; Long 1991; McLean 1984; Madsen 1989; Oldschool 1809; PHS 1976) (figure 12.2).

In his time, Hamilton was at the forefront of American botany, and he was as well known to his contemporaries as his near neighbor John Bartram. Hamilton's talents as a botanical cultivator and his extensive collection of rare and exotic plants housed in his impressive greenhouse complex were legendary (Boyd 1929; Fry 1995; Fussell and Long [1998–2009]; Graustein 1961; Jefferson 1944; Leighton 1976; Long 1991; McLean 1984; Madsen 1989; O'Malley 1996; PHS 1976; Schlereth 2007; Stetson 1949a; Ward 1879). Hamilton was considered an expert on the cultivation of exotic plants, and his advice and talent were sought out by many. Even before he was elected a member of the American Philosophical Society, the Society sought out Hamilton's botanical expertise, asking him to cultivate a box of seeds sent to them by the British East India Company in 1794. Thomas Jefferson himself ensured that Hamilton was one of the few individuals who received two boxes of seeds and cuttings from the Lewis and Clark expedition to cultivate (American Philosophical Society 1799; Jefferson 1944; Long 1991).

Hamilton spent most of his adult life either at The Woodlands or making plans to improve it, continually acquiring and cultivating botanical specimens in his greenhouse and landscape park. He employed a series of head gardeners to oversee the daily care of the greenhouse and grounds, including a few who went on to have successful careers as botanists and nurserymen, such as Frederick Pursh, and John Lyon (Boyd 1929; Ewan 1952, 1983; Ewan and Ewan 1963; Graustein 1961; Long 1991; PHS 1976; Pursh 1814). At the time of his death in 1813, The Woodlands had garnered international fame for its botanical collection both within the greenhouse

Figure 12.2. The greenhouse complex at the Elgin Botanic Gardens, New York, engraving, ca. 1801. Contemporary accounts suggest that this design was modeled directly on the greenhouse-hothouse complex at The Woodlands. Reproduced by permission from the Geographic Collection of the New York Historical Society.

complex and outside in the landscape park and pleasure grounds (Jacobs 2006; Long 1991; Stetson 1949; Schlereth 2007; Ward 1879). However, Hamilton's heirs were not particularly interested in continuing his botanical collection after his death, nor did they have the financial ability to do so, and parts of the estate were sold off to pay a variety of debts incurred by the family (Fisher 1929; Fry 1995; Fussell and Long [1998–2009]; Long 1991).

Various institutions and private citizens bought pieces of the estate throughout the early nineteenth century, with the first large parcel purchased in the 1820s for the construction of the Philadelphia Almshouse (Fry 1995; Fussell and Long [1998–2009]; Long 1991). Finally, in 1840, a group of men led by Eli K. Price purchased the historic core of the estate, which included the main house, greenhouse, stables, and 90 acres of Hamilton's original pleasure grounds, for the site of The Woodlands Cemetery Company (Fry 1995; Fussell and Long [1998–2009]; Long 1991; PHS 1976). The Cemetery Company converted the land into a private cemetery park while still maintaining many of Hamilton's original landscape features (Fry 1995; Fussell and Long [1998–2009]; Long 1991; Ward 1879; Weinberg and Lawrence 2006). During the Cemetery Company's early years, the greenhouse complex continued to be used by a series of nurserymen who rented the space in the early and mid-nineteenth century, but they were haphazard tenants, and the building soon fell into disrepair (Fry 1995; Fussell and Long [1998–2009]; H. 1840; Lockwood 1931; Long 1991). The condition of the greenhouse complex eventually became so poor that the Cemetery Company decided to tear it down in 1854 to make way for an octagonal carriage house to serve the cemetery's visitors (Fry 1995; Jacobs 2006; Long 1991).

Archaeology at The Woodlands

The Woodlands Cemetery Company continues to operate today, and the 54 acre core of Hamilton's original estate still stands in West Philadelphia, including the mansion house, stables, and the partial ruins of the octagonal carriage house under which lie the buried remains of the greenhouse complex. Completed in 1793, the complex measured approximately one hundred and forty feet in length, and consisted of a central two-story greenhouse flanked on either side by a single-story hothouse (Fry 1995; Fussell and Long [1998–2009]; H. 1840; Lockwood 1931; Long 1991). It was said to have contained anywhere from six to ten thousand separate plants, including a sunken pond specifically built for cultivating water lilies (Fry 1995; Fussell and Long [1998–2009]; Jacobs 2006; Jefferson 1944; Lockwood 1931; Long 1991; Oldschool 1809; PHS 1976; Schlereth 2007; Stetson 1949b; Ward 1879). Exploring both the structure of Hamilton's greenhouse complex and its physical relationship to the rest of the overall landscape design at The Woodlands has provided new insights into the development of natural history in eighteenth- and nineteenth-century America, as ideas about display and classification of plants and the ways in which they were cultivated and cared for changed over time.

More specifically, understanding the layout and design of Hamilton's greenhouse complex has shed light on the requirements of managing such a collection and what exactly was involved in the daily care and maintenance of a place devoted exclusively to the care of exotic plants outside their natural climates. As Hamilton's botanical collection at The Woodlands was on par with the most well-known estates and gardens in England, the opportunity to see the early achievements in American botany "on the ground" through the archaeological investigation of his greenhouse complex is unparalleled (Betts 1979; Cornett 2005; Jefferson 1944; Jacobs 2006; Leighton 1976; Lockwood 1931; Long 1991; Martin 1991; The Pennsylvania Horticultural Society 1976).

The first systematic archaeological study of The Woodlands was conducted by Joel Fry of Archaeological and Historical Consultants for the University City Historical Society in 1993. Financed through a grant from the Historic House Museum Challenge Grant Program, Fry's survey explored the archaeological integrity of the historic core of The Woodlands (Fry 1995; Weinberg and Lawrence 2006). Fry excavated a series of shovel test pits northwest and east of the nineteenth-century carriage shed, along with two separate five by five foot test units. Unit 1 was sited four feet east of the mansion's south portico, and Unit 2 was placed adjacent and east of the carriage shed ruins (Fry 1995; Weinberg and Lawrence 2006). Fry's shovel test pits revealed both historic and precontact artifacts indicating a lengthy history of human occupation of the site (Fry 1995; Weinberg and Lawrence 2006). The two test units produced a similar range of artifacts, along with several notable Hamilton-era features including evidence for the original portico stairs (Unit 1) and an unidentified brick and mortar feature (Unit 2) likely related to Hamilton's greenhouse complex (Fry 1995; Weinberg and Lawrence 2006). The area around Unit 1 was expanded and investigated again in 2005 by A. D. Marble and Associates, but no additional work was undertaken near Unit 2 (Weinberg and Lawrence 2006).

In the fall of 2008, curiosity and interest on the part of The Woodlands Cemetery Company led to further excavations near the greenhouse complex. In the spring of 2009, Dr. David Orr of Temple University and students in his Historic Sites class excavated two three by three foot test pits southwest of the greenhouse complex on an elevation break along a shallow ravine. Although the northern test pit showed signs of disturbance, both contained greenhouse-related artifacts, including hand-thrown, rounded rim flowerpot sherds and square cut nails (Deirdre H. Kelleher 2010, elec. comm.). The combined results of Fry's and Orr's surveys suggest that although the greenhouse complex is no longer standing, the archaeological integrity of the area has not been irredeemably compromised by any modern construction or landscaping activities. Therefore, the area surrounding the greenhouse foundation remains potentially significant and viable for a larger-scale excavation.

With this potential in mind, a group of archaeologists along with board members and staff of The Woodlands Cemetery Company gathered in early 2009 to begin planning some larger-scale testing of the area east of the ruins of a nineteenth-century carriage house in the general location of the late-eighteenth-century green-house complex. The plan for the 2009 excavation called for an exploratory trench near the projected south wall of the greenhouse complex based on conjectural draw-ings and earlier archaeological testing done in the same area (Fry 1995; Long 1991; Deirdre H. Kelleher 2010, elec. comm.; Weinberg and Lawrence 2006). The goal was to locate Joel Fry's original Unit 2 containing the brick and mortar feature and then expand outward from that feature to figure out how it related to the greenhouse complex and the overall landscape design of the estate.

In May 2009, a three-week exploratory excavation was opened just east of the carriage house wall. It was clear from the earlier 1993 excavations that the Hamilton-era occupational layer lay beneath a solid 5–6 feet of mostly sterile fill relating to various phases of construction and landscaping performed under the aus-pices of The Woodlands Cemetery Company (Fry 1995). Given the time and budget constraints of the project, it seemed prudent to narrow the focus of the investigation from the original 20 by 20 foot gridded area to just the eastern 10 by 10 foot unit (Unit 2), and within that, to focus primarily on the western half of the 10 by 10, creating a 10 by 5 foot exploratory trench.

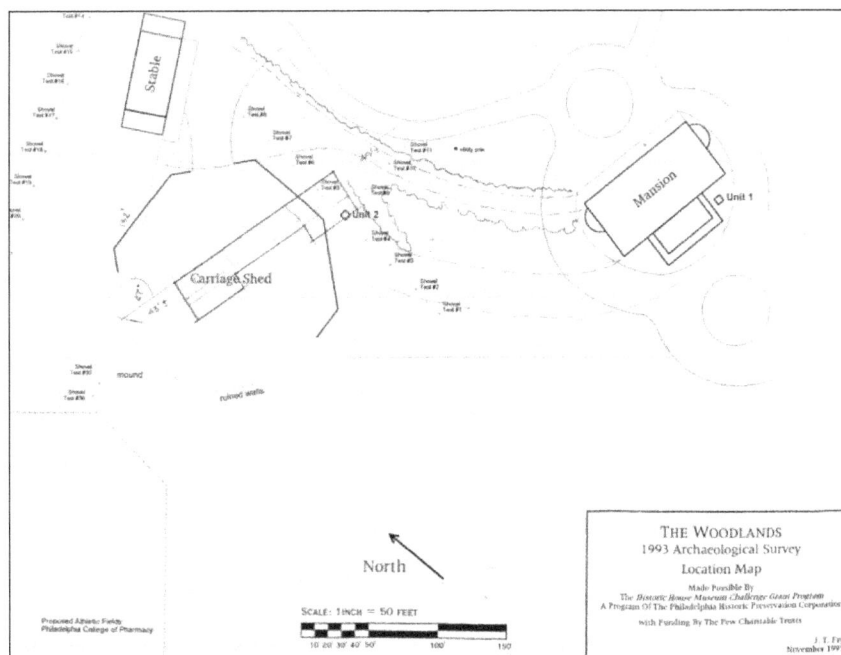

Figure 12.3. Composite map of the historic core of The Woodlands, showing the location of the 1993 archaeological testing by Joel T. Fry and the conjectural location of the greenhouse complex. Original map by Joel T. Fry, with additions by Timothy P. Long.

Two and half weeks of excavation through mostly sterile layers of nineteenth- and twentieth-century cemetery fill exposed what appeared to be the Hamilton-era occupational ground surface approximately 5 1/2 feet below grade. Immediately above this potential occupational level was a 6 inch thick layer of brick and mortar rubble (possibly related to the destruction of the greenhouse complex in the 1850s) and a small oval ash feature in the northeast corner of the trench. Below this feature along the eastern wall of the trench was a linear brick bed and a deliberate placement of large stones in the northern 5 by 5. Removing the three smaller stones revealed that they covered a circular opening about 2 feet in diameter, surrounded by angled brick and mortar that appeared to be a vertical access hole to a large brick and mortar cistern (figure 12.4).

The roof of the brick cistern slopes up towards the opening. The chamber itself is about 8 feet in diameter, 10 to 12 feet deep, and the inner surface of the cistern is faced with a dark colored material that may be cement or mortar of some kind. There were also what appeared to be a few access holes for pipes or something similar that would empty into (or perhaps out of) the cistern located near the floor in two places along the eastern half of the interior wall.

The discovery of a previously unknown cistern in close proximity to the location of Hamilton's greenhouse complex was entirely unexpected as there was no indication in the extant documents that any such structure existed. The presence of such a structure is not particularly surprising, however, given that the greenhouse complex held several thousand plants, including aquatic varieties (Boyd 1929;

Figure 12.4. Brick and mortar cistern at The Woodlands, showing the brick-lined access hole. Photograph by Jesse West-Rosenthal.

Lockwood 1931; Long 1991; McLean 1984; Madsen 1989; PHS 1976). Such an extensive botanical collection would have required a large quantity of water on a regular basis, so constructing a cistern right near the building would certainly make caring for the greenhouse plants that much easier.

But where did the water for the cistern come from? What appeared to be openings for pipes near the bottom of the structure could be seen heading north and east, but the angle of the cistern opening was such that any higher opening for pipes or drains along the shoulder of the cistern was impossible to make out. Although there is documentary evidence that Hamilton had an icehouse to the northeast of the greenhouse that may have drained into the cistern through these pipes (Timothy P. Long, pers. comm. 2009; Long 1991), their placement along the bottom edge of the cistern rather suggests that they may have been for draining water from the cistern rather than filling it up. Pipes heading north and east from the cistern may have led to the greenhouse itself.

Unearthing a cistern was only the beginning. Given its proximity to the conjectural location of the greenhouse complex, it was decided to return in May and June 2010 for a longer season at The Woodlands and expand the 2009 excavation area to search for the greenhouse foundations, but this time the plan was to employ mechanical excavation methods to remove the 4 feet of sterile clay fill (Tim P. Long 2009, elec. comm.).

On May 8, 2010, an entire 10 by 10 foot unit north of the original 2009 excavation was opened (10 feet north of the 2009 trench where the cistern was located, plus the 10 feet north of the 10 by 5 foot area not excavated in 2009). In the western half of the northern 10 by 10 (Unit 3), mechanical excavation revealed the expected thick layer of mostly sterile yellow clay fill, which was removed to a depth of about 4 feet. The removal of this clay fill exposed a 5–6 foot wide area of redeposited fill in the western wall of Unit 3 about 2.5 feet north of the cistern opening, which is almost certainly Joel Fry's original Unit 2 dug in 1993 (Fry 1995). Locating Fry's test unit had been one of the original goals of the project, and finding it just north of the cistern suggests that the brick and mortar feature found by Fry in the southwest corner of his unit is almost surely related to the greenhouse complex itself, rather than the brick and mortar path described by a visitor in 1806 (Fry 1995; Lockwood 1931; Long 1991).

In the eastern half of Unit 3, instead of sterile yellow clay, a dark silty rubble layer was revealed, sloping up toward the northeast corner of the unit. This layer was excavated by hand and found to be quite considerable, extending almost the entire length of Unit 3 along the eastern wall (about 8.5 feet) and sloping downward into the western half of the unit almost 6 feet along the northern wall. The slope consisted of multiple layers, which contained large numbers of late-eighteenth and early-nineteenth-century artifacts. This material appears to be a combination of artifacts related to the operation and subsequent destruction of the greenhouse, including a wide variety of construction debris, flowerpot remains, and copper wire as well as trash from the main house, specifically from the kitchen area, as there is a high number of whole oyster and clam shell halves, along with other faunal material. There are also large numbers of late-eighteenth and early-to-mid-nineteenth century ceramic wares that suggest the deposit existed at the time of the auction and clearing of the mansion at a Sheriff's sale in 1827, and that the area may have remained open through the destruction of the greenhouse in the mid-1850s (Fry 1995; Fussell and Long [1998–2009]; Long 1991).

As intriguing as the material discovered in this sloped deposit was the shape and existence of the feature itself. The sloping shape of this rubble deposit suggested that there might be an architectural feature below it (i.e. something against which this rubble mound had formed, or alternately, something that was keeping the rubble from spreading any further west), but the depth of this feature made it impossible to explore this possibility in the time remaining of the five week excavation. Rather than leave the excavation with so many unanswered questions, it was decided to come back for three weeks in August and September to further explore this slope deposit and the area just north of the cistern.

The excavation of Unit 3 resumed in mid-August, beginning with the exploration of the area just north of the cistern. The starting point was the northern half of the cistern roof, which was exposed by working back towards the northern end of the unit from the southern boundary with the 2009 trench. Removing a mix of red gravel and yellow clay fill along the eastern edge of the cistern revealed a row of bricks mortared into the slope of the cistern roof. The crew continued pulling back the gravel and clay mix until it became just the yellow clay fill, about 4 feet north of the southern edge of the unit. The removal of this fill revealed that the bricks mortared into the cistern formed a drain, which leads north through Unit 3 (figure 12.5). It is composed of coursed brick and marble fragments mortared to form a rectangular channel, with a single brick across the top to form the roof of the drain. The drain follows the slope of the cistern wall, beginning with one course at the neck of the cistern, and extending north along the shoulder of the tank to a full six courses. Once past the actual body of the cistern, the drain is less well preserved: only the southern 3 feet of the drain have the top brick; after 6 feet, only the bottom of the drain channel exists, and further north there is only a large indiscriminate mortar scatter.

While the discovery of a drain to the cistern indicates the complexity of water management that Hamilton employed in his greenhouse complex, the layout of the complex itself was still unclear. Was this upper drain for filling the cistern, while the lower openings seen in 2009 served to drain it? Where does this upper drain lead? Does it head down from Hamilton's icehouse or into the greenhouse for the plants? Given the length and direction of the drain, where, exactly is the greenhouse? Is this drain inside or outside the structure? What was needed was to find a foundation wall of some kind to help clarify the orientation of the buildings. So the excavation was expanded eastward from the cistern drain towards the rubble slope to look for other greenhouse features. About 1 foot east of the brick drain was a large piece of

Pennsylvania fieldstone, and upon widening the exploratory trench, it was discovered to actually be a number of fieldstone pieces mortared together and forming a straight southern edge about 4 feet south of the northeast corner of Unit 3, and just west of the edge of the rubble slope.

The excavation followed this fieldstone feature eastward until it hit the rubble mound. At that point a small trench in the rubble mound was opened up about 1.5–2 feet wide in line with the stone feature to see what lay directly under the rubble. Immediately below the artifact-heavy layers was a layer of brick and mortar rubble that also contained a high concentration of window glass—a good indication of a structure. Removal of the rubble layer revealed brick-in-course, mortared directly on top of the fieldstone to form a brick and stone foundation typical of the period (Joel T. Fry 2010, elec. comm.). Although the preservation of this foundation varies, it seems to have been well made originally, with both brick and stone placed neatly to form precise lines and angles. The foundation itself is a brick and a half wide (about 16 inches), with at least three brick courses above two stone courses. The entirety of the feature is only a little over 3 feet in length, extending west from the eastern wall of Unit 3 and stopping abruptly about a foot short of where it would have intersected the cistern drain. The location of this foundation, along with the presence of the brick, mortar, and glass rubble above it strongly suggest that we have—at last—located a section of Hamilton's greenhouse, most likely part of the southern, or front, foundation of the easternmost hothouse wing.

Finding both a section of the greenhouse foundation and a cistern drain in three weeks of "surgical strike" archaeology was a great piece of luck, and, as is often the case with archaeology, raises as many new questions as it answers. For instance, locating the foundation should answer many questions about the layout of the landscape. But there are a few oddities about this foundation, beginning with the fact that it seems to end abruptly about 1 foot east of where it would have intersected with the cistern drain (about 3 feet in from the eastern wall). It is possible that the foundation did originally continue to the drain and beyond, but either the brick and stone elements were removed at some later time, or were differentially preserved and crushed under the subsequent filling-in of the area by the Cemetery Company in the mid-nineteenth century (Fry 1995; Long 1991). The existing foundation does in fact line up with a trench feature found by Joel Fry in his 1993 test excavation (Fry 1995; 2010 pers. comm.), which could indicate that the foundation did continue, and may have arched over the cistern drain without leaving any indication of its presence in the surrounding soil.

Another possibility is that the greenhouse complex was of varying widths along the southern elevation, where the lean-to style hothouse wings may have stuck out farther than the central greenhouse section (Timothy P. Long, pers. comm. 2011) (figure 12.2). If this was the case, then the southern foundation would not be a straight line along the entire complex, and a break in the foundation may indicate where the edge of one hothouse wing met the central section. But this interpretation still leaves the question of the drain: did it continue into the greenhouse complex or not? Where did it end? As usual, the answers to these questions would have to wait for the next excavation season.

In the fall of 2011, another greenhouse-related feature was revealed, in part by Mother Nature. The summer and early fall of that year had seen several severe rainfalls in the Philadelphia area, with about 20 inches of rain in August alone (then the wettest month on record) (Callahan 2011). The effects of the unusually wet weather were felt all over the region, including The Woodlands where the saturated earth caused a partial collapse of the western wall of the 2010 excavation area (Unit 3). Although removing the collapsed fill had not been in the original plan for the fall of 2011, it proved to be fortuitous, as it provided a chance to pull back more of the sterile clay fill at the bottom of Unit 3 and examine the northern side of the cistern. In so doing, another discovery was made: a *second* covered rectangular brick drain, just like the one discovered in 2010, connected to the shoulder of the cistern, and heading diagonally northwest (i.e., towards the greenhouse and through Fry's original test unit from 1993).

The serendipitous discovery of this second drain in the fall 2011 cleanup has now brought the archaeological investigation of Hamilton's greenhouse complex full circle, as this drain is the same flat feature originally discovered by Fry in 1993

Figure 12.5. Overall photo of Unit 3 showing both brick drains, the cistern, and the partial foundation of the greenhouse. Photograph by Sarah Chesney.

that was seen cutting diagonally through his unit. The size, shape, and composition of this drain match the 1993 feature, and its orientation in Unit 3 is at the same diagonal angle.

Having two drains run into the cistern also helps to refine the interpretation of their use and connection to the greenhouse complex. From the layout and direction of the drains, they both appear to be heading to different parts of the greenhouse complex. But rather than cutting through the foundation as had been suggested by the evidence from 2010, the drains may actually be stopping at the edge of the building and be connected to a gutter system of some kind on the outside of the structure. Such a gutter-drain system would also explain the abrupt ending of the 2010 drain and why the northernmost section is uncovered. If the drain was designed to intersect a gutter pipe of some kind, it would stop at the edge of the building and possibly be open or have a different covering connecting it to a vertical section. Such a system may have been unusual, but not unheard of; other structures of this period were known to have gutters to pull the rain away from the building (Joel T. Fry, pers. comm. 2011). As an added benefit, a gutter system would allow Hamilton to capture all the rainwater and reuse it in his greenhouse—a very efficient water management system, which would certainly be advantageous to anyone managing the water needs of thousands of exotic greenhouse plants.

The discovery over the last few years of a cistern, two brick drains, and a partial foundation of Hamilton's greenhouse complex suggest that his botanical activities at The Woodlands were quite extensive and complex. The construction of a cistern with an extensive drain system is not particularly surprising given the vast numbers of plants said to have been housed within this structure (Boyd 1929; Lockwood 1931; Long 1991; McLean 1984; Madsen 1989; Oldschool 1809; PHS 1976). But the proximity of this cistern to the greenhouse and its drains to the north and northwest suggest that there was a complicated water management system designed to draw water directly from nature for the benefit of the greenhouse's exotic inhabitants. To go to the trouble of creating such a system, Hamilton's greenhouse must have been every bit as extensive as has been claimed—even if ten thousand plants may be an exaggeration.

The location and appearance of the cistern and its drains in relation to the foundation, while helping to settle any lingering doubts about the location of the greenhouse complex, also raises a number of interesting questions about the visual impact of this complex and the competing needs of utilitarian plant management. For example, how did the cistern and drain system potentially affect the picturesque nature of the greenhouse itself and the exotic appeal of the plants housed within its walls? There is a striking difference, for instance, between the appearance of the south side of the cistern (first exposed in 2009), which consists of neatly laid brick and mortar rows, and the north side, which consists of a messy, uneven mortar spread over the cistern bricks. The drains attached to the north side of the cistern are functional but not particularly neat, with some rows of bricks sticking out farther than others. Given the current interpretation of the partial foundation as being the southern wall of the easternmost hothouse, the cistern would be visible to any visitors to the greenhouse.

However, there would only be about 4 feet of space between the greenhouse complex itself and the south side of the cistern so it was likely that the only side of the cistern really visible was the neatly finished northern side, rather than the more utilitarian workmanship on the southern side. This combination of utilitarian innovations and exotic botanicals might seem a bit jarring, but it would suggest that Hamilton appreciated both the mundane necessities of caring for his botanical collection as much as the beauty such care produced. Unlike some other elites, whose appreciation for exotic plants was solely in their beauty and rarity (i.e. as status items), Hamilton showed off his greenhouse as both a utilitarian workspace and an art gallery—although even the utilitarian elements were required to be neat and clean where they were in full view of visitors. In some ways, Hamilton's multipurpose approach to his greenhouse complex anticipated the development of modern scientific botany with its shifting focus from the plant as an object of beauty complete in itself to understanding its place in the larger environment and its everyday needs.

Private Pleasure and Public Display

Although the archaeological investigation of Hamilton's greenhouse complex at The Woodlands is ongoing, the discoveries that have been made thus far suggest that Hamilton had a botanical collection and greenhouse operation that far surpassed the typical horticultural efforts found on other country estates of the Philadelphia elite. While men such as James Logan and William Bingham had beautifully landscaped gardens and grounds on their country estates—Logan even had a greenhouse at Stenton—neither one of them seems to have devoted the same kind of time and energy exclusively to botanical pursuits that Hamilton did. Logan and his heirs were interested in many related agricultural pursuits, of which cultivating exotics was only one, while Bingham seemed more interested in the public statement made by his landscaped grounds than in puttering around them himself (Brown 1937; Harshberger 1924; Jacobs 2006; Long 1991; McLean 1984; PHS 1976; Schlereth 2007; Ward 1879). But Hamilton was a man with a driving passion for—if not an obsession with—acquiring and cultivating new and exotic plant specimens, whose ambition and success rate more closely resembled that of business-oriented plant dealers like his neighbor John Bartram, rather than the more sedate horticultural collecting practiced by his fellow elites.

It was not just Hamilton's extensive botanical collection that set his estate apart from others of its kind; the way in which he attempted to use the estate as both a private and a public botanical space made The Woodlands unique. Many of Hamilton's actions and decisions concerning The Woodlands suggest that his primary role was that of a private collector of exotic botanicals, obsessed with limiting access to his collection and to various parts of his estate. Hamilton made The Woodlands his permanent home in 1767, at the age of 22, in order to pursue his botanical and architectural passions, and while living retired in the country on a full-time basis was not unheard of at this time, it was unusual in a young man who moved in the highest circles of Philadelphia society and might have been expected to participate in the endless swirl of city social events (Brown 1937; Fussell and Long [1998–2009]; Jackson 1932; Long 1991; Rasmusson 1966; Washington 1895a, 1895b). Hamilton's decision to forgo his town residence certainly suggests a desire for more privacy than could be found in an urban setting, or at least a desire for uninterrupted time to pursue his own interests. By 1793, Hamilton had made this move even more permanent, as that year saw not just himself, but his mother, nephews, and nieces permanently ensconced at The Woodlands as well (Jacobs 2006; Long 1991; 2010, elec. comm.). Making The Woodlands the permanent home for himself and his family increased both Hamilton's distance from the public life of Philadelphia and his control over every aspect of his estate as he was there to oversee every detail of estate management.

While Hamilton in his role as obsessed botanical collector clearly relished his privacy and complete control over his world like many other elites did on their country estates, he also played the role of public patron and host at The Woodlands on a scale that directly contradicted his seeming desire for privacy. On the surface, The Woodlands estate on the west bank of the Schuylkill River appeared to function just like any other early American country estate: a private retreat owned by a member of one of the most prominent families in Philadelphia, whose knowledge of English landscape design and interest in exotic plants made the gardens some of the most extensive and impressive on this side of the Atlantic (Betts 1979; Fisher 1929; Fussell and Long [1998–2009]; Jacobs 2006; Long 1991; Madsen 1989; Niemcewicz 1965; Oldschool 1809; PHS 1976; Rasmusson 1966; Scharf and Westcott 1884; Stetson 1949a). To a certain extent, this surface impression was true; numerous visitors to Hamilton's estate commented on the impressive nature of his grounds and his extensive greenhouses filled with exotic flora from all over the world. Even European visitors who were impressed by nothing else they had seen in America found Hamilton's gardens and botanical collections to be unparalleled, and fellow botanists were equally impressed. The Parisian botanist André Michaux claimed that Hamilton's collection was far more complete than any other he had seen, and he and his son drew extensively on Hamilton's botanical collection for their book on North American plants (Lockwood 1931; Long 1991; Niemcewicz 1965; Scharf and Westcott 1884; Schlereth 2007).

But the very fact that so many different individuals could testify to the magnificent character of The Woodlands estate suggests that Hamilton's country retreat was somewhat out of the ordinary, and not the model of privacy and exclusive access that one might expect. Visitors of all kinds seemed to be welcome to come and admire his estate though Hamilton was especially encouraging of those with an interest in and aptitude for botany. He had a long-standing arrangement with Dr. Benjamin

Smith Barton, a professor of *materia medica*, natural history, and botany at the University of Pennsylvania Medical School, to bring students out to The Woodlands to study Hamilton's extensive collection of plants—an experience which was impressive enough to stay with these young doctors for years afterward (Eaton 1951; Ewan 1983; Graustein 1961; Jacobs 2006; Long 1991; Ward 1879). Thomas Jefferson even wrote to Hamilton specifically requesting that he allow Jefferson's grandson, attending the University of Pennsylvania, access to his magnificent gardens and botanical collection (Cornett 2005; Jefferson 1944; Leighton 1976; Long 1991; Martin 1991).

In fact, rather than retreat into to a private world, Hamilton actively sought out botanical visitors to the Philadelphia area, and he encouraged them to come see his collections at The Woodlands (Cutler 1884, 1888; Stetson 1949a). When such visitors did arrive, Hamilton treated them as honored guests, and he dragged his botanical visitors through his greenhouse and along an extensive tour of his landscaped park. Hamilton was so anxious to show off his collection to his fellow botanical enthusiasts that he was blind to all else, including the ill health of the Reverend Menasseh Cutler on the occasion of his visit in 1803 (Betts 1979; Cutler 1884, 1888; Jacobs 2006; Long 1991; Madsen 1989; Stetson 1949a).

The sheer number of visitors that Hamilton received belied his estate's claim to privacy as the gates seemed to be open year-round for the convenience of the curious, much like the tradition of the "public days" of great English estates that Hamilton so admired (Betts 1979; Jacobs 2006; Long 1991; Madsen 1989; Niemcewicz 1965; Rasmusson 1966; Stetson 1949a). Certainly Hamilton's own decision to make The Woodlands his permanent residence reinforced this impression. Unlike other country estates along the Schuylkill River where families were only in residence during certain times of the year, visitors were likely to find Hamilton or his family at home year-round, and although outside the Philadelphia social hub, Hamilton kept up a busy social schedule at his supposed retreat (Cutler 1884; Rasmusson 1966; Stetson 1949a). He presided over weekly Thursday gatherings at The Woodlands that involved coffee, conversations, and sometimes entertainment for large numbers of friends and acquaintances, which were popular enough to become fixed engagements on the Philadelphia social calendar and remembered fondly by attendees long after they ended (Betts 1979; Franks 1899; Jacobs 2006; Long 1991; Madsen 1989; Rasmusson 1966; Stetson 1949a, 1949b). Visitors to Philadelphia often wrote of large dinner parties at The Woodlands, and Hamilton's hospitality was so well known that many visitors to his estate felt comfortable touring his gardens and grounds even when the owner himself was away from home (Fisher 1929; Manigault 1984; Niemcewicz 1965; Twining 1900). Such open hospitality at The Woodlands seems odd from the man who kept his greenhouse plants under lock and key and once yelled at a young woman for daring to disturb their contents (Carr 1861; Stetson 1949a).

Although Hamilton's constant struggle to negotiate both a private and a public life for The Woodlands made it highly unusual, it was not entirely unprecedented in late-eighteenth and early-nineteenth-century America, especially among the country estates and properties outside of Philadelphia. This was a time of growing garden enthusiasm on both sides of the Atlantic, raised to a frenzy by the constant imports of new plants and the creation of public gardens for the amusement of the general populace (Brockway 1979; Hix 1981; Long 1991; Niemcewicz 1965; Sarudy 1998; Schiebinger 2004; Schiebinger and Swan 2005; Woods and Warren 1988; Wulf 2009). In Philadelphia, as in other British colonial cities, these public gardens and nature displays were extremely popular. John Bartram, of course, had been operating his plant business and botanical gardens since the 1730s, and while the display of flora at Bartram's Garden was not in the same league as that of The Woodlands or the estates of other elites, it was open to visitors and prospective clients curious about the garden and plant collection of the man Linnaeus called "the greatest natural botanist of his time" (Eberlein and Hubbard 1944; Harshberger 1924; Jenkins 1933; The Pennsylvania Horticultural Society 1976; Prince 1957; Smith 1927; Stetson 1949a; Wulf 2009).

Philadelphia was also full of large public gardens modeled on the Vauxhall Gardens of London that were open to all and sundry and included, besides acres of gardens, refreshments and entertainments such as fireworks and other spectacles (Eberlein and Hubbard 1944; Long 1991; Scharf and Westcott 1884; Stetson 1949b). The most famous and successful of these Philadelphia public gardens was Grays Gardens at Lower (later Grays) Ferry on the west bank of the Schuylkill River just downriver from Hamilton's estate and just upriver from John Bartram's establishment (Eberlein and Hubbard 1944; Long 1991; Scharf and Westcott 1884; Stetson 1949a, 1949b). No doubt many of Hamilton's visitors assumed his grounds at The Woodlands were simply part of the tour of this botanical Mecca on the west bank of the Schuylkill.

It is Hamilton's dual, and sometimes conflicting, role of obsessive collector of exotic plants and enthusiastic host that makes both him and his estate—in particular his greenhouse complex—such a fascinating and important area of archaeological investigation. Eighteenth- and early-nineteenth-century Philadelphia was a center of international plant trade, counting as its inhabitants some of the most well-known and influential botanists and natural historians of the age, including John and William Bartram, Humphrey Marshall, William Young, Jr., Bernard McMahon, Benjamin Smith Barton, Thomas Nuttall, Frederick Pursh, and others (Boyd 1929; Graustein 1961; Harshberger 1924; Jacobs 2006; Long 1991; McLean 1984; Madsen 1989; O'Malley 1996; PHS 1976; Stetson 1949a, 1949b; Wulf 2009). But the vast majority of those who participated fully in this exchange were men who also–to varying degrees—did so as business professionals.

Well-off Philadelphia elites like Hamilton rarely devoted the same kind of time and energy to such endeavors as many of them also devoted their time to politics and other public activities (Bridenbaugh 1965; Brown 1937; Miller 1982; Nash 2002; Niemcewicz 1965; Rozbicki 2006). But Hamilton chose to devote his free time to his estate, to botany and architecture, which made both the man and the estate unique among others of their kind. Hamilton walked the line between typical divisions: public and private, elite dilettante and committed professional, obsessive collector and enthusiastic patron, trying to negotiate a middle ground for himself and his one-of-a-kind botanical collection. At the same time, botany itself was changing, becoming less exclusive, and more accessible to the general public. More and more individuals were entering the natural sciences from the middling classes and needed access to collections of material that formerly were only found on private estates (Brockway 1979; Drayton 2000; Ewan 1952, 1983; Ewan and Ewan 1963; Harshberger 1899; Leighton 1976). Hamilton's greenhouse complex at The Woodlands is a physical representation of this change and negotiation, as it was a space both public and private, where all of these people and plants came to interact.

It was also a space both utilitarian and aesthetic—a combination of beautiful exotics to be shown off and the necessary trappings required for their survival and maintenance. Like Hamilton himself, his greenhouse complex is a mass of contradictions that reflect the changing nature of nineteenth-century botany in which there was a growing divide between the "professionals" working in universities and botanic gardens, valuing the plants for their scientific (and sometimes economic) importance, and the so-called "amateurs" like Hamilton: collectors with a talent for cultivation and aptitude for scientific identification but for whom the aesthetic appeal remained most important. Hamilton and his greenhouse complex showcase botany at the beginning of this transition. Understanding the space where these conflicting desires were negotiated can shed light on the way in which the development of American botany played out "on the ground." In particular, it reveals how the practice of botany was experienced by an individual whose collection of plants was crucial to the growing scientific element of the field—the same element that threatened Hamilton's own position and reputation as a respected amateur botanist committed to collecting and cultivating for his own amusement.

The archaeological discoveries thus far have shed some light on the external elements of these negotiations between utilitarian and aesthetic needs as showcased directly in Hamilton's greenhouse complex. It is hoped that future excavations can reveal the internal negotiations made within the structure and provide further insight into the nature of early American botany and the individuals participating in its development.

References Cited

The American Philosophical Society

1799   Donations Received by the American Philosophical Society, since the
              Publication of Their Third Volume of their Transactions, with the
              Names of the Donors. *Transactions of the American Philosophical So-
              ciety* 4(1799): xvii–xxxvi.

Allen, James
1885   Diary of James Allen, Esq., of Philadelphia, Counsellor-at-Law, 1770–
                1778. *The Pennsylvania Magazine of History and Biography* 9(2):
                176–196.
Betts, Richard J.
1979   The Woodlands. *Winterthur Portfolio* 14(3): 213–234.
Boyd, James
1929   *A History of the Pennsylvania Horticultural Society, 1827–1927.* Penn-
                sylvania Horticultural Society, Philadelphia.
Bridenbaugh, Carl, and Jessica Bridenbaugh
1965   *Rebels and Gentlemen: Philadelphia in the Age of Franklin.* Galaxy
                Books, New York.
Brockway, Lucile
1979   *Science and Colonial Expansion: The Role of the British Royal Botanic
                Gardens.* Academic Press, New York.
Brown, Margaret L.
1937   Mr. and Mrs. Bingham of Philadelphia: Rulers of the Republican Court.
                The Pennsylvania Magazine of History and Biography 61(3): 286–324.
Callahan, Michael
2011   Lists! *Philadelphia Magazine*, December 2011: 68–79.
Carr, Robert.
1861   Introduction of the Lombardy Poplar into America. *The Gardener's
                Monthly* 3(1): 9.
Chesney, Sarah Jane
2009   Propagating Status: Gentleman Planters and Their Greenhouses in the
                Eighteenth-Century Chesapeake. Master's thesis, Department of An-
                thropology, College of William and Mary, Williamsburg, Virginia.
Cornett, Peggy
2005   Inspirations from The Woodlands: Jefferson's Enduring Ties to Phila-
                delphia's Botanical Riches. *Twinleaf* (January 2005): 9–17.
Cutler, Reverend Manasseh
1884   Notes and Queries: Visit of the Rev. Dr. Manasseh Cutler to William
                Hamilton of The Woodlands. *The Pennsylvania Magazine of History
                and Biography* 8(1): 109–111.
1888   New York and Philadelphia in 1787. *The Pennsylvania Magazine of
                History and Biography* 12(1): 97–115.
Drayton, Richard
2000   *Nature's Government: Science, Imperial Britain, and the "Improve-
                ment" of the World.* Yale University Press, New Haven, Connecticut.
Eaton, Leonard K.
1951   Medicine in Philadelphia and Boston, 1805–1830. *The Pennsylvania
                Magazine of History and Biography* 75(1): 66–75.

Eberlein, Harold Donaldson, and Cortlandt Van Dyke Hubbard

1944   The American "Vauxhall" of the Federal Era. *The Pennsylvania Maga-zine of History and Biography* 68(2): 150–174.

Ewan, Joseph

1952   Frederick Pursh, 1774–1820, and His Botanical Associates. *Proceed-ings of the American Philosophical Society* 96(5): 599–628.

1983   From Calcutta to New Orleans, or, Tales from Barton's Greenhouse. *Proceedings of the American Philosophical Society* 127(3): 125–134.

Ewan, Joseph, and Nesta Ewan

1963   John Lyon, Nurseryman and Plant Hunter, and His Journal, 1799–1814. *Transactions of the American Philosophical Society* New Series 53(2): 1–69.

Fisher, Joshua Francis

1892   Andrew Hamilton, Esq., of Pennsylvania. *The Pennsylvania Magazine of History and Biography* 16(1): 1–27.

1929   *Recollections of Joshua Francis Fisher, Written in 1864.* Edited by Sophia Cadwalader. Boston, Massachusetts.

Franks, Rebecca

1899   Letter of Miss Rebecca Franks to her sister, Abigail, the wife of Andrew Hamilton, Esq. 10 August 1781. *The Pennsylvania Magazine of His-tory and Biography* 23(3): 303–309.

Fry, Joel T.

1995   The Woodlands: An Archaeological Research and Planning Survey. Report to The University City Historical Society. Philadelphia, Pennsylvania.

Fussell, Catharine P., and Timothy Preston Long

[1998–2009] The Woodlands. Discovering Lewis and Clark. http://lewis-clark.org/content/content-article.asp?ArticleID=2666 (accessed October 2009).

Graustein, Jeannette E.

1961   The Eminent Benjamin Smith Barton. *The Pennsylvania Magazine of History and Biography* 85(4): 423–438.

H. [A Philadelphia Amateur]

1840   Notices of Green-houses and Hot-houses in and near Philadelphia, No. 1. *The Magazine of Horticulture, Botany, and All Useful Discoveries in Rural Affairs* 6(6): 201–203.

Harshberger, John W.

1924   Some Old Gardens of Pennsylvania. *The Pennsylvania Magazine of History and Biography* 48(4): 289–300.

Harshberger, John William

1899   *The Botanists of Philadelphia and their Work.* T. C. Davis & Sons, Philadelphia.

Heintzelman, Patricia L.

1972   Elysium on The Schuylkill: William Hamilton's Woodlands. Master's thesis, Department of Art History, University of Delaware, Newark, Delaware.

Hix, John

1981   *The Glass House.* The MIT Press, Cambridge, Massachusetts.

Huddleston, Eugene L.

1969   Poetical Descriptions of Pennsylvania in the Early National Period. *The Pennsylvania Magazine of History and Biography* 93(4): 487–509.

Jackson, Joseph

1932   Washington in Philadelphia. *The Pennsylvania Magazine of History and Biography* 56(2): 110–155.

Jacobs, James A.

2006   William Hamilton and The Woodlands: A Construction of Refinement in Philadelphia. *The Pennsylvania Magazine of History and Biography* 130(2): 181–210.

Jefferson, Thomas

1944   *Thomas Jefferson's Garden book, 1766–1824, with relevant extracts from his other writings.* Edited with Annotations by Edwin Morris Betts. The American Philosophical Society, Philadelphia.

Jenkins, Charles F.

1933   The Historical Background of Franklin's Tree. *The Pennsylvania Magazine of History and Biography* 57(3): 193–208.

Leighton, Ann

1976   *American Gardens in the Eighteenth Century: "For Use or For Delight."* The University of Massachusetts Press, Boston.

Leone, Mark P.

1984   Interpreting Ideology in Historical Archaeology: Using the Rules of Perspective in the William Paca Garden in Annapolis, Maryland. In *Ideology, Power, and Prehistory*, edited by Daniel Miller and Christopher Tilley, pp. 25–35. Cambridge University Press, Cambridge, United Kingdom.

1988   The Georgian Order as the Order of Merchant Capitalism in Annapolis, Maryland. In *The Recovery of Meaning: Historical Archaeology in the Eastern United States*, edited by Mark P. Leone and Parker B. Potter, Jr., pp. 235–261. Smithsonian Institution Press, Washington, D.C.

Lockwood, Alice G. B.

1931   *Gardens of Colony and State: Gardens and Gardeners of the American Colonies Before 1840.* Scribner's Sons, New York.

Long, Timothy Preston

1991   The Woodlands: A Matchless Place. Master's thesis, Historic Preservation Program, University of Pennsylvania, Philadelphia.

Madsen, Karen
1989   To Make His Country Smile: William Hamilton's Woodlands. *Arnoldia*
            49(2): 14–24.
Manigault, Margaret Izard
1984   Letter to Alice Delany Izard, 27 February 1808. *Manigault Papers*,
            South Carolina Historical Society & South Caroliniana Library, Spar-
            tanburg, South Carolina.
Martin, Peter
1991   *The Pleasure Gardens of Virginia: From Jamestown to Jefferson*. Prince-
            ton University Press, Princeton, New Jersey.
McLean, Elizabeth
1984   Town and Country Gardens in Eighteenth-Century Philadelphia. In
            British and American Gardens in the Eighteenth Century, edited by
            Robert P. Maccubbin and Peter Martin, pp. 136–147. The Colonial
            Williamsburg Foundation, Williamsburg, Virginia.
Miller, Richard G.
1982   The Federal City, 1783–1800. In *Philadelphia: A 300-Year History*, ed-
            ited by Russell F. Weigley, pp. 155–207. W.W. Norton, New York.
Nash, Gary B.
2002   *First City: Philadelphia and the Forging of Historical Memory*. The
            University of Pennsylvania Press, Philadelphia.
Neible, George W.
1908   Account of Servants Bound and Assigned before James Hamilton,
            Mayor of Philadelphia (continued). *The Pennsylvania Magazine of
            History and Biography* 32(2): 237–249.
Niemcewicz, Julian Ursyn
1965   *Under Their Vine and Fig Tree: Travels Through America in 1797–
            1799, 1805, with some Further Account of Life in New Jersey*, trans-
            lated by Metchie J. E. Budka, translator. Grassman Publishing, Eliza-
            beth, New Jersey.
Oldschool, Oliver [Joseph Dennie]
1809   American Scenery for the Port Folio: The Woodlands. *Port Folio
            (1801–1827)*, New Series, 2(6): 505–507.
O'Malley, Therese
1996   "Your Garden Must be a Museum to You": Early American Botanic
            Gardens *The Huntington Library Quarterly* 59(2/3): 207–231.
The Pennsylvania Horticultural Society
1976   *From Seed to Flower: Philadelphia, 1681–1876: A Horticultural Point
            of View*. Philadelphia.
Prince, Winifred Notman
1957   Notes and Documents. *The Pennsylvania Magazine of History and Bi-
            ography* 81(1): 86–88.

Pursh, Frederick
1814   *Flora Americae Septentrionalis, or A Systematic Arrangement and Description of the plants of North America: containing, besides what have been described by proceeding authors, many new and rare species collected during twelve years travels and residence in that country.* Printed for White, Cochrane, and Co., London.

Rasmusson, Ethel E.
1966   Democratic Environment-Aristocratic Aspiration. *The Pennsylvania Magazine of History and Biography* 90(2): 155–182.

Rozbicki, Michal Jan
2006   Between Private and Public Spheres: Liberty as Cultural Property in Eighteenth-Century British America. In *Cultural Identities in Colonial British America*, edited by Robert Olwell and Alan Tully, pp. 293–318. Johns Hopkins University Press, Baltimore, Maryland.

Sarudy, Barbara Wells
1998   *Gardens and Gardening in the Chesapeake, 1700–1805.* Johns Hopkins University Press, Baltimore, Maryland.

Scharf, J. Thomas, and Thompson Westcott
1884   *History of Philadelphia, 1609–1884.* 3 Vols. L. H. Everts & Company, Philadelphia.

Schiebinger, Londa
2004   *Plants and Empire: Colonial Bioprospecting in the Atlantic World.* Harvard University Press, Cambridge, Massachusetts.

Schiebinger, Londa L., and Claudia Swan (editors)
2005   *Colonial Botany: Science, Commerce, and Politics in the Early Modern World.* University of Pennslvania Press, Philadelphia.

Schlereth, Thomas J.
2007   Early North American Arboreta. *Garden History* 35 (Supplement 2: Cultural and Historical Geographies of the Arboretum): 196–216.

Smith, Edgar Fahs
1927   Early Science in Philadelphia. *The Pennsylvania Magazine of History and Biography* 51(1): 15–26.

Steiner, Bernard C.
1897   Andrew Hamilton and John Peter Zenger. *The Pennsylvania Magazine of History and Biography* 20(4): 405–408.

Stetson, Sarah P.
1946   American Garden Books Transplanted and Native, Before 1807. *William and Mary Quarterly*, Third Series III (3): 343–369.

1949a   William Hamilton and His "Woodlands." *The Pennsylvania Magazine of History and Biography* 73(1): 26–33.

1949b   The Philadelphia Sojourn of Samuel Vaughan. *The Pennsylvania Magazine of History and Biography* 73(4): 459–474.

Thayer, Theodore

1982   Town into City, 1746–1765. In *Philadelphia: A 300-Year History*, edited by Russell F. Weigley, pp. 68–108. W. W. Norton, New York.

Tinkcom, Harry M.

1982   The Revolutionary City, 1765–1783. In *Philadelphia: A 300-Year History*, edited by Russell F. Weigley, pp. 109–154. W.W. Norton, New York.

Twining, Thomas

1900   *Travels in America 100 Years Ago: Being Notes and Reminiscences.* Harper's Black and White Series. Harper & Brothers, New York.

Ward, Townsend

1879   A Walk To Darby. *The Pennsylvania Magazine of History and Biography* 3(2): 150–166.

Washington, George, and William S. Baker

1895a   Washington after the Revolution, 1784–1799 (continued). *The Pennsylvania Magazine of History and Biography* 19(4): 428–459.

1895b   Washington after the Revolution, 1784–1799 (continued). *The Pennsylvania Magazine of History and Biography* 19(2): 170–196.

Weinberg, David L., and John Lawrence

2006   The Woodlands: Limited Archaeological Survey. Prepared by A. D. Marble & Company for John Milner Architects, Inc., Conshohocken, Pennsylvania.

Woods, May, and Arete Swartz Warren

1988   *Glass Houses: A History of Greenhouses, Orangeries, and Conservatories.* Aurum, London, United Kingdom.

Wulf, Andrea

2009   *The Brother Gardeners: Botany, Empire, and the Birth of an Obsession.* Alfred A. Knopf, New York.

13

"He Will Be a Bourgeois American and Spend His Fortune in Making Gardens": An Archaeological Examination of Joseph Bonaparte's Point Breeze Estate

Richard Veit and Michael J. Gall

Introduction

Joseph Bonaparte, the elder brother of Napoleon Bonaparte and former King of Naples and Spain, fled from Europe following Napoleon's defeat at Waterloo and sought refuge in America. Despite an attempt to conceal his true identity, Joseph was soon recognized and requested asylum in the United States. With some misgivings, President James Madison allowed him to remain in the country. Joseph would reside in North America, with short interregna, from 1815 until 1839. He divided his time between a townhouse he rented in Philadelphia and his country estate, Point Breeze in Bordentown, New Jersey. At Point Breeze, he constructed one of the first picturesque gardens in the U.S., a pair of grand houses, as well as numerous outbuildings (figure 13.1). During his American sojourn, Joseph, who styled himself the Count de Survilliers, also became a major figure in the cultural life of the Delaware Valley.

From 2005 to 2012, the former Point Breeze Estate, also known as Bonaparte's Park, was the focus of Monmouth University's annual field school in historical archaeology and volunteer excavations by members of the Archaeological Society of New Jersey (figure 13.2). Through documentation of the former estate's extensive above-ground remains and selective subsurface testing of the property, new information about the design, meaning, and function of the property has come to light.

At Point Breeze, Joseph Bonaparte created an early American picturesque garden, which hearkened back to European antecedents, both English and French, and physically reproduced aspects of properties he had once owned in Europe (Weber 1986). The estate highlighted Joseph's great wealth and unusual social position as an exiled king. The substantial houses he built and the carefully designed but natural appearing landscape that Joseph created served as a grand stage where he could play the role of king in exile for visiting dignitaries, impress local residents, and serve as a cultural attaché, fostering the growth of fine art and landscape design in America. Furthermore, the lavish scale of Joseph's projects meant that he needed to employ large numbers of craftsmen, farmers, laborers, and servants. In so doing, he created

Figure 13.1. *Point Breeze on the Delaware*, Thomas Birch, 1818. Courtesy of the Newark Museum.

a network of individuals financially tied to him and his estate. Both symbolically, and economically, the estate served to strengthen these bonds. We argue that Joseph Bonaparte's Point Breeze estate was a multivocal landscape (Upton 1988), which embodied varying and indeed conflicting meanings for an assortment of individuals and disparate groups at different times. Furthermore, Point Breeze continues to be an evocative landscape of memory and promise.

Joseph Bonaparte at Point Breeze

Almost immediately upon arriving in the U.S., Joseph began searching for an appropriate estate. The estate needed to be suitable for a country gentleman, embody the landscape features necessary for the creation of a grand picturesque garden similar to those with which he was acquainted in Europe, and be located between Philadelphia and New York, enabling him to rapidly communicate with both friends and family abroad. Most importantly, it needed to command attention and communicate to the public an impression of the owner's wealth. In July 1816, Joseph found the property that he had longed for with the help of his land agent and interpreter James Carret.

Figure 13.2. Students excavating at Point Breeze. Courtesy of Peter Ackerman and the Asbury Park Press.

Joseph's initial purchase included an assemblage of seven contiguous tracts of land encompassing approximately 394.25 acres stretching 1.55 miles along the east side of the Crosswicks Creek in Chesterfield (now both Bordentown Township and Bordentown City), New Jersey (Burlington County Clerk's Office 1817). The purchased property also included a small island of 3 rods and 21 perches on Crosswicks Creek in Nottingham Township and a 3.5-acre town lot in Bordentown City containing a brick house. Nearly half of the purchased tract was composed of a roughly 125-acre estate called Point Breeze. Historically owned by the Farnsworth and Douglas families and just prior to Joseph's purchase by Stephen Sayre, former High Sheriff of London and briefly Benjamin Franklin's personal secretary, Point Breeze was a fine property prominently sited on a high bluff overlooking the confluence of Crosswicks Creek and the Delaware River. The remainder of the estate included a 198-acre plantation, an 8-acre house lot, and several other parcels.

Once ensconced at Point Breeze, Joseph immediately set about reshaping his properties into a single grand estate. By the time of his death in 1844, Joseph had purchased over 2,495 acres located in Nottingham, Mansfield, Lambertville, and Chesterfield Townships in Burlington County. By 1840, Joseph's Point Breeze estate in Chesterfield had been expanded to include approximately 1,517 contiguous acres containing several tenant homesteads and plantations. Joseph also owned an additional nine acres of town lots in the City of Bordentown adjacent to Point Breeze. The core of Joseph's Point Breeze estate, however, consisted of roughly 233 acres of undulating upland and marshland terrain. The land he purchased and new buildings he erected on the estate were financed with money and treasure that Joseph's secretary Louis Mailliard retrieved from a secret burial place in Switzerland (Stroud 2005:59). At Point Breeze, Joseph replaced Sayre's modest home with a "splendid mansion" (Gordon 1834:107) built partially of brick and wood. The former king, who was much more interested in art, architecture, and landscapes than he had been in power or military conquests, acted as his own general contractor during the construction of the house. Employing between 30 and 50 workmen, Joseph was able to make rapid progress on the estate.

A review of several contemporary paintings provides a unique chronological view of Point Breeze's evolution from Sayre's respectable Georgian home and grounds to Joseph's neo-classical mansion and extensive picturesque garden. Joseph also began a major landscaping campaign at Point Breeze. However, unlike so many of his contemporaries and predecessors in America, he eschewed formal Georgian geometric gardens and their grand illusions. Instead, he constructed one of North America's first picturesque gardens, modeled after European prototypes. Like the wealthy European gentleman he was, Joseph regularly opened his garden to the public. One happy result of this is an extensive body of contemporary commentary through which the meanings of this landscape for Joseph, his supporters, and detractors can be measured.

Lamentably, in January 1820, four years after construction began, Joseph's first mansion, the primary focus of our archaeological fieldwork, was destroyed by fire (Tower 1918:302). During the blaze, many of the mansion's furnishings were salvaged and removed to safety. As Joseph wrote a friend later that week, "All the furniture, statues, pictures, money, plate, gold, jewels, linen, books and in short everything that has not been consumed has been most scrupulously delivered into the hands of the people of my house" (Heston 1906:244–245). The remains of the ruined building were removed so that all that was left standing was a picturesque observation tower called the Belvedere (Berkley 1845:186).

Following the loss of the first house, Joseph constructed a second home on the site of his former stables (Berkley 1845:184) in the southern portion of the park (figure 13.3). It had a lawn and garden in front and in the rear was a large garden of rare flowers and plants, with statuary. Visitors described it as a "house built in the style of an Italian villa and with a flat terrace roof overlooking the park and woods. There was a large marble entrance-hall with [a] wide staircase at one end, the steps broad and very low. . . . The state rooms and picture gallery were on the ground floor" (Berkley 1845:184). Joseph's art collection, which was the largest in the U.S., included the works of many masters including David's painting of *Napoleon Crossing the Alps* and a reclining half-scale nude statue of his sister Pauline, which scandalized some of his visitors (Stroud 2005:66). A supporter of the arts, Joseph made the collection of sculptures and paintings available for display, where they could be viewed and studied by local amateur and professional artisans. Joseph also donated several European works of fine art to academies in Philadelphia, New York, and Charleston to promote the growth of the arts in America.

Near his second mansion, Joseph constructed a large home called the Lake House for his daughter the Princess Zenaide and her cousin-husband, Prince Charles Lucien Bonaparte. Charles was a noted naturalist (Stroud 2000). Both he and his father-in-law would become members of the Academy of Natural Sciences. Joseph

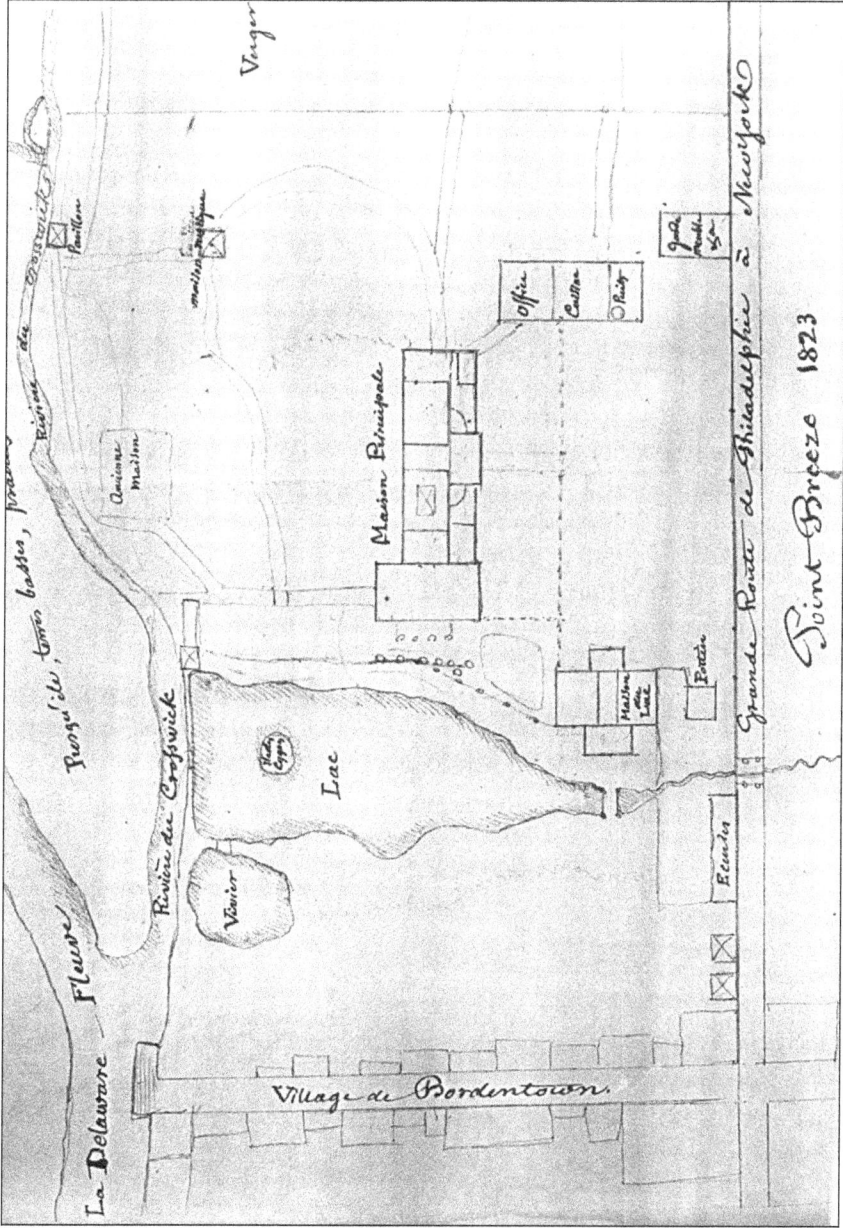

Figure 13.3. Anonymous "Point Breeze 1823." Courtesy of the Municipal Archives of Versailles.

also constructed a small guest house or lodge, later known as the Wash or Ice House, and a home for his gardener, the Garden or Gardener's House. Of these, only the Gardener's House still stands.

He also delighted in landscaping, and contemporary sources note that he had transformed his grounds "from a wild and impoverished tract into a place of beauty, blending the charms of woodland and plantation scenery" (Barber and Howe 1868:102). Joseph undertook several other major landscaping projects including bridging a number of small streams (Berkley 1845:186), throwing a dam across Thornton Creek, laying out 12 miles of drives through his property, building a boardwalk and wharves, installing tunnels, erecting statuary, planting vegetation, and creating a deer park.

Joseph lived much of his adult life in New Jersey. It was at Point Breeze that he learned of the death of Napoleon on St. Helena. Although his wife never joined him at his American estate, he fathered two daughters by his paramour Anne Savage. As he aged, he was drawn more and more to events abroad. In 1832, he returned to Europe hoping to install Napoleon's son Napoleon II on the throne of France. When this failed, he retreated to America. Finally, in 1838 he again visited France, and he reunited with his wife. The next year he suffered a massive stroke. Five years later, in 1844, he died in Florence (Stroud 2005).

After Joseph's return to Europe in 1838, Point Breeze was managed by and eventually willed to his eldest grandson, Joseph Lucien Charles Napoleon Bonaparte. Young Joseph sold off the contents of the house in a pair of auctions in 1847 and then conveyed the property to Thomas Richards (Woodward 1879). In 1850, Henry Beckett, the British Consul in Philadelphia, purchased the estate. He razed the famous Bonaparte House to build a more modern and more modest home (Woodward 1879:94). Essentially a private park, the estate served as a site for Grand Army of the Republic reunions during the 1890s. In the early 20th century, Harris Hammond, a wealthy industrialist, proposed to restore the property to its Bonaparte-era appearance and hired Everett Shinn, noted Ashcan artist, to reconstruct the landscape. However, the stock market crash and ensuing depression brought these plans to naught. Point Breeze has been owned by Divine Word Missionaries since the 1940s.

Landscape Archaeology and Archaeology in the Garden

Monmouth University's archaeological survey of Point Breeze is an example of landscape archaeology, a sub-sect of archaeology in which the cultural landscape, ranging in size from a house lot to a region, is the principal focus (Deetz 1990:2). Early landscape archaeologists focused much of their attention on settlement archaeology, carefully plotting the distribution of sites and their relationships to each other and to their geographical and environmental contexts (Chang 1972; Knapp and Ashmore

1999:2). Other scholars examined sacred landscapes and the symbolism that they embodied (Fritz 1987; Knapp 1996; Townsend 1992); while still other researchers focused on the interstitial areas, an area of study sometimes called non-site archaeology (Dunnell 1992; Foley 1981). Much of this work was influenced by the New Archaeology and cultural ecological approaches, which saw the environment as determinative (Kealhofer 1999:61). From these descriptive but productive approaches, researchers have increasingly moved towards a more reflexive understanding of landscapes as "something that not only shapes but is shaped by human experience" (Knapp and Ashmore 1999:4).

Historical archaeologists have been heavily influenced by post-processual ideational approaches and often strive to understand the meanings that landscapes embodied to those who inhabited and interacted with them. Although some historical archaeologists have examined large scale issues such as settlement patterns (South and Hartley 1980), other historical archaeologists, likely due to their close relationship with the historic preservation movement, have worked to uncover highly detailed information about the organization, function, and indeed contents of specific historic landscapes/ gardens (Yentsch 1996:xxv; Beaudry 1996). This archaeology, done in the service of restoration and interpretation, has provided considerable new information about historic horticultural practices (Yentsch 1996:xxv) and also the social implications of early gardens.

The publication of Mark Leone's 1984 article on the William Paca garden was one of the first explicitly theoretical forays into the study of American landscape archaeology (Hicks 2005:376). Leone and colleagues, influenced by such diverse thinkers as James Deetz (1977) and both Michael Shanks and Christopher Tilley (1982), argued that the formal garden reflected the status differences inherent in Annapolis society and that the Georgian Order influenced not just landscape design but also behavior, and indeed understandings of the world. Leone later expanded his argument to present the Georgian Order as a set of rules that influenced the material culture of the time and were internalized in a somewhat piecemeal pattern by individuals. He and others (Leone and Potter 1988:236–237; Leone, Ernstein, Kryder-Reid, and Shackel 1989; Leone and Shackel 1990; Miller, Yentsch, Piperno, and Paca 1987; Yentsch 1990; Wheaton 1989) explored the formal gardens of the eighteenth century and the cultural norms underlying their design. Their work has shown that gardens were status symbols with extraordinary resonance in early America.

Other scholars have explored issues of agency, layers of meaning, and narrative interpretations of Georgian gardens (Beaudry, Cook, and Mrozowski 1991; Yamin and Metheny 1996; Hicks 2005). Martin Hall approached the Georgian Order as part of a larger reading of material culture as personal statements (Hall 2000:374; Hicks 2005:379). For Hall, gardens were statements, objects of discourse (Hall 1992:377–378). Dan Hicks (2005:387) has presented a situational approach to historical archaeology, "operating at multiple scales and stances, with both familiar and unfamiliar." Indeed, historical archaeologists have moved beyond understanding the formal gardens of the late eighteenth century merely as status symbols reflecting a particular worldview and the social achievements and aspirations of their creators. Instead, these landscapes are interpreted as social statements embodying different meanings to the different groups of people who interacted with them and as cultural constructions that have meant different things to different groups of people at varying points through time (Heath and Gray 2012:1-19).

Point Breeze is a cultural landscape that was intentionally designed and created. In constructing his extensive garden, Bonaparte was following in a long European tradition of grand landscapes and adding to the still nascent American practice of landscape design. To quote Lisa Kealhofer (1999:70), "one conscious presentation of self was in the form of landscape gardens." One of the earliest in America is Governor Berkeley's 1649 plantation at Green Spring in Virginia, which was an early example of a naturalizing landscape, a style just becoming popular in England. It contrasted strongly with the geometric garden found at the nearby contemporary Bacon's Castle. While Bacon's Castle garden speaks to order and control, Berkeley's reflects his social and political interactions. "The style of garden, its meaning, and its social context, reveal choices made by men to define and legitimate their place in the world" (Kryder-Reid 1994).

Joseph Bonaparte's Point Breeze Estate

For Joseph Bonaparte, the former king turned American country gentleman, the creation of his Point Breeze picturesque garden assumed many roles and meanings. A lover of the arts, gardening offered Joseph a means to practice art, design, and architecture on a grand scale. Embellishing the natural environment by creating landscape scenes and views intended to be the subject of an artist's painting, Joseph focused his efforts, time, and money on designing a large picturesque garden at the core of his estate. The creation of gardens such as this one provided both the idle, wealthy, pleasure seeker and student of art an opportunity to tame the wild, create art from nature, exert dominance over the environment, and display wealth and status. It was a hobby suitable for an exceptionally wealthy landed gentleman such as Joseph.

To design a picturesque landscape, such as that at Point Breeze, the gardener used terrain, trees, shrubs, and flowers, elegantly winding paths, fields of crops, brooks, and broad vistas to create a setting with natural and ornamental views; views which could be contrasted against sections of the garden left wild (Watelet 2003:49). Like the author of a play or a novel, the gardener selected and employed these tools to construct theatrical scenes and set the stage for a journey on which a visitor or the gardener could embark. Both physical and emotive, the journey engaged the senses, challenged intellect, fostered reflection, and promoted hours of leisurely enjoyment (Watelet 2003:50).

Meandering paths through the garden were configured to offer changing scenery and views intended to inspire, surprise, indulge, awe, and delight. As if part of a game of intrigue, paths were placed to provide glimpses and lasting vistas of pleasing views (Watelet 2003:27). Shade cast by clustered trees allowed one to stop for a moment, observe, contemplate, and reflect on the scene, nature, and life before continuing on one's course. Some garden designers, like Joseph, even created large lakes where casual boat rides granted added enjoyment and changes in view and scenery (Watelet 2003:49). According to eighteenth-century French garden theorist Claude-Henri Watelet (2003:50), the garden's intent was to utilize elements of nature: wind, clouds, water, and vegetation, with architectural ruins, selectively placed statuary, and paths to create an impression of subtle, almost indiscernible landscape change and "arouse [one's] curiosity and compel [one] to move about with elements that fix[ed one's] attention and invite[ed one] to linger."

Joseph Bonaparte was no stranger to garden art and design. While living in Europe, he used his wealth to create and improve vast gardens at Mortefontaine, his French estate. He also made extensive improvements at his Swiss estate, Prangins (Stroud 2005:74). The former was adjacent to Ermonville, a famous garden park once owned by the eighteenth-century picturesque garden theorist the Marquis Rene-Louis Girardin. Girardin's design at Ermenonville was used as a model by Mortefontaine's initial owner, and Joseph likely continued to employ many of Girardin's landscape theories at Mortefontaine and later at Point Breeze (Stroud 2005:75).

Girardin designed his picturesque gardens with naturalistic views that would be pleasing to the eye, and which were intended to be the subject matter of paintings—hence picturesque, particularly scenes viewed from the estate mansion (Wiebenson 1978:74, 82). Girardin's interpretation of the picturesque garden, like those of contemporary garden theorist J. J. Rousseau (Watelet 2003; Wiebenson 1978:70, 72) were founded on the notion that landscapes should flow organically and be embellished only with agreeable, natural scenery and vernacular building styles. Nevertheless, Girardin did tastefully incorporate classical architecture, particularly temple ruins and villas, as well as altars, memorials, mills, a village, a tower, and even an obelisk into his Ermenonville garden. Girardin's pastoral themes stood in stark contrast to the *jardin anglo-chinois* picturesque style that characterized the gardens of wealthy French eccentrics, who wanted English gardens, but who designed them in their own style, often with exotic scenes, building types, and scenery that appeared inorganic and discontinuous (Wiebenson 1978:89). Though these styles had fallen out of vogue in France by 1789, they regained credence after Napoleon Bonaparte's coronation in 1804, when such luxuries were once again permitted (Wiebenson 1978:107).

Like his use of terrain at Mortefontaine to create natural, agreeable, and picturesque scenery, Joseph's Point Breeze estate contained similar qualities that enhanced its picturesque character. Even before Joseph acquired the Point Breeze property, the striking landscape was of interest to painters (Foster 1997: plate 39; Myers 2000:504). Complete with forests, farms, undulating terrain, meadows, and steep cliffs commanding a grand view of the confluence of the mighty Delaware River and

Crosswicks Creek, the core of the estate contained 233 acres well suited for creating a picturesque garden.

Point Breeze was typical of many contemporary French picturesque gardens (Weber 1986). Bonaparte's first mansion served as the focal, but not centrally located, point of the estate and was surrounded by a series of dispersed buildings, serving both functional and aesthetic purposes, including a boat house, a classical domed circular temple, an aviary house for imported European pheasants, a spring house, gardener's house, and servants' quarters. The lake and spring houses of later construction were located near the lake edge. The temple was sited adjacent to the first mansion along with the servant's house. Marble statuary in the form of deer, lions, gods, goddesses, and historical figures, such as Richard the Lion-Hearted, Ivanhoe, and Caesar Augustus could be found throughout the park either in plain sight or tucked away in a garden scene (Stroud 2005:79).

Joseph may have also embellished his garden scenery with non-formal, vegetative plantings, including white lindens, poplars, weeping willows, button-flowering locusts, and peach, apricot, and hazelnut trees (Stroud 2005:78–79). Other trees included chestnut, tulip, sassafras, ash, beech, oaks, pines, sweet gum, silver fir, acacia, dogwood, honey locust, and white birch. These too were planted as if their seeds were dispersed by the wind. Among the trees, shrubbery, artichoke plants, grasses, native flowers, and flowering plants, such as azalea, rhododendron, mock orange, and viburnum were planted. Rhododendrons still blanket many of the bluff slopes that bound small creeks on the estate, and vinca blanket low terraces adjacent to Crosswicks Creek.

The picturesque garden Joseph created at Point Breeze was among the first of its type in America and, in a region known for grand estates, e.g. Lansdowne, Andalusia, and the Woodlands, was one of the finest. Its prominent position on the high bluff overlooking the confluence of the Delaware River and the Crosswicks Creek enabled it to be clearly seen by travelers. Visible for over two miles up and down river, as well as from nearby Pennsylvania, Joseph's estate and mansion stood as a grand advertisement of his wealth, creativity, and sophistication. Writing in 1841 to Louis Mailliard, N. Chapman noted, "Two days ago, I went to Bordentown, the first time since you left us, and as the tower on the promontory of Point Breese came into view, I was really overpowered by the various recollections and associated, which were awakened" (Chapman 1841). The grandeur, elegance, and artistry in its creation were appreciated by dignified guests, family members, friends, local community members, and artists invited to utilize the pleasant views as subjects in their paintings. Still, many found it to be an ostentatious representation of wealth far beyond the means of the vast majority of Americans, even the Delaware Valley elite.

Archaeology

Archaeological investigations of Joseph Bonaparte's Point Breeze estate—conducted through Monmouth University's annual archaeological field school and the Archaeological Society of New Jersey—consisted of ground penetrating radar, magnetomerty, soil resistivity, subsurface testing, and careful mapping of above-ground landscape features. The subsurface testing focused primarily on the site of Joseph's first mansion (1817–1820). The surface survey concentrated on carefully identifying and mapping still visible landscape and structural features located in the southern portion of the estate at and near the first and second mansions and a preliminary examination of the remainder of the estate.

A series of historic maps of the estate, in particular an 1823 sketch map, an 1847 estate sale map, and a 1911 topographic and existing conditions map, were utilized to locate and document the condition of numerous exposed features between 2006 and 2012 (Anonymous 1823; Miller 1847; Thompson 1911) (table 13.1). Moreover, numerous early-nineteenth-century paintings by noted artists such as Thomas Birch, Charles Lawrence, and Charles Bodmer show the property during the Sayre and Bonaparte occupations. Furthermore, dozens of historic photographs and postcards survive that show the property in the post-Bonaparte era. His building ruins were of intense interest to local photographers, and their gradual decay was documented in considerable detail. The historical imagery provided an important chronology and context for the continuously changing appearance of the Point Breeze estate before, during, and after Joseph's occupation.

The remaining surface features provide physical evidence of Joseph's vision for his picturesque park at Point Breeze (figure 13.4). Landscape features, structures, and buildings served both an aesthetic and functional purpose. The only Bonaparte-era building currently standing on the former estate is a two-story gardener's house sited in the central eastern section of the property. Once surrounded by an orderly kitchen garden, the gardener's home, a critical component of the estate, was situated along a main thoroughfare away from the mansions, as were tenant farm houses. Though both mansion complexes were razed, a close examination of these locales provides strong evidence of the scale on which Joseph's park was constructed. Exposed clustered building foundations, such as the Lake House, wash house, kitchen, office, shed, well, and spring house associated with the second mansion, provided evidence of these once massive buildings, the foundations of which are now largely hidden by almost two centuries of vegetative growth and soil accumulation. Yet not everything in the park was intended to be obvious. To obscure its location, and perhaps remove servants as actors on the landscape, at least one deep well near Joseph's first mansion was constructed with an arched brick cover enabling it to be hidden below the ground surface. Abutting the mansion's foundation, evidence suggests that access to the well shaft was granted through a narrow window that connected to the mansion's cellar.

Garden paths, though clearly depicted on historic maps, were constructed as gently winding earthen mounds or horizontal cuts into undulating topography, only traces of which can still be seen. Some have been incorporated into the current functional use of the property and now serve as asphalt driveways. Others are now visible only as faint depressions or berms running through the heavily wooded property and along the edges of rhododendron-planted bluff slopes and knolls. The remains of a roughly 400-foot long boardwalk are only evinced by wooden pilings along Crosswicks Creek. Partially intact cut sandstone blocks along the bluff's edge, now almost completely covered with soil, once formed steps that snaked down steep bluffs to wharves and docks below the park's houses. The form and construction material used in a now crumbling stone and brick arched bridge spanning a natural divide and seasonal brook hints at its once elegant construction and Joseph's intent for such structures to blend into the natural scenery.

Huge, well-preserved, interlocking horizontally-laid timbers and vertical wooden pilings formed the foundation of two identified wharves at the base of the bluff near the first mansion's former location and a dock at the southern end of Joseph's earthen dam. Exposed only during low tide, the wharves and dock provided a platform from which goods and travelers could be unloaded from watercraft. The southern most of the two wharves was also associated with a boathouse at the base of the bluff.

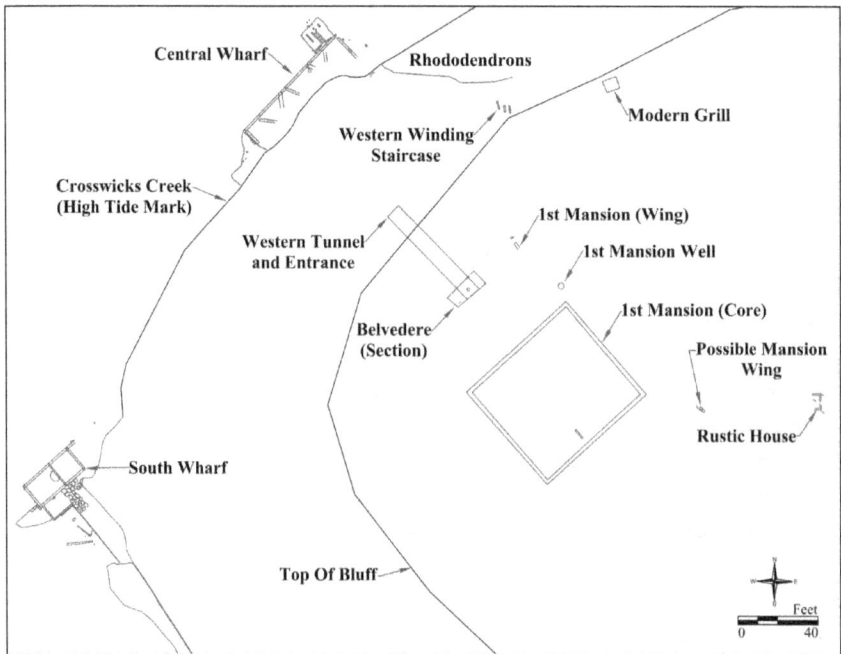

Figure 13.4. Surface and subsurface features identified near the site of the first mansion. Map by Michael Gall.

Table 13.1. Mapped and Identified Surface Features

Map/ Structure or Feature	1823 Map (Anonymous 1823)	1847 Map (Miller 1847)	1911 Map (Thompson 1911)	Surface Remains Identified
Southwestern Estate				
1st Mansion	X			
1st Mansion Well				X
Boardwalk		X		X
Boat House		X		
Belvedere	X	X		
Rustic House	X			
Detached House	X			
Western Winding Staircase				X
Dam Dock		X		X
South Wharf		X	X	X
Central Wharf		X	X	X
Western Tunnel Entrance				X
Western Tunnel				X
Rhododendron Covered Bluffs				X
Lake Dam	X	X	X	X
Southeastern Estate				
2nd Mansion	X	X		
Lake House	X	X	X	X
Wash House	X	X	X	X
Office	X			X
Kitchen	X	X		X
Stables		X		
Small Shed and Well		X		X
Stone and Brick Bridge		X	X	X
Stone Bridge				X
Wooden Dams				X
Spring House				X
Eastern Tunnel Entrance			X	X
Eastern Tunnel				X
Eastern Winding Staircase				X

Table 13.1. Mapped and Identified Surface Features *(cont.)*

Central Estate				
Gardener's House	X	X	X	X
Paths	X	X	X	X
Three Bridges		X	X	
Rhododendron Covered Bluffs				X
Northern Estate				
Paths		X	X	X
Farm House and Outbuildings		X		
North Wharf			X	

Among the most unusual features of Joseph's park are the remains of two massive stone and brick arched tunnels, or *cryptoportici*, associated with the first and second mansions (Mills 1902:296). A third unidentified tunnel also connected the second mansion to the lake house, where Joseph's daughter Zenaide, resided with her husband (Shippen 1954:215). The first identified tunnel was an arched brick-lined underground passageway approximately 7 feet wide, 7 feet high, and 50 feet long, which led from the cellar of his first mansion, through a side yard beneath an observation terrace, to a steep bluff bounded by the Crosswicks Creek (Heston 1906:242). When the first mansion burned, a tower called the Belvedere was erected above the tunnel (Shippen 1954:215). The second was a stone-lined tunnel, which granted access from the lake to his second mansion. This stone tunnel exhibited a tripartite arched opening. The triple arch, often seen in triumphal arches, was a feature commonly employed in picturesque gardens (Hunt 2002:26–35). Indeed, it resembles the entrance to the tunnels at Venus' Vale, a famous English garden at Rousham in Oxfordshire that was laid out in a painterly manner (Sambrook 1986:160). The tunnel system enabled goods, servants, residents, and guests to travel unnoticed from lake and river docks into buildings without altering the park ambiance overhead. Other grand estates in both Europe and America employed similar techniques, which served to render the landscape natural looking by hiding service functions (Moss 1998:71; Stroud 2005:81). Indeed, a similar method is used today in amusement parks such as Disney World.

While a number of structural and landscape features are still visible, many remain hidden, buried under two centuries of soil. An examination for such features was undertaken as part of the second stage of the investigation. Between 2007 and 2009, Monmouth University conducted three annual field schools that focused on the site of Joseph's first mansion. During the first season of fieldwork, a close-interval shovel test grid identified the site of Joseph's first house. Excavation units were employed to sample its contents. During the second season of fieldwork, additional excavation units and judgmentally placed shovel tests were used to better define the size and orientation of the mansion. Prior to the third year's fieldwork, a ground penetrating radar survey was commissioned to identify outbuildings and other subsurface features on the site. It identified six additional structures and several other features. Fieldwork in the summer of 2009 confirmed the presence of a deep shaft feature and at least four of the structures identified by the ground penetrating radar survey.

Fieldwork at the site is ongoing with a current focus on an outbuilding possibly containing a servants' quarters/kitchen associated with the Bonaparte-era occupation of the property. To date, over 100 shovel test pits and 23 excavation units, generally 5-foot square, have been excavated at the site. Just over 20,000 artifacts have been recovered. The bulk of the resources identified are historic, with most dating from the Bonaparte era. Earlier historic deposits dating to the eighteenth century as well as prehistoric deposits are also present. Although it is clear that block excavations would have allowed us an even finer-grained understanding of the site layout, the property's current use as a retirement community for Roman Catholic missionary priests and a desire to minimally impact the modern landscape and the archaeological deposits precluded such an approach.

Subsurface features include the filled cellar hole of the first mansion, what appears to be the filled cellar of a mid-eighteenth-century structure, an eighteenth-century sheet midden, foundations associated with either a wing of the main house or an outbuilding, foundations associated with the belvedere, a well, gravel paths, and a possible kitchen, containing Bonaparte-era deposits, and a second well. Minor features such as builders' trenches and interior division walls within the main house were also recorded but are not discussed here.

The foundation of the first mansion's core measures roughly 60 feet by 60 feet. Geophyiscal investigations suggest two rectangular additions each measuring approximately 45 feet by 100 feet flanked the north and south sides of the mansion core. These additions correspond with those depicted in several early nineteenth-century paintings of the estate. Ten excavation units were used to identify the parameters of the structure, and two were used to sample its contents. The building's core had a massive 18 inch thick cut stone foundation extending at least 6.5 feet below the current ground surface. It faced south/southwest towards the Delaware River. When the building burned, Joseph reported that nearly all of his possessions had been saved (Stroud 2005:63). Other contemporary sources noted that most of his possessions were lost (Shippen 1954:213). It appears that the cellar of the house was filled with much of the rubble from the building's destruction, including enormous quantities of broken brickbats—not cataloged, thousands of nails, large quantities of melted wine bottle glass, mirror glass, and very small quantities of French porcelain, furniture hardware, and personal items. Fragments of carbonized floorboards, joists, and even cloth, possibly from heavy tapestry wall hangings were also found. A single fragment of a compo picture frame was recovered. Bonaparte apparently undertook a rather massive salvage operation, removing most of the stone foundation from the northern and eastern walls of the structure. Nearly all of the recovered bricks are broken, likely indicating an attempt to salvage and reuse intact bricks.

Charred fragments of wooden tongue and groove flooring were also unearthed. Other artifacts of note include decorative bronze appliqués, possibly from pieces of furniture, butchered sheep bones, a sugar bowl lid, and a mendable, transfer-printed French porcelain bowl. The latter two exhibited fire damage, however, the pattern and inscription on the bowl, which reads, in French, Roman History, were clearly discernible (figure 13.5).

The marble floor fragments, silvered mirror fragments, compo picture frame chips, and bronze furniture appliqués show Bonaparte's desire to advertise his wealth in highly visible ways with items that were purely decorative. The frag-

Figure 13.5. A French earthenware plate with a fine transfer print. Photograph by Richard Veit.

mentary marble and wood floors encountered in Unit 2 is a study in contrasts, as the wood floor, which lined the cellar out of view from most visitors was austere and functional, while the marble floor, likely trodden upon by important guests, was primarily intended to impress with its stunning visual beauty, rather than its sturdy form as a surface. Similarly, ornamental porcelain vases were recovered from Excavation Units 1 and 2—fifty feet from each other. They probably once graced niches within the house.

The deposits encountered in Unit 1 and 2 provide information not only about the time of the fire but the aftermath of the clean-up as well. Non-architectural items such as wine bottles may have been present within the cellar at the time of the fire. Other items may have been introduced after the fire as the building collapsed and the cellar was filled with debris from the overlying structure. Documentary sources describe how movable valuables such as paintings and drapes were saved from the burning structure, while other more bulky items were left behind.

Within the mansion, the remains of truncated partition walls within the cellar were noted. These may have been used to divide off specialized areas within the larger structure. The large number of wine bottles found in this area suggests that this may have been a location where wine was stored. Bonaparte's nickname as King of Spain had been *Pepe Botellas* or colloquially Joe Bottles, a moniker that seems well supported by the archaeological evidence.

Three wells were identified. One is largely intact, one is buried, and one appeared to have been robbed out. The first was associated with the mansion but was much too deep to excavate as part of a field school. A second well dating to the mideighteenth century was identified near a possible mid-eighteenth-century cellar, associated with an earlier house on the estate. The third well was robbed out and backfilled. Testing there failed to reach intact cultural deposits. Next to and likely associated with the third well is a building with a stone foundation. It was not aligned with the mansion—but rather on a north/south axis. Very late-eighteenth- or nineteenth-century deposits associated with this structure include small quantities of burned artifacts, much like the mansion itself. However, the deposits consist primarily of ceramics: redware, creamware, and pearlware, with a small quantity of refined bisque earthenware decorated with cherubs involved in a bacchanal scene (figure 13.6). This structure may have served as a kitchen or in some other form of ancillary capacity.

Deeply buried brick walls near the first mansion's tunnel are likely associated with the Belvedere, which also housed servants on the property (Shippen 1954). Similarly, brick walls unearthed to the south of the house's main block may be the remains of the building's wings. Earlier domestic deposits and a filled cellar hole likely relate to the earlier Douglas or Farnsworth occupations of the property.

The catastrophic fire that destroyed the remains of Joseph Bonaparte's first mansion and the subsequent landscaping of the site served to preserve a rich deposit of early-nineteenth-century material culture, which reflects a truly extraordinary structure. An imposing brick building with what may have been a copper roof

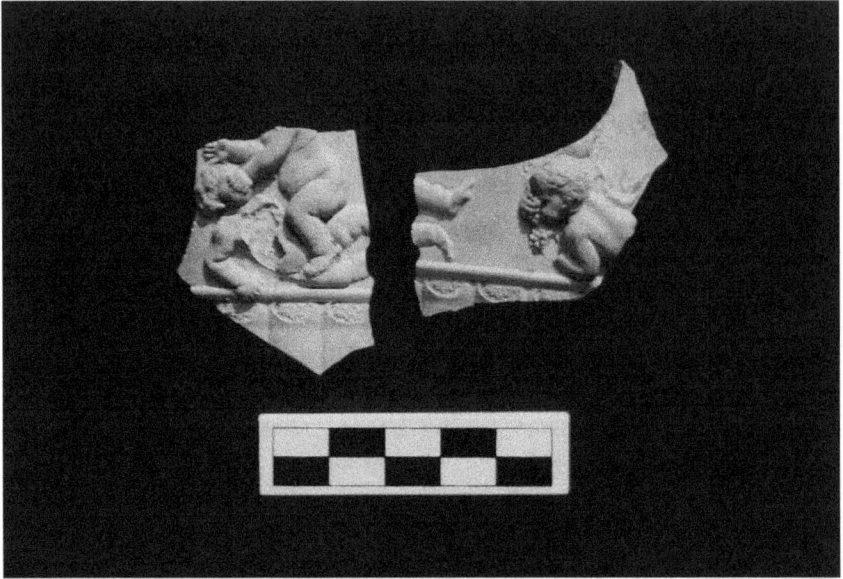

Figure 13.6. A fragment of an early-nineteenth-century teapot showing putti involved in a bacchanalian scene. Photograph by Richard Veit.

centered the property. Service functions were hidden. Upon entering the building, visitors would have trod upon black and white checkerboard marble floors, walked through well-lit rooms decorated with statuary and large mirrors, and if invited to eat, would have dined off imported French ceramics and consumed fine wines. It would have been a memorable experience. Joseph had recreated a bit of the splendor he had known in Europe in the Delaware Valley.

Understanding the Landscape

When asked to compare his own situation with that of Joseph, Napoleon wrote, the following telling line, "He will be a bourgeois American and spend his fortune in making gardens" (Girod de l'ain 1970:343). Napoleon knew his brother well. But what does Joseph's garden tell us about the former king and about landscapes in general? Thanks to the site's location on the main route across the state and Joseph's exceptional hospitality, it saw regular attention from travelers. A review of the guests who visited Point Breeze reads like a who's who of early-nineteenth-century America: John Quincy Adams, Henry Clay, the Marquis de Lafayette, Robert Stockton, and many others. Here he dazzled his guests and the general public with his knowledge of art, nature, politics, and culture; donated several fine works by European masters to art academies in Charleston, Philadelphia, and New York; and promoted the development and growth of fine art and landscape design in America.

While many visitors left Point Breeze suitably impressed, others were less kind. Edouard de Montule who visited in 1816 noted that "The house [was] not pretentious but the estate should someday be very comfortable" (Seeber 1951:197). A less sympathetic English traveler, William Harris, wrote that Joseph was "laying out some of the spoils of Europe in an elegant mansion and grounds" (Harris 1821:26–30). William Dalton, an English traveler, noted that Bonaparte's mansion had a "princely appearance but was surrounded by poor land (Dalton 1821:90). Two years later, in 1823, Scottish Botanist David Douglas called Bonaparte's mansion splendid and noted that he had pleasure grounds laid out in the English style (Douglas 1959:27–28). Perhaps the most intriguing description of the landscape was provided by Thomas Gordon (1834:106). He wrote:

> The attractions of the scene determined Joseph Buonoparte [*sic*], Count de Surveilliers, in his choice of a residence in this country; and this distinguished exile, who has filled two thrones, and has pretensions based on popular suffrage to a third, has dwelt here many years in philosophic retirement. He has in the vicinity about 1500 acres of land, part of which possessed natural beauty, which his taste and wealth have been employed to embellish. At the expense of some hundred thousand dollars, he has converted a wild and impoverished tract, into a park of surpassing beauty, blending the charms of woodland and plantation scenery, with a delightful water prospect. . . . With characteristic liberality, the County has opened his grounds to the public, we regret to perceive, that he has been ungratefully repaid, by the defacement of his ornamental structures and mutilation of his statues.

Clearly this was a landscape that could be read and interpreted in many different ways. Historical archaeologists have argued that gardens were a way for elites in the Chesapeake insecure in their power to demonstrate and convince others of their merit. Joseph's gardens may also have been an attempt to do this.

At the same time, Joseph's garden provided him with an appropriate setting for entertaining guests, acting the part of a king in exile, and fostering the appreciation for and growth of fine art in America. The estate enabled him to recreate his grand European lifestyle in a transformed picturesque garden that was enjoyed by estate residents, elite guests, artists, and the general public. His estate also functioned to bind Bordentown's residents to him through employment and perhaps some reflected glory. In constructing the gardens, Joseph hired large numbers of workmen. A recent mayor of Bordentown described Joseph as a one-man WPA program for Bordentown. This may not have been unintentional. Joseph, even today, is a revered figure in Bordentown, a local hero. A WPA mural in the local post office depicts him distributing oranges to delighted children on his frozen pond. While King of Spain Joseph was viewed as a despot, in America he was seen as a democratically inclined monarch.

Many of the visitors who came to the park went away impressed by the landscapes, plantings, statuary, and buildings. Others, as seen in these quotes, were clearly less impressed. While still others hunted without permission and even damaged Joseph's property. A thoughtless visitor or perhaps, as some believe, an arsonist burnt down his first home.

To date, we have succeeded in relocating the first mansion, the second mansion, and several outbuildings. We have begun mapping the extensive remains of the property. Although our study of Point Breeze is just beginning, it is clear that the site has tremendous archaeological potential. By documenting the site and understanding the varying contexts through which people experienced it, we can better understand how individuals, past and present, use landscapes as stages to perform their roles in society and how those landscapes continue to influence us today (figure 13.7).

Acknowledgements

A multi-year collaborative project is only possible with the help of numerous individuals. The invitation to work at Point Breeze tendered by the former Rector of Divine Word, Father Ray Lennon, S.V.D. and continued by his successors, Father Walter Miller, and most recently by Brother Paul Hogan, has been an extraordinary

Figure 13.7. An early-twentieth-century postcard showing the entrance to Joseph Bonaparte's Point Breeze estate. The former washhouse/tenant house stands in the background. Long after Joseph's departure from the property, the site remained an important landmark to local residents.

opportunity for which we are truly grateful. Dr. Andrew Cosentino, art historian and Divine Word Archivist, first alerted us to the opportunity to study this exceptional site. He also enlisted a crew of exceptional colleagues to help support the project including Andrew Bertolino, Michael Hanlon, Father Martin Padovani, S.V.D., Peter Tucci, and Ellen Wehrman. Mary Leck and Dan Aubrey from the Friends for the Bordentown-Trenton Marsh have also been generous in their support of our project. Their help is deeply appreciated. Monmouth University's support, particularly that of Stan Green, Dean of the School of Humanities and Social Sciences, and Fred McKitrick, Chair of the Department of History and Anthropology, was also invaluable. None of the fieldwork and labwork would have been possible without the help of our students and volunteers. Drs. Gerard P. Scharfenberger, who taught the graduate section of the field school in 2007 and William Schindler who explored the prehistoric components of the site in 2008 and 2009 were of tremendous assistance. Our field and lab assistants: Sean Bratton, Ed Carlson, Allison Gall, Adam Heinrich, Sean McHugh, Koorleen Minton, and Suzanne Moore were extraordinarily helpful. Generous funding was provided by the Descendants of the Founders of New Jersey and anonymous donors. The Cultural Resource Consulting Group and Richard Grubb and Associates, Inc. lent much-needed equipment which greatly increased the efficiency of our fieldwork. Vincent Haegele discovered the 1823 Map of Point Breeze and graciously shared it with us.

References Cited

Anonymous
1823   Point Breeze, 1823. Map on file in the Municipal Archives, Versailles, France.

Barber, John W., and Henry Howe
1868   *Historical Collections of New Jersey Past and Present.* John W. Barber, New Haven, Connecticut.

Beaudry, Mary C.
1996   Why Gardens? In *Landscape Archaeology: Reading and Interpreting the American Historical Landscape*, edited by Karen B. Metheny and Rebecca Yamin, pp. 3–6. University of Tennessee Press, Knoxville, Tennessee.

Beaudry, Mary, C., Lauren J. Cook, and Stephen Mrozowski
1991   Artifacts and Active Voices: Material Culture as Social Discourse. In *The Archaeology of Inequality*, edited by R. H. McGuire and R. Paynter, pp. 150–191. Blackwell, Oxford.

Berkley, Helen
1845   A Sketch of Joseph Bonaparte. *Godey's Lady's Book.* April 1845:181–185.

Burlington County Clerk's Office
1817   Deed from James Carret to George Reinholdt, April 13, 1817, Book
            of Deeds F2, pp. 269-275. Burlington County Clerk's Office, Mount
            Holly, New Jersey.

Chang, K. C.
1972   *Settlement Patterns in Archaeology*. Modules in Anthropology, 24.
            Addison-Wesley, Menlo Park, California.

Chapman, N.
1841   Letter to Louis Maillard, August 14, 1841. Manuscripts and Archives,
            Yale Univeristy Library, Mailliard Family Papers, Joseph Bonaparte,
            Correspondence, 1785–1856, File 0020016, Group 341, Box 2.

Dalton, William
1821   *Travels in the Unites States of America and Part of Upper Canada*.
            Appleby, n.p.

Deetz, James
1977   *In Small Things Forgotten: The Archaeology of Early American Life*.
            Anchor Books, New York.

1990   Prologue, Landscapes as Cultural Statements. In *Earth Patterns in Ar-
            chaeology*, edited by William M. Kelso and Rachel Most, pp. 1–6. Uni-
            versity of Virginia Press, Richmond.

Douglas, David
1959   *Journal Kept by David Douglas During his Travels in North America
            1823–1827*. Antiquarian Press, New York.

Dunnell, R. C.
1992   The Notion Site. In *Space Time, and Archaeological Landscapes*, ed-
            ited by J. Rossignol and L. Wandsnider, pp. 21–41. Plenum Press, New
            York.

Foley, R.
1981   Off-Site Archaeology: An Alternative Approach for the Short-Sited. In,
            Patterns of the Past: Studies in Honour of David Clarke, edited by Ian
            Hodder, G. Isaac, and N. Hammond, pp. 157–183. Cambridge Univer-
            sity Press, Cambridge, United Kingdom.

Foster, Kathleen A.
1997   *Captain Watson's Travels in America: The Sketchbooks and Diary of
            Joshua Rowley Watson, 1772–1818*. University of Pennsylvania Press,
            Philadelphia.

Fritz, J. M.
1987   Chaco Canyon and Vijayanagra: Proposing Spatial Meaning in Two
            Societies. In *Mirror and Metaphor: Material and Social Constructions
            of Reality*, edited by D. W. Ingersoll and G. Bronitsky, pp. 313–348.
            University Press of America, Lanham, Maryland.

Girod de l'Ain, Gabriel
1970   *Joseph Boanaparte: Le roi malgré lui.* Librarie Académique Perrin, Paris.

Gordon, Thomas F.
1834   *Gazetteer of the State of New Jersey.* Polyanthos, Cottonport, New Jersey.

Hall, Martin
1992   Small Things and the Mobile: Conflictual Fusion of Power, Fear, and Desire. In *The Art and Mystery of Historical Archaeology: Essays in Honor of James Deetz,* edited by Anne Elizabeth Yentsch and Mary C. Beaudry, pp. 373–399. CRC Press, Boca Raton, Florida.
2000   *Archaeology and the Modern World.* Routledge, London.

Harris, William Tell
1821   *Remarks Made during a Tour through the United States of America, in the Years 1817, 1818, and 1819.* Sherwood, Neely, and Jones, London.

Heston, Alfred
1906   The Usurper: Reflections on the Life of Joseph Bonaparte. Manuscript on file, the New Jersey History Society, Newark.

Hicks, Dan
2005   "Places for Thinking" from Annapolis to Bristol: Situations and Symmetries in "World Historical Archaeologies." *World Archaeology* 37(3):373–391.

Heath, Barbara J., and Jack Gray
2012   "Two Tracts of Land at the Poplar Forest": A Historical and Archaeological Overview of Thomas Jefferson's Plantation Retreat. In *Jefferson's Poplar Forest: Unearthing a Virginia Plantation*, edited by Barbara J. Heath and Jack Gray, pp.1-19. University of Florida Press, Gainesville.

Hunt, John Dixon
2002   *The Picturesque Garden In Europe.* Thames & Hudson, London.

Kealhofer, Lisa
1999   Creating Social Identity in the Landscape: Tidewater, Virginia, 1600–1750. In *Archaeologies of Landscape: Contemporary Perspectives*, edited by Wendy Ashmore and Arthur Knapp, pp. 58–82. Blackwell, Malden, Massachusetts.

Knapp, A. Bernard, and Wendy Ashmore
1999   *Archaeologies of Landscape: Contemporary Perspectives.* Blackwell, Malden, Massachusetts.

Knapp, A. Bernard
1996   The Bronze Age Economy of Cyprus: Ritual, Ideology, and the Sacred Landscape. In *The Development of the Cypriot Economy: From the*

Prehistoric Period to the Present Day, edited by V. Karagorghis, V. Karagoghis, and D. Michaelides, pp. 71–106. University of Cyprus and Bank of Cyprus, Nicosia.

Kryder-Reid, Elizabeth
1994   "As is the Gardener, so is the Garden": The Archaeology of Landscape as Myth. In *Historical Archaeology of the Chesapeake*, edited by Paul Shackel and Barbara Little, Washington, D.C.: Smithsonian Institution Press, 131–148.

Leone, Mark P., J. H. Ernstein, E. Kryder-Reid, and Paul A. Shackel
1989   Power Gardens in Annapolis. *Archaeology* 42(2):34–37, 74–75.

Leone, Mark P., and Parker Potter (editors)
1988   *The Recovery of Meaning in Historical Archaeology.* Smithsonian Institution Press, Washington, D.C.

Leone, Mark P. and Paul Shackel
1990   Plane and Solid Geometry in Colonial Gardens in Annapolis, Maryland. In *Earth Patterns, Essays in Landscape Archaeology*, edited by W. M. Kelso and Rachel Most, pp. 153–167. University of Virginia Press, Richmond.

Miller
1847   Map of the Residence & Park Grounds, near Bordentown, New Jersey, of the Late Joseph Napoleon Bonaparte, Ex-King of Spain, to be sold at auction, by Anthony J. Bleecker, on Friday, 25th, June, 1847, at 1 o'clock, P.M. on the Premises. Miller's Lithograph, New York.

Miller, Naomi F., Anne Yentsch, Dolores Piperno, and Barbara Paca
1990   Two Centuries of Landscape Change at Morven, Princeton, New Jersey. In *Earth Patterns in Archaeology*, edited by William M. Kelso and Rachel Most, pp. 257–276. University of Virginia Press, Richmond.

Mills, W. Jay
1902   *Historic Houses of New Jersey.* J. B. Lippincott, Philadelphia and London.

Moss, Roger W.
1998   *Historic Houses of Philadelphia.* University of Pennsylvania Press, Philadelphia.

Myers, Kenneth John
2000   Art and Commerce in Jacksonian America: The Steamboat Albany Collection. *The Art Bulletin* 82(3):503–528.

Sambrook, James
1986   *The Eighteenth Century: The Intellectual and Cultural Context of English Literature, 1700-1789.* Longman, New York.

Shanks, M. and C. Tilley
1982   Ideology, Symbolic Power, and Ritual Communication: A Reinterpretation of Neolithic Mortuary Practices. In *Symbolic and Structural Ar-*

chaeology, edited by Ian Hodder, pp. 129–154. Cambridge University Press, Cambridge, United Kindgom.

Seeber, Edward (translator and editor)

1951   *Travels in America, 1816–1817 by Edouard de Montule.* Indiana University Press, Indianapolis.

Shippen, Edward

1954   Reminiscences of Admiral Edward Shippen: Bordentown in the 1830s. *The Pennsylvania Magazine of History and Biography* 72(2):203–230.

South, Stanley, and Michael Hartley

1980   *Deep Water and High Ground: Seventeenth Century Low Country Settlement.* Institute of Anthropology and Archaeology, Columbia, South Carolina.

Stroud, Patricia Tyson

2000   *The Emperor of Nature: Charles-Lucien Bonaparte and His World.* University of Pennsylvania Press, Philadelphia.

2005   *The Man Who Had Been King: The American Exile of Napoleon's Brother Joseph.* University of Pennsylvania Press, Philadelphia.

Thompson, John W.

1911   Map of Bonaparte Park, Bordentown, New Jersey. John W. Thompson, Philadelphia.

Tower, Charlemagne

1918   Joseph Bonaparte in Philadelphia and Bordentown. *Pennsylvania Magazine of History and Biography* 42(4): 289–309.

Townsend, R. F. (editor)

1992   *The Ancient Americas: Art from Sacred Landscapes.* Art Institute of Chicago, Chicago.

Upton, Dell

1988   White and Black Landscapes in Eighteenth Century Virginia. In *Material Life in America 1600–1860*, edited by Robert Blair St. George, pp. 357–370. Northeastern University Press, Boston.

Watelet, Claude-Henri

2003   *Essays on Gardens: A Chapter in the French Picturesque.* University of Pennsylvania Press, Philadelphia.

Weber, Constance

1986   Bonaparte's Park: A French Picturesque Garden in America. *Journal of Garden History* 6(4):330–347.

Wheaton, Thomas

1989   Drayton Hall: Archaeological Testing of the Orangery. New South Associates Technical Report No. 11, Stone Mountain, Georgia.

Wiebenson, Dora

1978   *The Picturesque Garden in France.* Princeton University Press, Princeton, New Jersey.

Woodward, E. M.

1879   *Bonaparte's Park and the Murats*. MacCrellish and Quigley, Trenton, New Jersey.

Yamin, Rebecca, and Karen Bescherer Metheny

1996   Preface: Reading the Historical Landscape. In *Landscape Archaeology: Reading and Interpreting the American Historical Landscape*, edited by Rebecca Yamin and Karen Bescherer Metheny, pp. xiii–xxii. University of Tennessee Press, Knoxville.

Yentsch, Anne Elizabeth

1990   The Calvert Orangerie in Annapolis, Maryland: A Horticultural Symbol of Power and Prestige in an Early Eighteenth-Century Community. In *Earth Patterns in Landscape Archaeology*, edited by William M. Kelso and Rachel Most, pp. 169–188. University of Virginia Press, Richmond.

1996   Introduction: Close Attention to Place—Landscape Studies by Historical Archaeologists. In *Landscape Archaeology: Reading and Interpreting the American Historical Landscape*, edited by Rebecca Yamin and Karen Bescherer Metheny, pp. xxiii–xliii. University of Tennessee Press, Knoxville.

14

HISTORICAL ARCHAEOLOGY IN TRENTON: A THIRTY-YEAR RETROSPECTIVE

RICHARD W. HUNTER AND IAN BURROW

Context

Historically and geographically, Trenton, New Jersey, is a stereotypical Euro-American East Coast port city. Positioned at "the falls of the Delaware," at the head of navigation and head of tide, the settlement boasts more than three centuries of absorbing history, traces of which survive in abundance within and beneath the city's current urban landscape. A combination of circumstances has resulted in Trenton being the subject of multiple archaeological investigations, arguably more than in any other of the smaller historic cities in the eastern United States over the last three decades.

Trenton's first 100 years, beginning in the late 1670s, were those of a gradually emerging market town tied by the Delaware River to Philadelphia and by the King's Highway to New York. Important early industrial developments, notably the processing of iron and the production of steel, also took place during this time period. Two morale-boosting military successes in Trenton in the space of ten crucial days over Christmas and New Year's of 1776–77 helped turn the tide of revolutionary conflict in America's favor, while the town's port of Lamberton, also known as Trenton Landing, served as a critical transshipment point in the Continental Army's supply network. Postwar, Trenton emerged as a serious candidate for the permanent seat of Congress but settled ultimately, in 1790, for the lesser status of state capital (Raum 1871; Trenton Historical Society 1929; Turk 1964; Toothman 1977; Burrow and Hunter 1996).

In its second century, the city thrived first as a center of regional commerce and state government until a confluence of transportation and energy improvements (a bridge over the Delaware, turnpikes, a canal, water power development, and several major railroads) propelled its rise into an industrial powerhouse. After awkward forays into textile and paper making, Trenton blossomed in the second half of the nineteenth and early twentieth centuries as a manufacturing center for iron and steel, pottery, rubber, and a host of other specialized products ranging from oyster crackers to toy dolls to parachutes. Over the past century, Trenton's manufacturing might has waned, and the city has struggled economically, its dominant function today being administrative, judicial, and government services (Raum 1871; Trenton Historical Society 1929; Quigley and Collier 1984; Cumbler 1989; Stern 1994).

Trenton's archaeology, more prevalent and substantive in its survival and informational content than the casual observer might suppose, expresses many of the city's most important historical themes. The ground beneath the city holds valuable, tangible, educational, and in some instances economically sustainable historical assets—a subsurface condition that has been recognized gradually over the past quarter century. Some limited retrieval of archaeological data did take place in the city in the early twentieth century as new urban infrastructure, chiefly sewers and rail lines, was installed. This effort was concentrated primarily on Native American remains and the then-seething debate over human antiquity in North America spawned by Charles Conrad Abbott and his explorations in the so-called "Trenton gravels." The focus of these archaeological endeavors lay within what is today known as the Abbott Farm National Historic Landmark located just across the City of Trenton border in the Hamilton-Bordentown vicinity (Volk 1911; Cross 1956; Wall et al. 1996; Hunter Research, Inc. 2009).

It has taken the dictates of historic preservation law and regulation and the recently minted profession of cultural resource management to bring to the surface the extraordinary character and quality of Trenton's historical archaeological record. Since the late 1960s, federal legislation—notably Section 106 of the National Historic Preservation Act; various state laws, chiefly the New Jersey Register of Historic Places Act and Executive Order 215; and permitting procedures regulating development in waterfront and wetland settings—have resulted in the completion of more than one hundred historical and archaeological studies within the city limits. These studies include site assessments, surveys with and without subsurface investigation, data recovery excavations, and archaeological monitoring operations during construction. Referred to generically as cultural resource management archaeology, and framed in terms of work scope by the requirements of regulatory compliance, it is these endeavors, as opposed to research-based academic inquiries, that have laid bare Trenton's archaeological riches.

Funding in support of archaeological studies has come largely from the tax coffers of government and to a lesser extent from the pockets of private developers. The New Jersey Department of Transportation (NJDOT) has been in the vanguard of this work, required by law to take into account the effects of its numerous highway improvement projects on archaeological resources within the city. Other agencies actively involved in public archaeology in Trenton have included the Philadelphia District of the U.S. Army Corps of Engineers, the Division of Property Management and Construction (State of New Jersey Department of the Treasury), the Division of Parks and Forestry (New Jersey Department of Environmental Protection), the New Jersey State Building Authority, the New Jersey Water Supply Authority, the County of Mercer, and the City of Trenton. A small but important strand in Trenton's public archaeology has comprised studies supported by grants from the New Jersey Historical Commission and the New Jersey Historic Trust. Exercising oversight and quality control over all of this archaeological activity is the New Jersey Historic Preservation Office, a division of the New Jersey Department of Environmental Protection.

The archaeological investigation of Trenton has taken place against an ever-developing background of research and theoretical discussion about American urban archaeology. There is, as yet, no single-author overview of the subject comparable to that written by Martin Carver (1987) for English towns. Rather, the American literature is dominated by monographs on single cities, notably Philadelphia (Cotter et al. 1992; Yamin 2008), New York (Cantwell and Wall 2001), and Denver (Nelson et al. 2001); by edited collections of sometimes loosely related case and topic studies (Dickens 1982; Staski 1987; Young 2000); and by a myriad of individual papers on a wide range of broadly urban archaeological topics. More than 40 of the latter have, for example, been published in *Historical Archaeology*, the journal of the society of the same name, since 1975.

Numerous U.S. towns and cities have now been studied archaeologically. Prominent in the published literature east of the Mississippi are Pensacola and St. Augustine (Florida), Charleston (South Carolina), Jamestown and Alexandria (Virginia), Annapolis and St. Mary's City (Maryland), Wilmington (Delaware), Philadelphia (Pennsylvania), New Brunswick, Raritan Landing, and Paterson (New Jersey), New York City (New York), Newport and Providence (Rhode Island), Boston (Massachusetts), and Portsmouth (New Hampshire). There are several others where important work has also been done. Trenton is one of these.

To be added to this enumeration of published materials is the untold number of urban cultural resource compliance reports. Produced in response to the legal and regulatory requirements established from the late 1960s onwards, these documents contain large masses of data and some important research insights, but their impact on the discipline is less than it should be because of their limited accessibility, residing as they generally do in the repositories of the agencies that commission and review them (Mullins and Klein 2000:232, 238-239). Occasionally, one of these studies is selected for wider publication and circulation, the most notable in the mid-Atlantic being the magisterial and multi-disciplinary, six-volume study of the Five Points Site in Lower Manhattan (Yamin 2000).

The studies range from the most pragmatic and descriptive to the most abstrusely theoretical, the latter drawing on the strongly anthropological, processual and post-processual underpinnings of American archaeology. For this reason, it is difficult to discern any single dominant theme or concern in urban archaeological studies. Rather, two major and several other strands continue to dominate the discipline.

Primary among these is the study of consumer behavior, drawing on the frequently rich (or even overwhelmingly large) collections of artifacts from urban sites, and the possibilities for relating these to specific households, neighborhoods, and ethnic groups. This research domain speaks closely to the core aim of historical archaeology: to study and understand "the global nature of modern life" (Orser 2004:19).

The second major theme is what is termed the "Landscape Archaeology" approach. Although this can be defined broadly as the investigation of "the natural environment modified for permanent human occupation" (Zierden 2000:92), in urban archaeology it has come to be strongly and more narrowly associated with a specific theoretical stance that invests urban spaces with powerful symbolic meanings relating to social power relationships. This approach is exemplified in the work of Mark Leone, Paul Shackel, and others engaged in research at Annapolis and St Mary's City, Maryland (e.g. Leone et al. 1989, Leone 1994; Shackel 1994). There have also been similar, less polemical, overviews of the landscape archaeology of such places as Williamsburg, Virginia (Brown and Samford 1994); Boston; and Newport, Rhode Island (Mrozowski 1987).

Beneath, or embedded within, these dominant topics are more specific areas of research, most recently and succinctly summarized by Young (2000:5-13). Among these are dietary studies, the spatial design and use of house lots, the archaeological study of political and governmental institutions, the city-as-site concept (e.g., Cantwell and Wall 2001:12-14), the analysis of neighborhoods, and the investigation of gender roles and identity.

While having regard to these trends in urban archaeological studies, the approach to Trenton's historical archaeology has to some extent taken on a character of its own. This has in part resulted in the investigation of some topics in much more detail than in other cities (e.g., industrial, military, and governmental sites) and in relatively minor contributions to others (e.g., nineteenth-century consumer behavior). The approach has drawn strongly on the historical-geographical and diachronic "landscape" philosophy developed in the United Kingdom, and in which both authors of this paper were trained (see discussion in Burrow and Hunter 1996:32-34).

The City's Historical Archaeological Potential

The historical archaeology of any city is a moving target; its specificity determined by the city's life and its passage through time and space. In Trenton's case, a decade or so into the twenty-first century, redevelopment has compromised vast swaths of the city's buried heritage. Nonetheless, key areas where archaeological remains may survive can still be marked out, framed by the pre-urban topography of streams and streets and excluding the sites of buildings with deep basements and trenches dug for urban infrastructure.

Assessing the historical archaeology of the city has therefore been approached as a cartographic exercise, informed by an understanding of the settlement's geographic, geologic, and edaphic underpinnings and a detailed knowledge of past and current land use. Trenton originated and has evolved at a critical point of natural and transportational convergence in the cultural landscape. Human movement across the land has historically been drawn to the falls of the Delaware as the furthest downstream point where the river could be forded on foot or horseback—a crossing mechanism supplemented in the late seventeenth and eighteenth centuries by up to three local ferries. From 1804 onward, these were replaced by a succession of road and rail bridges, today numbering four. Movement on the water has been no less influential in Trenton's settlement growth. The geology of the falls, a series of innocuous-looking rapids formed on a band of gneiss and schist bedrock, presents an obstacle to watercraft moving upstream or downstream, forcing portage and encouraging the growth of transshipment facilities on the riverbank.

As far as Native American movement on and use of the landscape was concerned, trails converged on the ford at the falls and also ran along the fringes of the floodplain on both sides of the Delaware atop the terrace and bluff rims that overlook the river. At times of low water, canoes and dugouts were taken out and put back into the river upstream and downstream of the falls. Waterborne travel would also have extended upstream along the various tributaries feeding the left bank of the Delaware at and just below Trenton—along Assunpink Creek, Crosswicks Creek, Watson's Creek, and perhaps Petty's Run. The most potent influence on Native American activity in the local landscape, however, was the remarkable annual harvest of anadromous fish (principally sturgeon, shad, and alewife) that could be garnered from the Delaware below the falls and in the tidal marshes around the mouth of Crosswicks Creek. Along with other rich faunal and floral resources in the floodplain, the fish harvest fueled intensive seasonal occupation in the Middle Delaware Valley beginning around 5,000 years ago during the Late Archaic period. Seasonal occupation developed into year-round, village-based settlement during the Middle and Late Woodland periods (circa A.D. 1–A.D. 1600), which from around A.D. 900 was accompanied by horticulture.

Today, the former intensity of Native American occupation in the Middle Delaware Valley is most prominently acknowledged through the designation of the Abbott Farm National Historic Landmark (AFNHL), an entity in mixed public and private ownership located largely in Hamilton Township, Mercer County and Bordentown Township, Burlington County. The archaeological potential of the AFNHL has been heavily compromised as a result of suburban development, which took place with notably voracious speed between roughly 1880 and 1950. In recent decades, however, municipal, county, and state land acquisitions have led to more sensitive archaeological resource management practices on public lands (Hunter Research, Inc. 2009). In actuality, the intensity of Native American occupation that the AFNHL honors extended far beyond the limits of modern historic designation, including northward up the Delaware Valley at least to the mouth of Assunpink Creek, and south to at least the area of Fieldsboro.

The City of Trenton today obscures a zone of Native American archaeological potential, now much depleted but still sporadically intact in the form of "islands" of cultural deposits that have survived the deep intrusions of urban and suburban construction. Within the city, this zone of prehistoric archaeological potential, where evidence of sedentary and semi-sedentary occupation is most likely to be found, can be loosely defined as extending inland from the pre-urban left bank of the Delaware River for approximately 500 feet, expanding somewhat further from the river along the Assunpink stream corridor. Within this zone in the prehistoric and early historic periods was a complex mosaic of tributary drainage, wetlands, patches of fast land, floodplain terraces, and bluffs. Reconstructing the topography and hydrology of this mosaic—a task that challenges not only prehistoric archaeologists, but also geologists, geomorphologists, palynologists, and all manner of paleoenvironmental specialists—and comparing the result to modern land use characteristics are ultimately the key to understanding Trenton's buried Native American heritage, the ebb and flow of seasonal occupation, and the locations of camps and villages and places of sacred importance such as burying grounds (Stewart 1990; Schuldenrein 1994; Stewart 1994).

Just as water in the landscape profoundly influenced the pattern of Native American occupation and resource exploitation, it also framed early Euro-American settlement and economic activity. The first settlers from the Old World approached the falls of the Delaware by river; established plantations that placed a high value on river frontage, landings, and accessibility by boat; positioned farmhouses close to springs and sources of potable water; and sought out locations where water power could be harnessed. As the nucleus of what later became Trenton took root in the late seventeenth and early eighteenth centuries around Mahlon Stacy's gristmill on the Assunpink—with primary access to the outside world accomplished through the wharf and ferry at the foot of modern Ferry Street—the role of the settlement became cemented as a place where incoming and outgoing goods could be transshipped and traded.

By the mid-eighteenth century, "Trent's Town" was well established as a small market center, a commercial and administrative hub for the hinterland of West Jersey and its critical link to Philadelphia, the Caribbean, and Europe. Beginning in the 1720s, additional water-powered mills and water-dependent tanneries (and a brewery) were soon seated along the streams coursing through the town, supplemented in the 1730s and 1740s by iron and steel manufacturing facilities on Petty's Run. During the third quarter of the eighteenth century, the Ferry Street wharfage was supplemented with the satellite port community of Lamberton, with its river frontage extending downstream along the Delaware for almost half a mile below the mouth of the minor tributary known as Douglas Gut.

With water and transportation stimulating population growth, landowners subdivided property, and formal street grids were woven into the landscape. In Trenton proper, the Trent family and a handful of other property owners created a distinctive town plan between Assunpink Creek and Petty's Run. A new axial street (King, now Warren Street) was run southward for almost half a mile from the important intersection of the Indian trail (today's North Broad Street) and the Hopewell Road (the location of the Trenton Battle Monument). Toward the southern end of King, two cross-streets were laid out. The most important, Second (now State) Street was extended west to join awkwardly with River Road (another early route), and east to cross the Indian trail, named Queen (now Broad) Street where it ran through the town. Other cross-streets were grafted onto this layout as the century progressed. In Lamberton, the related Lambert and Cadwalader families laid out a more regular rectangular grid aligned parallel to the river.

The natural drainage (the Delaware River, Assunpink Creek, and Petty's Run), the street pattern, and the cadastral history provide the basic framework for understanding Trenton's archaeological potential for the early historic and pre-industrial era, a period extending from the late seventeenth through the mid-nineteenth century. Early plantation nuclei and landings, headed by the Stacy/Trent estate and its Ferry Street wharf, form one obvious set of high sensitivity archaeological locations. Farmsteads associated with other early settler families (Pettit, Emley, Lambert, Cadwalader, Beakes, and Douglas, to name a few), some of which have yielded archaeological remains, belong in this same category.

Within the historic cores of both Trenton and Lamberton, the street grids encase a zone of historical archaeological potential that is capable of producing evidence of occupation of town dwellings, workshops, stores, taverns, and hotels. Redevelopment has compromised much of this archaeology, particularly where actual buildings are concerned, but there are backyards, vacant lots, parks, and filled land where structural remains, artifacts, and environmental evidence frequently still survive. Historic religious and institutional properties offer a somewhat different archaeological prospect. Churches with their cemeteries, for example, are highly sensitive; schools, in contrast, with their less substantive buildings and ephemeral play areas, tend to offer thin archaeological pickings. The New Jersey State House complex has steadily expanded and redeveloped its building envelope to cover virtually the entire area of the historic State House Lot, and yet archaeological remains of the state's first office building dating from the mid-1790s were recently discovered beneath the sidewalk adjacent to the State Capitol's West State Street entrance.

The Trenton Barracks, a National Historic Landmark and a rare architectural survivor from the period of the French and Indian War, has a unique and still only partially explored archaeological expression. The sites of water-powered and water-using industrial facilities—mills, forges, furnaces, tanneries, breweries, distilleries—are a category of archaeological resource that has fulfilled its potential on more than one occasion in recent years. The stream corridors of Assunpink Creek and Petty's Run both conceal important buried remains that will shed light on Trenton's early industrial history.

Trenton's vital role in the Industrial Revolution is still very visible in the city's modern urban fabric. Factory buildings—a few still functional, several adaptively re-used (most often for warehousing and sometimes for offices or housing), and all too many of them ruinous—speak of past manufacturing endeavors. Extant row houses, corner stores, social clubs, schools, churches, and the like all speak of urban living in the late nineteenth and early twentieth centuries, Trenton's industrial heyday. Yet the city also has an exceptionally rich industrial archaeological heritage lurking at and below the ground surface. Substantial footings of nineteenth- and twentieth-century factories, especially those engaged in the pottery, iron and steel, and rubber industries, survive in abundance, and the sites where such remains survive are often well documented on maps, in photographs, and through the written and oral historical record. Archaeology has rather more to offer to our understanding of the city's manufacturing history through the discipline's recovery and analysis of discarded products and industrial waste. Trenton's industrial potteries, for example, prolific enough a century ago for the city to earn the sobriquet "the Staffordshire of America," are today largely invisible in architectural terms. A valuable history of this industry, nonetheless, may be gleaned from the kiln furniture and ceramic wasters that are strewn about the city, most notably along the banks of the Delaware and the Assunpink and in numerous filled-in canals, raceways, and swales.

Trenton's premier industrial archaeological resource is the Delaware and Raritan Canal, originally built from 1830–1834 (McKelvey 1975). The main canal heading south from its junction with the Feeder Canal was filled within the city in the 1930s and now supports New Jersey Route 129, while the stretch of the main canal heading north from the Feeder from Old Rose Street to Mulberry Street was obliterated in the 1950s by the construction of the Route 1 Freeway. In spite of this, the Feeder Canal itself and the main canal north of Mulberry Street are still intact and water-filled. Both form integral parts of the water supply and state park systems, run respectively by the New Jersey Water Supply Authority and the Delaware and Raritan Canal State Park. Less visible in the urban landscape but still intermittently surviving as an archaeological resource is the Trenton Water Power (Hunter 2005a; Hunter Research, Inc. 2011). A critical artery for water-powered industrial development in the city, this seven mile long raceway and exact contemporary of the Delaware and Raritan Canal mostly lies buried beneath New Jersey Route 29 and other city streets.

The archaeological potential along Trenton's canal corridors is substantial and includes, in addition to the waterway channels themselves, the sites of locks, bridges, lock and bridge tenders' houses, culverts, and waste weirs and basins. The many railroad corridors within the city offer a similar range of archaeological remains (with stations and rail yards being an important supplement) while other early infrastructure in the form of wooden water lines and brick sewers have both aroused interest as archaeological resources worthy of careful study. Commercial and institutional sites of the industrial period (hotels, stores, schools, and the like) can leave archaeological traces, most often in the form of building foundations, shaft features, and discarded waste. Similar evidence reflecting the occupation of workers' housing and the grander homes of merchants, industrialists, and professionals also abounds throughout the wards and neighborhoods of the city. Organized municipal refuse disposal, however, considerably complicates the interpretation of artifact assemblages from the late nineteenth century onwards.

Urban Archaeological Methods

The practice of historical archaeology within a built urban environment is always a challenge. The archival record, spoken history, and physical fabric of cities like

Trenton tend to be dense. Unlike archaeological sites in the countryside, where there may be relatively few pertinent documents, limited oral historical memory, and comparatively accessible buried evidence, urban historical archaeological resources can often be the subject of voluminous and confusing records as well as prolific recent memories. These resources may also lie deeply interred beneath buildings, fill, and hardscape surfaces.

Cartographic, documentary, and oral historical research, along with shrewd visual assessments of site conditions, are essential preludes to excavation, requiring time, effort, and considerable spatial intelligence for effective interpretation. Subsurface investigations invariably require mechanical excavation tools, shoring, fencing, and occasionally dewatering equipment. Space is usually at a premium when it comes to disposal of backdirt, and careful logistical planning is needed to ensure that areas of archaeological interest do not inadvertently end up being covered by spoil heaps created by the excavators themselves. Cultural stratigraphy within excavations may be complex—requiring great rigor in unraveling relationships within and between soils and structural remains and understanding differences between cumulative, depositional, erosive, and "cutting" processes. Numerous artifacts will usually be retrieved; each item demanding both accurate identification and a secure stratigraphic provenance if its full meaning is to be realized. Selective discarding of artifacts of minimal interest is a risky but necessary task if laboratories and museums are to avoid analyzing and storing vast quantities of marginally relevant material and data.

Trenton, like many east coast cities, has a broad range of cartographic sources that may be brought to bear on urban archaeological endeavors. These include manuscript maps accompanying land records, road surveys, surrogates records, and court records; Revolutionary War-era route maps and plans of military engagements and facilities; nineteenth-century wall maps; late-nineteenth- and twentieth-century city atlases and fire insurance maps; twentieth-century tax assessment records; and aerial photographs dating from the 1920s onwards. One might think that maps and plans of Trenton in the Revolutionary period would be of exceptional value to archaeologists, but unfortunately these are mostly too small-scale and lacking in accuracy to be of much use for the detailed site-specific research that typically supports archaeological excavations. Much more valuable are the rare manuscript maps and plans that accompany primary archival materials and the extraordinary wealth of information contained in the maps produced by the Sanborn and other insurance companies after the Civil War.

The written, as opposed to cartographic, record is a vital tool for urban historical archaeologists. Critical spatial data and other archaeologically relevant information lurk in land records (especially deeds and mortgages but also in tax ratable assessments and road returns), in property sale notices and advertisements in newspapers, in the industrial and population schedules of the federal censuses, and in a host of more personal archival materials such as surrogates records, diaries, travelers accounts, and letters. For the Trenton area, claims for compensation lodged with the American and British governments for damages and loss of property during the Revolutionary War (and related state and county records on the confiscation of Loyalist landholdings) can be especially pertinent to archaeological research. Interpreting the written archival record for archaeological purposes requires great care and discernment; what may seem like an obvious connection of archival and archaeological dots will often prove to be a mistaken linkage. The most fruitful archival materials, from an archaeological perspective, are usually those providing property-specific information or details of buildings and material culture.

A modern city contains many visible clues to what may lie beneath the surface of the urban landscape. Understanding these telltale traces of the past is an important precursor to excavation and helps greatly in archaeological interpretation. Modern walls and property boundaries will often follow historic alignments and sometimes include historic fabric. In Trenton, for example, the jigsaw of a retaining wall that holds back the south bank of Assunpink Creek just upstream of the South Broad Street bridge is composed to a large degree of the eighteenth-century foundations of the Trenton Mills, which occupy the site of Mahlon Stacy's gristmill, the town's first industrial facility. Telltale seams in the retaining wall at the southwest corner of the Thomas Edison State College campus provide valuable clues to the location of early industrial buildings deeply buried on the east side of Petty's Run. The course of the Trenton Water Power, a seven mile long, mid-nineteenth-century power canal, now almost entirely invisible above ground, is reflected in much of the right-of-way of Route 29 and adjoining property lines. Understanding surface clues such as these provides a head start to archaeological exploration.

In situations where archaeological investigations are to take place on urban sites still occupied by standing buildings, careful analysis of foundations, basements, crawlspaces, and other below-grade elements is essential. Whether archaeological excavation occurs before or after buildings are demolished, subsurface features and deposits must be clearly related to the upstanding architectural fabric to gain a full understanding of a site's land use history. The redevelopment of Trenton's "Dunhams Block" in the late 1980s provides a good illustration of this. Over the course of two centuries, the footprint of this city block within the historic core of the downtown had become completely built-up and displayed a complex mass of architectural styles and periods. Historians pieced together the development of the block from deeds and other primary archival materials while archaeologists inspected and mapped the basements. Portions of the block where basements were absent were identified as potential archaeological targets, and excavations took place within the interiors of buildings prior to their demolition. Carefully integrated historical, architectural and archaeological study was eventually focused on the Trenton House property, a nineteenth- and twentieth-century hotel in the northwest corner of the block, where a long and richly layered sequence of occupation was documented beginning in the early 1770s when cultivated land was replaced by a brick Georgian townhouse. One surprising outcome of this work was the recognition that the much-altered shell of this townhouse still survived both above and below ground (Hunter Research Associates 1989a).

While the opportunity to excavate within standing buildings may be preferable from the standpoint of archaeological interpretation, there are many drawbacks. Adequate lighting, finding space for screening and disposing of excavated soils, the need for respirators, and the ever-present danger of destabilizing walls and other structural elements are just a few of the difficulties. More often, archaeological testing and excavation in urban settings will take place following demolition on vacant, rubble-strewn or paved lots. Remote sensing, in particular ground-penetrating radar, may be a useful guide to excavation, not only in revealing potential anomalies of archaeological interest, but also to ensure avoidance of buried utilities. Geotechnical studies that involve core drilling can provide helpful information about groundwater levels and depth and gross composition of cultural and natural deposits and bedrock.

Traditional manual subsurface testing may be applicable in the urban environment in gardens, yards, and landscaped settings where soils and vegetation exist at the surface. However, shovel and posthole testing and hand-dug excavation units are frequently impractical on urban sites, and archaeologists will resort to a variety of mechanical excavation equipment to sample deeply buried and hard-to-access cultural deposits. The approach to mechanically excavated testing will typically be driven by the results of historical research and by localized site conditions such as the proximity of buildings, the character of the ground surface, the depth of fill, drainage issues, and buried infrastructure, most notably utilities such as water, gas, and sewer lines, and electric and fiber optic cables. A health and safety plan, developed by archaeologists in conjunction with an industrial hygienist, should be standard fare on all major urban archaeological excavations.

Prior to the reconstruction of Route 29 through south Trenton in the late 1990s and early 2000s, archaeological survey adopted a whole range of testing strategies, including archival study, geophysical and geomorphological analysis, and manual excavation and backhoe-assisted trenching. Even then, there were very deeply buried, inaccessible archaeological deposits that could be not be fully evaluated at the survey level prior to highway construction. As a result, mitigation of the effects of highway construction included not only formal data recovery excavations on prehistoric and historic sites that had been identified but also provision for evaluation through archaeological monitoring of other sites found during the course of construction. In this manner, archaeologists were able to document successfully exceptional remains of the port of Lamberton (also known as Trenton Landing) along the banks of the Delaware River. Among the most critical discoveries of this monitoring program were the remains of William Richards' stoneware pottery, circa 1774–1776, as well as a pair of brick bake ovens and the foundations of a fish-boiling house and several warehouses, all dating from the late eighteenth and early nineteenth centuries (Hunter 2005b; Hunter Research, Inc., forthcoming [a]).

Historical Archaeological Sites Investigated in Downtown Trenton

Belvidere-Delaware Railroad

Feeder Canal

Delaware and Raritan Canal

Perry Street

North Broad Street

South Broad Street

U.S. Route 1

West State Street

West Front St

Trenton

Warren St

East State Street

East Front Street

Assunpink Creek

N.J. Route 29

Delaware River

West Warren Street

Market

Bloomsbury

7

8

11

14

15

9   10   13

16

12

2
1
3   4

5
6

20   21
19

22

24

17

23   25

18

Pennsylvania

Falls of the Delaware

Ford

Colhoun Street Bridge

Trenton Water Power

"Trenton Makes" Bridge

Pennsylvania Railroad (AMTRAK)

Ferry Street

Camden and Amboy Railroad (River Line)

Legend (lines)
- Pre-Urban Shoreline
- Underground Stream
- Buried or Filled Canal
- Active Railroad
- Abandoned Railroad
- Road

Legend (symbols)
- ● Historic Landmark
- ○ Archaeological Site
- ◉ Historic Landmark/Archaeological Site

N

0   1,000
Feet

1. New Jersey State House
2. Offices of the Secretary of State and Clerk of the Supreme Court
3. Petty's Run Archaeological Site
   Harrow/Yard Plating Mill
   Trenton Steel Works
   Fithian Cotton Mill
   Front Street Paper Mill
4. Old Barracks
5. Golding & Company Works
6. Reynolds/Potts Paper Mill
7. Trenton Battle Monument
8. St. Michael's Church
9. Reynolds/DeKlyn/Houston House (Trenton House)
10. First Presbyterian Church
11. Quaker Meeting House
12. Douglass House
13. City Hall
14. Hanover Street Station (Camden and Amboy Railroad)
15. Federal Courthouse
16. Mercer Cemetery
17. William Trent House
18. Ferry Plantation Archaeological Site (Beakes House)
19. Trenton Cotton Factory
20. Eagle Factory
21. Trenton Mills
22. Mercer County Courthouse
23. Eagle Tavern (Rhodes Kiln Site)
24. Lock 6A (Delaware and Raritan Canal)
25. American Steel & Wire Company Works (Trenton Iron Company)

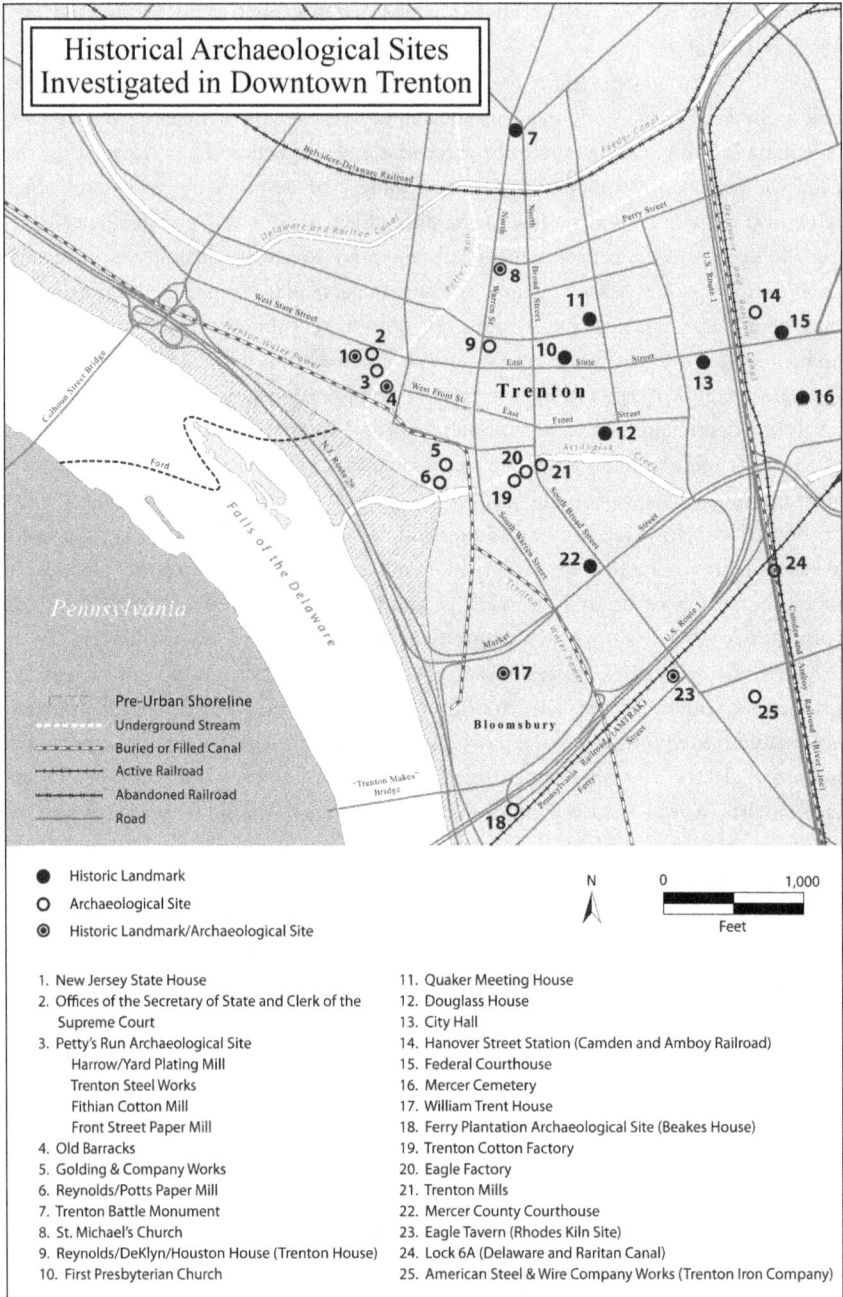

Figure 14.1a. Map showing historical archaeological sites investigated in downtown Trenton, ca. 1980–2010.

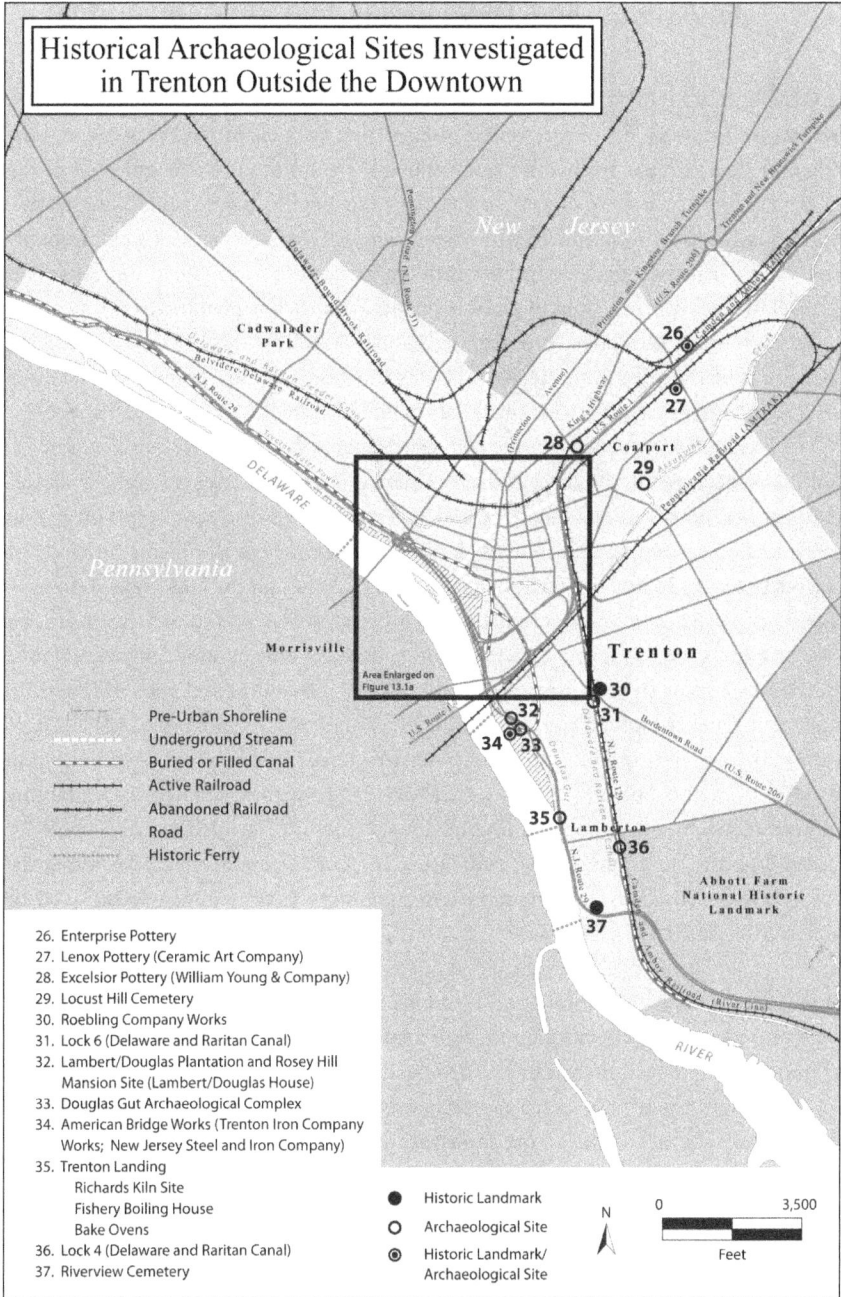

Figure 14.1b. Map showing historical archaeological sites investigated outside the downtown Trenton area, ca. 1980–2010.

Archaeological Discoveries

CONTACT PERIOD SITES

Seventeenth-century European sources suggest that the falls of the Delaware and the adjacent downstream freshwater tidal marsh were home to a recognizable group of the Lenape at the time of Dutch, Swedish, and English contact and initial settlement. Maps and manuscripts record a name whose original form was most probably *Sankhikan,* usually translated as "fire-drill" (a pump-drill for making fire). A map of the Delaware River prepared in 1616 by Captain Cornelius Hendricksen appears to show a grouping of Native American longhouses labeled "Stanke=kans" straddling the river near the falls. In the 1640s, Thomas Campanius Holm noted that there was an Indian settlement "in a wide plain" at the falls (Holm 1702:82 [Benedict 1920]).

The first extended contact between Native Americans and Europeans at the falls likely occurred in the context of a postulated Dutch initiative to establish a trading post here in the 1620s (Godfrey 1919). Trading post or not, it seems clear that there was intentional Dutch trade with Native Americans in the Trenton vicinity at least between 1623 and 1646 (Kalb et al. 1982:1). Although the falls formed the projected northern limits of the colony of New Sweden in 1642—and there were at least two proposals for European settlements at or near the falls in later decades—Native Americans appear to have remained in the falls vicinity up to and even well beyond the major Quaker immigration of the late 1670s (Hunter Research, Inc. 2011: Chapter 3). At least until the English Quaker settlement of West Jersey took firm hold in the 1680s, the Lenape on the Delaware showed considerable enterprise in adapting to both the incoming Europeans and to threats from the Susquehannocks—both by controlling the fur trade and by cultivating corn on a commercial basis along the river, including in areas near the mouth of Assunpink Creek in what would later be Trenton (Becker 1999).

Archaeological studies carried out in connection with the reconstruction of Route 29 produced a combination of archaeological and paleoenvironmental data that provided a tantalizing glimpse into Native American lifeways in the contact period in the Trenton area (Hunter Research, Inc. forthcoming [b]). In the 1600s, an almost flat, broad, open area dominated by tall, water-tolerant grasses extended south along the left bank of the Delaware from the mouth of Assunpink Creek. Grass and herb species known to have been growing here in late prehistoric times include goosefoot, pokeweed, smartweed, and knotweed, all of which were used either as food or for medicinal purposes by Native Americans. Hickory nuts, butternuts, acorns, and corn were also found in late prehistoric archaeological contexts, although no specific evidence for corn cultivation at this location was found to support the written seventeenth-century accounts.

This contact period landscape was thus already in part the product of human activity. Some areas had evidently been set aside specifically for burials, and one particular focus of settlement activity (which had in earlier centuries included wigwam-type houses) was identified just inland from the Delaware River in the area of Union and Federal streets. This latter occupation extended back at least 400 years and continued into the second quarter of the seventeenth century, if not later. Clear evidence of European contact was recovered from this site (referred to as the Chain Shop Site, a component of the Douglas Gut Archaeological Complex [28Me273]), both in the form of trade items, and as phytoliths from wheat or similar Eurasian grains. These materials were associated with a grouping of four pits in the northern part of the site.

In total, eight radiocarbon dates extending into the seventeenth century were obtained from features at the Riverview Executive Park, Chain Shop, and Cass Street sites along the Route 29 corridor. These dates, from carbonized materials in pits and other contexts, are consistent with a number of recovered trade items, such as beads and fragments of the distinctive Tidewater pipes of the seventeenth-century Chesapeake Bay area (Hunter Research, Inc. forthcoming [b]).

Indications of the persistence of Lenape lifeways in the Trenton area well into the eighteenth century were recovered from the Area D Site [28Me1-D] at the Abbott Farm National Historic Landmark just south of Trenton (Wall et al. 1995). A large and unusual pot from this site has been argued by Stewart (1998) as possibly being from a post-contact native cultural context, radiocarbon dated to A.D. 1780 plus or minus 60 years.

One striking feature of these contact period discoveries is their direct and consistent association with ceramic and lithic artifacts indistinguishable (at least at present) from those typically found on pre-contact Late Woodland sites in the Lower Delaware Valley. The implication is that the basic character of Lenape material culture remained largely unaffected by contact with Europeans for some considerable time. The disruption that this contact inflicted on the lives of the people themselves was of course much more profound, despite the relatively enlightened policy of the Quaker settlers towards Native Americans and their rights.

RESIDENTIAL SITES

Time has not been kind to Trenton's pre-Revolutionary domestic architecture. Although a number of colonial buildings survived into the mid-nineteenth century, just long enough for some of them to be drawn or photographed, almost all of them were torn down before the dawn of the twentieth century. Exceptions are the thrice-moved Douglass House, now entirely divorced from its archaeological context; the Eagle Tavern, which originated as a colonial dwelling; and the high-style mansion known today as the William Trent House, built in 1719.

The Trent House has been the subject of several regulatory compliance-driven archaeological studies as well as a number of educational archaeology programs.

The first formal archaeological investigations on the property were undertaken as part of repairs to the roof of a tunnel that connects the basement of the house with the early twentieth-century carriage house. This work effectively quashed any lingering hopes that this tunnel was the work of a smuggling William Trent (it actually dates to the 1930s), but it did demonstrate not only the survival of eighteenth- and nineteenth-century land surfaces but also the presence of a significant multi-period Native American occupation (Hunter Research, Inc. 1995a).

Recent restoration of the house itself was accompanied by excavations and extensive monitoring of the installation of new drains around the exterior. These encountered multiple foundations of nineteenth-century additions to the house (all removed by the restoration of the 1930s). More importantly, the foundations of the loggia leading from the house to the former detached kitchen of the 1740s were found to be in excellent condition, suggesting that the kitchen itself and its associated deposits are in place beneath the ground. During these investigations, a number of pieces of buff-yellow brick were encountered. These "Dutch" bricks are characteristic of seventeenth-century sites in the Delaware Valley (Veit 2000) and this quickly led to a realization that Trent's mansion was at approximately the same location as Ballifield, the plantation of one of Trenton's principal Quaker founders, Mahlon Stacy. An educational program of shovel testing over much of the present property has defined the areas of archaeological sensitivity where remains of the Stacy House may one day be found (Hunter Research, Inc. 2003a).

Knowledge about more vernacular buildings of the eighteenth century comes from the illustrative sources mentioned above, from the documentary research of Stephanie Toothman, and from some well-preserved archaeology at a small number of key local sites. One of the first substantive pieces of historical archaeological research to take place in Trenton ensued from cultural resource studies undertaken from 1979–1980 for the Route 1/Warren Street Ramps project, an intersection improvement by the New Jersey Department of Transportation (NJDOT). This work resulted in the identification of the Ferry Plantation Archaeological Site, the principal feature of which was the foundation of a house believed to have been erected by the Beakes family between 1710 and 1714. Burned in mid-December 1776 just prior to the First Battle of Trenton, NJDOT archaeologists documented a destruction deposit associated with this event sealing occupation layers of an earlier date. Quantitative artifact analyses and mean ceramic date calculations were an important factor in correctly pegging the remains as an early-eighteenth-century house foundation, as earlier studies of the site had mistakenly proclaimed it to be either a seventeenth-century Dutch trading post or early-eighteenth-century English blockhouse. The highway improvements underwent minor redesign to avoid destruction of the site, which still remains intact today (Kalb et al. 1982).

In the 1980s and 1990s, a major program of cultural resources investigation involving multiple archaeological surveys and data recovery excavations, again prompted by NJDOT highway improvements, focused on a segment of New Jersey

Route 29 extending south from U.S. Route 1 to the Route I-195/I-295 interchange in the Hamilton-Trenton-Bordentown marsh. As part of this work, the site of the plantation lying immediately south of the Beakes property was comprehensively examined. In 1999, data recovery excavations encountered the well-preserved cellar hole of a house built very early in the eighteenth century and torn down soon after the Revolution. Termed the Lambert/Douglas House, this interesting structure was probably erected for the use of a younger son of pioneer settler Thomas Lambert. The main portion of the house was 25 feet north-south by 22 feet east-west internally, probably of two stories, at least three rooms on the first floor, and had a kitchen wing adjoining to the west. Consistent dates of 1701 on a series of casement window leads indicate that the building was erected in the very early years of the eighteenth century. For about the next 60 years the building seems to have been largely unaltered. In the 1760s, the basement was modified, probably for the processing of shad and sturgeon, reflecting then owner John Douglas's livelihood as a "boatman" and the nearby Lamberton fishery. The demolition deposit filling the basement contained in excess of 25,000 eighteenth-century artifacts, of which the latest closely datable item is a New Jersey cent of 1787 (Burrow 2005a; Hunter Research, Inc. 2011).

Less than 100 feet to the south of the site of the Lambert/Douglas House was its successor, a late eighteenth/early nineteenth-century mansion named Rosey Hill, which remained standing until 1980. Excavation in 1999 of a stone-lined shaft feature, probably a double privy, at the rear of this building yielded an extraordinary domestic deposit of more than 11,000 early-nineteenth-century items, much of it fine china, glassware, and wine bottles. This material can be related to the household of John B. Sartori, the first papal diplomatic representative to the United States. From

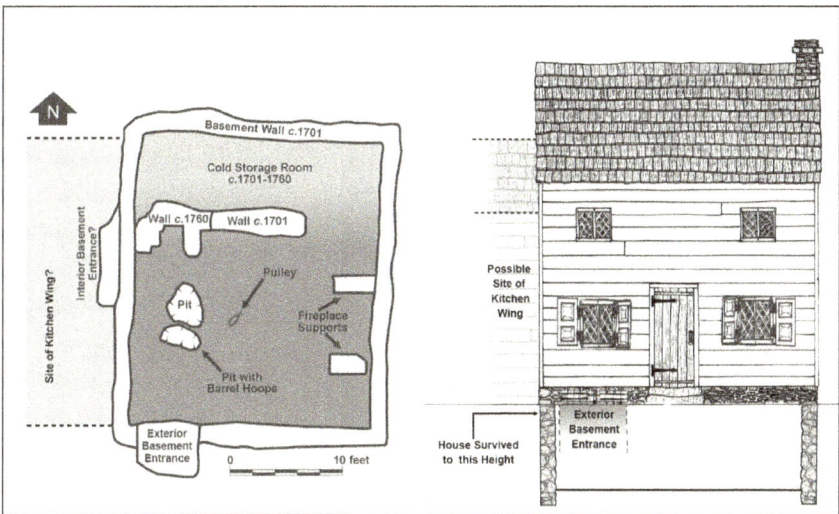

Figure 14.2. The Lambert/Douglas House, circa 1701–1790. *Left:* simplified plan view. *Right:* hypothetical reconstruction of the southern (front) elevation of the house.

1803 to 1832, Sartori and his large family lived at Rosey Hill, one of several Trenton-area riverside estates established in the early federal period by wealthy, recent European immigrants, some of whom were Catholic. The finds from the so-called "Sartori pit" are a rare instance of an archaeological assemblage that can be plausibly identified with a single household (Hunter Research, Inc. 2011).

While a number of farmhouses and mansions have been archaeologically examined in the Trenton area, all situated on the exurban fringes of the city, only one in-town house has received such treatment. This is the site of the Reynolds/DeKlyn/Houston House, which fronted on to King (modern Warren) Street in the core historic block defined by this street and Queen (North Broad), Second (East State), and East Hanover streets. Erected in the mid-1770s by the Morris family, perhaps as a speculative venture, this fine, five-bay, two-story, Georgian-style brick dwelling was owned by a succession of prominent local figures in the years during and following the Revolution: John Reynolds, a paper manufacturer; Barnt DeKlyn, a merchant; and William Churchill Houston, an attorney, politician, and member of the Continental Congress. In the mid-1820s, the house was converted into a hotel and subsequently expanded. Known for most of its existence as the Trenton House, this landmark facility was patronized by many national figures, among them Presidents Abraham Lincoln and William Howard Taft, William Jennings Bryan, Horace Greeley, and George B. McClellan (Woodward and Hageman 1883:69; Trenton Board of Trade 1889:69; Trenton Historical Society 1929:334, 666).

Archaeological excavations conducted on the Trenton House property in 1987 prior to demolition, inside what by this time was an abandoned Chinese restaurant, documented a more than four foot thick accumulation of cultural stratigraphy and a variety of structural features. These deposits reflected the intensive residential and commercial use of the site from the mid-1770s through to the present day: the construction of the original house, its major stages of expansion as a hotel, the remains of a massive mid-nineteenth-century ice house, a succession of garden features and yard soils, and an abundance of artifacts dating from the mid-eighteenth through early twentieth centuries. The archaeological work, through its combination of cartographic analysis, examination of basements and crawl spaces, and archaeological excavation, was especially valuable in clarifying the complex architectural development of this city block. Other excavations elsewhere within the interior of this block targeted patches of ground where basements had not been built and recorded a number of other backyard features, such as cistern and outbuilding foundations, dating from the late eighteenth century onwards (Hunter Research Associates 1989a).

MILITARY SITES

Trenton is also rich in military sites. The city is perhaps best known for its role in the Revolutionary War, as the setting for a pair of small but critically important military engagements referred to as the Battles of Trenton. One raged for a period of a few morning hours around much of the downtown on the day after Christmas in 1776, as Washington's Continental Army successfully surprised a Hessian force quartered in several of the buildings in and around the town. The second engagement was more narrowly focused on the crossing of Queen (South Broad) Street over Assunpink Creek as American troops held off a late afternoon British advance on January 2, 1777. While the basic configuration of the street network remains much as it was during 1776 and 1777, and a handful of colonial buildings (the William Trent House, the Old Barracks, the Quaker Meeting House, St. Michael's Church, the Eagle Tavern, and the Douglass House) still stand, it is difficult, even with the help of annual battle reenactments, to appreciate the ebb and flow of the battles in the modern urban surroundings.

Archaeological studies have produced occasional artifacts (weapon parts, munitions, military buttons, etc.) that may have a connection to the Battles of Trenton, and one may expect these types of finds to occur periodically as sites within the city are redeveloped. Cannon balls, for example, have been recovered on the Eagle Tavern property and from the Lambert/Douglas House Site. However, the Trenton battlefield locations, because of their urban setting and subsequent land alteration, are never going to yield meaningful distribution patterns of musket balls and other types of military hardware like the nearby rural Revolutionary War battlefield sites at Princeton and Monmouth Courthouse.

Yet, archaeology can still contribute usefully to the reconstruction of the cultural landscape as it would have existed at the time of the Trenton battles. This is especially the case for the Second Battle of Trenton, where archaeological investigations in and around the South Broad Street crossing of the Assunpink have identified substantial remains of the Trenton Mills on the south bank of the creek, upstream of the bridge, and revealed the topography of the swampy meadows and riverbank, on its downstream side. South of the Assunpink, beyond the limits of the colonial town, archaeological investigations have found ample evidence for the disruption and damage caused by both Hessian and American forces in December of 1776 at the Ferry Plantation Archaeological Site and the Lambert/Douglas Plantation and Rosey Hill Mansion Site. Evidence was also found during archaeological monitoring of the reconstruction of Route 29 in 2000 along the left bank of the Delaware River in Lamberton where the remains of war-ravaged fish houses, a pottery kiln, and other buildings on the property of Loyalist Daniel Coxe were discovered (see below).

The premier historic military site in Trenton is the Old Barracks, a National Historic Landmark and major regional heritage tourism attraction where much of the public programming is oriented toward schoolchildren (John G. Waite Associates 1998). Originally built in 1758 on the western edge of the town, this distinctive stone building began life as winter quarters for British regular forces fighting on the frontier during the French and Indian War. It served as a Continental Army hospital for much of the Revolution and then in 1792 was unceremoniously sliced in two when West Front Street was extended westward to the newly established State House Lot, where New Jersey's fledgling legislature set up for government business. After many subsequent years of mostly residential use, the two pieces of the Old Barracks were restored and recombined from 1914 to 1915 as part of a burst of *City Beautiful* improvements to the State House grounds that brought Mahlon Stacy Park into being (Trenton Historical Society 1929:984–988). In the late 1980s and early 1990s, another restoration campaign was mounted that aimed to restore the structure to its former colonial appearance with greater historical authenticity. Archaeology played a vital part in this most recent restoration effort.

Large-scale excavations from 1988 to 1989 under the direction of Ian Burrow and several smaller investigations in the early 1990s, helped guide the restoration of the building exterior and establish historic grades for landscaping purposes (Hunter Research Associates 1989b; Hunter Research, Inc. 1991a; 1996). Of particular note is the manner in which archaeological inquiry, through the exposure of stone footings, contributed to the reconstruction of the building's main entry stairway. Excavations also revealed traces of hitherto blocked door and window openings, the true elevation of the historic parade ground, post settings for the palisade fence that enclosed the barracks lot, and abundant evidence of pre-barracks Native American occupation. While many artifacts were recovered, relatively few items of colonial and Revolutionary War vintage were identified. One unique object found during this work is a ceramic or stone disk inscribed "Wilkes & Liberty No. 45," believed to date from around 1768 to 1770 and possibly a setting from a sleeve link or cufflink. This epigrammatic object, referencing English political radical John Wilkes and the well-known anti-monarchical issue of his London-published periodical magazine, the *North Briton*, can be viewed as a pointed reflection of political sentiment in Trenton in the years leading up to the Declaration of Independence (Burrow 2008).

INDUSTRIAL SITES

In addition to its intriguing military history, Trenton has a rich industrial heritage. Urban archaeology is a valuable tool in the pursuit of industrial history. Past production sites, besides containing structural remains of buildings and manufacturing equipment, will typically yield multitudes of discarded, often defective, artifacts and vast spreads of manufacturing debris. In Trenton's case, two of its foremost industries—metalworking and pottery making—have left an especially profound and tangible archaeological signature that pervades much of the city's underside. The mass production and related transportation and energy infrastructure wrought by the Industrial Revolution from the mid-nineteenth through the mid-twentieth centuries accounts for the bulk of this archaeological expression, but telling traces of earlier manufacturing endeavor, involving both metals and ceramics, have also been discovered in recent years.

Agricultural processing was Trenton's founding industry, as it was in many colonial towns. The site of Mahlon Stacy's gristmill, first developed between 1678

and 1679, persisted as a seat of water-powered industry deep into the second half of
the nineteenth century. While later mill remains exist at the site, substantial physical
evidence of the original mill is unlikely to have survived the many rebuilds, upgrades,
and reconfigurations that this site experienced, not to mention the periodic fires and
Assunpink floods that are documented. Likewise, the pair of colonial tanneries and
the early eighteenth-century brewery on Petty's Run, which marked the western edge
of the early town, have probably been decimated by later land use. It would be pre-
mature, however, to entirely exclude the possibility that deep-buried traces of these
facilities may be found in the future (Hunter Research, Inc. 2003b; AECOM 2010).
In 1999, during monitoring of the Route 29 tunnel construction in Lamberton, archaeologists discovered the foundations of a colonial and Revolutionary War–era
fishery boiling house—along with thousands of shad scales and a number of sturgeon
scutes—on the Delaware riverbank, demonstrating the surprising degree to which
one of Trenton's key early industries, fishing and fish processing, survived below
ground. In addition to the fishery-related remains, monitoring also exposed a pair of
conjoined bake ovens, probably also dating from the 1760s and 1770s, the wharf-
side location of which may indicate their use for baking hardtack, quite probably for
the Caribbean trade (Hunter Research, Inc. forthcoming [a]).

More recently, no less impressive and nationally significant remains of
Trenton's early involvement in iron and steel manufacture have been uncovered at
the Petty's Run Archaeological Site in the narrow strip of parkland wedged between
the New Jersey State House and the Old Barracks. Here, from 2008 to 2009, foundations of the Harrow/Yard plating mill (active from the early 1730s until the fall of
1777) and of a steel furnace and furnace house of the facility later became known as
the Trenton Steel Works (intermittently in operation from the late 1740s until 1784)
have been documented and are now displayed and interpreted for the visiting public
(figure 14.3). Among the most interesting artifacts from this site are several curved
cast-iron bars considered to be part of the fire grate at the base of the steel furnace.
The plating mill and steel works both played an important role as suppliers of metal
and munitions to the Continental Army during the Revolutionary War. Together, they
are emblematic of Trenton's mid-eighteenth-century emergence as a critical break-
in-bulk point and metal processing and fabrication center in the Delaware Valley,
midway between the iron mines, forges, and furnaces of northwestern New Jersey
and northeastern Pennsylvania and the ports and markets further downstream and
along the eastern seaboard (Hunter Research Associates 1989c; Hunter and Porter
1990; Hunter and Burrow 2010).

An exceptional story of archaeological revelation surrounds the identification and characterization of the stoneware products of Trenton potter James Rhodes,
who was active in south Trenton in the 1770s and 1780s (Hunter 2001; Liebeknecht
and Hunter 2003; Hunter Research, Inc. 2005a; Skerry and Hood 2009:204-208;
Hunter Research, Inc. forthcoming [a]). In 2000, again during archaeological monitoring of the Route 29 tunnel construction, the rectangular base of a pottery kiln,

Figure 14.3. The Petty's Run Archaeological Site: view from the roof of the New Jersey State House looking east toward the Old Barracks. The foundations in the foreground are part of the furnace house and cementation furnace at the Trenton Steel Works, circa 1745–1784; beyond are the wheel pit and foundations of the Front Street Paper Mill, circa 1827–1876, and the arched roof of the Petty's Run culvert, enclosed in the late 1870s.

14.5 by 8.5 feet in plan and up to four feet in height, was found set into the riverbank near the foot of Landing Street, along with more than 13,000 waster sherds and pieces of kiln furniture. Archival study established that this pottery had been set up around 1774 by William Richards, a Philadelphia merchant, apothecary, and ship owner, who, along with Moore Furman and Abraham Hunt, controlled most of the wharves and warehouses along the river frontage in Lamberton in the years leading up to, during, and immediately following the Revolutionary War. Richards' other riverfront operations included a store, bakery, and the Lamberton fishery, and he went on to serve the patriot cause as "Ship's Husband" (supplier of provisions) to the Pennsylvania Navy. His pottery, however, based on the claims of his Loyalist landlord Daniel Coxe to the British government after the war, was apparently destroyed by the Continental Army in the days leading up to the First Battle of Trenton in December 1776 during rebel raids on Hessian posts to the south of the town.

In 2005—in the course of a pair of unrelated archaeological projects focused on the Eagle Tavern, a Georgian-style brick building erected originally as a dwelling in the late 1760s at the corner of South Broad Street and Ferry Street—a second less well preserved stoneware pottery kiln was encountered. Initially, with the help of a grant from the New Jersey Historical Commission, Hunter Research reassessed field records and artifacts gathered from an unpublished archaeological field school conducted by Mercer County Community College in the mid-1970s. This activity resulted in the identification of waster sherds and kiln debris that very closely resembled the material found at the Richards kiln site. Since the Eagle Tavern is located three-quarters of a mile from the Richards kiln, it was felt that the kiln furniture and wasters indicated the former existence of a pottery on or near the Eagle Tavern property. In part because of this, archaeological monitoring was carried out for landscaping and utilities installation work then being performed in connection with the restoration of the tavern building. More waster sherds and kiln furniture were recovered, again resembling the materials found at the Richards kiln site. Further archival research established that this second pottery was set up and run by potter James Rhodes from 1778 until his death in 1784. Detailed comparison of the artifact assemblage from this second kiln with that from the Richards kiln indicated that Rhodes had likely worked earlier as Richards' master potter on the riverfront in Lamberton.

The primary linkage between the two kilns is provided by the pottery itself. A broad range of matching grey salt-glazed stoneware forms was being produced at both sites, often with distinctive incised, painted, rouletted, or molded decoration. Among the products are milk pans, plates, bottles, jugs, tankards, porringers, bowls, crocks, pipkins, and chamber pots, as well as some more unusual items, such as ointment pots, candlestick holders, a press-molded teapot with lion paw feet, and a coffee or chocolate pot. An inscribed and cobalt blue-painted lobed floral motif was noticeably in evidence. Also found at both kiln sites were examples of a signature mask-like stoneware face used as an applied decorative motif on the shoulders of jugs or large jars. All in all, there is little question that the same potter was at work at both kiln sites. On the basis of the archival record, and the absence of other documented potters in Nottingham Township (as this section of south Trenton was known at the time), there is little question that the potter was James Rhodes.

The recognition of James Rhodes and his ceramic output is of extraordinary value to archaeologists and historians, not to mention art historians and collectors. The Richards and Rhodes kiln sites represent two of only five archaeologically documented eighteenth-century stoneware pottery manufacturing sites on the eastern seaboard (the other three being in Yorktown, Virginia, and Cheesequake and Ringoes, both in New Jersey). Production at the two Trenton kilns was confined to a ten-year time frame from 1774 to 1784, which provides a tight chronological marker for Rhodes' wares when they turn up on archaeological sites or in museum collections and antique showrooms. The many telltale decorative traits and characteristic forms are also useful as an identifying mechanism. Rhodes' production seems to have been oriented toward a mid- to high-end market, different from contemporary redware producers, perhaps centered in cities and towns in the region or maybe further afield. William Richards' personal and merchant links with the Caribbean (he was a native of Barbados and traded extensively in the West Indies) and the kilns' proximity to the Lamberton waterfront suggest that Rhodes' wares may have been intended for a far flung export along the east coast, to the Caribbean islands and elsewhere in the New World. The finding and fingerprinting of Rhodes' wares is still recent; concerted attempts at tracing the distribution of this pottery type have yet to be made.

So far, James Rhodes is the earliest documented Trenton potter, although it is possible that he was preceded by other local redware potters, who would likely have pursued pottery making part-time, perhaps to supplement a livelihood in farming. In the immediate aftermath of the Revolution and the wake of James Rhodes, a redware proto-industry emerged in the heart of the city, largely as a result of the efforts of the McCully family. The McCullys operated kilns at a number of different locations, mostly in the Warren Street/Petty's Run area, and examples of their wares have occasionally been found on development sites. One tantalizing outcome of the recent Petty's Run excavations is that the abandoned steel furnace at the Trenton Steel Works may have been used for redware pottery manufacture in the mid-1780s, right around the time the McCully family began their business. Several generations of McCully pottery making saw Trenton redware manufacture continue into the late 1860s, overlapping with the much larger and more prolific industrial potteries for which the city is best known (see below). As with James Rhodes, future historical and archaeological research may be expected to provide new information and more artifacts associated with the McCully potting dynasty (Branin 1988:60-66).

In contrast to the scattered evidence of colonial and early federal industrial activity, Trenton contains an immensity of archaeological data reflecting the influence of the Industrial Revolution in the city. Underpinning Trenton's rise to manufacturing prominence in the mid- to late nineteenth century were major energy and transportation infrastructure improvements that still, to this day, frame evolving land use and redevelopment. Waterpower was an important early stimulus for industrial development, provided to the city first by its natural streams, Assunpink Creek and Petty's Run, at key points in the landscape where a suitable fall could be engineered. Archaeological remains of waterpower systems and mill building foundations are a staple of many North American cities, and Trenton is no exception in this regard.

As the new republic's manufacturing ambitions grew and hydropower technology improved during the early nineteenth century, both the Trenton Mills site at the South Broad Street crossing of the Assunpink and the iron and steel making locus on Petty's Run were reconfigured and put to new industrial uses. At the former site, where eighteenth- and nineteenth-century mill foundations and raceways may be seen upstream of the crossing, the Eagle Factory, a cotton manufacturing venture of the Waln family, was established in 1814. This entailed the conversion of the old gristmill for picking and cleaning cotton fiber and the construction of two new mill buildings. Another textile mill, the Trenton Cotton Factory, was built around the

Figure 14.4. William Richards' stoneware pottery kiln, circa 1774–1776. *Right:* the base of the double-flue rectangular kiln; *top left:* the signature applied molded face and incised cobalt-blue floral decoration of potter James Rhodes; *bottom left:* typical tankards produced at the Richards pottery.

same time, immediately downstream of the Eagle Factory and drawing on the same Assunpink hydropower system (Hunter et al. 2009). Subsurface testing downstream of the South Broad Street bridge in 2011, in connection with the planned "daylighting" of the Assunpink between South Broad and Warren streets, found minimal remains of the Eagle Factory and Trenton Cotton Factory, but the area immediately around and upstream of the bridge is believed to hold considerable archaeological potential (Hunter Research, Inc. 2003b; AECOM 2010). Still further downstream, at the mouth of the Assunpink, a glimpse of what may have been the foundation of the city's first paper mill, established by John Reynolds and Stacy Potts in 1778, was obtained during the construction of the Lafayette Yard Hotel in 2000. Additional remains of this mill, located on the edge of the hotel grounds, are likely to survive deeply buried beside the Assunpink.

Across town on Petty's Run, a short-lived cotton mill was erected by Josiah Fithian on the site of the old Harrow/Yard plating mill, also in 1814. This facility failed to survive the economic downturn of 1819 and was succeeded in 1827 by a paper mill, built just downstream on the site of the Trenton Steel Works. This latter mill, erected by Garret D. Wall, a U.S. Senator and prominent Trenton attorney, and originally managed by John Davison, remained in operation until 1876. Substantial foundations of the Fithian cotton mill were documented and reburied in 1996 during the expansion of the Thomas Edison State College main campus, while even more impressive masonry remains of the Wall/Davison paper mill, including a capacious wheel pit, were exposed during the Petty's Run excavations of 2008 and 2009. The paper mill ruins have been preserved and are now on display along with the Trenton Steel Works remains (Hunter Research Associates 1989c; www.pettysrun.org).

Although the Bloomsbury Mills, a large merchant gristmill erected around 1814 by Daniel W. Coxe adjacent to the William Trent House, drew power directly from the Delaware River via a wing dam, it was not until the early 1830s that the massive energy of the Delaware was more thoroughly harnessed for the benefit of the city's industrial entrepreneurs. This was achieved primarily through a seven mile long canal, built by the Trenton Delaware Falls Company from 1831 to 1834, which tapped the river at Scudders Falls, passed over the mouth of the Assunpink on an impressive stone and timber aqueduct, and emptied back into the Delaware south of town below the falls. This waterway fostered mill development in two main areas of the city. The first area, centered close to the downtown around the crossing of the Assunpink, was supplemented by a branch raceway that fed a series of mill sites along the Delaware riverbank adjacent to the William Trent House. Mill development also occurred at the downstream terminus of the canal on the former Rosey Hill Mansion property. The canal and its related mills experienced a somewhat checkered history and suffered during the economic downturn of the late 1830s. The system was revived in the mid-1840s by New York industrialist Peter Cooper as the newly named Trenton Water Power, becoming an integral part of the Cooper-Hewitt development of the Trenton Iron Company rolling mills complex on the riverbank between Federal Street and Cass Street. Much of the right-of-way and fabric of the Trenton Water Power is now buried beneath Route 29, but archaeological studies have documented the canal's cross-section in south Trenton and behind the New Jersey State House. Masonry from the Water Power's aqueduct abutments is still visible along the sides of Assunpink Creek to the rear of the Lafayette Yard Hotel on West Lafayette Street (Hunter 2005a; Hunter Research, Inc. 2011).

Early-nineteenth-century watermill construction and the Trenton Water Power merely got the ball of industrial growth rolling in Trenton. Transportation improvements—first, the turnpikes, then the Delaware and Raritan Canal and, not long after, a succession of railroad lines (the Camden and Amboy, the New Jersey Railroad, the Belvidere-Delaware, and the Delaware and Bound Brook)—quickly supplanted hydropowered energy development as the driving force behind the city's expansion into a manufacturing center. Furthermore, with the spread of steam power and the easy movement of coal into the city, the canal and railroads provided industrial facilities considerable freedom to locate beyond the main stream corridors. With these stimulants and the removal of critical siting constraints, industrial Trenton expanded rapidly over the landscape, simultaneously stretching and filling in the city's archaeological canvas.

Trenton's earliest turnpikes were chartered in the first decade of the nineteenth century (the Trenton and New Brunswick route in 1804; the Princeton and

Kingston Branch Turnpike in 1807; and the road southeast out of town to Borden-town in 1808). These do not lend themselves easily to archaeological research (the routes have been straightened, widened, and resurfaced many times over). Nonethe-less, the piers and abutments of the first bridge over the Delaware, erected from 1804 to 1806 as a southern extension of the Trenton and New Brunswick Turnpike into Pennsylvania, still survive as an important archaeological component within the present-day "Trenton Makes" bridge (Trenton Historical Society 1929:251, 275-280; Dale 2003:7-12).

The Delaware and Raritan Canal, on the other hand, is an omnipresent, partially functional element in Trenton's urban landscape and is an ongoing source of archaeological interest and concern. Built from 1831 to 1834, in tandem with the Trenton Water Power, the Delaware and Raritan Canal, so far as Trenton was concerned, was primarily conceived as a means of transportation, not as an indus-trial energy source. The city sits at the upper elevation of the canal, where the 22 mile long Feeder funnels water into the extended Trenton-to-Kingston stretch of the waterway's main line. Maintaining an adequate supply of water at this upper level severely limited the use of the canal for waterpower purposes (a function for which the Trenton Water Power compensated) and for this reason there is a notable paucity of water-powered mill sites along its route through the city, except along the Petty's Run stream corridor downstream of the Feeder crossing. However, in its role as a coal carrier, importer of raw materials, and exporter of finished products, the Dela-ware and Raritan Canal spurred the growth of numerous steam-powered factories along its banks in the mid- to late nineteenth century. In this way, the canal (and the rail lines that paralleled its route) supplies Trenton with a strong linear framework for much of its industrial archaeological heritage.

The canal route creates a distinctive trivet-like form in the Trenton land-scape with the Feeder approaching the city from the northwest along the left bank of the Delaware River and joining the main stem of the waterway at Old Rose Street. The canal's main line passes north-south through the city limits. The leg extending south from the junction with the Feeder toward Bordentown was filled in the 1930s and is now in use as the right-of-way for New Jersey Route 129. The segment head-ing north from the junction, like the Feeder, is water-filled. From Old Rose Street northward, it flows within a buried conduit built alongside the Route 1 Freeway in the 1950s, re-emerging and assuming its more traditional appearance at Mul-berry Street.

The Delaware and Raritan Canal is itself an archaeological resource of the highest caliber and has received a superior level of stewardship since being developed as a state park and admitted to the National Register of Historic Places in the mid-1970s. The waterway also serves a vital function as a supplier of potable water to much of the population of central New Jersey. With the safety net provided by a complex web of state and federal laws and regulations, the New Jersey Water Sup-ply Authority (NJWSA), the New Jersey Department of Environmental Protection, and the Delaware and Raritan Canal Commission have preserved, sustained, and enhanced what is effectively a "living" historic and archaeological property. As necessary capital improvement, maintenance dredging, and park development projects have proceeded, these have been accompanied by archaeological surveys, monitoring, and documentation. Critical components of the canal infrastructure (locks, spillways, culverts, bridges, basins), the canal prism or channel, and related canal-bank sites, such as lock and bridge tenders' houses, have all been examined in detail with much hitherto unappreciated information coming to light.

Within Trenton, revealing archaeological investigations were conducted along the segment of the canal's main line between U.S. Route 1 and the Hamilton Township border in advance of the construction of New Jersey Route 129 in the mid-1980s and early 1990s. This work, which included both archaeological survey and data recovery, was mostly focused on Locks 4 and 6A. Lock 4, just south of Lalor Street, was constructed in the early 1830s as part of the originally designed waterway, but it was rebuilt as a longer and deeper chamber in 1853 enabling it to receive larger boats. Lock 6A was installed in 1929 and represented a major modification of the canal brought about by upgrades to the Pennsylvania Railroad. Both locks were excavated and recorded in considerable detail, producing useful information about their construction, technology, and sequence of development. Lock 4 also yielded large quantities of Scammell china discarded as fill in the late 1930s when this section of the canal was abandoned and filled. A representative sample of Scammell products and kiln furniture, tightly dated to the years 1936 to 1938, was retrieved and published. The lock tender's house and other structures associated with Lock 4 were also recorded, while monitoring during construction of New Jersey Route 129 produced additional information on Lock 6, several bridges over the canal, and other canal-side features (Louis Berger & Associates, Inc. 1996).

Elsewhere in the city, the NJWSA, from 1989 to 1992, undertook archaeological surveys in connection with remedial work and drainage improvements along the section of the Delaware and Raritan Canal lying within Cadwalader Park, which led to detailed recording and analysis of the park's culvert and the Parkside Avenue aqueduct (Hunter Research, Inc. 1991b). NJWSA maintenance dredging along the waterway to improve water flow has also been accompanied by archaeological surveys to inventory and ensure the protection of buried and submerged remains from damage from dredging equipment and the use of staging areas (Hunter Research, Inc. 1991c). The same agency's elimination of stormwater and sediment from the 6,000 foot long conduit adjacent to the Route 1 Freeway was accompanied by a review of historic and archaeological properties along this section of the canal corridor (Hunter Research, Inc. 1991d).

Beginning with the completion in 1839 of the Camden and Amboy Trenton to New Brunswick branch line, the railroads dramatically quickened the pace of industrial development in the city. Together, the canal and railroads hastened the economic demise of Trenton's port community of Lamberton by siphoning off freight traffic from the Delaware River and turnpikes and encouraging development along these new transportation corridors. Relatively little attention has been given to Trenton's railroad-related archaeological resources, although the expansion of the federal courthouse on East State Street engulfed the site of the Hanover Street station, traces of which were found and recorded in pre-construction archaeological studies carried out in 1990. Among the features documented was a portion of a Camden and Amboy Railroad car house dating from the 1840s underlying the remains of a much larger Pennsylvania Railroad freight house of the early 1880s (Hunter Research, Inc. 1990a; 1990b).

Industrial archaeological resources from the mid-nineteenth through the mid-twentieth centuries abound throughout the City of Trenton with notable concentrations of properties along the canal and rail transportation corridors and along the Delaware River frontage from the mouth of the Assunpink downstream to Duck Island. Still functional, converted and ruined industrial buildings, bridges, and utilities infrastructure form a substantial part of the archaeological resource base in addition to the more traditional below-ground structural remains and production debris. Manufacturing sites and artifactual assemblages have been documented and sampled by archaeologists in many locations across the city, mostly in connection with cultural resources compliance actions required for highway and sewer improvements and urban redevelopment projects.

Mixed-use redevelopment of the sprawling Roebling wire rope complex and the neighboring American Steel & Wire works (formerly operated by the Trenton Iron Company) has taken place over the past quarter century producing a range of new uses (retail, offices, housing, and an arena). Located respectively on the east and west sides of the Delaware and Raritan Canal/Camden and Amboy Railroad corridor in the South Clinton Avenue/Hamilton Avenue section of South Trenton, these sprawling plants have experienced a variety of treatments—demolition, filling and grading, rehabilitation and adaptive re-use, and new construction. Relatively limited subsurface investigation was conducted at these two sites, but extensive documentation of buildings, structures, and equipment was carried out in accordance with the exacting standards of the Historic American Engineering Record.

Rather more archaeological energy was expended at the American Bridge/U.S. Steel site on the Delaware riverbank at the foot of Federal and Cass streets. In the 1980s and 1990s, during the course of this site being redeveloped for the Riverview Executive Plaza office complex, the Waterfront Park baseball stadium, related parking lots, and especially the reconstruction of Route 29, this nationally significant industrial property was studied in depth on a number of occasions. Initially developed for industrial purposes as a focus of textile manufacturing in the mid- to late 1830s, this site, critically situated at the downstream end of the Trenton Water Power, underwent a major reconfiguration in the mid- to late 1840s when Peter Cooper, Abram Hewitt, and Charles Hewitt appeared on the scene. Settling on Trenton as the main fabrication center for its regional web of iron and steel production, the Cooper-

Hewitt enterprise, trading as the Trenton Iron Company, established rolling mills on the riverbank at the looping terminus of the Water Power in 1845 and wire mills at the Hamilton Avenue plant beside the Delaware and Raritan Canal in 1849.

At the riverfront location, the company mass-produced in 1846 the first rolled wrought iron rails for the railroad industry and from 1854 to 1856 the first wrought iron structural I-beams for multi-story buildings. Its successor, the New Jersey Steel and Iron Company, went on in the late 1860s to perfect for the first time in America the Siemens-Martin open-hearth process for making steel, producing beams, girders, ships' anchors, and chains. Finally, the New Jersey Steel and Iron Company's successor, the American Bridge Company (a division of the U.S. Steel Corporation from 1901), produced steel for bridges and buildings, contributing structural components to many well-known architectural and engineering landmarks, including the Chrysler Building, the General Motors Building, Rockefeller Center, the United Nations Complex, and the Verrazano Narrows Bridge (all in New York City); the Tappan Zee Bridge over the Hudson River; and the Delaware Memorial, Walt Whitman, and Tacony-Palmyra bridges (all spanning the Delaware River) (Hunter 2005c; Hunter Research, Inc. 2011).

Despite the extensive redevelopment activity and the above-ground survival of only a single machine shop from the early 1870s (today a restaurant), the archaeology of the rolling mills site is still partially intact beneath the parking lots and roads. Archaeological excavations and monitoring at various times between 1981 and 2000 encountered the foundations of several of the pre-Trenton Iron Company textile mills and related buildings, the footings and furnace bases of the New Jersey Steel and Iron Company chain shop, traces of mill raceways, and of the Trenton Water Power. The foundations of the Rosey Hill Mansion, which served as Charles Hewitt's "ironmaster's residence" and as the company office, were investigated, along with the remains of a number of outbuildings. On-site acknowledgement of the historical importance of this industrial complex should someday be attempted through the installation of interpretive signage and other media.

Trenton's other fecund industry, rivaling and perhaps even exceeding iron and steel production in its number of manufacturing sites and volume of waste, was pottery making. From McCully's single traditional redware pottery in the downtown in 1850, the city's ceramic industry grew explosively through the second half of the nineteenth century and into the twentieth century to involve close to 50 potteries and related manufacturing sites at its peak between 1900 and 1920. For a century or more, a dizzying array of companies formed, dissolved, and re-formed under a multitude of corporate names (Stern 1994; Goldberg 1998).

Prior to the Civil War, the Trenton potteries mass-produced yellowware, Rockingham ware, whiteware (also referred to as white granite ware), and porcelain (including a winning line in door furniture items such as knobs and plates). Among the early leaders in the industry, all established in the 1850s, were firms and partnerships such as William Young & Company (later known as William Young & Sons and then William Young's Sons before being bought out by the Willet brothers in 1879, the works then becoming known as the Excelsior Pottery), Taylor and Speeler (later known as Taylor, Speeler and Bloor, and then the Trenton Pottery Company), Millington, Astbury & Poulson (operators of the Carroll Street Pottery), and William Rhodes and James Yates (operators of the City Pottery).

In the final third of the nineteenth century, production diversified to include sanitary earthenware (an industry trend led by Thomas Maddock and his sons and the Enterprise Pottery Company) and ironstone china mass-produced for hotels, restaurants, the Quartermaster's Department of the U.S. Army, and America's burgeoning middle classes (wares made, for example, by the Greenwood Pottery Company, the Mercer Pottery Company, John Moses' Glasgow Pottery, and several firms again involving members of the Maddock family). Other plants, such as Joseph Mayer's Arsenal Pottery, began by making Rockingham ware, but soon expanded their repertoire to include majolica and cut sponge-decorated ironstone china, while companies like Bloor, Ott & Brewer (later Ott & Brewer) produced high-end, finely decorated, and sculpted porcelain tablewares. Trenton's well-known specialty in art pottery had its origins during this period in the porcelain made at Ott & Brewer's Etruria Pottery, the Coxons' Empire Pottery, and the Willets' Excelsior Pottery, which spurred the formation of the Ceramic Art Company in 1889, which in turn morphed into Lenox Incorporated in 1906.

The 1890s saw considerable labor unrest, several strikes, and a trend toward consolidation among some of the potteries—all partly in response to a nationwide economic depression in 1892. In this year, the Trenton Potteries Company was formed, combining five major sanitary earthenware-producing plants (the Crescent, Delaware, Empire, Enterprise, and Equitable Potteries), which could then compete more successfully against the group of Maddock potteries. Both consortia went on to mass-produce hotel and restaurant china and other utilitarian wares, in addition to all manner of bathroom fittings (e.g., toilets, urinals, baths, basins, towel rails, and toilet roll holders). In the early twentieth century, diversification continued, and Trenton's ceramic production extended further into fine porcelain art pieces and sculpture, tile, electrical porcelain, and auxiliary specialties such as molds for the rubber industry (e.g., for gloves and condoms).

After World War I, the trend toward consolidation and the dominance of large pottery conglomerates was tempered by federal anti-trust legislation, which, along with continuing labor disputes, was a factor in the sale of the Maddock and Trenton Potteries Company holdings. The Maddock Pottery Company was sold to the Scammell China Company in 1923, while Thomas Maddock's Sons, after moving their sanitary earthenware plant out of Trenton to neighboring Hamilton Township, was purchased by the Standard Sanitary Manufacturing Company (an ancestor of today's American Standard) in 1929. The Trenton Potteries Company also changed hands in 1924, being acquired by the Crane Company, a large Chicago-based plumbing supply firm. Despite these changes, the Trenton potteries were hit hard by the Depression, the rise of plastics, and shifting consumer patterns, and the industry went into a slow and irrevocable decline from which it has never recovered.

From the standpoint of historical archaeology, a discipline that arguably thrives on the intellectual consumption of ceramics more than any other category of artifacts, Trenton's industrial potteries offer a veritable feast of process-related and processual data. Almost everywhere a major ground disturbance occurs in the city, spreads of ceramics and other artifacts connected with the pottery industry are to be found. Discarded bisque and glost-fired wasters, pieces of kiln furniture, kiln debris and plaster molds from the jiggering and jolleying machinery used in forming flat and hollow ware—these are just a few of the more common items recovered on a regular basis. Archaeological studies conducted in the course of projects complying with historic preservation laws over the past 40 plus years have encountered vast quantities of such materials. Professional archaeologists have been faced with an overwhelming prospect when it comes to documenting and processing these data, out of necessity resorting to only the most basic quantitative analyses and concentrating instead on studying the kiln sites and unique objects, and on the representative sampling of deposits and materials.

The pottery production sites have received little attention to date, in part because relatively few of them have been affected by redevelopment that has been subject to state and federal historic preservation oversight. The demolition of most of the buildings at the Ceramic Art Company/Lenox plant on Mead Street and St. Joe's Avenue in 2005, for example, was undertaken with private funds under municipal supervision without any provision for archaeological investigation and only limited architectural recording (Hunter 2005d). Admittedly, many of the pottery manufacturing sites are documented to some degree in corporate and municipal archives and in the many fire insurance maps, atlases, and historic photographs through which the city's industrial land use is recorded. Nonetheless, archaeological inquiry has much to offer in unraveling the layout and sequence of development of individual sites and providing detail about factory construction, pottery-making technology, and products. It is worth noting in this context that no known bottle kilns or tunnel kilns remain standing within the City of Trenton (tunnel kilns survive at the recently rehabilitated and adaptively re-used American Standard plant in Hamilton), leaving archaeology as the primary source for any future new information on these critical features of the industry.

The manufacturing sites of three industrial potteries have been studied by archaeologists in recent years, each with their own tale to tell. Archaeological survey and monitoring, along with Historic American Engineering Record documentation of the standing buildings, were performed at the Enterprise Pottery on New York Avenue from 1994 to 1995 in connection with NJDOT's construction of a new southbound exit ramp from U.S. Route 1. The ramp runs along the southeast side of the plant, along the Delaware and Raritan Canal corridor, before cutting northwestward across the sites of several kilns to join New York Avenue. The entire pottery lies within the Delaware and Raritan Canal Historic District, and construction of the ramp was judged to have an adverse effect on this contributing element of this National Register-listed property. Data recovery was ruled out as a means of mitigating the effects of construction on archaeological resources because of the hazard presented by radioactive soils resulting from the use of uranium in glazes. Instead, in addition to some limited archaeological monitoring during construction, a teachers' guide on the history of the Trenton's industrial potteries was produced, intended for use in the 4th through 8th grades, and a research database on the pottery sites was compiled (see below for more detail) (Hunter Research, Inc. 1995b; John Milner and Associates, Inc. 1995; Hunter Research, Inc. and Wilson Creative Marketing 1997; Madrigal and Hunter 1998).

Between 2000 and 2005, a series of archaeological investigations were performed in connection with the replacement of the Southard Street Bridge over the Route 1 Freeway/Delaware and Raritan Canal corridor, roughly a mile southwest of the Enterprise Pottery. Reconstruction of the northwestern end of the bridge affected the site of the Excelsior Pottery, which had its origins in the factory established between 1856 and 1857 by William Young & Company, and which again lay within the limits of the Delaware and Raritan Canal Historic District. Monitoring during construction along the Southard Street frontage of the Excelsior Pottery, where a packinghouse and decorating shop had stood in the late nineteenth century, resulted in the collection of a representative sample of ceramic wasters, chiefly porcelain hardware (knobs and pulls), ironstone china, and sanitary earthenware but also including several sherds with impressed or transfer-printed manufacturers' marks. Mitigation of the project effects on the Excelsior site also entailed updating and expanding the database developed as part of the Enterprise Pottery archaeological mitigation program (Hunter Research, Inc. 1999; 2005b).

The third manufacturing site subjected to archaeological study was not engaged in pottery production but instead provided an important auxiliary function within the industry—the grinding of flint and feldspar for inclusion in the clay body as a whitening and strengthening agent. Golding & Company (from 1885 Golding & Sons Company) established a flint and spar mill on the Trenton Water Power close to the mouth of Assunpink Creek in 1868. This site was subjected to archaeological monitoring during construction of the Lafayette Yard Hotel in 2000 and yielded a group of nine edge runner stones or "chasers" used in the grinding process and a small sample of flint nodules. The grinding stones were removed from the site and are stored in the rear yard of the Old Barracks awaiting some suitable form of display (Liebeknecht 2008).

Archaeological monitoring at the Lafayette Yard Hotel site in 2000 also resulted in the discovery and sampling of a yellowware waster dump sealed beneath deposits associated with the Golding & Company flint and spar mill. Analysis of the yellowware allowed for the attribution of this material to Charles Coxon's Clinton Street Pottery, located just over a mile to the northeast in the Coalport section of town. The date of its deposition was established as circa 1863–68 (White and Liebeknecht 2002a; 2002b). The collecting and analyzing of ceramic samples from deposits such as these are extraordinarily valuable as part of the ongoing effort at characterizing the production of Trenton's industrial potteries. Although this is a daunting task because there is simply so much discarded material out there, ultimately a body of sourced and dated ceramics can be built up which will provide a ready reference for archaeologists, historians, collectors, and the like throughout the country.

Ceramic waste deposits from the second half of the nineteenth century and the first half of the twentieth century abound throughout the city. Whether downtown redevelopment sites required grading, or clay pits on the fringe of the expanding town needed filling before construction could proceed (as was the case in the Calhoun Street/Princeton Avenue area), or canal rights-of-way needed filling prior to their re-use as highways, ceramic waste offered a convenient, permeable, and relatively stable fill matrix. In addition, prolific dumping by the potteries took place along riverbanks causing a narrowing of floodplains while at the same time expanding the area available for new building construction. For example, moving upstream along the Assunpink from the backyard of the Lafayette Yard Hotel, other ceramic waste deposits have been sampled between South Montgomery and South Stockton Streets (material attributable to the Assunpink Pottery Works of Henry Speeler & Sons [1860-71], the Speeler Pottery Company [1871-79], the International Pottery Company [1879-1936], and to the firm of Taylor & Davis [1871-75]) (Liebeknecht 2003). Pottery waste has also been found close to the site of the Chestnut Avenue bridge over the Amtrak Northeast rail corridor (material attributable to the late-nineteenth-century operation of the nearby Greenwood Pottery) (Abplanalp et al. 2006).

Other pockets of ceramic waste have been sampled at sites elsewhere along the Assunpink and Petty's Run stream corridors, but by far the deepest and most extensive pottery waster dumps occur along the Delaware River shoreline between Waterfront Stadium and the Trenton Marine Terminal. For most of the last quarter of the nineteenth century, and continuing up until the creation of the Sixth Ward Park in 1918–1919, potteries and other industrial facilities in south Trenton (as well as many factories situated elsewhere in the city) would dispose of their manufacturing waste by dispatching carts to Lamberton Street on the riverbank and tipping material over the terrace edge. In this manner, thick lenses and pockets of telltale sherds, kiln furniture, kiln debris, and other manufacturing items accumulated along the shoreline for a distance of almost three quarters of a mile and to depths in places that were in excess of ten feet.

The archaeological potential of the ceramic waste along this section of the Delaware riverbank in south Trenton first began to be appreciated in the late 1970s during archaeological surveys carried out as part of the planning studies for the reconstruction of Route 29. A pair of "china dumps," one tagged as the Maddock China Company Dump Site and the other as the Trenton China Company Dump Site, was identified, minimally sampled, and judged eligible for inclusion in the National Register of Historic Places. At the time, neither dump site was adequately defined in either horizontal or vertical terms, and the true extent of these deposits was obscured by vegetation, surface debris, and a few buildings.

It took a second, more accelerated public works project, the relocation and replacement of the Lamberton Interceptor, to provide the first real glimpse of the archaeological composition of the riverbank. The Lamberton Interceptor, a brick sewer main, was originally constructed from 1891 to 1892 down the center of Lamberton Street. Its reconstruction during 1980 and 1981 involved excavation of a deep linear trench into the shoreline fill deposits between the street and the river. Archaeological investigation and monitoring prior to and during installation of the new sewer allowed for some limited sampling of the two previously identified china dumps, which revealed some recognizable stratigraphic deposition and large quantities of diagnostic artifacts (Hunter 1982; Chesler 1983). The archaeological work, however, was confined to just a small number of discrete locations, and the true volume of the industrial waste still remained largely unappreciated.

The construction of the Route 29 tunnel in 1999 and 2000 finally exposed the riverbank in all its filled glory, revealing critical buried resources relating to the colonial port of Lamberton capped by swaths of late-nineteenth-century fill of variable thickness, within which lay swatches of ceramic waste. Through a combination of in-field sampling, stratigraphic observation, consideration of vessel forms and decorative styles, and, most especially, analysis of manufacturers' marks and the top and back marks of suppliers and corporate customers, many of the recovered artifacts could be broadly dated, typed, and traced back to specific pottery companies and clients (Liebeknecht 2000a; 2000b; 2001; Hunter Research, Inc. forthcoming [a]). Two potteries—the Arsenal Pottery of Joseph Mayer's Mayer Pottery Company (1876–circa 1905) and the Lamberton Works of the Maddock Pottery Company (1892–1923)—were especially well represented, dumping from the late 1870s until around 1918, when the Sixth Ward Park was created. Both potteries were located on Third Street, a short haul away from the riverbank. However, taken together, the Lamberton Interceptor and Route 29 archaeological work has documented dumping by several other potteries, including the Trenton China Company (1880-91), the predecessor at the Lamberton Works site, and also by a number of plants further north along the canal corridor (e.g., the Greenwood, Glasgow, Crescent, Excelsior, Mercer, Empire, and Anchor potteries). Certainly, dumping along the Delaware River in south Trenton was a cheap, easy, and widespread waste disposal solution for the pottery industry, perhaps undertaken by carters working for hire at multiple factories. Tellingly, this unsightly, environmentally unfriendly activity took place both downstream and downwind of the New Jersey State House complex and the upscale neighborhoods to the northwest of the downtown, but nevertheless was used as a basis for improved landscaping along the riverfront in the early twentieth century.

Just as the Delaware riverbank offered a hard-to-resist place to dispose of ceramic waste, so also was the Delaware and Raritan Canal a convenient receptacle for this material, when it came time to fill the canal in the mid-1930s after it had ceased commercial operation. The filled-in segment of the canal between Lock 2 and the junction with the Feeder Canal at Old Rose Street (now overlaid by Route 129 and the Route 1 Freeway) contains large quantities of ceramic debris that, for the most part, have received little study. One important exception is an assemblage of predominantly Scammell pottery that was gathered through a sampling operation at Lock 4 from 1987 to 1988 prior to the construction of Route 129. The Scammell China Company purchased the Maddock Pottery Company's Lamberton Works in 1923 and like the earlier owners generated vast amounts of ceramic waste. The recovered assemblage provides a useful representative sample of marked, decorated, bisque-fired, and glazed hotel and restaurant china, along with plaster molds, kiln props, and other kiln waste, all tightly datable to the years 1936–1938. Although the dinner wares had been discarded because they were defective, they still supply valuable data on mass-produced pottery forms and on Scammell's dealers and customers (Louis Berger & Associates, Inc. 1996:303-322).

Whether it is actual manufacturing sites being studied or the manifold sites of their waste products, the ceramics and iron and steel industries clearly dominate Trenton's industrial archaeological heritage and merit the bulk of archaeologists' ongoing attention. This work should not be conducted, however, to the exclusion of studying other aspects of Trenton's industrial and commercial past. For example, lumber, textiles, tanning, paper making, rubber manufacture, brewing, and bottling—these have all, at one time or another, been strongly in evidence in Trenton's history and may have left meaningful expressions in the urban landscape. The same is true of the city's transportation and utilities infrastructure, where two archaeological endeavors bear brief mention.

The Lamberton Interceptor, noted above, enjoyed its own moment of fame as an archaeological resource and recipient of a Senator William Proxmire "Golden Fleece Award," bestowed upon supposedly time- and money-wasting federal government involvements, in this instance caused by application of the National Historic Preservation Act. The original interceptor, despite intense antipathy, was deemed eligible for inclusion in the National Register of Historic Places in 1976, resulting in documentation and preservation of segments of its line within Lamberton Street and re-routing of the replacement sewer west of the street, closer to the river (Hunter 1982; Chesler 1983). In retrospect, the Proxmire award may arguably have been justified, although for resource-related reasons not recognized at the time. When the Route 29 tunnel was built in 2000, it became painfully apparent that the re-routed new sewer had wrought far greater damage on significant riverbank archaeological features and deposits than would have been the case had the original sewer merely been replaced on its original alignment. Such are the pitfalls of well-meaning cultural resources management, and we have a section of sand-filled, abandoned early 1890s sewer main to show for it.

Less contentious was the recovery in 2006 of portions of Trenton's early water supply system during reconfiguration of utilities in West State Street in connection with security improvements in front of the New Jersey State House. Archaeological monitoring and data recovery allowed for retrieval and documentation of a series of water logs (wooden pipes), cast-iron couplings, and wrought-iron bands dating from around 1820. These water pipes are thought to have been installed as part of a system upgrade carried out by the Trenton Water Works Company at a time when this firm was competing with the Trenton Aqueduct Company to fill the growing city's water supply needs (Hunter Research, Inc. 2007a).

GOVERNMENTAL SITES

In addition to its domestic, military, and industrial archaeological resources, Trenton has extensive archaeological remains that relate to its function as a seat of government. Indeed, as a seat of governments, local, county, and state, Trenton is home to several legislative, executive, and judicial buildings, many of which boast considerable history. Most have undergone rebuilding on the same site, which has destroyed or severely reduced their archaeological potential, although there are a handful of locations (e.g., the site of the original Hunterdon County Courthouse on South Warren Street) where one might still expect to find buried remains. Of these governmental buildings and complexes, one has yielded archaeological resources of unusual interest. This is the State House lot, today almost entirely built over by the New Jersey State House and Annex.

In the course of implementing security improvements along the West State Street frontage of the State House in 2006 (the same project that produced the water logs noted above), monitoring of the installation of an array of crash-proof bollards and related sidewalk replacement resulted in the discovery of substantial foundations and other features in the northeast corner of the historic State House lot (Hunter Research, Inc. 2007a). A limited program of archaeological data recovery ensued that confirmed the identification of the foundations as the remains of the offices of the Secretary of State and the Clerk of the Supreme Court, New Jersey's first public office building. The small one-story stuccoed stone structure, 46 by 28 feet in plan, was erected from 1795 to 1796 and in use until the mid-1840s. Forty-five feet away from the office building, directly under the present-day State House's West State Street portico, a brick-lined privy shaft was found. This was interpreted as the remains of the State House "necessary," built in 1797 to cater to the evacuative needs of legislators and bureaucrats, a vital receptacle for political waste of a most personal kind. The discovery of the office building prompted a minor redesign of the security improvements to minimize damage to the foundations after which the latter were preserved in place.

RELIGIOUS SITES

Trenton has dozens of churches and cemeteries, including several that date from the eighteenth and nineteenth centuries. A few have received archaeological attention. St. Michael's Church on North Warren Street, the oldest parts of which date from the

1740s, has been the subject of recent restoration efforts, and related archaeological work involved investigations beneath the floor of the adjoining parish house during 1997 and 1998 as well as an analysis of the church basement in 2007. The parish house was erected in 1892 over a portion of the churchyard, and archaeological testing in advance of the construction of new support piers for the floors within the building encountered the brick footings of the eighteenth-century bell tower and the partial remains of 15 burials. The latter work, combined with examination of the above ground facade, established the footprint of the 1740s building. This confirmed that the central portions of the north and south walls are from the original structure. Two substantial crypts were also found, one of which contained the grave of Sidney Paul Forman, who died in 1891. In addition to Ms. Forman's remains were found an almost intact funeral dress and other items of clothing, all preserved within a richly appointed casket. Following analysis and coordination with Forman descendants and the church administration, the remains and accoutrements were re-interred beneath the parish house. The analysis of the church basement a decade later was helpful in unraveling the building's sequence of development. This work established the location and dimensions of the eighteenth-century church and assessed which built-over portions of the property might yield further burials (Hunter Research, Inc. 1998; 2007b).

Elsewhere in the city, archaeological work conducted for the Route 29 reconstruction project included detailed study of the Riverview Cemetery, which had its origins in a late seventeenth-century Quaker burying ground (Hunter Research, Inc. forthcoming [a]). Archaeological testing along the highway alignment, which clipped the southwestern corner of the cemetery, encountered, rather than burials, a foundation that is thought to belong to a late-seventeenth-century house, perhaps once occupied by the Lambert family. Another, less well documented and largely invisible graveyard is Locust Hill Cemetery, an African American burying ground established in 1860 on what was then the fringe of the city (Hunter Research, Inc. 1997; Richard Grubb & Associates, Inc. 2011; Maser Consulting, P.A. 2012). Abandoned since the early years of the twentieth century and now partially built upon and surrounded by a later residential neighborhood, this cemetery has been extensively researched and is in the process of being reclaimed and acknowledged by the community as part of a broader city effort to restore the Assunpink Creek stream corridor. Limited archaeological investigation, focused on remote sensing to establish the locations of grave sites and monitoring during construction, may be expected in the years to come.

Beyond Compliance

The principal output of public archaeological endeavor in the United States is a vast and overwhelming "gray" literature—obtusely technical and often poorly written reports that, for the most part, are consigned to the shelves and servers of federal, state, county, and municipal agencies. Occasionally one may happen upon a report copy in a public library or local historical society; some can now be had in digital form. Simultaneously indigestible and soporific, these documents contain a sprawling mass and countless nuggets of historical and archaeological information, sometimes useful interpretations and, once in a while, an original idea. A miniscule proportion of these reports and their findings enjoy a life beyond the immediate needs of regulatory compliance. Few, however, are formally published or reworked for academic or public consumption.

Yet the product of public archaeological projects, and especially those dealing with historical archaeological resources, can be of great intellectual and social value. The data generated by these studies, when processed and applied appropriately beyond the narrow, short-term requirements of land use regulation and architectural or landscape restoration, can be a basis for academic research and publication. These report findings can also breathe life into communities through incorporation into presentations, exhibits, park design, school programming, and various forms of popular print and digital media. In this manner, the results of cultural resource management archaeology, when shared with the public, can be a vital part of the nation's connective educational tissue, whether it is providing grist for the ponderings of academe, nurturing skill in observation and inquiry within schoolchildren, or stimulating an interest in their surroundings among residents, visitors, and tourists. The issues, unsurprisingly, are firstly the lack of resources available to undertake this translation, and, more importantly, the general absence of regulatory, legal, or political stimuli to make it happen on a systematic basis.

The Trenton experience of public archaeology has seen the sprouting of a few seeds of an expanded and more enlightened historical output in the gray literary soil currently being cultivated by regulatory compliance. A handful of site-specific projects have spawned articles in academic journals, as with the Beakes homestead (Kalb et al. 1982), the Eagle Factory (Hunter et al. 2009), and the Petty's Run Archaeological Site (Hunter and Burrow 2010). In addition, an overview in the mid-1990s of Trenton's colonial archaeological potential drew extensively on cultural resource studies conducted up to that time (Burrow and Hunter 1996).

A broader distribution for a select group of reports on downtown historical archaeological projects has been achieved through their being posted on the Trenton Historical Society web site at trentonhistory.org (e.g., those connected with the redevelopment of the Dunhams/Capital Center block [Hunter Research Associates 1989a], planning for Mill Hill Park [Hunter Research, Inc. 2002], and the restoration of the Eagle Tavern [Hunter Research, Inc. 2005a]). The same digital outlet provides a report from a research project supported by a grant from the New Jersey Historical Commission that centered on the creation of a detailed map of Trenton as it existed in 1775 (Hunter Research, Inc. 2008). In this latter case, the research in question was prompted by archaeological work in the downtown and by an appreciation, after numerous site-specific studies, of the need for historically-based cartographic synthesis.

The "Trenton in 1775" mapping project, although incomplete in its coverage and in need of further expanded research, represented an ambitious attempt at using land records to reconstruct the topographic and cadastral shape of the town immediately prior to the Revolution. Probably unique for an American colonial settlement of its size, the resulting map is of tremendous potential utility to historic preservation planners and cultural resource managers, in addition to archaeologists, historians, and historical geographers.

No less ambitious in scope, and again an undertaking that will be ongoing for years to come, is the Trenton Potteries Database project. The database has its roots in the archaeological mitigation of a pair of recently completed NJDOT improvements—the construction of the Route 1/New York Avenue exit ramp and the replacement of the Southard Street bridge over Route 1—which impacted, respectively, the Enterprise and Excelsior potteries (Madrigal and Hunter 1998). This searchable and still growing database of basic information about Trenton's industrial potteries (dates of operation, types of products, owners and operators, makers' and customers' marks, maps, and images) is now maintained by the Potteries of Trenton Society (Hunter Research, Inc. 1999).

The bulk of the historic artifacts recovered during the course of public archaeological studies, it must be admitted, are seldom worthy of an exhibit. This is true, for example, of the masses of broken and incomplete ceramic wasters from Trenton's industrial potteries whose primary value is as a source of information for undertakings like the Trenton Potteries Database. However, very occasionally, an assemblage of artifacts and related archaeological data will merit display. This proved to be the case with the stoneware recovered from William Richards' kiln and other evidence of Richards' commercial enterprises found on the Lamberton waterfront during the construction of the Route 29 tunnel. This material and accompanying archival documentation formed the basis for an exhibit, *Remarkable For His Industry: William Richards, Trade & Manufactory in Revolutionary Trenton,* presented at the Old Barracks in 2007 and 2008. The pottery of James Rhodes (William Richards' master potter) has also gone on display in several other locations including the Trenton City Museum (Hunter et al. 2011), the New Jersey State Museum, the New Jersey Historical Society, and Colonial Williamsburg.

Trenton's historical archaeology has been adopted with enthusiasm by several local historical groups, notably the Trenton Historical Society, the Old Mill Hill Society, the Trenton Museum Society, the Trent House Association, the Old Barracks Association, and the Potteries of Trenton Society. These non-profit organizations have shown intense interest in public archaeology projects within the city and have applied for grants for research and educational programs that have made use of and built on the work undertaken by archaeologists and historians. They have orchestrated numerous presentations and tours of historic sites in the city, many of which have had an archaeological theme. The Old Barracks and Trent House, for example, have put on archaeological training programs that have been embraced wholeheartedly both by local schools and the community. Patriots Week, an annual celebration of the Battles of Trenton organized by the Trenton Downtown Association, routinely incorporates archaeological presentations and tours into its programming. The Potteries of Trenton Society holds an annual spring symposium to which archaeologists frequently contribute.

Nothing attracts the interest of a passer-by more than archaeologists sweatily plying their trade. Site tours and "open days" at in-progress archaeological excavations have been a powerful draw for residents, school groups, and visitors to the city. Coverage by local and regional print and television media has been a staple of these happenings. Such events were held successfully during the course of excavations at the Old Barracks and the William Trent House, along West State Street in the vicinity of the State House, and most recently at the Petty's Run Archaeological Site.

Brochures, posters, displays, and hand-outs have been a critical part of connecting public archaeological projects with the public. These materials have typically been distributed on-site during tours and open days or at public presentations. In a few instances, greater effort has been expended in the area of public outreach. In an attempt to bring Trenton's archaeology into the schools, local archaeologists have brought materials into the classroom and provided instruction. They have also created the teachers' guide *From Teacups to Toilets*, which was intended to introduce middle school students to the history of the city's industrial potteries (Hunter Research, Inc. and Wilson Creative Marketing 1997; Madrigal and Hunter 1998). Aimed more at the local adult population was a series of six popular booklets produced as part of the program of archaeological mitigation developed for the NJ-DOT's reconstruction of Route 29 (Burrow 2005a; 2005b; Hunter 2005a; 2005b; 2005c; Hunter and Ashton 2005).

The New Jersey Department of Transportation disseminated the proceeds of its Route 29 cultural resources investigations several steps further when it built the South River Walk Park atop the tunnel that now runs where the Lamberton waterfront formerly hosted wharves, warehouses, and other port facilities. Opened in 2004, this 6.5 acre county-owned amenity uses Trenton's history as its principal design theme, drawing extensively on the archival research and archaeological discoveries that accompanied the highway construction. At the core of the park is a "time tunnel" formed by a series of five paired arches whose mode of construction reflects the prehistory and history of the Middle Delaware Valley from the sixteenth through twenty-first centuries. Beneath each set of arches are grouped four bronze plaques devoted to historical topics, while a zigzagging path of inscribed granite date stones passes along the tunnel narrating landmark events in Trenton area history. A sequence of nine, more detailed historic interpretive signs lines the river edge of the park.

The incorporation of historical and archaeological material into outdoor exhibits is a growing feature of Trenton's efforts at establishing itself as a heritage tourism destination. Following the discovery of the remains of the first office of the Secretary of State and the Clerk of the Supreme Court, built in 1795 and 1796, the recently completed security improvements along the West State Street frontage of the New Jersey State House complex underwent a minor design change to allow for installation of a historic interpretive panel and a replication of the building footprint in the sidewalk. These now serve as a point of reference and interest for pedestrians, explaining a forgotten aspect of the origins of state government (Hunter Research, Inc. 2007a).

A much more elaborate, visible, and significant merging of archaeology into urban park design has recently taken shape less than 500 feet away at the Petty's Run Archaeological Site in the sliver of parkland wedged between the State House and the Old Barracks. Archaeological explorations conducted as part of the planning for the new Capital State Park revealed multiple, massive foundations from a cluster of water-powered mills dating from the early 1730s until the mid-1870s. This site presents a microcosm of Trenton industrial history and includes the exceedingly rare remains of an eighteenth-century steel furnace. The process of this site's archaeological excavation in 2008 and 2009, highlighted in numerous site tours, wide-ranging media coverage, and a web journal (www.pettysrun.org), aroused intense public interest. In 2010, when the State of New Jersey, for budgetary reasons, placed the Capital State Park project on hold and proposed backfilling the Petty's Run site, the public outcry was sufficient to prompt an intervention by the County of Mercer, which has resulted in the long-term stabilization, display, and interpretation of these remains. Trenton, as a result, now boasts a unique, visually appealing archaeological property in its downtown that will attract and educate visitors and help cement the city's important role in American history.

This example of the incorporation of serious and substantive archaeological content into park design—designer archaeology, as it might be termed—is several steps removed from the completion of a simple archaeological survey for the purpose of compliance with land use regulations. Such an outcome will only be viable on a few, very rare occasions, as determined by the quality of the resource and the consciousness of the host community. The Petty's Run site has been vigorously adopted by Trentonians and by historical groups throughout the region to the point where it will remain embedded in the modern urban landscape for many decades to come. This is an exceptional example of public archaeology enriching the everyday life and psyche of a city. The challenge going forward is how to stimulate a similar but broader-based and deeper-rooted appreciation for Trenton's archaeological remains in the face of a dwindling resource base and limited funding. As the city seeks to establish a future that draws in part upon its past and solicits visitors for its historic sites, the process and product of historical archaeology have a critical role to play—enticing interest, elucidating, educating, and encouraging responsible stewardship from public and private landowners alike.

References Cited

Abplanalp, Kathleen, Philip A. Hayden, Jennifer Leynes, Glenn R. Modica, and
        Gerard Scharfenberger
2006   Cultural Resources Investigation, Replacement of Chestnut Avenue
              Bridge (1149-163), East State Street Bridge (1149-164), and Mon-
              mouth Street Bridge (1149-165) over Amtrak, City of Trenton, Mercer
              County, New Jersey. Manuscript on file, (NJDEP), New Jersey.
AECOM
2010   Phase I/II Subsurface Archaeological Survey—South Broad Street (U.S.
              Route 206) Bridge Rehabilitation Project, City of Trenton, New Jersey.
              Manuscript on file, New Jersey Department of Transportation, Ewing,
              New Jersey.
Becker, Marshall
1999   Cash Cropping by Lenape Foragers: Preliminary Notes on Native
              Maize Sales to Swedish Colonists and Cultural Stability during the
              Early Colonial Period. *Bulletin of the Archaeological Society of New
              Jersey* 54:45–68.
Branin, Lelyn M.
1988   *The Early Makers of Handcrafted Earthenware and Stoneware in Cen-
              tral and Southern New Jersey*. Associated University Presses, Cranbury,
              New Jersey.
Brown, Marley R., and Patricia Samford
1994   Current Archaeological Perspectives on the Growth and Development
              of Williamsburg. In *Historical Archaeology of the Chesapeake*, edited
              by Paul Shackel and Barbara Little, pp. 231-246. Smithsonian Institu-
              tion Press, Washington, D.C.
Burrow, Ian
2005a   *A Tale of Two Houses: The Lambert/Douglas House and the Rosey
              Hill Mansion, 1700–1850*. History Traced by Route 29 Booklet Series.
              New Jersey Department of Transportation, Ewing, New Jersey.
2005b   *Ancient Ways: Native Americans in South Trenton, 10,000 B.C. to
              A.D. 1700*. History Traced by Route 29 Booklet Series. New Jersey
              Department of Transportation, Ewing, New Jersey.
2008   "Wilkes and Liberty"—Anglo-American Colonial Politics at the Old
              Barracks, Trenton, New Jersey. *Bulletin of the Archaeological Society
              of New Jersey* 63:76–80.
Burrow, Ian, and Richard Hunter
1996   Pretty Village to Urban Place: 18th Century Trenton and Its Archaeol-
              ogy. *New Jersey History* 114(3–4):32–52.
Cantwell, Anne-Marie, and Diana diZerega Wall
2001   *Unearthing Gotham: The Archaeology of New York City*. Yale Univer-
              sity, New Haven, Connecticut.

Carver, Martin
1987   *Underneath English Towns: Interpreting Urban Archaeology*. B.T. Batsford, London.

Chesler, Olga
1983   An Archaeological Investigation of the Maddock China Dump Site (28-Me-94) in Trenton, Mercer County, New Jersey. Manuscript on file, NJDEP, Trenton, New Jersey.

Cotter, John, Daniel G. Roberts, and Michael Parrington
1992   *The Buried Past: An Archaeological History of Philadelphia*. University of Pennsylvania Press, Philadelphia.

Cross, Dorothy
1956   *Archaeology of New Jersey, Volume II: The Abbott Farm*. The Archaeological Society of New Jersey and the New Jersey State Museum, Trenton, New Jersey.

Cumbler, John T.
1989   *A Social History of Economic Decline: Business, Politics and Work in Trenton*. Rutgers University Press, New Brunswick, New Jersey.

Dale, Frank T.
2003   *Bridges over the Delaware River: A History of Crossings*. Rutgers University Press, New Brunswick, New Jersey.

Dickens, Roy S., Jr.
1982   *Archaeology of Urban America: The Search for Pattern and Process*. Academic Press, New York.

Godfrey, Carlos E.
1919   *The Dutch Trading Post*. Pamphlet. Trenton Historical Society, Trenton, New Jersey.

Goldberg, David J.
1998   *Potteries, The Story of Trenton's Ceramic Industry: Preliminary Notes on the Pioneer Potters and Potteries of Trenton, New Jersey*. Trenton Museum Society, Trenton, New Jersey.

Holm, Thomas Campanius
1702 [circa   *A Short Description of the Province of New Sweden Now Called by*
1670–1702]   *the English Pennsylvania in America*. Memoirs of the Historical Society of Pennsylvania, vol. 3, part 1. Translated by Peter S. DuPonceau, pp. 1166. Also quoted in W. H. Benedict, 1920: New Jersey as it appeared to Early Observers and Travelers. *Proceedings of the New Jersey Historical Society* V(3):150–168.

Hunter Research Associates
1989a   Archaeological Investigations within the Dunhams Block in connection with the Capital Center Project, City of Trenton, Mercer County, New Jersey. Manuscript on file, NJDEP, Trenton, New Jersey.

1989b   Intensive Test Excavations at the Old Barracks, City of Trenton, Mer-
             cer County, New Jersey. 2 vols. Manuscript on file, NJDEP, Trenton,
             New Jersey.
1989c   Archaeological Investigations at the New Jersey State House, City of
             Trenton, Mercer County, New Jersey. Manuscript on file, NJDEP, Tren-
             ton, New Jersey.
Hunter Research, Inc.
1990a   Phase 1 Archaeological Investigations (Pre-Fieldwork Preparation and
             Preliminary Archaeological Reconnaissance) at the Trenton Federal
             Courthouse Annex, City of Trenton, Mercer County, New Jersey. Man-
             uscript on file, NJDEP, Trenton, New Jersey.
1990b   Phase 2 Archaeological Investigations (Intensive Archaeological Sur-
             vey) at the Trenton Federal Courthouse Annex, City of Trenton, Mer-
             cer County, New Jersey. Manuscript on file, NJDEP, Trenton, New
             Jersey.
1991a   Supplementary Archaeological Investigations at the Old Barracks, City
             of Trenton, Mercer County, New Jersey. Manuscript on file, NJDEP,
             Trenton, New Jersey.
1991b   Cultural Resource Studies for the Delaware & Raritan Canal Embank-
             ment Program in the Vicinity of the Cadwalader Park Culvert (Station
             1030+80), City of Trenton, Mercer County, New Jersey. Manuscript on
             file, NJDEP, Trenton, New Jersey.
1991c   Cultural Resources Investigations in Connection with the Proposed
             Maintenance Dredging of the Delaware and Raritan Canal, Prallsville
             Lock to Kingston Lock, Borough of Stockton, Delaware Township,
             City of Lambertville and West Amwell Township, Hunterdon County,
             Hopewell and Ewing Townships, City of Trenton and Lawrence, Prince-
             ton and West Windsor Townships, Mercer County, Plainsboro and
             South Brunswick Townships, Middlesex County, New Jersey. 2 vols.
             Manuscript on file, NJDEP, Trenton, New Jersey.
1991d   A Cultural Resources Investigation, Delaware and Raritan Canal, U.S.
             Route 1 Conduit, City of Trenton, Mercer County, New Jersey. Manu-
             script on file, NJDEP, Trenton, New Jersey.
1995a   Archaeological Investigations on the Tunnel at the William Trent
             House, City of Trenton, Mercer County, New Jersey. Manuscript on
             file, NJDEP, Trenton, New Jersey.
1995b   Cultural Resource Survey, U.S. Route 1 and New York Avenue Off-
             Ramp, City of Trenton, Mercer County, New Jersey. Manuscript on
             file, NJDEP, Trenton, New Jersey.
1996   Archaeological Investigations at the Old Barracks, Trenton, New
             Jersey 1994-5. Interior Monitoring and Further Investigation of the

Barracks Lot and Parade Ground. Manuscript on file, NJDEP, Trenton, New Jersey.

1997   A Historical Survey of the Locust Hill Cemetery, City of Trenton, Mercer County, New Jersey. Manuscript on file, NJDEP, Trenton, New Jersey.

1998   Archaeological Investigations in connection with the St. Michael's Parish House Restoration and Rehabilitation, City of Trenton, Mercer County, New Jersey. Manuscript on file, NJDEP, Trenton, New Jersey.

1999   The Trenton Potteries Database. Produced for the New Jersey Department of Transportation and maintained by the Potteries of Trenton Society, Trenton, New Jersey.

2002   The Assunpink Creek in Mill Hill: A History and Consideration of Historic Interpretive Opportunities. Manuscript on file, New Jersey Historical Commission, Trenton, New Jersey.

2003a   The William Trent House, City of Trenton, Mercer County, New Jersey: Archaeological Investigations, Research, Public Outreach, and Construction Monitoring 2000-2003. Manuscript on file, NJDEP, Trenton, New Jersey.

2003b   South Broad Street Bridge, Cultural Resources Assessment, City of Trenton, Mercer County, New Jersey. Manuscript on file, NJDEP, Trenton, New Jersey.

2005a   A Historical Account and Archaeological Analysis of the Eagle Tavern, City of Trenton, Mercer County, New Jersey. Manuscript on file, New Jersey Historical Commission and the Trenton Historical Society, Trenton, New Jersey.

2005b   Historical and Archaeological Investigations at the Excelsior Pottery Site, Southard Street Bridge Replacement Project, City of Trenton, Mercer County, New Jersey. Manuscript on file, NJDEP, Trenton, New Jersey.

2006   Cultural Resource Investigation of Ten Sites in the Hackensack Meadowlands: Hackensack Meadowlands Restoration Project, Hudson and Bergen Counties, New Jersey. Manuscript on file, NJDEP, Trenton, New Jersey.

2007a   Archaeological Monitoring and Data Recovery, West State Street Security Improvements, New Jersey State House, City of Trenton, Mercer County, New Jersey. Manuscript on file, NJDEP, Trenton, New Jersey.

2007b   St. Michael's Episcopal Church, Site Management Plan, City of Trenton, Mercer County, New Jersey. Manuscript on file, NJDEP, Trenton, New Jersey.

2008   The "Trenton in 1775" Mapping Project, City of Trenton, Mercer County, New Jersey. Manuscript on file, New Jersey Historical Commission and the Trenton Historical Society, Trenton, New Jersey.

2009   The Abbott Farm National Historic Landmark Interpretive Plan, Cultural Resource Technical Document, Hamilton Township, Mercer

County, Bordentown Township and the City of Bordentown, Burlington County, New Jersey. Manuscript on file, NJDEP, Trenton, New Jersey.

2011   Archaeological Data Recovery Excavations and Monitoring, New Jersey Route 29, City of Trenton, Mercer County, New Jersey. Vol. II. Lambert/Douglas Plantation and Rosey Hill Mansion Site. Manuscript on file (final draft), NJDEP, Trenton, New Jersey.

Forthcoming Archaeological Data Recovery Excavations and Monitoring, New Jersey Route 29, City of Trenton, Mercer County, New Jersey. Vol. III.
[a]   Historical Archaeology of the Lamberton/South Trenton Riverfront. Manuscript on file (draft), NJDEP, Trenton, New Jersey.

Forthcoming Archaeological Data Recovery Excavations and Monitoring, New Jersey Route 29, City of Trenton, Mercer County, New Jersey. Vol. I.
[b]   Prehistoric Sites. Manuscript on file (draft), NJDEP, Trenton, New Jersey.

Hunter Research, Inc., and Wilson Creative Marketing

2001 [1997] *From Teacups to Toilets: A Century of Industrial Pottery in Trenton, circa 1850 to 1940*. The Potteries of Trenton Society, Trenton, New Jersey.

Hunter, Richard W.

1982   Archaeological Monitoring of the Lamberton Interceptor, Lamberton Street, City of Trenton, Mercer County, New Jersey. Manuscript on file, NJDEP, Trenton, New Jersey.

2001   Eighteenth-Century Stoneware Kiln of William Richards Found on the Lamberton Waterfront, Trenton, New Jersey. In *Ceramics in America 2001*, edited by Robert Hunter, pp. 239–243. The Chipstone Foundation, Milwaukee, Wisconsin.

2005a   *Power to the City: The Trenton Water Power*. History Traced by Route 29 Booklet Series. New Jersey Department of Transportation, Ewing, New Jersey.

2005b   *Fish and Ships: Lamberton, the Port of Trenton*. History Traced by Route 29 Booklet Series. New Jersey Department of Transportation, Ewing, New Jersey.

2005c   *Rolling Rails by the River: Iron and Steel Fabrication in South Trenton*. History Traced by Route 29 Booklet Series. New Jersey Department of Transportation, Ewing, New Jersey.

2005d   Lenox Factory Buildings Demolished. *Trenton Potteries: Newsletter of the Potteries of Trenton Society* 6(2/3):1–9.

Hunter, Richard W., and Charles H. Ashton

2005   *Quakers, Warriors, and Capitalists: Riverview Cemetery and Trenton's Dead*. History Traced by Route 29 Booklet Series. New Jersey Department of Transportation, Ewing, New Jersey.

Hunter, Richard W., and Ian C. Burrow

2010   Steel Away: the Trenton Steel Works and the Struggle for American Manufacturing Independence. In *Footprints of Industry: Papers from* the 300th Anniversary Conference at Coalbrookdale, 3–7 June 2009, edited by Paul Belford, Marilyn Palmer, and Roger White, pp. 69–88. BAR British Series 523, Archaeopress, Oxford, United Kindgom.

Hunter, Richard W., and Richard L. Porter

1990 American Steel in the Colonial Period: Trenton's Role in a "Neglected" Industry. Canal History and Technology Proceedings IX:83–120.

Hunter, Richard W., Nadine Sergejeff, and Damon Tvaryanas

2009 On the Eagle's Wings: Textiles, Trenton, and a First Taste of the Industrial Revolution. New Jersey History 124(1):57-98.

Hunter, Richard W., Rebecca White, and Nancy Hunter

2011 Trenton Makes Pottery: The Stoneware of James Rhodes, 1774-1784. Trenton Potteries: Newsletter of the Potteries of Trenton Society 12(3/4):1–9.

John G. Waite Associates, Architects PLLC

1998 The Old Barracks: Historic Structure Report. Manuscript on file, NJDEP, Trenton, New Jersey.

John Milner and Associates, Inc.

1995 Historic American Engineering Record Documentation of the Enterprise Pottery, Route 1SB over New York Avenue, City of Trenton, Mercer County, New Jersey. Manuscript on file, NJDEP, Trenton, New Jersey.

Kalb, K. R., J. Kopleck, D. Fimbel, and I. J. Sypko

1982 An Urban Ferry Tale. Bulletin of the Archaeological Society of New Jersey 38:119.

Leone, Mark P.

1994 The Archeology of Ideology: Archaeological Work in Annapolis since 1981. In Historical Archaeology of the Chesapeake, edited by Paul Shackel and Barbara Little, pp. 219–229. Smithsonian Institution Press, Washington, D.C.

Leone, Mark P., Elizabeth Kryder-Reid, Paul Shackel, and Julie Ernstein

1989 Power Gardens of Annapolis. Archaeology 42(2):34–39, 74–75.

Liebeknecht, William B.

2000a Joseph Mayer's Arsenal Pottery Dump. Part 1: Yellow Ware. Trenton Potteries: Newsletter of the Potteries of Trenton Society 1(2):1–2.

2000b Joseph Mayer's Arsenal Pottery Dump. Part 2: Majolica. Trenton Potteries: Newsletter of the Potteries of Trenton Society 1(3):4–5.

2001 Joseph Mayer's Arsenal Pottery Dump. Part 3: Cut Sponge Decorated Ironstone China. Trenton Potteries: Newsletter of the Potteries of Trenton Society 2(3/4):1–5.

2003 Makers Marks from the Assunpink Pottery Works. Trenton Potteries: Newsletter of the Potteries of Trenton Society 4(3):6.

2008 Golding & Company Flint and Spar Mills, Trenton, New Jersey. Trenton Potteries: Newsletter of the Potteries of Trenton Society 9(1):1–5.

Liebeknecht, William B., and Richard W. Hunter

2003   The Richards Face—Shades of an Eighteenth-Century American Bel-
            larmine. In *Ceramics in America 2003*, edited by Robert Hunter, pp.
            259–261. The Chipstone Foundation, Milwaukee, Wisconsin.

Louis Berger & Associates, Inc.

1996   *Delaware and Raritan Canal (Site 28Me108), Historical and Archaeo-
            logical Studies.* Trenton Complex Archaeology: Report 11. The Cul-
            tural Resource Group, Louis Berger & Associates, Inc., East Orange,
            New Jersey.

Madrigal, Patricia A., and Richard W. Hunter

1998   Mitigating Effects on an Industrial Pottery. *CRM: The Journal of Heri-
            tage Stewardship* 9:25–26.

Maser Consulting, P. A.

2012   The History of the Locust Hill Cemetery. Manuscript on file, City of
            Trenton Department of Housing and Development, Trenton, New Jersey.

McKelvey, William J., Jr.

1975   *The Delaware and Raritan Canal: A Pictorial History.* Canal Press,
            York, Pennsylvania.

Mrozowski, Stephen A.

1987   Exploring New England's Evolving Urban Landscape. *Living in Cities:
            Current Research in Urban Archaeology*, edited by Edward Staski, pp.
            1–9. Society for Historical Archaeology, Pleasant Hill, California.

Mullins, Paul R., and Terry H. Klein

2000   Archaeological Views of Southern Culture and Urban Life. In *Archae-
            ology of Southern Urban Landscapes*, edited by Amy L. Young, pp.
            217–239. The University of Alabama Press, Tuscaloosa, Alabama.

Nelson, Sarah M., with K. Lynn Berry, Richard F. Carrillo, Bonnie J. Clark, Lori E.
            Rhodes, and Dean Saitta

2001   *Denver: An Archaeological History.* University of Pennsylvania Press,
            Philadelphia.

Orser, Charles E.

2004   *Historical Archaeology.* Pearson Education, Upper Saddle River, New
            Jersey

Quigley, Mary Alice, and David E. Collier

1984   *A Capital Place: The Story of Trenton.* Trenton Historical Society and
            Windsor Publications, Woodland Hills, California.

Raum, J. O.

1871   *History of the City of Trenton.* W. T. Nicholson & Co., Trenton, New
            Jersey.

Richard Grubb & Associates, Inc.

2011   *Three Centuries of African-American History in Trenton: A Prelimi-
            nary Survey of Historic Sites.* Trenton Historical Society, Trenton, New
            Jersey.

Schuldenrein, Joseph
1994   Alluvial Site Geoarchaeology of the Middle Delaware Valley: A Fluvial
            Systems Paradigm. *Journal of Middle Atlantic Archaeology* 10:1–21.
Shackel, Paul A.
1994   Town Plans and Everyday Material Culture: An Archaeology of Social
            Relations in Colonial Maryland's Capital Cities. In *Historical Archae-
            ology of the Chesapeake*, edited by Paul Shackel and Barbara Little, pp.
            85–96. Smithsonian Institution Press, Washington, D.C.
Skerry, Janine E., and Suzanne Findlen Hood
2009   *Salt-Glazed Stoneware in Early America.* The Colonial Williamsburg
            Foundation, Williamsburg, Virginia.
Staski, Edward (editor)
1987   *Living in Cities: Current Research in Urban Archaeology.* Society for
            Historical Archaeology, Pleasant Hill, California.
Stern, Marc Jeffrey
1994   *The Pottery Industry of Trenton: A Skilled Trade in Transition, 1850-
            1922.* Rutgers University Press, New Brunswick, New Jersey.
Stewart, R. Michael
1990   Archaeology, Sedimentary Sequences, and Environmental Change in
            the Delaware River Basin. Manuscript on file, Bureau for Historic Pres-
            ervation, Pennsylvania Historical and Museum Commission, Harris-
            burg, Pennsylvania.
1994   Stratigraphic Sequences and Archaeological Sites in the Delaware Val-
            ley: Implications for Paleoenvironmental Change in the Middle Atlantic
            Region. *Bulletin of the Archaeological Society of New Jersey* 49:99–105.
1998   *Ceramics and Delaware Valley Prehistory: Insights from the Abbott
            Farm.* Trenton Complex Archaeology: Report 14. The Cultural Re-
            source Group of Louis Berger & Associates, East Orange, New Jersey.
Toothman, Stephanie S.
1977   Trenton, New Jersey, 1719-1779: A Study of Community Growth and
            Organization. Unpublished Ph.D. dissertation, American Studies De-
            partment, University of Pennsylvania, Philadelphia.
Trenton Board of Trade
1889   *The Industries and Advantages of the City of Trenton.* The John L.
            Murphy Publishing Company, Trenton, New Jersey.
Trenton Historical Society
1929   *A History of Trenton, 1679–1929: Two Hundred and Fifty Years of
            a Notable Town with Links in Four Centuries.* Princeton University
            Press, Princeton, New Jersey.
Turk, Jessie R.
1964   Trenton, New Jersey, in the Nineteenth Century: The Significance of
            Location in the Historical Geography of a City. Unpublished Ed.D.
            thesis, Teachers College, Columbia University, New York.

Veit, Richard

2000   Following the Yellow Brick Road: Dutch Bricks in New Jersey, Fact
            and Folklore. *Bulletin of the Archaeological Society of New Jersey*
            55:70–76.

Volk, Ernest

1911   The Archaeology of the Delaware Valley. *Papers of the Peabody Mu-
            seum of American Archaeology and Ethnology 5*, Harvard University,
            Cambridge, Massachusetts.

Wall, Robert D., R. Michael Stewart, John Cavallo, and Virginia Busby

1995   *Area D Site (28Me1-D) Data Recovery.* Trenton Complex Archaeol-
            ogy: Report 9. The Cultural Resource Group of Louis Berger & Associ-
            ates. East Orange, New Jersey.

Wall, Robert D., R. Michael Stewart, John Cavallo, Douglas McLearen, Robert Foss,
            Philip Perazio, and John Dumont

1996   *Prehistoric Archaeological Synthesis.* Trenton Complex Archaeology:
            Report 15. The Cultural Resource Group of Louis Berger & Associ-
            ates, East Orange, New Jersey.

White, Rebecca, and William B. Liebeknecht

2002a   Rebekah at the Marriott: Marriott Site Yellow Ware Waster Dump,
            Circa 1863–1868, Trenton, New Jersey. *Trenton Potteries: Newsletter
            of the Potteries of Trenton Society* 3(1):1–4.

2002b   Rebekah at the Marriott: Marriott Site Yellow Ware Waster Dump,
            Circa 1863–1868, Trenton, New Jersey. *Trenton Potteries: Newsletter
            of the Potteries of Trenton Society* 3(2):1–4.

Woodward, E. M., and John F. Hageman

1883   *History of Burlington and Mercer Counties.* Everts and Peck,
            Philadelphia.

Yamin, Rebecca (editor)

2000   *Tales of Five Points: Working-Class Life in Nineteenth-Century New
            York.* 6 vols. John Milner Associates, Philadelphia.

2008   *Digging in the City of Brotherly Love: Stories from Philadelphia Ar-
            chaeology.* Yale University Press, New Haven, Connecticut.

Young, Amy L. (editor)

2000   *Archaeology of Southern Urban Landscapes.* University of Alabama
            Press, Tuscaloosa, Alabama.

Zierden, Martha

2000   Charleston's Powder Magazine and the Development of a Southern
            City. In *Archaeology of Southern Urban Landscapes*, edited by Amy L.
            Young, pp. 92–108. University of Alabama Press, Tuscaloosa, Alabama.

15

IT TAKES A VILLAGE: ARCHAEOLOGY AT TIMBUCTOO, BURLINGTON COUNTY, NEW JERSEY

CHRISTOPHER P. BARTON

Introduction

In recent years, scholars have gained a greater understanding of the heterogeneity of the African American historical experience through an explosion of archaeological investigation and documentary research. Though most research has been and continues to focus on sites associated with southeastern slavery, the subfield has shifted its gaze towards examining topics outside of slavery, ranging from northern antebellum free and "fugitive" black enclaves to post-emancipation life (Schuyler 1974; Giesmar 1982; Catts and Custer 1990; Wall, Rothschild and Copeland 2004; Sawyer 2004). This shift in concentration is important if the discipline is to maintain relevance as a viable subfield of historical archaeology. This is not to devalue the work that focuses on slavery, particularly that of plantation archaeology, as these studies have helped to establish archaeology pertaining to African Americans as a legitimate topic of archaeological and anthropological research (Orser 1998a; Wilkie 2004). However, to gain a better understanding of the dynamics and reflexivity of African American life, we must continue to shift our gaze towards other spatial and temporal landscapes. In exploring these other areas, such as the postbellum Delaware Valley, archaeology will add to anthropological discourses on everyday life.

This paper has several distinct but interrelated components. First, I briefly discuss the application of the Herskovits and Frazier debate on the origins of African American culture as investigated through historical archaeology. I examine the African American village of Timbuctoo, in present-day Westampton Township, New Jersey (figure 15.1). Finally, I discuss the recent archaeological work at Timbuctoo and contextualize the findings into broader discourses of African American heterogeneity.

The Archaeology of African Americans

Between the seventeenth and nineteenth centuries, as many as 600,000 Africans were forcefully imported into what has become the United States (Murphy 1994:147). The debate over enslaved African Americans' ability to retain African cultural practices has persisted for over 80 years (Orser 1998a). This scholarly debate has centered on two different theoretical models to explain the development of African American

Figure 15.1. Location of Timbuctoo. Map by Christopher Barton. Based on Google Earth image.

cultures. First, Melville Herskovits (1958) urged that dynamic elements of West African culture could be observed within the people of the African diaspora. Herskovits viewed these continuities as ethnic markers that could be ethnographically retraced from diaspora populations back to West Africa. According to Herskovits, these cultural continuities had resisted the effects of time, space, and acculturation; he further suggested that such "Africanisms" represent the cultural cornerstone for people of the African diaspora (Herskovits 1958).

By showing the persistence of African elements within the Americas, Herskovits was attempting to instill a sense of pride and admiration of Black culture, specifically among white intellectuals. Herskovits argued that, "when such a body of facts, solidly grounded, is established, a ferment must follow as a whole, will influence opinion in general concerning Negro abilities and potentialities, and thus contribute to a lessening of interracial tensions" (Herskovits 1958:32). The high admiration that Herskovits held for African diaspora communities is important to note, especially at a time when the prevalence of cultural evolutionist theories dominated academic discourses on cultural and biological hierarchy (Gershonhorn 2004: 23). As a result, these dominate and ethnocentric narratives characterized all sociocultural practices operating outside the bounds of white America as "primitive" and, thus, inferior (Orser 2004, 2007; Barton and Somerville 2012). Herskovits, like his mentor, Franz Boas, sought to challenge scientific claims to concrete categories of human races by arguing that ideologies of race were in fact social constructions that had no biological validity. These challenges to widely accepted ideologies must be contextualized in order to understand their importance.

From the turn of the twentieth century into the 1930s (and later), not only were academics still perpetuating ideologies of biological races but American society was fixated on ideas of racial superiority. Fear of the denigration of the white race through "mixing" resulted in the U.S. government's limitation and exclusion of immigrants from Southern and Eastern Europe and Asia (Gershonhorn 2004:60–61). The founding of the American Eugenics Society (AES) as well as developments in popular culture (e.g. minstrel shows, toys, radio programs) sought to underscore both the biological and cultural superiority of the white race (Hasian 1996:53; Barton 2012; Barton and Somerville 2012). The importance of discussing these structural practices of racism is that they help to contextualize the hostile environment endured by African Americans and demonstrate just how revolutionary Herskovits' search for cultural continuities was in the first half of the twentieth century (Gershonshorn 2004).

Leading the debate against Herskovits was sociologist Edward Frazier (1964) who argued a theory of "Negro cultural deprivation." For Frazier, the systematic tactics and strategies used within institutions of slavery, specifically the practice of selecting Africans from a wide array of ethnic groups had been purposefully employed in order to inhibit any collective resistance or identity among enslaved peoples. Thus, he argued, that the repressive networks and practices endured by diaspora populations starting from the Middle Passage to centuries of bondage and post-bellum racism had resulted in the inability for the continuation of African inspired practices within African American culture. For Frazier, this interpretation was specifically designed as social commentary on the contemporary socioeconomic position of African Americans in the United States. Quite simply, Frazier argued that the dehumanizing effects of slavery and centuries of continued racial- and class-orientated repression had not only inhibited any continuities between Africa and America but had resulted in the lasting sociopolitical and economic marginalization of African Americans (Cerroni-Long 1987:445–446). Frazier's goal was that by bringing attention to the repressive experiences endured by African Americans, he could garner public and government services to assist contemporary African Americans in need.

Though each model has it merits, they are not without their own shortcomings. For example, one of the difficulties associated with interpreting cultural continuities within the archaeological record is that, in some regards, artifact assemblages present spatially and temporally different cultures as tightly bound and static (Mullins 2000:32–33). Moreover, ethnic markers, such as inscribed colonoware, blue glass beads, etc., which have been viewed as identifiers of African cultural continuity in archaeological assemblages, may, in truth only represent isolated artifacts that have little bearing within the larger sociocultural network (Orser 2007:119). These observations question whether individual artifacts can be viewed as embodiments of widely held sociocultural beliefs or whether they are merely isolated objects that "lack the ability to reflect a social variable as complex as ethnic (or racial) identity" (Orser 2007:119).

Charles Orser (1998a, 1998b, 2004, 2007) argues that efforts should be focused on how African Americans used consumer tactics to both negotiate repressive landscapes and to construct collective and individual identities, rather than searching for isolated and individual markers of cultural continuities. Orser's arguments are important, given superficial assertions regarding the archaeology of the recent past in which archaeologists have stated that "the distribution of mass-produced goods across the United States produced amazing artifacts assemblage uniformity, and, therefore, the archaeological results rarely provide important new interpretive insights for the historical record" (Denton 1999:13, quoted in Barlie 2004:91–92). Such ill-advised statements fail to understand the importance of how people utilized mass consumption to improvise against repressive structures, specifically groups like African Americans who have been historically removed or slighted within documentary sources. As Paul Mullins (pers.comm. August 17, 2010) notes, "African American cultures revolves around the negotiation of racism and classism, which is reflected in the consumption of mass-produced commodities that have had distinctive and diverse symbolic meanings for people who had been collectively racially and economically marginalized." Thus, as Mullins (2000) and Orser (2004) correctly argue, archaeologies of race are inevitably archaeologies of socioeconomic class. As Orser argues (2007:46), to garner a better understanding of African American experiences archaeologists should investigate the confluence of race and class rather than the sole pursuit for cultural continuities to Africa.

Conversely, as Laurie Wilkie (2004:115) notes, one needs only to sample southern cuisine, listen to American music, or encounter herbal medical practices, to observe the continuity of African elements within contemporary African American culture. Indeed, many archaeologists in areas ranging from Florida (Davidson et al. 2006) to Texas (Brown: pers. comm. January 5, 2011) to Maryland (Leone 2005) to Connecticut (Sawyer 2003) have all proclaimed the presence of African-originated cultural practices among peoples of the African diaspora. Though such archaeological proclamations have continually been challenged (see Orser 1998a, 2001, 2004, 2007; Espenshade 2007), the material manifestations of African-inspired practices remain an unavoidable fact. What the archaeological investigations of cultural continuities have fostered are invaluable interpretations regarding the perseverance of people subjected to continual structural repression (Wilkie 2004:118–119; Fennel 2008).

Thus, it is my belief that any archaeology pertaining to African Americans should incorporate elements derived from both Herskovits' cultural continuities and Frazier's theory of response to socioeconomic subjugation. Reflexive improvisation and agency in the face of repression is the one common hallmark of an extremely heterogeneous African American culture. Whether such forms of improvisation and identity are embodied within individual artifacts as cultural continuities or manifested in consumer practices, they all reflect a uniquely African American experience. An experience that has be categorized by a legacy of perseverance against repression and marginalization.

Historical Background of Timbuctoo

It is from this brief discussion of how African American cultural development has been studied by archaeologists that I discuss the community of Timbuctoo. Founded circa 1825, the African American village of Timbuctoo has been in existence for almost 200 years. The village was situated on the outskirts of Mount Holly, a well-known Quaker stronghold in the eighteenth and nineteenth centuries (figure 15.2). Some scholars have argued that Timbuctoo's proximity to Mount Holly suggests white Quaker involvement in the creation of the community as a conscious action against slavery (Fishman 1997:195–196). Such social memory is rooted in collective history that emphasizes the path blazed by John Woolman, one of the most vocal Quaker abolitionists and a native of Mount Holly. Though Quaker denunciation of slavery developed in the early eighteenth century, it was Woolman's advocacy of abolition that led the 1774 Yearly Meeting to proclaim that slavery was irreconcilable with Quaker beliefs. This proclamation brought the controversial issue of slavery to the forefront of Quaker consciousness. However, Quakers' abhorrence of human

Figure 15.2. Recreated 1849 map of Timbuctoo and Mount Holly, New Jersey. Courtesy of Burlington County Historical Society.

bondage was based on morality and fear of their own eternal damnation in the afterlife, rather than condemning slavery because they saw African Americans as social equals (Hodges 1997:74–75; McDaniel and Julye 2009).

These perceptions of African American inferiority can be seen through the withheld admission of African Americans into local Friends' meetings. For example, it took William Boen, native of nearby Rancocas and close friend of Woolman, 51 years until he was finally accepted into the Mount Holly Meeting of the Society of Friends. Hodges (1997:75) notes, "Quaker unwillingness to accept African Americans in spiritual fellowship supports the view that their interest in manumission had more to do with their own souls than the souls or human conditions of black folk." African Americans were allowed to attend segregated Quaker services but were continuously denied membership into the Society of Friends (Cadbury 1936:168).

Despite this seeming lack of "Christian charity," Quakers were one of the most ardent and powerful abolitionist groups in New Jersey. So that while the majority of the white population continued at every turn to undermine both freed and enslaved African Americans, Quakers, as well as other abolitionists, brought their influence to bear through legislation to confront slavery and repression. For example, a legislative act in 1786 removed the £200 fee required for manumission by slaveholders, as long as the manumitted slave was over 35-years-old and able to economically provide for themselves. Another progressive legislation in 1786 required all slaveholders in the state to teach their slaves how to read and write, or be subjected to fines (New Jersey Legislature 1786:486–488). And yet, in the very same legislation, the law declared that freed African Americans from other states could not enter New Jersey, and the act required all freed persons living in state to carry certification of their legal status if traveling outside their hometown (Cooley 1896:33).

Such repressive measures arose in response to the ever-growing freed population of African Americans in the state. In fact, according to the 1800 census records, over two-thirds of the free African American population in the northern United States resided in New Jersey (Wright 1988). White male fear of women's and African Americans males' collective ability to influence elections resulted in the New Jersey constitution being amended in 1807 to limit voting privileges solely to white males (Klinghoffer and Elkis 1992:164). Understanding the dynamic histories of both progressive and repressive reactions to African Americans in New Jersey is paramount in order to contextualize the archaeology at Timbuctoo.

Timbuctoo was founded by former enslaved migrants from southern states (Paul Schopp, pers. comm. February 10, 2012). The population growth of the community centered on three factors: 1) the passage of New Jersey manumission laws; 2) the role of the community as a station along the underground railroad (Paul Schopp pers. comm. February 10, 2012); and 3) natural reproduction. In 1804, the Act for the Gradual Abolition of Slavery stated that enslaved African Americans born in New Jersey after July 4, 1804, would be granted their freedom after females had served their master for 21 years and males 25 years (Wright 1988: 25–26). Consequently, the first generation of enslaved African Americans who obtained their freedom through the act received their freedom around 1825, the same year that local history attest to the founding of Timbuctoo (Barton 2009; Barton and Markert, in review).

It has been argued (Wright 1988:39; Rizzo 2008; Barton 2009; Schopp pers. comm. February 10, 2012) that Timbuctoo operated as a destination along the Greenwich line of the underground railroad, which extended from Greenwich, New Jersey into New York City (figure 15.3). Much like Timbuctoo, other antebellum African American communities along the Greenwich line, such as Springtown, Guineatown, Small Gloucester, and Free Haven were located near towns such as Greenwich,

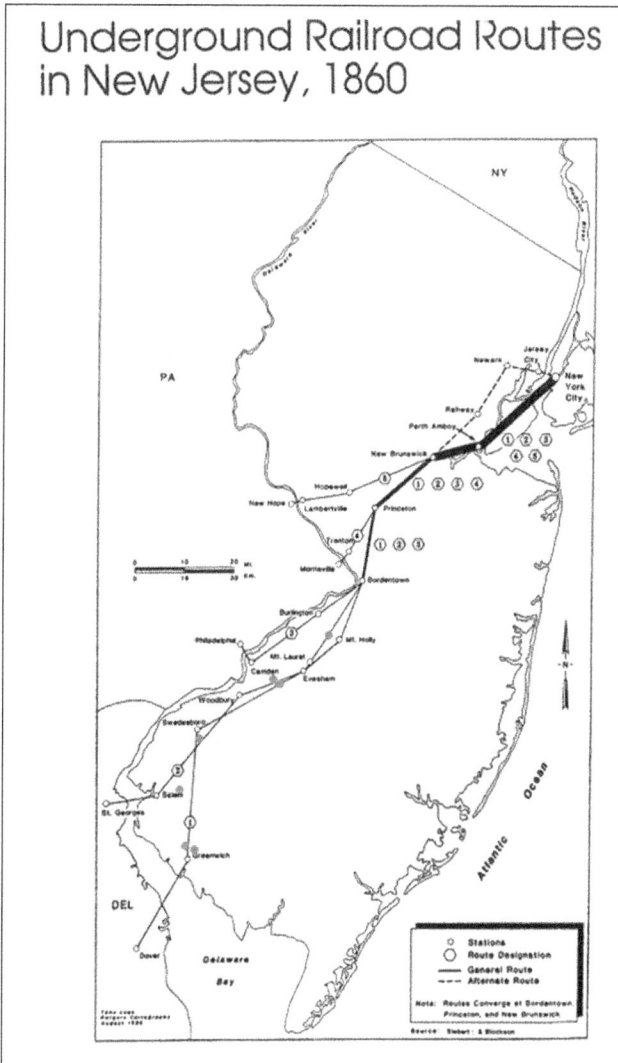

Underground Railroad Routes in New Jersey, 1860

Figure 15.3. Map of Greenwich Line of the Underground Railroad. The black dots indicate locations of known antebellum African American communities. Courtesy of the New Jersey Historical Commission.

Salem, Swedesboro, and Haddonfield, that had been heavily influenced by Quakers (Wright 1988; Barton 2009).

Although it has been argued that white Quakers provided financial support for the underground railroad (Interracial Committee of New Jersey 1932), it was largely African Americans who conducted the daily operations of this "network of freedom" (Wright 1988; LaRoche 2004). The presence of fugitive and formerly enslaved people has been well documented at Timbuctoo. For example, in 1860 slave catchers, aided by Caleb Wright, an African American and former Timbuctoo resident, attempted to apprehend Perry Simmons, a fugitive slave from Maryland, who had been living in Timbuctoo. Simmons, fearful of his pending return to human bondage, armed himself and hid in his loft. Amid the gunfire and cries for help, the residents of Timbuctoo came to Simmons's aid. This incident, known locally as the Battle of Pine Swamp (*New Jersey Mirror* 1860), is not only a sobering example of the racism and subjugation endured by African Americans in the antebellum period, but it is also a testament to the ability and willingness of African Americans to fight for their freedom (figure 15.4).

The omnipresent threat of slave catchers and their spies resulted in the people of Timbuctoo being highly suspicious of outsiders—white or black. For example, in 1858 shots were fired into the home of William Spry, an African American who was suspected of spying for slave catchers (*New Jersey Mirror* 1858). The newspaper attributed the shots to three Bucktonians: David "King" Parker, the informal leader of Timbuctoo, Perry Simmons, of the Battle of Pine Swamp, and William Chase.

Figure 15.4. The "Battle of Pine Swamp."

Specific examples, such as those detailed above, are only one illustration of the tactics that the residents used to protect themselves. One tactic of improvisation can be observed through residents' manipulation of the census records. For example, analysis of the census materials between 1850 and 1870, a time span that includes the abolishment of slavery, reveals that not only did the population of Timbuctoo grow in the years after the Civil War but the number of people claiming to have originated in former slave states increased as well (Turton 1999). In 1850, the total number of persons listed as originating from southern slave states was 10 percent, compared to 27 percent in 1870. In 1850 and 1860, when the fugitive slave laws were in effect, several residents claimed to have been born in New Jersey only to change their birth state in the 1870 census, saying that they had actually been born in slave states. For example in 1850, James Hill, age 40, told the census taker that his place of origin was New Jersey. Twenty years later, in 1870, Hill claimed that he had been born in Virginia. The inference here is that census takers represented possible threats, either as agents of a government that continuously debated the freedom of African Americans or as potential slave catchers in disguise. In an effort to secure their freedom, some residents of Timbuctoo manipulated the census by claiming freedom through the 1804 gradual emancipation act. This also shows that census records have the potential to provide information about individuals who escaped from slavery.

Following the end of the Civil War, the population of Timbuctoo reached its peak of around 125 persons (Turton 1999), an increase which was the result of both natural reproduction as well as continued migration. Even though the passage of the 13th Amendment, of which New Jersey did not ratify until 1866, ended slavery in the U.S., African Americans still had to operate within repressive landscapes. In New Jersey, the practice of institutionalized and everyday racism served to create distinct ideologies of sociocultural differences despite shared economic statuses among working-class white and black Americans.

Moving into the twentieth century, overt manifestations of racism, such as the presence of the Ku Klux Klan (KKK) and their actions toward the residents of Timbuctoo, have been detailed through the oral histories of several former residents. One resident remembers how, after a schoolyard fight between white and black children, members of the KKK descended upon the village. Even though the local authorities moved quickly to quell any potential violence, the fact remains that racism was a reality endured by residents well into the twentieth century (Interview with former resident, July 8, 2011).

Violence, of course, was not the only means of racial repression directed towards the people of Timbuctoo. The ruling in *Plessy vs. Ferguson* (1896) stated that Jim Crow laws mandating separate facilities for blacks and whites were constitutionally valid as long as the services provided were equal. In the oral history interviews, former residents remember attending colored schools in the 1940s. It was not until the local colored school burnt down that they were integrated with white students. Although there was one integrated school in late-eighteenth-century Mount Holly, likely a result of the 1786 act requiring masters to educate their slaves, the practice of institutionalized racism, as observed in racial segregation in some schools, continued in New Jersey until 1947 (New Jersey Constitution 1947, Article 1.).

Timbuctoo residents' lack of economic capital presented a daily struggle to be endured. Although some affluent African Americans resided in Burlington County (Irby 1976:2), black people, on the whole, faced the economic hardships associated with employment in low-paying occupations. According to the census records, beginning in 1850 and going forward throughout the community's existence, most of the village's residents obtained employment in some form of manual or domestic labor. Census records state that many of the residents held jobs in nearby brickyards and local farmsteads.

According to Paul Schopp (pers. comm. May 16, 2012), following the demise of slavery African Americans no longer needed the protection from slave catchers offered by rural communities like Timbuctoo, and thus many residents moved to more urban areas in search of employment. The population decline continued into the middle of the twentieth century. Today there are still residents who can trace their genealogy back to the town's founding, but the physical remains of the nineteenth-century village have almost completely vanished; the only aboveground markers denoting the community's presence are the 13 gravestones in the cemetery.

Archaeological Investigations at Timbuctoo

In the 1980s, Dave Orr and Bill Bolger, both employees of the National Park Service, were interested in the potential for archaeology at Timbuctoo; however, they were unable to garner support from the local community. In 2003, after a lengthy court case over disputed property rights, Westampton Township obtained title to roughly four of the total 40 acres comprising Timbuctoo.

In 2009, the township contracted with William Chadwick and Peter Leach of John Milner and Associates to conduct a geophysical study of the portion of the community now owned by Westampton Township. In that same year, the Timbuctoo Discovery Project, now chaired by Mary Weston and her son, Guy, was organized to begin investigations into the historical and archaeological dynamics of the community. The Westons are descendants of the Giles family, some of the first settlers of Timbuctoo. Utilizing the geophysical interpretations, Orr and myself, led a team of descendants, Temple University students, and volunteers into investigating the archaeological record of the community.

FEATURE 13

Further utilizing the geophysical reports, the Timbuctoo Discovery Project agreed that the first area for excavation was the lot of William and Rebecca Davis. According to the geophysicists interpretation, the Davis' lot contained the possible remains of a structure (Feature 13), outbuilding, and shaft feature. William Davis, an African American, was born free in Northampton Township (now part of Mount Holly), New Jersey, in 1836, and worked as a brick molder until he enlisted in the U.S. Colored Troops. He served in the 22nd regiment, and he was injured at the battle of Petersburg in 1864. After being honorably discharged, Davis returned to the Timbuctoo area, but he suffered from rheumatism and chronic back pain (Astle 2008). In 1879, he purchased the 20 by 100 foot plot from the executor of Mary Simmons' will for the sum of two dollars (Turton 1999). Upon acquiring the land, William and Rebecca built a 12 by 16 foot house (Feature 13). It was probably a one and a half story building atop a pier foundation. There, the Davis' raised five children. Davis continued to live in Timbuctoo until his death on April 4, 1914, at the age of 77, from pneumonia.

Through two field seasons, the team was able to uncover the foundation of the Davis home as well as over fifteen thousand artifacts. The temporal range for the artifacts recovered from the Davis' lot is between the 1860s and the 1940s. The interior of Feature 13 was used as a refuse pit and filled in the first half of the twentieth century (figure 15.5).

Preliminary interpretations reveal that the foundation of the Davis' home contains bricks that are either "salmon" or only partially vitrified. Such bricks were likely created using onsite wet clamps or at preindustrial brickyards. During the production process, the bricks further away from the heat source become pinkish or "salmon" and are often soft or brittle. These porous and fragile bricks, known as wasters or washers, may be the result of improper drying prior to kilning. Conversely, semi-vitrified bricks were located closer to or adjacent the heat source, resulting in such bricks becoming "burned" or partially vitrified along portions of the surface receiving maximum heat. Because salmon and semi-vitrified bricks lacked aesthetic uniformity, they were frequently used as noggin or insulation bricks rather than on the exteriors or faces of structures.

That said, the use of what were likely waster bricks for the construction of the foundation designated Feature 13 was an economical tactic to save on construction materials. While bricks were a relatively expensive commodity, they also offered a building strength that could not be matched by many other materials in the nineteenth century. What preliminary analysis suggests is that the use of discarded, inexpensive, or locally-fashioned bricks reflects an improvisation prompted by a lack of economic capital. This is further underscored by the fact that most of the bricks along the western side of Feature 13 were, at some time, removed. The evidence of a robber's trench and the discarded remains of either broken or extremely irregular bricks, with only the deepest course of whole brick left *in situ*, suggests that someone knew of a ready source for construction material. Rather than pay for expensive bricks, they simply dug up and took what they needed. These archaeological inferences again suggest a continued practice of improvisational tactics as a response to the lack of economic capital.

The bricks—coupled with an assortment of patent medicine bottles, immature oyster and clam shells, peanut butter jars, reused jelly jars as drinking glasses, Ball Mason jars, and low cost unmatched ceramics—suggest that the people using Feature 13 as a trash pit were constrained by a lack of economic capital. What these tactics of improvisation do suggest is that the people of Timbuctoo persevered despite limited economic resources. Some of the people may not have had a lot of money, but they were not "poor." Indeed, oral histories have recounted that residents established support networks for one another ranging from church services to one former resident serving as the community's midwife. Many former residents and descendants have conveyed a sense of pride in Timbuctoo.

Conclusions

In highlighting the applications of Herskovits' and Frazier's theories of African American cultural development through the 1960s and into the present day, this chapter briefly touched upon the problematic role of attempting to recover ethnic

Figure 15.5. Feature 13 after excavation. Photograph by Christopher Barton.

markers within African American archaeology as well as the danger of ignoring potential connections to a shared African past. Through discussing the preliminary historical and archaeological investigations of Timbuctoo, I have attempted to provide a better context for discussing the dynamics of the archaeological record pertaining to African Americans into broader discourses, debating both theories of Herskovits' cultural continuities and Frazier's Negro cultural deprivation.

The people of Timbuctoo were social agents who operated in a repressive world of shifting power relations. White people did not solely possess the social and political power at Timbuctoo and its surrounding area. The African American population wielded its own collective power as it sought to resist attempts at social and economic repression. Rather than simply being the subjects of oppression, the residents of Timbuctoo "pushed" back through tactics of improvisation developed in response to social and economical marginalization by the larger society. What preliminary interpretations suggest is that the archaeologies of Timbuctoo are a reflection of socioeconomic class, however, one cannot detach the tacit and explicit results of structural racism. For many African Americans, social, political, and economic marginalization in both the past and present are the result of a legacy of race and racism. This reality underscores that all archaeologies of race are in fact archaeologies of class—as can be observed at Timbuctoo. Though this chapter represents only a brief introduction to the history of the village and a preliminary analysis of archaeological work, what has been continually reflected in every facet of investigation is the ability of the residents of Timbuctoo to improvise and persevere.

Acknowledgements

First, I would like to thank the editors of this reader, David Orr and Richard Veit. I am deeply indebted to Paul Schopp, Bob Craig, and John Lawrence for their thorough reviews. I would like to thank Paul Mullins, Chuck Orser, Robert Schuyler, Kyle Somerville, Patricia Markert, Deirdre Kelleher and the anonymous readers for their comments in preparation of this article. I am forever indebt to the former residents and descendant community. I would especially like to thank the Westons for their love and support. Finally, to my wife, Jess, who had to deal with countless restless nights of my incoherent ramblings on Timbuctoo. Any shortcomings as a result of this article are the sole responsibility of the author.

References Cited

Astle, Gail
2008   Memorial Day Eulogy, Timbuctoo Cemetery, Westampton Township, New Jersey, May 25, 2008. http://www.rancocasnj.org/Reference/Timbuctoo.html (accessed June 6, 2011).

Baker, V. G.
1980   Archaeological Visibility of Afro-American Culture: An Example from
               Black Lucy's Gardens, Andover, MA. In *Archaeological Perspectives
               on Ethnicity in America: Afro-American and Asian American Culture
               History*, edited by Robert L. Schuyler, pp. 29–37. Baywood, New York.

Barile, Kerri S.
2004   Race, the National Register, and Cultural Resource Management: Cre-
               ating an Historic Context for Postbellum Sites. *Historical Archaeology*
               38(1):90–100.

Barton, Christopher P.
2009   Antebellum African American Settlements in Southern New Jersey.
               African Diaspora Archaeology Network Newsletter. December 2009,
               http://www.diaspora.uiuc.edu/news1209/news1209.html#4 (accessed
               June 4, 2010).

2012   Tacking Between Black and White: the Archaeology of Race Rela-
               tions in Gilded Age Philadelphia. *International Journal of Historical
               Archaeology*, 16(4):634–650.

Bourdieu, Pierre
1990   *The Logic of Practice*. Stanford University Press, Stanford, California.

Brown, Kenneth L.
1994   Material Culture and Community Structure: The Slave and Tenant
               Community at Levi Jordan's Plantation, 1848–1892. In *Working To-
               ward Freedom: Slave Society and Domestic Economy in the American
               South*, edited by Larry E. Hudson, pp. 95–118. University of Rochester
               Press, Rochester, New York.

Catts, Wade P., and Jay F. Custer
1990   *Tenant Farmers, Stone Masons, and Black Laborers: Final Archaeolog-
               ical Investigations of the Thomas Williams Site, Glasgow, New Castle
               County, Delaware*. Department of Transportation, Dover, Delaware.

Cerroni-Long, E. L.
1987   Benign Neglect?: Anthropology and the Study of Blacks in the United
               States. *Journal of Black Studies* 17(4):438–459.

Chadwick, William, and Peter Leach
2009   *Geophysical Survey of Timbucktoo, NJ*. John Milner and Associates:
               West Chester, Pennsylvania.

Cooley, Henry Scofield
1896   *A Study of Slavery in New Jersey*. Johns Hopkins University Press, Bal-
               timore, Maryland.

Davidson, James M., Erika Roberts, and Clete Rooney
2006   Preliminary Results of the 2006 University of Florida Archaeological
               Field School Excavations at Kingsley Plantation, Fort George Island,
               Florida. *The African Diaspora Archaeology Newsletter*. September

2006, http://www.diaspora.uiuc.edu/news0906/news0906.html#2 (accessed June 4, 2010).

Deetz, James
1996   *In Small Things Forgotten: An Archaeology of Early American Life.* Anchor Books, New York.

DeCorse, Christopher R.
1999   Africanist Perspectives on Diaspora Archaeology. In *"I, Too, am America" Archaeological Studies of African-American Life,* edited by Teresa A. Singleton, pp. 132–158. University of Virginia Press, Charlottesville.

Denton, Mark H.
1999   Dealing with Late-19th and Early-20th Century Sites. *Cultural Resource Management New and Views* 11(1):13–14.

Espenshade, Christopher
2007   A River of Doubt: Marked Colonoware, Underwater Sampling, and Questions of Inference. *The African Diaspora Archaeology Newsletter.* March 2007, http://www.diaspora.uiuc.edu/news0307/news0307.html#2 (accessed June 6, 2010).

Ferguson, Leland G.
1992   *Uncommon Ground: Archaeology and Early African Africa 1650–1800.* Smithsonian Institution Press, Washington, D.C.

Fishman, George
1997   *The African American Struggle for Freedom and Equality: The Development of a People's Identity, New Jersey, 1624–1850.* Garland, New York.

Fitts, Robert K.
1996   The Landscapes of Northern Bondage. *Historical Archaeology* 30(2):54–73.

Frazier, Edward F.
1964   *The Negro Church in America.* Schocken, New York.

Geismar, Joan H.
1982   *The Archaeology of Social Disintegration in Skunk Hollow: A Nineteenth-Century Rural Black Community.* Academic Press, New York.

Hasian, Marouf A.
1996   *The Rhetoric of Eugenics in Anglo-American Thought.* University of Georgia Press, Athens.

Herskovits, Melville J.
1990   *The Myth of the Negro Past.* Beacon Press, Boston.

Hodges, George R.
1997   *Slavery and Freedom in the Rural North: African Americans in Monmouth County, New Jersey, 1665–1865.* Madison House, Madison, Wisconsin.

Interracial Committee of New Jersey
n.d.   Survey of Negro Life in New Jersey. Community Reports, 11. In *New
                  Jersey Conference of Social Affairs, Interracial Committee*. Newark,
                  New Jersey.

Irby, James B.
1975   *Black Heritage in Central Burlington County*. J.B. Irby, Mt. Holly, New
                  Jersey.

Klinghoffer, Judith A., and Lois Elkis
1992   "The Petticoat Electors": Women's Suffrage in New Jersey, 1776–1807.
                  Journal of the Early Republic 12(2):159–193.

LaRoche, Cheryl J.
2004.   On the Edge of Freedom: Free Black Communities, Archaeology and
                  the Underground Railroad. Ph.D. dissertation, Department of Ameri-
                  can Studies, University of Maryland, College Park.

Leone, Mark P.
2005   *The Archaeology of Liberty in an American Capital: Excavations in
                  Annapolis*. University of California Press, Berkeley.

Mintz, Sydney W., and Richard Price
1976   *An Anthropological Approach to the Afro-American Past: A Caribbean
                  Perspective*. Institute for the Study of Human Issues, Philadelphia.

Mullins, Paul R.
1996   *The Contradictions of Consumption: An Archaeology of African
                  America and Consumer Culture*. Ph.D. dissertation, Department of
                  Anthropology, University of Massachusetts, Amherst.

1999a   "A Bold and Gorgeous Front": The Contradictions of African Ameri-
                  can and Consumer Culture. In *Historical Archaeologies of Capitalism*,
                  edited by Mark Leone and Parker Potter, pp. 169–193. Kluwer Aca-
                  demic Press, New York.

1999b   Race and Genteel Consumer: Class and African American Consump-
                  tion, 1850–1930. *Historical Archaeology* 33(1):22–38.

2000   *Race and Affluence: An Archaeology of African America and Con-
                  sumer Culture*. Springer, New York.

2001   Racializing the Parlor: Race and Victorian Bric-a-Brac Consumption.
                  In *Race and the Archaeology of Identity*, edited by C. Orser, pp. 158–
                  176. University of Utah Press, Salt Lake City.

2004   Ideology, Power, and Capitalism: The Historical Archaeology of Con-
                  sumption. In *A Companion to Social Archaeology*, edited by Lynn
                  Meskell and Robert W. Preucel, pp. 195–211. Blackwell, Malden,
                  Massachusetts.

Murphy, Joseph M.
1994   *Working the Spirit: Ceremonies of the African Diaspora*. Beacon,
                  Boston.

New Jersey Mirror
1858   Trouble Among the Darkies. April 15.
              Excitement at Timbuctoo, the Battle of Pine Swamp-the Invaders
              Forced to Retreat. December 6.
Orser, Charles E.
1998a   The Archaeology of the African Diaspora. *Annual Review of Anthro-
              pology* 27(1):63–82.
1998b   The Challenge of Race to American Historical Archaeology. *American
              Anthropologist* 100(3):661–668.
2001   Race and the Archaeology of Identity in the Modern World. In *Race
              and the Archaeology of Identity*, edited by Charles E. Orser, pp. 1–23.
              University of Utah Press, Salt Lake City.
2004   *Race and Practice in Archaeological Interpretation.* University of Penn-
              sylvania Press, Philadelphia.
2007   *The Archaeology of Race and Racialization in Historic America.* Uni-
              versity of Florida Press, Gainesville.
Sawyer, Gerald.
2001   New Salem plantation: continuing investigations into African captivity
              on an 18th century plantation in Connecticut. Presented at the Society
              for Historical Archaeology Conference, Long Beach, California, Janu-
              ary, 6.
Schuyler, Robert L.
1974   Sandy Ground: Archaeological Sampling in a Black Community in
              Metropolitan New York. *Papers of the Conference on Historic Sites
              Archaeology* 7(1):12–51.
Shackel Paul A.
2011   *New Philadelphia: An Archaeology of Race in the Heartland.* Univer-
              sity of California Press, Berkley.
Singleton, Theresa A.
1999   An Introduction to African-American Archaeology. In *"I, Too, am
              America" Archaeological Studies of African-American Life*, edited by
              Teresa A. Singleton, pp. 1–17. University of Virginia, Charlottesville.
Szwed, J. F.
1974   An American Anthropological Dilemma: the Politcs of Afro-American
              Culture. In *Reinventing Anthropology*, edited by Dell H. Hymes, pp.
              153–181. Vintage, New York.
Turton, Catherine
n.d.   *Timbuctoo: Burlington County, New Jersey.* National Park Service,
              Northeast Region, Philadelphia, PA.
Rizzo, Dennis
2008   *Parallel Communities: The Underground Railroad in South Jersey.* His-
              tory Press, New York.

Wall, Diana diZerega, Nan A. Rothschild, and Cynthia Copeland.
2008   Seneca Village and Little Africa Two African American Communities in
              Antebellum New York City. *Historical Archaeology.* 42(1):97–107.
Wilkie, Laurie A.
2000   *Creating Freedom: Material Culture and African American Identity at
              Oakley Plantation, Louisiana, 1840–1950.* Louisiana State University
              Press, Baton Rouge.
2004   Transcending Boundaries, Transforming the Discipline: African Dias-
              pora Archaeologies in the New Millennium. *Historical Archaeology.*
              38(1):109–123.
Wright, Giles R.
1988   *Afro-American History in New Jersey: A Short History.* New Jersey
              Historical Commission, Trenton, New Jersey.

CONTRIBUTORS

SHARON ALLITT is a private consultant. She specializes in faunal analysis and human skeletal anatomy. She intermittently teaches anthropology and anatomy courses as an adjunct professor. Her interests include stable isotope research, how the shift from hunting and gathering to cultivation impacted exploitation of local wildlife and the relationship between diet and disease. She received her doctoral degree in 2011 from Temple University where she studied a variety of prehistoric North American human and faunal skeletal collections including those from the Mohr Site in Pennsylvania. She was awarded the 5th Annual Middle Atlantic Archaeological Conference Graduate Student Paper Award for her preliminary dissertation research, which focused on using dog bone as a proxy for human bone in stable isotope analysis looking for the presence of maize at prehistoric archaeological sites.

CHRISTOPHER P. BARTON received his PhD in anthropology from Temple University and is the principal investigator at Timbuctoo, New Jersey. He received his BA from Rowan University and his MA in anthropology from the University of Pennsylvania. Additionally, he is currently an adjunct professor at Widener University.

CHARLES BELLO is an archaeologist currently employed by the Federal Emergency Management Agency (FEMA), stationed in Region VIII, Denver, Colorado, and is a member of the Colorado Council of Professional Archaeologists and the Wyoming Association of Professional Archaeologists. He attended graduate school at New York University.

JOSEPH BLONDINO is a graduate student in anthropology at Temple University. Although his research focuses primarily on pre-contact populations in the middle Atlantic region, he also has a great interest in military archaeology and early colonial sites, such as the Marcus Hook Plank Log House. He has worked on numerous sites in the region ranging from Paleoindian camps to historic period industrial sites in both the academic/research and compliance realms. He is interested in landscape and site formation and how geologic factors and processes affect both choice of site location by past populations and how cultural deposits are manifested in the archaeological record. He is also a proponent of public outreach and believes that an educated public is one of the most powerful tools at the disposal of the historic preservation community.

IAN BURROW studied history and archaeology at the universities of Exeter and Birmingham in England. From 1975 to 1988 he worked in several archaeological positions in England, including directing the Oxford Archaeological Unit. Since 1988 he has worked with Richard Hunter at Hunter Research, undertaking numerous projects in the Mid-Atlantic, New Jersey, and in Trenton. He has published papers on aspects of regional historical archaeology and teaches as an adjunct in several New Jersey colleges. He is a Fellow of the Society of Antiquaries of London and a Registered Professional Archaeologist. He has served as President of the Register of Professional Archaeologists and of the American Cultural Resources Association.

JOHN M. CHENOWETH received his MA in anthropology in 2006 from the University of Pennsylvania and his PhD in anthropology in 2011 from the University of California, Berkeley. His research uses historical archaeology to study how social identity is created through practice in daily life and how membership in a social group changes how people act and see the world. He has worked in the US Northeast and in the Caribbean, primarily studying religious, racial, and class identities, and in particular the Religious Society of Friends, better known as "Quakers." He is currently an assistant professor of anthropology at the University of Michigan–Dearborn.

SARAH CHESNEY is a PhD candidate in anthropology at the College of William and Mary in Williamsburg, Virginia. Her research focuses on the development of scientific botany in early federal Philadelphia and the historical archaeology of early American urban domestic sites. She received her MA in anthropology from William and Mary in 2009 and has done archaeological work in Maryland, Virginia, New Jersey, and Pennsylvania. Currently she is a Barra Foundation Dissertation in Art and Material Culture Fellow at the McNeil Center for Early American Studies in Philadelphia, Pennsylvania.

CAROLYN DILLIAN is an assistant professor of anthropology at Coastal Carolina University where she teaches courses in archaeological theory and method, regional seminars, and archaeological field schools. She has coauthored several articles on the life and work of Dr. Charles Conrad Abbott but also has research interests in North American prehistory, archaeological geochemistry, and prehistoric hunter-fisher-gatherers in Kenya. She currently directs research at Waties Island in South Carolina and is a Field Director with the Koobi Fora Field School in Kenya.

CHARLES FITHIAN is curator of archaeology with the Delaware Division of Historical and Cultural Affairs. He holds a master's degree in history with a concentration in colonial and revolutionary America from Salisbury University in Maryland. He is responsible for the curation of the extensive archaeological collections of the State of Delaware and for conducting historical and archaeological research. In addition to caring for the Division's archaeological collections, his current activities include directing the research and conservation of HM Sloop of War *DeBraak* and its collection and a survey of sites related to the War of 1812 in Delaware.

MICHAEL J. GALL is a senior archaeologist at Richard Grubb & Associates, Inc., a cultural resource management firm in Cranbury, New Jersey, and an adjunct professor in the History and Anthropology Department at Monmouth University. He is an executive board member of the Archaeological Society of New Jersey. He earned a BA in history and anthropology and later received an MA in history from Monmouth University. His research interests include farmstead, landscape, and early industrial archaeology in the middle Atlantic region; settlement patterns; and regional cultural development.

PATRICIA GIBBLE is a retired college instructor and assistant professor of anthropology, specializing in historic archaeology and gender studies. She received her PhD from American University in Washington, D.C., for her research into trends of red earthenware potting in the middle Atlantic region. At the present time she is the principal of her own contract archaeology firm. Her on-going public archaeology project at the Alexander Schaeffer Farm/Distillery focuses on the economics, craft manufacture, and gender roles of immigrant German Americans in south central Pennsylvania. Currently, she is authoring a case study entitled *Finding Esther: Gender and the Farm Economy at the Alexander Schaeffer Farm/Distillery.*

DANIEL GRIFFITH is retired from the State of Delaware after thirty-four years in cultural resource investigations and management, including six years as a state archaeologist, twelve years as deputy state historic preservation officer (SHPO), and sixteen years as Delaware's SHPO. He holds a master's degree in anthropology from The American University in Washington, D.C., with a concentration in archaeology. After retirement he was director of the Roosevelt Inlet Shipwreck Recovery Project in Lewes, Delaware, for two years. Currently he is project director of the Avery's Rest Site investigations (1675–1715) for the Archaeological Society of Delaware and, as a consultant, conducts analysis and research on American Indian archaeology of the middle Atlantic region.

WILLIAM HOFFMAN is a historical archaeologist with a research interest in material culture from both terrestrial and underwater sites. He earned his bachelor's degree from George Washington University and received his master's degree from Florida State University. From 2007–2011, he served as laboratory director of the Independence National Historical Park Archeology Laboratory. He is currently an archaeologist with the Department of the Interior, Bureau of Ocean Energy Management.

RICHARD W. HUNTER is president of Hunter Research, Inc., a historical and archaeological consulting firm in Trenton. He received a BA in archaeology and geography from Birmingham University (UK), an MA in archaeological science from Bradford University (UK), and a PhD in geography from Rutgers University. His doctoral research centered on water-powered industrial processing in the north branch of the Raritan River and Stony Brook/Millstone drainages of central New Jersey. He is a board member and past president of the Trenton Downtown Association, a former board member and president of Preservation New Jersey, a past member and chair of the Hopewell Township Historic Preservation Commission, and a trustee of the Trenton Museum Society. His many publications on New Jersey archaeology and history include *Hopewell: A Historical Geography*, coauthored with Ian Burrow, and "The Historical Geography and Archaeology of the Revolutionary War in New Jersey" in *New Jersey in the American Revolution*.

PATRICE L. JEPPSON received her PhD from Pennsylvania University, and has been active in historical archaeology for more than two decades. She has conducted archaeological research on sites in South Africa, in the American west, and the US mid Atlantic. Her first Delaware Valley archaeological experience was in 1984, at the Front and Dock Street site in Philadelphia (now the site of a Sheraton hotel). Later, between 2003 and 2005, she assessed the long history of archaeological research at the Independence Park site of Franklin Court for the Benjamin Franklin Tercentenary Consortium—an experience she writes about in this volume. Her current research involves how the public uses the archaeological sites in Independence National Historical Park for tourism needs and for national identity construction. Toward that end, she helped interpret archaeology to the public at the President's House Site (in 2007), and for two years she researched and blogged on the archaeological site documentation housed in the Independence Park archives. She recently completed a four-year project as part of a transdisciplinary team of NSF-funded, Drexel University–researchers using artifacts from Independence Park in the modeling of new 3D computer-vision technologies (2009–2012). She teaches as an adjunct assistant professor of anthropology at Cheyney University and West Chester University, both in Pennsylvania.

MARA KAKTINS is the ceramics and glass specialist at Ferry Farm, George Washington's boyhood home. She is a PhD candidate in Temple University's Anthropology Department, from which she also holds a master's degree in archaeology. Her dissertation research centers on the changing treatment of the poor throughout the colonial period, focusing on data recovered from her excavation of a privy associated with the first Philadelphia City Almshouse. Mara is also interested in the sociotechnic aspects of artifacts and is currently conducting an in depth study of Mary Washington's table and teawares, many of which contain glue residues that evidence historic mending.

WILLIAM B. LIEBEKNECHT holds a BA in anthropology from Beloit College in Wisconsin and an MA in public history from Rutgers University. He is an archaeological principal investigator employed by Hunter Research, Inc., located in Trenton, New Jersey. He has been an active member of the Archaeological Society of New Jersey from 1989 to the present and served as president from 2004 to 2007. He has over twenty-five years experience in prehistoric and historic archaeology in the middle Atlantic region where he has directed numerous archaeological investigations. He has developed an expertise in historical archaeology through working on pottery and early glass manufacturing sites in the Delaware Valley.

SEAN MCHUGH is an archaeologist at Richard Grubb & Associates, Inc., and has worked on numerous archaeological investigations (Phase I-III) for both historic and prehistoric resources in New Jersey, New York, Pennsylvania, Delaware, Maryland, and Virginia. He received his BA and MA in history from Monmouth University. His research interests include American military history and cartographical analysis. He also serves as an adjunct professor at Monmouth University and instructor at the university's archaeology field school.

DEBORAH MILLER is an archaeologist and laboratory director at Independence National Historical Park, consulting archaeologist at Stenton, and an adjunct faculty member at the University of the Arts graduate program in museum studies. She received her MA in American studies from The Pennsylvania State University and a BA in anthropology from Virginia Commonwealth University. She has more than ten years experience managing and analyzing diverse archaeological collections in the middle Atlantic region for federal, state, and non-profit institutions.

DAVID G. ORR is currently teaching full time at Temple University in the Department of Anthropology. A Fellow of the American Academy in Rome, he has worked in Pompeii and Cuma, Italy, as well as City Point, Valley Forge, Philadelphia, and numerous other sites in the United States. His interests include military, urban, battle-field, industrial, and landscape archaeology, as well as cultural resource management, material culture theory, and popular culture. He received his PhD from the University of Maryland.

TEAGAN SCHWEITZER graduated in May 2010 with a PhD in anthropology from the University of Pennsylvania with a focus on historical zooarchaeology and food studies. She currently works as a zooarchaeologist for the contract archaeology division of URS Corporation. She maintains a lab space in the Penn Museum. Her primary research interests center around the intersection of food and identity. She believes that what people ate had a lot to say about who they were, and she applies this theoretical orientation to her interpretations of historic faunal assemblages. Through better understanding the remnants of peoples' past meals, it is possible to more thoroughly understand the people themselves.

R. MICHAEL STEWART has a long record of research and publication dealing with the archaeology of American Indians ranging from the Paleoindian period through native contact and interaction with Europeans in the middle Atlantic and northeast regions. Specific interests include human ecology, trade, pottery technology, paleoenvironmental reconstruction, and the integration of archaeology and environmental sciences. He has degrees in anthropology from the University of Delaware (BA) and the Catholic University of America (MA, PhD). He currently teaches in the Department of Anthropology at Temple University and maintains ongoing field projects throughout the Delaware Valley.

Focusing on the built environment of the middle Atlantic region, DAMON TVARYANAS directs projects that integrate history, architectural history, archaeology, and material culture. He regards each of these pursuits as complementary facets of a single discipline, viewing them not as distinct professions but rather as differing strategies in the effort to develop a deeper understanding of our history and a more complete appreciation of the cultural patrimony that we all share. He holds a BA in art history from New York University and an MA in historic preservation from the University of Pennsylvania. He has over twenty years of experience working in the history and cultural resource management industries.

RICHARD VEIT is professor of anthropology and director of the Center for Excellence in Teaching and Learning at Monmouth University. He received his BA from Drew University in 1990, his MA in historical archaeology from the College of William and Mary in 1991, and his PhD in anthropology from the University of Pennsylvania in 1997. In 2007 he was the recipient of Monmouth University's distinguished teacher award. At Monmouth he teaches courses on archaeology, historical archaeology, New Jersey history, Native Americans, and historic preservation. He is the author of the award-winning book *Digging New Jersey's Past: Historical Archaeology in the Garden State* published by Rutgers University Press in 2002. He and Mark Nonestied co-authored the book *New Jersey Cemeteries and Tombstones History in the Landscape* (Rutgers, 2008) and, with Maxine Lurie, he edited *New Jersey: A History of the Garden State* (Rutgers, 2012). He serves on the boards of the Society for Historical Archaeology, Council for Northeast Historical Archaeology, and the Archaeological Society of New Jersey. His research interests include the archaeology of Native Americans in the colonial period, Dutch American farmsteads, early American gravemarkers, and early American industries. He is currently studying the Dr. John Vermeule house, a Dutch American farmstead in the Raritan Valley, and Point Breeze, Joseph Bonaparte's palatial New World estate.

INDEX

28Me1D, 11, 24. *See also* Area D
28Me273, 23

A

Abbott, Charles Conrad: archaeological
technique of, 49; graves and, 54,
61; historical archaeology and, 49,
53–54, 67; historical research of,
53–54; human evolution and, 49,
67; opera and, 55; poetry and, 55;
Trenton, New Jersey and, 324
Abbott Farm National Landmark: American Indians in, 324, 327; archaeological studies of, 15
abolition: Franklin, Benjamin and, 242,
243; in New Jersey, xx, 379, 383;
Quakerism and, 186, 379–380
acculturation: of enslaved Africans, 375–
76; of Germans in British colonial
America and, 126, 127; in housing
styles, 142–43; material culture and,
126, 139; models of, 125; resistance
to, 21–22, 27, 143; at Wistarburgh
Glasshouse, 111. *See also* culture
contact
Act for the Gradual Abolition of Slavery,
380–81, 383
Act of Toleration, 194
Acts of Trade, 177, 180
aerial photography, 64, 331, 350
African Americans: archaeological studies of, 375, 386–87; cultural continuity of, 377, 378; economic status
of, 384, 385–86; Franklin Court
and, 242, 243; freed population
in New Jersey of, 380–81; historical perceptions of, 380; literacy of,
380, 383–84; marginalization of,
379, 387; proof of freedom of, 380;
Quakers and, 379–380; religious
participation by, 380; voting and,
380
agency: African Americans and, 378; in
culture contact, 24, 27, 125, 126;
gardens and, 303; Georgian Order
and, 303; at Philadelphia City
Almshouse, 263; Quakerism and,
192; Schaeffer, Henry and, 143; of
subordinate groups, 125–26, 378

alcohol consumption, 129, 196
Alexander Schaeffer Farm/Distillery:
archaeological studies of, 130, 132;
artifact assemblage of, 133, 136; bio-
turbation of, 132; ceramic analysis
of, 136; ceramics from, 135–36; consumer choice on, 139, 144; dating of,
132, 133; description of, 128; documentary evidence of, 130, 131, 138,
139; expansion of, 142; history of,
128; housing style and, 142; occupation of, 132, 133, 134; ownership of,
129, 130, 131, 132; public outreach
at, 134; refuse disposal patterns on,
134–35; stratigraphy of, 132
Alloway Township, New Jersey, 93, 94
almshouses: admittance to, 250; Albany
Almshouse, 249, 254, 265–66;
archaeological studies of, 254;
architecture of, 266; badges from,
252, 261; Blockley Almshouse, 249,
256; ceramics of, 264, 265; changes
in, 250–51, 267–68; chocolate
consumption in, 267; Destitute
Asylum of Adelaide, Australia, 249;
donations to, 266; in early America,
251; escapes from, 251; Falmouth,
Massachusetts Almshouse, 249;
family styles of, 250, 251, 267–68;
Hudson poor farm cemetery, 249;
infirmaries of, 255–56; as last
resort, 251–52; Magdalen Society,
249; New York City Municipal
Almshouse complex, 249, 254, 259,
265–66, 267; out-relief by, 250,
251, 252, 267–68, 268; overseers of,
266; personal property at, 263, 266;
pewter artifacts found at, 255; in
Philadelphia, 256; purpose of, 250,
252; reformation of poor by, 252,
263; stigma of, 251, 252; teaware of,
265–66; uniforms of, 250, 251, 261;
workhouses and, 252, 254
Alricks, Peter, 52, 61
American Bridge Company, 352
American Eugenics Society, 376
American Indian archaeology: assumptions and, 15; Delaware Valley,
7–13; documentary evidence and,